Lecture Notes in Computer Scien

Edited by G. Goos and J. Hartmanis

T0238347

Advisory Board: W. Brauer   D. Gries   J. Sto

Oscar M. Nierstrasz (Ed.)

ECOOP '93 – Object-Oriented Programming

7th European Conference
Kaiserslautern, Germany, July 26-30, 1993
Proceedings

Springer-Verlag

Berlin Heidelberg New York
London Paris Tokyo
Hong Kong Barcelona
Budapest

Series Editors

Gerhard Goos
Universität Karlsruhe
Postfach 69 80
Vincenz-Priessnitz-Straße 1
D-76131 Karlsruhe, FRG

Juris Hartmanis
Cornell University
Department of Computer Science
4130 Upson Hall
Ithaca, NY 14853, USA

Volume Editor

Oscar M. Nierstrasz
Centre Universitaire d'Informatique, Université de Genève
24, rue Général-Dufour, CH-1211 Genève 4, Switzerland

CR Subject Classification (1991): D.1-3, H.2

ISBN 3-540-57120-5 Springer-Verlag Berlin Heidelberg New York
ISBN 0-387-57120-5 Springer-Verlag New York Berlin Heidelberg

This work is subject to copyright. All rights are reserved, whether the whole or part
of the material is concerned, specifically the rights of translation, reprinting, re-use
of illustrations, recitation, broadcasting, reproduction on microfilms or in any other
way, and storage in data banks. Duplication of this publication or parts thereof is
permitted only under the provisions of the German Copyright Law of September 9,
1965, in its current version, and permission for use must always be obtained from
Springer-Verlag. Violations are liable for prosecution under the German Copyright
Law.

© Springer-Verlag Berlin Heidelberg 1993
Printed in Germany

Typesetting: Camera-ready by authors
Printing and binding: Druckhaus Beltz, Hemsbach/Bergstr.
45/3140-543210 - Printed on acid-free paper

Preface

It is now more than twenty-five years since object-oriented programming was "invented" (actually, more than thirty years since work on Simula started), but, by all accounts, it would appear as if object-oriented technology has only been "discovered" in the past ten years! When the first European Conference on Object-Oriented Programming was held in Paris in 1987, I think it was generally assumed that Object-Oriented Programming, like Structured Programming, would quickly enter the vernacular, and that a conference on the subject would rapidly become superfluous. On the contrary, the range and impact of object-oriented approaches and methods continues to expand, and, despite the inevitable oversell and hype, object-oriented technology has reached a level of scientific maturity that few could have foreseen ten years ago.

Object-oriented technology also cuts across scientific cultural boundaries like perhaps no other field of computer science, as object-oriented concepts can be applied to virtually all the other areas and affect virtually all aspects of the software life cycle. (So, in retrospect, emphasizing just Programming in the name of the conference was perhaps somewhat short-sighted, but at least the acronym is pronounceable and easy to remember!) This year's ECOOP attracted 146 submissions from around the world — making the selection process even tougher than usual. The selected papers range in topic from programming language and database issues to analysis and design and reuse, and from experience reports to theoretical contributions.

The selection of papers was carried out during a two-day Programme Committee meeting in Geneva. All papers were reviewed in advance by at least three people. Papers were judged according to their originality, relevance and presentation quality. All papers were judged purely on their own merits, independently of other submissions. In most cases, authors of rejected papers received detailed comments on how to improve their manuscripts. In general, the quality of submissions was quite high, but we noted that many authors were making some common errors in the presentation of their results (such as not clearly demonstrating what was new or original). Authors who are in any doubt about how to prepare their papers for ECOOP are well advised to consult the excellent article by Alan Snyder in the January 1991 issue of the ACM OOPS Messenger on "How to Get Your Paper Accepted at OOPSLA." Although the article was not written with ECOOP in mind, it contains much good advice for authors submitting manuscripts to *any* conference!

This year's ECOOP is the first which is being run under the auspices of a formal international body rather than an ad hoc steering committee. AITO is the Association Internationale pour les Technologies Objets (the acronym is more pronounceable in French than in English — and turns out to mean "genuine" in Finnish!), and was founded during ECOOP 92 in Utrecht by a number of people who have been involved in various ways in running previous ECOOPs. AITO not only provides a formal mechanism for ensuring the continuation of ECOOP, but it also provides a legal (non-profit) entity that can facilitate the financing of future conferences. ECOOP 94 is now planned to be held in Bologna, Italy. Bids will be considered by AITO for hosting future ECOOPs. Please direct all inquiries to the AITO president, Pierre Cointe, (Ecole des Mines de Nantes, 3 rue Marcel Sembat 44049 Nantes Cedex 04, France. E-mail: cointe@emn.fr).

ECOOP consists not only of the technical programme represented in these proceedings, but also includes a strong tutorial programme covering both introductory and advanced object-oriented topics, a workshop programme mainly addressing the research community, a vendors' exhibition of new products and object-oriented literature, and a demonstration exhibition of innovative software. In addition to the programme committee and the referees, therefore, thanks must also go out to the conference chair, Gerhard Barth, and to those responsible for the organisation of the various ECOOP events: Walter Olthoff, Derek Coleman, Dieter Rombach, Jens Palsberg, Ansgar Bernardi and Walter Sommer, and the local organisation crew headed by Sabine Wagner and Reinhard Lafrenz.

Finally, I would like to thank the authors who all made valiant efforts to provide me with electronic copies of their papers conforming to common guidelines, despite the use of no less than seven different and incompatible document preparation systems (and even more variants). Their efforts have been very helpful in approaching a consistent appearance for these proceedings, in spite of the diverse origins of the papers.

May, 1993

Oscar Nierstrasz
ECOOP 93 Programme Chair

Organising Committee

Conference chair: Gerhard Barth (Germany)
Programme chair: Oscar Nierstrasz (Switzerland)
Organizing chair: Walter Olthoff (Germany)
Tutorials: Derek Coleman (United Kingdom)
Workshops: Dieter Rombach (Germany)
Panels: Jens Palsberg (Denmark)
Exhibition: Ansgar Bernardi (Germany)
Demonstrations: Walter Sommer (Germany)

Sponsors

AITO (Association Internationale pour les Technologies Objets)
DFKI (German Research Centre for Artificial Intelligence)
University of Kaiserslautern

Co-Sponsoring and Contributing Organisations

Gesellschaft für Informatik   Hewlett-Packard GmbH
ACM SIGPLAN   IBM Deutschland GmbH
Daimer Benz AG   Siemens-Nixdorf AG

Programme Committee

Mehmet Aksit	University of Twente
Pierre America	Philips Research Laboratories
Bruce Anderson	University of Essex
Jean Bézivin	Université de Nantes
François Bodart	Facultés Universitaires de Namur
Jean-Pierre Briot	University of Tokyo
Stefano Crespi Reghizzi	Politecnico di Milano
Elspeth Cusack	British Telecom
Klaus R. Dittrich	Universität Zürich
Simon Gibbs	Université de Genève
Chris Horn	Trinity College, University of Dublin
Ralph E. Johnson	Univ. of Illinois at Urbana-Champaign
Gerti Kappel	University of Vienna
Claus Lewerentz	Forschungszentrum Informatik (FZI)
Ole Lehrmann Madsen	Aarhus University
Boris Magnusson	Lund University
Bertrand Meyer	ISE Inc.
Birger Møller-Pedersen	Norwegian Computer Center
Max Mühlhäuser	University of Karlsruhe
Remo Pareschi	ECRC GmbH
Anna-Kristin Pröfrock	Siemens Nixdorf Software Eng. GmbH
Markku Sakkinen	University of Jyväskyä
Dave Thomas	Object Technology International Inc.
Mario Tokoro	Sony CSL / Keio University
André Weinand	Ubilab, Union Bank of Switzerland
Akinori Yonezawa	University of Tokyo
Roberto Zicari	Johann Wolfgang Goethe-Universität

Referees

Bruno Achauer
Peter Andersen
Jean-Marc Andreoli
Marc Andries
Marie-Jo Bellosta
Dag Belsnes
Andreas Birrer
Anders Björnerstedt
Peter Boehnlein
Marc Bourgois
Michael Bouschen
Søren Brandt
Christian Breiteneder
Rolf de By
Eduardo Casais
Shigeru Chiba
Hagen Conradi
Laurent Dami
Birgit Demuth
Roland Ducournau
Gregor Engels
Fabrizio Ferrandina
Oliver Frick
Harald Fuchs
Nobuhisa Fujinami
Philippe Gautron
Hans-Werner Gellersen
Andreas Geppert
Wolfgang Gerteis
Herbert Gold
Jan Goossenaerts
Thorsten Gorchs
Nicolas Graube
Rachid Guerraoui
Michel Habib
Görel Hedin
Martin Hofmann
Kohei Honda
Yasuaki Honda
Marianne Huchard

Yutaka Ishikawa
Dirk Jonscher
Karl-Heinz Köster
Jørgen Lindskov Knudsen
Hiroki Konaka
Shinji Kono
Dimitri Konstantas
Angelika Kotz-Dittrich
Stein Krogdahl
Michel Kuntz
Tsu-Min Kuo
Morten Kyng
Danny Lange
Doug Lea
Torsten Leidig
Lone Leth
Anund Lie
Frank J. van der Linden
Thomas Lindner
Ling Liu
Kim Jensen Møller
Kai-Uwe Mätzel
Gerhard Müller
Munenori Maeda
Satoshi Matsuoka
Shahrzade Mazaher
Jeff McAffer
Vicki de Mey
Sten Minör
Peter Axel Nielsen
Silvia Nittel
Jan Overbeck
Jens Palsberg
Michael Papathomas
Jean François Perrot
Steven Proctor
Georg Raeder
G.H.B. Rafsanjani
Stefan Rausch-Schott
Tim Regan

Werner Retschitzegger
Peter Roesch
Jean-Claude Royer
Andreas Rueping
Elmer Sandvad
Ichiro Satoh
Bruno Schäffer
Stefan Scherrer
Alex Schill
Joachim Schimpf
Duri Schmidt
Michael Schrefl
Michael Schwartzbach
Emil Sekerinski
Jon Skretting
Paal Soergaard
Markus Stumptner
Antero Taivalsaari
Akikazu Takeuchi
Takao Tenma
Bent Thomsen
Dave Thomson
Hideki Tsuiki
Stefan Vieweg
Juha Vihavainen
Andrei Voronkov
Shigeru Watari
Andrew Watson
Franz Weber
Clazien Wezeman
Helmut Wiegmann
Alan Wills
Jeremy Wilson
Mike Wilson
Philip Yelland
Peter Young
Andreas Zamperoni
Christian Zeidler
Walter Zimmer
Eddy G. Zondag

Contents

Keynote Address (Abstract)

Intimate Computing and the Memory Prosthesis: A Challenge for Computer
Systems Research? 1
  Michael G. Lamming (Rank Xerox EuroPARC)

Frameworks and Reuse

Active Programming Strategies in Reuse 4
  Mary Beth Rosson and John M. Carroll (IBM — T.J. Watson Research Center)

Frameworks in the Financial Engineering Domain: An Experience Report 21
  Andreas Birrer and Thomas Eggenschwiler (Union Bank of Switzerland)

Integrating Independently-Developed Components in
Object-Oriented Languages 36
  Urs Hölzle (Stanford University)

Concurrency and Distribution I

Encapsulating Plurality 57
  Andrew P. Black and Mark P. Immel (Digital Equipment Corporation)

Object Oriented Interoperability 80
  Dimitri Konstantas (University of Geneva)

Implementation of Distributed Trellis 103
  Bruno Achauer (University of Karlsruhe)

Types & Subtypes

A New Definition of the Subtype Relation 118
  *Barbara Liskov (MIT Lab for Computer Science) and Jeannette M. Wing
  (Carnegie-Mellon University)*

Attaching Second-Order Types to Methods in an Object-Oriented Language 142
  Yves Caseau (Bellcore) and Laurent Perron (Ecole Normale Supérieure)

Typed Sets as a Basis for Object-Oriented Database Schemas 161
  *Herman Balsters, Rolf A. de By (University of Twente) and Roberto Zicari
  (Johann Wolfgang Goethe-Universität)*

Invited Talk

The OSI Managed-Object Model 185
  Colin Ashford (Bell-Northern Research)

Languages and Inheritance

Nested Mixin-Methods in Agora 197

Patrick Steyaert, Wim Codenie, Theo D'Hondt, Koen De Hondt, Carine Lucas and Marc Van Limberghen (Free University of Brussels)

Solving the Inheritance Anomaly in Concurrent Object-Oriented
Programming...220

José Meseguer (SRI International)

Type Inference of SELF: Analysis of Objects with Dynamic and Multiple
Inheritance..247

Ole Agesen (Stanford University), Jens Palsberg and Michael I. Schwartzbach (Aarhus University)

Time-Dependent Behaviour

Predicate Classes..268

Craig Chambers (University of Washington)

TOOA: A Temporal Object-Oriented Algebra 297

Ellen Rose (University of Toledo) and Arie Segev (University of California)

A Timed Calculus for Distributed Objects with Clocks 326

Ichiro Satoh (Keio University) and Mario Tokoro (Sony CSL / Keio University)

Concurrency and Distribution II

A Language Framework for Multi-Object Coordination..346

Svend Frølund and Gul Agha (University of Illinois at Urbana-Champaign)

PANDA — Supporting Distributed Programming in C++...361

Holger Assenmacher, Thomas Breitbach, Peter Buhler, Volker Hübsch and Reinhard Schwarz (University of Kaiserslautern)

Transparent Parallelisation Through Reuse: Between a Compiler and a Library
Approach 384

Jean-Marc Jézéquel (IRISA)

OO Analysis and Design

Design Patterns: Abstraction and Reuse of Object-Oriented Design 406

Erich Gamma (Taligent, Inc.), Richard Helm (IBM - T.J. Watson Research Center), Ralph E. Johnson (University of Illinois at Urbana-Champaign) and John Vlissides (IBM - T.J. Watson Research Center)

ObjChart: Tangible Specification of Reactive Object Behavior...............................432

Dipayan Gangopadhyay (IBM - T.J. Watson Research Center) and Subrata Mitra (University of Illinois at Urbana-Champaign)

O-O Requirements Analysis: an Agent Perspective 458
Eric Dubois, Philippe Du Bois and Michaël Petit (Facultés Universitaires de Namur)

Reflection

Designing an Extensible Distributed Language with a Meta-Level
Architecture..482
Shigeru Chiba and Takashi Masuda (University of Tokyo)

MetaFlex: A Flexible Metaclass Generator 502
Richard Johnson and Muru Palaniappan (Aldus Engineering)

Panel Discussion (Position Statements)

Aims, Means, and Futures of Object-Oriented Languages: Programming Styles
and Tool Support...528
Mike Banahan (European C++ User Group), L. Peter Deutsch (Sun Laboratories), Boris Magnusson (University of Lund), and Jens Palsberg (Chairperson, Aarhus University)

Author Index 531

Intimate Computing and the Memory Prosthesis: A Challenge for Computer Systems Research?

(Abstract)

Michael G. Lamming

Rank Xerox EuroPARC

Cambridge, England

At EuroPARC we are trying to build a human *memory prosthesis* — a portable device to help individuals remember things. It will automatically capture and organise predefined classes of information and provide easy ways to recall it when needed, perhaps without even being asked. We call this device a memory prosthesis because it augments normal human memory. It differs from most other information systems in that it focuses on helping the user recall things *they once knew*. Our objective for the memory prosthesis is to assist users with everyday memory problems. Target tasks for the memory aid include: recalling names of people, places, and procedures, finding files, papers and notes, in whatever medium they are expressed, and remembering to perform tasks.

The memory prosthesis is an example of a new class of interactive system we envisage will be made possible by forthcoming advances in micro-electronics. Using cellular radio and infrared technology computers are able to communicate with each other without wires. This new development heralds the dawn of mobile computing. At present radio transceivers are large and power hungry, so much so that the machines to which the transceivers are attached are fairly large. We are looking a short while into the future when mobile computers will be somewhat smaller, indeed small enough to be worn rather than carried — perhaps resembling a watch or piece of jewellery. We look to a time when people don't have to remember to take their computer with them, they *wear* it and take it everywhere.

Such systems will have several fundamental capabilities not previously available on such a wide scale. They will dynamically connect and communicate, not only with each other, but with office equipment, domestic appliances and much of the other business and consumer electronic equipment that surrounds us.

The wireless communication technology used by these systems will be cellular — perhaps based upon the new digital cellular telephone standards. The low-power requirements of a tiny wearable computer will limit the range to a few meters and so communication cells will be small. The consequence of relying on small cells for communication is simple yet profound, mobile computers will know where they are. To find out their location they simply ask the nearest non-mobile object.

O.M. Nierstrasz (Ed.): ECOOP '93, LNCS 707, pp. 1-3, 1993.
© Springer-Verlag Berlin Heidelberg 1993

So to summarise: computers will be small enough to wear and take everywhere; they will be embedded in domestic appliances, office and consumer equipment; they will talk to each other using cellular wireless communications; and they will know where they are.

Taken together these facilities provide us with another view of mobile computing. Popular views of mobile computing regard it as a tool providing access to information and computation whilst the owner is away from his or her desk. We view it the other way round. Our computers can now gain continuous access to *us* and our immediate environment, wherever we are. In consequence, our personal computer will be able to find out much more about us, and like any other personal assistant, the more it knows the more useful it can be. To distinguish this style of system from *personal computing*, we have coined a new phrase: *intimate computing*.

Carrying a computer around *everywhere* offers almost limitless opportunities to capture useful information. Wherever we go, whatever we do, our tiny computer can *automatically* liaise with the equipment we use to do our work, with the portable computers belonging to the people we meet, and with the devices embedded in the building where we work, to construct a detailed personal cross-reference to much of the information with which we come into contact. Indeed, one of the most likely down-sides for intimate computing is the ease with which we may drown in the incoming tide of unstructured data — *unless it is filtered and organised automatically too.*

Most personal information systems, paper-based or computer-based, require some help from the user to construct a useful database. Typically the *user* has to recognise that an item of information might be required in the future; he or she must then make the effort to *capture* it; and lastly, and perhaps most importantly, he or she has to *organise* the information in a manner that makes it easy to find it again. But to do this, the user must be able to predict the situation in which the information will be needed and think up some indexing terms which he or she guesses might plausibly spring to mind the next time the information is sought. A common problem is to guess incorrectly! For example, Mary may choose to file a useful journal article by author or title, yet subsequently only manage to recall that it was the one her boss gave to her.

This example highlights a well established feature of the human memory system — people are particularly good at recalling activities from their own lives. Psychologists call this mechanism *episodic* or *autobiographical memory*. Experiments have shown that humans are not particularly good at remembering the *time* of an episode in their life, but they are much better at remembering *where* the episode occurred, *who* they were with, or *what* they were doing. We call this the *context*.

On the other hand, computers are excellent at recording the *exact* time an item of information was created, stored, communicated or processed in some way. For example, if Mary chooses to write a note about the journal article on her portable computer, the computer will almost certainly timestamp the note for her. In fact almost every computer transaction is timestamped in some way already. Electronic files are timestamped, telephone call-times are recorded for billing, faxes have the arrival time printed on them, and even each frame of a video sequence contains a time code. Moreover, computers are very good at searching through large bodies of data for items with a particular timestamp. So if we can give a computer system an exact timestamp it won't take very long to find all the items that are tagged with the same date and time. Yet as we have stressed already, context is fairly easy for humans to remember while exact timestamps are not. If only the context that gave rise to an item of useful information could be used by the computer to find the same item later on...

Previous work at EuroPARC has shown how this might be achieved with mobile technology. For example, Newman and his colleagues have demonstrated a technique called *episode recognition* [2]. Location data obtained from Active Badges can be used to construct automatically, a diary of an individual's life expressed in terms of their location and encounters with other members of staff and visitors. Experiments have shown that these chronicles are a powerful aid to recall, and can be used both to index, and retrieve other less memorable data collected automatically at about the same time. As a result it has been suggested that a more comprehensive diary containing richer descriptions of the user's activities might provide a useful indexing mechanism for navigating through a huge database of personal information [1]. We now believe it is possible to design a computer system in which imprecise informal yet personal memories we have for past events can be used as keys to recover detailed information about the event itself.

Clearly our primary motivation for building this system is to provide more effective support for human memory. But in doing so, we are encountering all sorts of technical problems for which we have no convenient solution. Nevertheless, our programme of work proceeds in anticipation of acceptable solutions becoming available shortly. By trying to build this demanding application we hope to create another small focus for research in computer science and engineering and highlight some of the technical challenges that lie ahead for all of us.

References

[1] Lamming, M. G., & Newman, W. M. (1992). *Activity-based Information Retrieval: Technology in Support of Personal Memory.* In F. H. Vogt (Ed.), Information Processing '92. Proceedings of the 12th World Computer Congress, Vol. III pp. pp 68-81. Madrid: Elsevier Science Publishers (North-Holland).

[2] Newman, W., Eldridge, M., & Lamming, M. (1991). *Pepys: Generating Autobiographies by Automatic Tracking.* In Proceedings of the second European conference on computer supported cooperative work. Amsterdam.

Active Programming Strategies in Reuse

Mary Beth Rosson and John M. Carroll

IBM T. J. Watson Research Center
Yorktown Heights, New York 10598, USA

Abstract. In order to capitalize on the potential for software reuse in object-oriented programming, we must better understand the processes involved in software reuse. Our work addresses this need, analyzing four experienced Smalltalk programmers as they enhanced applications by reusing new classes. These were *active* programmers: rather than suspending programming activity to reflect on how to use the new components, they began work immediately, recruiting code from example usage contexts and relying heavily on the system debugger to guide them in applying the borrowed context. We discuss the implications of these findings for reuse documentation, programming instruction and tools to support reuse.

1 Introduction

A key attraction of object-oriented programming languages is the potential they offer for the reuse of software components. A well-designed object class defines a tightly encapsulated bundle of state and behavior that can be "plugged into" a target application to fill some functional need — hence the popular metaphor of a "software IC" [4,5]. And while most of this potential has been asserted rather than demonstrated, empirical evidence documenting the advantages of an object-oriented language for code reuse is beginning to emerge [17]. At this point, however, we know very little about the *process* of component reuse and thus how we might best support reuse activities.

A programmer attempting to recruit existing software components for his or her current project must carry out two basic tasks. First, the candidate component(s) must be identified. This may be trivial in cases where the component was self-generated or is already familiar to the programmer (see, e.g., [6,16]). However, much of the missed potential in software reuse arises in situations where the programmer knows little or nothing about the component in advance. As component libraries increase in size, the difficulty of locating novel functionality increases commensurately. Not surprisingly, researchers have begun to apply a variety of classification and information-retrieval techniques to address the difficult problem of locating unknown functionality within large class libraries [12,21].

Once a candidate component has been identified, the programmer must incorporate the component into the ongoing project. Again, if the component is self-generated or already familiar, this process is simplified: the programmer already knows what it does and how it is used, and merely must apply this knowledge to the new situation. But for unfamiliar components, the programmer must engage in at

O.M. Nierstrasz (Ed.): ECOOP '93, LNCS 707, pp. 4-20, 1993.
© Springer-Verlag Berlin Heidelberg 1993

least some form of analysis, determining what the component does and how it can contribute to current needs, and then designing and implementing the code needed to extract the desired functionality [2, 10]. Researchers are only beginning to explore how one might document code intended for reuse (see, e.g., [14]). But from the perspective of a programmer considering reuse, one requirement is clear: understanding how to use a component must take less time and effort than (re)building the component itself. Indeed, given programmers' general preference for self-generated code, the cost of reusing a component should be considerably less than that of creating it.

This paper seeks to elaborate the requirements for reuse documentation and tool support through analysis of experts carrying out a reuse task. We observed Smalltalk programmers enhancing an application through the reuse of classes we provided. Most generally, our goal was to characterize the strategies and concerns of the programmers as they attempted to reuse the novel classes — by understanding what does and does not work well in the current reuse situation, we can begin to reason about possible modifications or enhancements. More specifically, however, we were interested in the role that examples might play in documenting reusable components. We have been researching example-based programming environments for learning and for reuse [3,13,20,22], and this empirical setting provides an opportunity to examine experts' natural strategies for finding and applying example information.

2 The Reuse Situation

Four experienced Smalltalk programmers participated in the study. All had been programming in Smalltalk/V® PM [8] for over two years, and had over 10 years of general programming experience. All had worked on user interface development in Smalltalk, largely on building components for advanced user interfaces (e.g., multimedia objects, direct manipulation techniques, visual programming).

Each programmer completed two reuse projects, in two separate sessions. The reuse situation approximated the application prototyping activities these programmers carry out in their normal work environment, in that both projects involved an enhancement to the user interface of an already-written interactive application. The applications were simple but non-trivial examples of Smalltalk projects; in debriefing sessions after the experiment, all of the programmers judged that these were representative reuse programming tasks. The order of the projects was counterbalanced — one project served as the first project for two of the programmers, the other as the first for the other two. During their second sessions, programmers were introduced to the Reuse View Matcher [22] and were allowed to use this tool while completing the project. Due to space limitations, this paper will not discuss the second set of sessions involving the Reuse View Matcher.

The programmers were read brief instructions at the beginning of each session, describing the application they were to enhance, and identifying the class they were to reuse in making this enhancement. They were told that they were not expected to spend "more than a couple of hours" on the project and that they should not worry if they did not complete it in this amount of time. Finally, the programmers were asked to "think aloud" while they worked, to vocalize their plans and concerns as they worked as much as possible without interfering with their activities [9].

After hearing these instructions, the programmers were given an extended introduction (approximately 20 minutes) to the application to be enhanced; this involved going over a hierarchical view of the major application classes, a design diagram of application objects and their connections, descriptions of typical interaction scenarios, as well as a comprehensive walk-through of the code. The intent was to familiarize them with the application enough so that their problem-solving efforts would focus on the reuse of the new class rather than on understanding how the existing application worked. No information other than the name was provided about the class to be reused.

During the reuse task, programmers worked at their own pace in a standard Smalltalk/V PM environment. The experimenters took notes and made videotapes of the programming activity on the display, occasionally prompting the programmer to comment on a plan or concern. All projects were completed within one and a half to two hours.

2.1 The Color-Mixer Project

One of the projects consisted of an enhancement to a color-mixer. The color-mixer converts rgb values input by the user to create custom colors; these colors are stored in and retrieved from a database of named colors. The original application has three buttons for red, green and blue (see Figure 1); clicking one of these buttons brings up a dialog box in which the user types an integer to manipulate a color component. The color being edited is displayed as a "swatch", and is flanked by the list of saved colors. Users can select colors from the list, as well as adding and deleting colors.

Because everything in Smalltalk is an object, and because objects typically inherit a good deal of their functionality, it is difficult to characterize the "size" of applications. However, the most important objects in the color-mixer are instances of six classes (see Figure 1): ColorMixer, ColorMixWindow, ButtonPane, ListPane, GraphPane and Dictionary. The last four classes in the list are components of the standard library. The number of methods in these six classes ranges from six to 54, with an additional 118 to 338 inherited methods.

The programmer's task was to replace the button+dialog box input style with horizontal sliders. No information was provided concerning the appearance or functionality of the slider, only that they were to use the new class HorizSliderPane. A typical solution involves the editing of the existing openOn: method (this is the method that creates and initializes the windows and subpanes, and the button creation code must be replaced with analogous code for the sliders), and the addition of four new methods (to handle activity in each of the sliders, and to draw any given slider).

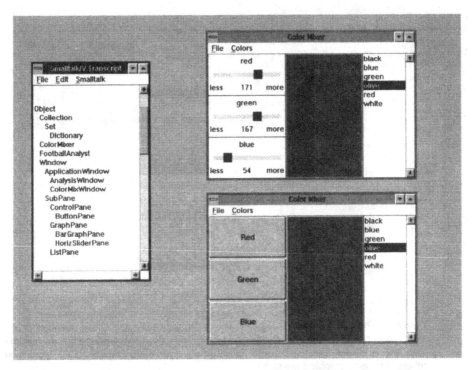

Figure 1. The Color-mixer Project: On the left is a listing of the major classes involved in the color-mixer and football analyst applications; indentation in the list signifies superclass-subclass relationships. In the upper right is the original color-mixer; beneath it is the application enhanced to use sliders as input devices.

The class library included an example application already making use of HorizSliderPane. The example usage was a football analysis program, in which five sliders are used to manipulate defensive player characteristics (e.g., speed, age, height), and the predicted consequences of the characteristics (e.g., sacks, interceptions, tackles) are graphed in a separate pane. This application uses five main classes (FootballAnalyst, HorizSliderPane, BarGraphPane, AnalysisWindow, and Dictionary; only Dictionary is part of the standard library; see Figure 1); method count ranges from five to 33, with from 118 to 363 inherited methods. Because one of our research goals was to examine experts' strategies for discovering and employing example usage information, the programmers were not told of the example application in advance.

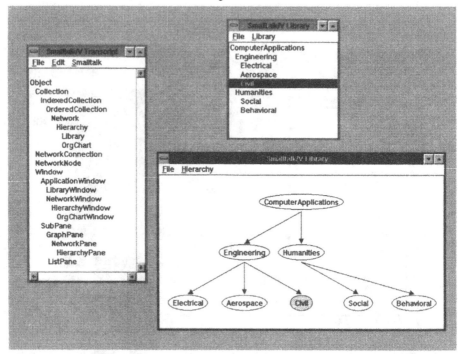

Figure 2. The Library Project: On the left is a listing of the major classes involved in the library and organization chart applications; indentation in the list signifies superclass-subclass relationships. In the upper right is the original library application; beneath it is the application enhanced to use a graphical hierarchy.

2.2 The Library Project

The second project consisted of enhancements to a library acquisitions application. This application manages a hierarchical collection of book categories (e.g., Computer Applications broken into Electrical Engineering, Aerospace Engineering, etc.); categories are annotated with information about acquisitions (e.g., number of books, titles). Hierarchical structure is conveyed via an indented list (see Figure 2), and users manipulate the categories by selecting a list item and making menu selections. In this way, they can add and delete categories, rename categories, and browse and edit the acquisitions information.

The library project uses five main classes (Library, NetworkNode, ListPane, NetworkConnection and LibraryWindow; only ListPane is part of the standard hierarchy, and the Library class inherits from two novel superclasses, Network and Hierarchy; see Figure 2). The method count for these five classes ranges from 4 to 54, with from 118 to 319 inherited methods.

Programmers were asked to enhance this project by using the new class HierarchyPane; again, they were told nothing of the appearance or functionality of the target class. An instance of this class is able to graph a hierarchical network of nodes (see Figure 2). It also can identify nodes or connections selected via a mouse click. Finally, the subpane allows users to name nodes by typing directly onto the graphed elements.

HierarchyPane differs from HorizSliderPane, in that much of its functionality is inherited from its superclass NetworkPane. Further, it was designed to work in concert with a number of other novel classes (HierarchyWindow, Node, NetworkNode and NetworkConnection), whereas HorizSliderPane is a relatively "standalone" component. A typical solution for reusing HierarchyPane in the library application involves creation of a new LibraryWindow class as a subclass of HierarchyWindow (thereby inheriting the ability to draw, select, and name nodes in the graph), and the updating of five methods from the original LibraryWindow class (the methods for adding, removing and showing acquisitions for a selected category, the method defining the menu, and the openOn: method).

As for the color-mixer project, the class hierarchy included an example usage of HierarchyPane — an organization chart, in which the nodes correspond to employees, and in which employees of various job descriptions (e.g., staff member, secretary, visitor) can be added to the hierarchy, given names, reassigned, and given project descriptions. The example uses seven main classes (OrgChart, OrgChartWindow, HierarchyPane, Node NetworkNode, NetworkConnection, and TextField; none of these are part of the standard hierarchy, and both OrgChartWindow and HierarchyPane inherit from novel superclasses; see Figure 2). The method count for these classes ranges from 1 to 37, with inherited methods ranging from 118 to 442. Programmers were not told in advance about the HierarchyPane usage example.

3 Reuse of Uses

In most discussions of component reuse in object-oriented systems, the focus has been on the class or classes reused. Design methodologies attempt to articulate characteristics of reusable classes [15,18] and tool builders develop techniques for classifying and retrieving useful classes [12,21] The dominant metaphor is "construction" — the programmer finds parts that can be reused, modifies them as necessary and connects them together (see, e.g., [4,5]).

Our observations suggest that this focus on components may be over-simplified. To develop the knowledge needed to reuse the components directly, the programmers would have had to stop work on their overarching goal — enhancing the project they had been given — and spend time analyzing and reflecting on the target class. These programmers were too focussed on their end goal to engage in protracted analysis. Instead, they made active use of all resources available in the environment, and began programming immediately. This led them to reuse the components only indirectly, through the reuse of "uses". That is, the main entity participating in the reuse programming was not the target class but rather the *example application of that class*. The programming consisted of finding and reusing the patterns of component reuse reified in the example application. As one programmer put it, on discovering the example application, "so there's a solution in the system!"

The extensive reuse of the example occurred despite mixed feelings expressed by the programmers. There was a sense that this wasn't the "right" way to reuse a class, that it was somehow cheating or taking the easy way out. One programmer said that he would look at the example only if all else failed, but then immediately began to work with it. Another viewed the example as a mixed blessing, because although it offered information on how to use the target class, it now required analysis itself: "Whenever you provide help, you provide trouble, now I have to understand this!" However, when probed about these feelings at the close of the experiment, the programmers indicated that the strategy of borrowing heavily from examples is one they use frequently in prototyping Smalltalk applications, and that their reservations were due to a perceived demand to use more conservative methods in this experimental situation.

Smalltalk provides explicit support for the identification and reuse of example usage context through its "senders" query which returns a list of methods in which a target message is sent. An experienced programmer can browse this list and make reasonable guesses as to which other classes if any are already using the class of interest; if motivated, they can then explore these other classes to discover why and how the target class is being used. All of the programmers made early and repeated use of the senders query; further, they showed an ability to discriminate among the various messages defined for the target class, asking for senders only on the more important methods (e.g., a method providing the contents for the subpane): "AnalysisWindow seems to be figuring prominently as a sender of interesting messages".

3.1 Reusing Pieces of an Example

The most common reuse of the example applications consisted of borrowing code used as the interface to the target class, both blocks of code copied out of methods and entire methods. For instance, all of the programmers borrowed code from the example applications' openOn: methods; by convention this is a message sent to a window which instantiates the various subpanes, defining their graphical and behavioral characteristics. The instantiation of subpanes in Smalltalk/V is often complex, and typically includes the definition of events that the subpane will handle. Thus copying an instantiation code snippet (8-15 lines of code) can save considerable time in working out exactly how a new kind of subpane needs to be initialized.

Sometimes the borrowed code was not directly reusable itself, but rather was used more as a functional specification. In working out slider event handling for the color-mixer project, the programmers copied over the sliderActive: method from the football program. This method does three things: first, the affected slider processes the mouse activity; second, the relevant player characteristic is updated; and third, predicted player performance is graphed. Only the first of these events maps directly to (and thus could be reused in) the color-mixer project. Nonetheless, the programmers were able to understand the code in **sliderActive:** as a specification of what they needed to do in their own version: process slider activity, re-set the model data (in this case, the color settings), and display the results (the new color swatch).

On a few occasions, the borrowed code came from work the programmers had just completed themselves (as in the "new code reuse" situation described in [6]). For example, both programmers working on the color-mixer first developed the code for one slider, then worked from that code to implement the other two. In these cases, the programmers knew exactly what needed to be changed, and the "programming" consisted simply of the physical edits.

In general, the copy/edit strategy worked quite well (see also [16]). It reduced the amount of typing required of the programmer, and helped to insure that the details of the code (e.g., placement of line separators) would be correct. More importantly, it removed the burden of analyzing the target class enough to generate the correct protocol for a particular usage situation, enabling a rapid programming progress. For many parts of the borrowed protocol (e.g., the event definitions in the **openOn:** method), the programmers knew what parts of the code needed to be edited and how to do this.

However, the copy/edit strategy did lead to some problems stemming from the novel parts of the target class' protocol, in that the programmers were now able to copy and "use" protocol that they didn't fully understand. A good example comes from one programmer's work on the color-mixer. In the football analyst example, each slider is instantiated with a different starting value. Because the slider instantiation code was copied from the football **openOn:**, instantiation of the **value** variable also became part of the color-mixer **openOn:**. The **value** attribute is not generic to subpanes, so the programmer did not know off-hand whether it was prerequisite to slider functioning, and if so, what a reasonable starting value would be for the color-mixer. The programmer did not know enough about the protocol for sliders to answer these questions, so he simply made a guess. Later on, this guess caused problems, as the initial positions of the sliders did not match the starting color (white). Subsequently, the programmer solved the problem not by going back and correcting the initialization code, but rather by adding code at a later point that simulated the selection of white in the color list pane.

In some cases there was a conflict between the component interface suggested by the example, and the current design of the project. In the football program, the activity of all the sliders is handled by a single method **sliderActive:**. Modeling on the example, one of the programmers began by copying over the method and modifying it to refer to color-mixer objects. However, in the course of doing this, he recognized that there would be a problem in discriminating among the different slider instances. Despite the suggestion by the football example that multiple sliders could be managed by one method, he decided to change his approach and work from the more familiar model of the buttons used by the original user interface. Noting that three separate methods had been written to handle button activity, he developed an analogous set of three slider activity methods.

The Smalltalk environment is very supportive of the copying/editing of example usage code. Programmers can open as many code browsers as they like, and can freely select and paste text among them. In this study, the programmers almost always had at least two browsers open (one for the example and one for the project) and often used more when the code involved a number of embedded messages. In this way, they could preserve their top-level context while going off to answer a question or to find additional relevant code in other classes or methods.

3.2 Reusing an Application Framework

All of the programmers' initial efforts to reuse the example application involved bringing methods or pieces of methods *from* the example application *into* the project. However, the two programmers working on the library project ultimately decided to create a new kind of library window, one that was a sibling of OrgChartWindow (i.e., had HierarchyWindow as a superclass, this was in fact the solution requiring least programming effort). In doing this, they were deciding to *inherit* rather than borrow from the example usage context. After this decision, their activity shifted, as they began bringing code from the original library window into the new window. This was in marked contrast to the programmers working on the color-mixer project, who appeared to never even consider inheriting functionality from the football example.

The decision to subclass reflects a desire to reuse more than just the snippets of code involving the target class; in this case, the programmers elected to adopt the entire application context of the example. In Smalltalk/V PM, this context is normally managed by a window; the window communicates with the underlying application objects (e.g., a hierarchical collection of employees) and with the subpanes used to display application information. Thus reuse of the context can be accomplished by subclassing the application window; reuse of this sort is often referred to as reuse of an "application framework" [7]. Framework reuse brings along the component of interest "for free" in some sense, in that it is already a component of the framework, and the example window already has the code needed to interface between the component and other application objects.

Deciding to reuse the example's application framework had a remarkable effect on the programmers' reuse efforts. What had at first been a rather complex process of tracking down individual methods and instance variables distributed across NetworkWindow, HierarchyWindow and OrgChartWindow, and copying and editing methods or pieces of methods, now became a straightforward process of copying over and updating the menu functions from the original LibraryWindow class. One of the programmers spent over an hour reaching the decision to subclass; once he did, he was rather frustrated at the thought of throwing away all the work he had done so far, but even so was able to complete the project in fifteen minutes.

The problems of tracking down functionality distributed throughout an inheritance hierarchy have been noted before; Taenzer, Ganti and Podar [23] refer to this as the "yoyo" problem. The Smalltalk/V class hierarchy browser offers little support for dealing with hierarchically distributed function, as programmers must navigate from superclass to superclass in search of methods. Taenzer et al. [23] point to this problem as an argument against reuse via inheritance, suggesting that understanding how to subclass an extensive hierarchy requires much more distributed code analysis than simply reusing a component. Our situation offers a new twist on considering whether to reuse functionality directly or through inheritance: when a component has already been incorporated into a rich application framework, programmers may find that indirect inheritance of the component's functionality (i.e., through subclassing the framework) will simplify enormously the task of reusing the component.

Several factors seemed to contribute to the programmers' decision to reuse the application framework for graphical hierarchies. One was simply the difficulties in tracking down, borrowing and integrating function. There seemed to be a sense that the process was more complicated than it should be, e.g., "I should probably be trying to inherit some of this...". When asked later, one of the programmers indicated that it was his realization of how many of his borrowed methods were inherited from superclasses of OrgChartWindow that made him decide to move the library window. For the other programmer, a critical incident was his effort to compile a key method (the one allowing selection of nodes in the graph), and discovering a instance variable of the example window that had no analog in the library application. Up to that point, he had seemed willing to work with the complexity of tracking down and borrowing example protocol, but adding a new (and mysterious) piece of state information was too much.

Another factor may have been the similarity between the example usage and the project. On first discovering the HierarchyWindow class, one programmer tried a simple experiment while voicing his belief that it would never work: he tried opening a HierarchyWindow "on" the library object (an instance of Library, part of the Collection hierarchy). To his (and our!) surprise, this experiment was successful. Of course, the LibraryWindow functionality was not present, but at least the book collection was displayed in a nice graphical hierarchy. This experiment may seem extreme, in that it has a rather low probability of pay-off. However, it was simple to do, and it provided the programmer with considerable insight into the example application that he was able to apply to his later efforts.

The subclassing strategy did simplify the reuse programming project. However, it also introduced some rather subtle problems. There was considerable overlap in the functionality of the example and of the library (e.g., both had facilities for adding and removing elements in a hierarchy, for renaming these elements). One of the programmers, having decided to subclass, wanted to inherit as much functionality as he could. So, when updating the menu selections, rather than copying over the methods from the original library window and editing them to work in this new context, he first tried simply inheriting the methods defined in the superclasses. On the surface, this strategy seemed to work — he was now able to add and delete library categories and rename them. He never realized that the underlying library structure was not being manipulated correctly (the relationships among categories weren't being specified). It may be that programmers following a subclassing strategy are more likely to satisfice, accepting generic inherited functionality that is almost but not quite right simply because it is there and is already working.

4 The Reuse Programming Process

The programmers were opportunistic in the objects of reuse — extensive recruitment of the example contexts reduced considerably the amount they needed to learn about the target class. But they were also opportunistic in how they went about doing the reuse task. They spent little time in deliberated analysis of the example, in understanding how it was going to help or interfere with their enhancement efforts. Rather they began using the code of the example immediately to make progress on their goal. These were *active users* of Smalltalk [1]: as has often been observed for human problem-solving [11[the process we observed was very locally driven, with specific features of the environment and the evolving solution determining each succeeding step.

4.1 Getting Something to Work With

An early goal for all of the programmers was to get an instance of the target class up and running, so that they could see what it looked like. One of the programmers working on the library project was able to use the organization chart example to do this. After discovering the example, he immediately took on the goal of starting it up. He found an OrgChart class method `fromUIIData`, the name of which signalled to him that it was a special "set-up" method, and that he could use it to create an appropriate OrgChart object and start up the application. By doing this, he was able to see what a HierarchyPane looked like, as well as to experiment with the interaction techniques it supported.

With respect to programming activities, the focus of initial efforts for all of the programmers was on modifying the project's `openOn:` method to include the new class: "I want to get one of these things as a subpane". However, while there was some browsing of the target class methods to see how to do this, the browsing tended to yield inferences about class functionality rather than usage protocol; as we noted earlier, the programmers seemed to resist carrying out an analysis of the target class comprehensive enough to allow them to write code to instantiate it for their project. Instead, they sometimes looked for clues in the code they were replacing. Thus the two programmers working on the color-mixer examined the code used to create the buttons, thinking about how they might modify it for sliders (e.g., what events a slider might handle in contrast to a button).

One programmer working on the color-mixer tried to take advantage of other code in the `openOn:` method as well. Noting that HorizSliderPane is a subclass of GraphPane, he examined the code instantiating the color swatch (an instance of GraphPane), thinking that he might be able to build a slider definition from it. This led to a variety of problems, as he began to hypothesize that the slider functionality was somehow built from the scroll bars present in every subpane, and that the protocol controlling these scroll bars for GraphPanes must be critical in creating sliders. This was certainly a reasonable hypothesis on functional grounds, but in fact was quite misleading.

The programmers seemed to feel that successfully instantiating the target class within the project context was a momentous event. It appeared that this was considered to be the major hurdle of the project, and now they could get on with business as usual, adding the remainder of the component's functionality (i.e., its event handling). One explanation for this is that the programmers could "see their end goal in sight" — a new and improved view of their project data. But another equally important factor is that by instantiating the new component as part of the project, the programmers could now rely much more on the environment to guide their programming. In a Smalltalk application, objects are created and code references are established only when the application is run, making the code alone inherently ambiguous and mental simulation of it difficult. In contrast, if the programmer is able to start up an application, all ambiguities in the code are resolved, and the programmer can use Smalltalk's sophisticated interactive debugging tools to analyze and modify the code.

4.2 Debugging into Existence

We have seen that the programmers relied heavily on code already in the environment in attacking the reuse projects. But they also relied heavily on the tools of the environment to locate and make sense of the relevant code. In particular, they repeatedly started up the application they were working on, and looked to see where it "broke" to plan their next move.

Smalltalk is particularly supportive of this debugging-centered style of program construction. The language is non-typed and compiled incrementally, which permits rapid and repeated experimentation with the code used to run an application. The debugger and inspector tools support such experimentation directly, providing flexible access to and manipulation of the runtime context for an application (i.e., objects and their state, messages in progress).

In some cases, the programmers knew something of the steps they would need to take, but used the debugger to help them in carrying these out. Thus, once they had copied the instantiation code from the example application's openOn:, they knew that certain modifications would be necessary: instance variable names needed to be changed, the menu name needed to be changed, the project would need a drawing method, etc. Some of the programmers even carried out some anticipatory activity, perhaps creating a method that they knew they would need, but that they also knew was not yet functional. However, for the most part, they relied on the system to detect the absence of methods or the inappropriate states of objects. In a typical scenario, the programmer would start up the project application, receive a "message not understood" error, return to the example in search of a method with that name, copy the method, perhaps making a few changes, try again and see how far it got, make some changes and try again. This sort of cycle might be repeated many times, but the programmers seemed comfortable with it, and seemed confident that they were making progress.

In other cases, the debugger was used to untangle more subtle problems. So, for example, the superclass HierarchyWindow uses the `network` instance variable to point to the main application object, whereas the original LibraryWindow class uses `library`. A thorough analysis of the example would have revealed the relevant mapping between these two variables. However, the two programmers working on this project simply borrowed the example code as-is and used the debugger to ascertain what role the `network` variable was playing and how to provide this information within their project.

The compiler was used in this opportunistic fashion as well. When dealing with complex pieces of borrowed code, the programmers often would attempt to compile the code before they had completed editing it. The system would flag variable names not defined for the class (e.g., the HierarchyWindow code refers to `graphPane`, while the LibraryWindow uses `pane`), and the programmers would then replace the unknown name with the name of the analogous variable. This minimized the amount to which they needed to read through and analyze the unfamiliar code.

5 Summary and Implications

Our observations describe a process of component reuse in which the component is reused only indirectly, through the reuse of its "uses" — bits of protocol or even entire application frameworks. The programmers we studied pursued this style of reuse piecemeal and opportunistically; they focused initially on getting a runnable albeit skeletal result which they could exercise and improve incrementally, relying heavily on interactive debugging. We have characterized these as "active" programming strategies, an orientation in which programmers directly and immediately enlist and transform their software materials in favor of withdrawing from such activity to analyze and plan.

5.1 Scope of Active Reuse

This work was exploratory empirical research in its scope and scale. It addressed a particular programming situation, application prototyping, which may differ significantly from other situations. However, at least some of our observations are consistent with studies of other reuse situations. Lange and Moher [16] observed that an experienced programmer extending a library of software components was quite likely to use existing components with related functionality as templates or models for the new components. Detienne [6] found that programmers designing and implementing new applications somtimes reused their own code as they worked. Interestingly, the programmers in this study chose not to borrow code from other applications, perhaps because the other applications available were only peripherally related to the problems being solved.

Further research is needed to assess the generality of the more specific strategies we observed. All four programmers relied extensively on the system tools to organize their work, using multiple browsers to maintain their context across different parts of the hierarchy, and using the debugger and inspector to track down and modify missing or inappropriate pieces of borrowed code. It is not clear though what the boundary conditions for such an approach might be — it may be that they are only likely to occur in a tool-rich interpreted environment like Smalltalk.

Some strategies were unique to a particular programmer. For example, only one programmer made the effort to "run" the example application before borrowing code from it. He felt that this gave him a chance to preview the functionality he would be incorporating; it may be that across a wider variety of reuse projects, perhaps involving more complex components, such a strategy would be more prevalent. In another case, one programmer experimented with opening a graphical HierarchyWindow "on" his application data. The success of this experiment conveyed a great deal to him about what the graphical network framework expected in terms of data structures. It is important to understand the generality of such techniques and strategies.

5.2 Consequences of Active Reuse

Beyond the question of generality, we can ask about the consequences of the active programming strategies we observed. For example, two of the programmers did not produce a perfectly correct result, and it is not clear whether or how their problems would have been detected and corrected given unlimited time, or given instructions that emphasized the accuracy of the result. Indeed, the active programming we observed may be inadvisable from a software engineering perspective, if the small errors or inefficiencies introduced by reliance on example code are very difficult to unearth subsequently. Further research is needed to determine what if any strategies experts have developed for minimizing this downside inherent in reuse by example.

It is important not to lose sight of the main benefit of this style of software reuse: these active strategies reflect a creative and effective resolution of the inherent tension between the need to distance oneself from one's own project to study someone else's code, and continuing to make concrete progress toward a desired result. Elsewhere we have characterized such a tension as the "production paradox" [1], wherein users are too focussed on the product they are creating to acquire the skills that will facilitate its creation. In this Smalltalk reuse setting, the programmers' borrowing of example code allowed them to quickly incorporate at least some approximation of the new functionality into their own project; they could then work within their own project context to "learn" the minimum necessary for successful reuse.

5.3 Training and Tools for Active Reuse

Our work has a variety of implications for how objected-oriented programming should be conceptualized, taught and supported. Most generally, it suggests the desirability of a broader view of component reuse: the pluggable "software IC" metaphor [4,5] is not the only way reuse has been conceptualized, but it is a dominant image in talking and thinking about reuse. Both of our target objects (the slider and the graphical hierarchy) could be used as pluggable components; the slider, in particular, is an interface widget and eminently pluggable. However, all four programming projects described here reused the target classes through use of some or all of their example usage contexts. This suggests a more situational view of reuse in which pluggable, context-free reuse is the simple and ideal case.

The programmers we studied invented the strategies we observed or learned them informally from colleagues. As we noted, they occasionally expressed some embarrassment at their own reluctance to fully analyze code they wanted to reuse and their predilection for "stealing" usage protocol. If these practices survive — indeed emerge from — the natural selection pressures of professional programming, we should at least consider that perhaps they should be the topic of instruction in (Smalltalk) programming.

This implication for instruction entrains a related implication for the documentation of software components. Our four programmers were able to find example uses of the target classes, but in many situations this would not be true, and hence an example-oriented reuse strategy would be thwarted. Of course, imagining example-based documentation on a large scale raises many consequent issues. Who will build the examples? One resource is the test programs built in the course of development, and often discarded afterward. Delivering these along with software components would provide some support for the example-oriented strategy at virtually no cost. Another question is what makes a good example. There is a literature on concept formation in cognitive psychology that addresses the issue of how examples are abstracted in comprehension [19]. It is an interesting and open question whether and how similar characteristics bear on reuse.

Finally, this work embodies three themes for tool support: the sequence of activities in reuse programming, recruitment of example usage code, and the use of the system debugger. Our four programmers seemed to follow a loose script: first they instantiated the component in the project context, then they successively elaborated it function by function. Throughout this process they made extensive use of example usage contexts and of the debugger. An obvious implication is to provide tools that more explicitly integrate and coordinate the information needed at each point along the way. Thus tool support might guide reuse activities through a reuse script (for example, a list of target class behaviors to instantiate in the project context), using this script to coordinate the programmer's work with the example usage code, the project code, and the interactive debugging facilities.

Acknowledgements

Important contributions to this work were made by Christine Sweeney and Dan Walkowski, who assisted in the design and development of the reusable components and the example usage contexts.

References

1. J.M. Carroll and M.B. Rosson. The paradox of the active user. In J.M.Carroll (Ed.), *Interfacing thought: Cognitive aspects of human-computer interaction* (pp. 80-111). Cambridge, Mass: MIT Press, 1987.

2. J.M. Carroll and M.B. Rosson. Deliberated evolution: Stalking the View Matcher in design space. *Human-Computer Interaction, 6,* 281-318, 1991.

3. J.M. Carroll, J.A. Singer, R.K.E. Bellamy, and S.R. Alpert. A View Matcher for learning Smalltalk. In *CHI'90 Proceedings* (pp.431-438), New York: ACM, 1990.

4. B.J. Cox. *Object oriented programming: An evolutionary approach.* Reading, Mass.: Addison-Wesley, 1986.

5. B.J. Cox. Building malleable systems from software 'chips'. *Computerworld* (March), 59-68, 1987.

6. F. Detienne. Reasoning from a schema and from an analog in software code reuse. In J.Koenmann-Belliveau, T.G.Moher & S.P.Robertson (Eds.), *Empirical studies of programmers: Fourth workshop.* (pp.5-22). Norwood, NJ: Ablex, 1991.

7. L.P. Deutsch. Design reuse and frameworks in the Smalltalk-80 system. In T.J.Biggerstaff & A.J.Perlis (Eds.), *Software reusability, volume 2: Applications and experience* (pp. 57-72). New York: Addison-Wesley, 1989.

8. Digitalk, Inc. (1989). *Smalltalk/V PM.* Los Angeles: Digitalk, Inc.

9. K.A. Ericsson and H.A. Simon. Verbal reports as data. *Psychological Review, 87,* 215-251, 1980.

10. G. Fischer. Cognitive view of reuse and redesign. *IEEE Software (July),* 60-72, 1987.

11. B. Hayes-Roth and F.A. Hayes-Roth. A cognitive model of planning. *Cognitive Psychology, 3,* 275-310, 1979.

12. R. Helm and Y.S. Maarek. Integrating information retrieval and domain specific approaches for browsing and retrieval in object-oriented class libraries. *Proceedings of OOPSLA'91* (pp. 47-61). New York: ACM, 1991.

13. S. Henninger. (1991). Retrieving software objects in an example-based programming environment. *Proceedings of SIGIR'91* (pp. 251-260). New York: ACM, 1991.

14. R.E. Johnson. Documenting frameworks using patterns. In *Proceedings of OOPSLA'92* (pp. 63-76). New York: ACM, 1992.

15. R.E. Johnson and B. Foote. Designing reusable classes. *Journal of Object-oriented Programming 1(2)*: 22-35, 1988.

16. B.M. Lange and T.G. Moher. Some strategies for reuse in an object-oriented programming environment. In *Proceedings CHI'89* (pp. 69-74), New York: ACM, 1989.

17. J.A. Lewis, S.M. Henry, D.G. Kafura, and R.S. Schulman. An empirical study of the object-oriented paradigm and software reuse. In *Proceedings of OOPSLA'91* (pp. 184-196). New York: ACM, 1991.

18. B. Meyer. *Object-oriented software construction*. New York: Prentice Hall, 1988.

19. R. Millward. Models of concept formation. In R.E.Snow, P.-A. Federico & Montague, W.E. (Eds.), *Aptitude, learning and instruction: Cognitive process analyses*. Hillsdale, NJ: Lawrence Erlbaum Associates, 1979.

20. L. Neal. A system for example-based programming. *Proceedings of CHI'89* (pp. 63-68). New York: ACM, 1989.

21. R.K. Raj and H.M. Levy. A compositional model of software reuse. In *Proceedings of ECOOP'89* (pp. 3-24), London: British Computer Society, 1989,

22. M.B. Rosson, J.M. Carroll, and C. Sweeney. A View Matcher for reusing Smalltalk classes. *Proceedings of CHI'91* (pp. 277-284). New York: ACM, 1991.

23. D. Taenzer, M. Ganti, and S. Podar. Problems in object-oriented software reuse. *Proceedings of ECOOP'89* (pp. 25-38). Cambridge: Cambridge University Press, 1989.

Frameworks in the
Financial Engineering Domain
An Experience Report

Andreas Birrer
Thomas Eggenschwiler

UBILAB
Union Bank of Switzerland
Bahnhofstrasse 45, CH-8021 Zurich, Switzerland
E-mail: {birrer, eggen}@ubilab.ubs.ch

Abstract: To supply the financial engineering community with adequate and timely software support we advocate a reusability oriented approach to software development. The approach focuses on frameworks and reusable building blocks. This paper presents a domain specific framework for a calculation engine to be used in financial trading software. It is as such an example of using frameworks outside their typical domain of graphical user interfaces.

1 Introduction

At UBILAB, the Information Technology Lab of Union Bank of Switzerland, the ET++Swapsmanager project [Egg92] is an effort to find a satisfying way to provide traders with sophisticated software support by employing a reusability-oriented approach based on object technology.

Financial engineering is concerned with the creation and valuation of financial instruments. To help understand the following architecture, we must look at some of the basics that drive financial markets.

The *primary financial markets* are the places (not necessarily physical) where supply of and demand for funds meet. For instance, if a corporation needs money to finance its operating expenses or some other investment – such as buying a subsidiary – there are roughly three sources of funds. The company could go to a bank and apply for a loan. The second possibility is to issue stock (equity securities) and thereby have investors participate in the investment's returns (and risks). The third approach is to issue some sort of bond (debt securities). In all of these cases the investors (suppliers of funds) expect a return to compensate for forgone opportunities. This return is usually in the form of interest payments. From the company's point of view it is the price it has to pay to temporarily dispose of the funds.

Besides the mere price there are other factors such as when the interest payments are due, how these are determined, the currency, the amount of security (collateralisation)

O.M. Nierstrasz (Ed.): ECOOP '93, LNCS 707, pp. 21-35, 1993.
© Springer-Verlag Berlin Heidelberg 1993

provided, etc. With all these variable factors considerable effort, and therefore cost, must be expended to match investors and borrowers and negotiate on the various characteristics of a potential deal. *Financial instruments* help reduce these costs by standardising the conditions under which financial transactions are carried out. Investors and borrowers can then choose the most attractive construction (instrument) available to them; typically with the aid of some intermediary. This is also eased by the fact that most financial instruments are highly fungible and traded anonymously.

Financial instruments have evolved from mere contracts for lending and borrowing to specialised means for transforming various characteristics of funds as corporations have learned how to use such instruments to manage all kinds of risks. Examples of the characteristics are determination of interest amount, interest payment schedules, exposure to market movements and currency conversion. It is therefore possible to customise a transaction by pipe-lining several financial instruments. The result, also called a *synthetic instrument*, is then sold as a package.

Each instrument and its associated practices of trade can be considered as defining one *financial market*. However, for a market to work efficiently, some system for *price indication* is needed. Active participants (especially traders) are the main source for this information. In the markets with high turnover volumes the prices at which deals are concluded are continuously published on electronic networks. We will refer to instruments for which the current price level is publicly known as *standard instruments*.

The price of a standard instrument is almost exclusively determined by supply and demand. But if a new instrument is engineered, how does one find its proper price? A widely accepted approach is to use the prices quoted in high volume financial markets for the derivation of a discount function. The higher the volume traded the more reliable is the price indication.

A *discount function* is used to assign to any cash flow in the future an equivalent value today. This is based on the observable fact that a Dollar received today is worth more than a Dollar received some time in the future; this is also known as the *time value of money*. Deriving a discount function effectively means expressing the time value of money in a market independent form. The present value, and hence the price, of an instrument is found by discounting all its associated (future) cash flows.

Valuation not only makes sense in the context of a single instrument. In effect, small and large collections of deals stemming from various instruments[1] are managed and evaluated on a portfolio basis. This is especially true for investment banks and broker houses that actively trade in these instruments. Exposure to market movements (price

---

[1] In object parlance: an instrument is a class of deals, a deal would be an instance of an instrument.

risk) and performance is measured with respect to an entire portfolio rather than on individual deals.

The rest of the paper is organised as follows: In section 2 we give an introduction to the swaps business and shed some light on the current situation concerning software support. In section 3 we go into the details of a calculation framework for financial instruments. In section 4 we summarise our experiences of the development and usage of the framework.

2 Swaps

Of the kaleidoscopic palette of today's financial instruments we will for the purpose of this paper only consider one genre of financial instruments, so-called *swaps*.

2.1 The Swap Product

Swaps are a fairly recent development. The most common of these structures is the *interest rate swap* where two parties agree to exchange, or swap, two sets of interest payments which are determined by two different interest rates [Kap90]. Hence there are two sides, or legs, to a swap. Typically, one of the interest rates is fixed at a certain percentage of some principal amount and the other is floating, i.e., pegged to some changing market index. Fig. 1 shows a situation where borrowers B and D engage in an interest rate swap. The rationale for doing this is that B can raise funds on floating rate terms comparatively cheaper than D can. Although B supposedly prefers to engage in a fixed rate liability it is still profitable to take on a floating rate debt and then swap it with D who has opposite preferences.

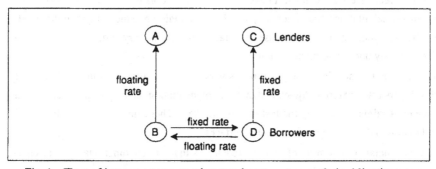

Fig. 1: Flow of interest payments when two borrowers swap their obligations through an interest rate swap

The other frequently met construction is the *currency swap* in which the flow of interest payments is identical to the interest rate swap but with the difference that the two sets of cash flows are denominated in different currencies.

At conclusion of a swap, the two sides must have equal value under the then prevailing market conditions. This possibly calls for a compensation payment by one of the counterparties. The value of one swap side is determined by present valuing each cash flow according to an appropriate discount function.

In trading situations it is not the present value of the two sides that is of most relevance to the trader or the customer. It is either the interest rate of the fixed side or the spread in excess to the floating side that are then referred to as the *price* of the swap (We will use price and rate interchangeably).

As market conditions (interest rates, exchange rates) change, the two sides of a swap perform differently and will eventually be misbalanced. Managing these misbalances on a portfolio basis is of paramount importance to the swaps trader.

2.2   Current Situation

The correct valuation of financial instruments in a trading situation depends on the availability of adequate software tools. Adequacy is needed with respect to both the user interface and the calculation support.

Innovation driven by competition among suppliers of financial instruments requires that software tools must constantly be extended to include calculation support for new financial products.

However, current approaches to the development of software tools in financial engineering are not satisfactory. Software tools are either built on top of a spreadsheet program or as a separate application. Both approaches have a number of deficiencies.

While spreadsheets allow for fast development of new tools they are often too slow for extensive calculations and almost impossible to maintain once the computational models become more complex. The user interface typically is very rudimentary and performs poorly under trading conditions.

Development of standalone applications is very costly and time consuming. Therefore developers often resort to "quick and dirty" implementation techniques in order to meet time constraints dictated by the fast moving markets. These time constraints have also led to minimalistic, menu driven, user interfaces.

A very crucial shortcoming of both approaches is that similar functionality is re-engineered for every new tool.

2.3 Towards better Solutions

Almost each instrument has its own trading practice and jargon. However, when looking at the instruments and the valuation procedures on a more abstract level one can
find many commonalties and interrelationships among them. Most notably:

- Each deal consists of a set of actual or potential cash flows.
- A cash flow has an associated business day on which it is realised.
- The value of any instrument is sensitive to changes in interest rates. Therefore the
  quantification and monitoring of the interest rate sensitivity is applicable to any instrument.
- Arbitrage between different markets tends towards consistent "time value of
  money"-profiles across markets which allows the valuation of one instrument in
  terms of the price structure of other instruments.
- Instruments can easily be expressed in terms of each other when adopting a LEGO®
  (or building blocks) approach in trying to understand financial instruments [Smi87].

These observations led us to the conviction that the domain of financial instruments is
ideally suited for the employment of a framework approach.

However, a framework can not be designed from scratch on paper. Rather, experience
suggests that it must grow bottom-up and successively mature by applying it to different problem (sub-)domains. Therefore, with the notion of a general framework for financial engineering in mind we set out with our first development in the domain of
swaps trading.

Fig. 2 shows a pilot application that was the result of a series of prototypes implemented in collaboration with trading specialists. The purpose of this endeavour was to
acquire initial domain know-how and experiment with various user interfaces.

The upper right window shows a domain specific desktop on which domain items are
depicted as icons. Relationships among the items may be edited through drag-and-drop
type manipulations on the icons. The bottom left window shows an editor in which data
can be modified directly via its graphical depiction by directly dragging a part of the
curve.

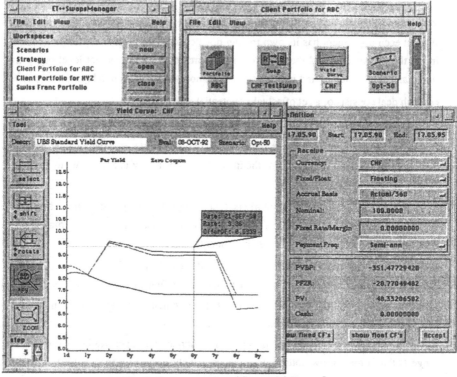

Fig. 2: Screen sample of Swaps Manager I

The following section describes the framework as it is being used in the context of a
swaps trading software.

3 The Architecture of the Calculation Engine Framework

Fig. 3 shows the structure of the framework and the most important objects. We will show the key abstractions in more detail, and then we will describe two scenarios which demonstrate their use.

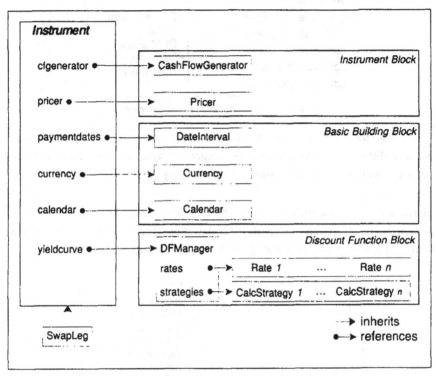

Fig. 3: The calculation engine objects

3.1 The Key Abstractions

As mentioned in section 1 standard instruments and the conventions to guide their trading define financial markets. The most important guidelines deal with the pricing of an instrument. The main problem here is achieving comparability of cash flows occurring at different dates. This is solved through the definition of a discount function which allows to calculate the present value of any cash flow due in the future [Mir91]. This leads to two key abstractions, the *instrument* and the *discount function*.

3.1.1 Instrument

An instrument represents any traded facility for generating cash flows in today's financial markets.

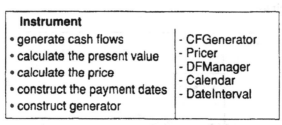

Instrument	
• generate cash flows	- CFGenerator
• calculate the present value	- Pricer
• calculate the price	- DFManager
• construct the payment dates	- Calendar
• construct generator	- DateInterval

Fig. 4: CRC-Card [Beck89] for an instrument

Every instrument has the ability to generate the cash flows from a description and a valid market environment by a discount function manager. It has a connection to objects encapsulating relevant market information (e.g., Currency, Calendar and DFManager).

Because we can't describe the algorithm for cash flow generation at an abstract level, we introduce objects which encapsulate this algorithm. This is a well known design pattern, called *strategy pattern* [Gam92], which we use in several situations.

CFGenerator	
• generate cash flows	- Instrument
	- DFManager
	- Currency
	- Calendar
	- Accrualbasis
	- DateInterval

Fig. 5: CRC-Card for a generator

The CRC-Card of Fig. 5 shows only one responsibility. This narrow set of tasks is typical for a strategy object. A specific implementation of a generator knows more about its instrument and is able to combine its parameters to achieve the results wanted, i.e., a list of cash flows. A similar technique is used for pricing an instrument. Fig. 6 shows the CRC-Card for a *pricer*.

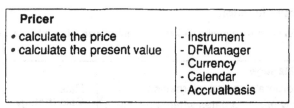

Pricer	
• calculate the price	- Instrument
• calculate the present value	- DFManager
	- Currency
	- Calendar
	- Accrualbasis

Fig. 6: CRC-Card for a pricer

Since Instrument is an abstract class, it can't decide which strategies are useful for a given implementation. It delegates their allocation to its subclasses by means of factory methods. A factory method is a method that is called by a base class to create a subclass dependent object. These are called *DoMakeGenerator* and *DoMakePricer*.

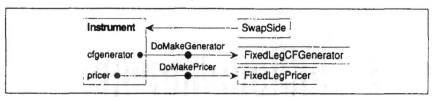

Fig. 7: Factory methods to generate customised strategies

An Instrument's interface is defined at the level of the abstract class, which allows to treat a collection of instruments. This collection generates cash flows as if it were a single instrument. Therefore a portfolio of instruments can itself be modeled as an instrument. Fig. 8 shows the class hierarchy for instruments.

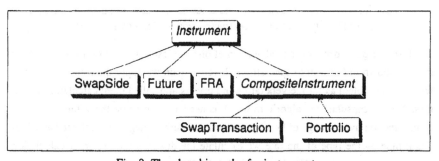

Fig. 8: The class hierarchy for instruments

3.1.2 Discount function

The discount function for a given market mix is implemented by a DFManager.

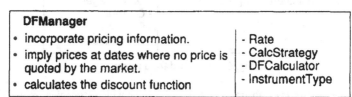

DFManager	
• incorporate pricing information.	- Rate
• imply prices at dates where no price is quoted by the market.	- CalcStrategy - DFCalculator
• calculates the discount function	- InstrumentType

Fig. 9: The CRC-Card for the DFManager

We calculate a discount factor for a given standard instrument by the method of zero-coupon pricing. For different kinds of standard instruments we use different formulas.

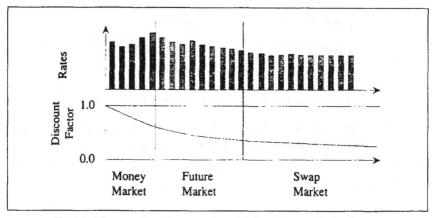

Fig. 10: Discount Function constructed from different kinds of rates

The DFManager forwards the calculation of discount factors (out of different kinds of rates as shown in Fig. 10) to specialised objects. Again we apply the same design pattern to this problem as for the generators and pricers and called them calculation strategies. They encapsulate the algorithm which is needed to compute the value of the discount function over a range of homogenous rates. These strategies are selected at calculation time by the type of the rate we calculate the discount factor for. A calculation strategy may depend on the discount factors at previous points to calculate a correct value. For every type of rate there must exist a calculation strategy.

Fig. 11 shows the structure of a DFManager object. The rates attribute consists of rate objects with each representing a standard instrument.

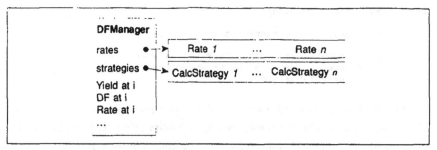

Fig. 11: The structure of a DFManager object

Currently, we support three kinds of standard instruments (Fig. 12).

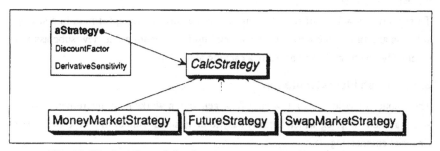

Fig. 12: The interface of the class `CalcStrategy` and it's sublcasses

Based on the above factorisations, the structure of the calculation context may be set-up at will. The `DFManager` inspects its structure when it has to calculate something for the first time and installs the needed strategies (through factory methods).

Consider a trader doing business in Swiss Franc Interest Rate Swaps. In these markets there exist several kinds of instruments which influence trading decisions. To achieve a better overview of the current market situation, several `DFManagers` can be in use at the same time. They differ in the mix of included prices. In this way we support the trader in integrating simultaneously accessible market information and arriving at a more accurate decision.

3.2 Scenarios

To illustrate the use of the classes, we present two scenarios which show the interaction among the actual objects involved.

3.2.1 Discount Factor Calculation

In the first scenario a `pricer` object starts a request for a discount factor at a date where a rate is defined, to calculate the present value of a cash flow (cf. Fig. 3).

This is processed in the following way:

```
double DFManager::DiscountFactor(Date theDate)
{
    Rate *theRate= rateslist->GetRate(theDate);
    CalcStrategy *cs= this->GetStrategy(theRate);
    return cs->DF(theDate);
}
```

What is the advantage of doing it this way? A DFManager relies only on the interface of the collaborator objects. It just uses the responsibilities defined in their abstract base class and manages them. We achieved a strong separation between structure information (Rate), selector knowledge (DFManager) and procedural knowledge (Strategy). To identify such a collaboration scheme we again use a design pattern, the *manager pattern*.

To support a new kind of rate, we implement the corresponding formula in a strategy subclass and define the new rate. So we end up implementing one new subclass with essentially one formula and possibly a caching algorithm.

3.2.2 Cash Flow Generation

The second scenario shows how cash flow generation works in an instrument. We describe a fixed swap leg which is fairly easy to understand without further knowledge in financial engineering.

A fixed swap leg is defined by several parameters, the most important being *principal*, *fixed rate*, and *accrual basis*:

- Principal denotes an amount of money which is the base for cash flow generation.

- Fixed rate is the interest rate used on the principal to calculate the amount paid in regular intervals.

- Accrual basis is the definition of the amount of days per year for which interest accrues.

These definitions are specific to one instrument, a fixed swap leg. To process the information correctly, a generator knows about the parameters supplied by its instrument. So a fixed leg generator accesses the information of a fixed swap leg by the specific swap leg interface.

Information that is common to more than one class is used through the interface of the abstract base class. The aim is to always use the most abstract interface possible.

In the scenario the swap leg collaborates with its generator to produce the cash flows. The generator obtains the necessary parameters from its instrument, in this case the fixed swap leg. The following shows a generic algorithm which implements the formula found in many swaps handbooks.

```
void FixedLegCFGenerator::GetCashFlows(List &theCFList)
{
    Interval *cashdate= swapleg->GetInterval();
    AccrualBasis *acb= swapleg->GetAccrualBasis();
    Date at,prev;
    double amount;

    //--- generate interest payments
    while (cashdate->Next(at)) {
        cashdate->Previous(prev);
        double accrual= acb->Alpha(prev, at);
        amount= Principal(prev) * Rate(prev) * accrual;
        theCFList.Add(new CashFlow(at, amount, ...));
    }
}
```

In the above code sample we use several parameter objects whose purpose we list briefly:

* `Interval` describes the structure of the payments over time.

* `AccrualBasis` is an object encapsulating the convention on how to calculate interest accrual periods.

To iterate over the payment periods, the generator uses `Interval`. This object generates in the loop all the dates necessary for the calculation. In each iteration one cash flow object is generated to store the information. The generator adds these to the list and returns the list to the instrument.

Evaluation

This example shows us not only the de-coupling of *what* and *how*, but also the co-operation of smaller abstractions. The `Interval` is defined by one object and used by another. The objects are solely connected by the interval object and its respective protocol. This is used in the swaps leg, for example, where one object knows how to specify the temporal structure, and the other needs to know the actual dates for the calculation.

The `AccrualBasis` calculates accrual factors with the accrual basis given by the swap leg.

To transfer cash flows as parameters we introduce a class `CashFlow` which stores all relevant data for later use.

Thus we achieved effective de-coupling by introducing fine grained abstractions that only define responsibilities. There are many different specific implementations which are all used homogeneously.

4 Experience

Our experience from developing the ET++SwapsManager and from earlier projects is that building, or better growing, a framework is hard work. It takes recurrent, conscious efforts to review a working design and improve it.

Typically, in developing a software system, functionality is added and tested incrementally. As a consequence the functionality of the system grows without much concern for the overall design. But, to really advance the design it has to be reworked periodically. Thus it is possible that, while preserving the monotonically increased functionality, the system decreases significantly in size, due to consolidation efforts.

Development of a framework starts with the implementation of a specific solution in a particular domain. Then the solution is successively reworked to cover a family of applications. For this process of generalising a design we found a few rules of thumb which were helpful in our project:

- Try to consolidate similar functionality found in different parts of the system and implement it through a common abstraction.

- Split up a large abstraction into several smaller abstractions such that a team of collaborating objects results. Each of these smaller abstractions then implements only a small set of responsibilities. A good example of this is separating pricing and cash flow generation from the instrument abstraction as described in section 3.1.1.

- Objectify abstractions that differ; implementing each variation of an abstraction as an object increases the flexibility of a design.

- Use composition instead of inheritance where possible. This reduces the number of classes in a system. Additionally, it relieves the (re-)user of the framework from having to deal with the inner workings of participating classes.

Especially the last rule seems crucial in the development of a highly flexible framework. The novice often tries to find class hierarchies in the problem domain and structures the needed responsibilities and code accordingly. The call for multiple inheritance is then merely a consequence when one is confronted with implementing an abstraction that is really a combination of already available sets of responsibilities. Structuring functionality along inheritance hierarchies, however, leads to static configurations. Frameworks draw their superiority from well designed collaborations among teams of objects.

Acknowledgements

We would like to thank Erich Gamma and André Weinand for their constructive comments on drafts of this paper and encouragement for redesigning it. We also thank Federico Degen and Jürg Gasser for their support on the financial engineering side of the project.

References

[Beck89]   K. Beck, W. Cunningham, "A Laboratory For Teaching Object-Oriented Thinking," In OOPSLA'89 *Conference Proceedings (October 1-6, New Orleans, Louisiana)*, published as, OOPSLA'89, ACM SIGPLAN Notices Notices, Vol. 24, No. 10, November 1989, pp. 1-6.

[Bro87]   F. P. Brooks Jr., *"No Silver Bullet - Essence and Accidents of Software Engineering," IEEE Computer*, Vol. 20, No. 4, April 1987.

[Egg92]   T. Eggenschwiler and E. Gamma, *"ET++SwapsManager: Using Object Technology in the Financial Engineering Domain,"* In OOPSLA'92 *Conference Proceedings (October 18-22, Vancouver)*, ACM SIGPLAN Notices Vol. 27, No. 10, pp. 166-177.

[Gam92]   E. Gamma, *Objektorientierte Software-Entwicklung am Beispiel von ET++ – Design-Muster, Klassenbibliothek, Werkzeuge*, Springer-Verlag, Berlin, 1992.

[Gam93]   E. Gamma, R. Helm, and J. M. Vlissides, *"Design Patterns: Abstraction and Reuse of Object-Oriented Designs,"* In ECOOP *Conference Proceedings (July 26-30, Kaiserslautern)*, Springer Verlag, 1993.

[Joh88]   R. E. Johnson and B. Foote, *"Designing Reusable Classes," The Journal Of Object-Oriented Programming*, Vol. 1, No. 2, 1988, pp. 22-35.

[Kap90]   K.R. Kapner and J.F.Marshall, *The Swaps Handbook - Swaps and Related Risk Management Instruments*, Institute of Finance, New York, 1990.

[Mir91]   Miron P, Swannell P, *Pricing and Hedging Swaps*, Euromoney Publications PLC, London, 1991.

[Smi87]   C.W. Smithson, *"A LEGO Approach to Financial Engineering: An Introduction to Forwards, Futures, Swaps and Options,"* In Midland Corporate Financial Journal, Winter 1987, pp. 64-86

[Wei89]   A. Weinand, E. Gamma, and R. Marty, *"Design and Implementation of ET++, a Seamless Object-Oriented Application Framework,"* Structured Programming, Vol. 10, No. 2, June 1989, pp. 63-87.

Integrating

Independently-Developed Components

in Object-Oriented Languages

Urs Hölzle

Computer Systems Laboratory
Stanford University
urs@cs.stanford.edu

Abstract. Object-oriented programming promises to increase programmer productivity through better reuse of existing code. However, reuse is not yet pervasive in today's object-oriented programs. Why is this so? We argue that one reason is that current programming languages and environments assume that components are perfectly coordinated. Yet in a world where programs are mostly composed out of reusable components, these components are not likely to be completely integrated because the sheer number of components would make global coordination impractical. Given that seemingly minor inconsistencies between individually designed components would exist, we examine how they can lead to integration problems with current programming language mechanisms. We discuss several reuse mechanisms that can adapt a component *in place* without requiring access to the component's source code and without needing to re-typecheck it.

1 Introduction

Object-oriented programming promises to increase programmer productivity through better reuse of existing code. In the ideal scenario envisioned by the object-oriented community, future programs would be mostly composed out of preexisting components rather than rewritten from scratch: "[Programmers will] produce reusable software components by assembling components of other programmers" [Cox86]. Reusing existing, tested code simultaneously reduces the effort needed to create new applications and improves the quality of the resulting programs.

However, this ideal scenario has not yet become reality: today, many programs are still mostly written from scratch, and there are few commercially available building blocks that could be reused in new applications. Clearly, the envisioned market for software ICs [Cox86] has not materialized yet. Writing reusable components and frameworks is hard [Deu83, OO88, OO90]. Furthermore, the few successful reusable components built so far (such as Interviews [LVC89] and ET++ [WGM88]) are relatively monolithic frameworks, and components are often hard to combine with other components [Ber90]. Why is this so? Why hasn't the dream of *pervasive reuse* been realized yet?

In this study we try to answer this question and come to the conclusion that one reason is that current programming languages (and programming environments) are not

O.M. Nierstrasz (Ed.): ECOOP '93, LNCS 707, pp. 36-56, 1993.
© Springer-Verlag Berlin Heidelberg 1993

very well equipped to handle the subtle integration problems likely to occur with pervasive reuse. To illustrate our point, we envision a futuristic world where reuse is indeed pervasive and where programs are mostly composed out of reusable components. We then argue that in such a world components would not be likely to be completely integrated because the sheer number of components would make global coordination impractical. Given that minor inconsistencies between individually designed components would always exist, we examine how these inconsistencies can lead to problems when combining the components, and how such problems could be overcome.

The paper is divided into two parts. In the first part, we clarify our assumptions and present a simple example of an integration problem caused by a few small inconsistencies. We then try to solve this problem using mechanisms present in many current object-oriented languages (composition, subtyping, and multiple dispatch) and show that none of these approaches completely succeeds in solving the problem.

In the second part, we argue that a broader view of reuse should be adopted, a view that includes an imperfect world where component interfaces are not completely coordinated. Programming languages and environments need to provide mechanisms that allow the programmer to make small changes to component interfaces without having access to the components' source code, and components should be delivered in a form that allows such modifications. We discuss several possible approaches that promise to solve integration problems and thus might bring us one step closer to a world of pervasive reuse.

2   Assumptions

Our study is based on four premises:
- that programs will be composed out of existing components,
- that such components were designed independently, and are sold by independent vendors,
- that a component's source code cannot or should not be changed, and
- that programs are written in a statically-typed language.

The first premise is one of the primary goals of object-oriented programming. We will assume that a large portion of new programs (say, more than 90%) consists of reused components. Thus, relatively little time is spent writing new code, and most of the programming effort lies in combining reusable components. Therefore, it is imperative that components can be combined easily so that programmer productivity is maximized.

The second premise follows from the first: if programs consist mainly of reused code, there must be many reusable components (thousands or tens of thousands), and, assuming a free market, these components must have been designed by many different organizations and vendors. Thus, it is very likely that many components were designed independently, without knowledge of each other. Even if a component vendor tried to be compatible (in some sense of the word) with other components, the sheer number of different components would make it impractical to verify compatibility for all combinations. Therefore, it may well be that a new application is the first application to combine two particular components, and that these two components are not perfectly well-integrated with each other. Many vendors will probably integrate their own components into frameworks, but this does not fundamentally change our assumption: there will be hundreds of frameworks, and as soon as an application reuses two or more independent frameworks, integration problems are likely to occur.

The third premise follows from the desire for incremental change: "Adding new code is good, changing old code is bad" [Lie88]. It is motivated by pragmatic necessity: vendors may not be willing to make their source code available to clients, and even if source code is available, it is desirable not to change the source in order to stay compatible with future versions of the component. If components become much more widely used than today, it will be even more important not to rely on any internal details of the components, or else tracking new versions of the tens or hundreds of components used by an application will become a software maintenance nightmare.

Finally, we are concerned only with statically-typed languages using subtype polymorphism [CW85], because these languages are so widely used and because static typing is often viewed as necessary for building reliable large systems (see, for example, [CC+89]). However, many of the problems we discuss also apply to dynamically-typed object-oriented languages (see section 5.1).

3   The Problem: Inconsistent Components

Assume that we are writing an application using the components A, B, and C, each of them bought from a different vendor. The simplified interfaces of the types offered by the components are shown below:

```
type BaseA {                    "BaseA is the supertype of all objects in component A"
    method print();
    methods mbase_{a1}, mbase_{a2}, ...
}


type SubA: BaseA {                        "One of many subtypes of BaseA"
    methods msub_{a1}, msub_{a2}, ...
}


type BaseB {              "BaseB is the supertype of all objects in component B"
    method printPart1();        "prints one part of a BaseB object"
    method printPart2();        "prints the other part of a BaseB object"
    methods mbase_{b1}, mbase_{b2}, ...
}


type SubB: BaseB {                        "One of many subtypes of BaseB"
    methods msub_{b1}, msub_{b2}, ...
}


type BaseC {              "BaseC is the supertype of all objects in component C"
    method drucke();                        "'drucke' is German for 'print'"
    methods mbase_{c1}, mbase_{c2}, ...
}
```

```
type SubC: BaseC {                          "One of many subtypes of BaseC"
    methods msub_{c1}, msub_{c2}, ...
}
```

Now suppose that we need to integrate objects derived from **BaseA**, **BaseB**, and **BaseC** in our application. For example, we would like to write a method that takes any object of the application and prints it on the screen. That is, we would like to create a common supertype **Printable** for **BaseA**, **BaseB**, and **BaseC**:

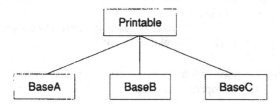

The three components are only superficially incompatible because the desired functionality is already present: BaseA has a print method, BaseB has two public print-Part methods that together would form a valid print method, and BaseC also has a printing method, albeit with a different name (component C was bought from a German supplier). However, since the components were developed independently of each other, they were not derived from a common supertype. Therefore, the three components cannot be integrated in a straightforward way in our application.

One might argue that the integration problem would not exist if the components were "well-designed" from the start, that is, if the component designer had created the "right" type hierarchy. However, we believe it is unlikely that such perfection would be common in the component market of the future. Even if some components achieved near-perfect status over time, users discovering flaws in the type factorization would still have to wait for the component provider to release a revised hierarchy. More importantly, *different users may well have conflicting requirements.* For example, in a type hierarchy representing cars, one user may want to have subtypes representing sports cars, off-road vehicles, vans, etc., whereas another user needs subtypes for US-built cars, Japanese cars, and European cars. If the component provider attempted to reify all possible types and type factorizations, users would be overwhelmed by a myriad of types, most of which they don't need. Finally, components cannot be viewed in isolation: even if all components are internally consistent and well-designed, their combination may not be consistent [Ber90]. Programs are likely to combine many different components or component frameworks, making perfect harmony unlikely.

However, it should be emphasized that we do not assume complete "anarchy" or lack of any standardization. On the contrary, we assume that developers will do their very best to make their components reusable and easy to integrate with other components. That is, we assume that the components we would like to reuse are *almost* compatible—but a few details are not: a method is missing, another method takes the "wrong" type of argument, etc. We believe that such minor inconsistencies are inevitable in any large-scale component market: a component provider simply cannot foresee all possible situations in which the component could be reused.

4   Integration Using Composition

Composition is a well-known approach to solve problems similar to our example. With composition, we define three *wrappers*, each of which contains a pointer to an object of the respective base type. For example, WrapperA would contain a BaseA object:

```
type WrapperA : Printable {
     a: BaseA;              "a holds the real object created by component A"
     method print();        "invokes a.print"
}
```

Instead of arranging the objects of the three components in a subtype relationship, we arrange the wrappers in the proper relationship:

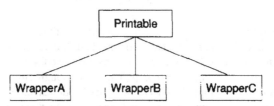

Each wrapper forwards the desired messages to the actual component object. In addition, WrapperC effectively renames the drucke method by calling it from its print method. Similarly, WrapperB synthesizes a print method using printPart1 and printPart2.

In essence, wrappers isolate the core of our application from the type hierarchies of the components. Using wrappers, we have created an alternate view of the type hierarchy presented by the components—instead of dealing with BaseA objects, the application only deals with the wrappers.

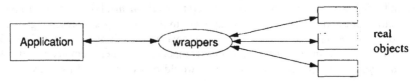

4.1   Problems with Wrappers

So far, we have considered only one side of wrappers, namely the *unwrapping* process that translates wrappers into component objects (arrows going from left to right). In addition, we also have to do the *wrapping*: whenever a component function returns an object, it has to be wrapped before it is passed back to the application (arrows going from right to left). Unfortunately, as in real life, wrapping is more difficult than unwrapping.

We could create a new wrapper whenever an object needs to be wrapped, independently of whether another wrapper for that particular object already exists or not. In this "functional style" of wrapping, multiple wrapper objects can exist for a single component object, which creates a problem in languages allowing pointer equality. Pointer equality cannot be used in the presence of "functional" wrappers because two wrappers may appear to be nonequal even though they denote the same object. Therefore, wrappers are no longer transparent unless pointer equality is strictly avoided. This restriction is simple to enforce in pure object-oriented languages like SELF [US87] where equality is a user-defined operation rather than a pointer comparison, so that we can define equality of wrappers to be equality of the wrapped objects. However, pointer equality is commonly used in many other languages (e.g., C++ [ES90]). In such languages, "functional" wrappers require strict coding discipline, thereby introducing the possibility of programming errors.

Also, functional wrappers can cause performance problems because a new wrapper object is allocated for every object returned by a component. If a certain component method is called a million times, a million wrappers will be created even if the method always returns the same component object.

To avoid these problems, wrappers could be canonicalized. With canonicalized wrappers, exactly one wrapper exists per component object, and thus only the minimum number of wrappers is created. Comparing the pointers of two wrappers gives the same result as comparing the component objects themselves, so that pointer equality does not create problems. Unfortunately, canonicalization is expensive: every time an object is returned by a component method, we have to check a dictionary to see if the object already has a wrapper. If the object is new, we must create a new wrapper and enter it into the dictionary. Thus, each invocation of a component function incurs at least one dictionary lookup, an overhead that will be unacceptable for many applications. Furthermore, both kinds of wrappers could introduce additional run-time overhead because each method invocation on a component object involves at least one additional call (to invoke the wrapper method itself).

Wrappers introduce additional redundancy into the system because they duplicate part of the interfaces of the components. Therefore, if a component interface changes, additional work is required to adapt the program. While this code duplication is undesirable, it is not as bad as it seems. Much of this duplication could be automated: the programming environment could construct the wrappers automatically (with some help from the programmer in case of renaming etc.) and keep track of the relationship between the components and their wrappers. When a component interface changes, the wrapper could be updated automatically.

4.2 Even more Problems with Wrappers

Even though the performance problems caused by wrappers can be severe, wrappers could still be practical if their use could be restricted to a few small areas in the program, so that the overall performance impact would be small. Unfortunately, this is not very likely to happen: wrappers have a tendency to spread, "infecting" everything they touch. An example will illustrate this point: suppose that a method defined in component A returns a list of objects rather than a single object. In this case, we are forced to *wrap the list* in order to prevent the application from seeing the "naked" component objects contained in the list! (The list wrapper would then wrap the individual component objects whenever they are retrieved from the list.)

It would appear that we would not need a wrapper for the list if we wrapped the list elements instead. However, this is not possible in general. For example, if a returned list represents the objects in a graphical editor, removing an element from the list would have no effect on the editor if we had copied the list and created a new list of wrapped objects rather than a wrapped list. (We need to create a new list because we cannot replace the objects with their wrappers in the original list since the wrappers are not subtypes of their respective component type.)

So, even though we wanted to wrap only the objects of component A, we ended up having to create a wrapper for a generic data type, the list. Even worse, if component B also used lists we would have to create a second wrapper for lists of BaseB objects. More realistic components probably would use many other data structures, all of which may have to be wrapped as well.

In languages without delegation (i.e., most current languages), wrappers have an additional limitation: they cannot be used to override a methods of the wrapped component object. For example, suppose in our application we needed to override print in BaseA to add a few blanks before the actual printout. This will work fine if print is only called from our own code, but not if it is called indirectly (as a result of invoking some other component method). That is, any existing component method that sends print will invoke the original print method because the receiver will be a component object, not a wrapper.

By now it should have become clear that our attempt to solve the integration problem with wrappers is not entirely satisfactory. Wrappers can solve some integration problems, but using them may require a large number of wrapper types and can introduce potentially severe run-time and space overheads. Inserting wrappers into a program can be a tedious process, and programs using wrappers are often harder to understand and therefore harder to maintain.

The problems with wrappers appeared because we tried to *hide* the real objects from the application in order to solve the typing inconsistencies between the components. But introducing separate wrapper objects for the real objects forced us to maintain the new invariant that the application must never interact directly with the real objects; all interactions must go through the wrappers. Maintaining this indirection is tedious and potentially expensive in terms of execution time or space. To eliminate these problems, we somehow have to unify the wrapper with the real object. In other words, we have to change a component object's type without losing the object's identity. The next section examines several such approaches.

5 Integration Using Typing Mechanisms

Typing mechanisms can be used to view an object from different viewpoints. For example, in any language with subtyping, an object of type SubA can also be viewed as being of type BaseA. To solve the integration problem, we would like to view, for example, a SubA object as being of type Printable. This chapter discusses how typing mechanisms of existing languages can be employed to this end.

5.1 Implicit Subtyping

Implicit subtyping, as used in some programming languages (e.g., POOL-I [AL90] and Emerald [RTK91]), can be very helpful in integrating different components. With implicit subtyping, the subtyping relationships need not be declared explicitly but are inferred by the system. In our example, Printable is a valid supertype of BaseA, and the system automatically detects this relationship. Therefore, we can pass a BaseA object as the actual parameter to a method expecting a Printable object.

In essence, implicit subtyping allows us to *extend* the *explicit* type lattice (i.e., the types created and named by the programmer) after the fact, without changing the actual *implicit* lattice (formed by all possible sub- and supertypes of all types occurring in the program). BaseA and SubA are two nodes in a much larger type lattice, and implicit subtyping allows us to reify and name any node in this lattice. For example, there is a type between BaseA and SubA whose interface contains $msub_{a1}$ but not $msub_{a2}$. The original designer of component A chose not to reify this type because it did not seem useful, but for our application it might very well be needed. Similarly, Printable is an implicit supertype of BaseA which the original component designer chose not to reify. It is well known that reusable class hierarchies tend to be factored into smaller and smaller pieces with each design iteration because users discover new possibilities for reuse if certain behaviors are factored out [OO90]. Implicit subtyping allows the (re)user of a component to perform this refactoring without waiting for the component provider to do so, and without changing the component itself.

The value of not having to explicitly name every possibly useful type becomes obvious as soon as one tries to name them. For example, Johnson and Rees propose to improve reusability through fine-grain inheritance by methodically splitting up the explicit class hierarchy into small pieces so that reusers can pick the pieces from which they want to inherit [JR92]. But in the example they present, a simple List class is split up into a complex multiple-inheritance hierarchy involving 25 different classes, only one of which (List) is usually needed. Implicit subtyping allows the programmer to avoid confusing the reusers with such a myriad of types while at the same time retaining all of the flexibility.

For all its benefits, implicit subtyping is only a limited solution to the integration problem. For example, it cannot overcome problems caused by misnamed methods (e.g., drucke in BaseC) or missing methods that could be synthesized out of existing methods (e.g., print for BaseB). Furthermore, implicit subtyping is not very popular: no major object-oriented language offers it, probably because it is often perceived as weakening type checking since it may establish a subtype relationship in cases where there is no semantic relationship (for example, Cowboy isn't a subtype of Drawable even though it has a draw method [Mag91]).

Interestingly, with respect to the integration problems discussed here, dynamically-typed languages are quite similar to statically-typed languages with implicit subtyping. In dynamically-typed languages, the subtyping relationships among objects are implicit and checked lazily (and a "message not understood" error is produced at runtime if an object does not have the required type). Therefore, a type like Printable implicitly exists (though it is not reified), and the programmer can write methods that take any "printable object" as an argument. Since the types are implicit and need not be statically checkable, dynamically-typed languages have a certain advantage. For example, types can be more flexible ("if the receiver is a positive number, the argument must be printable, otherwise it can be anything, since no message is sent to it"). More importantly, it is not possible for a programmer to accidentally *overconstrain* the type of an argument (e.g., to specify Integer where Number would suffice), and thus a dynamically-typed component will probably be somewhat more reusable. However, dynamically-typed languages usually cannot solve problems caused by misnamed or missing methods.

5.2   Multiple Subtyping

Multiple subtyping can ameliorate some integration problems even if the language uses explicit rather than implicit subtyping. The idea is similar to wrappers, except that we create a new subtype for every component type instead of creating a wrapper type. The subtype *mixes in* [Moo86, BC90] the desired interface in addition to inheriting the component type's interface. In our example, the type hierarchy would look as follows:

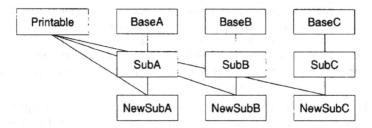

If our application created only NewSubA objects instead of SubA objects, we would have solved the integration problem: since NewSubA is a subtype of BaseA, the objects could be passed to all component methods expecting SubA or BaseA objects, and since NewSubA...C are subtypes of Printable we could also use the objects with all application methods expecting Printable objects.

While this solution appears to work for our simplistic example, it has a serious flaw that significantly reduces its usefulness in realistic applications: it requires that we create *only* NewSubA objects, and no SubA objects. Unfortunately, we do not have control over all object creations; usually, SubA objects would be created (and returned) by functions within component A, since the component was written before NewSubA was created. These objects would not fit into our type hierarchy and therefore could not be passed to methods expecting Printable objects. In essence, we are encountering the wrapping problem again, this time using subtyping rather than composition.

If the programming language allowed explicit type coercions, we could create "type wrapper" methods that coerce the result value to NewSubA for all component methods returning SubA objects. However, we are not aware of any popular object-oriented language that would allow this. In languages offering checked type narrowing (such as Eiffel [Mey91] and BETA [KM+87]), we cannot perform the narrowing because these operations check the object's true type (the creation type). That is, the narrowing tests if the object was *created* as a NewSubA object, not whether it *conforms to* the NewSubA type. Of course, such a test would fail because the object was created with type SubA. In fact, even in a language with implicit subtyping where the narrowing mechanism checked interface conformance, it would still not be sufficient. For example, NewSubB contains the print method which is not present in SubB, and thus a coercion from SubB to NewSubB would fail. Coercion mechanisms cannot solve our problem because we need to truly *extend* both the interface and (though trivially) the implementation of an existing component object, rather than just revealing more information about an object's preexisting interface and implementation.

5.3 Factory Objects

Multiple subtyping didn't solve our problems because we had no control over the objects created by component methods. Fortunately, there is a way to solve this problem at least partially. The idea is to introduce a level of indirection at every object creation. Instead of directly creating an object ("obj = new SubA"), every object is created via a call to a factory object ("obj = factory->createSubA()"). Linton originally proposed this technique to better encapsulate the InterViews library [Lin92], but it is also very useful to solve integration problems. If the factory object is exposed to the (re)user, we can replace the standard factory with our own version creating NewSubA objects rather than SubA objects. Since the object creation types are no longer hardwired in the code, we regain control over the objects created by component methods and can substitute our slightly modified types for the original ones.

However, this solution is still far from ideal. In our example, to make components "printable" we have to introduce a large number of classes (on per concrete component class). Each of these classes must duplicate the interface of corresponding component class: although the objects now have the correct creation type, we must still write "type wrapper" methods to convert returned objects. For example, if SubA has a method get that returns a SubA object, we need to override get in NewSubA to return a NewSubA object (the method just calls the original one and coerces the result object to NewSubA). Unfortunately, changing the result type of a method is impossible in some languages (notably C++), thus crippling the factory object approach in those languages.

Besides adding a considerable amount of code, factory objects may also slow down execution. Every object creation involves an additional dynamically-dispatched call, and most method invocations on component objects also involve an additional call through the "type wrapper" method and a type test for the result coercion (assuming checked coercions). Of course, all reusable components would have to use factory objects, but we assume that component vendors would be happy to enforce this programming convention since it makes their components more reusable.

This observation leads us to a serious problem. Suppose that vendor High sells a package that adds higher-level functionality to the more basic functionality of the SubA component sold by vendor Low. To smoothly integrate the Low objects into its code, vendor High has replaced Low's factory object as suggested above. But if we also need to replace Low's factory object for our own purposes, we are stuck: how can we merge High's changes to the original factory object with our changes? The table below shows the original factory (Low's), the changed factory (High's), and the factory we'd like to use ourselves. High has changed the entry for making SubA objects to solve an internal conflict in the High library, so now it returns HighSubA objects. This creates several in-

Entry	Low's factory	High's factory	Our factory
makeBaseA	BaseA	BaseA	Printable
makeSubA	SubA	HighSubA	NewSubA

tegration problems. For example, what should the new makeSubA entry be? High expects HighSubA objects, but we need NewSubA objects so that these objects have the Printable interface. The problem is that we may not know type HighSubA since it is probably a private type that High does not wish to expose, and even if we did we may not be able to use it because it may introduce conflicts into our type hierarchy (e.g., it may define its own print method with an incompatible signature).

In general, it will be hard to use more than one component that replaces Low's factory object because there may be no factory object simultaneously satisfying all component's needs for "replacement types." Furthermore, the order of changes to factory objects must be coordinated carefully so that no component overwrites the changes made previously by another component. In other words, though factory objects can solve some simple problems, they do not appear to scale well.

5.4   Multimethods

Multimethods (also called generic methods) [DG87] are relatively new in statically-typed languages [ADL91, Cha92]. With multimethods, the message lookup may involve all arguments, not just the receiver. Since multimethods are dispatched on multiple arguments, they are not "contained" in a single class, and thus are in some sense independent of the class or type hierarchy (but see [Cha92]). We can use this independence to modify a component without changing the component itself. For example, by defining a method print specialized for arguments of type BaseB we effectively add a print method to BaseB. By defining an additional print method specialized for BaseC arguments, we have a multimethod print for all component objects, solving our problem without introducing a new Printable type.

Unfortunately, we must pay a heavy price to avoid introducing the type Printable. Because the various component objects still have no common supertype, we need to write three versions of every method that conceptually takes an argument of type Printable—one version specialized for BaseA objects, one for BaseB and one for BaseC. That is, instead of writing one method we need to write three. Even worse, if we'd like to write a method that takes *two* arguments of type Printable, we must implement *nine* methods, one for each pair in the Cartesian product of the possible actual argument types. In addition to these code duplication problems, a solution with multimethods is not as readable as we'd like because the abstraction Printable is not reified in the program, making it harder to understand the resulting code.

If it were possible to create and name types that are sets of other types or classes and to specialize multimethods on types (not classes), the combinatorial explosion of multimethods could be avoided. For example, we could create the type Printable as the set containing BaseA, BaseB, and BaseC, and specialize the print multimethod on this type. However, we are not aware of any language that allows dispatching of multimethods on types.

Finally, multimethods also could not solve our problem if the underlying language allowed the *sealing* of types [App92]. A sealed class cannot be subclassed, and a sealed type cannot be specialized further. Sealing would prevent the programmer from creating new generic methods that dispatched on a sealed class or type. Sealing has mainly been proposed for implementation reasons [App92] to allow the compiler generate better code, but also as a software engineering mechanism to prevent "internal" classes from being subclassed [KM+87].

6   Discussion

Our study has led us to a surprising result: even our very simple example creates integration problems that cannot be solved easily with the language mechanisms present in current statically-typed object-oriented languages. Both traditional reuse mechanisms, composition and subtyping, do not fare well in our scenario. Composition (the wrappers approach) needs a significant amount of extra code and can lead to potentially serious performance problems. Subtyping, whether implicit or explicit, provides only a partial solution, and multimethods introduce code duplication. In other words, current statically-typed object-oriented languages do not appear to support reuse of independently developed components well.

This result can be (mis-)interpreted in several ways:

- "Pervasive reuse is only possible if all components are standardized so no integration problems occur." We believe that this conclusion would be equivalent to concluding that pervasive reuse is impossible. The complete integration of thousands of components into a coherent framework does not appear to be practical in the near future. The standardization of software components is sometimes being compared to the standardization of components in the building industry, or to standardized interfaces between HiFi components. We believe that this analogy is flawed because such interfaces are simple, self-contained, and "flat," whereas software interfaces are much more complicated, interrelated, and "deep." For example, a software component may be unusable if it is embedded in the "wrong" type hierarchy even though it offers the correct "flat" interface. Of course, this does not mean that standardization attempts are futile or undesirable, but such attempts are likely to be time-consuming and to eliminate only some (but not all) integration problems. If pervasive reuse of software is to become reality, we must find a more practical solution to the integration problem.

- "Editing the source code of components isn't so bad; after all, it's the only practical way to achieve pervasive reuse." This "pragmatic" interpretation contradicts one of our basic assumptions, and we feel that it is not justified. While editing the source code of components can solve the problems presented in this paper, it requires access to source code and produces a major software maintenance problem (tracking new revisions of the component). One of the goals of reuse is to reduce the cost of software development, and introducing such maintenance problems does not seem compatible with that goal.

- "Programs should be compact. Integration problems appear *between* (not within) programs, and such problems should be solved with systems integration languages, not programming languages." It is undoubtedly true that integration problems also occur on the inter-application level. However, if we cannot solve the integration problems *within* programs, overall productivity is unlikely to improve very much since most of the development effort lies in writing applications rather than in systems integration. Furthermore, if the inter-application interface is statically typed as well, application reusers will face the same problems that component reusers face—pushing the problem to a higher level doesn't make it disappear. However, application interfaces will probably be more standardized since they are coarser and fewer. Also, wrappers become more viable since the inter-application communication bandwidth is likely to be lower than the inter-component bandwidth so that the performance problems caused by wrappers are less severe.

We believe there is no single cause for the integration difficulties encountered with current languages and systems. However, the first and foremost culprit may be that the integration problem often is not acknowledged at all. Programming language designers seem concerned mostly with possibly large but well-integrated single applications rather than with applications composed out of a multitude of preexisting components. That is, they assume that component interfaces are well-coordinated and can be adjusted if necessary.

Another problem is that the traditional view of reuse overemphasizes *compiled-code reuse* ("Look, Ma, no changes!"), leading to several problems that can compromise widespread reuse. The unwillingness to recompile code can lead to rigid, less adaptable components and precludes many approaches that could modify a component without relying on internal implementation details. Because there is only one version of the object code, programmers face a dilemma between flexibility and performance. If the object code is kept flexible, it cannot be optimized as much; if it is highly optimized, flexibility suffers because many design parameters are hardwired in the code. For example, current compiled-code-oriented systems often use impure interfaces that expose implementation information in order to obtain better performance, thereby severely compromising reusability [HU92].

We wish to emphasize reuse in a broader sense, where reuse equals saved programming effort. Programming time is much more important than compilation time because the computational power needed for recompilation becomes cheaper and cheaper every year whereas the programmer's time does not.[†] Of course, reuse mechanisms must be practical in terms of the machine resources they require. But the overriding goal of reuse should be to increase programmer productivity, and we should not constrain our search for better reuse mechanisms *a priori* to mechanisms that preserve compiled-code reuse (see [Szy92] for a similar argument).

[†]   This is not to say that compilation time isn't an important factor influencing programming productivity. But even with today's hardware, a well-engineered compiler can compile several thousand lines of code per second [Tem90]. The problem is that most compilers are not tuned for compilation speed.

To summarize, we believe that a programming language / environment combination needs to provide the following functionality to be successful in a world of pervasive reuse:

- Component types and type hierarchies should be changeable within certain bounds so that component reusers can integrate one component with another. That is, it should be possible for the reuser to change the component types directly, without first introducing new subtypes or subclasses.

- This flexibility must be provided without requiring source code access to the component's implementation, and it should not compromise the efficiency of the resulting programs.

How this functionality is best provided, and whether it is provided directly by the programming language (type system) or by the programming environment, remains an open question.

7 Towards a solution

In view of this broader concept of reuse, this section discusses several possible approaches that promise to overcome the integration problem and to increase reuse.

7.1 Type Adaptation

A straightforward approach, which we call *type adaptation*, is to allow the programmer to change given interfaces in a restricted way *after* they have been delivered as a component. The interface changes must not invalidate the component's type structure (e.g., the subtype relationships must be preserved), but this restriction still allows many useful adaptations:

- New types can be added to the type hierarchy (for example, a common supertype Printable). As with implicit subtyping, this allows the programmer to reify types that are implicitly already present in the component's type lattice.

- Types can be complemented with new methods (e.g., a print method for BaseB calling printPartial1 and printPartial2) and new instance variables. Of course, the added methods do not have access to any internal implementation details of the component, and they may not conflict with existing public methods.[†] (In a language separating types and classes, complementing a type means adding the methods to all classes that implement the type.)

- Operations can be renamed to make the component compatible with others (in our example, drucke could be renamed to print).

[†] This also requires that the public (external) and private (internal) name spaces are kept separate. Then, adding a public method print does not create a name conflict even if the component's implementation already has a private method print. The two print methods are completely separate; no method added through type adaptation could call (or even name) the private print method, and no method in the component's implementation could call the new public print method (which didn't exist when the component implementation was written).

Since type adaptation augments types "in place," it causes none of the problems associated with wrappers or subtyping. No additional objects or type hierarchies are created, and all objects created within the component automatically have the augmented type (and no object has the original unchanged type). Furthermore, since the changes do not depend on internal component details (and vice versa), the component implementation could be replaced by the vendor with a newer version without causing adaptation problems for customers using type adaptation. Similarly, because the component's implicit type hierarchy does not change, the component implementation need not be re-typechecked after the changes. A variant of type adaptation would also be useful for dynamically-typed languages, where it would adapt objects (e.g., classes or prototypes) rather than types.

Adapting a component interface does not require access to the source code of the implementation. For example, a component could be distributed in an architecture-neutral intermediate format (such as ANDF [OSF91]) that contains all type information needed by a type adaptation system (but no source code) and could be translated into optimized machine code. In this intermediate form, the component's implementation need not hardwire the exact storage layout or dispatching mechanisms like machine code would. For example, introducing additional supertypes may change the optimal message dispatching strategy relative to the original component and would therefore be hard to implement if components were delivered as object code. With an intermediate format, the optimal dispatching strategy could still be used because machine-code generation is deferred until reuse time. Thus, we could eliminate the dilemma between flexibility and efficiency because the machine code can be customized for each application.

A more detailed discussion of the implementation of such an intermediate format is beyond the scope of this paper. More research is probably needed to investigate its practicality, but it appears that the implementation could leverage off already existing intermediate formats aimed at cross-architecture portability, such as the commercial ANDF format mentioned above.

7.2   Extension Hierarchies

Ossher and Harrison have proposed a mechanism called *extension hierarchies* [OH92] that is similar to type adaptation. Even though their description emphasizes extension rather than adaptation, extension hierarchies seem well suited to solving the integration problem. The basic idea is to combine a base hierarchy (= component) with sparse extension hierarchies containing changes, additions, and deletions. Extensions are modelled as operators and can be combined to form new extensions; both sequential combination (applying one extension, then another) and parallel combination (merging two extensions) are supported. Extension hierarchies are more general than type adaptation since they allow arbitrary changes that are not necessarily interface-preserving, and because they can be used to extend implementations as well as interfaces. Also, extension hierarchies are a programming environment mechanism rather than a language mechanism.

We believe that extension hierarchies hold much promise. While we do not agree with all aspects of the particular variation proposed in [OH92] (for example, the authors strictly avoid recompiling code after extensions are applied), extension hierarchies can solve many integration problems in a straightforward way. In our example, we could define an extension for each component to insert the Printable supertype. Since the extensions are kept separate from the base component, they can be reapplied automatically to newer versions of the components (as long as the component's interfaces do not change).

In general, extension hierarchies require full source-code access to apply an extension. To integrate a component, a programmer would change it, and the changes form the extension. Later, when a newer version of the component is delivered (ideally in the form of an extension to the previous version), the two extensions would be combined to form the new integrated component. However, the two extensions may conflict, and the conflicts will have to be resolved by the programmer, creating the maintenance problem we wished to avoid with our "no source changes to reused components" policy. That is, if extension hierarchies are used in their full generality, they can create problems similar to conventional change management systems. Therefore, we believe that an extension hierarchy system would have to be used in a restricted way to solve integration problems, so that extensions would only perform the modifications allowed by type adaptation. The system would probably contain an automatic "extension checker" to verify that an extension conforms to the rules of type adaptation. Passing this check would guarantee that an extension could be combined without conflicts with "update extensions" provided by the component's manufacturer, as long as the package's public interface is not changed by the manufacturer. In essence, the extension checker would thus represent a type adaptation subsystem implemented within an extension hierarchies system.

7.3   Other Related Work

A mechanism very similar to type adaptation (called *enhancive types*) was proposed by Horn [Hor87]. However, unlike type adaptation, enhancive types do not change types in place but instead allow a base type to be coerced into another type (the enhanced type) that offers additional operations implemented in terms of the base type's public methods. Horn's paper also discusses in more detail why the original methods of an enhanced type need not be re-typechecked. Unfortunately, the paper was couched in theoretical terms as an extension to constrained genericity, and the idea has largely been overlooked in programming language design.

Sandberg's *descriptive classes* [San86] are the first example of types that could be declared after the classes that were their subtypes. The usefulness of creating new superclasses for existing classes was discussed in detail by Pedersen [Ped89] and implemented in Cecil by Chambers [Cha93a]. *Predicate classes* [Cha93b] offer yet another way to extend objects, although this isn't their intended use. Opdyke [Opd92] defines a set of program restructuring operations (refactorings) that support the design, evolution and reuse of object-oriented application frameworks. Although Opdyke discusses the refactorings in terms of source code changes, most of them could be performed on a sourceless intermediate code format. In such a system, the refactorings would be very similar to the modifications allowed by type adaptation.

Palsberg and Schwartzbach have recognized a similar problem with traditional reuse mechanisms and have proposed a type substitution mechanism aimed at maximizing code reuse [PS90]. However, for the scenario outlined here, their solution is both too general and too restricted: too general because in the presence of subtype polymorphism it may require the re-typechecking of a component's implementation, and too restricted because it does not allow adding new methods or renaming methods. Thus, a system using type substitution could only partially solve the integration problems we encountered in this paper.

The Mjølner BETA fragment system [MPN89] is a grammar-based programming environment designed to customize and assemble program fragments. A fragment is any sequence of terminal and nonterminal symbols derived from a nonterminal symbol. Fragments may define interfaces or implementations, and in principle one interface fragment could have several implementation fragments. Most importantly, fragments can be plugged into empty "slots" of other fragments, providing for a very flexible program integration system. While the mechanisms of post-facto type adaptation and the fragment system are closely related, the underlying design and reuse philosophy of BETA / Mjølner is very different from ours since it is intended for *planned* reuse only. Extending the fragment system to incorporate type adaptation would be a promising area for future research.

The prototype of the Jade programming environment for Emerald described by Raj [RL89] is similar to BETA's fragment system. A piece of code can be left partially unspecified, and the code piece's *habitat* describes the required interface of the unspecified parts. Jade is interesting because the underlying programming language, Emerald, does not provide inheritance and thus does not by itself support code reuse. That is, the Emerald / Jade combination treats reuse at the level of the programming environment rather than at the language level. Like BETA / Mjølner, Jade emphasizes planned reuse only and therefore does not directly address the integration problem.

8   Conclusions

We have examined problems likely to occur in a world where reuse is pervasive and components are designed by independent organizations. In such a world, a large part of every application would consist of reusable components, and applications would combine many different components or frameworks. The interfaces and type hierarchies of components must be expected to be slightly inconsistent in relation to each other (even if the individual components are perfectly self-consistent) because the sheer number of different components would make perfect coordination impractical.

Today's programming languages and environments rely on components to be well-integrated and do not handle the integration of independently developed components well. Even slight inconsistencies can lead to integration problems that cannot be handled satisfactorily with the reuse mechanisms available in current languages. Wrappers create redundant type hierarchies and make programs harder to understand and change, and the wrapping and unwrapping of objects can incur performance problems. Typing mechanisms usually cannot solve the problems because existing component types and type hierarchies cannot be adapted; factory objects combined with multiple subtyping can solve simple problems but do not scale well. A language with multiple dispatch on argument types (not classes) could solve most adaptation problems at the expense of language complexity, but no current object-oriented language offers the combination of these features. Even dynamically-typed languages suffer from adaptation problems, although they are usually somewhat better off than their statically-typed counterparts.

We believe that it is helpful to adopt a broader view of reuse mechanisms that does not center around perfectly coordinated components and pure compiled-code reuse. Future programming language / environment combinations should allow the reuser to change component types and type hierarchies *in place* to integrate components with each other; component interfaces should not be completely frozen as they are today. Component implementations may best be delivered in an intermediate format so that the new flexibility can be combined with efficient execution.

We have proposed a new reuse mechanism, *type adaptation*, that is based on previous ideas by Horn, Sandberg, and Pedersen. It can adapt a component in restricted ways without requiring access to the component's implementation and without retypechecking it. With mechanisms such as type adaptation or Ossher and Harrison's extension hierarchies, we may come one step closer to reaching the dream of pervasive reuse.

Acknowledgments: I would like to thank David Ungar for his continuous guidance and support; I am also very grateful for the support provided by Sun Microsystems Laboratories. Ole Agesen, Lars Bak, Bay-Wei Chang, David Cheriton, Craig Chambers, John Maloney, Jens Palsberg, Clemens Szypersky, and the anonymous reviewers provided valuable comments on earlier drafts of this paper. Many thanks also go to Peter Kessler and Alan Snyder for discussions on the subject of integration.

References

[ADL91]   Rakesh Agrawal, Linda G. DeMichiel, and Bruce G. Lindsay. Static Type-Checking of Multi-Methods. In *OOPSLA '91 Conference Proceedings*, pp. 113-128, Phoenix, AZ, October 1991. Published as *SIGPLAN Notices 26(11)*, November 1991.

[AL90]   Pierre America and Frank van der Linden. A Parallel Object-Oriented Language with Inheritance and Subtyping. In *ECOOP/OOPSLA '90 Conference Proceedings*, pp. 161-168, Ottawa, Canada, October 1990. Published as *SIGPLAN Notices 25(10)*, October 1990.

[App92]   Apple Computer, Eastern Research and Technology. *Dylan, an object-oriented dynamic language*. Apple Computer, Cupertino, CA, April 1992.

[BC90]   Gilad Bracha and William Cook. Mixin-Based Inheritance. In *ECOOP/OOPSLA '90 Conference Proceedings*, pp. 303-311, Ottawa, Canada, October 1990. Published as *SIGPLAN Notices 25(10)*, October 1990.

[Ber90]   Lucy Berlin. When Objects Collide: Experiences with Reusing Multiple Class Hierarchies. In *ECOOP/OOPSLA '90 Conference Proceedings*, pp. 181-193, Ottawa, Canada, October 1990. Published as *SIGPLAN Notices 25(10)*, October 1990.

[CW85]   Luca Cardelli and Peter Wegner. On Understanding Types, Data Abstraction, and Polymorphism. *Computing Surveys 17(4)*, pp, 471-522, December 1985.

[Cha92]   Craig Chambers. Object-Oriented Multimethods in Cecil. In *ECOOP '92 Proceedings*, pp. 33-65, Utrecht, The Netherlands, June 1992. Published as *Springer Verlag LNCS 615*, Berlin, Germany 1992.

[Cha93a]   Craig Chambers. *The Cecil Language—Specification and Rationale.* Technical Report 93-03-05, Computer Science Department, University of Washington, Seattle 1993.

[Cha93b]   Craig Chambers. Predicate Classes. In *ECOOP '93 Conference Proceedings*, Kaiserslautern, Germany, July 1993.

[CC+89]   Peter Canning, William Cook, Walter Hill, and Walter Olthoff. Interfaces in strongly-typed object-oriented programming. In *OOPSLA '89 Conference Proceedings*, pp. 457-468, New Orleans, LA, October 1989. Published as *SIGPLAN Notices 24(10)*, October 1989.

[Cox86]   Brad Cox. *Object-Oriented Programming: An Evolutionary Approach.* Addison-Wesley, Reading, MA 1986.

[DG87]   Linda G. DeMichiel and Richard P. Gabriel. The Common Lisp Object System: An Overview. In *ECOOP '87 Conference Proceedings*, pp. 223-233, Paris, France, June 1987. Published as *Springer Verlag LNCS 276*, Berlin, Germany 1987.

[Deu83]   L. Peter Deutsch. Reusability in the Smalltalk-80 Programming System. Proceedings of the *Workshop on Reusability in Programming*, p. 72-76. Newport, RI, September 1983.

[ES90]   Margaret A. Ellis and Bjarne Stroustrup. *The Annotated C++ Reference Manual.* Addison Wesley, Reading, Ma 1990.

[Hor87]   Chris Horn. Conformance, Genericity, Inheritance and Enhancement. In *ECOOP '87 Conference Proceedings*, pp. 223-233, Paris, France, June 1987. Published as *Springer Verlag LNCS 276*, Berlin, Germany 1987.

[HU92]   Urs Hölzle and David Ungar. The Case for Pure Object-Oriented Languages. In *Proceedings of the OOPSLA '92 Workshop on Object-Oriented Languages: The Next Generation.* Vancouver, Canada, October 1992.

[JR92]   Paul Johnson and Ceri Rees. Reusability through Fine-grain Inheritance. *Software—Practice and Experience 22(12)*, pp. 1049-1068, December 1992.

[KM+87]   B. B. Kristensen, O. L. Madsen, B. Møller-Pedersen and K. Nygaard. The BETA Programming Language. In B. Shriver and P. Wegner (eds.), *Research Directions in Object-Oriented Programming*, pp. 7-48. MIT Press, Cambridge, MA 1987.

[Lie88]   Henry Lieberman. Position Statement in the Panel on Varieties of Inheritance. In *Addendum to the OOPSLA '87 Proceedings*, p. 35. Published as *SIGPLAN Notices 23(5)*, May 1988.

[LVC89]   Mark A. Linton, John Vlissides, and Paul Calder. Composing user interfaces with Interviews. *IEEE Computer Magazine*, February 1989.

[Lin92]   Mark A. Linton. Encapsulating a C++ Library. *Proceedings of the 1992 Usenix C++ Conference*, pp. 57-66, Portland, OR, August 1992.

[Mag91]   Boris Magnusson. Position statement during the ECOOP '91 Workshop on Types, Geneva, Switzerland, July 1991.

[MPN89]   Ole Lehrmann-Madsen, Birger Møller-Pedersen, and Kristen Nygaard. *The BETA Programming Language—A Scandinavian Approach to Object-Oriented Programming*. OOPSLA '89 Tutorial Notes, New Orleans, LA, October 1989.

[Moo86]   David A. Moon. Object-Oriented programming with Flavors. In *OOPSLA '86 Conference Proceedings*, pp. 1-8, Portland, OR, October 1986. Published as *SIGPLAN Notices 21(11)*, November 1986.

[Mey91]   Bertrand Meyer. *Eiffel—The Language*. Prentice Hall, New York 1991.

[OH92]   Harold Ossher and William Harrison. Combination of Inheritance Hierarchies. In *OOPSLA '92 Conference Proceedings*, pp. 25-43, Vancouver, Canada, October 1992. Published as *SIGPLAN Notices 27(10)*, October 1992.

[OO88]   Panel: Experiences with reusability. In *OOPSLA '88 Conference Proceedings*, pp. 371-376, San Diego, CA, September 1988. Published as *SIGPLAN Notices 23(11)*, November 1988.

[OO90]   Panel: Designing Reusable Designs: Experiences Designing Object-Oriented Frameworks. In *Addendum to the OOPSLA/ECOOP '90 Conference Proceedings*, pp. 19-24, Ottawa, Canada, October 1990.

[Opd92]   W. F. Opdyke. *Refactoring Object-Oriented Frameworks*. Ph. D. Thesis, Department of Computer Science, University of Illinois, Urbana-Champaign 1992. Published as Technical Report UIUCDCS-R-92-53097.

[OSF91]   Open Systems Foundation. *OSF Architecture-Neutral Distribution Format Rationale*. Open Systems Foundation, June 1991.

[Par72]   David Parnas. On the criteria to be used in decomposing systems into modules. *Communications of the ACM, 15(12)*, December 1972.

[Ped89]   Claus H. Pedersen. Extending ordinary inheritance schemes to include generalization. In *OOPSLA '89 Conference Proceedings*, pp. 407-417, New Orleans, LA, October 1989. Published as *SIGPLAN Notices 24(10)*, October 1989.

[PS90]   Jens Palsberg and Michael Schwartzbach. *Type substitution for object-oriented programming*. In *ECOOP/OOPSLA '90 Conference Proceedings*, pp. 151-160, Ottawa, Canada, October 1990. Published as *SIGPLAN Notices 25(10)*, October 1990.

[RL89]   Rajendra K. Raj and Henry K. Levy. A Compositional Model for Software Reuse. *Computer Journal 32(4)*, pp. 312-322, 1989.

[RTK91]   Rajendra K. Raj, Ewan Tempero, and Henry K. Levy. Emerald: A General-Purpose Programming Language. *Software—Practice and Experience 21(1)*, pp. 91-118, January 1991.

[San86]   David Sandberg. An Alternative to Subclassing. In *OOPSLA '86 Conference Proceedings*, pp. 424-428, Portland, OR, October 1986. Published as *SIGPLAN Notices 21(11)*, November 1986.

[Szy92]   Clemens Szypersky. Extensible Object-Orientation. In *Proceedings of the OOPSLA '92 Workshop on Object-Oriented Languages: The Next Generation.* Vancouver, Canada, October 18, 1992.

[Tem90]   Josef Templ. Compilation Speed of the SPARC Oberon Compiler. Personal communication, April 1990.

[US87]   David Ungar and Randall B. Smith. SELF—The Power of Simplicity. In *OOPSLA '87 Conference Proceedings*, pp. 227-242, Orlando, FL, October 1987. Published as *SIGPLAN Notices 22(12)*, December 1987.

[WGM88]   André Weinand, Erich Gamma, and Robert Marty. ET++—An Object-Oriented Application Framework in C++. In *OOPSLA '88 Conference Proceedings*, pp. 168-182, San Diego, CA, October 1988. Published as *SIGPLAN Notices 23(11)*, November 1988.

Encapsulating Plurality

Andrew P. Black and Mark P. Immel

This paper describes the *Gaggle*, a mechanism for grouping and naming objects in an object-oriented distributed system. Using Gaggles, client objects can access distributed replicated services without regard for the number of objects that provide the service. Gaggles are not themselves a replication mechanism; instead they enable programmers to construct their own replicated distributed services in whatever way is appropriate for the application at hand, and then to encapsulate the result.

From the point of view of a client, a Gaggle can be named and invoked exactly like an object. However, Gaggles can be used to represent individual objects, several ordinary objects, or even several other Gaggles. In this way they encapsulate plurality. If a Gaggle is used as an invokee, *one* of the objects that it represents is chosen (non-deterministically) to receive the invocation.

1. Introduction

When designing a distributed object-oriented system, particular choices must be made for the implementation of each object in the system, and for the location of each object. These decisions can have a profound effect on the performance of the system as a whole, and they are therefore likely to be revisited and changed as the system evolves.

A good programming language and development environment will make it easy to encapsulate system components so that the effects of any changes in their implementation are localized. This is true even in centralized environments. Distributed programming environments, of which Emerald will be used as an example, go a step further: they also encapsulate distribution [5]. That is, the syntax and semantics (modulo failures) of the basic computational step, the invocation of a named operation on a receiver object, are independent of the location of the receiver.

A particular choice must also be made for the *number* of objects used to implement a particular abstraction. This choice can have a profound effect on the availability and reliability of the system as a whole. However, ordinary objects do not provide a way of encapsulating such a choice. This paper introduces the *Gaggle*, a facility for "encapsulating plurality", i.e., for hiding from a client the *number* of objects that implement a service. Simply put, Gaggles provide a way of treating a plurality of objects as if they were a single object.

Authors' electronic mail addresses: black@crl.dec.com; immel@husc.harvard.edu.

Contact address: Dr A. P. Black, Digital Equipment Corporation, Cambridge Research Laboratory, One Kendall Square, Bldg. 700, Cambridge, Massachusetts 02139, U.S.A.

Mark Immel was supported by the Division of Applied Sciences of Harvard University while this work was undertaken.

O.M. Nierstrasz (Ed.): ECOOP '93, LNCS 707, pp. 57-79, 1993.
© Springer-Verlag Berlin Heidelberg 1993

The context of this paper is the Emerald programming language, but we believe that the concept of the Gaggle is equally applicable to other environments for the programming of distributed applications.

1.1. An Example

To clarify the problem caused by replicated services, consider a highly available file service. High availability is achieved by using multiple servers.

Suppose that there are three servers and that the quorum consensus algorithm is used to ensure consistency [8]. Any object that wishes to read a file must therefore know both the identities of the servers and the algorithm for reading a file. We will refer to this information as the access data (shown as the small circle labeled "A" in Figure 1.)

It is possible for every client to have a separate and independent copy of the access data. This has the advantages of simplicity and robustness; provided a quorum of servers is available, the client will be able to obtain service (see Figure 1a). However, this arrangement has serious maintainability and transparency problems. First, the client must treat replicated files in a different way from non-replicated files. Second, if the replication algorithm is changed, perhaps to the available copies algorithm [2], then every client must be found and modified to reflect that change. In a wide-area distributed system this is infeasible.

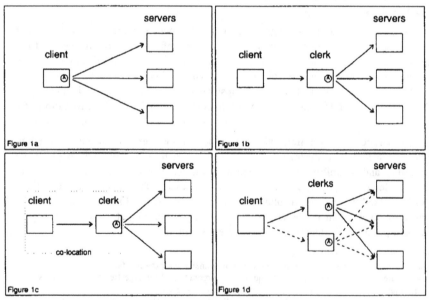

Figure 1: Four ways of accessing a replicated service.

The obvious solution to this problem is to encapsulate the access data in a clerk object, as shown in Figure 1b. When a client object needs to read a file, it invokes a clerk, which then executes the *read* algorithm on its behalf. Now only the clerk need be modified if the access data change. Moreover, if the same clerk interface is used to read non-replicated files, then the representation of a file can be changed from non-replicated to replicated without necessitating any changes in the client. Schroeder [13] discusses the Clerk paradigm in more detail.

Unfortunately, using a single clerk reintroduces a single point of failure into the system: if the clerk fails, then the client cannot read its file, even though the file servers may all be available. There are two ways to avoid this loss of availability: *co-location* of the clerk and the client, and *replication* of the clerk.

- If the client and the clerk are *co-located* in the same address space, the clerk is unlikely to fail separately from the client, and the existence of the clerk does not compromise availability. This arrangement is shown in Figure 1c, where the dotted line encloses the co-located objects. Although Emerald provides various facilities for requesting that objects be co-located, it is not always appropriate to solve the availability problem in this way.

  If the client is running in a small machine (perhaps a laptop computer), or if it obtains its services over a low-bandwidth link (perhaps a dial-up telephone line or a radio modem), then there are obvious load- and traffic-reduction reasons for locating the clerk near the servers. It is also advantageous to allow many clients to share a data cache kept by a single clerk; in this situation the clerk cannot be local to all of the clients. In addition, initializing a clerk may be time consuming, so that clients that expect to interact only briefly with the service will be best served by an existing clerk.

- An alternative is to *replicate* the clerk, and to allow clients to invoke any clerk that is available, as shown in Figure 1d. A client might pick a clerk essentially at random, or in a way that minimizes response time or that shares the load on the clerks. If the clerk used in the initial invocation is no longer available on a subsequent invocation, the client transparently "fails over" to one of the other clerks.

The Gaggle was conceived as a mechanism for transparently invoking one of a number of clerk objects. The problem that it solves is fitting the notion of transparent fail-over within a group of essentially equivalent clerks into an object-oriented computation. To understand this problem better, we must briefly look at the primitive mechanisms of such a computation.

1.2. Characteristics of Distributed Object-Oriented Computation

For the purposes of this paper, we can characterize distributed object-oriented computation by the collaboration of several active *objects* through the exchange of *invocation messages* and replies. Such computations proceed by means of invocations such as

$$buffer \leftarrow file.read\,[offset,\; length\,];$$

this invocation has four parts. *file* names some object, which we call the invokee; this is the object that will actually carry out the computation. *read* is the name of the operation that the invokee is requested to perform. [*offset, length*] is the argument list; the values of the arguments (i.e., the names of the objects that *offset* and *length* denote) are sent to the invokee along with the operation name, so that the invocation request can be parameterized. When the invocation completes, a result object has been generated, and the result variable *buffer* will name it.

In this computational model, the object that is to receive and execute the invocation cannot be distinguished from the object named in the invocation statement. In Emerald, objects are named using network unique identifiers, so the invokee *file* can be anywhere on the network. Moreover, *file* can move from one Emerald node to another: the invocation machinery will track it down. But Emerald does not enable one to express the idea that the invokee should be a plurality of objects.

1.3. Gaggles

A Gaggle behaves very much like an object: it can be named and invoked in the same way as an object. However, because a Gaggle can represent an individual object, several ordinary objects, or even several other Gaggles, a Gaggle encapsulates plurality. If a Gaggle is invoked, *one* of the objects that it represents is chosen to receive the invocation.

We designed Gaggles to be a flexible low-level tool, useful as a basis for experimentation, rather than as a finished solution to a particular problem. Their advantages are that they fit into our object-oriented computational model, including our rather rigid view of typing, and that the costs of the implementation fall only on those objects that use them.

The remainder of this paper is organized as follows. Section 2 discusses other work related to our proposal. Section 3 shows some of the ways in which Gaggles can be used, and illustrates their use in solving real problems of distributed computation. Section 4 looks at the design space for Gaggles, and discusses why we feel that our particular design choices are appropriate. Section 5 describes some possible implementations of Gaggles for systems of various scales. Section 6 summarizes the work and gives its current status.

2. Relationship with other work

2.1. Group Communication amongst Objects

Pardyak [12] has proposed a general model of group structure for the interaction of clients and replicated services in an object-oriented environment. Figure 2 shows his model; for consistency, we have re-labeled Pardyak's "group objects" as "clerk objects". The "member" objects are the servers that actually provide the replicated service; they can communicate amongst themselves using the member channel, or

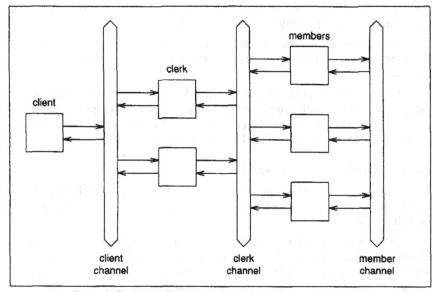

Figure 2: Pardyak's General Model of Group Structure (after [12])

with both members and clerks using the clerk channel. The clients access the service by using a client channel to communicate with several clerk objects.

Pardyak's implementation is less general than this model; it deals only with the special case in which there is a single clerk object. This restriction permits the client communications channel to be a traditional object invocation. Gaggles provide the tool to generalize his work so that multiple clerk objects are permitted. (Remarkably, we were not aware of this synergy until after the initial design of the Gaggle had been completed.)

2.2. ISIS Process Groups

ISIS, to quote its developers, is "a system for building applications consisting of cooperating, distributed processes. Group management and group communication are two basic building blocks provided by ISIS" [15]. The system has generated significant interest and is in use at several sites. ISIS presents users with a sharp set of tools for building one particular kind of fault-tolerant system, but it is not particularly useful if other kinds of system organization are preferred.

In the most recent formulation of ISIS [15, 16], the sender of a message must itself be a member of a group in order to send a message to that group. This means that an ISIS process group cannot replace an existing single server process directly. If a client wishes to make a request of a server group to which it does not belong, it must send the request to a particular member of the group called the contact, which will generally multicast the request to the whole group. If the contact fails, the client must somehow choose a new contact and and retry the request. Thus the client must be aware of the fact that it is making use of a group of processes rather than a single process: plurality is not encapsulated.

The previous formulation of ISIS [3] had special support for clients of groups. However, this gave rise to significant implementation complexity, and was hard to make secure.

It should be emphasized that Gaggles do not compete with ISIS process groups; the two ideas are complementary. Gaggles provide encapsulation; process groups provide fault tolerance. Gaggles can be used to encapsulate any replication mechanism; ISIS process groups can be used with or without encapsulation.

2.3. Replicated Objects in Emerald

In existing Emerald systems, although great care is taken to present the illusion that each object has a unique representation, some objects are actually replicated by the implementation.

Emerald distinguishes immutable objects from mutable objects. Immutable objects are often small objects like integers, strings, or types; if a remote node wishes to access such an object, it makes sense to create a local copy on that node. Because the state of an immutable object does not change, the implementation can create many copies of an immutable object without affecting Emerald's shared object semantics.

User-defined objects can also be declared to be immutable; the implementation may choose to replicate such objects too. Emerald requires only that the *abstract* state of an immutable object not change; it is legal for an immutable object to change its *concrete* representation. For example, an immutable object that represents a function could memoize its results and still be immutable. If a programmer erroneously declares as **immutable** an object whose abstract state changes, then the result of a computation will depend on the number of copies that the implementation chooses to create.

Gaggles may be viewed as an extension of this mechanism. Invoking a Gaggle is like invoking an immutable object: one of the representative objects will be chosen to receive the invocation, and the semantics of the computation should be oblivious to this choice.

2.4. Fragmented Objects

The SOS system designed at INRIA [14] supports "Fragmented Objects"; fragments of a single object can be located on separate machines. To clients, the whole Fragmented Object appears to be a single object. However, each fragment can view the other fragments as if they are self-contained objects, and the failure of one fragment does not cause the failure of the whole Fragmented Object.

A client accesses a Fragmented Object through a fragment in its own address space, which plays a rôle similar to that of a stub in an RPC system. This stub fragment in turn accesses other fragments using a lower-level fragmented object called a channel. Any particular message is delivered to either a single fragment or to multiple fragments, depending on the nature of the channel (which is under the control of the Fragmented Object). The channels and the fragments may run a membership protocol so that they are constantly aware of changes in availability. Before a client can use a Fragmented Object for the first time, it must go through a binding process to create an appropriate channel and encapsulate it in the stub fragment.

Compared to Gaggles, Fragmented Objects provide the programmer with much more flexibility, and associated complexity. provide one very simple way to invoke a plurality of objects; Fragmented Objects provide a collection of mechanism out of which the object designer can build his or her own robust invocation mechanism.

3. Using Gaggles

Gaggles are quite flexible, and can be used in many different ways. First we describe some of the usage paradigms or "idioms" that we have encountered; then we sketch some examples of more complete applications.

3.1. Usage Paradigms

A Gaggle of Independent Objects.

This is the most obvious way of using a Gaggle. A number of equivalent and independent objects are placed in the Gaggle; the client invokes the Gaggle directly for service. A Gaggle of independent objects might be used to access one of a number of equivalent time servers or name servers.

The Consistent Gaggle.

Although Gaggles do not themselves provide any consistency, they can be used to encapsulate the interface to a group of objects that do collaborate to maintain consistency. The replicated file service described in the introduction illustrates one way of achieving consistency. An ISIS-style process group is another way. Because the members of the Gaggle can refer to each other by their own names, any consistency algorithm of the implementor's choice can be used. Clients of the consistent Gaggle invoke it using the name of the Gaggle invokee.

A Gaggle of Workers.

A Gaggle of objects can be used to encapsulate a pool of worker processes that provide computational cycles for a client. Suppose a Gaggle of n objects is created and located on various hosts in order to distribute the computational load. A client object would invoke the Gaggle to initiate work on a particular subtask. Such a request would be received by an arbitrary member of the Gaggle. However, because each member of the Gaggle would be aware of the rule used to share tasks, it would be a trivial matter for the receiver to forward the task to the appropriate worker. For example, the convention might be to assign task k to worker object k **mod** n.

If the amount of data associated with the task is large, this arrangement has the disadvantage that the data must be sent to the receiver and then forwarded to the worker. This can be avoided by not sending the data in the request message; instead the client's name is sent. Once the worker is selected, it can then invoke the client to request its share of the data directly.

Multiple Names per Object.

Gaggles can be used to provide multiple names (object identifiers) for a single object. The object simply creates several Gaggles, and then makes itself a member of each. Each Gaggle will have a distinct name. So long as it is the only member, all invocations on the Gaggles will arrive at the creating object.

To allow an object to have different behaviours when it is invoked by its various names, we have added a new keyword (**invokee**) that permits an object to ascertain the name used by the invoker (see section 4.3).

Hiding Object Identity.

It has long been assumed that because the *concept* of object identity is essential to describing the semantics of object-oriented languages, the ability to *test* the identity of two object references is similarly essential. Recently, this assumption has been questioned. The ANSA system [1] does not provide a built-in way of testing object identity at all; if the application demands the ability to test the identity of a certain class of objects, then this can be provided by adding an explicit *getIdentity* operation to the code that defines those objects.

In a system like Emerald that *does* provide testable object identity, Gaggles can be used to hide it. This is done by creating multiple names for an object, as described in the previous section. Indeed, the very *possibility* that an object might be known by multiple names means that programmers cannot assume that distinct names refer to distinct objects. Thus, if it is essential that a reliable identity test be available on a particular class of object, the programmer should provide those objects with a *getIdentity* operation.

3.2. Some Applications of Gaggles

Accessing a Name Service.

Lampson has described a highly available large scale name service [11] with many servers, each supporting some fragment of the naming tree. A given directory may be replicated on several servers. Each server also keeps information on how to access the servers that store the parents of its directories.

In order to resolve a name one typically accesses a local server. If that server stores the appropriate directory, it will return the value associated with the name in question. Otherwise, it will return information that will help the requester find an authoritative name server.

Updates are made in a similar way. Because there may be multiple copies of a single directory, and two updates to the same subtree may be received by different servers, it is possible for different servers to present inconsistent views of the namespace. Various algorithms are run on the servers to ensure that all changes will *eventually* be reflected at all concerned servers. However, clients may see temporary inconsistencies, such as a newly-created sub-directory not yet being visible in an ennumeration of the parent directory.

A client of the name service typically uses an object (a clerk) to provide a single access point for the service. The clerk encapsulates information about the service, such as which servers support various parts of the namespace, and may also cache the results of previous queries. The name server clerk deals with an enquiry by first searching its own cache, and if possible returning a result without ever contacting a name server. If no match is found in the cache, the clerk makes a corresponding inquiry of a nearby name server. The clerk can keep information about the responsiveness and location of several servers to improve performance. Updates are first reflected in the cache, and then forwarded to a server for the appropriate naming domain.

The advantage of this arrangement is that while the clerk improves responsiveness, it keeps no vital data. There is no need for the clerk to be persistent. If it crashes, the client can use a new clerk. In fact, there typically will be several clerks active at a give time; it does not matter which one the client uses.

This sort of application can be implemented conveniently by making the clerks a Gaggle of independent objects. Using a sufficiently-large Gaggle helps to ensure that a clerk is always available. Since using the same clerk in successive operations is not necessary for correctness, the fact that successive Gaggle invocations may be dealt with by different receivers is not a concern.

Causally Consistent Name Service.

Although the weak consistency of a Lampson-style name service helps to ensure high-availability and low latency, Ladin has observed that sometimes this semantics is inadequate [10]. For example, suppose a system administrator wishes to create a new sub-directory and then to populate it with information about printers. If the update that creates the directory goes to one server and the request to add the first printer goes to another, the operation to add the printer may fail because the directory does not exist. In this situation, high availability doesn't help: the perceived behaviour does not meet the user's requirements.

Ladin describes a mechanism that lets the client obtain whatever degree of consistency it requires. Each update to the namespace returns an identifier. Enquiries and updates may require that the state on which they operate is "later" than the state created by a certain set of updates; this set is identified *explicitly* by providing the set of update identifiers as an argument to the name server request. Using this mechanism it is possible to state that the various additions to the printer directory must be "later" than the update that created the directory. If such an addition happened to be sent to a server that has not yet seen the creation of the directory (i.e., it arrives too "early"), the addition will be delayed until the server has been able to obtain and apply the update that created the directory. In this way the algorithm achieves tighter consistency, possibly at the expense of increased response times.

A Gaggle of independent objects can be used to provide an interface to a Ladin-style name service just as effectively as to a Lampson-style name service, and in the same way. However, in a small-scale Ladin-style name service, where all directories are fully replicated, the rôle of the clerk in finding an authoritative server for a given operation disappears. Any server will do. In this situation, all the servers can be made members of a consistent Gaggle that can *itself* be the receiver of the updates and queries.

Mail dispatch.

When sending mail, the user agent needs to contact a message transfer agent that is willing to store and forward its messages. Any of a number of message transfer agents will serve.

This problem can be solved by constructing a Gaggle of independent message transfer agents, and by invoking the Gaggle to deposit outgoing mail. This Gaggle invocation will succeed if any one of the transfer agents can be found.

One Object, Many Rôles.

Sometimes a single object may play several rôles. For example, in a hierarchic file system the rôles of the various directory objects might all be implemented by a single B-tree object, rather than by having a separate object for each directory.

Reference 4 discusses a similar situation: a file that can be read by multiple clients simultaneously. A current file position index must be kept for each reader. The file object might create a channel sub-object for each reader; in this case the current file position would be implicit. Alternatively, the file might service all of the readers itself, and require that each read request supply a channel identifier.

A system designer ought to be able to use a single object playing multiple rôles, or to use a separate object for each rôle, depending on the costs and constraints of a particular situation. It might even be desirable to try both design alternatives. Unfortunately, in an object-oriented system in which each object has a single name, the two alternatives present different interfaces to the client. For example, if the operation to read from a channel relies on the identity of the channel object to determine which stream is to be read, then it would not be possible to combine several streams into a single multi-channel object, since an additional parameter would be required to select the required stream.

As we showed in Section 3.1, Gaggles provide a mechanism for giving an object multiple names. This enables each client to invoke a receiver specific to its channel, while still allowing the implementor to choose between the above strategies. A single file object known by multiple names could use the value of the invokee to choose the correct channel. Alternatively, the multiple names could be used to refer to genuinely distinct open file objects.

Type Restriction.

Hutchinson has experimented with an extension to Emerald in which it is possible to restrict the dynamic type of an object[†]. In this extension, the statement

restrict *e* **to** *t*

denotes a new object that has the same value as *e* but whose type is *t*. It is legal whenever **typeof** *e* – the dynamic type of the object denoted by *e* – conforms to *t*. This means that **typeof** *e* must be more general than *t*; *e* contains more operations, or the operations return more general results. Type restriction is not part of the standard Emerald language, but the same functionality can be obtained using Gaggles.

In Emerald, the dynamic type of an object will always conform to the syntactic type of any expression that evaluates to it. If $\mathcal{E}[\![\, expr\,]\!]$ denotes the value of *expr*, and $\mathcal{T}[\![\, expr\,]\!]$ denotes the *syntactic* type of *expr*, we have

$$\mathcal{E}[\![\, \textbf{typeof}\; n\,]\!] \succ \mathcal{T}[\![\, n\,]\!]\; .$$

The Emerald type checker guarantees this invariant, and also ensures that for every invocation *n.op*, the operation *op* is contained in the type $\mathcal{T}[\![\, n\,]\!]$ [7]. This means that if *n* is a variable that names an object *b*, only a subset of *b*'s operations will in general be available for invocation on *n*.

It is tempting to use this mechanism to restrict the operations that certain clients may perform on a particular object. However, such a restriction can always be circumvented, because an explicit widening coercion (a **view** expression) can be used to transform *n* into an expression with wider type on which all of *b*'s operation can be invoked.

However, Gaggles can be used to achieve the effect of secure narrowing. Consider a Gaggle invokee *B* whose type is a restriction of the dynamic type of an object *b*, and which has *b* as its only member. If the **typeof** primitive is applied to *B*, the result will be the restricted type (as explained in section 4.2), and any attempt to **view** it as a wider type will fail. Any invocations sent to *B* will be received by *b*, since it is the only member of the Gaggle.

4. The Design of Gaggles

This section presents the current design of Gaggles and discusses some of the alternatives we considered.

4.1. Syntax

One of the last issues that we dealt with is how Gaggles should appear in the Emerald language. In some ways, Gaggles are similar to other forms of collection, like Array and Vector, which are already in the language. Constructors for these collections are presented as Emerald objects. Much of their implementation is also in Emerald, although some operations must be implemented by system primitives. It seemed desirable to present Gaggles in the same manner. This approach minimizes changes to the language itself; the only additions are system primitives.

---

† Norman Hutchinson, *Personal Communication.*

The object *Gaggle* is similar to *Array*; it is immutable and has the following interface:

function *of* [*AType* : *Type*] → [*result* : *GaggleType*] .

The result of *Gaggle.of*[*AType*] is an immutable object with the following interface (which we will call *GaggleType*)

function *getSignature* [ ] → [*Signature*]
operation *new* [ ] → [*GaggleManager*] .

There are two ways of viewing a Gaggle. A *GaggleManager* represents the management interface of the Gaggle, and exports operations to add members and to access the service interface:

operation *addMember* [*AType*] → [ ]   % *the only management operation*
function *invokee* [ ] → [*AType*]   % *returns the service interface* .

The result of *invokee* looks like an ordinary object of the type given in the *of* operation. In particular, it can be invoked; for this reason we call this entity the GaggleInvokee.

The following code fragment shows how a Gaggle might be populated and used.

const *aGaggleManager* ← *Gaggle.of*[*NSClerk*].*new*
aGaggleManager.*addMember*[*NS*.*lookup*["*primary clerk*"]]
aGaggleManager.*addMember*[*NS*.*lookup*["*alternate clerk*"]]
aGaggleManager.*addMember*[*NS*.*lookup*["*backup clerk*"]]
const *aClerk* : *NSClerk* ← *aGaggleManager*.*invokee*[ ]

After this sequence, *aClerk* is bound to the Gaggle's service interface, which can be treated like an object of type *NSClerk*.

4.2. Semantics

In order to make a GaggleInvokee like an object, every aspect of the language that involves objects must be defined for GaggleInvokees.

In Emerald, a program may **move** an object to a location, **fix** an object at a location, **unfix** an object, **refix** an object at a new location, determine the **typeof** an object, **view** an object as having another type, determine whether an object is **isfixed**, invoke an object, and **locate** an object. We have devised ways of handling all of these primitives.

- The Emerald **move** primitive is actually a hint; the implementation is not required to perform the move suggested. Thus, one alternative is to say that move applied to a GaggleInvokee does nothing. But, it is conceivable that the Gaggle would like to take some action when an object tries to move it, such as creating a new member at the specified location. For this reason, members of a Gaggle may provide an operation *move_handler* which takes the appropriate action.

The semantics for move, when applied to a GaggleInvokee, is to invoke the operation *move_handler* on the GaggleInvokee. If the chosen receiver does not have such an operation, no action is taken.

- The **fix** statement fixes the location of an object; this prevents the object from moving until it is unfixed. Often, rather than specifying a location by means of a node object, the programmer specifies a second object at which to fix the first. In this case, the location of the second object is ascertained, and the first object is fixed at the same location. The **fix** statement fails if the object is already fixed.

  Since immutable objects are copied rather than moved, fixing an immutable object is a null operation. The location of an immutable object is always "here" (it is co-located with the enquirer), so fixing an object at an immutable object has the same effect as fixing an object at the current location. (At one time we considered creating a special object **everywhere** to represent the location of immutable objects; however, this was never implemented.)

  We considered imitating these semantics for Gaggles, but decided against it. Because the number and location of the members of a Gaggle are chosen by its manager, not by the system, there is no guarantee that there will always be a member at a particular location, and it seemed inappropriate to allow the statement **fix** *g* **at** *l* to succeed in spite of the fact that no member of the Gaggle *g* is at location *l*.

  The same objection can be raised against another alternative: treating **fix** like **move**, i.e., to say that members of a Gaggle may provide an operation *fix_handler*. Since **move** is a hint, the (user-defined) implementation cannot be "wrong". But **fix**, unlike **move**, is not a hint.

  We finally decided to make it an error to **fix** a GaggleInvokee, or to fix an object at a GaggleInvokee. With hindsight, it might also be wise for it to be an error to fix an immutable object.

- Since it is not an error to **unfix** an object which is not currently fixed, it is not an error to **unfix** a GaggleInvokee.

- The **refix** construct is an atomic **unfix** and **fix**; like **fix** it fails if either the object or location is a GaggleInvokee.

- The **typeof** a GaggleInvokee is the type that was used as argument to the *Gaggle.of* [· · ·] invocation that built the Gaggle manager. **typeof** does not return the type of any particular member, which might contain more operations). This is because the meaning of the statement "object *o* has type *T*" is that all the operations in *T* can be invoked on *o* without danger of a "Message-Not-Understood" error. In the case of a Gaggle, we can offer this guarantee only for the type specified as the argument to *Gaggle.of* [· · ·].

- The expression **view** *o* **as** *t* has syntactic type *t*. At execution time, the system checks that **typeof** *o* $\geqslant$ *t*. If it does, the view expression succeeds (and returns the *o*); otherwise, the view expression fails. This rule needs no modification for GaggleInvokees.

- The **isfixed** predicate tests whether or not a particular object is fixed. Since a GaggleInvokee cannot be fixed, **isfixed** applied to a GaggleInvokee is always false.

- Invocation of a GaggleInvokee is defined to be the invocation of some member of the Gaggle, if a member can be found. If no member can be found with reasonable effort, the GaggleInvokee is considered unavailable. The implementation is free to invoke any member, and need not choose the same object on consecutive invocations. Our reasons for this choice are discussed in Section 4.4.

- The expression **locate** o returns the current location of the object o. Evaluation of a **locate** expression requires running the object-finding algorithm normally used for invocation; **nil** is returned if the object cannot be found. For GaggleInvokees, an attempt is made to find some member of the Gaggle, and return its location. If no member can be found with reasonable effort, **nil** is returned.

  At first glance, this may seem like a rather peculiar semantics for **locate**. Two consecutive **locate** statements could return locations on different continents. But the same possibility exists without Gaggles, because objects are mobile.

4.3. Other Language Constructs

Emerald contains one other primitive, **self**, that must be clarified in the presence of Gaggles. In addition, we have added two new primitives, denoted by the keywords **isplural** and **invokee**.

- **self** always denotes the current object, i.e., the one that evaluates **self**. In the case of a member of a Gaggle, it does not refer to the Gaggle but to the member itself.

- **invokee** denotes the name of the current invokee. An object may need to know if it has been invoked as a member of a Gaggle (and if so, of which Gaggle) or if it is has been invoked under its own name. **invokee** returns the GaggleInvokee if the object was invoked as part of a Gaggle, and **self** otherwise.

  This keyword is permitted only within the bodies of operations. Inside an initially, recovery, or process section the object has not been invoked and thus **invokee** has no meaning.

- **isplural** is a primitive predicate; **isplural** o returns **true** if o is a GaggleInvokee, and **false** otherwise. Although a client cannot violate the encapsulation of plurality and see the members of a Gaggle, it may occasionally be necessary to know whether or not an object is a GaggleInvokee. The provision of **isplural** is in the same spirit as the provision of **locate**; we expect that it will be used infrequently, but that sometimes it will be required.

4.4. Semantics of Gaggle Invocation

Like objects, GaggleInvokees can be invoked. When this happens, the invocation could conceivably be sent to one, some, or all of the members of the Gaggle.

Sending the invocation to all members is an unwise choice, because if one member is unavailable the invocation must fail, and one of our goals was to increase availability. A more reasonable choice is to send the invocation to all *available* members; this is the option chosen by the ISIS process group mechanism. However, this means that the implementation must keep a list of currently available members, and that the delivery of invocations must be consistent with this list. In other words, it requires a full implementation of causally consistent groups. Our intention is that the Gaggle should be a lighter-weight mechanism that can be used to *build* causally consistent groups.

Another possibility is to invoke *many* of the members: not necessarily all, but several. This is not very useful; consistency cannot be achieved by this mechanism alone, and having all members that receive the invocation communicate it to all other members would generate an unnecessarily large number of messages.

The remaining alternative is to invoke a single member object. There are motivations for this choice besides the process of elimination: this is all that many applications require (see Section 3), and the other invocation protocols can be built on top of this mechanism. This alternative maintains the property that the users of a service are the only ones who pay for them. In addition, it results in simpler semantics and implementation.

4.5. Failure Semantics

With the above semantics for invocation, one should not interpret the fact that the GaggleInvokee is unavailable to indicate that every member of the Gaggle is broken. Indeed, given two simultaneous invocations of the same GaggleInvokee, one may fail while the other succeeds.

We have considered allowing an object to retry a failed invocation, while indicating to the system that it should try harder. Objects could thus try increasingly expensive levels of invocation before deciding that the GaggleInvokee is unavailable. Another possibility is to allow invoking objects to indicate the "permissible expense" of an invocation directly. Then, the implementation would try no harder than instructed to locate the object.

4.6. Ownership vs. Multiple Interfaces

We explored various alternatives for providing the management and service interfaces before settling on the scheme described above. One alternative was that one member of the Gaggle would be special: it would be the "owner". execute management operations. Unfortunately, if the owner crashed, the Gaggle would be incapacitated. We therefore considered allowing the owner to pass ownership rights to other objects.

The ownership concept implied that the owner of a Gaggle would not have the same type as other members of the Gaggle, since it would have additional operations for management. What, then, would be the type of a GaggleInvokee? This problem prompted us to conceive our present solution, which uses two distinct object identifiers to name the two distinct interfaces.

4.7. Types

The type of each member of a Gaggle must conform to the type of the GaggleInvokee. This does not imply that each member must have the same concrete type, or even the same abstract type. This typing rule is the most lenient possible: it is the minimum requirement on the members that ensures that sending an invocation to any one of the members will not result in a "Message-Not-Understood" error.

4.8. Removal and Enumeration

We do not provide these services for Gaggles. To do so would require maintaining a list of all members of a Gaggle and running consistency protocols. The price we pay for our light-weight Gaggles is that these operations are not possible. However, if they are required, these operations can be implemented at the user-level as follows.

An object can forward invocations to another object by making the body of each of its operations invoke the corresponding operation on the other object. Similarly, it may forward invocations to a set of objects by maintaining a list of the objects and forwarding invocations to each. The forwarding object can provide a list of the objects to which it currently forwards; these are the members. If it accepts instructions to update the list, it can also export operations to add and remove members.

However, the forwarding object is a single point of failure. If it breaks, the entire group is unavailable. This can be remedied by making the forwarding object a Gaggle. The Gaggle can also provide the desired removal and enumeration facilities; the members of the Gaggle run their own consistency protocol to ensure that membership changes are seen by all members of the Gaggle. Users of the group invoke the Gaggle, which forwards the invocation to the members of the group.

4.9. Gaggles as members of Gaggles

Since Gaggles are designed to be treated as objects, there is no reason why Gaggles should not be members of other Gaggles. An invocation of a Gaggle can be forwarded to any member, including a member that is a Gaggle. The consequence is that the invocation must eventually be delivered to a member of the transitive closure of the Gaggle that was initially invoked. Since Gaggles have no membership list, we cannot prevent a Gaggle from being (indirectly) a member of itself. This implies that the invocation protocol must detect cycles.

5. Implementation Considerations

Although do not yet have a complete implementation of Gaggles, we have considered many possible implementation strategies and their suitability for systems of varying scale. We are pleased that the design of Gaggles has not made implementation inflexible; indeed, we often found ourselves dazzled by the array of alternatives. Just as it is hard to imagine a single object finding algorithm suitable for systems of vastly differing scale, it is unlikely that a single Gaggle invocation algorithm will suffice in all situations. Given some basic constraints, such as the inclusion of protocol version numbers in the headers of messages, there is no reason why the implementation of Gaggles could not be different on different nodes, or be changed dynamically while the system is running.

There are two major primitives to be implemented: adding a member to a Gaggle, and invoking a gaggleInvokee. It seems that there is a tradeoff between work done at the time a member is added and at the time an invocation is made. At one extreme, we could tell every node in the network about every new member. Then, every node would have a complete membership list and invocation would easy. At the other extreme, we could tell no other node about the new member, and to perform an invocation we could ask every node if it knows of any member of the Gaggle.

There is no parallel to the Gaggle *addMember* operation in an ordinary Emerald system. However, we do have experience with various algorithms for finding (singular) objects. An understanding of these algorithms will form the basis on which we can build a Gaggle finding algorithm.

5.1. Algorithms for Finding Objects

Emerald combines the process of finding an object with the process of invoking it. This is done for efficiency (objects are usually found at their previous location) and for correctness (an object might move between the two stages of an algorithms that first found an object and then invoked it).

The Broadcast Algorithm.

The original Emerald system ran over a five-node local area network at the University of Washington. The identities of the nodes were static and well-known.

If a node needed to invoke an object not present locally, it checked to see if it had a forwarding pointer to the object (a last known location of the object). If it did, the invocation was sent to that node. If the object was still there, the invocation would succeed. Otherwise, the forwarding chain would be followed until either the object was found and invoked or the chain broke.

If the object was found, the invoking node received a new forwarding pointer so that it could update its local tables. If the invoking node had no initial forwarding pointer, or if the forwarding chain had broken, the invoking node used broadcasts and, if they failed, a series of reliable point-to-point messages to all other nodes in the network. The object would either be found, or it would be determined to be unavailable.

Although this algorithm was suitable for a small scale local area area network, it is clear that it will not scale to the wide area.

The Hermes Algorithm.

The Hermes location algorithm was designed for the wide area and does not require broadcasts [6]. Forwarding pointers are still used, but in the event of a broken forwarding chain, the location of the object is obtained from stable storage.

Each Hermes object has a current location and a storesite, both of which may change. The storesite is a stable storage device that preserves a record of the object's state. When an object moves, the node from which the object is moving keeps a forwarding pointer to the new location; in addition, the storesite is informed of the new location. The forwarding pointers are appropriately timestamped so that one can tell which of two forwarding pointers is newer. Whenever a reference to an object is passed from one node to another, a pointer to its last known location is passed as well. Thus, when one object invokes another, the Hermes algorithm always has a forwarding pointer to follow. If the chain of forwarding pointers is broken, the location of the object is retrieved from stable storage.

Since the object can change its storesite, finding the current storesite is not trivial. The name of the object's initial storesite is encoded in its identifier. When the object chooses a new storesite, the old storesite is required to keep a forwarding pointer to the new one; the name service is also informed. When the location of the new storesite has become stable in the name service, the old storesite can forget the forwarding pointer.

Modifying the finding algorithms for Gaggles.

It is clear that following forwarding pointers will not work one object identifier can refer to many objects. This is precisely the situation we have created with Gaggles.

One solution is to break the problem into two pieces. First, when a node invokes a gaggleInvokee, it selects a particular member to invoke. Then the Hermes algorithm is used to find and invoke that member. Unfortunately, this gives up the advantages of the Gaggle's non-deterministic invocation semantics. If the particular member chosen happens to be at the end of a long forwarding chain, the invocation will be slow, even though some of the nodes that participated in the forwarding process might host other members of the Gaggle.

The alternative approach – invoking all known members in parallel – violates the semantics of Gaggles. Finding all known members in parallel and then invoking the one that is found first is correct but potentially expensive. We are forced to see a compromise.

If a member of the invoked Gaggle is local to the invoking node, the invocation can be performed without further ado. If there is no local member, one of the known members is selected (using the best information that is available locally) and the forwarding chain for that object is followed. However, the invocation message contains not only the identifier of the selected object, but also a tag indicating that this is a Gaggle invocation, and the identifier of the gaggleInvokee. Now the recipient of this message has more freedom of action. If the selected member of the Gaggle is local, the invocation can be performed. If it is not, but some other member of the Gaggle is local, the invocation can *still* be performed. Failing these happy eventualities, the recipient can either follow the forwarding chain for the initially selected object, or it can substitute some other known member of the Gaggle and forward the invocation to it.

Some care must be taken to ensure that this algorithm terminates. It is sufficient to record in the invocation message the most recent timestamped forwarding pointers to all of the members on which invocation has been attempted. In the case of nested Gaggles, this will also serve to detect membership cycles.

The effectiveness of this algorithm depends on the care with which we select the particular member to which the invocation is forwarded at each step. The selection is assisted by keeping as much information as possible about the various members. In addition to timestamped forwarding pointers, we might keep information about network topology, system loads, and response times measured on previous invocations.

The initial invoker (indeed, any node on the invocation path) can also limit the flexibility that it grants to other nodes later in the chain by setting a maximum number of forwarding steps; when the maximum is reached, the invocation is forwarded no further, but instead a progress report is returned to the initial invoker containing updated membership information and forwarding pointers. The initial invoker can then decide whether to continue with its first choice of member or to try a different member. (A similar facility appears in the Hermes algorithm under the name of a hop-count; however, since in Hermes the invoked object is singular, the initial invoker has no freedom of choice. However, limiting the length of forwarding chains does increase robustness.)

In general, there are two parameters for the location algorithm: the topology of the network, and the members of the Gaggle. Given complete information about both, it would be easy to select the best member to invoke. But we do not have such information. Our response is twofold: first, we try to propagate as much information as we can, as cheaply as possible; second, we recognize that our information will never be complete, and strive do as well as possible with what we have.

Stable Storage.

The Hermes object-finding algorithm uses stable storage as a last resort. We can increase the robustness of Gaggles by using the name service to provide a form of stable storage for the gaggleManager.

Whenever a member is added to a group, it is possible to immediately update the (global) name-service. Alternatively, the updates can be batched. Now, if a node cannot find those members of a Gaggle that it knows about, it can ask the name server for a membership list and see if there are additional members. Since the name server is not up-to-date, it cannot be relied on to supply the names of all members; since it is a global service, it is relatively expensive, and should be used only as a last resort. However, since members are never removed from a Gaggle, the information received from the name service, while incomplete, will never be incorrect.

Thus, stable storage for a Gaggle is implemented a little differently than for an ordinary object, but not inelegantly. Just as objects that exist in a single place store their state at a single storesite, objects that exist in a plurality of places store their state in a "distributed storesite": a name service.

The *addMember* operation.

When a member is added to a Gaggle, it is not clear to whom that information should be propagated. The membership table on the node where the *addMember* invocation occurred should certainly be updated. In addition, a name server update might be made or queued, as mentioned above. Beyond this, various alternatives are possible.

The reason to propagate membership information is to reduce the message traffic necessary to implement an invocation. Any propagation strategy that uses extra messages is therefore suspect. However, piggybacking Gaggle membership information onto existing node to node communication is promising. For example, nearby machines could be notified of new Gaggle members when status and load information are exchanged. Or, the next time an invocation for the gaggleInvokee is seen by the adding node, the membership update could be returned.

5.2. The Emerald implementation of Gaggles

The code for the Emerald run-time library that implements Gaggles is given in Figure 3. The only necessary additions to the Emerald language are the system primitives that implement *addMember* and that generate a new name (an object identifier) for the gaggleInvokee. This name is the only state in a gaggleManager; it is constant and assigned at object creation time, so the gaggleManager is immutable. Thus, when the name of agaggleManager is passed from one object to another, giving another object the ability to manage the Gaggle, the gaggleManager can be passed by value. Thus, if the name of the gaggleManager is passed to several objects on different nodes, the gaggleManager has been automatically replicated.

6. Current Status

The original implementation of Emerald generated highly efficient native code for a network of microVAX[TM] II workstations [9]. It has been ported to networks of SUN[TM] workstations. However, both the generation of native code and the history of the implementation have made the compiler and run time support for this version of the system hard to maintain.

[TM] VAX is a trademark of Digital Equipment Corporation. SUN is a trademark of SUN microsystems, Inc.

```
const Gaggle ←
  immutable object Gaggle
    export function of [ memberType : type ] → [ result : gaggleType ]
      where gaggleType ←
        typeobject gaggleType
          function getSignature [ ] → [ Signature ]
          operation new [ ] → [ gaggleManager ]
        end gaggleType
      where gaggleManager ←
        typeobject gaggleManager
          operation addMember [ memberType ] → [ ]
          function invokee [ ] → [ memberType ]
        end gaggleManager

      result ←
        immutable object gaggleCons
          export function getSignature [ ] → [ s : Signature ]
            s ← gaggleManager
          end getSignature
          export operation new [ ] → [ aGaggleManager : gaggleManager ]
            aGaggleManager ←
              immutable object manager
                initially
                  const theInvokee ← % a system primitive generating
                                     % a new object identifier
                end initially
                export operation addMember [ newMember : memberType ] → [ ]
                  % A system primitive handling member addition
                end addMember
                export operation invokee [ ] → [ gaggleInvokee : memberType ]
                  gaggleInvokee ← theInvokee
                end invokee
              end manager
          end new
        end GaggleCons
  end Gaggle
```

Figure 3: Emerald implementation of Gaggles

To promote the use of Emerald as a teaching and research tool, Norman Hutchison created a portable version of the Emerald compiler (written in Emerald), and a portable run-time system (written in portable C). However, this version of the language was restricted to a single address space.

During the summer of 1992, the present authors started to add distribution to the portable version of Emerald. As this work progressed, we began to consider the extensions described here. We hope that Gaggles will be implemented as part of our ongoing work to complete the distributed portable implementation of Emerald.

We have not come to any definite conclusion about the relative merits of one Gaggle finding algorithm over another; only benchmarks run on real implementations can definitively decide that question. However, we have highlighted some of the problems involved, examined many of the choices, and presented some plausible solutions.

Acknowledgements

We wish to thank the Cambridge Research Laboratory of Digital Equipment Corporation for providing computing resources and for the support of the first author, and the Division of Applied Sciences of Harvard University for the support of the second author while the work reported here was undertaken. We also wish to thank Norman Hutchinson and Eric Jul for helpful discussions while Gaggles were being designed, Robbert van Renesse for his assistance in obtaining information about ISIS, and Marc Shapiro and Messac Makpangou for information about SOS.

References

[1]   Architecture Projects Management Ltd. "ANSA: An Application Programmer's Intro-duction to the Architecture". TR.017, APM Ltd, November 1991.

[2]   Bernstein, P. A. and Goodman, N. "An Algorithm for Concurrency Control and Recovery in Replicated Distributed Databases". *Trans. Database Systems* **9**, *4* (December 1984), pp.596-615.

[3]   Birman, K. P., Schiper, A. and Stephenson, P. "Lightweight Causal and Atomic Group Multicast". *Trans. Computer Systems* **9**, *3* (August 1991), pp.272-314.

[4]   Black, A. P. "Supporting Distributed Applications: Experience with Eden". *Proc. 10th ACM Symp. on Operating Systems Prin.*, December 1985, pp.181-193.

[5]   Black, A. P., Hutchinson, N., Jul, E., Levy, H. M. and Carter, L. "Distribution and Abstract Types in Emerald". *IEEE Trans. on Software Eng.* **SE-13**, *1* (January 1987), pp.65-76.

[6]   Black, A. P. and Artsy, Y. "Implementing Location Independent Invocation". *IEEE Trans. on Parallel and Distributed Syst.* **1**, *1* (January 1990), pp.107-119.

[7]   Black, A. P. and Hutchinson, N. "Typechecking Polymorphism in Emerald". Tech. Rep. CRL 91/1 (Revised), DEC Cambridge Research Lab., Cambridge, MA, July 1991.

[8]   Gifford, D. K. "Weighted Voting for Replicated Data". *Proc. 7th ACM Symp. on Operating Systems Prin.*, December 1979, pp.150-159.

[9]   Jul, E.   *Object Mobility in a Distributed Object-Oriented System.* Ph.D. Thesis, University of Washington, Dept. of Computer Science, December 1988. (Tech. Rep. 88-12-06).

[10] Ladin, R., Liskov, B. and Shrira, L. "Lazy Replication: Exploiting the Semantics of Distributed Services". *Proc. of the 9th ACM Symp. on Prin. of Distributed Computing*, Quebec City, Quebec, August 1990, pp.43-57.

[11]   Lampson, B. W. "Designing a Global Name Service". *Proc. 5th ACM Symp. on Prin. Distributed Computing*, August 1986, pp. 1-10.

[12]   Pardyak, P. "Group Communication in an Object-Based Environment". *Proc. International Workshop on Object-Orientation in Operating Systems*, Paris, France, September 1992.

[13]   Schroeder, M. S. "Software Clerks". *Proc. ACM SIGOPS Workshop on Models and Paradigms for Distributed System Structuring*, Le Mont Saint-Michel, France, September 1992.

[14]   Shapiro, M., Gourhant, Y., Narzul, J. L. and Makpangou, M. "Structuring Distributed Applications as Fragmented Objects". Rapport de Recherche 1404, INRIA, Le Chesnay Cedex, France, January 1991.

[15]   van Renesse, R., Birman, K., Cooper, R., Glade, B. and Stephenson, P. "Reliable Multicast between Microkernels". *Proc. of the USENIX workshop on Micro-Kernels and Other Kernel Architectures*, Seattle, Washington, April 1992, pp. 269-283.

[16]   van Renesse, R., Cooper, R., Glade, B. and Stephenson, P. "A RISC Approach to Process Groups". *Proc. ACM SIGOPS Workshop on Models and Paradigms for Distributed System Structuring*, Le Mont Saint-Michel, France, September 1992.

Object Oriented Interoperability

Dimitri Konstantas

University of Geneva[1]

Abstract. Object Oriented Interoperability is an extension and generalization of the Procedure Oriented Interoperability approaches taken in the past. It provides an interoperability support frame by considering the object as the basic interoperation unit. This way interoperation is based on higher level abstractions and it is independent of the specific interface through which a service is used. A prototype implementation demonstrates both the feasibility of the ideas and the related implementation issues.

1 Introduction

An important issue in today's large heterogeneous networks is the support for *interoperability*, that is the ability of two or more entities, such as programs, objects, applications or environments, to communicate and cooperate despite differences in the implementation language, the execution environment or the model abstractions. The motivation in the introduction of interoperation between entities is the mutual exchange of information and the use of resources available on other environments.

1.1 Procedure Oriented Interoperability

The problem of interface matching between offered and requested services has been identified by many researchers [3][9][14][15][16][17][20] as an essential factor for a high level interoperability in open systems. Nevertheless, most of the approaches taken in the past [9][14][16][20] are based on the Remote Procedure Call (RPC) paradigm and handle interoperability at the point of procedure call. We call this type of interoperability support approach *Procedure Oriented Interoperability (POI)*. In Procedure Oriented Interoperability support it is assumed that the functionality offered by the server's procedures matches exactly the functionality requested by the client. Thus the main focus of the interoperability support is the adaption of the actual parameters passed to the procedure call at the client side to the requested procedures at the server side. An example of this approach is the one taken in the *Polylith* system [16]. The basic assumption of the approach is that the interface requested by the client (at the point of the procedure call) and the interface offered by the server "fail to match exactly". That is the offered and requested parameters of the operation calls differ. A language called *NIMBLE* has been developed that allows programmers to declare how the actual parameters of a procedure call should be rearranged and transformed in order to match the formal parameters of the target procedure. The supported parameter transformations include coercion

---

1. *Author's address:* Centre Universitaire d'Informatique, University of Geneva, 24, rue Général-Dufour, CH-1211 Geneva 4, Switzerland.
E-mail: dimitri@cui.unige.ch. *Tel:* +41 (22) 705.76.47. *Fax:* +41 (22) 320.29.27.

O.M. Nierstrasz (Ed.): ECOOP '93, LNCS 707, pp. 80-102, 1993.
© Springer-Verlag Berlin Heidelberg 1993

of parameters, as for example five integers to an array of integers, parameter evaluation, as for example the transformation of the strings "male" and "female" to integer values, and parameter extensions, that is, providing default values for missing parameters. The types of the parameters that are handled are basic data types (integers, strings, booleans etc.) and their aggregates (arrays or structures of integers, characters etc.). The programmer specifies the mapping between the actual parameters at the client side and the formal parameters at the server side using NIMBLE and the system will then automatically generate code that handles the transformations at run time.

Whereas NIMBLE focuses in bridging the differences between the offered and requested service interfaces, the *Specification Level Interoperability (SLI)* support of the *Arcadia* project [20] focuses on the generation of interfaces in the local execution environment through which services in other execution environments can be accessed. The major advantage of SLI is that it defines type compatibility in terms of the properties (specification) of the objects and hides representation differences for both abstract and simple types. This way SLI will hide, for example, the fact that a stack is represented as a linked list or as an array, making its representation irrelevant to the interoperating programs sharing the stack. In SLI the specifications of the types that are shared between interoperating programs are expressed in the *Unifying Type Model (UTM)* notation. UTM is a unifying model in the sense *"that it is sufficient for describing those properties of an entity's type that are relevant from the perspective of any of the interoperating programs that share instances of that type"*[20]. SLI provides a set of language bindings and underlying implementations that relate the relevant parts of a type definition given in the language to a definition as given in the UTM. In SLI the implementer of a new service will need to specify in UTM the service interface and provide any needed new type definitions for the shared objects and language bindings that do not already exist. In doing so the user will be assisted by the *automated assistance tools* which allow him to browse through the existing UTM definitions, language bindings and underlying implementations. Once a UTM definition for a service has been defined the *automated generation tool* will produce the necessary interface in the implementation language selected plus any representation and code needed to affect the implementation of object instances. This way the *automated generation tool* will always produce the same interface specification from the same UTM input. However SLI can provide different bindings and implementations for the generated interface allowing a service to be obtained from different servers on different environments, provided that they all have the same UTM interface definition.

A similar approach to SLI has been taken in the *Common Object Request Broker Architecture* (CORBA) [14] of the Object Management Group (OMG). The Object Request Broker (ORB) *"provides interoperability between applications on different machines in distributed environments"*[14] and it is a common layer through which objects transparently exchange messages and receive replies. The interfaces that the client objects request and the object implementations provide, are described through the *Interface Definition Language (IDL)*. IDL is the means by which a particular object implementation tells its potential clients what operations are available and how they should be invoked. An interface definition written in IDL specifies completely the interface and each operation's parameters. The IDL concepts are mapped accordingly to the client languages depending on the facilities available in them. This way given an IDL interface, CORBA will generate interface stubs for the client language through which the service can be accessed using the predefined language bindings. In the current status of ORB, language bindings exist only for the C language.

Although the above approaches can provide interoperability support for a large number of applications, they have a number of drawbacks that severely restrict their interoperability support power. The first drawback is the degeneration of the "interface" for which interoperability support is provided to the level of a procedure call. A service is generally provided through an interface that is composed of a set of inter-related procedures. What is of importance is not the actual set of the interface procedures but the overall functionality they provide. By reducing the interoperability "interface" to the level of a procedure call, the inter-relation of the interface procedures is lost, since the interoperability support no longer sees the service interface as a single entity but as isolated procedures. This will create problems in approaches like Polylith's that bridge the differences between the offered and requested service interface, when there is no direct one-to-one correspondence between the interface's procedures (interface mismatch problem).

Interoperability approaches like SLI and CORBA on the other hand do not suffer from the interface mismatch problem, since the client is forced to use a predefined interface. Nevertheless, the enforcement of predefined interfaces (that is, sets of procedures with specified functionality) makes it very difficult to access alternative servers that provide the same service under a different interface. This is an important interoperability restriction since we can neither anticipate nor we can enforce in a open distributed environment the interface through which a service will be provided. With the SLI and CORBA approaches, the service's interface must also be embedded in the client's code. Any change in the server's interface will result in changes in the client code.

Another common characteristic and restriction of the above interoperability approaches is that they require the migration of the procedure parameters from the client's environment to the server's environment. As a result only *migratable* types can be used as procedure parameters. These are the basic data types (integers, strings, reals etc.) and their aggregates (arrays, structures etc.), which we call *data types*. Composite non migratable abstract types, like a database or keyboard type, cannot be passed as procedure parameters. This however is a reasonable restriction since the above approaches focus in interoperability support for systems based on non-object oriented languages where only data types can be defined.

1.2   Object Oriented Interoperability

Although Procedure Oriented Interoperability provides a good basis for interoperability support between non-object oriented language based environments, it is not well suited for a high level interoperability support for environments based on object oriented languages. The reason is that in an object oriented environment we cannot decompose an object in a set of independent operations and data and view them separately, since this will mean loss of the object's semantics. For example, a set of operations that draw a line, a rectangle and print characters on a screen, have a different meaning if they are seen independently or in the context of a window server or a diagram plotting object. In object oriented environments it is the overall functionality of the object that is of importance and not the functionality of the independent operations. That means that the same functionality can be offered with a different interface[1] from different objects found either on the same or in different environments. Interoperability support in an object oriented environment should bridge the interface differences between the various objects offering the same service, while preserving the overall object semantics. We call this kind of interoperability support *Object Oriented Interoperability* (*OOI*).

Object Oriented Interoperability is a generalization of Procedure Oriented Interoperability in the sense that it will use, at its lower levels, the mechanisms and notions of POI. However OOI has several advantages over POI. First of all it allows the interoperation of applications in higher level abstractions, like the objects, and thus supports a more reliable and consistent interoperation. A second advantage is that it supports fast prototyping in application development and experimentation with different object components from different environments. The programmer can develop a prototype by reusing and experimenting with different existing objects in remote (or local) environments without having to change the code of the prototype when the reused object interfaces differ. A last advantage is that since OOI is a generalization of POI, it can be used to provide interoperation between both object oriented and conventional (non-object oriented) environments. Furthermore when OOI support is used for non-object oriented environments it provides a more general frame than POI and can also handle cases where the requested and offered service interfaces do not match.

In this paper we present the concept of Object Oriented Interoperability and describe our prototype implementation. In section 1 we give a brief overview of the previous interoperability approaches and outline the Object Orient Interoperability ideas. In section 2 we present in detail the Object Oriented Interoperability concepts and ideas and in section 3 we describe the prototype implementation. Finally in section 4 we give our conclusions, open issues and further research directions.

2 Overview of Object Oriented Interoperability

We identify two basic components necessary for the support and implementation of object oriented interoperability: *Type Matching* and *Object Mapping*. Type matching provides the means for defining the relations between types on different execution environments based on their functionality abstraction and object mapping provides the run time support for the implementation of the interoperability links.

2.1 Terminology

In the rest of this section we use the term *client interface* to specify the interface through which the client wishes to access a service, and the term *server interface* to specify the actual interface of the server. In addition we will use the term *node* to specify the execution environment of an application (client or server), as for example the Hybrid [4] execution environment or the Smalltalk [2] execution environment. In this sense a node

---

1. From here on we will use the term "interface" to signify the set of public operations and instance variables, through which functionality and data of an object are accessed.

can span over more than one computer and more than one node can co-exist on the same computer. Although we will assume that the client is in the *local* node and the server in the *remote* node, local and remote nodes can very well be one and the same. With the term *parameter* we mean the operation call parameters *and* the returned values, unless we explicitly state differently. Finally we should note that by the term *user* we mean the person that is responsible for the management of the application.

2.2 Type Matching

In a strongly distributed environment [19] a given service will be offered by many servers under different interfaces. As a result a client wishing to access a specific service from more than one server will have to use a different interface for each server. Although we can develop the client to support different interfaces for the services it access, we might not always be able to anticipate all possible interfaces through which a service can be offered, or force service providers to offer their services via a specific interface. Object Oriented Interoperability approaches this problem by handling all interface transformations, so that a client can use the same interface to access all servers offering the same service. The Type Matching problem consists of defining the bindings and transformations from the interface that the client uses, to the actual interface of the service.

2.2.1 Towards a solution to the Type Matching problem

Ideally we would like to obtain an automatic solution to the Type Matching problem. Unfortunately in the current state of the art this is not possible. The reason is that we have no way of expressing the semantics of the arbitrary functionality of a service or an operation, in a machine understandable form. In practice the best we can do is describe it in a manual page and choose wisely a name so that some indication is given about the functionality of the entity. Nevertheless, since nothing obliges us to choose meaningful names for types, operations or their parameters, we cannot make any assumptions about the meaning of these names. Furthermore even if the names are chosen to be meaningful, their interpretation depends in the context in which they appear. For example a type named *Account* has a totally different meaning and functionality when found in a banking environment and when found in a system administrator's environment. Thus any solution to the Type Matching problem will require, at some point, human intervention since the system can not automatically deduct either which type matches which, or which operation corresponds to which, or even which operation parameter corresponds to which between two matching operations. What the system can do is assist the user in defining the bindings and generate the corresponding implementations.

We distinguish three phases in providing a solution to the Type Matching problem. In the first phase, which we call the *functionality phase,* the user specifies the type or types on the remote environment providing the needed functionality (service). The system can assist the user in browsing the remote type hierarchy and retrieving information describing the functionality of the types. This information can be manual pages, information extracted from the type implementation or even usage examples.

In the second phase, which we call the *interface phase,* the user defines how the operations of the remote type(s) should be combined to emulate the functionality represented by the client's operations. This can a be a very simple task if there is a direct correspondence between requested and offered operations, or a complicated one if the operations from several remote types must be combined in order to achieve the needed result. As in the functionality phase the system can assist the user by providing information regarding the functionality of the operations.

The third phase is the *parameter phase*. After specifying the correspondence between the requested and remote interface operations the user will need to specify the parameters of the remote operations in relation to the ones that will be passed in the local operation call. This might require not only a definition of the correspondence between offered and requested parameters, but also the introduction of adaption functions that will transform or preprocess the parameters. The system can assist the user by identifying the types of the corresponding parameters, reusing any information introduced in the past regarding the relation between types and standard adaption functions, and prompt the user for any additional information that might be required.

2.2.2   Type Relations

In OOI we distinguish three types of type relations, depending on how the local type can be transformed to the remote type. Namely we have *equivalent, translated* and *type matched* types.

Migrating an object from one node to another means moving both of its parts, that is data and operations, to the remote node, while preserving the semantics of the object. However, moving the object operations essentially means that a new object type is introduced on the remote node. This case is presently of no interest to OOI since we wish to support interoperability through the reuse of existing types. Thus in OOI migrating an operation call parameter object means moving the data and using them to initialize an instance of a pre-existing equivalent type. This is most commonly the case with data types, like integers, strings and their aggregates, where the operations exist on all nodes and only the data need to be moved. In OOI when this kind of a relation exists between a type of the local node and a type of the remote node we say that the local type X, has an *equivalent* type X′ on the remote node and we denote it as

$X \Rightarrow X'$; *Local type X has X′ as equivalent type on the remote node.*

Although data types are the best candidates for equivalency relation, they are not the only ones. Other non-data types can also exist for which an equivalent type can be found on a remote node. For example a raster image or a database type can have an equivalent type on a remote node and only the image or database data need to be moved when migrating the object. In general two types can be defined as equivalent if their semantics and structure are equivalent and the transfer of the data of the object are sufficient to allow the migration of their instances. In migrating an object to its equivalent on the remote node, the OOI support must handle the representation differences of the transferred data. In this sense type equivalency of OOI corresponds to representation level interoperability [20].

In an object oriented environment we are more interested in the semantics of an object rather than its structure and internal implementation. For example, consider the Hybrid [13] type string and the CooL [1] type ARRAY OF CHAR. In the general case the semantics of the two types are different: the string is a single object, while the ARRAY OF CHAR is an aggregation of independent objects. Nevertheless when in CooL an ARRAY OF CHAR is used for representing a string, it becomes semantically equivalent and can be transformed to a Hybrid string, although the structure, representation and interfaces of the two types are different. In OOI this type relation is defined as *type translation* and it is noted as

X +> X´ : translationFunction ; *The local type X is translated to type X´ on the remote node, via the defined translation function.*

Translation of the local type to the remote type is done with a user definable translation function. This way the particularities of the semantic equivalency can be handled in case specific way. The user can specify different translations according to the semantics of the objects. For example if the local node is a CooL node and the remote a Hybrid node then we can define two different translations for an ARRAY OF CHAR:

ARRAY OF CHAR +> string : array2string ;
ARRAY OF CHAR +> array of integer : array2array ;

Where in the first case the ARRAY OF CHAR represents a character string, while in the second a collection of characters that need to be treated independently (in Hybrid characters are represented via integers).

Type translation can be compared to Specification Level Interoperability [20], where the interoperability support links the objects according to their specifications. Nevertheless, type translation is more flexible than SLI since it allows multiple translations of the same type according to the specific needs and semantics of the application.

A local type for which bindings to a remote type or types have been defined, as a solution to the Type Match problem, (that is, bindings and transformations from the interface that the client uses, to the actual interface of the service) is said to be *type matched* to the remote node. We can have two kinds of type matched types: multi-type matched and uni-type matched types. Multi type-matched types are the ones that are bound to more that one type on the remote node, and uni-type matched types are the ones that are bound to a single type on the remote node. In OOI we denote that a type X is type matched to types X´ and X´´ on the remote cell as

X –> X´ ; *Local type X is type-matched to remote type X´ .*

X –> < X´, X´´ > ; *Local type X is type-matched to remote types X´ and X´´.*

The target of OOI is to allow access to objects on remote nodes. The basic assumption being that the object in question cannot be migrated on the local node. However, the access and use of the remote object will be done with the exchange of other objects in the form of operation call parameters. The parameter objects can, in their turn, be migrated on the remote node or not. Parameter objects that cannot be migrated on the remote node are accessed on the local node via a type match, becoming themselves servers for objects on the remote node.

Type relations are specific to the node for which they are defined and do not imply that a reverse type relation exists, or that they can be applied for another node. For example, if the local node is a Hybrid node and the remote is a C++ node, the Hybrid type boolean has as equivalent in the C++ node an int (integer) (booleans in C++ are presented by integers), while the reverse is, in general, false.

2.2.3   To Type-Match or not to Type-Match?

Type matching is a general mechanism for interoperability support and it can be used in all cases in place of equivalency and translation of types. However, the existence of translation and equivalency of types is needed for performance reasons since accessing objects through the node boundary is an expensive operation. If an object is to be accessed frequently on the remote node, then it might be preferable to migrate it, either as equivalent or translated type. For example, it is preferable to migrate "small" objects, like the data types, rather than access them locally. Nevertheless the user has always the possibility to access any object locally, even an integer if this is needed, as it might the case with an integer that is stored at a specific memory address which is hardwired to an external sensor (like a thermometer) and which continuously updated. This can be done by defining a type match and using it in the parameter's binding definitions.

A typical scenario we envisage in the development of an application with OOI support is the following. The user (application programmer) will first define a set of type matchings for accessing objects on remote nodes. These will be used in the development of the application prototype. When the prototype is completed the user will measure the performance of the prototype and choose for which types a local implementation is to be provided. For these types an equivalency of translation relation will also be established, possibly on both nodes, so that they can be migrated and accessed locally. This way the performance of the prototype will be improved. This process can be repeated iteratively until the performance gains are no longer justifiable by the implementation effort.

One of the major advantages of the OOI approach is that in the above scenario the application prototype will not be modified when local implementations of types are introduced[1] and the type relations change. The new type relations are introduced in the OOI support and do not affect the application programs.

2.3   Object Mapping

Whereas type matching maintains the static information of the interoperability templates, object mapping provides the dynamic support and implementation of the interoperability links. We distinguish two parts in object mapping: the static and the dynamic. The static part of object mapping is responsible for the creation of the classes that implement the interoperability links as specified by the corresponding type matching. The dynamic part on the other hand, is responsible for the instantiation and management of the objects used during the interoperation.

2.3.1   Inter-Classes and Inter-Objects

The essence of object mapping is to dynamically introduce in the local node the services of servers found on other nodes. This however must be done in such way so that the access of the services is done according to the local conventions and paradigms. In an object oriented node this will be achieved with the instantiation of a local object that represents the remote server, which in OOI we call an *inter-object*. An inter-object differs

---

1. With the exception of a possible recompilation if dynamic linking is not supported.

from a proxy, as defined in [18], in three important points. First in contrast with a proxy, an inter-object and its server can belong to different programming and execution environments and thus they follow different paradigms, access mechanisms and interfaces. The second difference is that while a proxy provides the only access point to the actual server, that is the server can be accessed *only* via its proxies, this is not the case with inter-objects. Objects on the same node with the server can access it directly. An inter-object provides simply the gateway for accessing the server from remote nodes. Finally while a proxy is bound to a specific server, an inter-object can dynamically change its server or even access more than one server combining their services to appear as a single service on the local node.

An inter-object is an instance of a type for which a type match has been defined. The class (that is, the implementation of a type) of the inter-object is created by the object mapper from the type match information and we call it *inter-class*. An inter-class is generated automatically by the object mapper and it includes all code needed for implementing the links to the remote server or servers.

2.3.2 Dynamic Support of the Object Mapping

After the instantiation of an inter-object and the establishment of the links to the remote server, the controlling application will start calling the operations of the inter-object passing other objects as parameters. OOI allows objects of any type to be used as a parameters at operation calls. The object mapper will handle the parameter objects according to their type relations with the remote node. This way objects whose type has an equivalent or translated one on the remote node, will be migrated, while objects for which a type match exists will be accessed through an inter-object on the remote node.

In the case where no type relation exists for the type of a parameter object, the object mapper will invoke the type matcher and ask the user to provide a type relation. This way type relations can be specified efficiently taking into account the exact needs and circumstances of their use. In addition the dynamic definition of type relations during run time relieves the user from the task of searching the type hierarchy for undefined type relations. Also the incremental development and testing of a prototype becomes easier since no type relations need to be defined for the parts of the prototype that are not currently tested.

3 Prototype Implementation

A prototype implementation of Object Oriented Interoperability support was designed and developed for the Hybrid cell [5]. In this section we present the prototype implementation and discuss the related issues. In our presentation we are using interoperability examples for Hybrid and CooL. Hybrid is an object oriented language designed [13][7] and implemented [4] at the University of Geneva, whereas CooL is a an object oriented language designed and implemented in the ITHACA Esprit [1] project and which is now a product from Siemens-Nixdorf Inf. AG.

The implementation of the OOI support was part of the Cell prototype implementation [8]. The Cell is a frame for the design of strongly distributed object based systems [6]. In the Cell frame each node is transformed to a *cell* composed by a *nucleus* and a *membrane*. The nucleus is the original execution environment while the membrane surrounds the nucleus and is responsible for all external (to the nucleus) communication. The main goal of the Cell frame is to allow the objects of a node (nucleus) to transparently access and use services found on other heterogenous nodes, without introducing any changes to the nucleus.

3.1 Type Matching on the Hybrid cell

In order to provide support for type matching in the Hybrid cell, we designed and implemented a *Type Matching Specification Language (TMSL)* that allows the user to express type relations in a syntax very similar to the Hybrid language syntax. Although the design of the Hybrid TMSL (which we will refer as *H-TMSL*) has been influenced by the interface language NIMBLE [16], H-TMSL is more general since it allows any type to be used as parameter of an operation. In the following we describe the H-TMSL using examples of how the type relations for a CooL cell can be expressed. The full grammar of the H-TMSL is given in Annex I.

In the Hybrid cell the type relations defined in H-TMSL are stored in membrane objects. Nevertheless, in order to allow easier access from the UNIX environment (for debugging and verification) the definitions are also stored and kept synchronized in a UNIX file in H-TMSL syntax. At initialization of the membrane the file containing the type relation definitions is opened and all information is loaded into the membrane objects.

3.1.1 Type Relations

A type relation in H-TMSL is defined for a specific remote cell which is identified by its name.[1] For the examples given bellow we assume that the local Hybrid cell is named HybridCell and the remote CooL cell is named CooLCell. The general syntax of a type relation on the Hybrid cell is

IdOfRemoteCell :: <TypeRelation> ;

where TypeRelation can be either equivalent, translated or type matched and IdOfRemoteCell is the id of the remote cell, which in the case of the CooL cell is CooLCell.

Equivalent and Translated types.

In both CooL and Hybrid integers and booleans are equivalent types. On the Hybrid cell this is expressed as

CooLCell :: integer => INT ;
CooLCell :: boolean => BOOL ;

Although the notion of a *string* exist in both languages, in CooL strings are represented as arrays of characters while in Hybrid they are *basic data types*. Thus the relation between them is of a translated type

CooLCell :: string +> ARRAY OF CHAR : string2arrayOfChar ;

In the CooL cell the corresponding definitions will be:

HybridCell :: INT => integer ;

---

1. The names of the cells are managed by the membranes and are specific to it.

```
HybridCell :: BOOL => boolean ;
HybridCell :: ARRAY OF CHAR +> string : arrayOfChar2string ;
```

In the definition of translated types we specify a translation function, like string2array-OfChar and arrayOfChar2string, which performs the data translation.

Because type equivalency and translation imply knowledge and ability to access the internal representation of the objects, we do not allow, in the present implementation, the dynamic introduction of equivalent and translated types by the user. All information about equivalent and translated types is defined statically and loaded at initialization.

Type Matched types.

In contrast to equivalent and translated types, type matchings can be defined dynamically at run time by the user. A type can be matched to either a single remote type or to a collection of remote types (*multi-type match*). For example if we have on the local Hybrid cell a type windowServer, which is matched to the type WINDOW_CONTROL of the remote cell, the type match will be expressed as

```
CooLCell :: windowServer -> WINDOW_CONTROL {<operation bindings>} ;
```
while a multi-type match will be expressed as

```
CooLCell :: windowManager -> < WINDOW_CONTROL, SCREEN_MANAGER >
            { <operation bindings>} ;
```

When an object of the local nucleus in its attempt to access a service creates an instance of a type matched type (an inter-object), a corresponding instance of its type matched type will be created on the remote cell. However, there are cases where we do not want a new instance to be created on the remote cell but we need to connect to an existing server. This for example can be the case with a data-base object. We do not want an instance of an empty data-base but we want to use the existing one with all its stored data. In H-TMSL this is noted with the addition of @ at the of remote type name:

```
CooLCell :: personnel -> PERMANENT_PERSONEL_DB @
            { <operation bindings>} ;
```

If there are more than one instances of type PERMANENT_PERSONEL_DB at the CooL cell then it is up to the membrane to choose which one will be used. However in the case of an instantiation of an inter-object due to a parameter mapping, the object mapper will always bind the inter-object to the corresponding (pre-existing) parameter object.

In the rest of this section we describe the H-TMSL type matching syntax using as examples a Hybrid type windowServer, which defines in the Hybrid cell the interface through which a window server is to be accessed (requested interface), and a CooL type WINDOW_CONTROL which provides an implementation of the a window server (offered interface). For simplicity we assume that the operation names of the two types describe accurately the functionality of the operations. For example the operation named newWindow creates a new window, while the operation get_Position returns the position pointed by the pointing devices (i.e. mouse, touch-screen etc.).

The Hybrid type windowServer (Figure 1) has five operations. Operations newWindow and newSquareWin return the id of the newly created window or zero in case of failure. Operation refreshDisplay returns true or false signifying success or failure. Operation readCoordinates returns the coordinates of the active point on the screen as read

```
type windowServer : abstract {
      newWindow : (integer #{ : topLeftX #}, integer #{ : topLeftY #},
                   integer #{ : botRightX #}, integer #{ : botRightY #})
               -> integer #{: windowId #} ;
      newSquareWin : (integer #{ : topLeftX #}, integer #{ : topLeftY #},
                   integer #{ : side #} ) -> integer #{ : windowId #} ;
      refreshDisplay : (display ) -> boolean ;
      readCoordinates : ( mouse, keyboard, touchScreen, integer #{ : scaleFactor #} )
               -> point ;
      windowSelected : (mouse, keyboard, touchScreen ) -> integer ;
} ;
```

Figure 1   Hybrid Type windowServer.

from the pointing devices and operation windowSelected returns the id of the currently selected window or zero if no window is selected.

The CooL type WINDOW_CONTROL (Figure 2) has 4 methods. The methods cre-

```
TYPE WINDOW_CONTROL =
      OBJECT
            METHOD create_win ( IN botRightX : INT, IN botRightY : INT,
                         IN topLeftX : INT, IN topLeftY : INT, IN color : INT ) : INT
            METHOD redisplay_all (IN  display : DISPLAY) : INT
            METHOD get_Position (IN inDevices : IO_DEVICES, IN scaling : INT)
                   : POSITION
            METHOD select_Window (IN position : POSITION) : INT
      BODY
      ...
      END OBJECT
```

Figure 2   CooL Type WINDOW_CONTROL

ate_win and select_Window return the id of the newly created window and of the window into which the specific position is found, or -1 in case of an error. Method redisplay_all returns 0 or 1 signifying failure or success, and method get_Position returns the position pointed by the I/O devices (i.e. keyboard, mouse, touch-screen etc.) as adapted by the scaling factor.

3.2   Binding of Operations

Although type WINDOW_CONTROL provides all the functionality that type windowServer requires, this is done via an interface different to the one that windowServer expects. In general in H-TMSL we anticipate two levels of interface differences. First in the required parameters (order, type etc.) and second in the set of supported operations, that is, different number of operations with aggregated, segregated or slightly[1]

---

1. The term is used loosely and it is up to the user to define what constitutes a minor (slight) difference in functionality.

different functionality. The resolution of these differences corresponds to the parameter and interface phases of the type matching definition.

3.2.1 Parameters phase

Assuming that the functionality of the provided operation corresponds to the requested functionality, the differences between the parameters passed to the local operation call (offered parameters) and of the parameters required by the remote operation (requested parameters) can fall into one or more of the following categories:

- Different order of parameters. For example the first parameter of the local operation might correspond to the second on the remote operation.

- Different representation of the information held by the parameter. For example a boolean condition TRUE or FALSE can be represented locally by an integer while on the remote operation the string "TRUE" or "FALSE" might be expected.

- Different semantic representation of the information. For example if we have a Hybrid array with ten elements indexed from 10 to 19, an equivalent array in CooL will be indexed 1 to 10. Thus an index, say 15, of the Hybrid array should be communicated as 6 to the CooL cell.

- Different number of parameters. The requested parameters might be more or less than the offered ones. In this case the parameters offered might include all information needed or more information might be required.

H-TMSL anticipates all the above differences and allows the user to specify the needed transformations for handling them.

Migrated parameters

In our example we consider first the operations newWindow and create_win which have the same functionality specification. The binding of newWindow to create_win is expressed in H-TMSL as

newWindow : create_win(3, 4, 1, 2, int17()) ^ RET ;

Operation newWindow offers four parameters which are identified by their position with a positive integer (1 to 4). Method create_win will be called with these parameters transposed. Its first parameter will be the third passed by newWindow, the second will be the fourth and so on. The fifth parameter of create_win specifies the color of the new window. This information does not exists in the offered parameters. Nevertheless, in this case, we can use a default value with the use of an *adaption function*, like int17(). (Adaption functions are described in the next paragraphs.) The returned value from create_win, noted as RET in H-TMSL, is passed back to the Hybrid cell and becomes the value that newWindow will return.

In the above operation binding definition we assume that a relation for the CooL and Hybrid integers exists. That is we assume that on the Hybrid cell we have

CooLCell :: integer => INT ;

and on the CooL cell

HybridCell :: INT => integer ;

This way the migration of the parameters and returned values will be handled automatically.

Operation newSquareWin does not exist in the interface of WINDOW_CONTROL but its functionality can be achieved by operation create_win called with specific parameter values. That is we can have

newSquareWin : create_win (bottomRX(1, 3), bottomRY(2, 3),1, 2, int17()) ^ RET;

where functions bottomRX and bottomRY are adaption functions. Adaption functions are user defined functions, private to the specific type match. They provide the means through which the user can adapt the offered parameters to a format compatible to the requested parameters. They can be called with or without parameters. The parameters to be passed to the adaption functions can be any of the offered parameters or even the result of another adaption function. In the type matching definition of H-TMSL the adaption functions are included at the end of the type match definition between @{ and @}. Thus for the previous example we have the following adaption functions:

```
@{
      bottomRX : (integer : topLeftX, side ) -> integer ;
            { return (topLeftX + side ) ; }

      bottomRY : (integer : topLeftY, side ) -> integer ;
            { return (topLeftX - side ) ; }

      int17 :  -> integer ;
            { return (17) ; }
}@
```

The adaption functions will be invoked locally (that is, in our example, in the Hybrid cell) and their result will be passed as parameter to the remote call (create_win). An adaption function is effectively a private operation of the inter-class and as such it can access its instance variables or other operations.

Mapped Parameters

When the parameter cannot be migrated to the remote cell, that is when there is no corresponding equivalent or translated type, it should be accessed on the local cell. This will be done via a *mapping* of a remote object to the local parameter according to an existing type match. In our example this will need to be done for the refreshDisplay operation and redisplay_all method.

The parameter passed to refreshDisplay is an object of type display which cannot be migrated to the CooL cell. Thus it must be accessed on the Hybrid cell via a mapping on the CooL cell. For this a type match must exist on the CooL cell to the Hybrid display type.

HybridCell :: DISPLAY -> display { .... } ;

This way the binding of refreshDisplay to redisplay_all is expressed as

refreshDisplay : redisplay_all (1 : display <- DISPLAY) ^ int2bool(RET) ;

meaning that the first parameter of the method redisplay_all will be an object mapped to the first parameter passed to the operation refreshDisplay, according to the specified type match on the CooL cell. In addition the returned value of redisplay_all, which is an integer, is transformed to a boolean via the adaption function int2bool which is defined as following:

```
@{
     int2bool : ( integer : intval ) -> boolean ;
          {
               if ( intval ?= 0 )   { return (FALSE) ; }
               else                 { return ( TRUE ); }
          }
@}
```

Multi-type mapped parameters

In H-TMSL we also anticipate the case where the functionality of a type is expressed by the composite functionality of more than one type on the remote cell. In our example this is the case for the CooL type IO_DEVICES, which corresponds to the composite functionality of the Hybrid types mouse, keyboard and touchScreen.

HybridCell :: IO_DEVICES -> < keyboard @, mouse @, touchScreen @ > { ... } ;

Note that in this example the IO_DEVICES inter-object will be connected to the existing keyboard, mouse and touchScreen objects on the Hybrid cell.

The definition of multi-type match operation bindings is similar with that of single type match bindings, but with the definition of the operation's type. If for example we assume that type IO_DEVICES has a method read_keyboard which corresponds to the operation readInput of the Hybrid keyboard type, the binding would be expressed as

read_keyboard : keyboard.readInput (...) ^ ... ;

In fact this syntax is the general syntax for the definition of an operation binding and can be used in both single or multi type matchings. Nevertheless for simplicity in single type matchings the definition of the corresponding type can be omitted since there is only one type involved.

In our original example, the binding of the Hybrid operation readCoordinates to the operation get_Position will be expressed as

readCoordinates : get_Position (< 2,1, 3 > : < keyboard, mouse, touchScreen >
                              <- IO_DEVICES, 4) ^ RET

assuming that we have on the CooL cell the relation

HybridCell :: POSITION +> point ;

3.2.2   Interface adaption

When defining the operation bindings between two types from different environments there will be cases where the functionality of the local operation is an aggregation of the functionality of more than one remote operations. Adapting a requested operations interface to an offered one might require anything from simple combinations of the operations up to extensive programming. In order to simplify the user's task, H-TMSL allows the definition of simple operation combinations in the type match specification. For example the functionality of the Hybrid operation windowSelected can be obtained with the combination of the CooL methods get_Position and   select_Window. The operation binding is thus:

windowSelected : select_Window (WINDOW_CONTROL.get_Position (
     < 2,1, 3 > : < keyboard, mouse, touchScreen > <- IO_DEVICES, 4)) ^ RET ;

This defines that the method get_Position will first be called on the remote CooL cell and its result will not be returned to the calling Hybrid cell but it will be used as the first parameter to the select_Window method. Since the result of the get_Position method is not returned to the Hybrid cell, there is no need for a type relation of the CooL type PO-SITION to exist on the Hybrid cell.

To be noted that the remote operation call is defined as WINDOW_CONTROL.get_-Position, that is *with* the type that it belongs to, so that it be can distinguished from the adaption functions.

3.3 Object Mapping

Once a complete type match definition has been specified, the information is passed to the object mapping service (object mapper) which is responsible for the run-time support of the OOI. The object mapper will generate dynamically an inter-class for the local matched type, which in our example is the windowServer, and add it into the Hybrid workspace. The operations of the inter-class are generated from a general template and their task is to forward the operation call to the remote server [8]. When an instance of the type is requested, an inter-object will be instantiated connected to the remote server object, that is the instance of the WINDOW_CONTROL, with its operation bound to the corresponding server's operations. The object mapping service is responsible for locating the target cell and establishing and maintaining the communication channel(s). We then say that the instance of the WINDOW_CONTROL in the CooL cell is mapped into the Hybrid cell (Figure 3).

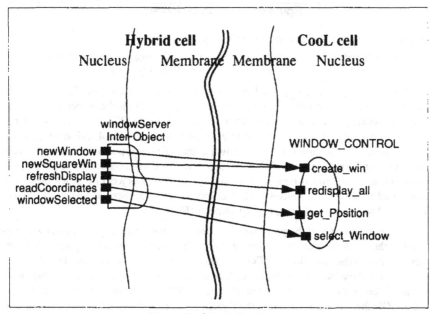

Figure 3 Object Mapping.

In order to outline the functionality of the object mapping service we will describe the actions taken when an operation of the windowServer inter-object is called. For our example we consider the operation readCoordinates, which is called with four parameters: a keyboard object, a mouse object, a touchScreen object and an integer (Figure 4)

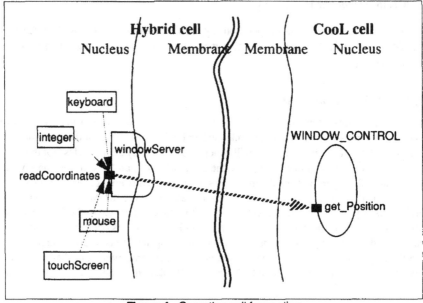

Figure 4 Operation call forwarding

and which is bound to the method get_Position.

readCoordinates : get_Position (< 2,1, 3 > : < keyboard, mouse, touchScreen >
<- IO_DEVICES, 4) ^ RET

From the 4 parameters passed to operation readCoordinates, the first three ones (keyboard, mouse and touchScreen) cannot be migrated to the CooL cell but must be accessed locally via a multi-type match of the CooL type IO_DEVICES. The fourth parameter is an integer for which an equivalent type exists on the CooL cell and thus it can be migrated to it. This information is known to the object mapper since it is included in the type match specifications. The local object mapper will contact the remote object mapper and request the instantiation of two object: an inter-object of type IO_DEVICES connected to the Hybrid objects keyboard, mouse and touchScreen and an INT object initialized to the value of the integer parameter (Figure 5).

When the transfer of the parameters has been completed the object mapper will proceed in the invocation of the remote operation. The remote object mapper will be instructed to call the operation get_Position passing it as parameters the IO_DEVICES inter-object and the INT object (Figure 6). The CooL object mapper will invoke the method and receive the result, an object of type POSITION. Because for the CooL type POSITION there is a translation to the Hybrid type point, the CooL object mapper will instruct the Hybrid object mapper to instantiate an object of type point which it will in-

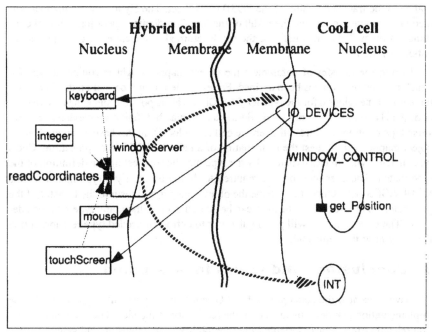

Figure 5 Parameters' transfer

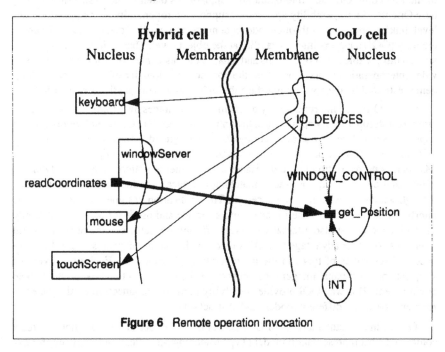

Figure 6 Remote operation invocation

itialize to the translated value of the POSITION object. The Hybrid object mapper will then be instructed to receive the result of the readCoordinates operation call in the instance of point. This will finally be the result returned to the caller of the readCoordinates operation.

During the transfer of parameters the object mapper might encounter a type for which no type relation has been defined. For example it might be that on the CooL cell there is no type relation for the type IO_DEVICES. This is possible since the type matcher of the Hybrid cell does not verify during a type match definition the existence of reverse type relations (i.e. from the remote cell to the local). In this case when the Hybrid object mapper will request the instantiation of an IO_DEVICES inter-object, the CooL type matcher will invoke dynamically the type matcher requesting the definition of the type match. The user will then be required to define on the fly a type match for the IO_DEVICES type. Once this is done the object mapper will resume the transfer of the parameters. This way an application can be started even without any type relations defined. The object mapper will prompt the user to define all needed type relation during the first run of the application.

4 Conclusions and issues to be studied

We have presented the concept of Object Oriented Interoperability and our prototype implementation that demonstrates both the feasibility of the ideas and the implementation related issues. Object Oriented Interoperability is an extension and generalization of the Procedure Oriented Interoperability approaches taken in the past. While Procedure Oriented Interoperability approaches support interoperability at the operation call level, linking applications through independent operation call, Object Oriented Interoperability (OOI) supports interoperability at the object level. That is, it considers the object, an inseparable set of operations and data, as the basic interoperation unit. OOI provides interoperation support based on the abstract functionality of the objects without being restricted by the specific interface through which their functionality is offered.

Object Oriented Interoperability offers many advantages over traditional Procedure Oriented Interoperability approaches. In contrast to Procedure Oriented Interoperability approaches which require parameter objects to be migrated to the remote environment, OOI allows parameter objects to access locally if they cannot be migrated. As a result OOI places no restriction to the interfaces used in interoperation. A second advantage is that OOI does not require exactly matching interfaces nor does it force the interface through which a service must be accessed. The application designer can decide on the interface that he wants to use for accessing a service and use it for accessing not only the target server but also alternative servers offering the same service under different interfaces. Another advantage of OOI is that it makes no assumptions about the existence and semantics of types in the interoperating environments. Each type, even the simplest and most banal integer type, must be explicitly related to a type on the remote environment. This way OOI provides flexibility in the interconnection of diverse environments based on different models and abstractions.

One of the "disadvantages" of OOI comes from the fact that it does not enforce a common global representation model (Type Matching Specification Language) for expressing the interoperability bindings. Each execution environment is free to choose its own language. As a result the interoperability type matching specifications for a server need to be defined independently by the user for each execution environment. However, bilateral mappings can offer a higher flexibility when the interoperating languages support special features. For example, a common interface definition language, like the CORBA IDL, does not include the notion of a *transaction*; thus, even when the interoperating languages support transactions, like Argus [11] and KAROS [2], their IDL based interoperation will not be able to use transactions.

Our prototype implementation for OOI support allowed us to identify several issues that need further studying. A first issue concerns the security aspects of OOI support. That is, not only the authorization and verification of the interoperating entities but also, and most important, the implications of allowing a remote user to define new type relations in the local environment and then instantiate the resulting inter-classes. The questions in this issue are who has the right to create new type relations and how this can be controlled. A second security aspect concerns the inter-relations with third parties. A user can define a type match and establish links for a type of a second cell that is itself type-matched to a third cell. In this case we access the third cell indirectly via the second cell, using accesses privileges that we might not have locally.

A second issue that needs to be studied concerns the public instance variables in the interconnection of application developed in different programming languages. The issue here is dual: first whether the public instance variables of a local type are meaningful to an inter-object and if so how they are bound and used, and second how do we handle the public instance variables of two applications written in different languages where one supports public instance variables while the other does not.

A last issue concerns the refinement of the TMSL syntax. For example, the choice of using numbers for expressing the parameter correspondence was not an optimal one. A better choice would have been to use a code, like #1, #2 etc., so that it would be easier to use integers for parameter extensions and not adaption functions. The syntax refinement will also allow us to define a TMSL framework that can adaptedable to more than one language.

We plan to continue our research by refining the Object Oriented Interoperability specifications and studying the open issues presented. In parallel we plan to design and develop OOI support prototypes for different executions environments, based on both Object Oriented and non-Object Oriented languages. Once the OOI support prototypes are developed we will use them for interconnecting different applications, both existing and specially developed, and study the related issues and problems.

References

[1]   Denise Bermek and Hugo Pickardt, "HooDS 0.3/00 Pilot Release Information", ITH-ACA.SNI.91.D2#4, August 28, 1991, Deliverable of the ESPRIT Project ITHACA (2705).

[2]   Rachid Guerraoui, *"Programmation Repartie par Objets: Etudes et Propositions"* Ph.D. Thesis, Universite de Paris-Sud, October 1992.

[3]   Adele Goldberg "Smalltalk-80", Addison Wesley 1984.

[4]   Yoshinori Kishimoto, Nobuto Kotaka, Shinichi Honiden, "OMEGA: A Dynamic Method Adaption Model for Object Migration", Laboratory for New Software Architectures, IPA Japan (Working Paper)

[5]   D. Konstantas, O.M. Nierstrasz and M. Papathomas, "An Implementation of Hybrid," in *Active Object Environments*, ed. D. Tsichritzis, pp. 61-105, Centre Universitaire d'Informatique, University of Geneva, 1988.

[6]   Dimitri Konstantas, "Cell: A model for Strongly Distributed Object Based Systems", in *Object Composition* ed. D. Tsichritzis, CUI, University of Geneva, 1991. Also presented in the ECOOP 91 Workshop *"Object-Based Concurrent Computing"*.

[7]   Dimitri Konstantas, "Design Issues of a Strongly Distributed Object Based System," Proceedings of 2nd International Workshop for Object-Orientation in Operating Systems (I-WOOOS '91), IEEE, Palo-Alto, October 17-18, 1991.

[8]   Dimitri Konstantas, "Hybrid Update" in *Object Frameworks*, ed. D. Tsichritzis, Centre Universitaire d'Informatique, University of Geneva, 1992.

[9]   Dimitri Konstantas , "Hybrid Cell: An Implementaiton of an Object Based Strongly Distributed System", Proceedings of the *International Symposium on Autonoums Decentralized Systems ISADS 93*, Kawasaki, Japan, March 30, 1993. Also in *Object Frameworks*, ed. D. Tsichritzis, CUI, University of Geneva, 1992 under the title "The Implementation of the Hybrid Cell".

[10]   Jintae Lee and Thomas W. Malone, "How can Groups Communicate when they use Different Languages? Translating Between Partially Shared Type Hierarchies", Proceeding of the *Conference on Office Information Systems*, March 1988, Palo Alto CA.

[11]   Barbara Liskov, Dorothy Curtis, Paul Johnson and Robert Scheifler, "Implementation of Argus," in *Proceedings of the 11th ACM Symposium on Operating Systems Principles*, pp. 111–122, ACM, Austin TX (USA), November 1987.

[12]   Oscar M. Nierstrasz, "Active Objects in Hybrid", in *Object-Oriented Programming Systems Languages and Applications (OOPSLA)*, N. Meyrowitz (ed.), Special Issue of SIGPLAN Notices, Vol. 22, No. 12, Dec. 1987 243-253

[13]   *The Common Object Request Brocker: Architecture and Specification*, Object Management Group and X Open, Document Number 91.12.1 Revision 1.1

[14]   Xavier Pintado, "Gluons: Connecting Software Components", in *Object Composition* Technical report ed. D. Tsichritzis, Centre Universitaire d'Informatique, University of Geneva, 1991.

[15]   James M. Purtilo and Joanne A. Atlee, "Module Reuse by Interface Adaption", *Software Practice & Experience*, Vol. 21 No 6, June 1991.

[16]   Ken Sakamura, "Programmable Interface Design in HFDS", Proceedings of the Seventh TRON Project Symposium, Springer-Verlag 1990, Tokyo, 1990.

[17]   Marc Shapiro, "Structure and Encapsulation in Distributed Systems: The Proxy Principle," 6th International Conference on Distributed Computing Systems, Boston, Massachusetts, May 1986.

[18]   Peter Wegner, "Concepts and Paradigms for Object Oriented Programming.," ACM OOPS Messenger, vol. 1, no. 1, August 1990.

[19]   Jack C. Wileden, Alexander L. Wolf, William R. Rosenblatt and Peri L. Tarr, "Specification Level Interoperability," Communications of ACM, vol. 34, no. 5, May 1991.

Annex I: Type Matching Programming Language.

typeMatchDef	: remoteCellId ':::' typeMatch ';'
typeMatch	: localType '->' remoteTypes typeMatchSpec | localType '=>' remoteType [':' transFunction] | localType '+>' remoteType [':' transFunction]
remoteTypes	: '<' remoteTypeList '>'
remoteTypeList	: remoteType ['@'] [',' remoteTypeList]
typeMatchSpec	: '{' operMatchList '}' [adaptDefList]
adaptDefList	: '@{' Program '}@' [adaptDefList]
operMatchList	: operMatch [operMatchList]
operMatch	: localOpName ':' remoteOpDef '(' argMatchList ')' '^' returnValDef ';'
remoteOpDef	: remoteType '.' remoteOpName
argMatchList	: argMatch [',' argMatchList]
argMatch	: localArgId | adaptFunct '(' localArgId ')' | localArgId ':' localType '<-' remoteType | '<' localArgIdList '>' ':' '<' localTypeList '>' '<-' remoteType | remoteOpDef '(' argMatchList ')'
returnValDef	: RET | adaptFunct '(' RET ')' | RET ':' localType '->' remoteType
localArgIdList	: localArgId [',' localArgIdList]
localTypeList	: localType [',' localTypeList]
localArgId	: SMALL_INTEGER
localType	: STRING
remoteType	: STRING
remoteOpName	: STRING
remoteCellId	: STRING
transFunction	: STRING
adaptFunct	: STRING
Program	: *Program code in Hybrid.*

Annex II: Type Match definition example

```
CooLCell :: windowServer -> WINDOW_CONTROL {
      newWindow : create_win(3, 4, 1, 2, int17() ) ^ RET ;
      newSquareWin : create_win ( bottomRX(1, 3), bottomRY(2, 3),1, 2, int17() )
                  ^ RET ;
      refreshDisplay : redisplay_all ( 1 : display <- DISPLAY ) ^ int2bool(RET) ;
      readCoordinates : get_Position
                  (< 2,1, 3 > : < keyboard, mouse, touchScreen > <- IO_DEVICES, 4 )
                  ^ RET
      windowSelected : select_Window (
                  WINDOW_CONTROL.get_Position
                  ( < 2,1, 3 >  : < keyboard, mouse, touchScreen > <- IO_DEVICES,
int1() )
                  ) ^ RET ;
}
@{
      bottomRX : (integer : topLeftX, side ) -> integer ;
            { return (topLeftX + side ) ; }

      bottomRY : (integer : topLeftY, side ) -> integer ;
            { return (topLeftX - side ) ; }

      int17 :  -> integer ;
            { return (17) ; }

      int1 :  -> integer ;
            { return (1) ; }

      int2bool : ( integer : intval ) -> boolean ;
            {
                  var boolval : boolean ;
                  if ( intval ?= 0)      { boolval := FALSE ; }
                  else                   { boolval := TRUE ; }
                  return (boolval) ;
            }
@} ;
```

Implementation of Distributed Trellis

Bruno Achauer

Computer Science Department, Telecooperation Group
University of Karlsruhe, D-76128 Karlsruhe, Germany

Abstract. DOWL is an extension of the Trellis language supporting distribution. It allows programmers to transparently invoke operations on remote objects and to move objects between the nodes of a distributed system. A few primitives permit the programmer to take full advantage of distribution and to tune performance; most notably by restricting the mobility of objects and specifying which objects should move together. This paper describes the implementation of these extensions: the object format, communication system and the mechanism to invoke operations on remote objects. Performance figures are also presented.

1 Introduction

Object-oriented systems are well-suited for distributed processing: in the object-oriented paradigm, flow of both control and data is performed by sending messages between objects. Provided that there is an appropriate addressing mechanism, these messages can be sent over a network; thus, operations on objects can be invoked regardless of their actual location. Moreover, location-independent invocation allow movement of objects at run time, providing opportunities for dynamic reconfiguration and load adaption.

In contrast to remote procedure call (RPC), the distributed object-oriented paradigm is not bound to client/server architectures and provides full syntactical and semantical equivalence between local and remote operation invocation: in both cases, arguments can be passed as object references.

However, complete distribution transparency is not desirable. For several reasons, there have to be mechanisms to make distribution visible. First, distributing an application obviously requires means for object placement. Second, even though there is no semantic difference between local and remote invocation, there are differences in performance. A mechanism to keep related objects closely together is therefore essential to keep the communication overhead tolerable. A related topic is parameter passing. Depending on the intended usage of arguments passed to an operation on a remote object, it might be beneficial to migrate arguments to the object instead of simply passing object references. Finally, there is a need to restrict the mobility of some objects, either because they are communicating heavily with entities outside the application or because they are bound to local resources.

This paper describes the implementation of DOWL, an extension of the Trellis language [12] to support transparent distribution. Rather than inventing a

O.M. Nierstrasz (Ed.): ECOOP '93, LNCS 707, pp. 103-117, 1993.
© Springer-Verlag Berlin Heidelberg 1993

new language, we wanted to extend a strongly typed, commercially available language to support distributed applications. One of our primary goals was upward compatibility; existing Trellis applications should run on the extended system without any changes.

Specifically, we have chosen to support fine-grained distribution because coarse-grained distribution models (e.g. by clustering objects at the language level) tend to destroy the uniform object model. Moreover, experience has shown that coarse-grained distribution usually introduces an additional abstraction level, which can create problems for the application programmer. For example, in the Argus system [10] there are two different object models, guardians and clusters, with different semantics: Clusters are data types living entirely within a guardian; they are accessed using local procedure calls. Guardians are similar to virtual nodes; they are accessed by remote procedure calls (with different parameter passing semantics). While building a distributed application based on Argus, Greif and others noticed that the semantic differences in this model can force the programmer to use a guardian where a cluster might be more appropriate [8].

The Trellis extensions to support distribution are: [1]

- An addressing mechanism allowing object references to span node boundaries and to invoke operations on remote objects. This is invisible at the language level; the only difference between a local and a remote invocation is a difference in performance.
- The (logical) nodes of the distributed system are represented by $Node objects. Besides containing information peculiar to the runtime system, they can also answer inquiries about the topology of the distributed system.
- An object's $location component contains the object's current location. Its initial value is the node on which the object was created, and it changes whenever the object moves.
  Assignment to the $location component causes the object to move (*migrate*) to the assigned object's location; thus, two objects can be brought together by simply specifying the first object's location to be the second object. Migration is possible even if the moving object currently has one of its operations activated; in this case, the operation is suspended and the operation's context moves along with the object to the target location where it is resumed. Finally, operation results are transmitted back to the caller of the operation.
- To prevent migration of an object, it can be *fixed* at a node. There are two mechanisms available: instances of a type declared with the $fixed attribute cannot migrate at all; their location is always the node on which they were created. Any attempt to unfix them will result in an error. The inverse attribute, $mobile states that instances of this type are able to migrate (this is the default).
  An object's $fixed_at component contains the node at which the object is fixed or the constant Nil if the object is able to migrate. For instances of a fixed type, this component cannot be altered. For others, assigning a node

to it atomically unfixes the object and migrates it to the specified location where it becomes fixed again. Assigning Nil unfixes the object.

- Although both local and remote operation invocation have identical semantics, they have different performance: Using today's technology, a local operation is several orders of magnitude faster than a remote one. It is therefore crucial to keep related objects closely together to reduce communication costs. DOWL provides two mechanisms to achieve this: explicit migration requests using the $location components, and attaching objects.

  To specify which objects should move together, objects can be *attached* [9] to other objects. Whenever an object migrates, all mobile objects attached to it will also move. Attachment is transitive; any object attached to a moving object will move also. However, attachment is not symmetric; an attached object can migrate without affecting any objects to which it is attached.

- Normally, arguments to an operation are passed as simple references to objects. In addition, DOWL offers two alternative mechanisms: *call-by-move* and *call-by-visit* [3], causing argument objects to migrate either permanently or temporarily to the location where invocation takes place.

Finally, there are two low-level primitives allowing which allow the programmer to violate distribution transparency: the $replicated type attribute forces instances of a (mutable) type to be replicated, and the $local_operation attribute requests an operation to be performed on the local representative regardless of the real object's actual location. These attributes are DOWL's equivalent to the asm statement in C; a programmer should use them only if he knows exactly what he is doing.

Prototypes of DOWL run on DEC's VAX and MIPS architecture workstations, and experience with the Trellis Programming environment (a large, non-distributed application [5]) suggests that we have achieved a high degree compatibility: Adapting the programming environment to DOWL required only minor changes to existing code (most of them were necessary to tell the compiler about the special treatment required for builtin types). In particular, there was only a single operation which required call-by-move.

The rest of this paper describes how these extensions are implemented: The next section presents DOWL's object format and the mechanisms supporting object references across node boundaries. Communication in DOWL is achieved by sending objects between the nodes; section 3 details the mapping of this communication model to facilities provided by the supporting operating system. Section 4 shows how remote object invocation and the parameter passing mechanisms work. Section 5 gives performance information. We conclude with a comparison with related work.

2 Object Format

Trellis distinguishes between constant and mutable objects. Constant objects cannot change their state once they are created and thus can be distributed by simple replication. In contrast, mutable objects can change during their lifetime. These objects can be used to share data; it is therefore important that only a single copy of a mutable object exists, to ensure that changes to the object made on one node are seen by all nodes. DOWL ensures this by distributing mutable objects as *proxies* [2, 7, 11]. A proxy is a (local) representative for some object residing on a remote node; it behaves exactly like the object it represents: invoking an operation on it is trapped by the runtime system and forwarded to the real object, which carries out the computation. Any results returned or exceptions raised are then transmitted back and delivered to the (local) caller.

Internally, an object is represented by a pointer to an object header, followed by several slots containing the object's instance variables (cf. figure 1). There are two kinds of slots: *Refs* are references to other objects, and *bytes* hold any kind of data that is not to be interpreted as an object reference (e.g. the individual characters of a string).

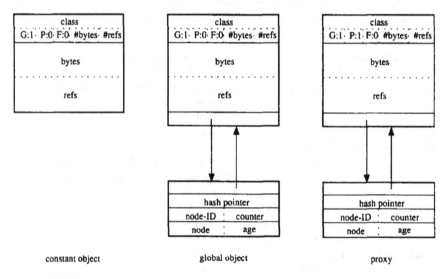

Fig. 1. DOWL object formats.

The object header consists of several subfields describing the object's type and its precise memory layout (i.e. the number of byte and ref slots present). Three flag bits contain information related to distribution:

- The *G-bit* distinguishes *global* objects (which can be referenced across node boundaries) from *local* objects (which are distributed by replication). Its value is determined by the object's type attributes; it never changes.

The other bits are significant for global objects only:

- The *P-bit* indicates whether the structure represents a resident object or a proxy; it is set and cleared as the object enters and leaves the node.

– The *F-bit* determines whether the object is currently fixed. For instances of a fixed type, its value cannot change; for others, it is set and cleared when the object is fixed and unfixed.

Finally, the slot part of a global object is followed by a pointer to a *global object descriptor*, a structure containing information required to implement inter-node references:

– The *global object identifier (GOID)* uniquely identifies the object. It consists of two parts: an identifier for the node that created the object and the value of a counter which is incremented whenever a new GOID is fabricated.
– A *forwarding address* [9] indicates the location of non-resident objects. It consists of two parts: an identifier for the node on which the object is believed to reside, and a counter showing how often the object has migrated so far. The counter is used to disambiguate conflicting forwarding addresses; a greater value indicates more recent location information.
– Each node maintains a hash table mapping GOIDs to object descriptors. A *hash pointer* chains all descriptors hashing to the same table slot.
– Finally, an *object pointer* points to the structure allocated for the object.

Descriptors only exist for proxies and resident objects that are referenced from remote nodes; all other objects may have a NULL descriptor pointer, meaning that no external references to the object exist. The descriptor is created only when the object or a reference to it leaves the node for the first time. On the other hand, object structures are only needed when the object is actually referenced; either locally or remotely through its descriptor. There is no need to retain the object for proxies that are not referenced locally; it is sufficient to have the descriptor which can forward all incoming requests. Eventually, the address information on nodes referring to these lone descriptors will be updated, and the descriptor can be reclaimed by the garbage collector.

The real object denoted by a proxy is located by following a chain of forwarding addresses until the object is found. This process is explained best by an example (cf. figure 2):

An object originally created on node A migrated to node B and then finally to node C. Both A and C still have local references to the object, but there are no more references to it on B and the storage allocated for the object structure has already been reclaimed by the garbage collector. Accessing the object from A now proceeds as follows:

1. The P-bit is set, identifying the object structure as a proxy. Consulting the object descriptor gives the object's global identifier (A-4711) and the information to look on node B for it.
2. B's descriptor table contains an entry for object A-4711, but there is no associated object structure (the object pointer is NULL). This identifies the descriptor as part of another proxy. (If the structure were still present, the proxy nature would be revealed by a set P-bit). Since forwarding addresses are consistent (B-0 vs. C-1), the search continues on node C.

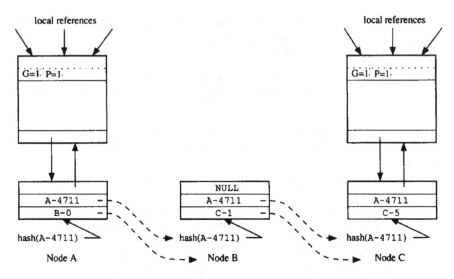

Fig. 2. Forwarding addresses.

3. Now, C has both a descriptor and a structure for object **A-4711**. Moreover, the structure's P-bit is clear, indicating that the object actually resides on C. Thus, the desired access can be performed and C sends the result directly to the original requester, A.

4. A receives both the result and a new location for the object which is more recent than its current address (**C-5** vs. **B-0**). Consequently, it updates the object's descriptor to point directly to node C. If updating the descriptor destroys the last reference to the descriptor on B, it will eventually be reclaimed by garbage collection.

The primary drawback of this object structure is the extra space required for proxy structures; each proxy must provide enough space to accommodate the real object just in case the real object should migrate to a node which has a proxy. This is not a severe problem since Trellis objects are rather small (the average object size is less than 40 bytes); moreover, for permanently fixed objects even this space can be saved because these objects will never migrate and thus can never replace one of their proxies.

On the other hand, representing both proxies and resident objects by the same structure increases efficiency; no indirection is required to access a slot of an object and there is also no need to convert between pointers to proxies and pointers to resident objects or to find and update any pointers. Furthermore, both local and remote objects are implemented by the same object layout, which allows the compiler and runtime support routines to deal with only a single kind of object structures.

A final advantage is the separation of object structures (manipulated by compiler-generated code and a few runtime support routines) and object descriptors (maintained entirely by the runtime system); this allows separation of local garbage collection (reclaiming object structures within a node) from distributed GC (reclaiming object descriptors).

3 Communication

Communication in DOWL is based on message passing. The communication system is implemented as two layers to hide the ultimate transmission method provided by the supporting operating system: a lower layer maintains connections between nodes; it provides functions to send or receive byte streams to or from any node in the system. The upper layer sends objects (more specifically, object graphs) to receivers denoted by arbitrary objects (usually proxies), using the lower layers's functionality for actual transmission. Communication between the layers is achieved by several FIFO queues to allow concurrent operation of both layers.

Besides converting messages between the object graph and byte streams format, the upper layer maintains the object descriptors (notably forwarding addresses and the P- and F-bits) and implements the attachment functionality. It is implemented as two procedures: linearization and delinearization.

Linearization is invoked by sending an object; it traverses the object graph to convert it into a byte stream that will finally be handed to the lower layer for delivery. For each object encountered during the traversal, it decides whether the object has to be included in the byte stream or whether it is sufficient to include the object's GOID and addressing information: Objects to be included are the root object, all local objects and all attached objects which are both resident and mobile. A side effect of the traversal is to allocate and initialize an object descriptor for each global object encountered (unless there is already a descriptor).

Encoding of an object consists of the the object's class, its storage layout and all slot values. Object references are encoded as offsets into the generated byte stream. For global objects, both the GOID and forwarding address from the object descriptor are also included. If the object itself is to be included into the byte stream, the forwarding address in the descriptor is updated to point to the the target node, and the age counter in the passed object is incremented.

A few objects are known to the runtime system and must be present on every node; examples are constants like True, False or Nil, types and methods. These objects are encoded specially and will be mapped to their remote counterparts.

Attached objects are recognized by *attachment maps*. The compiler creates one map for every type and every operation processed. Type maps identify those slots in the object structure containing attached objects, and operation maps show the location of attached variables in the operation's activation record.

Finally, the linearized structure is handed to the lower layer for actual transmission. Additional parameters (determined from the original object's type and from the way linearization was invoked) shows how the message must be dispatched on arrival:

- *Invocation messages* are sent by a thread trying to invoke an operation on a proxy. They are handed to the target node's *distribution server*, which will spawn a new thread to perform the operation.
- Results of remote operation are returned in *result messages*. They are passed to the thread that invoked the operation.
- All other messages are caused by object migration. Depending on how linearization was invoked, the object either becomes fixed or remains mobile.

At the target node, the byte stream is received by the lower layer and handed to the upper layer to reconstruct the object graph (delinearization). A major side-effect of this process is the updating of the descriptor table: in particular, descriptors are allocated for all unknown global objects found in the message and the received forwarding addresses are compared to the data from the descriptor table. If the received information is more recent, the descriptors are updated.

Reconstructing the object graph is done in two passes. The first pass locates all special objects and finds (reusing already existing proxies) or allocates storage for all others. The second pass initializes the slots in the non-special objects.

Finally, the reconstructed object is handed to the designated receiver: invocation messages are put on a queue from where they finally will be picked up by the distribution server. Result messages are handed directly to the thread awaiting completion of its remote invocation. All other messages request object migration; they are completely processed after the object graph is reconstructed.

The lower layer is responsible for reliable transmission of byte streams between nodes, using communication primitives provided by the supporting operating system. Its implementation in the current prototypes is based on TCP (stream sockets), which already provides reliable transmission. The actual implementation is therefore very simple. Every pair of nodes is connected by a bi-directional communication channel, which is operated by two activities on each side:

- A *write server* waits for byte streams to be put on a queue by the upper layer. It removes them and sends them asynchronously over the channel.
- The *read server* waits to receive byte streams from the channel. After receiving a message, it hands it to the upper layer for delinearization and dispatching to its receiver.

Finally, a *connection server* is used to implement system startup: A new node wishing to join the network first queries the connection server of an existing node about the topology of the system. Next, it contacts the connection server of every node, asking it to create the communication channel and to spawn the servers operating the channel. Finally, the new node creates its own server activities to access the channel and joins the system.

All servers are written in Trellis itself, backed up by a few builtin routines to access operating system services. Communication within a node is based on FIFO queues, which are part of the predefined library.

Implementation of the $location and $fixed_at components takes advantage of the migration primitives and the fact that invoking an operation on an object takes place at the object's actual location:

```
TYPE_MODULE Object

        COMPONENT ME.$location: OBJECT
        GET IS (Local_Node($Node))
        PUT IS BUILTIN ("Object_PutLocation", "trellis$image");
```

Since both operations are guaranteed to be performed at the object's actual location, the **get** operation is implemented by returning the node on which the operation takes place. Likewise, the **put** operation simply calls an entry point which checks whether the object to be moved is fixed. If so, it returns silently; otherwise, it moves its (resident) argument to the specified location.

$Fixed_at is implemented similarly[1], using a different entry point:

```
TYPE_MODULE Object

        COMPONENT ME.$fixed_at: $Node|Null
        GET IS BUILTIN ("Object_GetFixedAt", "trellis$image")
        PUT SIGNALS (is_fixed)
        PUT IS BUILTIN ("Object_PutFixedAt", "trellis$image");
```

4 Remote Invocation and Parameter Passing

The basic idea to implement operations on remote objects is borrowed from Amber [6]: Whenever there is a chance that an operation's controlling object (**self** in Smalltalk parlance) might be a proxy, check whether the operation operates on a resident object. If so, invocation can proceed; else, the operation is suspended, its context is migrated to the controlling argument's actual location where the operation is resumed. After the operation has returned, its results are sent back to the caller. Another benefit of this scheme is that objects can be moved even if they have one of their methods activated; the invocation context will follow the object as soon as it tries to access the object.

For operations on local objects, the residency check can be omitted because these objects are guaranteed to be always resident. For all others, it must be performed in three situations:

1. when invoking an operation (its controlling argument might be a proxy),
2. when returning from an operation (which might have migrated the controlling argument) and
3. after a context switch (another thread might have moved the controlling argument).

Implementing the check is cheap for the first two cases; on the VAX, it requires only two machine instructions (one of which is hardly ever executed):

```
        BBC     #34,me(LP),5    ; is controlling argument a proxy?
        JSB     GoOn_Remote     ; yes, trap to the run time system
```

---

[1] Here, the get operation is implemented by a builtin routine to avoid atomicity problems; builtin routines are guaranteed to be never interrupted.

In the current version of Trellis, context switches can occur only at predefined sequence points which are already covered by the other two checks, so the check for the third case can be omitted; it could be implemented by making the interrupt return sequence check for a proxy controlling argument.

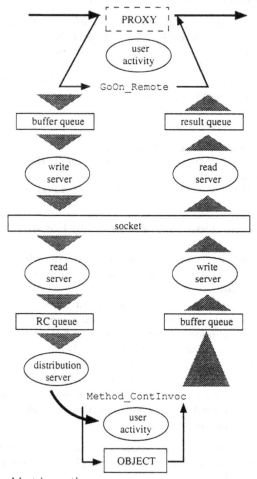

Fig. 3. Remote object invocation.

After a failed residency check, a run time support routine (GoOn_Remote) takes control. This routine causes the interrupted operation's context to migrate to its caller before being resumed. Specifically, the following steps are performed (cf. figure 3):

1. **GoOn_Remote** encapsulates the operation context into an invocation message object which is sent to the controlling object. **GoOn_Remote** then waits for a result message to arrive.

The encapsulated context consists of:
- the thread awaiting the result of the remote invocation,
- the name of the interrupted operation,
- the exact position where the operation was interrupted,
- the values of all other registers used by the operation,
- the size and contents of the operation's activation record and
- the activity's global context (e.g. its default I/O streams).

2. On the target node, the byte stream is received, the invocation message is reconstructed and passed to the node's distribution server.

3. The distribution server creates a new thread to resume the interrupted operation. The new thread executes **Method_ContInvoc** as its first routine; its argument is the operation context from the invocation message.

4. **Method_ContInvoc** restores the context of the suspended operation from the passed context: First, it allocates stack space to accommodate the operations activation record and initializes it from the original context. Next, it restores the values of all registers in use. Finally, the suspended operation is resumed by jumping to the residency check whose failure triggered the remote invocation.

   When restoring the stack frame, **Method_ContInvoc** pushed the address of the instruction after the jump instead of the original return address. This way, the stacks looks as if **Method_ContInvoc** had called the suspended operation and it will regain control when the operation finally returns.

   Finally, **Method_ContInvoc** encapsulates the operation's result and the global context into a result message which is sent back to the original thread. At this point, **Method_ContInvoc** returns, causing its thread to terminate.

5. When the result message finally arrives, the original thread is resumed. It pops the interrupted operation's frame (which completed on the remote node), extracts its result from the message and returns it to the operation's caller.

The **$replicated** type attribute is implemented by suppressing the residency checks for all operations owned by this type. **$Local_operation** suppresses the check for a single operation only.

Call-by-move and call-by-visit are implemented by marking the associated argument slots in the activation record as attached; this ensures that these arguments are always attached to the operation's controlling argument. In addition, the compiler generates additional code to migrate the argument objects to the invocation node. For example, the following code fragments compile to (roughly) the same machine code [2]:

```
OPERATION foo (ME, arg: $MOVE some_type)
IS BEGIN ...

OPERATION foo (ME, arg: $ATTACHED some_type)
```

---

[2] Colocate is a runtime support routine that tries to migrate its first argument to the second argument's location. It returns the initial location of the first argument if migration succeeded, **Nil** otherwise.

```
IS BEGIN
    colocate (arg, me);
    ...
```

If arguments are passed by visit, the generated code must also remember the object's original location; thus,

```
OPERATION foo (ME, arg: $VISIT some_type)
IS BEGIN
    ...
    RETURN;
    ...
```

is equivalent to

```
OPERATION foo (ME, arg: $ATTACHED some_type)
IS BEGIN
    VAR arg_loc: Object := colocate (arg, me);
    ...
    IF arg_loc ~= Nil THEN arg.$location := arg_loc END IF;
    RETURN;
    ...
```

5 Performance

We have performed several experiments to evaluate the performance of DOWL. All figures presented here were obtained by measuring the time required to execute the following operation:

```
OPERATION time (me, x: Dummy, n: Integer)
IS BEGIN
    LOOP EXIT WHEN (n <= 0);
        foo (x);
        n := n - 1;
    END LOOP;
END; !time
```

where foo is a null operation which returns immediately. Overhead introduced by checking for proxies and by performing remote operation invocation was determined by varying the characteristics (mutable vs. constant) and the relative locations of x and me (the object executing the loop). All experiments were conducted on two unloaded DECstation models 5000/240 connected by our departmental ethernet.

In the first experiment, both me and x were constant objects. Thus, neither the calling loop nor the called operation contained any proxy checks and the generated code was effectively the same as that generated by plain Trellis. The time required for one iteration was 3.8 microseconds.

In the second experiment, both me and x were mutable objects residing on the same node, which added four additional proxy checks to each iteration (three in the loop body and one in foo's entry code). Executing one iteration now required 4.9 microseconds, an overhead of 29% compared to Trellis.

However, this test models the worst case possible: a very tight loop doing no useful work. For real programs we've encountered much smaller performance degradations. For instance, a program creating a large graph and rearranging it several times was found to run about 9% slower under DOWL than it did under Trellis. This difference occurs because all user-defined objects are ultimately defined in terms of primitive types provided by the system, and a substantial amount of time is spent in operations on these building blocks. Since most primitive types are either constant or replicated, no proxy checks are required.

Proxy checking overhead could further be reduced by changing the strategy employed to place the checks: Instead of placing a proxy check at operation entry and after every operation invocation to guarantee that the controlling object is *always* resident, the checks could be placed before each access to an instance variable to ensure that the object is resident only when it is *necessary*. Flow analysis could reduce the number of proxy checks even further (e.g. there is only one check required for two instance variable accesses without an intervening operation invocation). This strategy will eliminate *all* checks from the timing loop above; its effect on real programs is currently under investigation.

To determine the performance of remote operation invocation, both me and x were fixed on different nodes. The time required to perform one iteration was 14.1 milliseconds, of which about 2.4 milliseconds were spent doing the actual TCP/IP transmission. In contrast, a null remote procedure call to a multithreaded server takes only 5.5 milliseconds using DCE RPC.

We suspect that a large fraction of DOWL's remote invocation overhead is caused by the message queues and servers connecting the two communication system layers, because performing a remote invocation requires at least seven activity context switches (there are even more if a large amount of data is transferred), which have a high latency in our implementation. Providing a procedural interface between the two layers could eliminate four of them and should thus increase performance significantly.

6 Related Work

Over the past years, several new object-based languages and extensions to existing languages with support for distribution have been presented. Some well-known examples are Emerald [3, 4, 9], Distributed Smalltalk [7, 2, 11] and Amber [6]. All systems provide location-independent invocation and migration of objects at run time.

Emerald is an object-based language. Its major features include a uniform object model, linguistic support for mobility control and for expressing object relationships.

Several implementations of Distributed Smalltalk allow interaction between Smalltalk images on different nodes. None of these systems supports mobility control or mechanisms to express object relationships; however, [2] addresses issues like access control, remote debugging and connecting heterogeneous nodes.

Amber augments a subset of C++ with primitives to manage concurrency and distribution. The system is designed to maximize performance by exploiting concurrency in short-lived applications. This is achieved by providing a network-wide shared virtual memory. There are no declarative mechanisms to restrict object mobility or to specify which objects are related; however, objects can be attached at run time. Both Amber and Emerald locate remote objects using forwarding addresses.

Most of the DOWL extensions have been inspired by Emerald. However, the appearance of the location primitives differs: Emerald uses predefined language constructs, while DOWL implements them in the standard library. Our approach allows individual types to redefine and customize these operations, e.g. to do type-specific cleanup or initialization when an object leaves or enters a node.

Emerald represents a global object as pointers to a descriptor containing addressing information and a pointer to the object's storage area which is only valid if the object is resident. Local objects are direct pointers to the storage. This scheme consumes less memory than DOWL's object structure (the descriptor usually is much smaller than the actual data), but it is less efficient because any access to an instance variable requires double indirection.

Proxies in Distributed Smalltalk are full-fledged objects that know about the location of the object they represent. Remote object invocation is implemented based on the doesNotUnderstand mechanism. Conversion between objects and proxies is achieved by exchanging object table entries, an option not available to systems like Emerald and DOWL where objects are represented by pointers.

Amber's base architecture is a shared virtual memory; thus, objects are represented by their addresses which are valid on every node. Remote object invocation is implemented using residence checks on operation invocation and return; after a failed check, the invocation context is migrated to the object and the operation is resumed.

When invoking an operation on a global object, Emerald checks a bit in the object descriptor to determine whether the object is resident. If this check fails, the parameters are sent to the object's actual location to perform the operation. To allow the migration of an object which has active operation invocations, the run time system searches all stacks for activation records corresponding to invocations on the migrating object. Any activation records found are moved along with the object and copied onto a new stack at the target node. The top part of the original stack (corresponding to operations called by the migrating context) is copied to a new stack on the original node. The boundaries of the three stacks are finally modified to appear as if remote operations were performed instead of local invocations.

DOWL's scheme migrates an operation context only if it absolutely has to; in particular, moving an object temporarily away from a node (which might happen frequently if call-by-visit is employed) need not result in any overhead except for migrating the object.

7 Conclusion

We have presented the runtime system of DOWL, an extension of the Trellis language to support transparent distribution: the object format, the structure of the communication system and the mechanism to invoke operations on remote objects. We believe that the performance of the system is acceptable, even though no tuning efforts have been implemented so far. DOWL is not radically different from the (few) other known distributed object-oriented systems, but excels by several subtle features, e.g. the possibility to circumvent distribution transparency if required, an object format allowing efficient instance variable access, decoupling local from global garbage collection and finally the sophisticated type system and programming environment inherited from Trellis.

Acknowledgments

I would like to thank Lutz Heuser for many instructive discussions during the design of DOWL and Max Mühlhäuser for providing helpful comments on a draft version of this paper. Special thanks go to Wulf Becherer. He designed and implemented key components of the runtime system.

This work was supported by Digital Equipment Corp. and was performed in part at the Computer Science Department at the University of Kaiserslautern.

References

1. Achauer, B.: Distribution in Trellis/DOWL. Proc. TOOLS USA '91
2. Bennet, J.: The Design and Implementation of Distributed Smalltalk. Proc. OOPSLA '87
3. Black, A., Hutchinson, N., Jul, E., Levy, H.: Object Structure in the Emerald System. Proc. OOPSLA '86
4. Black, A., Hutchinson, N., Jul, E., Levy, H., Carter, L.: Distribution and Abstract Types in Emerald. IEEE Trans. Software Engineering SE-13, 1987
5. O'Brien, P., Halbert, D., Kilian, M.: The Trellis Programming Environment. Proc. OOPSLA '87
6. Chase, J., Amador, F., Lazowska, E., Levy, H., Littlefield, R.: The Amber System: Parallel Programming on a Network of Multiprocessors. Proc. 12th ACM Symp. Operating Systems Principles, 1989
7. Decouchant, D.: Design of a Distributed Object Manager for the Smalltalk-80 system. Proc. OOPSLA '86
8. Greif, I., Seliger, R., Weihl, W.: A Case Study of CES: A Distributed Collaborative Editing System Implemented in Argus. Programming Methodology Group Memo 55, MIT, 1987.
9. Jul, E., Levy, H., Hutchinson, N., Black, A.: Fine-Grained Mobility in the Emerald System. ACM Trans. Computer Systems 6(1), 1982
10. Liskov, B.: Overview of the Argus Language and System. Programming Methodology Group Memo 40, MIT, 1984.
11. McCullogh, P.: Transparent Forwarding: First Steps. Proc. OOPSLA '87
12. Schaffert, C., Cooper, T., Bullis, B., Kilian, M., Wilpolt, C.: An Introduction to Trellis/OWL. Proc. OOPSLA '86

A New Definition of the Subtype Relation

Barbara Liskov[1] and Jeannette M. Wing[2]

[1] MIT Laboratory for Computer Science
Cambridge, MA 02139, USA
[2] School of Computer Science, Carnegie Mellon University,
Pittsburgh, PA 15213, USA

Abstract. The use of hierarchy is an important component of object-oriented design. Hierarchy allows the use of type families, in which higher level supertypes capture the behavior that all of their subtypes have in common. For this methodology to be effective, it is necessary to have a clear understanding of how subtypes and supertypes are related. This paper presents a new definition of the subtype relation that ensures that any property proved about supertype objects also holds for subtype objects. It also discusses the ramifications of the definition on the design of type families.

1 Introduction

What does it mean for one type to be a subtype of another? We argue that this is a semantic question having to do with the relationship between the specifications of the two types. In this paper we give a precise definition of the subtype relation in terms of the behavior of types as described by their specifications. Our definition extends earlier work by providing for subtypes that have more methods than their supertypes, and by allowing for sharing of mutable objects among multiple users. We also discuss the ramifications of the definition with respect to various kinds of subtype relationships and give examples of type families that satisfy the definition.

To motivate our notion of subtyping, consider how subtypes are used in object-oriented programming languages. In strongly typed languages such as Simula 67, C++, Modula-3, and Trellis/Owl, subtypes are used to broaden the assignment statement. An assignment

x: T := E

is considered to be legal provided the type of expression E is a subtype of the declared type T of variable x. Once the assignment has occurred, x will be used according to its "apparent" type T, with the expectation that if the program performs correctly when the actual type of x's object is T, it will also work correctly if the actual type of the object denoted by x is a subtype of T.

Clearly subtypes must provide the expected methods with compatible signatures. This consideration has led to the formulation by Cardelli of the contra/covariance rules [5]. However, these contra/covariance rules are not strong

O.M. Nierstrasz (Ed.): ECOOP '93, LNCS 707, pp. 118-141, 1993.
© Springer-Verlag Berlin Heidelberg 1993

enough to ensure that the program containing the above assignment will work correctly for any subtype of T, since all they do is ensure that no type errors will occur. It is well known that type checking, while very useful, captures only a small part of what it means for a program to be correct; the same is true for the contra/covariance rules.

For example, consider stacks and queues. These types might both have a *put* method to add an element and a *get* method to remove one. According to the contravariance rule, either could be a legal subtype of the other. However, a program written in the expectation that x is a stack is unlikely to work correctly if x actually denotes a queue, and vice versa.

What is needed is a stronger requirement that constrains the behavior of subtypes: the subtype's objects must behave "the same" as the supertype's as far as anyone using the supertype's objects can tell. This paper is concerned with obtaining a precise definition of this "subtype requirement." Our definition is applicable to a particularly general environment, one that allows multiple, possibly concurrent, users to share mutable objects; the environment is discussed further in Section 2. Although the states of objects in such an environment may reflect changes due to the activities of several users, we still want individual users to be able to make deductions about the current states of objects based on what they observed in the past. These deductions should be valid if they follow from the specification of an object's presumed type even though the object is actually a member of a subtype of that type and even though other users may be manipulating it using methods that do not exist for objects of the supertype.

In other words, we want the subtype to preserve *safety* properties ("nothing bad happens") that hold for the supertype. There are two kinds of safety properties: *invariant* properties, which are properties true of all states, and *history* properties, which are properties true of all sequences of states. For example, for a stack, an invariant property we might want to prove is that its size is always greater or equal to zero; a history property is that its bound never changes. We might also want to prove *liveness* properties ("something good eventually happens"), e.g., an element pushed onto a stack will eventually be popped, but our focus here will be just on safety properties. Our definition of subtype will guarantee that all the invariant and history properties that hold for objects of the supertype also hold for objects of the subtype.

Our approach lets programmers reason directly in terms of the specifications rather than the underlying mathematical models of types, be they algebras, categories, or higher-order lambda expressions. Our definition is motivated by pragmatic concerns: we wanted to make our ideas accessible to everyday programmers. We provide a simple checklist that can be used by programmers in a straightforward way to validate a proposed design of a type hierarchy. In this paper, we use informal specifications; see [20] for formal ones.

This paper makes two important technical contributions:

1. It provides a very general yet easy to use definition of the subtype relation. Our definition extends earlier work, including the most closely related work done by America [3], by allowing subtypes to have more methods than their supertypes.

2. It discusses the ramifications of the subtype relation and shows how interesting type families can be defined. For example, arrays are not a subtype of sequences (because the user of a sequence expects it not to change over time) and 32-bit integers are not a subtype of 64-bit integers (because a user of 64-bit integers would expect certain method calls to succeed that will fail when applied to 32-bit integers). We show in Section 4 how useful type hierarchies that have the desired characteristics can be defined.

The paper is organized as follows. We describe our model of computation in Section 2. In Section 3 we present and discuss our formal definition of subtyping, motivating it informally with an example relating stacks to bags. Section 4 discusses the ramifications of our definition on designing type hierarchies. We describe related work in Section 5, and then close with a summary of contributions.

2   Model of Computation

We assume a set of all potentially existing objects, *Obj*, partitioned into disjoint typed sets. Each object has a unique identity. A *type* defines a set of *legal values* for an object and a set of *methods* that provide the only means to manipulate that object. An object's actual representation is encapsulated by its set of methods.

Objects can be created and manipulated in the course of program execution. A *state* defines a value for each existing object. It is a pair of two mappings, an *environment* and a *store*. An environment maps program variables to objects; a store maps objects to values.

$$State = Env \times Store$$
$$Env = Var \rightarrow Obj$$
$$Store = Obj \rightarrow Val$$

Given an object, x, and a state ρ with an environment, e, and store, s, we use the notation x_ρ to denote the value of x in state ρ; i.e., $x_\rho = \rho.s(\rho.e(x))$. When we refer to the domain of a state, dom(ρ), we mean more precisely the domain of the store in that state.

We model a type as a triple, $< O, V, M >$, where $O \subseteq Obj$ is a set of objects, $V \subseteq Val$ is a set of legal values, and M is a set of methods. Each method for an object is a *constructor*, an *observer*, or a *mutator*. Constructors of an object of type τ return new objects of type τ; observers return results of other types; mutators modify the values of objects of type τ. A type is *mutable* if any of its methods is a mutator; otherwise it is *immutable*. We allow "mixed methods" where a constructor or an observer can also be a mutator. We also allow methods to signal exceptions; we assume termination exceptions, i.e., each method call either terminates normally or in one of a number of named exception conditions. To be consistent with object-oriented language notation, we write x.m(a) to denote the call of method m on object x with set of arguments a.

Objects come into existence and get their initial values through *creators*. Unlike other kinds of methods, creators do not belong to particular objects, but rather are independent operations. They are the "class methods"; the other methods are the "instance methods." (We are ignoring other kinds of class methods in this paper.)

A *computation*, i.e., program execution, is an alternating sequence of states and statements starting in some initial state, ρ_0:

$$\rho_0 \ S_1 \ \rho_1 \ \cdots \ \rho_{n-1} \ S_n \ \rho_n$$

Each statement, S_i, of a computation sequence is a partial function on states. A *history* is the subsequence of states of a computation. A state can change over time in only three ways[3]: the environment can change through assignment; the store can change through the invocation of a mutator; the domain can change through the invocation of a creator or constructor. We assume the execution of each statement is atomic. Objects are never destroyed:

$$\forall \ 1 \le i \le n \ . \ dom(\rho_{i-1}) \ \subseteq \ dom(\rho_i).$$

Computations take place within a universe of shared, possibly persistent objects. Sharing can occur not only within a single program through aliasing, but also through multiple users accessing the same object through their separate programs. We assume the use of the usual mechanisms, e.g., locking, for synchronizing concurrent access to objects; we require that the environment uses these mechanisms to ensure the atomicity of the execution of each method invocation. We are interested in persistence because we imagine scenarios in which a user might create and manipulate a set of objects today and store them away in a persistent repository for future use, either by that user or some other user. In terms of database jargon, we are interested in concurrent transactions, where we are ignoring aborts and the need for recovery. The focus of this paper is on subtyping, not concurrency or recoverability; specific solutions to those problems should apply in our context as well.

3 The Meaning of Subtype

3.1 The Basic Idea

To motivate the basic idea behind our notion of subtyping, let's look at a simple-minded, slightly contrived example. Consider a bounded bag type that provides *put* and *get* methods that insert and delete elements into a bag. *Put* has a pre-condition that checks to see that adding an element will not grow the bag beyond its bound. *Get* has a pre-condition that checks to see that the bag is non-empty. Informal specifications [19] for *put* and *get* for a bag object, b, are as follows:

---

[3] This model is based on CLU semantics.

put = **proc** (i: int)
    requires The size of b is less than its bound.
    modifies b
    ensures Inserts i into b.

get = **proc** () **returns** (int)
    requires b is not empty.
    modifies b
    ensures Removes and returns some integer from b.

Here the **requires** clause states the pre-condition. The **modifies** and **ensures** clauses together define the post-condition; the **modifies** clause lists objects that might be modified by the call and thus indicates that objects not listed are not modified.

Consider also a bounded stack type that has, in addition to *push* and *pop* methods, a *swap_top* method that takes an integer, i, and modifies the stack by replacing its top with i. Stack's *push* and *pop* methods have pre-conditions similar to bag's *put* and *get* and *swap_top* has a pre-condition requiring that the stack is non-empty. Informal specifications for methods of a stack, s, are as follows:

push = **proc** (i: int)
    requires The height of s is less than its bound.
    modifies s
    ensures Pushes i onto the top of s.

pop = **proc** () **returns** (int)
    requires s is not empty.
    modifies s
    ensures Removes the top element of s and returns it.

swap_top = **proc** (i: int)
    requires s is not empty.
    modifies s
    ensures Replaces s's top element with i.

Intuitively, stack is a subtype of bag because both are collections that retain an element added by *put/push* until it is removed by *get/pop*. The *get* method for bags does not specify precisely what element is removed; the *pop* method for stack is more constrained, but what it does is one of the permitted behaviors for bag's *get* method. Let's ignore *swap_top* for the moment.

Suppose we want to show stack is a subtype of bag. We need to relate the values of stacks to those of bags. This can be done by means of an *abstraction function*, like that used for proving the correctness of implementations [13]. A given stack value maps to a bag value where we abstract from the insertion order on the elements.

We also need to relate stack's methods to bag's. Clearly there is a correspondence between the stack's *put* method and bag's *push* and similarly for the *get* and *pop* methods (even though the names of the corresponding methods do not match). The pre- and post-conditions of corresponding methods will need to relate in some precise (to be defined) way. In showing this relationship we need to appeal to the abstraction function so that we can reason about stack values in terms of their corresponding bag values.

Finally, what about *swap_top*? There is no corresponding bag method so there is nothing to map it to. However, intuitively *swap_top* does not give us any additional computational power; it does not cause a modification to stacks that could not have been done in its absence. In fact, *swap_top* is a method on stacks whose behavior can be explained completely in terms of existing methods. In particular,

s.swap_top(i) = s.pop(); s.push(i)

If we have a bag object and know it, we would never call *swap_top* since it is defined only for stacks. If we have a stack object, we could call *swap_top*; but then for stack to still be a subtype of bag, we need a way to explain its behavior so that a user of the object as a bag does not observe non-bag-like behavior. We use an *extension map* for this explanation. We call it an extension map because we need to define it only for new methods introduced by the subtype.

The extension map for *swap_top* describes what looks like a straight-line program. A more complicated program would be required if stack also had a method to *clear* a stack object of all elements:

clear = **proc** ( )
    modifies s
    ensures Empties s.

This method would be mapped to a program that repeatedly used the *pop* method to remove elements from the stack until its size is zero (assuming there is a way to determine the size of a bag and stack, e.g., a more realistic specification of *get* would signal an exception if passed an empty bag).

Here then is our basic idea: Given two types, σ and τ, we want to say that σ is a subtype of τ if there exist correspondences between their respective sets of values and methods. Relating values is straightforward; we use an abstraction function. Relating methods is the more interesting part of our notion of subtyping. There are two main ideas. Informally, we require that:

- σ must have a corresponding method for each τ method. σ's corresponding method must have "compatible" behavior to τ's in a sense similar to its signature being "compatible" according to the usual contra/covariance rules. This boils down to showing that the pre-condition of τ's method implies that of σ's and the post-condition of σ's implies that of τ's. (We will see later that our actual definition of subtyping is slightly weaker.)
- If σ adds methods that have no correspondence to those in τ, we need a way to explain these new methods. So, for each new method added by σ to τ, we

need to show "a way" that the behavior of the new method could be effected by just those methods already defined for τ. This "way" in general might be a program.

3.2 Formal Definition

Our definition relies on the existence of specifications of types. The definition is deliberately independent of any particular specification language, but we do require that the specification of a type $\tau = < O, T, N >$ contain the following information:

- A description of the set of *legal* values, T.
- A description of each method, m $\in$ N, including:
  - its signature, i.e., the number and types of the arguments, the type of the result, and a list of exceptions.
  - its behavior, expressed in terms of a pre-condition, m.pre, and a post-condition, m.post. We assume these pre- and post-conditions are written as state predicates. We write m.pred for the predicate m.pre $\Rightarrow$ m.post.

The pre- and post-conditions allow us to talk about a method's side effects on mutable objects. In particular, they relate the final value of an object in a post state to its initial value in a pre state. In the presence of mutable types, it is crucial to distinguish between an object and its value as well as to distinguish between its initial and final values. We will use "pre" and "post" as the generic initial and final states in a method's specification. So, for example, x_{pre} stands for the value of the object x in the state upon method invocation.

To show that a subtype σ is related to supertype τ, we need to provide a *correspondence mapping*, which is a triple, $< A, R, E >$, of an *abstraction* function, a *renaming* function, and an *extension* mapping. The abstraction function relates the legal values of subtype objects to legal values of supertype objects, the renaming function relates subtype methods to supertype methods, and the extension mapping explains the effects of extra methods of the subtype that are not present in the supertype. We write $\sigma < \tau$ to denote that σ is a subtype of τ. Figure 1 presents our definition of the subtype relation.

Figure 2 illustrates the last clause of our definition, the diamond rule, which is key to handling extra mutators of the subtype. This diagram, read from top to bottom, is not quite like a standard commutative diagram because we are applying subtype methods to the same subtype object in both cases (m and E(x.m(a))) and then showing the two values obtained map via the abstraction function to the same supertype value.

3.3 Discussion

There are two kinds of properties that must hold for subtypes: (1) all calls to methods of the supertype have the same meaning when the actual call invokes a method of the subtype; (2) all invariants and history properties that hold for objects of the supertype must also hold for those of the subtype.

Definition of the subtype relation, $<$:

$\overline{\sigma = <O_\sigma, S, M>}$ is a *subtype* of $\tau = <O_\tau, T, N>$ if there exists a correspondence mapping, $<A, R, E>$, where:

1. The abstraction function, $A : S \to T$, is total, need not be onto, but can be many-to-one.
2. The renaming map, $R : M \to N$, can be partial and must be onto and one-to-one. If m_τ of τ is the corresponding renamed method m_σ of σ, the following rules must hold:
   - *Signature rule.*
     - *Contravariance of arguments.* m_τ and m_σ have the same number of arguments. If the list of argument types of m_τ is α_i and that of m_σ is β_i, then $\forall i.\alpha_i < \beta_i$.
     - *Covariance of result.* Either both m_τ and m_σ have a result or neither has. If there is a result, let m_τ's result type be γ and m_σ's be δ. Then $\delta < \gamma$.
     - *Exception rule.* The exceptions signaled by m_σ are contained in the set of exceptions signaled by m_τ.
   - *Methods rule.* For all $x : \sigma$:
     - *Pre-condition rule.* $m_\tau.pre[A(x_{pre})/x_{pre}] \Rightarrow m_\sigma.pre$.
     - *Predicate rule.* $m_\sigma.pred \Rightarrow m_\tau.pred[A(x_{pre})/x_{pre}, A(x_{post})/x_{post}]$
   where P[a/b] stands for predicate P with every occurrence of b replaced by a. Since x is an object of type σ, its value (x_{pre} or x_{post}) is a member of S and therefore cannot be used directly in the pre- and post-conditions for τ's methods (which relate values in T). A is used to translate these values so that the pre- and post-conditions for τ's methods make sense.
3. The extension map, $E : O_\sigma \times M \times Obj* \to Prog$, must be defined for each method, m, not in *dom(R)*. We write E(x.m(a)) for E(x, m, a) where x is the object on which m is invoked and a is the (possibly empty) sequence of arguments to m. E's range is the set of programs, including the empty program denoted as ϵ.[4]
   - *Extension rule.* For each new method, m, of $x : \sigma$, the following conditions must hold for π, the program to which E(x.m(a)) maps:
     - The input to π is the sequence of objects $[x]||a$.
     - The set of methods invoked in π is contained in the union of the set of methods of all types other than σ and the set of methods *dom(R)*.
     - *Diamond rule.* We need to relate the abstracted values of x at the end of either calling just m or executing π. Let ρ_1 be the state in which both m is invoked and π starts. Assume m.pre holds in ρ_1 and the call to m terminates in state ρ_2. Then we require that π terminates in state ψ and
     $$A(x_{\rho_2}) = A(x_\psi).$$
     Note that if $\pi = \epsilon, \psi = \rho_1$.

Fig. 1. Definition of the Subtype Relation

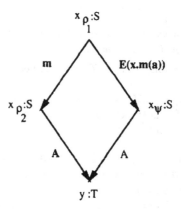

Fig. 2. The Diamond Diagram

The renaming map defines the correspondence between methods of the sub-type and supertype. It allows renaming of the methods (e.g., the *put* method of bag can be renamed to *push*) because this ability is useful when there are multiple supertypes. For example, two types might use the same name for two different methods; without renaming it would be impossible to define a type that is a subtype of both of them.

The requirement about calls of individual methods of the supertype is satisfied by the signature and methods rules. The first two signature rules are the usual contra/covariance rules for "syntactic" subtyping as defined by Cardelli [5]; ours are adapted from America [3]. The exception rule says that m_σ may not signal more than m_τ since a caller of a method on a supertype object should not expect to handle an unknown exception. The pre-condition rule ensures the subtype's method can be called in any state required by the supertype as well as other states. The predicate rule when expanded is equivalent to:

$$(m_\sigma.pre \Rightarrow m_\sigma.post) \Rightarrow ((m_\tau.pre \Rightarrow m_\tau.post)[A(x_{pre})/x_{pre}, A(x_{post})/x_{post}])$$

which is implied by the stronger conjunction of the following separate pre- and post-condition rules that America uses:

Pre-condition rule. $m_\tau.pre[A(x_{pre})/x_{pre}] \Rightarrow m_\sigma.pre$
Post-condition rule. $m_\sigma.post \Rightarrow m_\tau.post[A(x_{pre})/x_{pre}, A(x_{post})/x_{post}]$

These two rules are the intuitive counterparts to the contravariant and covariant rules for signatures. The post-condition rule alone says that the subtype method's post-condition can be stronger than the supertype method's post-condition; hence, any property that can be proved based on the supertype method's post-condition also follows from the subtype's method's post-condition. Our pre-and-predicate rule differs from America's pre-and-post rule only when the subtype's method's pre-condition is satisfied and the supertype's method's pre-condition is not. In this case we do not require that the post-condition of the subtype's method imply that of the supertype's method; this makes sense because specifications do not constrain what happens when a pre-condition is not satisfied. Our weaker formulation gives more freedom to the subtype's designer. (A similar formulation is used by Leavens [17].)

The requirement about invariants holding for values of objects of the supertype is satisfied by requiring that the abstraction function be defined on all legal values of the subtype and that each is mapped to some legal value of the supertype.

Preservation of history properties is ensured by a combination of the methods and extension rules; they together guarantee that any call of a subtype method can be explained in terms of calls of methods that are already defined for the supertype. Subtypes have two kinds of methods, those that also belong to the supertype (via renaming) and those that are "extra." The methods rule lets us reason about all the non-extra methods using the supertype specification. The extension rule explains the meaning of the extra methods in terms of the non-extra ones, thus relating them to the supertype specification as well. Note that interesting explanations are needed only for mutators; non-mutators always have the "empty" explanation, ϵ.

The extension rule constrains only what an explanation program does to its method's object, and not to other objects. This limitation is imposed because the explanation program does not really run. Its purpose is to explain how an object could be in a particular state. Its other arguments are hypothetical; they are not objects that actually exist in the object universe.

The diamond rule is stronger than necessary because it requires equality between abstract values. We need only the weaker notion of *observable equivalence* (e.g., see Kapur's definition [14]), since values that are distinct may not be observably different if the supertype's set of methods (in particular, observers) is too weak to let us perceive the difference. In practice, such types are rare and therefore we did not bother to provide the weaker definition.

3.4 Applying the Definition of Subtyping as a Checklist

Let's revisit the stack and bag example using our definition as a checklist. Here $\sigma = < O_{stack}, S, \{push, pop, swap\_top\} >$, and $\tau = < O_{bag}, B, \{put, get\} >$. Suppose we represent a bounded bag's value as a pair, $< elems, bound >$, of a multiset of integers and a fixed bound, requiring that the size of the multiset, elems, is always less than or equal to the bound. E.g., $< \{7, 19, 7\}, 5 >$ is a legal value for bags but $< \{7, 19, 7\}, 2 >$ is not. Similarly, let's represent a bounded stack's value as a pair, $< items, limit >$, of a sequence of integers and a fixed bound, requiring that the length of items is always less than or equal to its limit. We use standard notation to denote functions on multisets and sequences.

The first thing to do is define the abstraction function, $A : S \to B$, such that for all st: S:

$$A(st) = < mk\_elems(st.items), st.limit >$$

where the helping function, mk_elems, maps sequences to multisets. It is defined such that for all integer sequences, sq, and integers, i:

$$mk\_elems([\,]) = \{\,\}$$
$$mk\_elems(sq \,||\, [i]) = mk\_elems(sq) \cup \{i\}$$

([ ] stands for the empty sequence and { } stands for the empty multiset; || is concatenation and $\cup$ is a multiset union operation that does not discard duplicates.)

Second, we define the renaming map, R:

R(push) = put
R(pop) = get

Checking the signature rule is easy and could be done by the compiler.

Next, we show the correspondences between *push* and *put*, and between *pop* and *get*. Let's look at the pre-condition and predicate rules for just one method, *push*. The pre-condition rule for *put/push* requires that we show:

The size of b is less than its bound.	*Put*'s pre-condition.
$\Rightarrow$	
The height of s is less than its bound.	*Push*'s pre-condition.

or more formally[5],

$$size(A(s_{pre}).elems) < A(s_{pre}).bound$$
$$\Rightarrow$$
$$length(s_{pre}.items) < s_{pre}.limit$$

Intuitively, the pre-condition rule holds because the length of stack is the same as the size of the corresponding bag and the limit of the stack is the same as the bound for the bag. Here is an informal proof with slightly more detail:

1. *A* maps the *items* sequence to the *elems* multiset by putting all elements of the sequence into the multiset. Therefore the length of the sequence $s_{pre}.items$ is equal to the size of the multiset $A(s_{pre}).elems$.
2. Also, *A* maps the limit of the stack to the bound of the bag so that $s_{pre}.limit = A(s_{pre}).bound$.
3. From *put*'s pre-condition we know $length(s_{pre}.items) < s_{pre}.limit$.
4. *push*'s pre-condition holds by substituting equals for equals.

---

[5] Note that we are reasoning in terms of the *values* of the object, s, and that b and s refer to the same object.

Notice the role of the abstraction function in this proof. It allows us to relate stack and bag values, and therefore we can relate predicates about bag values to those about stack values and vice versa. Also, note how we depend on A being a function (in step (4) where we use the substitutivity property of equality).

The predicate rule requires that we show *push*'s predicate implies *put*'s:

$$\text{length } (s_{pre}.items) < s_{pre}.limit \Rightarrow$$
$$s_{post} = < s_{pre}.items \parallel [i], s_{pre}.limit > \wedge \textbf{modifies } s$$
$$\Rightarrow$$
$$size(A(s_{pre}).elems) < A(s_{pre}).bound \Rightarrow$$
$$A(s_{post}) = < A(s_{pre}).elems \cup \{i\}, A(s_{pre}).bound > \wedge \textbf{modifies } s$$

To show this, we note first that since the two pre-conditions are equivalent, we can ignore them and deal with the post-conditions directly. (Thus we are proving America's stronger post-condition rule in this case.) Next, we deal with the **modifies** and **ensures** parts separately. The **modifies** part holds because the same object is mentioned in both specifications. (Recall that the modifies clause indicates that all objects other than those listed cannot be modified.) The **ensures** part follows directly from the definition of the abstraction function.

Finally, we use the extension mapping to define *swap_top*'s effect. As stated earlier, it has the same effect as that described by the program, π, in which a call to *pop* is followed by one to *push*:

$$E(s.swap\_top(i)) = s.pop(); \; s.push(i)$$

Showing the extension rule is just like showing that an implementation of a procedure satisfies the procedure's specification, except that we do not require equal values at the end, but just values that map via A to the same abstract value. (In fact, such a proof is identical to a proof showing that an implementation of an operation of an abstract data type satisfies its specification [13].) In doing the reasoning we rely on the specifications of the methods used in the program. Here is an informal argument for *swap_top*. We note first that since s.swap_top(i) terminates normally, so does the call on s.pop() (their pre-conditions are the same). *Pop* removes the top element, reducing the size of the stack so that *push*'s precondition holds, and then *push* puts i on the top of the stack. The result is that the top element has been replaced by i. Thus, $s_{\rho_2} = s_\psi$, where ρ_2 is the termination state if we run *swap_top* and ψ is the termination state if we run π. Therefore $A(s_{\rho_2}) = A(s_\psi)$, since A is a function.

In the arguments given above, we have taken pains to describe the steps of the proof. In fact, most parts of these proofs are obvious and can be done by inspection. The only interesting issues are (1) the definition of the abstraction function, and (2) the definition of the extension map for the new methods that are mutators. The arguments about the methods and extension rules are usually trivial.

4   Type Hierarchies

The constraint we impose on subtypes is very strong and raises a concern that it might rule out many useful subtype relations. To address this concern we applied our method to a number of examples. We found that our technique captures what people want from a hierarchy mechanism (the so-called "is-a" relation in the literature), but we also discovered some surprises.

The examples led us to classify subtype relationships into two broad categories. In the first category, the subtype extends the supertype by providing additional methods and/or additional "state." In the second, the subtype is more constrained than the supertype. We discuss these relationships below.

4.1   Extension Subtypes

A subtype extends its supertype if its objects have extra methods in addition to those of the supertype. Abstraction functions for extension subtypes are onto, i.e., the range of the abstraction function is the set of all legal values of the supertype. The subtype might simply have more methods; in this case the abstraction function is one-to-one. Or its objects might have more "state," i.e., they might record information that is not present in objects of the supertype; in this case the abstraction function is many-to-one.

As an example of the one-to-one case, consider a type intset (for set of integers). Intset objects have methods to *insert* and *delete* elements, to *select* elements, and to provide the *size* of the set. A subtype, intset2, might have more methods, e.g., *union*, *is_empty*. Here there is no extra state, just extra methods. Explanations must be provided for the extra methods using the extension map E, but for all but mutators, these are trivial. Thus, if *union* is a pure constructor, it has the empty explanation, ϵ; otherwise it requires a non-trivial explananation, e.g., in terms of *insert*.

Sometimes it is not possible to find an extension map and therefore there is no subtype relationship between the two types. For example, intset is not a subtype of fat_set, where fat_set objects have only *insert*, *select*, and *size* methods; fat_sets only grow while intsets grow and shrink. Intuitively intset cannot be a subtype of fat_set because it does not preserve various history properties of fat_set. For example, we can prove that once an element is inserted in a fat_set, it remains forever. More formally, for any computation, c:

$$\forall s : fat\_set, \rho, \psi : State \ . \ [\rho < \psi \wedge s \in dom(\rho)] \Rightarrow$$
$$[\forall x : int \ . \ x \in s_\rho \Rightarrow x \in s_\psi]$$

where $\rho < \psi$ means ρ precedes ψ in c. This theorem does not hold for intset. The attempt to construct a subtype relation fails because no extension map can be given to explain the effect of intset's *delete* method.

As a simple example of a many-to-one case, consider immutable pairs and triples. Pairs have methods that fetch the first and second elements; triples have these methods plus an additional one to fetch the third element. Triple is a subtype of pair and so is semi-mutable triple with methods to fetch the first, second, and third elements and to replace the third element. Here, $E(x.replace(e)) = \epsilon$ because the modification is not visible to users of the supertype. This example shows that it is possible to have a mutable subtype of an immutable supertype, provided the mutations are invisible to users of the supertype.

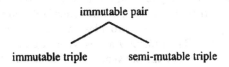

Fig. 3. Pairs and Triples

Mutations of a subtype that would be visible through the methods of an immutable supertype are ruled out. For example, an immutable sequence, which allows its elements to be fetched but not stored, is not a supertype of mutable array, which provides a *store* method in addition to the sequence methods. For sequences we can prove elements do not change; this is not true for arrays. The attempt to construct the subtype relation will fail because there is no way to explain the *store* method via an extension map.

Many examples of subtypes that are extensions are found in the literature. One common example concerns persons, employees, and students. A person object has methods that report its properties such as its name, age, and possibly its relationship to other persons (e.g., its parents or children). Student and employee are subtypes of person; in each case they have additional properties, e.g., a student id number, an employee employer and salary. In addition, type student_employee is a subtype of both student and employee (and also person, since the subtype relation is transitive). In this example, the subtype objects have more state than those of the supertype as well as more methods.

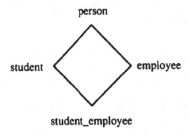

Fig. 4. Person, Student, and Employee

Another example from the database literature concerns different kinds of ships [12]. The supertype is ordinary ships with methods to determine such things as who is the captain and where the ship is registered. Subtypes contain more specialized ships such as tankers and freighters. There can be quite an elaborate hierarchy (e.g., tankers are a special kind of freighter). Windows are another well-known example [11]; subtypes include bordered windows, colored windows, and scrollable windows.

Common examples of subtype relationships are allowed by our definition provided the *equal* method (and other similar methods) are defined properly in the subtype. Suppose supertype τ provides an *equal* method and consider a particular call x.equal(y). The difficulty arises when x and y actually belong to σ, a subtype of τ. If objects of the subtype have additional state, x and y may differ when considered as subtype objects but ought to be considered equal when considered as supertype objects.

For example, consider immutable triples $x =< 0, 0, 0 >$ and $y =< 0, 0, 1 >$. Suppose the specification of the *equal* method for pairs says:

equal = **proc** (q: pair) **returns** (bool)
    ensures Returns true if p.first = q.first and p.second = q.second; false, otherwise.

(We are using p to refer to the method's object.) However, for triples we would expect the following specification:

equal = **proc** (q: triple) **returns** (bool)
    ensures Returns true if p.first = q.first, p.second = q.second, and p.third = q.third; false, otherwise.

If a program using triples had just observed that x and y differ in their third element, we would expect x.equal(y) to return "false." However, if the program were using them as pairs, and had just observed that their first and second elements were equal, it would be wrong for the *equal* method to return false.

The way to resolve this dilemma is to have two *equal* methods in triple:

pair_equal = **proc** (p: pair) **returns** (bool)
    ensures Returns true if p.first = q.first and p.second = q.second; false, otherwise.

triple_iequal = **proc** (p: triple) **returns** (bool)
    ensures Returns true if p.first = q.first, p.second = q.second, and p.third = q.third; false, otherwise.

One of them (*pair_equal*) simulates the *equal* method for pair; the other (*triple_equal*) is a method just on triples.

The problem is not limited to equality methods. It also affects methods that "expose" the abstract state of objects, e.g., an *unparse* method that returns a string representation of the abstract state of its object. x.unparse() ought to return a representation of a pair if called in a context in which x is considered to be a pair, but it ought to return a representation of a triple in a context in which x is known to be a triple (or some subtype of triple).

The need for several equality methods seems natural for realistic examples. For example, asking whether e1 and e2 are the same person is different from asking if they are the same employee. In the case of a person holding two jobs, the answer might be true for the question about person but false for the question about employee.

4.2 Constrained Subtypes

The second type of subtype relation occurs when the subtype is more constrained than the supertype either in what its methods do or in the values of objects or both. In this case, the supertype specification will always be nondeterministic; its purpose is to allow variations in behavior among its subtypes. Subtypes constrain the supertype by reducing or eliminating the nondeterminism. The abstraction function is usually into rather than onto. The subtype may extend those supertype objects that it simulates by providing additional methods and/or state.

A very simple example concerns elephants. Elephants come in many colors (realistically grey and white, but we will also allow blue ones). However all albino elephants are white and all royal elephants are blue. Figure 5 shows the elephant hierarchy. The set of legal values for regular elephants includes all elephants whose color is grey or blue or white. The set of legal values for royal elephants is a subset of those for regular elephants and hence the abstraction function is into. The situation for albino elephants is similar.

elephant

royal   albino

Fig. 5. Elephant Hierarchy

Though the value sets are different, the specifications for the *get_color* method for the supertype and its subtypes might actually be the same:

get_color = **proc** () **returns** (color)
    ensures Returns the color of e.

where e is the elephant object. If e is a regular elephant then the caller of *get_color* should expect one of three colors to be returned; if e is a royal elephant, the caller should expect only blue. Alternatively, the nondeterminism in the specification of *get_color* for regular elephants might be made explicit:

get_color = **proc** () **returns** (color)
    ensures Returns grey or blue or white.

Then we would need to change the specification for the method for royal elephants to:

get_color = **proc** () **returns** (color)
      ensures Returns blue.

Notice that it would be wrong for the post-condition of *get_color* for regular elephants to say just "Returns grey" because then the predicate rule would not hold when showing that royal elephant is a subtype of elephant.

Not only must the specifications of corresponding methods relate appropriately, but any invariant property that holds for supertype objects must hold for subtype objects. Suppose we removed the nondeterminism in the specification for regular elephants, defining the value set for regular elephants to be just those elephants whose color is grey. Then the theorem stating all elephants are grey:

$$\forall e : elephant \; \forall \rho : State \; . \; [e \in dom(\rho) \Rightarrow e_\rho.color = grey]$$

would hold of all regular elephants but not for any of its subtype objects. Instead, our weaker theorem does hold for regular elephants and its subtypes:

$$\forall e : elephant \; \forall \rho : State \; . \; [e \in dom(\rho) \Rightarrow$$
$$e_\rho.color = grey \lor e_\rho.color = blue \lor e_\rho.color = white]$$

This simple example has led others to define a subtyping relation that requires non-monotonic reasoning [18], but we believe it is better to use a nondeterministic specification and straightforward reasoning methods. However, the example shows that a specifier of a type family has to anticipate subtypes and capture the variation among them in a nondeterministic specification of the supertype.

Another similar example concerns geometric figures. At the top of the hierarchy is the polygon type; it allows an arbitrary number of sides and angles of arbitrary sizes. Subtypes place various restrictions on these quantities. A portion of the hierarchy is shown in Figure 6.

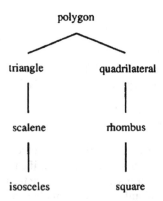

Fig. 6. Polygon Hierarchy

The bag type informally discussed in Section 3.1 is nondeterministic in two ways. As discussed earlier, the specification of *get* is nondeterministic because it does not constrain which element of the bag is removed. This nondeterminism allows stack to be a subtype of bag: The specification of *pop* constrains the nondeterminism. We could also define a queue that is a subtype of bag; its *dequeue* method would also constrain the nondeterminism of *get* but in a different way than *pop* does.

In addition, since the actual value of the bound for bags was not constrained, it can be any natural number, thus allowing subtypes to have different bounds. This nondeterminism shows up in the specification of *put*, where we do not say what specific bound value causes the call to fail. Therefore, a user of *put* must be prepared for a failure unless it is possible to deduce from past evidence, using the history property that the bound of a bag does not change, that the call will succeed. A subtype of bag might constrain the bound to a fixed value, or to a smaller range. Several subtypes of bag are shown in Figure 7; largebags are essentially unbounded bags since their bound (fixed at creation) is ∞, and mediumbags have various bounds, so that this type might have its own subtypes, e.g., bag_150, containing all bags with bound equal to 150.

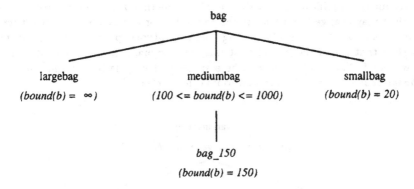

Fig. 7. A Type Family for Bags

The bag hierarchy may seem counterintuitive, since we might expect that bags with smaller bounds should be subtypes of bags with larger bounds. For example, we might expect bag_150 to be a subtype of largebag. However, the specifications for the two types are incompatible. For largebags we can prove that the bound of every bag is ∞, which is clearly not true for bag_150. Furthermore, this difference is observable via the methods: It is legal to call the *put* method on a largebag whose size is greater than or equal to 150, but the call is not legal for a bag_150. Therefore the pre-condition rule is not satisfied.

Although the bag type can have subtypes with different constraints on the bounds, it is not a valid supertype of a dynamic_bag type where the bounds of the bags can change dynamically. Dynamic_bags would have an additional method, *change_bound*, for object b:

change_bound = **proc** (n: int)
>   **requires** n is greater than or equal to the size of b.
>   **modifies** b
>   **ensures** Sets the bound of b to n.

Change_bound is a mutator for which no explanation via an extension map is possible. Note that we can prove that the bound of a bag object does not vary; clearly this is not true for a dynamic_bag object.

If we wanted a type family that included both dynamic_bag and bag, we would need to define a supertype in which the bound is allowed, but not required, to vary. Figure 8 shows the new type hierarchy where the *change_bound* method for varying_bag looks like:

change_bound = **proc** (n: int)
>   **requires** n is greater than or equal to the size of b.
>   **modifies** b
>   **ensures** Either sets b's bound to n or keeps it the same.

Not only is this specification nondeterministic about the bounds of bag objects, but the specification of the *change_bound* method is nondeterministic: The method may change the bound to the new value, or it may not. This nondeterminism is resolved in its subtypes; bag (and its subtypes) provide a *change_bound* method that leaves the bound as it was, while dynamic_bag changes it to the new bound. Note that for bag to be a subtype of varying_bag, it must have a *change_bound* method (in addition to its other methods).

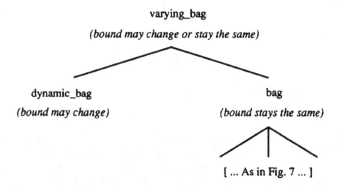

Fig. 8. Another Type Family for Bags

In the case of the bag family illustrated in Figure 7, all types in the hierarchy might actually be implemented. However, sometimes the supertypes are not intended to be implemented. These *virtual types* serve as placeholders for specific subtypes that are intended to be implemented; they let us define the properties all the subtypes have in common. Varying_bag is an example of such a type.

Virtual types are also needed when we construct a hierarchy for integers. Smaller integers cannot be a subtype of larger integers because of observable differences in behavior; for example, an overflow exception that would occur when adding two 32-bit integers would not occur if they were 64-bit integers. However, we clearly would like integers of different sizes to be related. This is accomplished by designing a nondeterministic, virtual supertype that includes them. Such a hierarchy is shown in Figure 9, where integer is a virtual type. Here integer types with different sizes are subtypes of integer. In addition, small integer types are subtypes of regular_int, another virtual type. Such a hierarchy might have a structure like this, or it might be flatter by having all integer types be direct subtypes of integer.

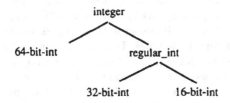

Fig. 9. Integer Family

5 Related Work

Research on defining subtype relations can be divided into two categories: work on the "syntactic" notion of subtyping and work on the "semantic" notion. We clearly differ from the syntactic notion, formally captured by Cardelli's contra/covariance rules [5] and used in languages like Trellis/Owl [24], Eiffel [21], POOL [2], and to a limited extent Modula-3 [23]. Our rules place constraints not just on the signatures of an object's methods, but also on their semantic behavior as described in type specifications. Cardelli's rules are a strict subset of ours (ignoring higher-order functions).

Our semantic notion differs from the others for two main reasons: We deal with mutable abstract types and we allow subtypes to have additional methods. We discuss this related work in more detail below. We also mention how our work is related to models for concurrent processes.

Our work is most closely related to that of America [3] who uses the stronger pre- and post-condition rules as discussed in Section 3. (Meyer also uses these rules for Eiffel [21], although here the pre- and post-conditions are given "operationally," by providing a program to check them, rather than assertionally.) It is also related to work by Cusack [7] who defines subtyping in terms of strengthening state invariants. However, neither author considers the problems introduced by extra mutators. Thus, by not considering history properties at all, they allow certain subtype relations that we forbid (e.g., set could be a subtype of fat_set in these approaches).

Our work is also similar to America's in its approach: We expect programmers to reason directly in terms of specifications; we call this approach "proof-theoretic." Most other approaches are "model-theoretic"; programmers are expected to reason in terms of mathematical structures like algebras or categories. We believe a proof-theoretic approach is better because it is much more accessible to programmers.

The emphasis on semantics of abstract types is a prominent feature of the work by Leavens. We go further by addressing mutable abstract types. In his Ph.D. thesis [15] Leavens defines a model-theoretic semantic notion of subtyping. He defines types in terms of algebras and subtyping in terms of a *simulation relation* between them. Further work by Leavens and Weihl showing how to verify programs with subtypes uses Hoare-style reasoning as we do [16]. Again, their work is restricted to immutable types. Their *simulation relations* map supertype values down to subtype values; hence, they do reasoning in the subtype value space. In contrast we use our abstraction function to map values up to the supertype value space. We can rely on the substitutivity property of equality; they cannot. Indeed, in our proofs we depend on A being a function.

Bruce and Wegner give a model-theoretic semantic definition of subtyping (in terms of algebras) but also do not deal with mutable types [4]. Like Leavens they model types in terms of algebras; like us they define *coercion functions* with the substitution property. They cannot handle mutable types and are not concerned with reasoning about programs directly.

In his 1992 Master's thesis [9], Dhara extends Leavens' thesis work to deal with mutable types. Again, his approach is model-theoretic and based on simulation relations; moreover, because of a restriction on aliasing in his model, his definition disallows certain subtype relations from holding that we could allow. Dhara has no counterpart to our extension rule for extra mutators, and no techniques for proving subtype relations.

To our knowledge, Utting is the only other researcher to take a proof-theoretic approach to subtyping [25]. His formalism is cast in the refinement calculus language [22], an extension of Dijkstra's guarded command language [10]. Utting makes a big simplifying assumption: he does not allow data refinement between supertype and subtype value spaces. Our use of abstraction functions directly addresses this issue, which intuitively is the heart of any subtyping relation.

Finally, our extension rule is related to the more general work done on relating the behaviors of two different concurrent processes. Cusack has investigated the meaning of subtyping for CSP processes [6] and (with Rudkin and Smith) LOTOS processes [8], but takes a model-theoretic approach. Abadi and Lamport's *refinement mappings* [1] are akin to our extension mappings, but have not yet been applied in the context of subtyping.

6 Conclusions

In this paper we have defined a method for reasoning about whether one type is a subtype of another based on the semantic properties of the two types. An object's type determines both a set of legal values and an interface with its environment (through calls on its methods). Thus, we are interested in preserving properties about supertype values and methods when designing a subtype. We are particularly interested in an object's observable behavior (state changes), thus motivating our focus on mutable types and mutators. Ours is the first approach to provide a way of determining the acceptability of the "extra" mutators.

Our approach guarantees that the subtype preserves all the invariant and history properties of the supertype. This very strong definition ensures that if one user reasons about a shared object using properties that hold for its apparent type, that reasoning will be valid even if the object actually belongs to a subtype and is manipulated by other users using the subtype methods. Our definition of subtyping works even in a very general environment in which possibly concurrent users share mutable objects.

The constraint we impose on subtypes is very strong and raises a concern that it might rule out many useful subtype relations. To address this concern we applied our method to a number of examples. We found that it is not difficult to define useful type hierarchies that fit our constraint, and identified two kinds of type families, those in which the subtypes extend the supertype by adding extra state and methods, and those in which the subtypes constrain the supertype by removing or eliminating nondeterminism.

In developing our definition, we were motivated primarily by pragmatics. Our intention is to capture the intuition programmers apply when designing type hierarchies in object-oriented languages. However, intuition in the absence of precision can often go astray or lead to confusion. This is why it has been unclear how to organize certain type hierarchies such as integers. Our definition sheds light on such hierarchies and helps in uncovering new designs. It also supports the kind of reasoning needed to ensure that programs that work correctly using the supertype continue to work correctly with the subtype.

We believe that programmers will find our definition relatively easy to apply and expect it to be used primarily in an informal way. The essence of a subtype relationship is expressed in the mappings. We hope that the mappings will be defined as part of giving type and subtype specifications, in much the same way that abstraction functions and representation invariants are given as comments in a program that implements an abstract type. The proofs are usually trivial and can be done by inspection. Such a property is necessary if we expect formal definitions to be applied in daily use.

Acknowledgments

We thank Gary Leavens for a helpful discussion of subtyping and pointers to related work. In addition, Gary, Mark Day, Sanjay Ghemawat, John Guttag,

Deborah Hwang, Greg Morrisett, Eliot Moss, John Reynolds, Bill Weihl, Amy Moormann Zaremski, and the referees gave useful comments on earlier versions of this paper.

This research was supported for Liskov in part by the Advanced Research Projects Agency of the Department of Defense, monitored by the Office of Naval Research under contract N00014-91-J-4136 and in part by the National Science Foundation under Grant CCR-8822158; for Wing, by the Avionics Lab, Wright Research and Development Center, Aeronautical Systems Division (AFSC), U. S. Air Force, Wright-Patterson AFB, OH 45433-6543 under Contract F33615-90-C-1465, ARPA Order No. 7597.

References

1. Abadi, M., Lamport, L.: The existence of refinement mappings. Digital Equipment Corp. Sys. Research Ctr. Tech Rpt. 29, 1988.
2. America, P.: A parallel object-oriented language with inheritance and subtyping. ACM SIGPLAN 25 (1990) 161-168.
3. America, P.: Designing an object-oriented programming language with behavioural subtyping. Foundations of Object-Oriented Languages, REX School/Workshop, Noordwijkerhout, The Netherlands, Springer-Verlag Lec. Notes in Com. Sci. 489 (1991) 60-90.
4. Bruce, K. B., Wegner, P.: An algebraic model of subtypes in object-oriented languages (draft). ACM SIGPLAN Notices 21 (1986).
5. Cardelli, L.: A semantics of multiple inheritance. Info. and Computation 76 (1988) 138-164.
6. Elspeth Cusack: Refinement, conformance, and inheritance. Formal Aspects of Computing. 3(2), (1991), 129-141.
7. Elspeth Cusack: Inheritance in object oriented Z. Proceedings of ECOOP '91, 1991.
8. Elspeth Cusack, Steve Rudkin, and Chris Smith: An object oriented interpretation of LOTOS. Formal Description Techniques, II, S.T. Vuong (ed.). Elsevier Science Publishers B.V. (North-Holland) (1990), 211-226.
9. Dhara, K. K.: Subtyping among mutable types in object-oriented programming languages. Iowa State University Ames, Iowa, 1992.
10. Dijkstra, E. W.: A Discipline of Programming. Prentice Hall, New York, 1976.
11. Halbert, D. C., O'Brien, P. D.: Using types and inheritance in object-oriented programming. IEEE Software (1987) 71-79.
12. Hammer, M., McLeod, D.: A semantic database model. ACM Trans. Database Systems 6 (1981) 351-386.
13. Hoare, C. A. R.: Proof of correctness of data representations. Acta Informatica 1 (1972) 271-281.
14. Kapur, K.: Towards a theory of abstract data types. Tech. Rpt. 237, MIT Lab. for Computer Science, Cambridge, MA, 1980.
15. Leavens, G.: Verifying object-oriented prograsm that use subtypes. Tech. Rpt. 439, MIT Lab. for Computer Science, Cambridge, MA, 1989.
16. Leavens, G., Weihl, W. E.: Reasoning about object-oriented programs that use subtypes. ECOOP/OOPSLA '90 Proceedings, 1990.
17. Leavens, G., Weihl, W.E.: Subtyping, modular specification, and modular verification for applicative object-oriented programs. (forthcoming).

18. Lipeck, U.: Semantics and usage of defaults in specifications. Foundations of Information Systems Specification and Design, Hans-Dieter Ehrich and Joseph A Goguen and Amilcar Sernadas Dagstuhl Seminar 9212, Rpt. 35, 1992.
19. Liskov, B., Guttag, J.: Abstraction and Specification in Program Design. McGraw Hill and MIT Press, 1985.
20. Liskov, B., Wing, J. M.: Family Values: A Semantic Notion of Subtyping. MIT-LCS-TR-562, Tech. Rpt., December 1992. Also published as CMU-CS-92-220 TR.
21. Meyer, B.: Object-oriented Software Construction. Prentice Hall, New York, 1988.
22. Morgan, C.: Programming from Specifications. Prentice Hall, New York, 1990.
23. Nelson, G. (Ed.): Systems Programming with Modula-3. Prentice Hall, New York, 1991.
24. Schaffert, C., Cooper, T., Wilpolt, C.: Trellis: object-based environment language reference manual. Dig. Equip. Corp. Eastern Research Lab., Tech Rpt. 372, 1985.
25. Utting, M.: An object-oriented refinement calculus with modular reasoning. University of New South Wales, Australia, 1992.

Attaching Second-Order Types to Methods in an Object-Oriented Language

Yves Caseau
Bellcore, 445 South Street
Morristown, NJ 07960, USA
(201) 829 44 71
caseau@bellcore.com

Laurent Perron
Ecole Normale Supérieure
45 rue d'Ulm
75005 Paris, France
perron@clipper.ens.fr

Abstract

This paper proposes an extension of the notion of method as it is currently used in most object-oriented languages. We define polymethods as methods that we can attach directly to types, as opposed to classes and that we can describe with a second-order type. Two benefits result from this extension; first, the expressive power of the language is improved with better modeling abilities. Next, second-order types yield a more powerful (precise) type inference, which extends the range of static type checking in a truly extensible object-oriented language. We first show that extensible object-oriented languages present many difficulties for static type-checking and that second-order types are necessary to get stronger type-checking. We illustrate how to combine polymethods through *type* inheritance and propose a technique based on abstract interpretation to derive a second-order type for new polymethods.

1. Introduction

Object-oriented languages have two interesting features that distinguish them from other programming languages: they are *order-sorted* and *extensible*. By order-sorted we mean that their data structures (objects) are organized into a (class) hierarchy, with implicit inclusion polymorphism (inheritance). By extensible we mean that new classes can be added at any time, including dynamically with some languages. Some languages (Smalltalk [GR83], LAURE[Ca91]) are more extensible than others (C++[Str86]), since new methods can also be added dynamically. Another interesting feature of some of those languages is the *reflection* [MN88] of the organization, when classes (Smalltalk) or types (LAURE) are first-class objects. This enables (Section 2.3) the definition of light-weighted parametric polymorphic objects, using classes or types as object attributes. Generally speaking, these languages are very convenient for prototyping and yield a substantial reduction in the prototype development time.

However, the same languages often suffer from a lack of static type-checking necessary to achieve efficiency through compilation. As a consequence, these languages are rarely used for large software. Much work has been done to palliate this situation, starting at the two ends of the problem. In one case, features of object-oriented programming have been added to safe, strongly typed languages (e.g., QUEST [Car89]). In the second case, new type systems and their type inference procedures have been developed for object-oriented languages (e.g., Typed Smalltalk [GJ90]). Still, many problems remain when we want to apply static type-checking to a truly extensible, order-sorted language (e.g., the long discussion in the newsgroup *comp.object*, initiated by C. Chambers, about the *min* function, also in Section 2.1). It must be emphasized that

O.M. Nierstrasz (Ed.): ECOOP '93, LNCS 707, pp. 142–160, 1993.
© Springer-Verlag Berlin Heidelberg 1993

our goal is not to identify a new language that can be statically type-checked, but to find a way to do as much static type inference/checking as possible in a knowledge representation language that already exists (knowledge representation *demands* flexibility and extensibility).

Here, we describe the solution that we have implemented in the LAURE language, based on the type system T described in [CP91] and the notion of abstract interpretation over a function space. If one looks at type inference as an abstract interpretation of the semantics, poor type inferences are due to an oversimplification in the image lattice when an ambiguous situation occurs. Our idea is to delay this reduction and to carry an abstract expression (a type function) instead, which will be applied to the right context, thus yielding a better decision. We have extended the usual notion of a *method* with three features (resulting in *polymethods*). First, a second-order type (a function on types from T) is attached to each method. Second, methods are inserted directly in the type hierarchy, instead of using the class hierarchy, and some additional relations among method parameters can be specified.

The paper is organized as follows. Section 2 deals with our motivations for introducing polymethods. We present a set of examples that are hard to type using current techniques proposed for object-oriented languages. Section 3 recalls the necessary properties of our underlying type system, developed in [CP91]. We define polymethods and present a language for second-order types. Section 4 gives a practical description of polymethods and shows how they can be used. We also give an informal description of the technique used for second-order type inference. Section 5 first gives an algorithm for inheritance conflicts and then proposes an inference procedure to compute the second-order type of each new method. The last section illustrates how polymethods solve some of the problems presented earlier.

2. Motivations

2.1 Strong Type-Checking

We consider a set of classes *integer, number, string* .... with an ordering feature $\leq$. Since we need to make a distinction between the property $\leq$ and its definition on the various classes $\leq@integer, \leq@string$ ... we shall call the first a *feature* (following the OSF notations [Smo89] [AP90]) and the others *methods* (as in any object-oriented language [Mit90]). We suppose two important hypotheses :

- $\leq$ supports inclusion polymorphism (e.g., *integer* $\subset$ *number*),
- $\leq$ is extensible (new classes c can be added with a method $\leq@c$).

A correctly typed definition of the *min* feature has already been given when *one* of the hypotheses holds (e.g., ABC[GMP90], Eiffel[Me89]). If we consider the following method definition, which represents the *min* feature (*entity* is the set of everything).

Example:[1] [**define** min(x:entity, y:entity) **method** -> object => [**if** (x $\leq$ y) x **else** y]]

---

[1] All examples are given using LAURE syntax. We hope that the simplicity of the examples will make the syntax self-evident. Keywords are in boldface, -> means range, => precedes the definition of a method. Messages are written using a functional syntax.

This method will not yield static type-checking, since it is defined on the class *object* (the top of the hierarchy). If it is applied to an object that doesn't have the feature ≤, a dynamic error will occur that was not detected by the compiler. If we have a truly extensible language, we can do better, we can create a class *ordered_set*, and define a method ≤@ordered_set to be sure that every member of an ordered set has the feature ≤.

Example: [define ordered_set **class** subsets (number string),
  with method(≤(x:ordered_set) -> boolean
                      => [error "≤ is not defined on ~S and ~S", self, x])]

Assuming this is allowed by the language (which is rare), this is still not enough, since we will not catch an error as simple as *min(1,"john")*. Because of the inclusion polymorphism, the solution proposed for the Eiffel language, which is to declare the two arguments *self* and *x* of *min* as having the *same* type, doesn't work here : min(1,3.5) is a valid instruction. Similarly, we cannot represent the type of *min* with a disjoint union like

$$min : \ (integer \times integer \rightarrow integer) \ \cup \ (number \times number \rightarrow number) \ \cup \ ...$$

because this would miss the link between *min* and ≤, any new class can potentially use the *min* feature. A complex solution would be to store an explicit disjunction and a graph of dependencies, which would be used to re-compute the methods' type dynamically. We have found the use of second-order types to be a much more elegant way to represent the intimate relationship between the two methods ≤ and *min* in the type system.

2.2 Order-Sorted and Heterogeneous Sets

The question of heterogeneous structures, such as sets, yields many interesting questions when we try to develop static type-checking inference for a knowledge representation object-oriented language, because of the inclusion polymorphism [CW85]. Here, we consider the case of lists as an example; roughly speaking, there are two ways of grasping the problem.

- Typed lists: each list $(a_1 ... a_n){:}t$ has a given type t such that all members a_i of the list are of type t . This is the solution of ML [HMM86], or Machiavelli [OBB89], because it is easier to get type safety on list operations this way. As a consequence, there are many empty lists $():integer, ():string$ ... that are all different.

- Untyped lists: a list has no given type, except the generic type *list*. If we have a type lattice, we can always associate the type $\bigvee_{i=1}^{i=n} t_i$ to the list $(a_1 ... a_n)$, where t_i is the type of each member a_i. As a consequence, there is a unique empty list $()$. This is a simpler solution, and it gives a simpler semantics to set operations (as opposed to the special meaning of set union in Machiavelli [OBB89]).

Although the first solution is simpler, it is not relevant for knowledge representation object-oriented languages, as is illustrated by the following example. Suppose that we have two classes, *person* and *employee*, and that John and Mary are employees and Peter is just a person (*employee* is a subclass of *person*). What happens if we delete Peter in the list (John Mary Peter):*person*? If we define delete with the following parametric signature.

delete: $list[t] \rightarrow list[t]$,

delete(Peter,*add*(Peter,(John Mary)) is different from (John Mary), because they have different types. If we give a finer description such as

$$delete: \; list[t] \rightarrow list[t']with \; t \prec t',$$

then there is no reason why *delete*(John,(John)) would be of type list[*person*]; we are back to the second solution, where there is a unique empty list and where lists have no fixed types. Therefore, we chose the second solution for an object-oriented solution because it is more natural. However, this will make static type-checking more difficult since list[*integer*] and list[*string*] are no longer disjoint, their intersection is {()}. Our solution is to attach methods directly to types, so that the case of the empty list can be singled out, and to use second-order types to capture parametric type inference.

2.3 Optimization and Parametric Polymorphism

Let us now consider the stack example, as can be written with a reflective object-oriented language such as LAURE. We attach a slot *of* to each stack object, which represents a type for all objects stored in the stack (the rest of the representation is as usual: an *index* and an array *content*).

```
[define stack class
    with     slot( of -> type, default ∅),
             slot( index  -> integer, default 0),
             list_slot(content),
             method( top => last(content(self))),
             method( push(x:entity)
                => [if (x ∈ of(self)) [do  (content(self) put_at  index(self) x]
                                           (index(self) is (index(self) + 1))]
                    else range_error( arg  x, set  of(self))]), ...

[define my_stack  stack of integer]
```

This example shows how a simple polymorphic stack can be implemented with such a language, which entirely relies on dynamic typing. Here, types are seen as sets (hence the test *(x ∈ of(self))* for checking if *x* is of type *of(oself)*) and a type error is created when the test fails. More details about the power of exceptions as first-class objects can be found in [Do90].

However, this leaves us with two problems. First, we want to introduce parametric type inference [CW85], such as in [OB89], so that we can deduce that *top(my_stack)* is an integer. In addition, we would like to perform static type checking to improve safety, and we would like to generate better code (compiler optimization) when the argument types are found to be correct. This implies that the test*(x ∈ of(self))* must be taken out of the code and placed in the method's type definition. We prefer to extend the method notion as opposed to extending the object model with class parameters [CP91].

3. Background: The LAURE Type System

3.1 A Set-Based Type System

In this section we recall some of the interesting properties of the type system presented in [CP91], which are necessary to build polymethods. We see objects as nodes in a *semantic network*, without any structure (such a network, which represents the state of the object system, is denoted by a function v of the set S).[2] Objects are organized into a class lattice[3] $(C,<)$, which is *reified* [FW84] (the set of classes C is included into the set of objects O). Each class c represents a set of objects, written $\chi_v(c)$. Classes are used as types, but we also add the following type constructions: finite enumerations $(\{o_1,...,o_i\})$ allow the compiler to perform optimizations based on recognition of constants; disjunctive types permit type inference without loss of information; powerset types (*set_of*) are introduced to optimize set operations and parametric types (*p:e*, where p is a parameter from a set P, is the set of objects whose parameter p belongs to e). We define types through a type expression language E, where each expression represents a set.

<type:E > :: $\{o_1,...,o_i\}$ | C | **set_of**(<E>) |
                  <E> $\cup$ <E> | <E> $\cap$ <E> | <E> -$\{o_1,...,o_i\}$ | <P>:<E>

Example: • *{string} $\cup$ integer}* represents the sets of strings or integers,
• *{list - {()}}* represents the set of non-empty lists.

Similarly, we write $\chi_v(e)$ the set of objects represented by the type expression e in the object system $v \in S$. In [CP91] we define the notion of a licit evolution of a system, which gives a precise meaning to the term *extensibility*. We have shown that we can define a type *normal form* from N, which supports two syntactical operations $\prec$ and $\wedge$, that represent, respectively, subtyping and type combination. We define our type system **T** to be the quotient of N by the equivalence relation $\approx$ $\left(t_1 \approx t_2 \Leftrightarrow (t_1 \prec t_2) \& (t_2 \prec t_1)\right)$ and we get the following result.

Theorem: *(T, $\prec$, $\wedge$) is a complete lattice and subtyping is inclusion:*
$\forall t_1, t_2 \in T, t_1 \prec t_2 \Leftrightarrow$ *for every licit system* $v, \chi_v(t_1) \subset \chi_v(t_2)$

In addition [CP91], we have defined two interesting functions on types: ε and ρ. Informally, ε is a meta-type extraction procedure ($\varepsilon(t)$ is a valid type for all members of a set of type t) and ρ is a parameter-extraction procedure ($\rho(p,t)$ is a valid type for the object y as soon as $y = v(p)(x)$ and x is an object of type t). These functions are necessary to build the lattice structure, but also play an important role for type inference.

3.2 Features and Polymethods

Objects are described with *features*, which represent relationships among objects and operations that can be performed on those objects. The set of features F has a distinguished subset A of *attributes*, which are binary relations among objects stored in the object system v. A itself has a distinguished subset P that represents a set of *parameters* (introduced previously), which associates one unique value to each object.

We can now introduce *polymethods*, used to define features from F.

---

[2] The set S contains functions that associates binary relations on O to each attribute [CP91].

[3] We assume that the taxonomy $(C,<)$ is a lattice, without any loss of generality since we can efficiently extend any hierarchy into a complete lattice. Notice that this does not preclude classes from being mutually exclusive [CP91].

Definition: *A polymethod is a tuple $m = (r(m) \in F, \sigma(m), f(m), \kappa(m))$:*
- *$r(m)$ is the feature that m is defining,*
- *$\sigma(m) = t_1 \times \dots \times t_n$, and is called the **signature** of m, where $t_i \in T$.*
- *$f(m)$ is a function (the **definition**) from $S \times O^{n-1} \to S \times O$ such that:*

$$\forall v \in S, \ \forall \ a_1 \dots a_{n-1} \in O,$$
$$\forall i, \ (a_i \in \chi_v(t_i)) \ \& \ f(m)(a_1 \dots a_{n-1}) = (v',y))$$
$$\Rightarrow v' \text{ is a licit system } \& \ y \in \chi_v(t_n).$$

- *$\kappa(m)$ is a **second-order type** for m:*

$$\forall v \in S, \ \forall \ x_1, \dots, x_{n-1} \in T, \ \forall a_1, \dots, a_n \in O,$$
$$(\forall i, \ (x_i \prec t_i) \ \& \ (a_i \in \chi_v(x_i))) \wedge f(m)(a_1, \dots, a_{n-1}) = (v',y)) \Rightarrow$$
$$y \in \chi_v(\kappa(m)(x_1, \dots, x_{n-1}))$$

The signature tells when the polymethod can be used to compute a given feature. Each polymethod is a restriction of the feature $r(m)$ ($t_1 \times \dots \times t_{n-1}$ is called the domain of the restriction, t_n is called its range) and is responsible to know when it is valid.[4] This definition is an extension over the usual notion of a method in two ways: we attach polymethods to types as opposed to classes only and we complete the polymethod definition by a second-order type, which supports better type inference.

Example: • Identity is a feature defined with one polymethod (Id, σ, f, κ):

$$f = (\lambda x.x),$$
$$\sigma = \text{Object} \times \text{Object},$$
$$\kappa = (\lambda x.x).$$

• Fibonacci is a feature defined with two polymethods

$$(\text{fib}, \{0,1\} \times \text{Integer}, (\lambda x.1), (\lambda t.\{1\}))$$
$$(\text{fib}, \text{Integer} \times \text{Integer}, (\chi.(\text{fib}(x-1) + \text{fib}(x - 2))), (\lambda t.\text{Integer}))$$

Definition: *A feature f is a collection of polymethods m with same arity and $r(m) = f$. A feature is well-defined if for any tuple of object $(x_1, \dots, x_n)$ there exists a unique smaller restriction to apply (restrictions are naturally ordered by the inclusion product order on their domains).*
In this case, f represents a function from $S \times O^{n-1} \to S \times O$ obtained by applying to each object tuple the unique smallest polymethod that applies.

The underlying assumption is that a restriction on a smaller domain overrides a more general restriction.[5] Transforming any collection of polymethods into a well-defined feature is the goal of multiple inheritance conflict resolution, as described in Section 5.1.

3.3 Second-Order Types

Second-order types are type functions (usually lambda-abstractions) attached to polymethods to represent the relations among the types between the input parameters and the result of the polymethod. A second-order type is a finer type description than a signature. This means if we apply $\kappa(m)$ to a type tuple $(x_1, \dots, x_{n-1})$ that contains an

---

[4] As opposed to each class knowing which feature can be used; this separation between organization and description makes organizing simpler.

[5] For instance, if we say $f(x) = x + 1 \wedge f(0) = 0$, the second equation is used to define $f(0)$ rather than the first.

object tuple $(a_1, ..., a_{n-1})$, we will get a type that must contain the result of applying m to the object tuple. Fore instance, we can always use the canonical second-order type $(\lambda x_1 ... x_{n-1}.range(m))$ obtained from the signature. Here are some other valid second-order types.

Examples:

$\lambda X.X$ which is a second-order type of the *identity* polymethod,

$\lambda X. \varepsilon(X)$ which is the second-order type of the *car* polymethod (first member of a list),

$\lambda X. \rho(of,X)$ which is the second-order type of the *top* polymethod.

Our first motivation to introduce second-order types is to associate them with primitive polymethods to get better type inference. For instance, with the previous information, the compiler will know that the type of Id(e) is the same as the type of the instruction e.

However, we also want to infer such second-order types for new polymethods. For this purpose, we define a language of functional types $\Lambda(T)$ as lambda-abstractions over the set of types T, using the operations introduced in the previous sections and a type inference function ψ. This function is defined in [CP91] so that $\psi(f, t_1, ..., t_n)$ is a type that will contain the type of the result of applying the feature f to objects of types $t_1, ..., t_n$. We will give an informal description of ψ in the next section.

$\Lambda :: \lambda x_1 ... x_n . <exp(x_1, ..., x_n)>.$

$<exp(x_1, ..., x_n)> :: x_i \mid T \mid \text{if}(<test(x_1, ..., x_n)>, <exp(x_1, ..., x_n)>, <exp(x_1, ..., x_n)>) \mid$	
$\psi(<F>, <exp(x_1, ..., x_n)>, ..., <exp(x_1, ..., x_n)>) \mid$	feature inference
$\varepsilon(<exp(x_1, ..., x_n)>) \mid$	powertype inference
$\rho(<P>, <exp(x_1, ..., x_n)>) \mid$	parametric inference
$<exp(x_1, ..., x_n)> \wedge <exp(x_1, ..., x_n)> \mid$	lattice join
$<exp(x_1, ..., x_n)> \vee <exp(x_1, ..., x_n)>$	lattice meet
$<test(x_1, ..., x_n)> :: <exp(x_1, ..., x_n)> = <exp(x_1, ..., x_n)> \mid$	type equality
$<exp(x_1, ..., x_n)> \prec <exp(x_1, ..., x_n)>.$	type subsumption

Each lambda-abstraction of Λ with n variables represents a function from $T^n \rightarrow T$. Such a function is a second-order type for a polymethod m, if it can be used to predict the type of the result of applying m. to a set of arguments with known types.

4. Informal Description of Polymethods

In this section we explain why polymethods are a useful extension from methods. We also give an informal description of the inference strategy to derive second-order types for new methods. A more precise description will follow in Section 5.

4.1 Attaching Methods to Types

The first original feature of polymethods is to be attached to a type as opposed to a class. Since classes are types, this is a generalization of method attachment, which is made possible because our type system has the same inclusion lattice structure as the class lattice. The practical advantage is that we can attach the method more precisely where it is needed, which yields shorter code (in a traditional method we would have to add some code to test that the first argument satisfies some extra condition) and better readability. Here are some examples that show how we can now use the type hierarchy to define methods.

- *Attaching a method to a union.* With a traditional OO language, sharing code in only performed through inheritance. If we have two separate classes A and B that could share a method, we need either to duplicate the code, or create an additional class C from which A and B will inherit and to which we attach the method. This situation has two major drawbacks; first, it is not always possible to insert the new class C. Let us consider a toy example where we want to define a new method *very_long?* which applies both to strings and lists. Since the two classes *string* and *list* have been created previously, neither C++ or Smalltalk will allow the definition of a new class from which they would inherit (in a simple manner). The second drawback is that code sharing yields the definition of multiple classes, which confuse the initial design of the taxonomy. Because the taxonomy is the backbone of software organization in an OO language, this sort of "overloading" should be avoided. Using a polymethod is a simpler solution,

```
[define very_long(x:{string + list}) polymethod -> boolean, => length(x) > 80],
```

which allows sharing without useless complexity.

- *Attaching a method to a single object or a given collection of objects.* Another problem that we have encountered frequently while writing LAURE applications is methods that apply to a single object. This occurs either because the object is one-of-a-kind (e.g., a keyword), or because it needs a special behavior. The usual solution is to create a special class in the first case and to insert a conditional test in the generic method when the second case occurs. We already mentioned the drawbacks associated with the creation of a new class that is not necessary from a design point of view. Similarly, treating exceptional situations with conditional statements is not an optimal solution and becomes confusing if there are many such "special" objects. Since finite collections are types in LAURE, we may attach a polymethod to one object or to a collection of objects (*a la* MODULA2) as in

```
[define fact(x:{0}) polymethod -> integer, => 1]
[define fib(x:{0,1}) polymethod -> integer, => 1].
```

- *Handling exceptional objects.* The previous example showed how exceptional objects could be handled positively (by saying how to deal with them). Type difference can be used to deal with them negatively. For instance, we can define inversion on non-zero numbers.

```
[define inverse(x:{float - {0.0}}) polymethod -> float, => (1 / x)].
```

Dealing with the exception (0) in such a way is safer than relying on a specialized method defined on {0} and is more elegant than using a conditional statement.

- *Attaching a method to a parameterized type.* Last but not least, we may now attach methods to complex type expressions that represent subsets of a generic class. For instance, the sum feature should be defined only on lists that contains numbers (integer, float ...). This is captured easily with a polymethod

```
[define sum(l:{list & {number set_of}}) polymethod -> number,
=> [let n as 0, [for x in l, n <- (n + x)], n]]
```

The same example would hold with {stack & {of in {number}}}.

Such an improvement in expressive power is bound to entail additional complexity. The two main issues are the resolution of multiple inheritance conflicts and the efficient compilation of polymethods. The efficient evaluation is actually a sub-problem of the compilation, which we consider less important since our focus with LAURE is to bring flexibility in the interpreted mode but deliver performance in the compiled mode (actually LAURE's interpreter is faster than equivalent COMMONLISP interpreters).

Inheritance conflicts are more frequent with polymethods since the type lattice is more complex and there is a greater chance for two polymethods to have signatures with a non-empty intersection. However, we can re-use the strategy that was developed for LAURE previously [Ca89], where resolution is done by applying a commutative and associative combination operator over the lattice structure. We used to rely on the class lattice structure of LAURE, but the solution still works with a more complex lattice structure (cf. Section 5.1).

We deal with the compilation issue in the same way, using the techniques that were developed to compile methods. When LAURE tries to compile a message using the feature f, it uses the type inference module to determine a type for each sub-expression. If the feature f is closed [Ca89] (which really means that we allow static binding), LAURE will search if the types of the arguments yield a unique method m for the feature f. This is the case when

(1) the argument signature is included in the method m's signature,

(2) the argument signature has an empty intersection with the signature of any other method that is not bigger than m according to order defined in Section 3.2 (f is well-defined).

Practically, this is often the case, which explains why compilers such as Typed Smalltalk [GJ90] or LAURE can improve performance up to C++ level. However, when this does not occur, we must rely on dynamic binding and determine at run-time which method to call. The only way to get rid of this last case is to build a statically-typed language, but this creates a large set of problems as we have seen in the first section, and does not seem relevant for a prototyping/ knowledge representation language. By combining a powerful type inference mechanism (such as the one we are describing) with the flexibility of dynamic typing/binding (when required), we can combine advantages and win on both aspects.

4.2 Attaching Type Expression to Methods

The second original feature of polymethods is the ability to receive a second-order type. In the rest of the paper, we will concentrate on how such a type can be derived automatically. Here we would like to show that second-order types can be used directly by an (advanced) user to help the compiler. When defining a polymethod, the user writes an expression introduced by the keyword =>, with an implicit lambda-abstraction; it is also possible to write another expression, introduced by the keyword :=>, which represents the type of the result using the method variables to represent the types of the parameters. Let us consider an example where we define addition over lists, sets and strings. We also want the compiler to detect errors (one cannot add a string and a set) and to make polymorphic type inference (adding two strings will produce a string). Thus we write the following definition:

```
[define plus(x:{set + {list + string}} y:{set + {list + string}}) polymethod -> {set + {list + string}},
    => [case x    set  (x + y),
                  list (copy(x) append y),
                  string (x append y)],
    :=> [if (x ≤ set) [if (y ≤ set) set else {}]
    else_if (x ≤ list) [if (y ≤ list) list else {}]
```

```
else_if (x ≤ string) [if (y ≤ string) string else ()]
else entity])
```

In the second expression (after :=>) the variable x and y represent the types of the two arguments. Here we only use conditional expression and the type lattice order (≺), but we could build more complex type expressions using the operators *in*: and @ (in(x) is the LAURE equivalent of ε(x) and (x @ p) the equivalent of ρ(x,p)). We can use LAURE to write second-order types because types are first-class objects in LAURE.[6]

Indeed, the goal of second-order type inference is to produce the type function automatically for such an example. However, there are still cases when the user must give the second-order type, because it could not be deduced. This is, for instance, the case for primitive methods or for methods that use heterogeneous data structures, such as in the two examples

```
[define car(l:list) method -> entity, => #'car_list , :=> in(l)]
[define top(x:stack) method -> entity, => last(content(x)), :=> (x @ of)]
```

Second-order types are used at compile-time during type inference. If we remember from the last section how messages were compiled, the second-order type will be used when the compiler has found which method to apply. If such a method m has a second-order type κ(m), the compiler will apply this function to the tuple of types of the arguments in the message to compute the type inferred for the result of the message, as opposed to simply using the range of the method. Thus, if we compile the message plus("aa","bb"), the compiler will infer the type *string* and not simply {set + {list + string}}. The combined process of finding which method of the feature f to apply for a set of arguments $(x_1, x_2, \dots x_n)$ with given types $(t_1, t_2, \dots t_n)$ and of computing the predicted type of the result is embodied in the function ψ (i.e., $\psi(f, t_1, t_2, \dots t_n)$ is the type inferred for the expression $f(x_1, x_2, \dots x_n)$.

4.3 Second-Order Type Inference

In this section we would like to describe informally the principles used to build automatically second-order types for methods. A more precise description will follow in the next sections. A type inference procedure is an abstraction mechanism, that can be seen formally as an abstract interpretation. This means that we abstract values into set of values and we predict the result of an expression with a set that will contain the actual result. For instance, a usual abstraction of a method is to check if the types of the arguments are correct and return the range of the method as the type inferred for the result.

Precision in type inference is lost when the abstraction is performed at a coarse level. For instance, if the identity method (λx.x) is abstracted into *Entity* → *Entity*, then the type inferred for identity(1) is *Entity* (as opposed to *integer* or {1}). To get better type inference, we need a better abstract domain that can carry more information. We

---

[6]This idea that the user would like to help the compiler with a second-order type has actually been extended in the LAURE language to a further degree. When the user gives the type function, this function may either return a type, in which case it is understood as a second-order type, but it can also return a method, in which case the function is seen as an optimization rule. The method returned by the type expression is substituted to the original method in the compilation process. This allows to perform optimizations based on type information in a way that is (somehow) elegant and extensible (the user can add his own rules).

can also see that a better inference for Identity(1) depends both on the abstraction for the identity method but also from the actual type of the argument.

Thus, using functions over types as an abstraction domain is a natural method to improve the precision of type inference. This is the principal intuition behind the use of second-order types. We want to abstract each method into a lambda-abstraction that gives the type of the result as a function of the type of the arguments. Since a method is defined by an expression of the language, this means that the type inferred for an expression e must not be a simple type (e.g., *Entity* in the case of the identity method) but rather a type expression that uses the types of the method arguments as its own arguments (e.g., x for the same identity method). Then we can obtain a second-order type by lambda-abstraction (e.g., $\lambda x.x$ for the identity method).

Using a functional domain allows some typing decision to be delayed until the type is actually applied, thus we can describe it as a lazy abstraction since part of the work is done later. For instance, type inference on the message Identity(1) will return $\{1\}$, when the type of the identity method ($\lambda x.x$) is applied to the type of the argument 1 (which is $\{1\}$).

Practically, we use an abstraction method Ξ which translates an instruction on values into an instruction on types, using the basic type constructors and some type inference methods (such as ψ). This method is implemented on each kind of LAURE instruction (all LAURE instructions are first class objects). The result of each method is another LAURE instruction, which represents an expression from $\Lambda(T)$.

5. Using Polymethods

5.1 Framework for Inheritance Conflict Resolution

In order to get *well-defined* features, we need to solve "multiple inheritance conflicts". To do so, we assume the existence of a combination property, which takes two methods of the same feature and creates a third.

> **Proposition:** *There exists a commutative and associative combination operation, written $\otimes$, which takes two methods of the same feature and returns a new method whose domain is the intersection of the domains.*

The actual combination operation that we use in the language depends on the degree of description that we have for each method. For instance, if a set value is returned by m_1 and m_2, a natural convention is to return the union of the two sets for the method $m_1 \otimes m_2$.[7] Another common rule is to choose m_1 over m_2 if the domain of m_1 is included in m_2's domain. The more information we have on each method, the better the resolution conflict (thus, *reflection* is interesting, because we can enrich the description of a method). Last, we need to introduce an *error* value, which is the only way to deal with some situations (e.g., $\forall x \in \{1,2\}\ f(x) = 1\ \&\ \forall x \in \{2,3\}\ f(x) = 2$). We now use the combination operation to solve all virtual conflicts.

---

[7] This point of view comes from a knowledge representation and AI background. Conflict resolution is a semantic problem that does not have a unique well-founded solution. What is described here is a framework which allows us to build a consistent conflict resolution strategy from a few semantic rules given by the user [Ca89].

Strategy: *If f is a feature with two methods, whose domains have a non-empty intersection D such that there is no other restriction with domain D, we add a new method obtained by combining two such methods with ⊗. We repeat this process until there are no such pairs of methods. The result of the iteration is independent of the choice of a particular pair at each step. The result is a well-defined feature.*

The Church-Rosser property results from associativity and commutativity of ⊗. This strategy has many advantages. First, we get a truly declarative semantics for multiple inheritance, which is more satisfying than operational ones based on the order in which the taxonomy is explored. Because of the lattice structure, each conflict is solved once at the "higher" possible level. Moreover, the conflict resolution strategy can be enriched with new rules for method combination. An important corollary is that for each well-defined feature, the set of method's domains is closed by intersection, which is close to the condition imposed in OBJ2 [GM86].

5.2 Type Inference and Abstract Interpretation

The LAURE language is an imperative language, built around the notion of message passing, which associates a function written $[e]$ from $S \rightarrow O \times S$ to each expression e of the language. The input parameter is the state of the system and the output is a pair (resulting value, resulting state). We have developed a type inference procedure as an *abstract interpretation* [CC77] of the semantics [AM91] [CP91]. We abstract each semantics function $[e]$ as a type $[e]_r{}^*$ from T, which represents the type expected for the result of evaluating e. The fact that each variable is typed in LAURE is represented by the context $\Gamma = \{a_i : X_i, i = 1... n\}$, where a_is are variables and X_i are types. The definition of the abstraction is given by the fact that the type lattice is a sub-lattice of O's powerset. The consistency of the abstract interpretation [CC77] guarantees that $\forall v \in S, [e]_1 \in \chi([e]_r{}^*)$. This standard abstraction is shown as *type inference* in Figure 1.

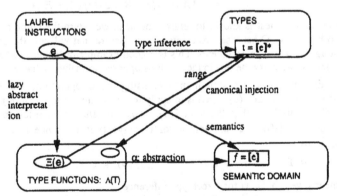

Figure 1: Two Schemes of Abstract Interpretation

However, the problems that we have presented in the first section can be characterized as an oversimplification in the abstraction process. Our abstract domain is too limited to reflect the complex type information needed for such tricky problems. This is why we have introduced second-order types, as a more complex abstract domain (the canonical second-order type presented previously can be seen as a canonical injection from the simpler abstract domain to the other, as in Figure 1). We call this a *lazy* abstraction because representing the type of an instruction as a function over types avoids making simplifications too soon and delays the decision until a finer context Γ is known. For instance, the type obtained for the identity will be $(\lambda t.t)$ as opposed to Object $\rightarrow$ Object. The abstraction arrows from the TYPE FUNCTION abstract domain to the semantics domain in Figure 1 reflects the fact that each second-order type is an abstraction of the semantics (cf. the definition of a second-order type in Section 3.2)

5.3 Lazy Abstract Interpretation with $\Lambda(T)$

The key step to second-order type inference is to "abstract" the abstract interpretation rules into functions from $\Lambda(T)$. If e is an expression with free variables $a_1, \ldots a_n$, we consider the types $x_1, \ldots x_n$ of those variables as meta (type) variables and we look to express $[e]^*$ as a function of $x_1, \ldots x_n$, using $\Lambda(T)$. Therefore, we shall build a function Ξ from the set of LAURE expression to $\Lambda(T)$ such that

$$\forall\, t_1,\ldots,t_n \in T,\ \Xi(e)(t_1,\ldots,t_n) = [e]_\Gamma^*,\ where\ \Gamma = \{a_i : t_i,\ i = 1\ldots n\}.$$

We have extended the class lattice with two additional sets: *error* and *ambiguous* = *error* $\vee$ *object* . $[e]_\Gamma^* = error$ means that the execution of e produces an error; $[e]_\Gamma^* = ambiguous$ means that the execution of e may produce an error.

Ξ is built by structural induction over the LAURE language, in a similar manner as the abstract interpretation is defined in [CP91]. We know a bound for each type variable x_i (since $x_i \prec X_i$), so we carry the context $\Gamma = \{a_i : X_i,\ i = 1\ldots n\}$. Here is a first (simplified) example for applying Ξ to a conditional statement[8].

$$\Xi_\Gamma([if\ e_1\ e_2\ then\ e_3\ ]) =\ if\ [e_1]_\Gamma^* \leq boolean$$
$$then\ (B \wedge C)\ |\ B = \Xi_\Gamma(e_2),\ C = \Xi_\Gamma(e_3)$$
$$else\_if\ [e_1]_\Gamma^* \leq error\ then\ \ error$$
$$else\ \ if(A \cap boolean = \emptyset,\ error,\ B \wedge C)$$
$$|\ A = \Xi_\Gamma(e_1),\ B = \Xi_\Gamma(e_2),\ C = \Xi_\Gamma(e_3)$$

This means if the test is known to return a boolean we return the union of the types of the two branches. Otherwise, we create an *if* structure that will test the correctness of the test against the type arguments. This is a good example of laziness: when there is some ambiguity, we carry the test in the result as opposed to making a hasty decision.

We handle messages in a similar manner using the ψ operation. The semantics associated with a message $f(a_1,\ldots,a_n)$ is to apply the restriction of the feature f, which is relevant (f is well-defined) to the tuple $[(a_1, \ldots,a_n)]$ (evaluated from left to right). In [CP91], we have defined a function ψ for message type inference and shown the following result

$$\forall\, t_1, \ldots,\ t_n \in T,\ \forall\, a_i \in t_i,\ \forall\, v,\ [\ f(a_1,\ldots,a_n)\ ](v)_1 \in \psi(f,\ t_1,\ \ldots,\ t_n).$$

This means we can use ψ for direct type inference

$$[\ f(a_1,\ldots,a_n)\ ]_\Gamma^* = \psi(f,\ [a_1]_\Gamma^*,\ [a_2]_\Gamma^*,\ \ldots,\ [a_n]_\Gamma^*).$$

Since ψ was introduced as a symbol of $\Lambda(T)$, we can define

---

[8] In the rest of the paper, we write $E(x,y,\ldots)\ |\ x = a,\ y = b,\ \ldots$ for the expression E from $\Lambda(T)$ obtained by substitution.

$$\Xi_\Gamma(f(e_1 ,e_2 ... ,e_n)) = \psi(f, A_1, ... , A_n) \mid A_i = \Xi_\Gamma(e_i).$$

Thus, instead of simply associating to the message a type that would contain its results, *we associate an expression that we can use to compute a better type for each variable context Γ.* The previous definition has been extended in our current system to catch finer inference (e.g., using the test in an *if* statement).

5.4 Application to New Polymethod Definitions

We can use the function Ξ for classic type inference and compiler optimization [CP91]. In addition, we can also use it to infer a second-order type for a new method defined by some variables and a LAURE expression, according to the following result

Theorem: *If $(a_1,..., a_n)$ are some variables, $X_1,...,X_n$ are some types and $e(a_1,...,a_n)$ an instruction made from these variables, we can define a method m from e with:*
- $f(m)(x_1,x_2,...,x_n,\vee) = [\![e(x_1,x_2,...,x_n)]\!](\vee),$
- $\kappa(m) = \Xi_\Gamma(e)$ *with* $\Gamma = \{a_i : X_i, i = 1... n\}$
- $\sigma(m) = X_1 \times ...\times X_n \times \kappa(m)(X_1,...,X_n).$

The important point is that $\kappa(m)$ $(= \kappa(e))$ can be represented by a function from Λ which is "compiled" from the expression e. Here is a short example that shows how a second-order type is inferred

Example: • Add1 is defined by one variable *self* and one instruction (*self* + 1) :

  f(m) = (λx.x+1),

  σ(m) = Number $\times$ Number,

  κ(m)(x) = $[\![$ (self+1) $]\!]_{\{self:x\}}$* = ψ(+, x, {1}).

  This second order type means that Add1 returns an integer when applied to an integer and a number when applied to a number.

To avoid problems, we use the canonical second-order type when we need it inside a recursive definition of a method. A better solution is to produce a fix-point upper bound of the second-order type, which we are currently experimenting.

From a practical perspective, $\Lambda(T)$ is included in the LAURE language through reflection of the type system (all type operations, such as ψ, are methods implemented on objects that represent LAURE types). This means that the result $\kappa(m)$ of the type inference procedure is simply a LAURE instruction, from which a function is made by lambda-abstraction. This means that the procedure for second-order type inference, which is given a LAURE object representing the instructions (*self* + *1*), will not produce a complex term but rather another LAURE expression (as an object) which is used to produce the second-order function. Here are some example of such a transformation:

  self $\rightarrow$ self

  (self+ 1) $\rightarrow$ range_message(+,self,{1})

  [if (self $\leq$ x) self else x] $\rightarrow$ [if ((range_message($\leq$,self,x) glb boolean) = {}) {} else (self lub x)]

The transformation is implemented by structural recursion as an abstract interpretation. Because we do not deal with recursive functions yet, the complexity of type inference is linear in the size of the program and polynomial in the size of the class taxonomy.

6. Application to Common Problems

6.1 The Min Method

We can now consider the *min* feature and see how second-order types can be used to get a proper type description. We assume here that ≤ is a primitive feature, defined by methods whose second-order types are derived from their signatures. The second-order type inferred by LAURE for the *min* method will be

$\Xi($ *[if* $(self \le x)$ *self else x])* $_{\{self:entity,\ x:entity\}}.$

Since ⟦ $(self \le x)$ ⟧*$_{\{self:entity,\ x:entity\}}$ = ψ (≤,entity,entity) = *ambiguous*, we get

$\lambda(x,y).$ *iff* $\psi(\le, x, y)$ ∩ *boolean = ∅, error, x ∨ y)).*

With this second-order type, the compiler can both perform polymorphic type inference and detect errors, while the user may extend the feature ≤ by new methods (such as a lexicographic order on lists introduced in the next section). Here are some of the strong points.

- Strong type checking is possible: *min*(1,"a") or *min*("a",2.3) will be detected as errors because ψ(≤, *integer*, *string*) = *error*. This would, of course, be also true for a message *min*(x,y) where we simply know that x and y belong to two types that are not comparable.

- *Min* is a truly polymorphic function: if we find the expression *min*(x,y) in an environment where the type of x and y is very imprecise (e.g., Object), the inferred type will simply be Object. If x and y are known to be integers, the inferred resulting type will be integer.

- This is an extensible description: if ≤ is augmented by a new method, the type for *min* is still valid without any re-computation. The dependency between ≤ and *min* is represented in the second-order type.

6.2 List Operations and Polymethods

Let us now consider the case of lexicographic order on lists, as defined the following method.

```
Example:   [define (l:list ≤ x:list) method -> boolean,
           => [    if  (l = {}) true
               else_if  (x = {}) false
               else [or (car(l) ≤ car(x)), [and (car(l) = car(x)), (cdr(l) ≤ cdr(x))]]]]
```

The second-order type inferred by the system will not detect that the expression (x ≤ y), where x is of type {*list* ∧ *set_of(integer)*} and y is of type {*list* ∧ *set_of(string)*}, is a type error. Actually it is not ! x and y could be two empty lists (cf. Section 2.2) and the message (x ≤ y) is legitimate. This means that we lose some safety in type-checking when we take a "truly object-oriented, extensible" point of view on lists. On the other hand, [MMM91] shows that if the good type-checking properties of ML are kept, some aspects of object-orientation must be simplified. However, here we can get a better typing if we use polymethods to distinguish the case of the empty list.

Let us consider the following definition.

Example: [define (x:{()} ≤ y:list) polymethod -> boolean, => true]
[define (x:{list - {()}} ≤ y:{()}) polymethod -> boolean, => false][9]
[define (x:list ≤ y:list) polymethod -> boolean,
  => [or (car(x) ≤ car(y)), [and (car(x) = car(y)),(cdr(x) ≤ cdr(y))]]]]

The second-order type inferred for the last method is

$$\lambda(x,y).if(\ \psi(\leq,\varepsilon(x),\ \varepsilon(y))\ \cap\ boolean\ =\ \varnothing,\ error,\ boolean)$$

This allows the system to detect typing errors such as

$$((1\ 2\ 3)\ \leq\ (\text{"aa"}))\ ;\ (((1\ 2)\ (2\ 3))\ \leq\ (((1))))\ ;$$

Obviously, this only happens when the compiler can find out if the list is empty or not. This is done by extending the type inference rules and by defining primitive methods, such as cons or append, with more detailed signature.

6.3 Stacks

The last feature of polymethods is the ability to add preconditions on methods' arguments that bind the type of one argument to another. The preconditions that can be added are of the form $(x \in p(y))$, where x and y are two methods arguments and *p* is a parameter. Syntactically, the special form p(y) is used in place of a type in the definition of the typed variable x. For instance, here is the revised stack example, using polymethods

```
[define of parameter]
[define stack class with slot(of -> type, default ∅) ...]
[define top(s:stack) polymethod -> integer, => last(content(s)), :=> (s ● of)]
[define push(self:stack, x:of(self)) polymethod -> void,
     => (content(self) put_at index(self) x),
        (index(self) is (index(self) + 1))]
```

The second-order type for the method *top* is given explicitly here and enables parametric type inference on stacks. The argument *x* of the method *push* is typed with the special form *of(self)*, which means that the precondition $(x \in$ of(self)) must be verified before applying the method.

This is a major improvement over the code presented in the first section of this paper. Not only do we get a more concise definition, but the condition $(x \in$ of(self)) can be checked automatically *by the compiler*. The key result for checking such statements at compile-time is the following [CP91]

$$[x]^* \leq \rho(p,[y]^*)\ \Rightarrow\ (x \in p(y))\ is\ always\ satisfied$$

Thus, if the message *push(s,x)* is compiled, and if we know that *s* is a stack of integer and that *x* is an integer, the test $[x]^* \leq \rho(p,[y]^*)$ will be verified at compile-time and the run-time code will not include any type-checking. Thus we obtain the same efficiency as a statically type-checked language, with the flexibility of a dynamically type-checked language, since we can still have heterogeneous stacks.

---

[9] If the domain of the second method was *list*, the system will complain about a conflict on {( )} × {( )}. This is another example that justifies the introduction of type difference.

6.4 Comparison with Related Works

This work is one among many attempts to introduce complex type inferences, such as those performed by ML [Mil78][HMM86], into an object-oriented language. Various type systems have been proposed to efficiently compile such languages [Wan87] [Red88] [CP89], but none of them was found to be adequate for LAURE [CP91] (Section 2). In fact, there are two families of approaches. The first tries to develop a statically strongly-typed language, such as Machiavelli [OBB89] or extended ML [HMM86]. Usually the problems that we presented in our motivations are solved, but there are restrictions on object-orientation or set operations. The second family [JGZ89] [CHC90] [PS91] tries to adapt more closely to object-oriented languages, but leaves the same problems open. We have found that the only way to escape this dilemma is to use second-order types. Another very important distinction in this family of work is the philosophy behind the objects. Most of the type-safe, completely static inference procedures that have been proposed recently use a notion of object that is more like a *value* than an object in the database sense (with real updates, side-effects and identity). For instance, although more powerful, the QUEST [Car89] type system (which subsumes our goals) could not be used for a language like LAURE.

Using second-order types for getting better type inference [Sce90][HM91] helped us to solve some very practical problems. The main difference with similar work comes from our order-sorted, extensible domain. What makes LAURE's type inference simpler is that abstract interpretation is only an approximation (and is still consistent [CC77]), which allows some simplification in the difficult cases, instead of running into complexity problems [HM91]. Using abstract interpretation to define type inference is a common idea, which is also applied to a simpler dynamically typed language in [AM91]. The reason we can afford to leave some difficult case out is that we use a dynamically typed language, which allows the compiler to generate type-ambiguous code if everything else failed. A last promising line of work is *safety analysis* [PA92], from which our work borrows some ideas.

Another distinction between the various works is the use of a set-based semantics, which offers many advantages from a data modeling perspective [SZ87] [LR89]. Although this is a controversial issue [CHC90], we believe that our model, based on sets and on a separation between taxonomy and methods, prevents some hard problems related in [PS91] to occur and provides a better foundation for method specialization and inheritance than [Mit90] in the case of an extensible and reflective object-oriented language.

7. Conclusion

In this paper we have shown how to extend methods in an object-oriented language into polymethods to solve some problems related to type-checking. Polymethods are extended into three directions: they are typed with a second-order type, which captures parametric and inclusion polymorphism in a complete and elegant manner; polymethods are attached directly to types instead of classes, which permits a finer description; last, some tests can be attached to methods' arguments that are verified at compile time by type inference. We have shown the benefits of a set-based type system for the LAURE language, from which we can derive a second-order type language and second-order type inference based on abstract interpretation.

The type system and its inference procedure have been implemented in the LAURE language, together with the second-order types. We have found them very practical since they allow type optimizations that used to be hard-coded into the compiler to be described in a formal and elegant manner. We are now implementing the second-order type inference procedure, to derive those types automatically (in the current version of the language, they are entered explicitly as a lambda expression from $\Lambda(T)$).

Acknowledgments

We would like to thank Guy Cousineau and Michel Bidoit for their comments on an earlier version of this paper. We are also grateful to all the contributors to the newsgroup *comp.object* who helped us in our thinking of a practical solution to the *min* problem. Last, we thank the anonymous referees for their detailed comments and suggestions.

References

[AM91] A. Aiken, B. R. Murphy: *Static Type Inference in a Dynamically Typed Language*. Proc. of the 18th Symposium on Principles of Programming Languages, 1991.

[AP90] H. Ait-Kaci, A. Podelski. *The Meaning of Life*. PRL Research Report, DEC, 1990.

[Car89] L. Cardelli: *Typeful Programming*. DEC SRC report #5, 1989.

[Ca89] Y. Caseau: "A Model For a Reflective Object-Oriented Language," *Sigplan Notices, Special Issue on Concurrent Object-Oriented Programming*, 1989.

[Ca91] Y. Caseau: *An Object-Oriented Language for Advanced Applications*. Proc. of TOOLS USA 91, 1991.

[CC77] P. Cousot, R. Cousot: *Abstract Interpretation : A Unified Model for Static Analysis of Programs by Constructions or Approximation of Fixpoints*. Proc. Fourth ACM symposium of Principles of Programming Languages, 1977.

[CHC90] W. Cook, W. Hill, P. Canning: *Inheritance is not Subtyping*. Proc. of the 17th ACM Symposium on Principles of Programming Languages, San Francisco, 1990.

[CP89] W. Cook, J. Palsberg: *A Denotational Semantics of Inheritance and its Correctness*. Proc. of OOPSLA-89, New Orleans, 1989.

[CP91] Y. Caseau, L. Perron: *A type System for Object-Oriented Database Programming and Querying Languages*. Proc. of International Workshop on DataBase Programming Languages, 1991.

[CW85] L. Cardelli, P. Wegner: *On understanding types, data abstraction, and polymorphism*. ACM Computing Surveys, vol 17 n. 4, 1985.

[Don90] C. Dony: *Exception Handling and Object-Oriented Programming: Towards a Synthesis*. Proc. of OOPSLA'90, Ottawa, 1990.

[FW84] D.P. Friedman, M. Wand: *Reification: Reflection without Metaphysics*. ACM Symposium on LISP and Functional Programming, Austin, August 1984.

[GJ90] J. Graver, R. Johnson: *A Type System for Smalltalk*. Proc. of the 17th ACM Symposium on Principles of Programming Languages, San Francisco, 1990.

[GM86] J. Goguen, J. Meseguer: *Eqlog: Equality, Types and Generic Modules for Logic Programming*. In Logic Programming, Functions, Relations and Equations, Eds. D. DeGroot, G. Lindstrom, Prentice Hall, 1986.

[GMP90]   L. Geurts, L. Meertens, S. Pemberton: *ABC Programmer's Handbook*. Prentice-Hall, 1990.

[GR83]   A. Goldberg, D. Robson: *Smalltalk-80: The language and its implementation*. Addison-Wesley, 1983.

[HM91]   F. Henglein, H. G. Mairson: *The Complexity of Type Inference for Higher-Order Typed Lambda Calculi*. Proc. of the 18th Symposium on Principles of Programming Languages, 1991.

[HMM86]   R. Harper, D.B. MacQueen, R. Milner : *Standard ML*. Report ECS-LFCS-86-2, Dept. of Computer Science, University of Edimburgh, 1986.

[JGZ89]   R. Johnson, J, Grauer, L. Zurawski: *TS: An Optimizing Compiler for Smalltalk*. OOPSLA-89, New Orleans, 1989.

[LR89]   C. Lecluse, P. Richard: *Modelling Complex Structures in Object-Oriented Databases*. Proc. of ACM PODS, 1989.

[Me89]   B. Meyer : *Static Typing for Eiffel*. Interactive Software Engineering, July, 1989.

[Mil78]   R. Milner: *A theory of type polymorphism in programming*. In j. Computer and System Sciences vol 17 n. 3, 1978.

[Mit90]   J. Mitchell: *Towards a Typed Foundation for Method Specialization and Inheritance*. Proc. of the 17th ACM Symposium on Principles of Programming Languages, San Francisco, 1990.

[MMM91]   J. Mitchell, S. Meldal, N. Madhav: *An Extension of Standard ML modules with subtyping and inheritance*. Proc. of the 18th Symposium on Principles of Programming Languages, 1991.

[MN88]   P. Maes, D. Nardi: *Meta-level Architecture and Reflection*. Elsevier Science Publication (North Holland), 1988.

[OB89]   A. Ohori, P. Buneman: *Static Type Inference for Parametric Classes*. OOPSLA-89, New Orleans, 1989.

[OBB89]   A. Ohori, P. Buneman, V. Breazu-Tannen: *Database Programming in Machiavelli - a Polymorphic Language with Static Type Inference*. ACM SIGMOD Conf. on Management of Data, May 1989.

[PS91]   J. Palsberg, M. I. Schwartzbach: *Static Typing for Object-Oriented Programming*. DAIMI PB-355, June 1991.

[PS92]   J. Palsberg, M. I. Schwartzbach: *Safety Analysis versus Type Inference for Partial Types*. DAIMI PB-404, July 1992.

[Red88]   U. Reddy: *Objects as Closures: Abstract Semantics of Object-Oriented Languages*. Proc. ACM Conference on LISP and Functional Programming, 1988.

[Sce90]   A. Scedrov: *A Guide to Polymorphic Types*. Logic and Computer Science, Academic Press, 1990.

[Smo89]   G. Smolka: *Logic Programming over Polymorphically Order-Sorted Types*. PhD Thesis, Universität Kaiserslautern, May 1989.

[Str86]   B. Stroustrup: *The C++ Programming Language*. Addison-Wesley, 1986.

[SZ87]   A. Skarra, S. Zdonik: *Type Evolution in an Object-Oriented Database*. In Research Directions in Object Oriented Programming, ed. B. Schriver and P. Wegner, MIT press, 1987.

[Wan87]   M. Wand: *Complete Type Inference for Simple Objects*. Proc. IEEE Symposium on Logic in Computer Science.

Typed Sets as a Basis for Object-Oriented Database Schemas*

Herman Balsters[1], Rolf A. de By[1], Roberto Zicari[2]

[1] Computer Science Department, University of Twente,
P.O. Box 217, 7500 AE Enschede,
The Netherlands
[2] Fachbereich Informatik, Johann Wolfgang Goethe-Universität,
Robert Mayerstraße 11–15,
D–6000 Frankfurt am Main,
Germany

Abstract. The object-oriented data model TM is a language that is based on the formal theory of FM, a typed language with object-oriented features such as attributes and methods in the presence of subtyping. The general (typed) set constructs of FM allow one to deal with (database) constraints in TM.

The paper describes the theory of FM, and discusses the role that set expressions may play in conceptual database schemas. Special attention is paid to the treatment of constraints, and a three-step specification approach is proposed. This approach results in the formal notion of database universe stated as an FM expression.

Keywords: object-oriented databases, constraint specification, sets, type theory.

1 Introduction

The language TM is a (high-level) object-oriented data model that has been developed at the University of Twente and the Politecnico di Milano. It contains the basic elements that one would expect from a state-of-the-art OO model, but with *important new features*, two of which we will discuss in this paper:

1. predicative description of sets (predicative sets as complex values), and
2. static constraints of different granularity (object level, class level, database level).

The language TM is a language for describing conceptual schemas of object-oriented databases. As it stands, TM is not a database programming language, like for instance Galileo [3] or that of O_2 [21], although the provisions to make

---

* This work has been partially funded by the Commission of The European Communities under the ESPRIT R&D programme: project 2443 STRETCH. Our E-mail addresses are, resp.: balsters@cs.utwente.nl, deby@cs.utwente.nl, zicari@informatik.uni-frankfurt.de.

it one are fairly straightforward. The strength of TM stems from its richness as a specification language and its formal, type-theoretic, background.

The expressiveness of the language is best characterized by a list of its typical features. It has

- complex objects, formed from arbitrarily nested records, variant records, sets, and lists[3];
- object identities (oid's);
- multiple inheritance;
- method and method inheritance;
- composition links that allow to refer from one object type to another; and
- static type-checking.

The paper does not present the full syntax of TM, but instead presents significant examples to illustrate the main features of the model.

The language TM is not unique in that it is based on a formal theory; other notable examples are IQL [1], Iris [22], LIFE [2], Logres [11], Machiavelli [24, 25], and F-logic [19]. However, we know of no other language that is formally capable of dealing with arbitrary set expressions and (their) powertypes (or set types) in the context of subtyping and multiple inheritance. In fact, TM is a syntactically sugared version of its underlying Formal Model, FM. Aspects of FM are treated in Sect. 3. The aim of this paper is to illustrate the importance of sets for conceptual schemas, and, indeed, for object-oriented database systems in general.

The essential novelty of TM is that it allows arbitrary set expressions as well-typed expressions. Like existing systems such as ORION [7, 20], O_2 [21] and GemStone [15], TM allows to handle expressions that denote enumerated sets. Moreover, it also allows to use set expressions that are formed by *set comprehension*. Such expressions take the form $\{ x : \sigma \mid \phi(x) \}$, where $\phi(x)$ is a boolean expression in which the variable x may occur. A set expression of this form is called a *predicative set*. Together with the (well-founded) introduction of logical constructs it allows to formally deal with such necessary elements in conceptual schemas as constraints and the collection of allowed database states.

In TM, set expressions are either enumerated sets or predicative sets. If the elements of some set are of type σ then that set is of type $\mathbb{P}\sigma$, the powertype of σ as defined in Sect. 3.3. In systems like O_2 and ORION, this type is denoted by $\{ \sigma \}$. Like all other expressions, set expressions are typed within a context of subtyping, which means that expressions may have many types.

The topic of this paper concerns general set constructs and (static) constraints in an object-oriented model, both at the level of a TM specification and at the level of its formal FM counterpart. Dynamic aspects such as method specification and method invocation, updates, and dynamic constraints will not be discussed. Dynamical issues are, of course, important, but treatment of these

---

[3] In the rest of the paper we will not deal with variant records and lists for reasons of a clean exposition.

issues is beyond the scope of this paper. We refer to [33] for full coverage of TM and FM supplied with methods and views.

The TM language is currently being implemented as a high-level database interface. With respect to the topic of this paper, it is important to remark which problems arise for implementing constraints, and predicative sets in general. Constraint specifications can be used in many ways, for instance, to define the notion of transaction safety, or to deduce properties of the database application. Our first prototype generates testing code from the constraint specification to determine whether the constraint is satisfied. We are currently investigating less naive and more efficient ways to do so, following lines as were set out by [26, 28].

This paper is organized as follows. A small example application, involving (the recurring) employees, managers, secretaries, and departments, is described in Sect. 2. The formal theory of FM, which is based on the Cardelli type system [13], is described in more detail in Sect. 3 and in the Appendix. We refrain from offering denotational semantics for this extended Cardelli type system solely for lack of space; we refer the interested reader to [5, 6, 32]. To define the mathematical meaning of TM in terms of FM we translate the structural concepts of TM into elements of FM where the mathematical meaning is precisely given. This translation is described in Sect. 4.

2 Motivation with Examples

We will demonstrate the new features of the TM language by means of an example. We do not describe in this paper the full syntax of the language but rather present significant examples in order to illustrate the main features of the underlying model.

In this section we show two features of the TM language, namely the possibility to:

- use predicative descriptions of sets and
- express static constraints with different granularity (i.e., for objects in isolation, class extensions, and database states).

2.1 Predicative Sets

Most of the theoretical proposals and system implementations of object-oriented data models are restricted to the possibility of defining only enumerated sets [1, 8, 9, 21, 24]. Besides enumerated sets, we allow the definition of predicative sets in TM.

Example 1. Let us consider the following three class declarations (which also show the possibility to define inheritance and composition links in TM):

```
Class Employee with extension EMP
    attributes
        name    : string
```

```
        age     : integer
        spouse  : Employee
        gender  : string
end  Employee
```

Class Manager ISA Employee with extension MAN
  attributes
```
        friends : IPEmployee
```
end **Manager**

Class Secretary ISA Employee with extension SEC
  attributes
```
        boss : Manager
```
  end Secretary □

The three classes are related to each other by an inheritance relationship. Before defining the predicative sets feature, we first discuss our notion of inheritance. TM's inheritance is based on an extension of Cardelli's subtyping relation ≤ [13]. In this paper, it is extended to powertypes (powertypes start with the type constructor IP). A formal definition of the notion of subtyping in TM can be found in Sect. 3.

We give an example of a predicative set in the context of the declarations given above. Consider the following **Manager** object with attributes **name**, **age**, **spouse**, **gender** and **friends**:

⟨ name="Martin", age=40, spouse=Martin's_Wife, gender="Male",
  friends={x: Employee |(x·name = "Black" or x·name = "Smith") and
$$x \cdot age < 40\} \ ),$$

where **Martin's_Wife** is some **Employee** object.

What is relevant here is the definition of the values of the set of friends of Martin which is given by a predicate without enumerating all values of the set.

In the example x is a member of the extension of class **Employee**. This means that the set of friends is a subset of the existing employees stored in the database. That is, Martin's friends are solely those employees (stored in the database) with name Black or Smith and who are younger than 40.

Another interesting point here is that whenever the extension associated to class **Employee** changes (e.g. by addition/deletion of employees in it) the set of friends of Martin is automatically derived by the definition of the associated predicate and its definition need not be changed. That is, the set-valued attribute **friends** is a derived attribute and depends on the actual state of the extension of class **Employee**. Such attributes can be compared to the approach taken in [31], where query statements can be used as attribute values.

In general, TM's predicative sets can be defined using a full first-order logic with typed variables and special boolean expressions. The general format of a predicative set is

$$\{ \ x : \sigma \,|\, \phi(x) \ \} \ ,$$

where $\phi(x)$ is a boolean expression, and σ is a class name or a type. If σ is a class name, x is implicitly taken to range over σ's class extension.

The boolean expressions of TM are either

- *constants:* **true** and **false**
- *logical formulas*, built up as follows:
  - if e is a boolean expression, then so is **not** e
  - if e and e' are boolean expressions, then so are $(e$ **or** $e')$, $(e$ **and** $e')$, $(e$ **implies** $e')$
  - if e is a boolean expression, x is a variable and σ is a type, then so are **forall** $x : \sigma \bullet (e)$ and **exists** $x : \sigma \bullet (e)$
- *special boolean expressions:* if e and e' are TM-expressions then so are the expressions $(e$ **isa** $e')$, $(e = e')$, $(e$ **in** $e')$, $(e$ **sin** $e')$, and $(e$ **subset** $e')$.

The special boolean expressions are treated in more detail in Sect. 3, but we offer a few words of comment here so that the reader can get an idea of what is intended by these constructs.

- $(e = e')$: this expression holds if both expressions e and e' evaluate to the same value.
- $(e$ **isa** $e')$: this expression holds if e is a specialization of e'. An example of such a (well-typed and true) boolean expression is

  $$\langle \text{age=3, name="Jones", salary=5000} \rangle \text{ isa } \langle \text{age=3, name="Jones"} \rangle \ ,$$

  since there are two respective types of these (record-)expressions that are in the subtype relation and, furthermore, the first expression is indeed a specialization of the first one.
- $(e$ **in** $e')$: this expression holds if the element e evaluates to a member of the evaluation of the set e'.
- $(e$ **sin** $e')$: this expression holds if there exists an element e'' such that both $(e$ **isa** $e'')$ and $(e''$ **in** $e')$ evaluate to true. In other words, e can be considered a specialization of an element of e'.
- $(e$ **subset** $e')$: this expression holds if the evaluation of the set e is contained in the evaluation of the set e'.

In the remainder of this section we will offer some examples employing these special boolean expressions. We note that we have also used some arithmetical relations (like $\leq$ and $>$) in these examples. Strictly speaking, we should have also listed these relations above when discussing our logical formulas, but we will tacitly assume that reader knows how to incorporate such constructs in the language.

Example 2. Suppose we want to modify the original predicative definition of the set of friends of Martin, such that now all Martin's friends have to be married with an employee younger than 35. We will not repeat the other attribute values, and focus only on that of **friends**:

friends=$\{x$: Employee | $(x\cdot$name $=$ "Black" or $x\cdot$name $=$ "Smith") and
$\quad\quad\quad\quad x\cdot$age $<$ 40 and
$\quad\quad\quad\quad$ exists y:Employee $\bullet$ $(x\cdot$spouse $= y$ and $y\cdot$age $<$ 35)$\}$

The additional condition (exists y:Employee $\bullet (x\cdot$spouse $= y$)), now implies that all of Martin's friends are married to employees younger than 35. $\square$

We give another example of a predicative set definition in TM.

Example 3. Let us consider again Martin's friends (recall that Martin is a manager), and suppose we want an additional condition which imposes that his friends are all married to secretaries. In TM we write:

friends= $\{x$: Employee | $(x\cdot$name $=$ "Black" or $x\cdot$name $=$ "Smith") and
$\quad\quad\quad\quad x\cdot$age $<$ 40 and
$\quad\quad\quad\quad$ exists y:Secretary $\bullet$ $(y$ isa $x\cdot$spouse and $y\cdot$age $<$ 35)$\}$ $\square$

The last condition contains the special boolean expression (y isa $x\cdot$spouse) between two typed expressions: $x\cdot$spouse of type Employee and y, which is of type Secretary. This isa-expression tests whether the value of y, viewed as an Employee, is equal to that of a spouse (who is an employee). Informally this means comparing the common attrinutes of a secretary object and an employee object to decide whether they are equal. This possibility of "viewing" objects at different levels of abstraction according to their position in the type hierarchy is called *object context* in TM.

To be correct, the above definition would require some additional constraints on the gender of spouses (e.g., the gender of two married employees must be different). We will introduce them later in this section, when introducing the TM mechanism to specify constraints.

We conclude this informal introduction to TM's predicative sets giving a last example.

Example 4. We want to add yet another condition to the set of friends of Martin: every spouse of Martin's friends (who are all married to secretaries by previous conditions) is also a friend of a manager. We write:

friends= $\{x$: Employee | $(x\cdot$name $=$ "Black" or $x\cdot$name $=$ "Smith") and
$\quad\quad\quad\quad x\cdot$age $<$ 40 and
$\quad\quad\quad\quad$ exists y:Secretary $\bullet$ $(y$ isa $x\cdot$spouse and $y\cdot$age $<$ 35 and
$\quad\quad\quad\quad\quad\quad$ exists z:Manager $\bullet y$ sin $z\cdot$friends)$\}$ $\square$

The last condition in the above predicate contains the boolean expression y sin $z\cdot$friends). Informally speaking this expression implies the object y (our secretarial spouse) to be at least in one manager's set of friends.

Just as '$=$' has an accompanying notion in isa to deal with subtypes, in has sin as an analogous notion. This means that e sin e' holds whenever e isa e'' holds for some e'' for which e'' in e'.

We turn now our attention to the mechanism of specifing constraints in TM.

2.2 Constraints

In TM it is possible to incorporate static constraints at three different levels:

- Objects,
- Class extensions, and
- Database states.

In this paper, we are interested in the specification of constraints rather than in their evaluation or enforcement. We will illustrate each type of constraint by means of an example.

Object and Class Constraints. Constraints can be associated to objects (i.e., they should hold for *each* individual object of a certain class; we call them *object constraints*), and to class extensions (i.e., they should hold for each extension of a certain class; we call them *class constraints*). Both object and class constraints are defined within the corresponding TM class definition. Our language makes a syntactical distinction between the two kinds of constraints because of notational conciseness: object constraints need not be explicitly (universally) quantified over all possible objects. These features are demonstrated by an example.

Example 5. Consider the class hierarchy as defined in Example 1. Suppose we want to define some object and class constraints for the class Employee as follows:
Object constraints (added to the definition of class **Employee**) :

- "the gender of an employee is either Male or Female". In TM we write:

  c_1 : (gender = "Male" or gender = "Female")

- "Married employees have different gender":

  c_2 : (spouse·gender $\neq$ gender)

- "For each employee x the spouse of the spouse of x is x":

  c_3 : (spouse·spouse = self) □

An object constraint is always implicitly quantified over the objects of the class, e.g. the class **Employee** in the above example. Validation of object constraints can be performed for one object at a time. We remark that the example constraints are very simple; arbitrarily complex constraints are actually allowed.

Object constraints defined in a class are also inherited by the objects of its subclasses. These "inherited" constraints will be in conjunction with the constraints defined for each subclass. For an example of object constraint inheritance we refer to Sect. 4.

Typical class constraints (though not all[4]), in contrast to object constraints, involve two quantifications over the objects of that class. To validate such a constraint the least one needs is the class extension as a whole.

Example 6. We specify a class constraint for the class **Employee**:

---

[4] Class constraints *not* involving two explicit quantifications are, for instance, those that use aggregate functions like *sum*, *count*, etc.

– Class constraints are also added to the definition of class Employee:
  • "If two male employees have different names, also their respective spouses will have different names" (This is a rule by Dutch law, as the woman gets the husband's name.):
    c_4 : forall x_1, x_2 •
       $((x_1 \cdot \text{name} \neq x_2 \cdot \text{name}$ and $x_1 \cdot \text{gender} = \text{"Male"}$ and $x_2 \cdot \text{gender} = \text{"Male"})$
       implies $x_1 \cdot \text{spouse·name} \neq x_2 \cdot \text{spouse·name})$

The complete specification of the class Employee thus becomes:

Class Employee with extension EMP
  attributes
      name   : string
      age   : integer
      spouse : Employee
      gender : string
  object constraints
      c_1 : gender = "Male" or gender = "Female"
      c_2 : spouse·gender $\neq$ gender
      c_3 : spouse·spouse = self
  class constraints
      c_4 : forall x_1, x_2 •
         $((x_1 \cdot \text{name} \neq x_2 \cdot \text{name}$ and $x_1 \cdot \text{gender} = \text{"Male"}$ and $x_2 \cdot \text{gender} = \text{"Male"})$
         implies $x_1 \cdot \text{spouse·name} \neq x_2 \cdot \text{spouse·name})$
  end   Employee □

Database Constraints. In TM it is also possible to define constraints between different classes. This is expressed by the so-called TM database constraints. Database constraints are defined in a separate section after the definition of the classes. Typical database constraints (though not all) involve quantifications over the objects of at least two different classes.

Example 7. For example, we may specify the following constraints:

– Database constraints (defined after the class definitions):
  • "A secretary and a manager cannot be the same employee" (i.e., the intersection of the Secretary and Manager extensions is empty):
    c_5 : forall x : Manager forall y : Secretary •
                   (not exists z : Employee • x isa z and y isa z)
  • "Each manager has at least one secretary":
    c_6 : forall x : Manager exists y : Secretary • $y \cdot \text{boss} = x$

3   Formal Language Features

The formal semantics of the TM language are based on those of FM, a formal model that is extensively described in [5, 6, 32]. The semantics of TM is precisely determined by describing a mapping from TM expressions to FM expressions. This mapping is described in Sect. 4. Here, we focus on FM.

FM is an extension of the theory described in [13, 14]. The extension consists of introducing set constructs and logical formalism. A major aim is to incorporate a general set construct into the language involving first-order logical predicates; the format of such a set is $\{\ x : \sigma \mid \phi(x)\ \}$.

The intention of this section is to give an outline of syntactical aspects of the type theory of FM; for further details and semantical issues we refer to [5, 6]. Semantical issues are, of course, important, but (solely due to reasons of lack of space) we refer the interested reader to the two articles mentioned above for a full treatment of the semantical part of our theory. For readers interested in other issues regarding subtyping in type theory we refer to [12, 16, 19, 25, 30, 34].

3.1 Cardelli Type Theory

In this section we give a brief summary of the system described in [13, 14]. For the base system, we restrict ourselves to basic types and record types. Full details of syntactical and proof-theoretical aspects can be found in the Appendix.

Expressions and Types. Types in our simplified version of the Cardelli system are either

1. *basic types*: such as integer, real, bool, string, or
2. *record types*: such as ⟨age:integer, name:string⟩, and
   ⟨address:string, date:⟨day:integer,month:integer,year:integer⟩⟩.

Record types have field names (*labels* or, as you wish, *attribute names*), and type components; records are permutation invariant under field components. Note that types can have a complex structure.

Expressions in our version of Cardelli type theory are either

1. *variables*: such as $x_{integer}, y_{string}, z_{\langle name:string,\ sal:real\rangle}$ or
2. *constants*: such as $1_{integer}, 2.0_{real}, True_{bool}$, or
3. *records*: such as ⟨name="john", age=17⟩, or
4. *projections*: such as ⟨name="john", sal=1.2⟩·name.

We note that variables and constants are typed. Type subscripts in variables and constants are usually dropped, for purposes of readability, when it is clear from the context what the type of the variable or constant is. Expressions of the form $e \cdot a$, where e is supposed to be some record expression, denote the projection of the record e on one of its attributes a.

All (correct) expressions in our language are typed according to (inductively defined) typing rules. If an expression e has type σ then this is written as $e : \sigma$.

Example 8. For example, the expression

$$\langle age=3, name=\text{``john''}, date=\langle day=27, month=2, year=1991\rangle\rangle$$

is typed as

⟨age:integer,name:string,date:⟨day:integer,month:integer,year:integer⟩⟩. □

Subtyping. The set of types T is equipped with a subtyping relation $\leq$. We speak of subtyping when there exists a partial order $\leq$ on the set of types, and the typing rules are extended to the effect that an expression e that has type σ may occur at a position where an expression of supertype τ of σ is expected. Or, in other words,

$$e : \sigma,\ \sigma \leq \tau \Rightarrow\ e : \tau \ .$$

Subtyping represents specialization/generalization characteristics of expressions and types.

Example 9. We have

$$(\texttt{age:integer, name:string, address:string}) \leq (\texttt{age:integer, name:string}) \ ,$$

because the former type has all of the properties (here reflected by the (suggestive) attribute names **age** and **name**) of the latter type, but also has an extra property, namely that it has the additional field component tagged **address**. Hence any expression of the first type can also be typed as the second type. □

The subtyping relation introduces polymorphism into the language, in the sense that expressions can now have more than just one type. We shall now describe a way of attaching a *unique* type to a correctly typed expression by means of so-called *minimal typing*.

Minimal Typing. As we have seen above, subtyping allows expressions to have many types. It turns out, however, that every correctly typed expression has a unique so-called *minimal type* [5, 27]. An expression e has minimal type τ, if $e : \tau$ and there is no type σ such that $e : \sigma$ and $\sigma \leq \tau$. If σ is the minimal type of e then we write $e :: \sigma$. Another important property of minimal typing is that if $e :: \sigma$ and $e : \tau$, for some type τ, then it is always the case that $\sigma \leq \tau$. The minimal type of an expression, say e, conveys the most detailed type information that can be attached to e; any other type that can be attached to e will be a generalization (supertype) of the minimal type and will thus have filtered out certain information regarding e's components. We will make frequent use of minimal typing in our language, since it is very handy to have a unique type available for expressions in the presence of subtyping polymorphism. We note that this language, as well as the extended language with predicates and sets, is statically type checkable [5, 6, 13]. Exact typing rules are given in the Appendix.

3.2 Adding Predicates – The Logical Formalism

The actual extension of the language that we would like to achieve, is that we wish to incorporate predicatively described sets, of which the general format is $\{\ x\ :\ \sigma\ |\ \phi(x)\ \}$, where $\phi(x)$ is a boolean expression. It is the purpose of this section to describe what the expressions $\phi(x)$ look like.

Let e, e' be boolean expressions and σ be some type. Then so are $\neg (e), (e \Rightarrow e')$ and $\forall x : \sigma \bullet (e)$ boolean expressions, with the obvious intuitive meanings. (We note that the other propositional connectives like ∧, ∨ and ⇔, as well as the existential quantifier ∃, can be defined in terms of the above mentioned constructs in the usual way.)

Furthermore, we have boolean constructs of the form $(e = e')$ and $(e \triangleleft e')$. The boolean construct $(e = e')$ is used to test whether the expressions e, e' are *equal*, and the second construct is used to test whether expression e is a *specialization* of the expression e'. We shall now discuss these two constructs in more detail.

The expression $(e = e')$ is correctly typed if the expressions e, e' are correctly typed and, moreover, both expressions have exactly the same typing possibilities. This is the same as saying that the minimal types of e, e' are the same.

The expression $(e \triangleleft e')$ is correctly typed if the expressions e, e' are correctly typed and, moreover, expression e has at least the same typing possibilities as expression e'. This can also be expressed by saying that the minimal type of e is a subtype of the minimal type of e'.

Example 10. The expression

⟨age=3, name="john", registered=True⟩ ◁ ⟨name="john", registered=False⟩ ,

is correctly typed because the first record has a minimal type that is smaller than the minimal type of the second record. The expression evaluates, however, to *false*, because the left hand side subexpression is not a specialization of the right hand side. □

3.3 Adding Powertypes and Sets

Set Membership and Subtyping. If σ is a type then $\mathbb{P}\sigma$ denotes the powertype of σ. Intuitively, a powertype $\mathbb{P}\sigma$ denotes the collection of all sets of expressions e such that e satisfies $e : \sigma$. Note that a powertype as well as elements thereof can be infinite, depending on the particular type. The powertype constructor resembles the construction of the powerset $\mathcal{P}(V)$ of a set V in ordinary set theory. An expression e in our language is called a *set* if it has a powertype as its type; i.e. $e : \mathbb{P}\sigma$, for some type σ. We stress here that a set in our theory is an *expression* and not a type; i.e. we add to the set of types special types called powertypes, and, in addition, we add to the set of expressions special expressions called sets. Powertypes obey the following rule regarding subtyping: if $\sigma \leq \tau$ then $\mathbb{P}\sigma \leq \mathbb{P}\tau$. Typing rules for sets are given, for reasons of simplicity, in terms of minimal typing.

Set membership is denoted by ∈ and indicates that an element occurs, modulo the =-relation, in some set. We have the following rule for typing of set-membership

$(e \in e') :: \text{bool}$, whenever $e' :: \mathbb{P}\sigma$ and $e :: \sigma$.

We also have a *specialized* version of set membership, denoted by ε, indicating that an element occurs, modulo the ◁-relation, in some set. We have the following typing rule for specialized set membership

$(e \varepsilon e') :: \text{bool}$, whenever $e' :: \mathbb{P}\sigma', e :: \sigma$ and $\sigma \leq \sigma'$.

Intuitively, $e \varepsilon e'$ holds if for some e'' we have $e \triangleleft e''$ and $e'' \in e'$.

Consider, as an example, the constants 1.0 and 2.0 of type real and the integer constant 2, and postulate that integer $\leq$ real. We then have that 2.0 ∈ {1.0, 2.0} is correctly typed and evaluates to true, whereas the expression 2 ∈ {1.0, 2.0} cannot even be evaluated for the simple reason that it is wrongly typed. It does hold, however, that 2 ε {1.0, 2.0}, since 2 ◁ 2.0.

Enumerative and Predicative Sets. The first set construct that we have is *set enumeration*. To get a clean typing of enumerated set terms, all of the form $\{e_1, \ldots, e_m\}$, we will only allow expressions $e_1, \ldots, e_m$ that have exactly the same typing possibilities; i.e. the expressions $e_1, \ldots, e_m$ must have the same minimal type. We have the following rule for the typing of enumerated sets:

$$\{e_1, \ldots, e_m\} :: \mathbb{P}\sigma, \text{ whenever } e_k :: \sigma, \text{ for all } k\, (1 \leq k \leq m) \ .$$

This rule might seem like a rather severe restriction, but we have some very good reasons for doing so, which we now explain by means of an example.

Example 11. First, consider an alleged enumerated set like {1, 2.0}, in which an integer and a real element occur. As in ordinary set theory, we would like this set to be in the =-relation with the predicatively described set $\{x : \sigma \,|\, x = 1 \vee x = 2.0\}$, where we still have to decide on the choice of the type σ. Obviously, we have only two choices for σ: it is either integer or real. But no matter which of the types is chosen for σ, we always get a type inconsistency, which a quick look at the two components $x = 1$ and $x = 2.0$ in the latter predicative set reveals. Since the minimal type of x can only be either integer or real, one of the two components will be incorrectly typed, hence yielding the type inconsistency. (Note that if the integer 1 in the set {1, 2.0} is replaced by the real number 1.0 then we would not have such a type inconsistency.) □

We now describe *predicative sets*. A predicative set is of the form $\{x : \sigma \,|\, e\}$, where e is some boolean expression possibly containing the variable x. Intuitively, such a set denotes the collection of all those expressions of type σ satisfying the predicate e.

For example, $\{x : \text{real} \,|\, (x = 1.0) \vee (x = 2.0)\}$ is the set corresponding to the expression {1.0, 2.0}. We have the following rule for the typing of predicative sets:

$$\{x : \sigma \,|\, e\} :: \mathbb{P}\sigma, \text{ whenever } e :: \text{bool} \ .$$

We now come back to some remarks made above concerning the (rather severe) typing of enumerated sets. In order to make our theory of sets intuitively acceptable, we would, of course, want to have the enumerated set {1.0, 2.0} to be in the =-relation with the predicative set $\{x : \text{real} \,|\, (x = 1.0) \vee (x = 2.0)\}$. (Intuitively these two constructs describe exactly the same set). Now, the only way to achieve this is to assure that the minimal types of these two sets are exactly the same. It is for this reason, and our definition of set membership, that we have chosen for our strict rule of only allowing expressions, occurring in some enumerated set, that have exactly the same minimal type.

Union, Intersection and Set Difference. Given two sets e and e', we can also form the union, intersection and difference of these two sets.

Consider the two, very simple, sets $\{1\}$ and $\{2.0\}$. If we denote the union of these two sets by $\{1\} \cup \{2.0\}$, then we, intuitively, would expect this union to be in the $=$-relation with the set $\{1,2.0\}$. But then, we get erroneous results: the latter, enumerated, set is not correctly typed since it contains both an integer and a real element, while both elements should have had the same minimal type. So, somehow, the union of the two mentioned sets should not be allowed. It would be allowed, however, either if the first set had been the real set $\{1.0\}$, or if the second had been the integer set $\{2\}$. This suggests that of two sets the union can be taken only if those sets have the same minimal type, and this is indeed the choice that we will make when taking the union of two sets: $e \cup e'$ is correctly typed if e and e' have the same minimal powertype. We emphasize that this choice is not at all arbitrary; complete coverage of all aspects regarding this matter is, however, beyond the scope of this paper. For full details the reader is referred to [6] and [32]. Analogous arguments pertain to taking set intersection and set difference.

We now state our rules for the typing of union, intersection, and difference of sets.

$$(e \cup e'), \ (e \cap e'), \ (e - e') \ :: \ \mathbb{P}\sigma, \text{ whenever } e, e' :: \mathbb{P}\sigma \ .$$

We mention, finally, that we also have a subset relation between sets, denoted by $(e \subseteq e')$, with the following typing rule

$$(e \subseteq e') :: bool, \text{ whenever } e, e' :: \mathbb{P}\sigma \text{ (for some type } \sigma) \ .$$

(We note that we can define a specialized form $\sqsubseteq$ of the subset relation $\subseteq$, analogous to $\in$ and $\varepsilon: e \sqsubseteq e'$ holds if, for some e'', it holds that $e \triangleleft e''$ and $e'' \subseteq e'$.)

4 Mapping Higher-order OO Concepts

4.1 Introductory Remarks

The purpose of the present section is to show how to give a formal meaning to a database schema specified in TM. We will do so by supplying a mapping of TM constructs to FM constructs. As FM is a language with a complete type theory (as well as a formal semantics) we will, in the end, have supplied a semantics for TM.

Providing the precise meaning of a database schema means to characterize the allowed database states and the allowed operations on such states. Operations are not the topic of this paper. A full translation of the example of Sect. 2 is not given here; the interested reader is referred to [4].

4.2 Three-level Methodology

The methodology that we adopt here to describe the set of allowed states of our database is essentially that of [10], where it was used to give a set-theoretic foundation of relational databases.

The methodology consists of three levels of description, each of which makes use of the earlier level(s), if any. At level 0 we start off by describing the object types associated with the classes of interest to the database schema. At this level we also describe the set of allowed (possible) objects of those types. Actually, at each level we will describe a type, and a set of instances of that type. This set describes a further restriction on the possible instances by taking constraints into account. In the following, by *class extension* of a certain class we will mean a collection of objects of the class' associated type.

The three levels that are used in our methodology are

0. the **object level**, in which the object types of interest are described *as well as,* for each object type, the set of allowed objects of that type,
1. the **class extension level**, in which the set of allowed class extensions for each class is described, and
2. the **database level**, in which the set of allowed database states is described.

Each of the above mentioned sets of allowed instances will be a set expression in FM. For a class C we will, at the object level, identify C's object type, which we call γ. Then, we define the expression C_Universe :: $\mathbb{P}\gamma$ such that C_Universe is the set of allowed objects of class C. At the class extension level, we will proceed with identifying C_ClassUniverse :: $\mathbb{P}\mathbb{P}\gamma$ as the set of allowed class extensions for class C. An element of C_ClassUniverse is thus a possible class extension of class C. At the database level, finally, we will define DatabaseUniverse as the collection of allowed database states. We have chosen to view a database state as a record, such that its attributes denote class extension names. As a consequence, a typical type for DatabaseUniverse is

$$\text{DatabaseUniverse} :: \mathbb{P}(C_1 : \mathbb{P}\gamma_1, \ldots, C_n : \mathbb{P}\gamma_n) \ ,$$

where C_1 up to C_n denote the classes in the database schema. Note that the type of DatabaseUniverse is determined to be a minimal type; hence, the database cannot contain more class extensions than C_1 up to C_n. Similar observations need to be made about the variables in the table below.

We give the following tabular overview of our specification strategy.

Next, we should also be more precise as to the forms of the definitions of the sets of allowed instances. To that end, we give definition schemes for each kind of set occurring in the three levels. The class universe of a class C has a rather straightforward definition scheme:

$$\text{C\_Universe} = \{x : \gamma \mid \phi(x)\} \ .$$

The predicate $\phi(x)$ determines which objects of type γ are allowed objects; $\phi(x)$ is typically the predicate to describe attribute and object constraints.

Table 1. Overview of specification strategy

level	type	allowed instances
level 0	γ	C_Universe :: $\mathbb{P}\gamma$
level 1	$\mathbb{P}\gamma$	C_ClassUniverse :: $\mathbb{P}\mathbb{P}\gamma$
level 2	$\langle C_1 : \mathbb{P}\gamma_1, \ldots, C_n : \mathbb{P}\gamma_n \rangle$	DatabaseUniverse::$\mathbb{P}\langle C_1 : \mathbb{P}\gamma_1, \ldots, C_n : \mathbb{P}\gamma_n \rangle$

The set of allowed class extensions for class C can now schematically be defined as

$$\texttt{C\_ClassUniverse} = \{\ X : \mathbb{P}\gamma \mid X \subseteq \texttt{C\_Universe} \land \phi'(X)\ \}\ .$$

Each class extension X should obviously contain allowed instances for C only, and should thus be a subset of C_Universe. The predicate $\phi'(X)$ is be used to state further constraints on the class extension like, for instance, the requirement that at least ten objects should be in any extension of this class. In $\phi'(X)$ the class constraints are described. The expression DatabaseUniverse should finally be defined:

$$\begin{aligned}
&\texttt{DatabaseUniverse} = \\
&\quad \{\ DB : \langle C_1 : \mathbb{P}\gamma_1, \ldots, C_n : \mathbb{P}\gamma_n \rangle \mid \\
&\quad\quad \bigwedge_{i=1}^{n} DB \cdot C_i \in C_i\_\texttt{ClassUniverse} \land \Phi(DB)\ \}\ .
\end{aligned}$$

By the generalized conjunction, this definition first of all requires each class extension in an allowed database state DB to be an allowed class extension. Furthermore, it may pose additional requirements on the database state by means of $\Phi(DB)$. This predicate is the place for all remaining structural constraints like, for instance, referential integrity between distinct class extensions. We refer the reader to Sect. 4.3 for specific examples.

4.3 Modelling of TM concepts in FM.

The class concept. Most of TM's constructs can be mapped straightforwardly to FM constructs. In general, a type associated with some class of TM will become a type in FM. TM's object constraints, class constraints, and database constraints correspond (or are mapped) to the three levels just discussed.

The TM features of Class, ISA-relationship, persistency, implicit quantification, and advanced attribute specification can all be dealt with in our approach as we map from *class specifications* in TM to *(set) expressions* in FM, thereby giving an indirect semantics of those class specifications.

Recursive data types and self. To deal with the TM features of recursive data types and the **self** concept in FM we postulate the existence of the *basic type* **oid** (see Sect. 3.1). The type **oid** is meant to capture the notion of *object identity* [18]. This type is not visibly a part of TM, but it rather allows to 'mathematically implement' TM's features in FM.

This implementation comes rather naturally by augmenting each associated type of a class with the **id** attribute of type **oid**. The obvious idea about this attribute is that it will uniquely identify an object in the class extension and that it is immune to user modifications.

We therefore have the following (FM) types associated with the classes of the examples in Sect. 2. Note that we show here the first step of the object level:

Example 12. Translation of types associated with classes.

```
employee  = ⟨id:oid, name:string, age:integer, spouse:oid, gender:string⟩
manager   = ⟨id:oid, name:string, age:integer, spouse:oid, gender:string,
            friends:Poid⟩
secretary = ⟨id:oid, name:string, age:integer, spouse:oid, gender:string,
            boss:oid⟩ □
```

As is illustrated here, TM's recursive type structures are broken down in non-recursive structures by changing the type of recursive attributes, like **spouse**, to **oid**. In addition, it is required that the **id**-values are unique and referential integrity holds. In other words, the **spouse**-values should be existing **id**-values in the relevant class extension. To deal with the recursive attribute **spouse:Employee** of that class the following changes have been made:

1. **employee** is augmented with the **id:oid** attribute,
2. **employee**'s **spouse** attribute is changed to be of type **oid**, and
3. allowed class extensions (i.e., each element of **Employee_ClassUniverse**) obey:
   (a) **id**-uniqueness, and
   (b) referential integrity with respect to the **spouse** attribute.

Let us first show how the above requirements on the class extension are dealt with. We complete the object level as far as employees are concerned:

Example 13. Translation of set of allowed employee objects; declaration and definition.

```
Employee_Universe :: Pemployee
Employee_Universe = {x:employee | x·gender = "Male" ∨ x·gender = "Female"}  (c₁)
□
```

Now we can deal with the two requirements at the class extension level. First, the set of allowed employee class extensions is declared, and then it is defined:

Example 14. Translation of **Employee** class extension; declaration and definition.

```
Employee_ClassUniverse :: PPemployee
Employee_ClassUniverse =
    {X : Pemployee |
        X ⊆ Employee_Universe ∧                                    (object level)
        ∀ x : employee • ∃ y : employee • (x ∈ X ⇒ (y ∈ X ∧ x·spouse = y·id)) ∧
                                                              (referential integrity)
        ∀ x : employee • ∀ y : employee • (x ∈ X ∧ y ∈ X) ⇒
            ((x·id = y·id ⇒ x = y) ∧                              (oid uniqueness)
             (x·spouse = y·id ⇒ x·gender ≠ y·gender) ∧                  (c'_2)
             (x·spouse = y·id ⇒ x·id = y·spouse) ∧                     (c'_3)
             (∀ x' : employee • ∀ y' : employee •
              (x ∈ X ∧ y ∈ X ∧ x' ∈ X ∧ y' ∈ X ∧ x'·id = x·spouse ∧ y'·id = y·spouse)
              ⇒ x'·name ≠ y'·name))                                    (c_4)
    } □
```

The set of allowed employee objects, i.e. **Employee_Universe**, should typically deal with the object constraints of the class **Employee**. The constraint c_1 is dealt with in the above, but the other two (i.e. c_2 and c_3) are *not*. The reason for this is that these two constraints make use of TM's specific feature of recursive data types, and although they are proper object constraints in TM, they should be considered class constraints in FM. This is why they occur in a slightly altered version as c'_2 and c'_3 in the definition of **Employee_ClassUniverse**. Thus, we see that constraints that may conceptually be at TM's object level can be at FM's class extension level. In fact, it is even possible that one of TM's object constraints will be translated to a database constraint in FM. We will in the sequel call such a situation a *level shift*. In case of a level shift, quantifiers that were implicit in TM need to be made explicit.

The **self** concept becomes a trivial notion now. It simply denotes the **id** value of the object at hand. Thus, the constraint

$$c_3 : (\text{spouse·spouse} = \textbf{self})$$

will become a formula of the form

$$c_3 : (\text{spouse·spouse} = \text{id}) \ .$$

However, by the introduction of object identities we have also introduced a form of indirection, since no longer can we use an expression of the form **spouse·spouse** in the context of an object of the class **employee**. This is because **spouse** is no longer an expression of some record type (where we may apply attribute selection), but now it is of type oid. To obtain the **spouse** of one's **spouse** we now need to (conceptually) query the class extension. This form of indirection is also provided for in the translation.

ISA-relationships and inheritance. A word should also be said about the translation of **ISA**-relationships. This translation concerns aspects of inheritance. The aspects that are relevant in the present context are

1. inheritance of attributes,
2. inheritance of object constraints, and
3. the fact that the subclass extension can be seen as a subset of the class extension at any time.

We remark that inheritance of class constraints should *not* take place. To understand why this is the case, consider the example constraint that employees should *on average* earn more than some specific amount. This typical class constraint may well hold for the class of managers, but need not hold for that of secretaries. Thus, class constraints should not be inherited.

Object constraints should be inherited. The reason for this is that all variables that range over the class extension are universally quantified, and thus the constraint could be inherited. Actually, the translation takes care of its inheritance regardless of whether it has been explicitly specified. The constraint for ISA-inclusion in the definition of **DatabaseUniverse** is the reason for this.

The inheritance of attributes is straightforward: all attributes are inherited and sometimes their types may become more specific types as indicated in the subclass definition. This has already been illustrated in Example 12.

The inheritance of object constraints can be performed directly when there is no level shift. It takes place from the object universe of the supertype to that of the subtype. The type over which the implicit variable ranges needs to be adjusted. See for an example the translation of c_1 in the sets **Employee_Universe** and **Manager_Universe**:

Example 15. Translation of set of allowed manager objects.

Manager_Universe :: $\mathbb{P}$**manager**
Manager_Universe $= \{\ x$:**manager** $\mid x \cdot$**gender** $=$ "Male" $\vee x \cdot$**gender** $=$ "Female" $\}$
$\hfill (c_1 \text{ inherited}) \ \square$

In case of a level shift of an object constraint, it is also inherited but now only the type over which the original implicit variable ranged needs adjustment, and none of the other types.

As has been discussed, object constraints (including those that get a level shift (c_2' and c_3')) should be inherited. However, to express them properly for the **manager** and **secretary** class universes, we need to refer to the class universe of **employee**, and then by definition the constraints become a database constraint. For instance, the c_3 version for **manager** should read something like "The employee that is the spouse of some manager, should have that manager as her/his spouse". Consequently, the constraints c_2 and c_3 are getting *two* level shifts. They take effect at the database level, which is illustrated below.

Example 16. Translation continued; definition of the database universe.

DatabaseUniverse :: $\mathbb{P}$(EMP:$\mathbb{P}$**employee**, MAN:$\mathbb{P}$**manager**, SEC:$\mathbb{P}$**secretary**)
DatabaseUniverse $=$
$\quad \{$ DB : (EMP:$\mathbb{P}$**employee**, MAN:$\mathbb{P}$**manager**, SEC:$\mathbb{P}$**secretary**) $\mid$
$\qquad$ DB·EMP $\in$ **Employee_ClassUniverse** $\wedge$

DB·MAN $\in$ Manager_ClassUniverse $\land$

DB·SEC $\in$ Secretary_ClassUniverse $\land$ (class level)

$\forall x:$manager $\bullet \exists y:$employee $\bullet (x \in$ DB·MAN $\Rightarrow (y \in$ DB·EMP $\land x \lhd y)) \land$

$\forall x:$secretary $\bullet \exists y:$employee $\bullet (x \in$ DB·SEC $\Rightarrow (y \in$ DB·EMP $\land x \lhd y)) \land$

         (ISA-inclusions)

$\forall x:$manager $\bullet \forall y:$oid $\bullet$

  $(x \in$ DB·MAN $\land y \in x \cdot$friends$) \Rightarrow$

  $\exists z:$employee $\bullet (z \in$ DB·EMP $\land z \cdot$id $= y) \land$

$\forall x:$secretary $\bullet \exists y:$manager $\bullet$

  $(x \in$ DB·SEC $\Rightarrow (y \in$ DB·MAN $\land y \cdot$id $= x \cdot$boss$)) \land$

         (referential integrities)

$\forall x:$manager $\bullet \forall y:$employee $\bullet$

  $(x \in$ DB·MAN $\land y \in$ DB·EMP$) \Rightarrow$

  $(x \cdot$spouse $= y \cdot$id $\Rightarrow x \cdot$gender $\neq y \cdot$gender$) \land$ (c_2'' for manager)

$\forall x:$secretary $\bullet \forall y:$employee $\bullet$

  $(x \in$ DB·SEC $\land y \in$ DB·EMP$) \Rightarrow$

  $(x \cdot$spouse $= y \cdot$id $\Rightarrow x \cdot$gender $\neq y \cdot$gender$) \land$ (c_2'' for secretary)

$\forall x:$manager $\bullet \forall y:$employee $\bullet$

  $(x \in$ DB·MAN $\land y \in$ DB·EMP$) \Rightarrow (x \cdot$spouse $= y \cdot$id $\Rightarrow x \cdot$id $= y \cdot$spouse$) \land$

         (c_3'' for manager)

$\forall x:$secretary $\bullet \forall y:$employee $\bullet$

  $(x \in$ DB·SEC $\land y \in$ DB·EMP$) \Rightarrow (x \cdot$spouse $= y \cdot$id $\Rightarrow x \cdot$id $= y \cdot$spouse$) \land$

         (c_3'' for secretary)

$\forall x:$manager $\bullet \forall y:$secretary $\bullet$

  $(x \in$ DB·MAN $\land y \in$ DB·SEC$) \Rightarrow \neg \exists z:$employee $\bullet (z \in$ DB·EMP $\land x \lhd z \land y \lhd z) \land$

         (c_5)

$\forall x:$manager $\bullet \exists y:$secretary $\bullet x \in$ DB·MAN $\Rightarrow (y \in$ DB·SEC $\land x \cdot$id $= y \cdot$boss$)$

         (c_6)

} $\square$

5 Conclusions and future work

In this paper, the language TM, which is used to describe conceptual schemas of object-oriented databases, is discussed. The strength of the language stems from its conceptual richness and its firm basis in a type theory that allows subtyping and multiple inheritance. One particular feature of TM, its (typed) predicative sets, are introduced and their (elementary) role in giving a formal database description is illustrated.

TM can be compared to other languages described in the literature, for instance Machiavellli [24, 25]. Machiavelli does not fully support Cardelli and Wegner's view of inheritance [12], and the authors of Machiavelli themselves also consider this somewhat unsatisfactory. Another drawback is that Machiavelli only allows for enumerated sets as set-valued objects.

We have only discussed TM's features for handling constraints in this paper. Views and methods can also be defined in TM [33]. Other research underway concerns both implementation and theoretical aspects of the language. One specific problem, which is well-known from the area of program synthesis, is that our language allows the specification of so-called non-constructive predicative sets. Such sets do not allow a straightforward translation to program code, typically because of the use of quantifiers. The use of techniques from the area of program synthesis in our context will be the topic of another paper.

We are currently investigating the following issues in the context of TM:

- a TM-based DBMS prototype,
- a logical query language for TM-databases,
- further conceptual primitives for dealing with synchronization,
- the specification of general dynamic constraints,
- application development on top of TM, and
- the problem of schema updates, [7, 8, 29, 36, 37, 38], and that of object updates [35] in the presence of TM's three-level constraints.

6 Acknowledgements

We would like to express our thanks to Peter Apers, René Bal and Chris de Vreeze for their remarks made on an earlier version of this paper.

References

1. Object identity as a query language primitive, S. Abiteboul & P. C. Kanellakis, Proceedings of ACM-SIGMOD 1989 International Conference on Management of Data, Portland, OR, May 31–June 2, 1989, J. Clifford, B. Lindsay & D. Maier (eds.), ACM Press, New York, NY, 1989, pp. 159–173.

2. H. Aït-Kaci, An Algebraic Semantics Approach to the Effective Resolution of Type Equations, Theoretical Computer Science 45, 1986, pp. 293–351.

3. A. Albano, L. Cardelli & R. Orsini, GALILEO: A strongly-typed, interactive conceptual language, ACM Transactions on Database Systems 10, 2, June, 1985, pp. 230–260.

4. H. Balsters, R. A. de By & R. Zicari, Sets and Constraints in an Object-Oriented Data Model, Technical Report INF-90-75, University of Twente, Enschede, December, 1990, ISSN 0923-1714.

5. H. Balsters & M. M. Fokkinga, Subtyping can have a simple semantics, Theoretical Computer Science 87, September, 1991, pp. 81–96.

6. H. Balsters & C. C. de Vreeze, A semantics of object-oriented sets, The Third International Workshop on Database Programming Languages: Bulk Types & Persistent Data (DBPL-3), August 27–30, 1991, Nafplion, Greece, P. Kanellakis & J. W. Schmidt (eds.), Morgan Kaufmann Publishers, San Mateo, CA, 1991, pp. 201–217.

7. J. Banerjee, H. T. Chou, J. F. Garza, W. Kim et al. Data model issues for object-oriented applications, ACM Transactions on Office Information Systems 5, 1, January, 1987, pp. 3–26.

8. J. Banerjee et al., Semantics and implementation of schema evolution in object-oriented databases, Proceedings of ACM-SIGMOD 1987 International Conference on Management of Data, San Francisco, CA, May 27–29, 1987, U. Dayal & I. Traiger (eds.), ACM Press, New York, NY, 1987, pp. 311–322.

9. D. Beech, A Foundation for Evolution from Relational to Object Databases, Advances in Database Technology — EDBT '88, J. W. Schmidt, S. Ceri & M. Missikoff (eds.), Springer-Verlag, New York–Heidelberg–Berlin, 1988, pp. 251–270.

10. E. O. de Brock, Database Models and Retrieval Languages, Technische Hogeschool Eindhoven, Eindhoven, 1984, Ph.D. Thesis.

11. F. Cacace, S. Ceri, S. Crespi-Reghizzi, L. Tanca & R. Zicari, Integrating object-oriented data modeling with a rule-based programming paradigm, Proceedings of ACM-SIGMOD 1990 International Conference on Management of Data, Atlantic City, NJ, May 23-25, 1990, H. Garcia-Molina & H. V. Jagadish (eds.), ACM Press, New York, NY, 1990, pp. 225–236.

12. L. Cardelli & P. Wegner, On understanding types, data abstraction, and polymorphism, Computing Surveys 17, 4, December, 1985, pp. 471–522.

13. L. Cardelli, A semantics of multiple inheritance, in: Semantics of Data Types, G. Kahn, D. B. Macqueen & G. Plotkin (eds.), Lecture Notes in Computer Science #173, Springer-Verlag, New York–Heidelberg–Berlin, 1984, pp. 51–67.

14. L. Cardelli, A semantics of multiple inheritance, Information and Computation 76, 1988, pp. 138–164.

15. G. Copeland & D. Maier, Making Smalltalk a Database System, Proceedings of ACM-SIGMOD 1984 International Conference on Management of Data, Boston, MA, June 18–21, 1984, B. Yormark (ed.), ACM, New York, NY, 1984, pp. 316-325.

16. Y. C. Fuh & P. Mishra, Type inference with subtypes, Proceedings Second European Symposium on Programming (ESOP88), H. Ganzinger (ed.), Lecture Notes in Computer Science #300, Springer-Verlag, New York–Heidelberg–Berlin, 1988, pp. 94–114.

17. S. E. Hudson & R. King, Cactis: a self-adaptive, concurrent implementation of an object-oriented database management system, ACM Transactions on Database Systems 14, 3, 1989, pp. 291–321.

18. S. N. Khoshafian & G. P. Copeland, Object identity, Proceedings of the First International Conference on Object-oriented Programming Systems, Languages, and Applications (OOPSLA86), N. Meyrowitz (ed.), Portland, Oregon, 1986, pp. 406–416.

19. M. Kifer & G. Lausen, F-logic: a higher-order language for reasoning about objects, inheritance, and scheme, Proceedings of ACM-SIGMOD 1989 International Conference on Management of Data, Portland, OR, May 31–June 2, 1989, J. Clifford, B. Lindsay & D. Maier (eds.), ACM Press, New York, NY, 1989, pp. 134–146.

20. W. Kim et al., Integrating an object-oriented programming system with a database system, Proceedings of the Second International Conference on Object-oriented Programming Systems, Languages, and Applications (OOPSLA88), San Diego, CA, September, 1988.

21. C. Lécluse & P. Richard, The O_2 database programming language, Proceedings of Fifteenth International Conference on Very Large Data Bases, Amsterdam, The Netherlands, August 22–25, 1989, P. M. G. Apers & G. Wiederhold (eds.), Morgan Kaufmann Publishers, Palo Alto, CA, 1989, pp. 411–422.

22. P. Lyngbaek & V. Vianu, Mapping a semantic database model to the relational model, Proceedings of ACM-SIGMOD 1987 International Conference on Management of Data, San Francisco, CA, May 27–29, 1987, U. Dayal & I. Traiger, ACM Press, New York, NY, pp. 132–142.

23. D. Maier, A logic for objects, Workshop on Foundations of Deductive Databases and Logic Programming, Washington, DC, August, 1986, pp. 6–26.

24. A. Ohori, P. Buneman & V. Breazu-Tannen, Database programming in Machiavelli — a polymorphic language with static type inference, Proceedings of ACM-SIGMOD 1989 International Conference on Management of Data, Portland, OR, May 31–June 2, 1989, J. Clifford, B. Lindsay & D. Maier (eds.), ACM Press, New York, NY, pp. 46–57.

25. A. Ohori, Semantics of types for database objects, Theoretical Computer Science 76, 1, October, 1990, pp. 53–92.

26. X. Qian, The Deductive Synthesis of Database Transactions, Ph.D. Thesis, Department of Computer Science, Stanford University, Stanford, CA, November, 1989.

27. J. C. Reynolds, Three Approaches to Type Structure, in: Mathematical Foundations of Software Development, H. Ehrig et al. (eds.), Springer-Verlag, New York-Heidelberg-Berlin, 1985, Lecture Notes in Computer Science # 185, pp. 97–138.

28. T. Sheard & D. Stemple, Automatic verification of database transaction safety, ACM Transactions on Database Systems 14, 3, September, 1989, pp. 322–368.

29. A. H. Skarra & S. B. Zdonik, Type Evolution in an Object-Oriented Database, in: Research Directions in Object-Oriented Programming, MIT Press series in Computer Systems, B. D. Shriver & P. Wegner (eds.), MIT Press, Cambridge, MA, 1987, pp. 393–416.

30. R. Stansifer, Type inference with subtypes, Proceedings Fifteenth Annual ACM Principles of Programming Languages (POPL88), 1988, pp. 88–97.

31. M. Stonebraker, E. Anderson, E. Hanson & B. Rubenstein, QUEL as a data type, Proceedings of ACM-SIGMOD 1984 International Conference on Management of Data, Boston, MA, June 18–21, 1984, B. Yormark (ed.), ACM, New York, NY, pp. 208–214.

32. C. C. de Vreeze, Extending the Semantics of Subtyping, accommodating Database Maintenance Operations, Universiteit Twente, Enschede, The Netherlands, Doctoraal verslag, August, 1989.

33. C. C. de Vreeze, Formalization of inheritance of methods in an object-oriented data model, Technical Report, INF-90-76, December, 1990, University of Twente, Enschede.

34. M. Wand, Complete type inference for simple objects, Proceedings Second Annual Symposium on Logic in Computer Science (LICS87), 1987, pp. 37–44.

35. S. B. Zdonik, Can objects change type? Can type objects change?, Proceedings of the Workshop on Database Programming Languages, Roscoff, France, September, 1987, (extended abstract), pp. 193–200.

36. R. Zicari, Primitives for schema updates in an object-oriented database system: A proposal, X3/SPARC/DBSSG OODB Task Group Workshop on Standardization of Object Database Systems, Ottawa, Canada, October 23, 1990.

37. R. Zicari, A framework for schema updates in an object-oriented database system, Proceedings of Seventh International Conference on Data Engineering, Kobe, April 8–12, 1991.

38. R. Zicari, A framework for schema updates in an object-oriented database system, in: Building an Object-oriented Database System-The Story of O_2, F. Bancilhon, C. Delobel & P. Kanellakis (eds.), Morgan Kaufmann Publishers, San Mateo, CA, 1992, pp. 146–182.

A   Appendix

In the following appendix we give the syntax of FM, as discussed in the main body of the text. Throughout this appendix, T denotes the set of types and E denotes the set of expressions. We let σ and τ vary over T, and let e vary over E. C denotes a set of constants, V a set of variables. Also, we let c vary over C and x over V. The symbol L, finally, denotes a collection of labels (or attribute names). We let a and b vary over L. A set of basic types B, including for instance **integer**, **real**, and **string**, is postulated.

We have used the following abbreviations in our meta-syntax: $\mathbf{E}\sigma \in T(\ldots)$ for "there exists a $\sigma \in T$ such that ...", $\mathbf{A}\sigma \in T(\ldots)$ for "for all $\sigma \in T \ldots$", $\longrightarrow$ for "implies", and $\leftrightarrow$ for "if and only if".

1. **Types and expressions**

$T \ ::= \ B \mid \langle L:T,\ldots,L:T\rangle \mid \mathbb{P}T$

basic types, record types, power types

$E \ ::= \ V_T \mid C_T \mid \langle L=E,\ldots,L=E\rangle \mid E{\cdot}L \mid \{E,\ldots,E\} \mid \{V_T|E\} \mid$
$\quad (E=E) \mid (E\triangleleft E) \mid (E\in E) \mid (E\,\varepsilon\,E) \mid (E\subseteq E) \mid (E\sqsubseteq E) \mid$
$\quad \neg(E) \mid (E\Rightarrow E) \mid \forall V_T \bullet (E)$

typed variables, typed constants, records, record projection, enumerated sets, predicatively described sets, extra boolean constructs, and logical expressions

2. **Typing rules**

(a) $x_\tau : \tau$

(b) $c_\tau : \tau$

(c) $e_1 : \tau_1, \ldots, e_m : \tau_m \longrightarrow \langle a_1 = e_1, \ldots, a_m = e_m\rangle : \langle a_1 : \tau_1, \ldots, a_m : \tau_m\rangle$

(d) $\langle a_1 = e_1, \ldots, a_m = e_m\rangle : \langle a_1 : \tau_1, \ldots, a_m : \tau_m\rangle \longrightarrow$
$\qquad \langle a_1 = e_1, \ldots, a_m = e_m\rangle {\cdot} a_j : \tau_j$

(e) $e_1 : \tau, \ \mathbf{A}\sigma \in T((\mathbf{E}j \in [1 .. m](e_j : \sigma)) \longrightarrow$
$\qquad \mathbf{A}i \in [1 .. m](e_i : \sigma)) \longrightarrow \{e_1, \ldots, e_m\} : \mathbb{P}\tau$

(f) $e : \mathtt{bool} \longrightarrow \{x_\tau|e\} : \mathbb{P}\tau$

(g) $\mathbf{E}\tau \in T(e : \tau), \ \mathbf{A}\sigma \in T(c : \sigma \leftrightarrow e' : \sigma) \longrightarrow (c = e') : \mathtt{bool}$

(h) $\mathbf{E}\tau \in T(e : \tau), \ \mathbf{A}\sigma \in T(e : \sigma \longrightarrow e' : \sigma) \longrightarrow (e' \triangleleft e) : \mathtt{bool}$

(i) $\mathbf{E}\tau \in T(e' : \mathbb{P}\tau), \ \mathbf{A}\sigma \in T(e' : \mathbb{P}\sigma \leftrightarrow e : \sigma) \longrightarrow (e \in e') : \mathtt{bool}$

(j) $\mathbf{E}\tau \in T(e' : \mathbb{P}\tau), \ \mathbf{A}\sigma \in T(e' : \mathbb{P}\sigma \longrightarrow e : \sigma) \longrightarrow (e\,\varepsilon\,e') : \mathtt{bool}$

(k) $\mathbf{E}\tau \in T(e' : \mathbb{P}\tau), \ \mathbf{A}\sigma \in T(e' : \mathbb{P}\sigma \leftrightarrow e : \mathbb{P}\sigma) \longrightarrow (e \subseteq e') : \mathtt{bool}$

(l) $\mathbf{E}\tau \in T(e' : \mathbb{P}\tau), \ \mathbf{A}\sigma \in T(e' : \mathbb{P}\sigma \longrightarrow e : \mathbb{P}\sigma) \longrightarrow (e \sqsubseteq e') : \mathtt{bool}$

(m) $e : \mathtt{bool}, e' : \mathtt{bool} \longrightarrow \neg(e) : \mathtt{bool}, (e \Rightarrow e') : \mathtt{bool}, \forall x_\tau \bullet (e) : \mathtt{bool}$

3. **Subtyping rules**

Postulate a partial order $\leq_B$ on B.

The relation $\leq$ is defined by

(a) $\beta \leq_B \beta' \longrightarrow \beta \leq \beta'$

(b) $\tau_1 \leq \tau'_1, \ldots, \tau_n \leq \tau'_n \longrightarrow$
$\quad \langle a_1 : \tau_1, \ldots, a_n : \tau_n, b_1 : \sigma_1, \ldots, b_m : \sigma_m\rangle \leq \langle a_1 : \tau'_1, \ldots, a_n : \tau'_n\rangle \ (m, n \geq 0)$

(c) $\tau \leq \tau' \longrightarrow \mathbb{P}\tau \leq \mathbb{P}\tau'$

4. **Minimal typing rules**

(a) $x_\tau :: \tau$

(b) $c_\tau :: \tau$

(c) $e_1 :: \tau, \ldots, e_m :: \tau_m \longrightarrow \langle a_1 = e_1, \ldots, a_m = e_m\rangle :: \langle a_1 : \tau_1, \ldots, a_m : \tau_m\rangle$

(d) $e :: \langle a_1 : \tau_1, \ldots, a_n : \tau_n\rangle \longrightarrow e{\cdot}a_i :: \tau_i \ (1 \leq i \leq n, n \geq 1)$

(e) $e : \mathtt{bool} \longrightarrow e :: \mathtt{bool}$

(f) $e_1 :: \tau, \ldots, e_m :: \tau \longrightarrow \{e_1, \ldots, e_m\} :: \mathbb{P}\tau$

(g) $\{x_\tau|e\} :: \mathbb{P}\tau$

(h) $e :: \tau, \ e' :: \tau \longrightarrow (e = e') :: \mathtt{bool}$

(i) $e :: \tau, \ e' :: \tau', \ \tau \leq \tau' \longrightarrow (e \triangleleft e') :: \mathtt{bool}$

(j) $e :: \tau, e' :: \mathbb{P}\tau \longrightarrow (e \in e') :: \mathtt{bool}$

(k) $e :: \tau, \ e' :: \mathbb{P}\tau', \ \tau \leq \tau' \longrightarrow (e\,\varepsilon\,e') :: \mathtt{bool}$

(l) $e, e' :: \mathbb{P}\tau \longrightarrow (e \subseteq e') :: \mathtt{bool}$

(m) $e :: \mathbb{P}\tau, \ e' :: \mathbb{P}\tau', \ \tau \leq \tau' \longrightarrow (e \sqsubseteq e') :: \mathtt{bool}$

(n) $e :: \mathtt{bool}, \ e' :: \mathtt{bool} \longrightarrow \neg(e) :: \mathtt{bool}, (e \Rightarrow e') :: \mathtt{bool}, \forall x_\tau \bullet (e) :: \mathtt{bool}$

The OSI Managed-object Model

Colin Ashford

Bell-Northern Research
P.O. Box 3511, Station C,
Ottawa, Canada,
K1Y 4H7

Abstract. The challenge facing the International Organization for Standardization (ISO) in the early eighties, in developing Open Systems Interconnection (OSI) protocol standards for network management, was to ensure that such protocols should, on the one hand, be standardised but, on the other, be capable of managing a myriad of resource types. ISO met the challenge by developing a single internationally-standardised carriage protocol (CMIP), and tools to produce information models that would reflect the resources being managed. Such an approach makes it possible for the same carriage protocol to carry management messages for many different types of resources. In developing its information modelling tools and services, ISO has adopted an object-oriented approach: the resources to be managed are modelled as managed objects or aggregates of managed objects. The managed-object model is similar to popular object-oriented programming-language models but it includes a number of features that reflect the special requirements of network management. These requirements include: asynchronous operation, active resources, a distributed environment, compatibility, and feature optionality. Fulfilling these requirements lead to the inclusion of concepts such as event-notification, multiple object-selection, packages, and allomorphism. The next generation of network-management standards will need to address the demands of large, multi-protocol, mutable networks. How these requirements might affect the evolution of the managed-object model and services is considered.

1 Introduction

Over the last half-dozen years, the International Organization for Standardization (ISO) has progressed a number of Open Systems Interconnection (OSI) network-management standards to international standards status. These standards define an architecture, protocols, information modelling and notation tools, and functional models "...which enable managers to plan, organise, supervise, control, and account for the use of interconnection services..." [ISO89a]. In developing these standards, ISO took an object-oriented approach to information modelling and, as a consequence, developed an object model for network management—the OSI managed-object model. Recently there has been interest in the object model both from the standpoint of systems implementation [NMF93] and application integration [HoTh93].

The purpose of this paper is: to introduce the important aspects of the OSI managed-object model and associated services; to present some of the design requirements and

O.M. Nierstrasz (Ed.): ECOOP '93, LNCS 707, pp. 185-196, 1993.
© Springer-Verlag Berlin Heidelberg 1993

indicate how they were met; and to consider how the model and services might evolve to meet the needs of the next generation of network-management systems.

The layout of the paper is as follows: §2 gives some background concerning OSI network management and the OSI Reference Model; §3 presents the OSI management architecture and services; §4 considers the evolution of the model and services; and §5 offers some conclusions.

2   Background

In this section we try to answer the questions: "What is OSI network management?" and "How should network-management protocols be designed in the context of OSI?"

2.1   What is OSI Network Management?

Figure 1(a) gives a pictorial representation of a typical network management environment: *managing* systems (stylised as work stations) communicate with *managed* systems (stylised as equipment cabinets) across a *management network*. Figure 1(b) shows a single instance of communication between a managing and a managed system.

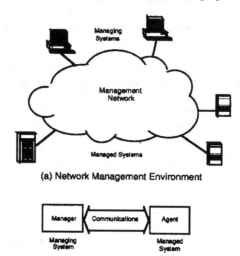

(a) Network Management Environment

(b) A Single Instance of Communication

Figure 1   OSI Network Management

The purpose of the OSI network-management standards is to standardise the management information that flows across the interface between the managing and managed systems. To develop the actual messages that will flow across the interface, the model shown in Figure 1(b) needs to be further refined (by, for example, the addition of managed objects). It should be noted that this refinement simply helps in the specification of the messages; it in no way constrains implementors in their choice of development techniques. In particular, implementors are not required to use an object-oriented approach to systems development (although they might well chose to do so). Implementors are free to implement real systems as they choose—their implementations only have to conform to the specification of the "bits on the wire".

ISO/IEC 7498-4 [ISO89a] forms the basis for the standardisation of OSI network-management. It categorises the requirements for management in five functional areas: fault management, configuration management, performance management, security management, and accounting management. See Figure 2 for more details.

The question is: "How can these broad requirements be translated into messages between systems?" To answer the question, we will have to take a short detour to review the basic elements of the OSI Reference Model.

Fault Management	The detection, isolation, and correction of abnormal network operation.
Configuration Management	The configuration of the network or components to meet changing user needs or alleviate congestion.
Performance Management	The monitoring and tuning of the performance of the network.
Security Management	The management of facilities required to support network security.
Accounting Management	The determination and allocation of costs for the use of network services.

Figure 2 OSI Management Functional Areas

2.2 A Crash Course on the OSI Reference Model

The OSI Reference Model [ISO84], see Figure 3, is a layered communications model in which the (n)-layer of the model provides services to the (n+1)-layer by means of (n)-layer protocols. For example the Network Layer of a particular implementation might provide routing services to the Transport Layer by means of X.25 packets. Figure 4 illustrates how this is done: each (n)-layer Protocol Data Unit (PDU) contains a slot, normally labelled "User Data", in which the (n+1)-layer PDU is carried; the (n+1)-layer PDU has a slot in which the (n+2)-layer PDU is carried, and so on. (N)-layer protocol design, then, is a question of providing (n)-layer services by means of (n)-layer PDUs with "holes" in them for (n+1)-layer PDUs. Except, of course, at the Application Layer where there is no (n+1)-layer.

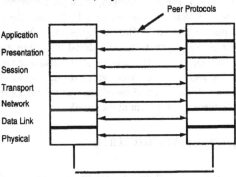

Figure 3 OSI Reference Model

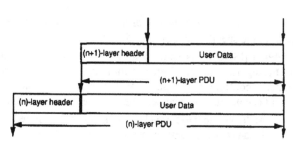

Figure 4 Protocol Data Units

The Application Layer is modelled as a "tool-box" of service elements such as Remote Operations Service Element [ISO89b; ISO89c] or Distributed Transaction Processing Service Element [ISO92d; ISO92e; ISO92f]. Service elements are combined into various *application contexts* to carry the application's messages.

2.3 Application-layer Message Development

It was recognised at a fairly early stage that, for OSI network-management, the application functionality was essentially open-ended—it would not be possible for one group to develop a set of messages that would accommodate all resource types. An open-ended message design was required. The design would have to cleanly separate the generic aspects (such as carriage protocol and access control) from the resource-specific aspects (such as message parameters and code points). Two design approaches were considered—a *functional approach* and a *model approach*.

The **functional approach** consists of designing generic messages to reflect the five functional areas and of refining these messages on a resource-by-resource basis. Such refinements would take the form of optional parameters or extensions to parameter lists.

The **model approach** consists of designing a set of messages to reflect a model of the resources to be managed and of refining the model on a resource-by-resource basis.

The latter approach offered the best method of separating the generic from the resource-specific and the best method of allowing multiple standards-groups to develop management message-sets independently—essentially by modelling the resources to be managed in terms of managed objects. The only question left was: "Which modelling paradigm?" A number of paradigms were considered including data-store, relational, and object-oriented. The object-oriented notions of encapsulation, object state, and inheritance were attractive and resonated well with evolving ideas of network-management modelling. Thus an object-oriented paradigm was adopted although the full ramifications of the choice were not apparent at the time!

3 OSI Management Architecture

The OSI management architecture consists of the managed-object model and a number of supporting object services and features.

3.1 OSI Managed-object Model

The managed-object model is similar to those found in many popular programming languages but it has a number of features that reflect the special requirements of network management.

3.1.1 Managed objects

A managed object is defined as "...an abstraction of real resource..." [ISO89a] (e.g. a modem or a user service) and, as such, it should support the requirements of:

- attributes (e.g. usage statistics, configuration parameters);
- operations (e.g. reset and start test);
- asynchronous events (e.g. over temperature and loss of power);
- behaviour (resources are intelligent and have state); and
- implementation hiding (as far as possible, irrelevant differences in implementation should be hidden).

To meet these requirements, ISO/IEC 10165-1 [ISO92a] defines the managed-object model and associated services. Managed objects are characterised by:

- the *operation invocations* they accept;
- the *event notifications* they emit;
- the *attributes* (state) they make available; and
- the *behaviour* they exhibit.

Managed objects support three generic operation-invocations:

set   request a change in the value of one or more attribute values; and

get   request the retrieval of one or more attribute values; and

delete   request the deletion of an object.

In addition managed objects support a parameterised operation-invocation *action* and a parameterised event-notification *notify*. These operation-invocations and event-notifications allow the object model to support an open-ended set of operations and events.

As shown in Figure 5, object invocations and notifications are modelled as acting directly on the surface of the managed objects. As we shall show later in this section, these object invocations and notifications will be carried between managing and managed systems by means of a carriage protocol.

3.1.2 Managed-object Structuring

The need to structure resources within a managed systems was considered important both for the naming and the selection of resources. The structure of the *Management Information Base (MIB)* reflects this need. The MIB can be regarded as a number of 1:n containment relationships that form a tree of managed objects. The containment relationships define the hierarchical naming-structure of managed objects and may also specify required behaviour of members of the relationship. The MIB also provides the object structuring on which multiple-object selection is based.

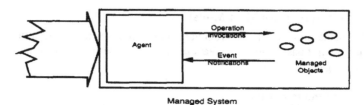

Managed System

Figure 5 Invocations and Notifications

3.1.3   Managed Relationships

Relationships between resources, such as that of back-up, switching, connecting, and existence, can be as important as the resources themselves from the point of view of network management. It was regarded as important to be able to discover and to manage such relationships, but, by using the existing carriage protocol.

A managed relationship is defined as "...a semantic binding between one or more managed objects which affects the behaviour of the bound objects" [ISO93a]. A managed relationship is characterised by:

- the semantics of the relationship (how the bound objects affect one another);
- the roles of the managed objects bound in the relationship; and
- the reification of the relationship.

In order to manage relationships using the existing carriage protocol, relationships may be reified in terms of managed objects, attribute pointers, or MIB containment.

3.2   Managed-object Services

The managed-object model is supported by an infrastructure of services and tools.

3.2.1   Managed-object Life Cycle

In order to reflect real resources, the managed-object model needs to support the concept of multiple instances of a class. Thus all managed objects are instances of a class and all objects have unambiguous names. Managed objects can be created remotely by conceptually applying a set of instantiation rules to a managed-object specification. The rules control the initial values of attributes and the naming of the created object instance.

An important concept in OSI protocol specifications is that of optionality. The features of protocol specifications are often subsetted into functional units: to be conformant, implementations must support at least a kernel functional unit and, in particular circumstances, may be required to support additional functional units. The OSI managed-object model supports a similar concept—*packages*. Managed-objects are defined in terms of packages of characteristics (operations, events, attributes, and behaviour) that are included on either a mandatory or conditional basis. Real resources are often designed with a large number of optional features and the mechanism of packages helps limit the combinatorial explosion that would occur if sub-classing alone were used to model the feature combinations.

3.2.2 Managed-object Specification

Protocol standards are the first (and most important) step towards interoperability and it is crucial that the specifications be both clear and unambiguous. The formal (in the sense of unambiguous) specification of the syntax of the characteristics of managed objects is accomplished by the use of a template language [ISO92b] and a data-typing language, ASN.1 [ISO90].

ISO has not agreed on a mechanism for the formal specification of the behaviour of managed objects; at the moment natural language is used. A number of attempts at using various formal description techniques for the specification of the behaviour of managed objects have been reported [SiMa91; ISO92g]; ISO is currently reviewing this issue.

In order to permit re-use, class specifications are arranged in a specialisation/generalisation hierarchy linked by multiple inheritance.

3.2.3 Carriage Protocol

The carriage protocol, CMIP [ISO91a] supports the messaging needs of the managed and managing systems and the need for access control, multiple and conditional object-selection, and asynchronous operation.

CMIP is an object-based, asynchronous, request/reply carriage protocol between managing and managed systems. It provides two types of service:

1. the carriage of event notifications asynchronously emitted by managed objects; and

2. the carriage of operation invocations directed towards managed objects.

The event-notification PDU provides fields for identifying:

- the managed object associated with the event;
- the event type;
- the time of the event; and
- an extensible parameter field to carry event-specific or object-specific information.

The operation-invocation PDU provides fields for:

- identifying the target object or objects;
- identifying the operation;
- enabling access to objects;
- correlating the reply with the invocation; and
- an extensible parameter field to carry object-specific or operation-specific information.

The identification of the target managed-object can be based on either:

- its name;
- its position in the Management Information Base;
- a predicate referring to its attributes; or
- a combination of all three.

These features allow a managing system to affect a number of objects with a single operation-invocation (termed *scoping*) and to select objects for operation invocations depending on their dynamic state (termed *filtering*).

3.3   Summary of OSI Network Management Architecture

The complete OSI network management architecture is shown in Figure 6. The *manager*, in the managing system, communicates with an *agent*, in the managed system by means of CMIP. The agent notionally:

- imposes access constraints;
- performs object selection for in-coming operation invocations; and
- provides dissemination for out-going event notifications.

Managed objects are arranged in a singly-rooted tree that serves as a basis for naming and multiple-object selection.

We emphasise again that the internal structuring of the managed system is purely illustrative and does not constrain actual implementations.

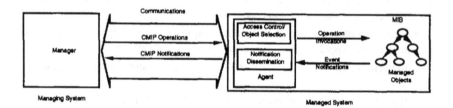

Figure 6   OSI Network Management Architecture

3.4   Managed-object Compatibility

Class inheritance is viewed as a mechanism that can improve interoperability between managed and managing systems in the face of asynchronous system-updates and vendor specialisation. A managing system may not have full understanding of certain specialised object classes but could, to some useful degree, manage instances of such classes as instances of more generalised classes of which it does have full understanding. Such interoperability can be achieved by the managing system essentially ignoring information it receives but does not understand—although ignoring information is potentially dangerous. Interoperability can also be achieved by the managed system through object substitutability [WeZd88] or object and service mutation.

It has been recognised that the managed-object subclassing hierarchy is not a subtyping hierarchy [Ame87] and thus instances of subclasses cannot be safely substituted for (and subsequently managed as) instances of their superclasses. This unfortunate state of affairs is because the inheritance rules [ISO92a] permit:

- invocation and result signatures to be extended;
- attribute ranges to be changed; and
- new notification-types to be added.

ISO/IEC 10165–1 [ISO92a] therefore specifies additional compatibility constraints on the inheritance rules to improve substitutability. It also imposes additional requirements on objects and object services to dynamically alter their behaviour to further improve substitutability. The combination of compatibility constraints and the requirements for dynamic alteration of object and service behaviour to improve substitutability is termed **allomorphism**.

4 Next-generation Network Management Standards

The current generation of OSI network-management standards is based on a model of a single managing-system communicating with a single managed-system using a single carriage protocol. Although these standards are an important and necessary first step to practical network-management solutions, the model and services must be evolved to meet the challenges of large, multi-protocol, mutable networks. In this section we give our views on the demands to be met by the next generation of network management standards and how the managed-object model and associated services may need to evolved.

4.1 Requirements

The next generation of network management standards must, we believe, reflect the following broad trends in network management:

1. **distributed** management—the managed and managing functions will be distributed throughout the management network;

2. **inter-networking**—multi management-protocols are a fact of life and have to be accommodated; and

3. **interoperability evolution**—management networks will be required to dynamically adapt to new object classes and new versions of existing object classes.

ISO is committed to an evolutionary approach to the further development of OSI network-management standards enabling the maximum degree of compatibility with existing implementations. A key tool in this regard is the ability to enhance protocol services by combining, rather than altering, existing protocols. Protocol standards are combined in new application contexts to provide enhanced capabilities. This permits a "mix-and-match" approach to standards development.

4.2 Distributed Management Architecture

The current OSI network-management architecture draws a clear distinction between the managing and managed functionality and where each resides. In practice, such distinctions are not so clear and will become more blurred as networks increase in size.

Management functionality will increasingly be distributed amongst peer and subordinate management systems on a functional, geographical, or operational basis. Similarly managed objects may be aggregated or fragmented over multiple managed-systems and managed relationships may span multiple managed-systems. In some cases the direct management of individual managed objects may be impractical and it will be necessary to provide standardised mechanisms for abstracting the characteristics of a number of managed objects into a higher-level surrogate object. For similar reasons it will be necessary to standardise mechanisms to define and manage *domains* of objects that are subject to the same *policy*. In fact the whole notion of distinct managing and managed systems will become blurred as intermediate systems provide run-time abstraction, delegation, and domain functions. The OSI managed-object model and services will need to be evolved to support such changes.

In order to obtain knowledge of the features of managed systems, the current standards require managed systems to be interrogated individually; as networks increase in size this will become impractical to carry out on a routine basis. Private caching of such knowledge can help, but this could be provided publicly in systems such as traders [ISO93c] and name servers [ISO91b]. It is likely that access to these services will be available by means of new application-contexts rather that by the enhancement of existing protocols.

There will be an increasing need for transactions involving multiple managed-systems and exhibiting so-called ACID properties (Atomicity, Consistency, Isolation, and Durability). ISO is currently developing an application context to combine Distributed Transaction Processing with CMIP [ISO93b].

4.3   Inter-network Management

Multiple management-protocols, difficult though they are for implementors to deal with, are a fact of life. Protocol mapping schemes have been proposed [NMF92] but such schemes require on-going enhancement to support evolving object-class libraries. Other proposal include adapter objects [OMG91], multiple interfaces to objects [ISO92c], and common object models [HoTh93]. A promising approach seems to be *federation* [Gor92], where management domains agree to federate by means of high-level inter-domain interfaces.

4.4   Interoperability Evolution

In the long term, we believe that management systems will have to accommodate new classes of resource and relationships dynamically. Thus formal notations describing the syntax and semantics of managed objects, aggregates of managed objects, and managed relationships will be required. Such descriptions will allow valued-added applications such as load-balancing, dynamic routing, and surveillance to automatically accommodate new resource types. For similar reasons we believe that managed object versioning and compatibility rules will need to evolve.

5   Conclusions

The managed-object model adopted by ISO to help in the development of network-management protocol standards nicely separates the generic from the resource-specific and permits a decentralised, but disciplined, approach to the development of resource-specific management messages. The model supports features, such as event notification and scoping, to meet requirements peculiar to network management. Object substitutability is complicated by the particular rules governing inheritance, however, a useful degree of interoperability is provided by means of allomorphism. The carriage protocol, CMIP, reflects network-management concerns of security, asynchronous operation, and bandwidth conservation.

The next generation of network-management standards will need to reflect the requirements of managing large, multi-protocol, mutable networks. The managed-object model and its related services will need to evolve to meet these requirements.

References

[Ame87] Inheritance and Subtyping in a Parallel Object-Oriented Language. In *Proceedings of European Conference on Object-Oriented Programming* (Oslo, Norway, August 1988). LNCS 322, Springer-Verlag, New York, 1988.

[Gor92] Goranson, H.T. Services in the SIRIUS-BETA Inter-Integration Domain. In *Enterprise Integration Modelling, Proceedings of the First International Conference.* Ed. Petrie, C.J. The MIT Press, Cambridge, Mass, 1992.

[HoTh93] Hodges, R. and Thompson, C. *Workshop Report, Workshop on Application Integration Architectures.* Texas Instruments, Dallas, Texas. 1993.

[ISO84] International Organization for Standardization and International Electrotechnical Commission. *Information Technology — Open Systems Interconnection — Basic Reference Model.* International Standard ISO/IEC 7498 : 1984.

[ISO89a] International Organization for Standardization and International Electrotechnical Commission. *Information technology — Open Systems Interconnection — Basic Reference Model — Part 4: Management Framework.* International Standard ISO/IEC 7498–4 : 1989.

[ISO89b] International Organization for Standardization and International Electrotechnical Commission. *Information Processing Systems — Text Communications — Remote Operations — Part 1: Model, Notation and Service Definition.* International Standard ISO/IEC 9072-1 : 1989.

[ISO89c] International Organization for Standardization and International Electrotechnical Commission. *Information Processing Systems — Text Communications — Remote Operations — Part 2: Protocol Specification.* International Standard ISO/IEC 9072-2 : 1989.

[ISO90] International Organization for Standardization and International Electrotechnical Commission. *Information Technology — Open Systems Interconnection — Specification of Abstract Syntax Notation One (ASN.1).* International Standard ISO/IEC 8824 : 1990.

[ISO91a] International Organization for Standardization and International Electrotechnical Commission. *Information Technology — Open Systems Interconnection — Common Management Information Protocol Specification.* International Standard ISO/IEC 9596 : 1991.

[ISO91b] International Organization for Standardization and International Electrotechnical Commission. *Information technology — Open Systems Interconnection — Management Information Services — The Directory.* International Standard ISO/IEC 9594 : 1991.

[ISO92a] International Organization for Standardization and International Electrotechnical Commission. *Information Technology — Open Systems Interconnection — Management Information Services — Structure of Management Information — Part 1: Management Information Model.* International Standard ISO/IEC 10165-1 : 1992.

[ISO92b] International Organization for Standardization and International Electrotechnical Commission. *Information Technology — Open Systems Interconnection — Management Information Services — Structure of Management Information — Part 4: Guidelines for the Definition of Managed Objects.* International Standard ISO/IEC 10165-4 : 1992.

[ISO92c] International Organization for Standardization and International Electrotechnical Commission. *Information Technology — Basic Reference Model for Open Distributed Processing — Part: 2 Descriptive Model.* Committee Draft ISO/IEC 10746-2. Dec. 1992.

[ISO92d] International Organization for Standardization and International Electrotechnical Commission. *Information technology — Open Systems Interconnection — Distributed transaction processing — OSI TP Model.* International Standard 10026-1 : 1992.

[ISO92e] International Organization for Standardization and International Electrotechnical Commission. *Information technology — Open Systems Interconnection — Distributed transaction processing — OSI TP Service.* International Standard 10026-2 : 1992.

[ISO92f] International Organization for Standardization and International Electrotechnical Commission. *Information technology — Open Systems Interconnection — Distributed transaction processing — OSI TP Protocol.* International Standard 10026-3 : 1992.

[ISO92g] International Organization for Standardization and International Electrotechnical Commission. Use of Z to Describe the Management Information Model. USA National Body Contribution, ISO/IEC JTC1/SC21/WG4 N1587. 1992.

[ISO93a] International Organization for Standardization and International Electrotechnical Commission. *Information Technology — Open Systems Interconnection — Management Information Services — Structure of Management Information — Part 2: General Relationship Model.* Committee Draft ISO/IEC 10165-7. Jan. 1993.

[ISO93b] International Organization for Standardization and International Electrotechnical Commission. *Information Technology — Open Systems Interconnection — Application Context for Systems Management with Transaction Processing.* Committee Draft ISO/IEC 11587, Jan. 1993.

[ISO93c] International Organization for Standardization and International Electrotechnical Commission. *Information Technology — Basic Reference Model for Open Distributed Processing — Part: 1 Overview and Guide to Use.* ISO/IEC JTC1/SC21/WG7 N755, Jan. 1993.

[NMF92] The Network Management Forum. *ISO/CCITT and Internet Management: Coexistence and Interworking Strategy,* Bernardsville, NJ, 1992.

[NMF93] Network Management Forum. *Comparison of the OMG and ISO/CCITT Object Models,* Bernardsville, NJ, 1993.

[OMG91] Object Management Group, *The Common Object Request Broker: Architecture and Specification,* Boulder, CO, 1991.

[SiMa91] Simon, L. D. and Marshall, L. S. Using VDM to Specify OSI Managed Objects. In *Proceedings of the IFIP TC6/WG6.1 Forth International Conference on Formal Description Techniques* (FORTE '91), Sydney, Australia, November 1991. Eds. G. A. Rose and K. R. Parker, Elsevier, 1991.

[WeZd88] Wegner, P. and Zdonik, S.B. Inheritance as an Incremental Modification Mechanism. In *Proceedings of European Conference on Object-Oriented Programming* (Oslo, Norway, August 1988). LNCS 322, Springer-Verlag, New York, 1988.

Nested Mixin-Methods in Agora

Patrick Steyaert[*], Wim Codenie, Theo D'Hondt,
Koen De Hondt, Carine Lucas, Marc Van Limberghen

Programming Technology Lab
Computer Science Department
Vrije Universiteit Brussel
Pleinlaan 2, B-1050 Brussels BELGIUM
email: {prsteyae | wcodenie | tjdhondt | kdehondt |
clucas | mvlimber}@vnet3.vub.ac.be

Abstract: Mixin-based inheritance is an inheritance technique that has been shown to subsume a variety of different inheritance mechanisms. It is based directly upon an incremental modification model of inheritance. This paper addresses the question of how mixins can be seen as named attributes of classes the same way that objects, methods, and also classes in their own right, are seen as named attributes of classes. The general idea is to let a class itself have control over how it is extended. This results in a powerful abstraction mechanism to control the construction of inheritance hierarchies in two ways. Firstly, by being able to constrain the inheritance hierarchy; secondly, by being able to extend a class in a way that is specific for that class. Nested mixins are a direct consequence of having mixins as attributes. The scope rules for nested mixins are discussed, and shown to preserve the encapsulation of objects.

1. Introduction

The need to control and to make abstraction of the construction of inheritance hierarchies has been expressed by several authors. On the one hand it seems an obvious extension of the "incremental changes" philosophy of the object-oriented paradigm to be able to incrementally change entire inheritance hierarchies. On the other hand there is a need to control the complexity arising from the use of multiple inheritance [Hendler86] [Hamer92].

A notable example of the first is that given by Lieberman in [Cook87]. The question is how an entire hierarchy of black and white graphical objects can be incrementally changed so that the initially monochrome graphical objects can be turned into coloured objects. In

The following text presents research results of the Belgian Incentive Program "Information Technology" - Computer Science of the future, initiated by the Belgian State - Prime Minister's Service - Science Policy Office. The scientific responsability is assumed by its authors.

* The first author is supported by the above research program.

O.M. Nierstrasz (Ed.): ECOOP '93, LNCS 707, pp. 197-219, 1993.
© Springer-Verlag Berlin Heidelberg 1993

present day systems, one either has to destructively change the root class of this hierarchy by adding a colour attribute, or one has to manually extend each class in the hierarchy with a colour subclass.

The second need stems from the observation that unconstrained multiple inheritance hierarchies often end up as tangled hierarchies. Multiple inheritance is less expressive than it appears, essentially in its lack to put constraints on multiple inheritance from different classes [Hamer92]. For example, one would like to put a mutual exclusion constraint on the triangle and rectangle classes, registering the fact that a graphical object can not be both a triangle and a rectangle, and, as such, a class cannot (multiply) inherit from both the triangle and rectangle class.

This article describes a tentative answer to both needs. An extension of mixin-based inheritance [Bracha&Cook90] is proposed. In this extension mixins[1] can be applied dynamically and hence combined flexibly by making use of the available control structures. In addition, the applicability of a mixin can be restricted to a limited, but extensible, set of classes.

Mixins provide the extra abstraction that is needed to be able to construct an entire inheritance hierarchy in a building block fashion. The statement that mixins provide exactly the right building blocks for constructing inheritance hierarchies is supported by the results obtained in [Bracha&Cook90], where it is shown that mixin-based inheritance subsumes the different inheritance mechanisms provided by Smalltalk, Beta and CLOS. In contrast with [Bracha&Cook90] the emphasis of our work is on the dynamic applicability of mixins.

Mixins, as in CLOS for example, add to the solution of the first problem, while adding to the problems of the second. Mixins allow unanticipated combinations of behaviour to be made [Stein,Lieberman,Ungar89]. But, when uncontrolled, one faces an explosion of possible combinations of mixins [Lang&Pearlmutter86]. A mechanism to control this combinatorial explosion is needed.

Essential to our approach is that each class knows how to extend itself. A class is asked to extend itself by sending it a message. Each class responds to a limited set of "mixin messages". "Mixin methods" correspond to mixin messages. A mixin method implements an extension for a certain class. Of course mixin methods can be inherited and "late binding" also applies to mixin methods. So, extension of a class is obtained in a very object-oriented way.

---

1 To avoid confusion it's important to note here that there is a difference in emphasis in mixins as used in e.g. CLOS and mixins as used in mixin-based inheritance. In the former a mixin is "mixed in" by means of multiple inheritance and linearization, whereas in the latter a mixin is explicitly applied to a class. We will come back to this in the next section.

A related issue is the dichotomy between encapsulated and non-encapsulated inheritance [Snyder86]. We will show how the nesting of mixin-methods gives rise to a kind of nested scoping that addresses this issue. Typical for this kind of scoping is that visibility of identifiers is *not* directed towards the visibility of variables that are shared by different objects, but rather towards the visibility of inherited variables in the class hierarchy. This difference can best be illustrated by the observation that in an object-oriented programming language it is possible to have two sorts of "omnipresent" variables: 1) a Smalltalk-like global variable, 2) a variable declared in the root class of the class hierarchy. The former is a variable shared by all objects in the system, the latter amounts to an instance variable that is present in each object in the system.

The first part of the paper introduces all concepts in a language independent way. In the second part these concepts are illustrated by means of examples written in Agora. Agora is an object-oriented language under development. One of its hallmarks is the consistent use of mixins for inheritance. Although typing is considered important in Agora, the examples are presented in an untyped version of Agora.

The structure of the paper is as follows. In section 2, we introduce mixin-based inheritance, and the necessary terminology for the rest of the paper. In section 3 we describe mixin-attributes and address encapsulated/non-encapsulated inheritance in this context. Section 4 shows how mixins are introduced in Agora. Section 5 provides a thorough discussion on the scope rules of nested mixins. Section 6 describes how classes are seen as attributes, and the difference between class nesting and mixin nesting. In section 7, the full power of mixin-methods and dynamic application of mixins is explored. The status of mixin-methods is discussed, and a preliminary evaluation is given in section 8. Section 9 discusses related work. Section 10 concludes.

2. Mixin-based Inheritance

In a simplified form[2], inheritance can be modeled as a hierarchical incremental modification mechanism [Wegner&Zdonik88]. A parent P (the superclass) is transformed with a modifier M to form a result R = P + M (the subclass); the result R can be used as a parent for further incremental modification.

Typically the parent, result and modifier are collections of named attributes. From the viewpoint of the result R, the attributes defined in the parent P are referred to as the "inherited" attributes. Attributes defined in the modifier M are referred to as the "proper" attributes of R. Furthermore, in object-oriented languages where encapsulation is

---

2 One important aspect we do not address here is the deferred binding of self-reference in inheritance.

promoted, two sorts of attributes exist: private, or encapsulated attributes, and public attributes. Public attributes can be accessed freely; access to the encapsulated attributes is restricted to (the body of) the definition of the public and encapsulated attributes. On top of this, in class-based languages we can distinguish class-attributes from instance-attributes[3].

An attribute, either public or private, is selected by name. The result of this can be, amongst others, a computed value, or side effect (e.g. in the case of a method), or simply a stored value (e.g. in the case of an instance variable), or a combination of these, depending on the type of attribute. Each type of attribute can have its own attribute selection rule.

The result R is truly an extension of the parent P (to contrast with e.g. aggregation). Access to the inherited attributes in R is exactly the same as access to the proper attributes of R, though the proper attributes of R take precedence over the inherited attributes in case of name conflicts.

The above incremental modification model of inheritance is a simplification. In most common object-oriented languages, modifiers themselves, also have access to the attributes of the parent being modified. For example, a subclass can invoke operations defined in the superclass (hereafter called parent operations). To model this, a modifier M is parameterized by a parent P that can be referred to in the definitions of the attributes of M. The actual parent is supplied to a modifier when a modifier is composed with a parent. Composing a parent P and a modifier M now takes the form $P \Delta M = P + M(P)$, where the modifier M is no longer a simple set of attributes, but is now a function from a parent to a set of attributes.

The above model is the essence of the model of inheritance in [Bracha&Cook90] where it is used as a basis for the introduction of mixin-based inheritance. It is shown that mixin-based inheritance is a general inheritance model subsuming the inheritance mechanisms provided in Smalltalk, Beta and CLOS.

Whereas in classical single or multiple inheritance the modifier M has no existence on its own (generally it is more or less part of the result R); the essence of mixin-based inheritance is that the modifier M is an abstraction that exists apart from parent and result. Modifiers are called "mixins". The composition operation Δ is called "mixin application". The class to which a mixin is applied is called the base class. In practice a mixin does not have its base class as an explicit parameter, but, rather, a mixin has access to the base class through a pseudo-variable, in the same way that a subclass has access to a superclass via a pseudo-variable. In a statically typed language, though, this means that a mixin

---

3 In the paper we only consider mixins as class attributes.

must specify the names and associated types of the attributes a possible base class must provide. This is why mixins are sometimes called "abstract subclasses".

In order to build a new class, first, a mixin is defined; then, this mixin is applied to a base class. One and the same mixin can be used to specialize different (unrelated) base classes. A typical example is that of a colour mixin which adds a colour attribute and the associated accessor methods, and can be applied to classes as different as vehicles and polygons. A typical example involving the invocation of parent operations is that of a "bounds" mixin that constrains the movements of points. The move method attribute defined in the bounds mixin checks for the boundary conditions, and relies on the base class to actually move the point. The actual base class can be a class that implements points by means of cartesian coordinates, or one that implements points by means of polar coordinates.

```
class-based inheritance
class R
 inherits P
 extended with NamedAttribute₁ ... NamedAttributeₙ
endclass

mixin-based inheritance
M is mixin
    defining NamedAttribute₁ ... NamedAttributeₙ
endmixin
class R1 inherits P1 extended with M endclass
class R2 inherits P2 extended with M endclass
```

If it were not for this usage of parent operations the application of a mixin to a base class could easily be mimicked by multiply inheriting from both the base class and the mixin. The parameterization of a mixin with a base class is what makes mixin-based inheritance fundamentally different from multiple inheritance, with the exception of for example CLOS where the inheritance graph is linearized.

A mixin in CLOS is a class that has no fixed superclass and as such can be applied to ("mixed in") different superclasses. In CLOS terminology, this means that a mixin class can do a Call-Next-Method, even though it has no apparent superclass. Mixin-classes in CLOS depend directly on multiple inheritance, and more specifically linearization. Contrary to this, in our work, a mixin is not a class (a mixin can not be instantiated for example), and multiple inheritance is a consequence of, rather than the supporting mechanism for, the use of mixins. In contrast with CLOS, in which mixins are nothing but a special use of multiple inheritance, mixins are promoted as the sole abstraction mechanism for building the inheritance hierarchy.

Mixin-based inheritance gives rise to explicitly linearized inheritance. The order in which mixins are applied is significant for the external visibility of public attribute names.

Attributes in the mixin override base class attributes with the same name. In absence of any name conflict resolution mechanism, attribute name look up is determined by application order.

Given a suitable name conflict resolution mechanism mixin-based inheritance can be used to mimic (most forms of) multiple inheritance. With multiple inheritance one and the same class can be reused different times as a parent class in different combinations with other parent classes; with mixin-based inheritance one and the same mixin can be reused in different combinations with other mixins (or base classes). The ability to form "chains" of mixins is appropriate in this case. An evaluation of how mixin-based inheritance addresses multiple inheritance problems is beyond the scope of this paper. The reader is referred to [Bracha92] and [Bracha&Cook90].

Apart from this explicit linearization, duplication of sets of attributes of shared parent classes (mostly used for duplication of instance variables) can be controlled explicitly by the programmer as well: not by the order of application, but by the number of applications of one and the same mixin. The inability of, for instance, graph-oriented multiple inheritance to control the duplication of shared parent classes has been shown to lead to encapsulation problems [Snyder86].

3. Mixins as Attributes

Applying the orthogonality principle to the facts that we have mixins and that a class consists of a collection of named attributes, one must address the question of how a mixin can be seen as a named attribute of a class. The adopted solution is that a class lists as mixin attributes all mixins that are applicable to it. The mixins that are listed as attributes in a certain class can only be used to create subclasses of that class and its future subclasses. Furthermore, a class can only be extended by selecting one of its mixin attributes. In much the same way that selecting a method attribute from a certain object has the effect of executing the selected method-body in the context of that object, selecting a mixin attribute of a certain class has the effect of extending that class with the attributes defined in the selected mixin. So, rather than having an explicit operation to apply an arbitrary mixin to an arbitrary class, a class is asked to extend itself.

Inheritance of mixins plays an important role in this approach. If it were not for the possibility to inherit mixins, the above restriction on the applicability of mixins would result in a rather static inheritance hierarchy and in duplication of mixin code (each mixin would be applicable to only one class). A mixin can be made applicable to more or less classes according to its position in the inheritance tree. The higher a mixin is defined the more class that can be extended with it. In a programming language such as Agora, where mixin-based inheritance is the only inheritance mechanism available, this means that all generally applicable mixins (such as a mixin that adds colour attributes) must be defined in some given root class.

```
inheritance of a mixin-attribute
--- Root class attributes ---
ColourMixin is mixin
  defining colour
endmixin

CarMixin is mixin
  defining enginetype
endmixin

Car is class obtained by CarMixin extension of Root
--- class Car inherits ColourMixin defined in the Root class
ColouredCar is class obtained by ColourMixin extension of Car
```

Note that classes can be attributes too. The meaning is analogous to having a plain object as attribute; there need not be a special relation between a class that is an attribute of a containing class and its containing class. Typically, much more meaning is attributed to nesting of classes [Madsen87]. This will be considered later.

3.1 Applicability of Mixins

What defines applicability of a mixin to a class ? There is no decisive answer to this question. The possible answers accord to the possible varieties of incremental modification mechanisms (e.g. behavioural compatible, signature compatible, name compatible modification, and modification with cancellation) used for inheritance [Wegner&Zdonik88]. If nothing but behaviour compatible modifications are allowed, then only the mixins that define a behaviour compatible modification of a class are applicable to that class.

To put it another way, restricting the applicability of mixins puts a constraint on the possible inheritance hierarchies that can be constructed. The desirability of constraining multiple inheritance hierarchies has already been noted [Hendler86] [Hamer92]. One such constraint is a mutual exclusion constraint on subclasses. The following example is taken from [Hamer92].

Consider a Person class with a Female and a Male subclass. A mutual exclusion constraint on the Female and the Male subclasses expresses the fact that it should not be possible to multiple inherit from Female and Male at the same time. In terms of mixin-based inheritance, we have a Person class, with two mixin-attributes: Female-Mixin, and Male-Mixin. Once the Female mixin is applied to the person class, the Male mixin should not be applicable to the resulting class, and vice versa. This mutual exclusion constraint is realized simply by canceling the Male-Mixin in the Female-Mixin, and by canceling the Female-Mixin in the Male-Mixin.

```
mutual exclusion constraint on classes
--- MarriedPerson class attributes ---
  Female-Mixin is mixin
     defining husband
     canceling Male-Mixin
  endmixin

  Male-Mixin is mixin
     defining wife
     canceling Female-Mixin
  endmixin
```

This solution relies on the ability to cancel inherited attributes. A more elegant solution, and one that should be provided in a full-fledged programming language, would be to have some declarative means to express the fact that two mixins are mutually exclusive. Classifiers [Hamer92] play this role for class-based (non mixin-based) languages. A similar mechanism is imaginable for mixins. The reason why the example is given without resorting to such a declarative construction is to show that mixins provide a good basis — and a better basis than classes — to express this sort of constraints on the inheritance hierarchy.

3.2 Mixins and Encapsulated Inheritance

In most object-oriented languages a subclass can access its superclass in two ways. Firstly, by direct access to the private attributes of the superclass (direct access to the implementation details). Secondly, by access to the public attributes of the superclass (parent operations). A mixin is applicable to a class if this class provides the necessary private and public attributes for the implementation of the mixin. This puts an extra restriction on the applicability of a mixin.

The tradeoff between direct access to the implementation details of a superclass and using parent operations is discussed in [Snyder87]. If a mixin depends directly on implementation details of the class it is applied to, then modifications to the implementation of the base class can have consequences for the mixin's implementation. A mixin that uses parent operations only is likely to be applicable to a broader set of classes (it is more abstract). Mixins that make use of the implementation details of a superclass are said to inherit from their superclass in a non-encapsulated way; mixins that make use of parent operations only are said to inherit from their superclass in an encapsulated way

One solution to this problem is to have all superclass references made through parent operations. This implies that for each class, two kinds of interfaces must be provided: a public interface destined for classes (= instantiating clients) that use instances of that class and, a so called private interface for future subclasses (= inheriting clients).

The solution we adopt is to differentiate between mixins that don't and mixins that do rely on implementation details of the base class they are applied to, recognizing the fact that in some cases direct access to a base class's implementation details is needed. To put it differently: a mixin is applicable to a class if this class provides the necessary private attributes for the implementation of the mixin, but not all mixins that are applicable to a class need access to the private attributes of that class (for example the above colour mixin). Essentially, mixins are differentiated by how much of the implementation details of the base class are visible to them. As we will show the solution relies heavily on the ability to inherit mixins. The degree to which a mixin has access to the implementation details of a base class is solely based on whether this mixin is either a proper or rather an inherited attribute of this base class.

Consider a class C that was constructed by application of a mixin MC to a given base class. There are two sorts of mixins that can be used to create subclasses of C: mixins that are proper attributes of C (defined in the mixin MC) and inherited mixins. A mixin that is a proper attribute of the class C, has, by definition, access to the proper private attributes of that class C, and to the same private attributes that the mixin MC has access to. An inherited mixin has no access to the proper private attributes of the class it is applied to. Note that this leads naturally to, and is consistent with, nested mixins. For a mixin to be a proper attribute of the class C, it must be defined in (and consequently nested in) the mixin MC. According to lexical scope rules, it then has access to the names of the attributes defined in the mixin MC.

```
nested mixin-attributes
--- BaseClass attributes ---
 MC is mixin
    defining
    properToC       --- e.g. an instance variable
    PMC is mixin
        defining
            --- properToC is visible here
    endmixin --- PMC ---
 endmixin   --- MC ---

 NotPMC is mixin
    defining
    --- properToC is NOT visible here
 endmixin --- NotPMC ---

C is class obtained by MC extension of BaseClass
PC is class obtained by PMC extension of C
NotPC is class obtained by NotPMC extension of C

--- both PC and NotPC are subclasses of C; only PC has access to C
proper attributes ---
```

So, the amount of detail in which a subclass depends on the implementation aspects of its superclass is determined by the relative nesting of the mixins used to create the sub- and superclass. Not only are a mixin's proper instance variables visible for the method declarations in that mixin, but also those of the surrounding mixins. A mixin can be made more or less abstract according to its position in the inheritance tree.

Complete abstraction in mixins can be obtained by not nesting them in other mixins (i.e. defining all mixins on the root class), resulting in a totally encapsulated form of inheritance, as is proposed in [Snyder87]. If abstraction is not required, exposure of inherited private attributes in mixins can be obtained by making the nesting and inheritance hierarchy the same, i.e. by nesting the mixin provided to create the subclass in the mixin provided to create the superclass. This corresponds to Smalltalk-like inheritance.

Of course, combinations between full and no nesting at all are possible. The higher in the hierarchy a mixin is defined, the more objects that can be extended with this mixin, the more abstract the mixin has to be.

A brief comparison between nested mixins and encapsulated inheritance where only parent operations are used to access a superclass, is in place here. In the latter it is the superclass that takes the initiative to determine how much of the implementation will be exposed to inheritors by differentiating between private (visible to inheritors) from public (visible to all) attributes. No distinction is made between inheritors that do make use of the exposed implementation and inheritors that don't. With nested mixins there *is* a distinction between subclasses that do and subclasses that don't rely on a superclass's implementation details. Exposure of implementation details to an inheritor is on initiative of both the ancestor and the inheritor !

4. Mixin-based Inheritance in Agora

4.1 Some Agora Syntax

Agora syntax resembles Smalltalk syntax in its *message-expressions*. We have unary, operator and keyword-messages. Message-expressions can be imperative (statements) or functional (expressions). For clarity, keywords and operators are printed in italics.

aString *size*	unary message
aString1 *+* aString2	operator message
aString *at:*index *put:*aChar	keyword message

A second category of message-expressions is the category of *reify messages*[4]. Reify

---

4 In a reflective variant of Agora it is possible to add reifier methods, hence the name. Reifier methods are executed 'at the level of the interpreter' in which all interpreter parameters (context and such) are 'reified'.

messages have the same syntax as message expressions; in the examples they are differentiated from message expressions by having bold-styled keywords/operator. Reify expressions collect all "special" language constructs in one uniform syntax (comparable to lisp special forms). They correspond to syntactical constructs such as assignment statements, variable declarations and many other constructs used in a more conventional programming language. Reify expressions help in keeping Agora syntax as small as possible. Special attention must be paid to the precedence rules. Reify expressions have, as a group, lower precedence than regular message expressions. In each category unary messages have highest precedence, keyword messages have lowest precedence.

```
a <- 3                       assignment reifier

c define                     variable declaration reifier

c define: 3                  same, but with initial value
```

Message-expressions can be grouped to form blocks.

```
[c1 define: Complex new ;
 c2 define: Complex new ;
 c1 real:3 imag:4 ;
 c2 <- c1]
```

4.2 Mixins & Methods

The following is an example mixin method. This method adds a `colour` attribute and its access methods to the object it is sent to. In all the examples that follow, mixin definitions standing free in the text (top-level mixins), are presumed to be defined on the root class called `object`. So, in the example below, the root class `Object` is extended with colour attributes by invoking its *addColour* mixin (sending the message *addColour* to it). The resulting `ColourObject` class is a subclass of class `Object`.

```
addColour Mixin:
           [ colour define ;
             colour:newColour Method:[colour <- newColour] ;
             colour Method: colour
           ] ;
ColourObject define: Object addColour
```

`Object` is extended with an instance variable "`colour`" and two methods: an imperative method `colour:` and a functional method `colour`. The body of a method can be either a block or, as can be the case for functional methods, a single expression. To the left of the **Method:** reifier keyword is the pattern to invoke the method; it has the form of an ordinary message expression, except that it has no receiver and the arguments to the keywords are replaced by the names of the formal arguments.

5. Introducing Block Structure in Object-Oriented Languages

Most object-oriented languages define the scope of identifiers more or less ad hoc. In those languages (including Smalltalk), scope rules do not emerge from nesting. Rather, a different look up strategy is defined for each kind of "variable". Smalltalk, for example, offers a blend of variables (class variables, class instance variables, global variables, pool variables, instance variables, arguments, local variables, block arguments) each with its own visibility rule.

While designing Agora, we were aiming to unify all these variants of scoping and to define a simple, uniform strategy to describe the scope of an "identifier". Agora is a block structured language. Blocks and nested structures have come into disfavour in object-oriented languages (with the notable exceptions of Simula and its descendant BETA). Block structures provide locality. The lack of locality in e.g. Smalltalk, where all classes reside in one flat name space, has its drawbacks to structure large programs. Block structures are a natural way to hierarchically structure name spaces. Accordingly scope rules can be imposed. In Agora the visibility of an identifier is solely based on the relative nesting of the block in which this identifier is declared. Nesting results from the declaration of mixins within mixins, methods within mixins, and usage of blocks within methods (for e.g. control structures). Hence, no a priori distinction is made between local variables and e.g. instance variables, nor is there any special provision to declare a global or class variable.

Introducing block structure in an object-oriented system is a very delicate operation [Buhr&Zarnke88]. This is because the "natural" form of scoping that emerges from the nesting of blocks -- identifiers declared in some context are visible in blocks declared in the same context -- can seriously interfere with the notion of encapsulation.

Scope rules can be seen as a mechanism to structure name spaces, whereby a name space is defined as a collection of identifiers with the same scope. One must take care, however, since in an object-oriented language in which objects are considered to be encapsulated, this encapsulation implies that each object has a separate name space; similarly strictly encapsulated inheritance implies that each sub-object[5] within an object has a separate name space. As is shown earlier, the scope rules for nested mixins structure the name space within a single object. The intention is to regulate the sharing of name spaces of sub-objects. While this breaks the encapsulation of sub-objects, objects are still considered as totally encapsulated, i.e. access to the encapsulated part of an object is reserved to the implementation of the public part of that object, but one sub-object can access the encapsulated part of another sub-object within the same object (mediated by the aforementioned rules).

---

5 Each object is composed out of sub-objects according to the inheritance hierarchy.

In the following section we focus on name space sharing for sub-objects. Sometimes there is a need to share name spaces between objects, rather than sub-objects. The above mentioned class variables and global variables, as found in Smalltalk, are examples of such name spaces shared by a number of (or all) objects. In the same way that the scope rules for nested mixins regulate the sharing of name spaces of sub-objects, it is obvious that another set of scope rules can regulate the creation of shared name spaces for objects. This is normally what is accomplished with nested classes in other work, and will be discussed in the section on class nesting versus mixin nesting.

5.1 An Example of Mixin Nesting in Agora

As said before, a mixin is either nested in another mixin, or not nested at all, to control the amount of detail to which a subclass depends on the implementation of a superclass. This is illustrated in the two following examples.

The general idea in the first example is to have turtles which are, in our case, a sort of point that can be moved in a "turtle-like" way (no drawing is involved at the moment). The essence is that a turtle user does not manipulate the location and heading of the turtle directly but uses the home/turn/forward protocol.

```
--- root-class (Object) attributes ---
MakeTurtle Mixin:
  [ location define: Point rho:0 theta:0*pi ;
    heading define: 0*pi ;
    position Method: location ;
    home Method:
          [ location <- Point rho:0 theta:0*pi; heading <- 0*pi ];
    turn:turn Method: [heading <- heading + turn] ;
    forward:distance Method:
          [ location <- location +
                        (Point rho:distance theta:heading) ] ;

  MakeBounded Mixin:
   [ bound define: Circle m:location r:infinite ;
     home Method:
           [ bound <- Circle m:location r:infinite ; super home ] ;
     newBound:maxRho Method:
           [ bound <- Circle m:location r:maxRho ] ;
     forward:distance Method:
           [ newLocation define ;
             newLocation <- location + (Point rho:distance
                                             theta:heading) ;
           (newLocation - (bound center)) rho > bound r
              ifTrue:
              [super forward:
                     (((LineSeg p1:location p2:newLocation)
                            intersect:bound) - location)rho ]
            ifFalse: [ super forward:distance ] ] ] ] ;
```

```
Turtle define: Object MakeTurtle ;
BoundedTurtle define: Turtle MakeBounded ;
aBoundedTurtle define: BoundedTurtle new ;
aTurtle define: Turtle new ;
aBoundedTurtle forward:1 ;
aTurtle forward:3
```

Once the turtle is defined, the next step is to create a subclass that puts boundaries on the movements of the turtle. In the example turtles are restricted to move within the bounds of a circle. For this purpose the forward method is overridden in the subclass that implements this boundary checking. This overridden forward method uses direct access to the turtle instance variables location and heading in its implementation.

For the construction of the classes Turtle and BoundedTurtle, two mixins, MakeTurtle and MakeBounded respectively, are defined. To make sure that the class BoundedTurtle inherits from class Turtle in a non-encapsulated way, the MakeBounded mixin is nested in the MakeTurtle mixin. Notice that, since the MakeBounded mixin is defined only for Turtle, it can only be used to extend the Turtle class and its subclasses. Not only is it impossible to extend the root class Object with the MakeBounded mixin since it is not defined for the root class but also since Object does not define the location/heading instance variables that are required by the MakeBounded mixin.

Each instance of Turtle and each instance of BoundedTurtle has its own set of location/heading instance variables. Furthermore, if in the MakeBounded mixin an instance variable were to be declared with a name that collides with a name in the MakeTurtle mixin (e.g. an instance variable with the name "heading"), then each BoundedTurtle would have two instance variables with this name. One instance variable would only be visible from within methods defined in the MakeTurtle mixin, the other instance variable would only be visible from within methods defined in the MakeBounded mixin. There is a "hole in the scope" of the instance variable defined in the MakeTurtle mixin. So, there is no merging going on for instance variables with equal names, neither is it an error to have an instance variable with the same name in a subclass (as is the case in Smalltalk). Notice that identifier lookup is a static operation: The instance variable that is referred to in an expression can be deduced from looking at the nested structure of the program. No dynamic lookup strategies are applied. Similar observations can be made for non-nested mixins. Encapsulating the names of instance variables in this way is an important aid in enhancing the potential for mixin composition. This is all the more important if mixins are used to create/emulate multiple inheritance hierarchies.

Thus, if a mixin is nested in another mixin, classes created by the innermost mixin are always (not necessarily direct) subclasses of classes defined by the outermost mixin. However, the reverse statement is not always true. Nesting is not a requirement for subclasses.

```
--- root-class (Object) attributes ---
MakeDrawingTurtle Mixin:
  [ penDown define: true ;
    togglePen Method: [penDown <- penDown not] ;
    forward:distance Method:
            [ newPosition define ;
              oldPosition define: self position ;
              super forward:distance ;
              newPosition <- self position ;
              penDown ifTrue:
                    [… draw line from old position to new position …]
            ] ;
    MakeDashed Mixin:
      [ dashSize define: 1 ;
        setDashSize:newSize Method: [dashSize <- newSize] ;
        forward:distance Method:
          [penDown
             ifTrue:
               [ 1 to: (distance div: dashSize)
                     do:     [ super forward: dashSize ;
                               self togglePen ] ;
                   super forward: (distance mod: dashSize) ;
                   penDown <- true
               ]
             ifFalse: [ super forward:distance ]
          ]
      ]
  ] ;


DrawingTurtle define: Turtle MakeDrawingTurtle ;
DashedDrawingTurtle define: DrawingTurtle MakeDashed ;
```

The goal in the above example is to extend the Turtle class so that it draws, or does not draw (depending on the status of the pen), on the screen where the turtle is heading. The drawing capabilities can be added fairly independently of the implementation of the turtle. Once again the forward method is overridden. But all that is needed in the implementation of the overridden forward method is the old forward method and a method that returns the current location of the turtle. Notice that, even though the location of the turtle must now be made public (to read), the heading instance variable is still encapsulated. The MakeDrawingTurtle mixin that implements this extension does not have to be nested in the Turtle mixin, resulting in a MakeDrawingTurtle mixin that can be applied to other sorts of turtle classes that respect the forward/position protocol.

Earlier on we said that the MakeBounded mixin could only be applied to the Turtle class and its subclasses. DrawingTurtle is such a subclass. We now have two ways to create bounded drawing turtles. On the one hand, by applying the MakeDrawingTurtle to a BoundedTurtle (DrawingBoundedTurtle define: BoundedTurtle MakeDrawingTurtle), on the other hand, by applying the MakeBounded mixin to a DrawingTurtle (BoundedDrawingTurtle define:DrawingTurtle MakeBounded). In this example both results are the same; the forward method in the

`MakeDrawingTurtle` mixin is such that it only draws a line up to the position where the turtle has moved, even if it moved a shorter distance than was intended.

It is important to note that the order of mixin application has no effect on the exposure of implementation details of the applied mixins to each other. This is important since this greatly enhances the reusability of mixins. The order in which the mixins *MakeDrawingTurtle* and *MakeBounded* are applied has no effect on the respective exposure of implementation details of the turtle base class to the inheriting clients `DrawingBoundedTurtle` or `BoundedDrawingTurtle`. The `makeBounded` and the `makeDrawingTurtle` cannot access each other's encapsulated part (independently of which mixin is applied first), and in both cases only the `MakeBounded` mixin has access to the `turtle` class's implementation details. It is coincidental in the example that we can choose in which order the mixins *MakeDrawingTurtle* and *MakeBounded* are applied, and that both results exhibit the same *behaviour*. In cases where this choice is not available, any dependence of the exposure of implementation details on the order of mixin application would seriously restrict the reuse of mixins.

6. Classes as Attributes, Class Nesting Versus Mixin Nesting

Even though the emphasis, up until now, was put on mixins as attributes, a class can also be considered as an attribute of an object. The main difference with having mixins as attributes (and classes as attributes in non mixin-based inheritance) is that this does not introduce a new set of scope rules. Since the definition of a class is nothing but the application of a mixin to a base class, having classes as attributes does not imply nested classes, as illustrated below.

```
makeA Mixin:
  [ B define: Object makeB ; -- local class
    ...
  ] ;
makeB Mixin:
  [...] ;

A define: Object makeA
```

In this example, a class A is defined, that keeps a reference to a local class B. The description of B however is not nested in A, since B is created with a mixin defined on the root class `Object`. Normal scope rules apply to the identifier B.

In most object-oriented languages, classes reside in a name space shared by all objects. Indeed, in most cases a class should be visible for all objects. Due to the lack of global variables in Agora this can only be realized by inheriting attributes that refer to classes, rather than by having a global name space for classes. Classes that should be globally visible must be defined as attributes of the root class. Since all classes are derived from the root class, and the mixins to derive these classes are de facto nested in this root class, each class inherits and has direct access to these attributes. Of course this results in each object having all globally visible classes as instance variables. In a practical implementation this need not be a problem.

For non mixin-based inheritance the ability to have classes as attributes normally implies class nesting. The major difference between nesting of classes and nesting of mixins lies in their respective relation to encapsulation. As was amply discussed, nested mixins respect the encapsulation of objects.

When nesting classes, the nesting is used to create shared name spaces for objects. Although nested classes can be very useful (as is shown in both [Madsen87] and [Buhr&Zarnke88]), this mechanism can be used by a programmer to break the encapsulation of objects. The next example is an example of class nesting. Both b1 and b2 can access the same variable "i" (instance variable of class A), i.e. they share the same variable "i" in their name space. Modification of this variable in, let's say b1, has an effect on the variable seen by a and b2. Instance variables (i.e. the variable "i") of an instance of class A (i.e. a) can directly be accessed by instances of class B (i.e. b1,b2) , even if there is no relation (sub or super) between these two classes.

```
class A extends SuperOfA
 i : Integer ;
 class B extends SuperOfB
  -- i is visible here !
 end B ;
end A ;
a : A ;
b1 : a.B ;
b2 : a.B
```

The two different forms of scoping (nested mixins and nested classes) do not mix very well. This is apparent when one uses class nesting and a non encapsulated form of inheritance at the same time (as is the case in BETA). Then, identifier look up is ambiguous, because in every class, two different contexts can be consulted: the surrounding block context or the context of the superclass. In the above class nesting example this ambiguity would be apparent if an instance variable with the name "i" were defined in the superclass of B. This problem is resolved by giving priority to one of both name spaces in case of a name conflict, e.g. by first looking in the superclass chain and then in the surrounding scope (here again the superclass chain must be searched and so on ...).

7. Mixin Methods

The fact that mixin application is realized by mere message passing, and that mixins can be applied dynamically has clear advantages. In this section we will give a simple example of dynamic mixin application, an example of late binding of mixins, and the role of the self pseudo-variable in mixin-methods.

Mixins can be combined to form chains of mixins that can be applied as a whole. Chains of mixins are useful to abstract over the construction of complex class hierarchies. A simple example is given making use of the Turtle classes shown earlier on. The idea is to construct different sorts of dashed drawing turtles without having to explicitly create a simple drawing variant, and a dashed drawing variant for each sort of turtle. This is, of course, the simplest example of how dynamic mixin application is used to abstract over the construction of an inheritance hierarchy.

```
MakeDashedDrawing Method: self MakeDrawingTurtle MakeDashed ;

DashedDrawingTurtle define: Turtle MakeDashedDrawing ;
DashedDrawingBoundedTurtle define: BoundedTurtle MakeDashedDrawing
```

In the example a chain of mixins is constructed as a method that successively applies two mixins. A declarative operator (as in [Bracha&Cook90]) to construct chains of mixins (or even entire hierarchies) could prove useful.

To illustrate the use of late binding of mixin attributes, consider a program in which two freely interchangeable implementations of point objects exist; one implementation based on polar coordinates and one based on cartesian coordinates. In some part of the program, points must be *locally* (for this part of the program only) restricted to bounded points, i.e. points that can not move outside given bounds. To do this, every point must have a mixin attribute to add methods and instance variables that implement this restriction. Each of the point implementations can have its own version of this mixin in order to take advantage of the particular point representation. For example, the mixin defined on polar coordinate represented points, can store its bounding points in polar coordinates in order to avoid excessive representation transformations. An anonymous point class (one of which we don't know whether it is a polar or a cartesian point; typically a parameter of a generic class) can now be asked to extend itself to a bounded point by selecting the bounds mixin by name. The appropriate version will be taken.

```
MakeCartesianPoint Mixin:
  [ x define: 0 ; y define: 0 ;
    move:aPoint Method: … ;

    MakeBounded Mixin:
            [ bound define: CartesianBasedBounds new;
              move:aPoint Method: …
            ]
  ] ;
```

```
MakePolarPoint Mixin:
  [ rho define: 0 ; theta define: 0*pi ;
    move:aPoint Method: … ;

    MakeBounded Mixin:
          [ bound define: PolarBasedBounds new;
            move:aPoint Method: …
          ]
  ] ;

--- suppose Point is bound to either a Polar or Cartesian Point
BoundedPoint define: Point makeBounded
```

The self pseudo-variable plays an important role in mixin methods. The receiver of a message that caused the execution of a mixin is the class that is being extended. Motivated by convenience, but somewhat different from the meaning of the self pseudovariable in a method and from what could be expected, the self pseudo variable used in the execution of a mixin-method contains a reference to the new class that is being defined (rather than to the old base class that is being extended). The contents of this variable can be stored for later use by instances of this class. Instances of a class often create other instances of the same class (e.g. recursive data structures). In a class-based language this is simply done by referring to the class's name. Since a mixin can be applied to a set of different base classes, there is no single name it can refer to.

Consider the definition of the cartesian and polar point classes. Suppose a method to add points was not included in the definition of these classes, and you do not want to destructively change these classes to add this method. What normally should have been defined in some abstract superclass of the two different point classes, you now want to define as an afterthought. The obvious thing to do is to make a mixin that adds the addition method so that it can be applied to both classes. The idea is to let the result of the addition method be a point of the same kind as the receiver point. This can be done by making use of the self pseudo variable in the mixin method that adds this extra behaviour. The contents of the self pseudo variable is used as initial value for the instance variable AddablePoint so that every instance of class AddablePolarPoint / AddableCartesianPoint has an instance variable referring to the class itself.

```
MakePointAddable Mixin:
  [ AddablePoint define: self ;
    sum:argument Method: AddablePoint x:(…) y:(…)
  ] ;

AddableCartesianPoint define: CartesianPoint MakePointAddable ;
AddablePolarPoint define: PolarPoint MakePointAddable
```

Note that the meaning of the self pseudo variable in a mixin-method is different from (and also has a slightly different purpose than) a construct such as "self class" in Smalltalk. In a situation where the sum message is sent to a subclass X of e.g. AddablePolarPoint, with the above construct the sum method still yields instances of class AddablePolarPoint. In a construct where a Smalltalk-like "self class" would be used this would yield instances of the subclass x.

8. Status, Evaluation, and Future Work

An implementation of Agora exists, built on top of Smalltalk. Agora is an experimental language, hence the implemented language differs on some points from what is described in the paper. However, mixin-methods are implemented according to the description given in the paper.

One important aspect omitted in this paper is the reflective architecture of Agora. This is an important issue since some of the features that one expects to find built into the programming language, we intend to introduce by making use of reflective facilities (in the style of [Kiczales,des Rivières&Bobrow91], [Jagannathan&Agha92]). This includes, but is not limited to, features such as resolution of name collisions, abstract methods, declarative combination and mutual exclusion of mixins. Experiments in this direction are under way.

Experience with the use of mixin-methods in Agora is somewhat limited to small scale experiments. The performance, both in time and memory, of the Smalltalk implementation is such that no large experiments have been attempted. Still some observations can be made.

Although the scope rules seem unfamiliar, newcomers (in our limited experience, of course) to Agora quickly take up the scope rules. The choice of the relative nesting of mixins is seen as an incentive to think about how abstract a mixin must be made.

Another observation is that due to the use of mixin-methods, different functionalities that are normally found in one class tend to be split up into different mixins. One could say that a class tends to be split up into different "views" or "perspectives". Also, there is a trade-off between overriding of mixin-methods and overriding of "ordinary" methods, i.e. a generic print method can be defined by overriding this method in each possible class, or by having a print mixin that is overridden in each class. The latter then corresponds to a printing view on each class. It has the advantage that otherwise unrelated classes can be extended with the same printing "view". The net effect is that programs are written by first defining all kinds of mixins, and then combining these mixins to classes as needed. Larger experiments are needed to further determine how mixin-methods will be used in practice.

It should be stressed that we think the importance of mixin-methods is in their ability to express otherwise tangled inheritance hierarchies in a more intelligible way. Central to this is the notion of applicability of mixins. In its current form, however, the applicability of a mixin can only be based on the absence or presence of implementation details in possible base classes. Further work to see how other sorts of constraints on the applicability of mixins can be (declaratively) expressed, is needed.

9. Related Work

Our work is an extension of mixin-based inheritance as was introduced in [Bracha&Cook90]. To their work we add dynamic application of mixins, mixins as attributes and the resulting scope rules for nested mixins. The extra polymorphism gained by viewing mixins as attributes seems to us an important enhancement to mixin-based inheritance. In contrast with [Bracha&Cook90] the mixin-methods used in Agora remain untyped at the moment.

The relation to nested classes [Buhr&Zarnke88][Madsen87] has been discussed above. The correspondence between so called virtual superclasses [Madsen&Møller-Pedersen89] in BETA, and mixins has already been noted [Bracha92]. The same remarks as in the previous paragraph apply to the relation between mixin-methods and virtual superclasses.

Agora was primarily designed as a prototype-based language. Mixin-based inheritance can also be applied to prototype-based programming languages. New prototypes are created by taking an existing object and extending it with a set of variables and methods. Similar to mixins in a class based language we can identify a base-object and a set of extensions. Here as well, extensions can be considered as separate abstractions. The terminology mixins and mixin-application from the class-based case can be retained.

Once again, we must consider the fact that a mixin can be seen as an attribute of an object (or an instance attribute of a class). In this case too, an object (the prototype) is extended by selecting one of its mixin-attributes. So, in contrast with other prototype-based languages (e.g. Self [Ungar&Smith87]) an object plays a more "active" role in the extension process. This is especially important if one considers the possibility to override inherited mixin-attributes. The full extent of combining mixins and prototypes is outside the scope of this paper.

Having mixins as instance attributes is very similar to "enhancements" described in [Hendler86]. We agree that being able to associate functionality with instances rather than classes has several advantages. The advantages of dynamic classification have also been discussed in the classifier approach of [Hamer92]. Both approaches lack the equivalent of late binding of mixin attributes. Although our approach lacks the equivalent of having classifiers as first-class values (which would amount to first class mixin "patterns").

10. Conclusion

Mixin-methods are proposed as a uniform framework to control and make abstraction of the way inheritance hierarchies are constructed. Central to this are the notions of applicability of mixins and dynamic application of mixins. Due to the treatment of mixins as attributes, mixins can be inherited and overridden. This introduces an extra level of abstraction in the way classes are extended that is not available (to the authors' best knowledge) in present day object-oriented languages.

The scope rules for nested mixins were discussed. On the one hand having mixins as attributes naturally leads to nested mixins, on the other hand an important factor in the applicability of a mixin to a base class is the availability of the necessary implementation details in this base class. The scope rules for nested mixins integrate both concerns. They are such that an Agora programmer has a fine-grained control over the amount of implementation details of the base class a mixin has access to.

While similar issues have been discussed elsewhere, no work has been found that discusses all of the above issues in one single framework.

11. Acknowledgments

The paper benefited from discussions with Franz Hauck and Michel Tilman. The authors thank Karel Driesen and Serge Demeyer for giving useful comments on an earlier version of the text, and Geert Bollen for proofreading. We also thank the anonymous referees for their helpful comments.

12. References

[Bracha&Cook90] G. Bracha and W. Cook. Mixin-based Inheritance. In Proc. of ACM Joint OOPSLA/ECOOP'90 Conference Proceedings, pp.303-311, ACM Press 1990.

[Bracha92] G. Bracha. The Programming Language Jigsaw: Mixins, Modularity and Multiple Inheritance. PhD thesis, Department of Computer Science, University of Utah, March 1992.

[Buhr&Zarnke88] P.A. Buhr, C.R. Zarnke. Nesting in an Object-Oriented Language is NOT for the Birds. In Proc. of ECOOP'88 European Conference on Object-Oriented Programming, pp.128-143, Springer-Verlag 1988.

[Cook87] S. Cook. Panel Varieties of inheritance. In OOPSLA'87 Addendum to the proceedings, pp.35-40, ACM Press 1987.

[Hamer92]   J. Hamer. Un-Mixing Inheritance with Classifiers. In Proc. of
ECOOP'92 Workshop on Multiple Inheritance and Multiple
Subtyping, available as Working Paper WP-23 Dept. of Computer
Science and Information Systems, Univ. of Jyväskylä, pp.6-9,
1992.

[Hendler86]   J. Hendler. Enhancement for Multiple Inheritance. In Proc. of
Object-Oriented Programming Workshop 86, Sigplan Notices Vol
21 (10), pp.98-106, October 1986.

[Jagannathan&Agha92] S. Jagannathan, G. Agha. A Reflective Model of Inheritance. In
Proc, of ECOOP'92 European Conference on Object-Oriented
Programming, pp.350-371, Springer-Verlag 1992.

[Kiczales,des Rivières&Bobrow91] G. Kiczales, J. des Rivières and D.G. Bobrow. The
Art of the Meta-Object Protocol. MIT Press, 1991.

[Lang&Pearlmutter86] K. J. Lang and B. A. Pearlmutter. Oaklisp: an Object-Oriented
Scheme with First Class Types. In Proc. of ACM Conf. on Object-
Oriented Programming, Languages, and Systems, pp.30-37, ACM
Press 1986.

[Madsen87]   O. L. Madsen. Block Structure and Object-Oriented Languages.
Research Directions in Object-Oriented Programming B. Shriver and
P. Wegner (eds), pp 113-128, MIT Press 1987.

[Madsen&Møller-Pedersen89] O. L. Madsen B. and B. Møller-Pedersen. Virtual Classes,
A powerful mechanism in object-oriented programming. In Proc. of
ACM Conf. on Object-Oriented Programming, Languages, and
Systems, pp.397-406, ACM Press 1989.

[Snyder87]   A. Snyder. Inheritance and the Development of Encapsulated
Software Components. In Research Directions in Object-Oriented
Programming B. Shriver and P. Wegner (eds), pp 165-188, MIT
Press 1987.

[Stein,Lieberman,Ungar89] L.A. Stein, H. Lieberman and, D. Ungar. A Shared View of
Sharing: The Treaty of Orlando. In Object-Oriented Concepts,
Databases, and Applications, Won Kim, Frederick H. Lochovsky
Eds, pp.31-48, ACM Press 1989.

[Ungar&Smith87]   D. Ungar & R. B. Smith. Self: The Power of Simplicity. In Proc.
of ACM Conf. on Object-Oriented Programming, Languages, and
Systems, pp 227-242, ACM Press 1987.

[Wegner&Zdonik88] P. Wegner, S. B. Zdonik. Inheritance as an Incremental
Modification Mechanism, or What Like is and Isn't Like. In Proc.
of ECOOP'88 European Conference on Object-Oriented
Programming, pp.55-77, Springer-Verlag 1988.

Solving the Inheritance Anomaly in Concurrent Object-Oriented Programming*

José Meseguer

SRI International, Menlo Park, CA 94025, and
Center for the Study of Language and Information,
Stanford University, Stanford, CA 94305

Abstract. The *inheritance anomaly* [23] refers to the serious difficulty in combining inheritance and concurrency in a simple and satisfactory way within a concurrent object-oriented language. The problem is closely connected with the need to impose *synchronization constraints* on the acceptance of a message by an object. In most concurrent object-oriented languages this synchronization is achieved by *synchronization code* controlling the acceptance of messages by objects. Synchronization code is often hard to inherit and tends to require extensive redefinitions. The solutions that have appeared so far in the literature to alleviate this problem seem to implicitly assume that better, more reusable, mechanisms are needed to create and structure synchronization code. The approach taken in this paper is to consider the inheritance anomaly as a problem *caused* by the very presence of synchronization code. The goal is then to completely eliminate synchronization code. This is achieved by using order-sorted rewriting logic, an abstract model of concurrent computation that is machine-independent and extremely fine grain, and that can be used directly to program concurrent object-oriented systems. Our proposed solution involves a distinction between two different notions of inheritance, a type-theoretic one called *class* inheritance, and a notion called *module* inheritance that supports reuse and modification of code. These two different notions address two different ways in which the inheritance anomaly can appear; for each of them we propose declarative solutions in which no explicit synchronization code is ever used.

1 Introduction

The term "inheritance anomaly" has been coined by Satoshi Matsuoka and Akinori Yonezawa [23] to describe what is widely recognized as a serious difficulty in combining inheritance and concurrency in a simple and satisfactory way within a concurrent object-oriented language. Early references pointing out serious difficulties in this area include [20, 32, 35, 6].

* Supported by Office of Naval Research Contracts N00014-90-C-0086 and N00014-92-C-0518, and by the Information Technology Promotion Agency, Japan, as a part of the R & D of Basic Technology for Future Industries "New Models for Software Architecture" sponsored by NEDO (New Energy and Industrial Technology Development Organization).

O.M. Nierstrasz (Ed.): ECOOP '93, LNCS 707, pp. 220-246, 1993.
© Springer-Verlag Berlin Heidelberg 1993

The problem is closely connected with the need to impose *synchronization constraints* on the acceptance of a message by an object. A well-known example is a bounded buffer, where a **put** message should be accepted only if the buffer is not full, and a **get** message should be accepted only if the buffer is not empty.

In most concurrent object-oriented languages this synchronization is achieved by special code controlling how the messages will be accepted. The code performing such control is called *synchronization code*. The problem is that often this kind of synchronization code is hard to inherit and tends to require extensive redefinitions. This difficulty has been illustrated by a number of examples in the literature. Indeed, the problem is considered so thorny that a number of well-known concurrent object-oriented languages such as POOL/T [6], Act1 [22], and ABCL/1 [37] have given up supporting inheritance as a basic language feature.

A number of proposals to alleviate this problem have appeared in the literature, including [20, 35, 33, 7, 31, 36, 23, 19, 9]. It seems fair to say that, although some good progress has been made, the problem is considered far from solved. Matsuoka and Yonezawa [23] present an excellent analysis and survey of the anomaly by means of a series of increasingly more difficult examples that show where some of the proposed solutions break down. We adopt those examples in this paper to illustrate the characteristics of our own solution.

Somehow implicit in all the solutions that have appeared in the literature is the assumption that better, more reusable, mechanisms are needed to create and structure synchronization code. Indeed, what the different languages and solutions proposed so far seem to have in common is the presence of two different kinds of code, namely usual code for changing the state of an object by the reception of a message, and synchronization code to control the invocation of the usual code. The default assumption is that if no synchronization code is given the usual code can always be invoked.

The approach taken in this paper is to consider the inheritance anomaly as a problem *caused* by the very presence of synchronization code. The logical solution if we take this hypothesis seriously is to *completely eliminate* synchronization code. This is done by adopting a declarative style of programming in which the effects of messages on objects are described by logical axioms called *rewrite rules*. Each rewrite rule characterizes circumstances under which a concurrent change can take place in the system, as well as the appropriate change in such circumstances. Since change can only take place by application of rewrite rules, the appropriate conditions for the reception of messages are indeed *implicit* in the rewrite rules themselves. Therefore, no explicit synchronization code is ever needed, and the problem of how to inherit such code—which constitutes the inheritance anomaly—disappears. In this way, no difficulty remains for having a fully satisfactory integration of inheritance and concurrency in an object-oriented language. Therefore, rather than talking about *solving* the inheritance anomaly it would have been more accurate to speak of *eliminating* the anomaly.

Our proposed solution involves a distinction between two different ways in which the inheritance anomaly can appear, namely:

1. the case in which the behavior of messages previously defined in superclasses is not contradicted by their behavior in a subclass (adding a new message get2—to get two elements at once—in a subclass of the bounded buffer class is a typical example), and

2. the case in which the behavior of messages previously defined is in fact modified (adding a gget message that acts just as a get message, except that it cannot be accepted if the last message received was a put is a typical example).

These two cases can be best distinguished by introducing a precise distinction between two different notions of inheritance which, unfortunately, tend to be conflated in the common use of this term:

1. a type-theoretic one, whose purpose is the taxonomic *classification* of objects and in which the behavior of messages in a superclass is never contradicted by their behavior in a subclass (although additional behavior can be exhibited by subclasses, including the introduction of new rules, new messages, and new attributes); we call this notion *class* inheritance, and restrict the notion of *subclass* only to pairs of classes for which this relation holds;

2. a notion called *module* inheritance that supports reuse and modification of code and in which the behavior of messages previously defined in a class can indeed be modified. The key idea is to view the two *modules* in which the relevant old and new classes were introduced as standing in a (module) inheritance relation, not the classes themselves.

For each of the two cases in which the inheritance anomaly can manifest itself, these two inheritance mechanisms plus the use of rewrite rules provide a respective declarative solution in which no explicit synchronization code is ever used. The case solved by class inheritance is clearly the simplest. In the rewriting logic abstract model of concurrent computation [25, 26], the code for a class is an unstructured *set* of rewrite rules, with each rule acting independently of the others. For a subclass in our sense, this set of rules is typically enlarged by adding some new rules, but this in no way alters the previously given rules which remain exactly as before and are inherited from the superclass or superclasses.

The structure of the paper is as follows. In Section 2 the semantic framework used throughout the paper, namely rewriting logic, is introduced informally by means of examples (a precise definition of the rules of rewriting logic is given in Appendix A). In Section 3 the syntax of Maude's object-oriented modules [26] used to present the examples discussed in the paper is first used; it is shown how such modules are just sugared versions of theories in rewriting logic and their de-sugared versions are presented. In Section 4 the semantics of *class inheritance* is presented in terms of the order-sorted type structure of rewriting logic and shown to completely eliminate any anomalies that can be described in terms of such a notion inheritance. Section 5 discusses module inheritance and examples that fit within that category and shows how they can be solved in a way that does not involve any synchronization code nor, more generally, any concurrency considerations whatsoever. Section 6 recapitulates and summarizes the key characteristics of the solution that we propose. Section 7 discusses implementation issues, and Section 8 makes some concluding remarks.

2 Rewriting Logic as a Semantic Framework for Concurrent Object-Oriented Programming

We informally introduce rewriting logic by means of a simple example and explain how it provides a language-independent semantic framework for concurrent object-oriented programming and, more generally, for concurrent programming. A precise definition of the rules of rewriting logic is given in Appendix A; a detailed account of rewriting logic and its semantics, and of how it unifies many existing models of concurrency can be found in [25].

Rewriting logic is a logic to reason correctly about the evolution in time of a concurrent system. The distributed state of a concurrent system is represented as a *term* whose subterms represent the different components of the concurrent state. Typically, however, the *structure* of the concurrent state may have a variety of equivalent term representations because it satisfies certain *structural laws*. For example, in a concurrent object-oriented system the concurrent state, which is usually called a *configuration*, has typically the structure of a *multiset* made up of objects and messages. Therefore, we can view configurations as built up by a binary multiset union operator which we can represent with empty syntax as

```
subsorts Object Msg < Configuration .
op __ : Configuration Configuration -> Configuration
                                [assoc comm id: null] .
```

where the multiset union operator __ is declared to satisfy the structural laws of associativity and commutativity and to have identity null. The subtype declaration[2]

```
subsorts Object Msg < Configuration .
```

states that objects and messages are singleton multiset configurations, so that more complex configurations are generated out of them by multiset union.[3]

As a consequence, we can abstractly represent the configuration of a typical concurrent object-oriented system as an equivalence class [t] modulo the structural laws of associativity, commutativity and identity obeyed by the multiset union operator of a term expressing a union of objects and messages, i.e., as a multiset of objects and messages.

---

[2] For our treatment of the inheritance anomaly it is very important to use a typed version of rewriting logic that supports subtypes; typing aspects are further explained in Sections 3 and 4.

[3] Of course, we do not want two different objects with the same name in any such configuration, but this can be easily enforced (see [26, Section 4.4]).

An *object* in a given state is also represented as a term

$$\langle O : C \mid a_1 : v_1, \ldots, a_n : v_n \rangle$$

where O is the object's name or identifier, C is its class, the a_i's are the names of the object's *attribute identifiers*, and the v_i's are the corresponding *values*. The set of all the attribute-value pairs of an object state is formed by repeated application of the binary union operator $\_,\_$ which also obeys structural laws of associativity, commutativity, and identity; i.e., the order of the attribute-value pairs of an object is immaterial.

For example, a bounded buffer whose elements are numbers can be represented as an object with three attributes: a `contents` attribute that is a list of numbers of length less than or equal to the bound, and attributes in and out that are numbers counting how many elements have been put in the buffer or got from it since the buffer's creation. For example, a typical bounded buffer state can be

```
< B : BdBuff | contents: 9 5 6 8, in: 7, out: 3 >
```

Concurrent interaction with the buffer can be achieved by means of put and get messages, with an appropriate reply message from the buffer after a get. We can for example assume the syntax

```
put_in_ : Nat OId -> Msg .
getfrom_replyto_ : OId OId -> Msg .
to_elt-in_is_ : OId OId Nat -> Msg .
```

for puts, gets, and replies, respectively, where Nat is the type of natural numbers, and OId is the type of object identifiers, and where in each message's syntactic form each underbar must be filled with an element of the appropriate type as indicated by the list of types after the ":" and with the entire message being of course of type Msg.

In rewriting logic sentences are rewrite rules of the form

$$[t] \longrightarrow [t']$$

or, more generally, conditional rewrite rules of the form

$$r : [t] \longrightarrow [t'] \quad \text{if} \quad [u_1] \longrightarrow [v_1] \wedge \ldots \wedge [u_k] \longrightarrow [v_k].$$

What those sentences axiomatize are the basic *local transitions* that are possible in a concurrent system. For example, in a concurrent object-oriented system including bounded buffers that communicate through messages the local transitions of bounded buffers are axiomatized by rewrite rules of the form

```
(put E in B) < B : BdBuff | contents: Q, in: N, out: M > =>
   < B : BdBuff | contents: E Q, in: N + 1, out: M >
   if (N - M) < bound .
```

```
(getfrom B replyto I)
   < B : BdBuff | contents: Q E, in: N, out: M > =>
   < B : BdBuff | contents: Q, in: N, out: M + 1 >
   (to I elt-in B is E) .
```

where E, N, M range over natural numbers and Q over lists. The first rule specifies the conditions under which a put message can be accepted (namely, that N - M is smaller than bound) and the corresponding effect; the second rule does the same for get messages (note that the requirement that the buffer must not be empty is implicit in the pattern Q E for the contents attribute).

What the rules of deduction of rewriting logic support is sound and complete reasoning about the concurrent transitions that are possible in a concurrent system whose basic local transitions are axiomatized by given rewrite rules. That is, the sentence $[t] \longrightarrow [t']$ is provable in the logic using the rewrite rules that axiomatize the system as axioms if and only if the concurrent transition $[t] \longrightarrow [t']$ is possible in the system. A precise account of the model theory of rewriting logic fully consistent with the above system-oriented interpretation, and proving soundness, completeness, and the existence of initial models is given in [25].

The intuitive idea behind the rules of rewriting logic in Appendix A is that proofs in rewriting logic exactly correspond to concurrent computations in the concurrent system being axiomatized, and that such concurrent computation can be understood as concurrent rewritings *modulo* the structural laws obeyed by the concurrent system in question. In the case of a concurrent object-oriented system such structural laws include the associativity, commutativity and identity of the union operators __ and _,_, and this means that the rules can be applied regardless of order or parentheses. For example, a configuration such as

```
(put 7 in B1) < B2 : BdBuff | contents: 2 3, in: 7, out: 5 >
< B1 : BdBuff | contents: nil, in: 2, out: 2 >
(getfrom B2 replyto C)
```

(where the buffers are assumed to have a large enough bound) can be rewritten into the configuration

```
< B2 : BdBuff | contents: 2, in: 7, out: 6 >
< B1 : BdBuff | contents: 7, in: 3, out: 2 >
(to C elt-in B2 is 3)
```

by applying concurrently the two rewrite rules[4] for put and get modulo associativity and commutativity.

Intuitively, we can think of messages as "traveling" to come into contact with the objects to which they are sent and then causing "communication events" by application of rewrite rules. In rewriting logic, this traveling is accounted for in a very abstract way by the structural laws of associativity, commutativity and identity. This abstract level supports both synchronous and asynchronous

---

[4] Note that rewrite rules for natural number addition have also been applied.

communication [25, 26], and provides great freedom and flexibility to consider a variety of alternative implementations at lower levels.

For the purposes of the present paper rewriting logic should be regarded as a language-independent semantic framework which, by itself, does not make any commitments to specific features or synchronization styles, and in which many different concurrent object-oriented languages could be given a precise mathematical semantics. However, to ease the exposition and make our discussions concrete, the examples used will be written in the syntax of the Maude language. Since, as we shall see, Maude modules are nothing but sugared versions of theories in rewriting logic, this does not matter much. Nevertheless, for purposes of efficient implementation Maude's language design introduces specific syntactic restrictions that are discussed in Section 7.

3 Maude's Object-Oriented Modules and their Translation into Rewrite Theories

We illustrate the syntax of object-oriented modules with a module for bounded FIFO buffers; we then make explicit the rewrite theory of which the module is a sugared version. We assume as previously defined a parameterized data type[5] LIST that is instantiated to form lists of natural numbers. We assume bound to be a natural number, but we do not care which one[6]

```
omod BD-BUFF is
  protecting NAT .
  protecting LIST[Nat] .
  class BdBuff | contents: List, in: Nat, out: Nat .
  initially contents: nil, in: 0, out: 0 .
  msg put_in_ : Nat OId -> Msg .
  msg getfrom_replyto_ : OId OId -> Msg .
  msg to_elt-in_is_ : OId OId Nat -> Msg .
  vars B I : OId .
  vars E N M : Nat .
  var Q : List .
  rl (put E in B) < B : BdBuff | contents: Q, in: N, out: M > =>
       < B : BdBuff | contents: E Q, in: N + 1, out: M >
       if (N - M) < bound .
  rl (getfrom B replyto I)
```

---

[5] Algebraic data types are also regarded as rewrite theories; their equations are assumed to be Church-Rosser and are used as rewrite rules. In Maude, such data types are declared in *functional modules* [26] and belong to a functional sublanguage very similar to OBJ3 [16]. By contrast, rules in object-oriented modules typically fail to be Church-Rosser, and in some cases may never terminate.

[6] In Maude this module should be most naturally parameterized by two parameters, namely the type of data elements and the size bound; however, to simplify the example we avoid parameterization.

```
        < B : BdBuff | contents: Q E, in: N, out: M > =>
        < B : BdBuff | contents: Q, in: N, out: M + 1 >
        (to I elt-in B is E) .
  endom
```

After the keyword **class**, the name of the class—in this case **BdBuff**—is given, followed by a "|" and by a list of pairs of the form **a:** S separated by commas, where **a** is an attribute identifier and S is the type inside which the values of such an attribute identifier must range in the given class. In this example, the attributes are the **contents**, and the **in** and **out** counters. The **initially** clause states that when buffers are created they are empty and have their two counters set to 0. The messages and rewrite rules are identical to those in Section 2, but the type of the variables in the rules has now been made explicit.

We give below the essential aspects[7] of the translation of this module into a rewrite theory. Since in Maude rewrite theories themselves correspond to what are called *system modules* with keywords **mod** and **endm**, we express this translation in a system module notation.

```
mod BD-BUFF# is
   extending CONFIGURATION .
   protecting NAT .
   protecting LIST[Nat] .
   sorts <BdBuff BdBuff .
   subsort BdBuff < Object .
   subsort <BdBuff < CId .
   subsorts Nat List < Value .
   op BdBuff : -> <BdBuff .
   op put_in_ : Nat OId -> Msg .
   op getfrom_replyto_ : OId OId -> Msg .
   op to_elt-in_is_ : OId OId Nat -> Msg .
   var X : <BdBuff .
   vars B I : OId .
   vars E N M : Nat .
   var Q : List .
   var ATTS : Attributes .
   sct < B : X | contents: Q, in: N, out: M, ATTS > : BdBuff .
   rl (put E in B) < B : X | contents: Q, in: N, out: M, ATTS >
        => < B : X | contents: E Q, in: N + 1, out: M, ATTS >
        if (N - M) < bound .
   rl (getfrom B replyto I)
        < B : X | contents: Q E, in: N, out: M, ATTS > =>
        < B : X | contents: Q, in: N, out: M + 1, ATTS >
        (to I elt-in B is E) .
  endm
```

---

[7] We omit the rewrite rules for object initialization associated with the **initially** clause; on the matter of object creation see [26, Section 4.4].

In the translation process, the most basic structure shared by all object-oriented modules is made explicit by the CONFIGURATION system module which they all import. The details of that module can be found in [26, Section 4] and need not concern us here. It is enough to say that they make precise the essential properties of configurations already discussed in Section 2, namely that they are multisets of objects and messages, that objects have the special syntax already discussed and each has a set of attribute-value pairs whose values are in a sort Value, etc. In addition, appropriate messages and rewrite rules to query the attributes of an object are also included in the CONFIGURATION module.

We assume that rewrite theories have an *order-sorted* type structure [14]; this means that they are typed (we call their types *sorts*), that types can have subtypes (which can be declared by *subsort* declarations) and that operation symbols (which are declared with the types of their arguments and the type of their result) can be overloaded. In addition to the order-sorted syntax, a rewrite theory declares the relevant structural laws so that rewriting can take place modulo those axioms, and of course the rewrite rules of the theory. In the CONFIGURATION module the operators __ and _,_ for forming unions of configurations and of attribute-value pairs respectively have both been declared with structural laws of associativity, commutativity, and identity.

The translation of a given object-oriented module extends the basic structure of configurations with the classes, data sorts, messages and rules introduced by the module. In particular, this extension gives rise to a series of subsort declarations. All sorts originally declared as values of attributes are now included as subsorts of the Value sort. Similarly, all classes, in this case BdBuff, are declared as subsorts of the Object sort. Note that, in addition, a subsort <BdBuff of the sort CId of *class identifiers* has been introduced. The purpose of this subsort is to range over the class identifiers of the subclasses of BdBuff. For the moment, no such subclasses have been introduced; therefore, at present the only constant of sort <BdBuff is the class identifier BdBuff. Notice the slight ambiguity introduced by this notation, since now BdBuff denotes *two different things*: a *sort name* in the sort structure of a module, and a *data element* in a subsort of a data type of class identifiers. However, this ambiguity is harmless— the context will always make explicit the intended sense—and could in any case be easily avoided by an appropriate notational convention; for example, by adopting quotes for the identifier use.

Objects of sort BdBuff are defined by a predicate called a *sort constraint* and introduced by the keyword sct which they must satisfy. In this case the sort constraint requires that the class identifier must have sort <BdBuff and that it must have among its attributes an attribute called contents whose value must be a list of natural numbers, and attributes called in and out whose values must be natural numbers. For more on sort constraints see [27, 26].

A trivial observation that is however key to our solution of the inheritance anomaly is that

If a variable x is declared to have a sort s, then it can range over elements of that sort or of any of its subsorts.

This observation is used crucially in the above translation of the rewrite rules, so that the translated rules become fully *general* in the sense that they can apply not only to objects in the original class where they were defined, but also—as further explained in Section 4—to objects in its subclasses. For example, the rewrite rules originally introduced in the **BD-BUFF** module have been modified to make them applicable not only to objects whose class identifier is exactly **BdBuff**, but also to other objects with class identifiers for subclasses of **BdBuff**, which may in addition have other attributes, i.e., indeed to all the objects of the class **BdBuff**.

Specifically, whenever a class identifier C appears in the lefthand side of a rule declared in an object-oriented module, in its translation we understand that a variable ranging over <C—which can match the constant C and any other constants C' that could be introduced later in subsorts <C' of <C for subclasses C' of C—is meant instead.[8] In addition, in the translated form of the rules variables of the form **ATTS**, which match a set of additional attribute-value pairs, have been added to the patterns of objects. In this way the translated rules will also apply in subclasses where more attributes have been declared.

4 Class Inheritance

Our generalization of rewrite rules in the previous translation so that they can apply not only to objects in the original class but also to objects in any of its subclasses is motivated by a sharp distinction between two different notions of inheritance: *class inheritance* and *module inheritance*. At a type-theoretic level of data sorts and object classes, sort and class inheritance provides a means of *classifying* data and objects into taxonomic *hierarchies*. At the level of modules, module inheritance supports modularity, reuse, and ease of evolution by arranging modules into hierarchies and by providing a rich algebra of module compositionality operations.

Class inheritance is directly supported by the order-sorted type structure of rewriting logic. As we shall see in this section, a subclass declaration C < C' in an object-oriented module is just a particular case of a subsort declaration C < C'. As a consequence of the order-sorted type structure, the effect of a subclass declaration is that the attributes, messages and rules of all the superclasses as well as the newly defined attributes, messages and rules of the subclass characterize the structure and behavior of the objects in the subclass. An object in the subclass behaves exactly as any object in any of the superclasses, but it may exhibit additional behavior due to the introduction of new attributes, messages and rules in the subclass.

This notion of class inheritance is considerably more restrictive than, and should be sharply distinguished from, the notion of inheritance adopted in prac-

---

[8] This way of generalizing rules so that they can be inherited was pointed out in Section 4.4 of [24]; I am indebted to Timothy Winkler for later suggesting to me the elegant sort structure of the sorts <C as a better alternative to a more cumbersome identifier data type definition.

tice by most object-oriented languages, where the behavior of a message (sometimes also called a *method*) in a subclass may be different form its behavior in a superclass and where mechanisms to change message behavior by what is called message (or method) "specialization" or "derivation" are typically provided.

The need for such message specializations often appears in practice. However, in our approach the mechanisms for message specialization that change the previous behavior in a superclass belong to module inheritance and are cleanly separated for the more restrictive notion of class inheritance that we propose. The advantages of this separation are many; some will become apparent in this paper, others are discussed in [26], and still others will be the subject of a future paper.

For the moment we can point out that in this way we avoid doing violence to class inheritance by forcing upon it the job of modifying code. As a consequence, we can have great flexibility of code reuse *and* a precise and satisfactory *order-sorted* semantics for subclasses that respects the intuitions of what it means to *classify* objects. By contrast, in approaches that conflate these two equally laudable goals, flexibility of code reuse is achieved at the heavy price of emptying the notion of class of most of its conceptual value.

One important advantage of our notion of class inheritance is that *rewrite rules are always inherited downwards* in the class hierarchy. We can illustrate this point by defining a subclass of BdBuff with a new message get2 to get two elements of the buffer at once. We can introduce such a subclass in the module

```
omod BD-BUFF2 is
  extending BD-BUFF .
  class BdBuff2 .
  subclass BdBuff2 < BdBuff .
  msg get2from_replyto_ : OId OId -> Msg .
  msg to_2elts-in_are_ : OId OId List -> Msg .
  vars B I : OId .
  vars E E' N M : Nat .
  var Q : List .
  rl (get2from B replyto I)
      < B : BdBuff2 | contents: Q E' E, in: N, out: M > =>
      < B : BdBuff2 | contents: Q, in: N, out: M + 2 >
      (to I 2elts-in B are E E') .
      ***the requirement of having at least two elements
      ***in the buffer is implicit in the pattern Q E' E
  endom
```

The translation into a rewrite theory is given by the system module

```
mod BD-BUFF2# is
  extending BD-BUFF# .
  sorts <BdBuff2 BdBuff2 .
  subsort BdBuff2 < BdBuff .
  subsort <BdBuff2 < <BdBuff .
```

```
op BdBuff2 : -> <BdBuff2 .
op get2from_replyto_ : OId OId -> Msg .
op to_2elts-in_are_ : OId OId List -> Msg .
var Y : <BdBuff2 .
vars B I : OId .
vars E E' N M : Nat .
var Q : List .
var ATTS : Attributes .
sct < B : Y | contents: Q, in: N, out: M, ATTS > : BdBuff2 .
rl (get2from B replyto I)
    < B : Y | contents: Q E' E, in: N, out: M, ATTS > =>
    < B : Y | contents: Q, in: N, out: M + 2, ATTS >
    (to I 2elts-in B are E E') .
endm
```

The consequence of this definition is that buffers in BdBuff2 will react to put
and get messages exactly like buffers in BdBuff. This is because the rewrite rules
in BD-BUFF# have a variable X ranging over class identifiers in <BdBuff, and in
the module BD-BUFF2# there is a subsort declaration

```
subsort <BdBuff2 < <BdBuff .
```

Therefore, the variable X can match the constant BdBuff2 of sort <BdBuff2, so
that the rules in BD-BUFF# also apply to objects in BdBuff2.

The only difference between both classes is that, unlike buffers in BdBuff,
buffers in BdBuff2 can react to get2 messages by sending the two rightmost
elements if they exist. Note that, due to the fact that Y has sort <BdBuff2, the
above rule will *not* match bounded buffers in BdBuff that are not in BdBuff2.

In the same vein, we could have defined additional messages, such as for
example a message empty? that checks whether the buffer is empty or not, and
could have introduced additional attributes, which could appear in the rules for
those new messages without any problem.

An interesting example involving *multiple* class inheritance is that of a lockable bounded buffer. The idea is to have a class of lockable objects in general,
and then define lockable bounded buffers by multiple inheritance from bounded
buffers and from lockable objects. When the object is locked no messages except
unlock should have any effect. Unlike the standard solution, which would add a
Boolean-valued attribute to ascertain the locked or unlocked state of an object
and would violate class inheritance in our sense, our solution is simpler and fully
respects our notion of class inheritance. The standard solution could be achieved
by means of module inheritance mechanisms to be discussed in Section 5.

The basic idea is to view the locking of an object as a kind of *metamorphosis*
that changes the nature of the object. This suggests that the class of the object
in fact *changes* when being locked. This can be easily accomplished by assuming
that the sort CId of class identifiers has subsorts UCId, and QCId of unquoted
and quoted identifiers together with quote and unquote operators

```
'_ : UCId -> QCId
unquote: QCId -> UCId
```

each inverse of the other, and by adopting the syntactic convention that the
class identifiers introduced by users are always unquoted.[9] We can then define a
module

```
omod LOCKABLE is
  class Lockable .
  msgs lock, unlock : OId OId -> Msg .
  var O : OId .
  var ATTS : Attributes .
  rl lock(O)
        < O : Lockable | ATTS > => < O : 'Lockable | ATTS > .
        ***the class changes from Lockable to 'Lockable
  rl unlock(O)
        < O : 'Lockable | ATTS > => < O : Lockable | ATTS > .
        ***the class changes from 'Lockable to Lockable
endom
```

whose corresponding translation into a rewrite theory is

```
mod LOCKABLE# is
  extending CONFIGURATION .
  sorts <Lockable Lockable .
  subsort Lockable < Object .
  subsort <Lockable < UCId .
  op Lockable : -> <Lockable .
  ops lock, unlock : OId -> Msg .
  var Z : <Lockable .
  vars O : OId .
  var ATTS : Attributes .
  sct < O : Z | ATTS > : Lockable .
  rl lock(O) < O : Z | ATTS > => < O : 'Z | ATTS > .
  rl unlock(O) < O : 'Z | ATTS > => < O : Z | ATTS > .
endm
```

Now we can define lockable bounded buffers by multiple inheritance as follows

```
omod LOCKABLE-BD-BUFF is
  extending LOCKABLE .
  extending BD-BUFF .
  class LckblBdBuff .
  subclasses LckblBdBuff < Lockable BdBuff .
endom
```

---

[9] Therefore, if this convention were to be followed, all the previous occurrences of the
sort CId should be replaced by UCId.

We can pause for a moment and ask how rewriting logic and the notion of class inheritance that we have proposed contribute to solving the inheritance anomaly in the case where the behavior of messages in superclasses is not modified. An answer to this question can be summarized as follows:

1. Programming a class with rewrite rules completely eliminates any need for special code to enforce synchronization constraints. We only need to give rewrite rules specifying the desired behavior. The effect of synchronization is obtained *automatically* and *implicitly* by the very definition of deduction in the logic.

2. If a class C is a subclass of other previously defined classes in the precise sense that we have given to class inheritance in our framework, then all the rewrite rules defining messages in the superclasses are automatically inherited without any change whatsoever. Therefore, for cases of inheritance that fall within our precise technical notion of class inheritance, the inheritance anomaly *completely vanishes*.

We now need to consider cases where the inheritance anomaly appears in the context of message (or method) "specializations" that change the original behavior. In our framework those cases fall outside class inheritance and are dealt with by different mechanisms of module inheritance.

5 Module Inheritance and Message Specialization

In programming practice one often wants to *modify* the original code of an application to adapt it to a different situation. The class inheritance mechanism as we have defined it will *not* help in such cases: it is not its purpose, and forcing it to modify code would only muddle everything and destroy its semantics. Instead, what we propose is to provide different *module inheritance* mechanisms to do the job of code modification. This distinction between a type-theoretic level of classes (more generally sorts) and a level of modules which, in our case, are theories in rewriting logic was already clearly made in the FOOPS language (besides the original paper [12], see also [17] for a very good discussion of inheritance issues and of the class-module distinction in the context of FOOPS), and indeed goes back to the distinction between sorts and modules in OBJ [16].

In Maude, code in modules can be modified or adapted for new purposes by means of a variety of module operations—and combinations of several such operations in *module expressions*—whose overall effect is to provide a very flexible style of software reuse that can be summarized under the name of *module inheritance*. Module operations of this kind include:

1. *importing* a module in a **protecting**, **extending**, or **using** mode;
2. *adding new rewrite rules* to an imported module;
3. *renaming* some of the sorts or operations of a module;
4. *instantiating* a parameterized module;
5. *adding modules* to form their union;

6. *redefining* an operator—for example a message—so that its syntax and sort requirements are kept intact, but its semantics can be changed by discarding previously given rules involving the operator so that new rules or equations can then be given in their place;

7. *removing* a rule or an equational axiom, or removing an operator or a sort altogether along with the rules or axioms that depend on it so that it can be either discarded or replaced by another operator or sort with different syntax and semantics.

The operations 1–5 are all exactly as in OBJ3 [16]. The operations 6–7 are new and give a simple solution to the thorny problem of *message (or method) specialization* without complicating the class inheritance relation, which remains based on an order-sorted semantics. The need for message specialization, i.e., for providing a different behavior for a message, arises frequently in practice. Consider for example a message **gget** which behaves just as **get**, except that it cannot be accepted if the last message received was a **put**. This means that now bounded buffers must be *history sensitive*, that is, they must remember more about their past than was previously necessary. Specifically, for **gget** to behave correctly, not only must **put** leave somehow a trace of being the last message received, but any message other than **put** must, when accepted, erase such a trace. This of course requires redefining the messages in question.

Therefore, our solution is to understand this as a module inheritance problem, and to carefully distinguish it from class inheritance. In this case, it is the *modules* in which the classes are defined that stand in an inheritance relation, not the classes themselves. The *redefine* operation, with keyword **rdfn**, provides the appropriate way of modifying and inheriting the BD-BUFF module as shown below. To illustrate the differences between class and module inheritance, we define a module **BD-BUFF+HS-BD-BUFF** in which the old class of bounded buffers and the new, history-sensitive, class both coexist.

```
omod BD-BUFF+HS-BD-BUFF is
   protecting BOOL .
   extending BD-BUFF .
   using BD-BUFF*(class BdBuff to HSBdBuff, rdfn(msg put_in_,
       msg getfrom_replyto_)) .
   att after-put: Bool in HSBdBuff .
   initially contents: nil, in: 0, out: 0, after-put: false .
   msg ggetfrom_replyto_ : OId OId -> Msg .
   vars B I : OId .
   vars E N M : Nat .
   var Q : List .
   var Y : Bool .
   rl (put E in B)
       < B : HSBdBuff | contents: Q, in: N, out: M, after-put: Y >
       => < B : HSBdBuff | contents: E Q, in: N + 1, out: M,
           after-put: true > if (N - M) < bound .
       ***put acts as before, but after-put is set to true
```

```
  rl (getfrom B replyto I)
    < B : HSBdBuff | contents: Q E, in: N, out: M,
      after-put: Y > =>
    < B : HSBdBuff | contents: Q, in: N, out: M + 1,
      after-put: false > (to I elt-in B is E) .
    ***get acts as before, but after-put is set to false
  rl (ggetfrom B reply to I)
    < B : HSBdBuff | contents: Q E, in: N, out: M,
      after-put: false > =>
    < B : HSBdBuff | contents: Q, in: N, out: M + 1,
      after-put: false > (to I elt-in B is E) .
    ***gget acts like get, but only if after-put is false
endom
```

The module expression

```
  using BD-BUFF*(class BdBuff to HSBdBuff, rdfn(msg put_in_,
      msg getfrom_replyto_)) .
```

declares that a new copy of the BD-BUFF module is created[10] and imported in such a way that the class BdBuff is renamed to HSBdBuff and the messages (msg put_in_) and (msg getfrom_replyto_) are both *redefined*, i.e., their syntax and sort information are maintained, but, within this new copy of the BD-BUFF module, the original rules defining their behavior are discarded. Their new behavior is then defined by the new rules for put and get given later in the module. In addition, the gget message is introduced and a rule defining its behavior is given. Notice that all the rules for objects in HSBdBuff use the newly defined attribute after-put, introduced by the statement

```
  att after-put: Bool in HSBdBuff .
```

Space limitations preclude giving a detailed account of the rdfn and rmv (remove) commands; this will be done elsewhere.

The essential point to bear in mind about the module BD-BUFF+HS-BD-BUFF is that, although the classes BdBuff and HSBdBuff are both subsorts of Object, the class HSBdBuff is *not* a subclass of BdBuff. Therefore, in the context of the new module, the old rules for put and get messages and the new rules for put, get, and gget *coexist without interference*, because they apply to different objects in two different classes that are *incomparable* in the class hierarchy.

The distinction between class inheritance and module inheritance can be illustrated in this example by means of the diagrams in Figure 1, where the diagram on the left expresses the class inheritance relation between the three classes involved, and the diagram on the right expresses the module inheritance relation between the modules used to define those classes. Note that the arrows in the subclass relation have a very specific meaning, namely that of a

---

[10] However, submodules below BD-BUFF, such as the implicitly given CONFIGURATION module, are not copied: they are *shared*.

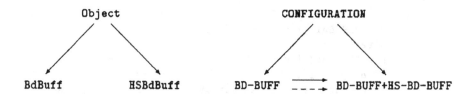

Fig. 1. Class inheritance vs. module inheritance for bounded buffers.

subsort relation, whereas the inheritance arrows between modules can have a much more flexible—yet precise—variety of meanings, because of the variety of module operations that can be involved. In this case, the solid arrows correspond to inheritance by **extending** importation, whereas the dotted arrow involves sort renaming, message redefinition, and a **using** importation; note also that the module **BD-BUFF** is inherited in *two* different ways by the module **BD-BUFF+HS-BD-BUFF**.

6 The Cheshire Cat

We can now attempt to summarize our discussions in previous sections and try to explain the nature and specific characteristics of the solution to the inheritance anomaly that we have proposed, and why it provides in our view a satisfactory solution to the problem.

The main goal, as already mentioned in the Introduction, is to solve the problem by making it disappear completely. In this sense, we should hope that the inheritance anomaly becomes like the Cheshire cat in Alice in Wonderland, which first disappears leaving its grin behind, and then the grin also disappears with the cat never coming back again.

In order to gain some feeling for how close we have been able to get to reaching such a goal, we should first point out that our treatment of the problem has in any case eliminated completely any need for special code for enforcing synchronization constraints. In fact, it seems to us that it is precisely the low level of abstraction involved in such synchronization constraints and the associated and necessary involvement of a language user under those circumstances into implementation decisions of which he should have been spared by a compiler and a higher level language that give rise to the "anomaly" in the first place. This does not imply in any way a lack of awareness of how useful and important it may be to give the advanced user of a concurrent language adequate ways of controlling and modifying the concurrent execution of his or her programs. However, there are disciplined ways of achieving such control by methods such as metaobject protocols [21] and other reflective methods [34].

Secondly, we should point out that—by introducing a clear distinction between class and module inheritance—our analysis has revealed that what is usually grouped together as a single problem can be fruitfully decomposed into two problems:

1. the case in which, as in the **get2** and the lockable bounded buffer examples discussed in Section 4, the behavior of messages previously defined in superclasses is not contradicted by their behavior in a subclass, and
2. the case in which, as in the **gget** example, the behavior of messages previously defined is in fact modified.

Regarding case 1, the semantics of class inheritance that we have proposed makes the inheritance anomaly problem disappear completely *without having to do anything*. Besides, the notion of class inheritance sheds light on when solutions based on the notion of a *guard* [23, 9], which have some similarities with rewrite rules, are likely to be most successful.

Case 2 involves an ineliminable need to *modify* the original behavior of some messages in ways that, in principle, would be hard if not impossible to foresee in advance. Therefore, *something* must necessarily be done. Our proposed solution is based on using module inheritance mechanisms that redefine the appropriate messages or remove some rules, and that create new classes with different behavior that are unrelated in the class inheritance hierarchy to the old classes that exhibited the original behavior. This solution has in our view the following advantages:

- it is fully general and gives complete flexibility for redefining the behavior of messages;
- it is achieved in a disciplined way by means of well-structured module operations which can be given a precise semantics as operations on logical theories;
- leaves intact the order-sorted semantics of class inheritance, and in fact operates outside the framework of class inheritance in our sense;
- *has nothing to do with concurrency*, and as before does not involve nor requires any special code for enforcing synchronization constraints.

In summary, the alleged incompatibility between inheritance and concurrency, the feeling that, somehow, it is problematic or very difficult to have both concurrency and inheritance coexisting in a satisfactory way within the same language, seems in ultimate analysis a mirage.

An area where fruitful research could be done is in devising more refined module inheritance mechanisms that reduce even more the work needed to modify the code in modules. As already pointed out, such techniques have nothing to do with concurrency and would in any case be very useful for many other languages, not necessarily object-oriented, and not necessarily concurrent.

A worthwhile research topic is transferring the ideas that have been developed here by means of rewriting logic techniques to other concurrent languages. This might cast new light on the strengths and limitations of existing inheritance techniques, and might suggest new language design solutions.

Yet another area where very useful research could be done is in devising efficient language implementation techniques that—when applied to languages supporting a high enough level of abstraction—avoid altogether the inheritance anomaly. Section 7 below further discusses this last topic.

7 Implementation Issues

It could perhaps be objected that, although rewriting logic and its order-sorted type structure together with the module inheritance mechanisms seem to make the inheritance anomaly go away, this has only been accomplished at the *specification level*, and that therefore we are after all somehow still left with the problem at the *implementation level*.

To answer this objection, we must clarify an implicit ambiguity between our use of rewriting logic as a language-independent semantic framework, and as a programming language with the Maude syntactic conventions. Indeed, in this paper rewriting logic has actually been used for *both* purposes. However, it would not be reasonable to implement rewriting logic in its fullest generality for programming purposes. This is because, in its most general form, rewriting can take place *modulo* an arbitrary equational theory E that could be undecidable. Therefore, for programming purposes rewriting logic must be carefully restricted in order to allow reasonably efficient implementations. We discuss below specific restrictions under which parallel implementations could be developed. Therefore, although our ideas are still preliminary, we intend our solution of the inheritance anomaly to work at both the specification and the implementation levels.

We consider two subsets of rewriting logic. The first subset allows rewriting modulo any combination of a few commonly occurring structural axioms such as associativity, commutativity and identity for which matching algorithms exist. This subset gives rise to Maude—in the sense that Maude modules are executable rewriting logic theories in it—and, although it can in some cases be inefficient, can be supported by an interpreter implementation adequate for rapid prototyping, debugging, and executable specification. The second, smaller subset gives rise to Simple Maude, a sublanguage meant to be used for concurrent programming purposes for which a wide variety of machine implementations can be developed. Figure 2 summarizes the three levels involved.

7.1 Simple Maude as a Machine-Independent Parallel Language

Simple Maude represents our present design decisions about the subset of rewriting logic that could be implemented efficiently in a wide variety of machine architectures. In fact, we regard Simple Maude as a *machine-independent parallel programming language*, which could be executed with reasonable efficiency on many parallel architectures.

Communication in Simple Maude is performed by asynchronous message passing. The restriction from Maude to Simple Maude is obtained by restricting the form of the rewrite rules that are allowed. We refer the reader to [30] for more

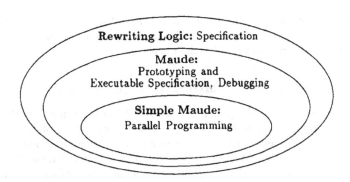

Fig. 2. Maude and Simple Maude as subsets of Rewriting Logic.

details about Simple Maude and concentrate only on the case of object-oriented modules, where we only allow conditional rules of the form

$$
\begin{aligned}
(\ddagger) \quad &(M) \; \langle O : F \mid atts \rangle \\
&\longrightarrow (\langle O : F' \mid atts' \rangle) \\
&\quad \langle Q_1 : D_1 \mid atts_1'' \rangle \ldots \langle Q_p : D_p \mid atts_p'' \rangle \\
&\quad M_1' \ldots M_q' \\
&\quad if \; C
\end{aligned}
$$

involving only one object and one message in their lefthand side, where $p, q \geq 0$, and where the notation (M) means that the message M is only an optional part of the lefthand side, that is, that we also allow *autonomous objects* that can act on their own without receiving any messages. Similarly, the notation $(\langle O : F' \mid atts' \rangle)$ means that the object O—in a possibly different state—is only an optional part of the righthand side, i.e., that it can be omitted in some rules.

Specifically, the lefthand sides in rules of the form $(\ddagger)$ should fit the general pattern

$$
M(O) \; \langle O : C \mid atts \rangle
$$

where O could be a variable, a constant, or more generally—in case object identifiers are endowed with additional structure—a term. Under such circumstances, an efficient way of realizing rewriting modulo associativity and commutativity by communication is available to us for rules of the form $(\ddagger)$, namely we can associate object identifiers with specific addresses in the machine where the object is located and send messages addressed to the object to the corresponding address.

A declarative version of the Actor model [2, 1] can be obtained by only allowing rules of the form $(\ddagger)$ with the additional restrictions of necessarily involving a message in the lefthand side and of being *unconditional* (see Section 4.6 of [26] for a discussion of the actor model and its rewriting logic semantics). Therefore, in spite of the restrictions imposed on it, Simple Maude is still quite expressive and is in particular more expressive than actors.

7.2 MIMD, SIMD, and MIMD/SIMD Implementations

Although we are still in the planning stages of language implementation, the ample experience that already exists on efficient compilation of rewriting for functional languages, and our past experience on parallel compilation of rewrite rules for the Rewrite Rule Machine [4] lead us to believe that Simple Maude can be implemented with reasonable efficiency on a wide variety of parallel architectures, including MIMD, SIMD, and MIMD/SIMD architectures.

Each of these architectures is naturally suited for a different way of performing rewriting computations. Simple Maude has been chosen so that concurrent rewriting with rules in this sublanguage should be relatively easy to implement in any of these three classes of machines. The paper [30] discusses this matter in greater detail; here we limit ourselves to a brief sketch.

In the MIMD (multiple instruction stream, multiple data) case many different rewrite rules can be applied at many different places at once, but only one rule is applied at one place in each processor. The implementation of object-oriented rules of the form (‡), involving a message and an object, can be achieved by *interprocessor communication*, sending the message to the processor in which the addressee object is located, so that when the message arrives the corresponding rules can be applied.

The SIMD (single instruction stream, multiple data) case corresponds to applying rewrite rules one at a time, possibly to many places in the data. The implementation of rules of the form (‡) will require special SIMD code for message passing in addition to the SIMD code for performing the rewriting.

The MIMD/SIMD case is at present more exotic; the Rewrite Rule Machine (RRM) [15, 5, 4, 3] is an architecture in this class in which the processing nodes are two-dimensional SIMD arrays realized on a chip and the higher level structure is a network operating in MIMD mode. This case corresponds to applying many rules to many different places in the data, but here a single rule may be applied at many places simultaneously within a single processing node. The message passing required for rules of the form (‡) can be performed in a way entirely similar to the MIMD case. From the point of view of maximizing the amount and flexibility of the rewriting that can happen in parallel, the MIMD/SIMD case provides the most general solution and offers the best prospects for reaching extremely high performance in many applications.

8 Concluding Remarks

This paper has presented a solution to the inheritance anomaly based on rewriting logic that eliminates the need for explicit synchronization code and removes any obstacles to the full integration of concurrency and inheritance within a concurrent object-oriented language. This work suggests further work ahead on language design for concurrent object-oriented languages and on efficient implementation techniques supporting the level of abstraction desirable for concurrent languages that aim at avoiding altogether the inheritance anomaly.

In particular, it might be fruitful to investigate how the ideas presented here could be used in other languages whose syntax may be quite different from that of rewrite rules. The semantic framework of rewriting logic is very general, can support both synchronous and asynchronous communication, and could probably be usefully applied to many of those languages precisely for this purpose. The work presented here offers a solution from a particular perspective, namely one that views programs as collections of rewrite rules. In order to exploit the techniques available from this perspective in the context of other concurrent object-oriented languages more research clearly needs to be done.

Of the previous proposals in the literature, the closest in spirit to the present one are those by Matsuoka and Yonezawa [23] and by Frolund [9]. We comment briefly on their relationships to the present work. Both Matsuoka and Yonezawa and Frolund advocate *guards* as a useful and fairly reusable way of writing synchronization code. Although, as already pointed out, our approach completely eliminates the need for any special synchronization code, the *implicit effect* of guards is obtained by the patterns in rewrite rules and by the conditions in conditional rewrite rules and therefore there is some similarity between those two approaches and ours. Roughly speaking, our notion of class inheritance identifies a type of inheritance situation where guards can work very well.

The relationship with the work of Frolund [9] could be summarized by saying that, although Frolund allows more general cases of (class) inheritance than we do—so that some of his examples would in our case be treated by means of module inheritance techniques—however, his approach is somewhat more restrictive in the sense that, for safety reasons, he adopts the position that a method's synchronization constraints should increase monotonically as we go down in the inheritance hierarchy. By contrast, when defining a subclass with our treatment of class inheritance, we can not only add new rules for new messages, but we can also add new rules for messages previously defined in some superclasses, and this can have the effect of extending the behavior of those previously defined messages. In terms of guards, this would correspond to relaxing for a subclass the conditions under which a message can be invoked, whereas in Frolund's treatment those conditions should become more restrictive.

Yet another point of similarity is Matsuoka's and Yonezawa's [23] goal of reducing synchronization code to the minimum, a goal fully consistent with the complete elimination of such code that we advocate. Finally, a different solution proposed by Matsuoka and Yonezawa [23] based on the use of *reflection* bears some resemblance to our use of module inheritance for cases where the behavior of messages has to be modified. The point is that, very roughly speaking, one could regard the module inheritance techniques that we have proposed as a very well structured form of static reflection where the code is modified at compile time.

Acknowledgements

I thank Akinori Yonezawa and Satoshi Matsuoka for kindly explaining to me the difficulties involved in the "inheritance anomaly" and their solutions to those difficulties along several very fruitful and illuminating conversations that, along with the reading of their clear and insightful paper [23], have stimulated my work on this topic. I also thank Satoshi Matsuoka and Svend Frolund for their very helpful comments to a previous version that have suggested improvements and clarifications in the exposition.

I thank my fellow members of the Declarative Languages and Architecture Group at SRI International, especially Timothy Winkler, Narciso Martí-Oliet and Patrick Lincoln, for the many discussions with them on object-oriented matters, and for their technical contributions to Maude that have benefited this work. In addition, Narciso Martí-Oliet deserves special thanks for his very helpful suggestions after carefully reading the manuscript.

I thank Joseph Goguen for our long term collaboration on the OBJ, Eqlog and FOOPS languages [16, 11, 12], concurrent rewriting [10] and its implementation on the RRM architecture [13, 4], all of which have influenced this work, and Ugo Montanari for our joint work on the semantics of Petri nets [28, 29] that was an important early influence on rewriting logic.

References

1. G. Agha. *Actors*. MIT Press, 1986.
2. G. Agha and C. Hewitt. Concurrent programming using actors. In A. Yonezawa and M. Tokoro, editors, *Object-Oriented Concurrent Programming*, pages 37–53. MIT Press, 1988.
3. H. Aida, J. Goguen, S. Leinwand, P. Lincoln, J. Meseguer, B. Taheri, and T. Winkler. Simulation and performance estimation for the rewrite rule machine. In *Proceedings of the Fourth Symposium on the Frontiers of Massively Parallel Computation*, pages 336–344. IEEE, 1992.
4. Hitoshi Aida, Joseph Goguen, and José Meseguer. Compiling concurrent rewriting onto the rewrite rule machine. In S. Kaplan and M. Okada, editors, *Conditional and Typed Rewriting Systems, Montreal, Canada, June 1990*, pages 320–332. Springer LNCS 516, 1991.
5. Hitoshi Aida, Sany Leinwand, and José Meseguer. Architectural design of the rewrite rule machine ensemble. In J. Delgado-Frias and W.R. Moore, editors, *VLSI for Artificial Intelligence and Neural Networks*, pages 11–22. Plenum Publ. Co., 1991. Proceedings of an International Workshop held in Oxford, England, September 1990.
6. Pierre America. Synchronizing actions. In *Proc. ECOOP'87*, pages 234–242. Springer LNCS 276, 1987.
7. Denis Caromel. Concurrency and reusability: from sequential to parallel. *Journal of Object-Oriented Programming*, pages 34–42, September/October 1990.
8. N. Dershowitz and J.-P. Jouannaud. Rewrite systems. In J. van Leeuwen, editor, *Handbook of Theoretical Computer Science, Vol. B*, pages 243–320. North-Holland, 1990.

9. Sven Frolund. Inheritance of synchronization constraints in concurrent object-oriented programming languages. In O. Lehrmann Madsen, editor, *Proc. ECOOP'92*, pages 185–196. Springer LNCS 615, 1992.

10. Joseph Goguen, Claude Kirchner, and José Meseguer. Concurrent term rewriting as a model of computation. In R. Keller and J. Fasel, editors, *Proc. Workshop on Graph Reduction, Santa Fe, New Mexico*, pages 53–93. Springer LNCS 279, 1987.

11. Joseph Goguen and José Meseguer. Eqlog: Equality, types, and generic modules for logic programming. In Douglas DeGroot and Gary Lindstrom, editors, *Logic Programming: Functions, Relations and Equations*, pages 295–363. Prentice-Hall, 1986. An earlier version appears in *Journal of Logic Programming*, Volume 1, Number 2, pages 179–210, September 1984.

12. Joseph Goguen and José Meseguer. Unifying functional, object-oriented and relational programming with logical semantics. In Bruce Shriver and Peter Wegner, editors, *Research Directions in Object-Oriented Programming*, pages 417–477. MIT Press, 1987. Preliminary version in *SIGPLAN Notices*, Volume 21, Number 10, pages 153–162, October 1986.

13. Joseph Goguen and José Meseguer. Software for the rewrite rule machine. In *Proceedings of the International Conference on Fifth Generation Computer Systems, Tokyo, Japan*, pages 628–637. ICOT, 1988.

14. Joseph Goguen and José Meseguer. Order-sorted algebra I: Equational deduction for multiple inheritance, overloading, exceptions and partial operations. *Theoretical Computer Science*, 105:217–273, 1992.

15. Joseph Goguen, José Meseguer, Sany Leinwand, Timothy Winkler, and Hitoshi Aida. The rewrite rule machine. Technical Report SRI-CSL-89-6, SRI International, Computer Science Laboratory, March 1989.

16. Joseph Goguen, Timothy Winkler, José Meseguer, Kokichi Futatsugi, and Jean-Pierre Jouannaud. Introducing OBJ. Technical Report SRI-CSL-92-03, SRI International, Computer Science Laboratory, 1992. To appear in J.A. Goguen, editor, *Applications of Algebraic Specification Using OBJ*, Cambridge University Press.

17. Joseph Goguen and David Wolfram. On types and FOOPS. To appear in *Proc. IFIP Working Group 2.6 Working Conference on Database Semantics: Object-Oriented Databases: Analysis, Design and Construction, 1990*.

18. Gerard Huet. Confluent reductions: Abstract properties and applications to term rewriting systems. *Journal of the Association for Computing Machinery*, 27:797–821, 1980.

19. Yutaka Ishikawa. Communication mechanism on autonomous objects. In *OOPSLA '92 Conference on Object-Oriented Programming*, pages 303–314. ACM, 1992.

20. Dennis Kafura and Keung Lee. Inheritance in actor based concurrent object oriented languages. In *Proc. ECOOP'89*, pages 131–145. Cambridge University Press, 1989.

21. Gregor Kiczales, Jim des Riviers, and Daniel G. Bobrow. *The Art of the Metaobject Protocol*. MIT Press, 1991.

22. Henry Liebermann. Concurrent object-oriented programming in Act 1. In A. Yonezawa and M. Tokoro, editors, *Object-Oriented Concurrent Programming*, pages 9–36. MIT Press, 1988.

23. Satoshi Matsuoka and Akinori Yonezawa. Analysis of inheritance anomaly in object-oriented concurrent programming languages. Dept. of Information Science, University of Tokyo, January 1991; to appear in G. Agha, P. Wegner, and A. Yonezawa, editors, *Research Directions in Object-Based Concurrency*, MIT Press, 1993.

24. José Meseguer. A logical theory of concurrent objects. In *ECOOP-OOPSLA '90 Conference on Object-Oriented Programming, Ottawa, Canada, October 1990*, pages 101–115. ACM, 1990.

25. José Meseguer. Conditional rewriting logic as a unified model of concurrency. *Theoretical Computer Science*, 96(1):73–155, 1992.

26. José Meseguer. A logical theory of concurrent objects and its realization in the Maude language. To appear in G. Agha, P. Wegner, and A. Yonezawa, editors, *Research Directions in Object-Based Concurrency*, MIT Press, 1993.

27. José Meseguer and Joseph Goguen. Order-sorted algebra solves the constructor-selector, multiple representation and coercion problems. *Information and Computation*, 103(1):114–158, 1993.

28. José Meseguer and Ugo Montanari. Petri nets are monoids: A new algebraic foundation for net theory. In *Proc. LICS'88*, pages 155–164. IEEE, 1988.

29. José Meseguer and Ugo Montanari. Petri nets are monoids. *Information and Computation*, 88:105–155, 1990.

30. José Meseguer and Timothy Winkler. Parallel Programming in Maude. In J.-P. Banâtre and D. Le Mètayer, editors, *Research Directions in High-level Parallel Programming Languages*, pages 253–293. Springer LNCS 574, 1992.

31. Christian Neusius. Synchronizing actions. In Pierre America, editor, *Proc. ECOOP'91*, pages 118–132. Springer LNCS 512, 1991.

32. M. Papathomas. Concurrency issues in object-oriented programming languages. In D. Tsichritzis, editor, *Object Oriented Development*, pages 207–246. Université de Geneve, 1989.

33. Etsuya Shibayama. Reuse of concurrent object descriptions. In *Proc. TOOLS 3, Sydney*, pages 254–266, 1990.

34. Brian Smith and Akinori Yonezawa, editors. *Proc. of the IMSA '92 Workshop on Reflection and Meta-Level Architecture, Tama-city, Tokyo*. Research Institute of Software Engineering, 1992.

35. Chris Tomlinson and Vineet Singh. Inheritance and synchronization with enabled sets. In *OOPSLA '89 Conference on Object-Oriented Programming*, pages 103–112. ACM, 1989.

36. Ken Wakita and Akinori Yonezawa. Linguistic support for development of distributed organizational information systems. In *Proc. ACM COCS*. ACM, 1991.

37. A. Yonezawa, J.-P. Briot, and Etsuya Shibayama. Object-oriented concurrent programming in ABCL/1. In *OOPSLA '86 Conference on Object-Oriented Programming, Portland, Oregon, September-October 1986*, pages 258–268. ACM, 1986.

A Rewriting Logic

This appendix gives the rules of deduction of rewriting logic.

A.1 Basic Universal Algebra

For the sake of simplifying the exposition, we treat the *unsorted* case; the many-sorted and order-sorted cases can be given a similar treatment. Therefore, a set Σ of function symbols is a ranked alphabet $\Sigma = \{\Sigma_n \mid n \in \mathbb{N}\}$. A Σ-algebra is then a set A together with an assignment of a function $f_A : A^n \longrightarrow A$ for each $f \in \Sigma_n$ with $n \in \mathbb{N}$. We denote by T_Σ the Σ-algebra of ground Σ-terms, and by $T_\Sigma(X)$ the Σ-algebra of Σ-terms with variables in a set X. Similarly, given a set E of Σ-equations, $T_{\Sigma,E}$ denotes the Σ-algebra of equivalence classes of ground Σ-terms modulo the equations E (i.e., modulo provable equality using the equations E); in the same way, $T_{\Sigma,E}(X)$ denotes the Σ-algebra of equivalence classes of Σ-terms with variables in X modulo the equations E. Let $[t]_E$ or just $[t]$ denote the E-equivalence class of t.

Given a term $t \in T_\Sigma(\{x_1, \ldots, x_n\})$, and terms $u_1, \ldots, u_n$, $t(u_1/x_1, \ldots, u_n/x_n)$ denotes the term obtained from t by *simultaneously substituting* u_i for x_i, $i = 1, \ldots, n$. To simplify notation, we denote a sequence of objects $a_1, \ldots, a_n$ by $\overline{a}$. With this notation, $t(u_1/x_1, \ldots, u_n/x_n)$ can be abbreviated to $t(\overline{u}/\overline{x})$.

A.2   The Rules of Rewriting Logic

A *signature* in rewriting logic is a pair (Σ, E) with Σ a ranked alphabet of function symbols and E a set of Σ-equations. Rewriting will operate on equivalence classes of terms modulo the set of equations E. In this way, we free rewriting from the syntactic constraints of a term representation and gain a much greater flexibility in deciding what counts as a *data structure*; for example, string rewriting is obtained by imposing an associativity axiom, and multiset rewriting by imposing associativity and commutativity. Of course, standard term rewriting is obtained as the particular case in which the set E of equations is empty. The idea of rewriting in equivalence classes is well known [18, 8].

Given a signature (Σ, E), *sentences* of the logic are sequents of the form $[t]_E \longrightarrow [t']_E$ with t, t' Σ-terms, where t and t' may possibly involve some variables from the countably infinite set $X = \{x_1, \ldots, x_n, \ldots\}$. A *theory* in this logic, called a rewrite theory, is a slight generalization of the usual notion of theory—which is typically defined as a pair consisting of a signature and a set of sentences for it—in that, in addition, we allow rules to be labelled. This is very natural for many applications, and customary for automata—viewed as labelled transition systems—and for Petri nets, which are both particular instances of our definition.

Definition 1. A *(labelled) rewrite theory* $\mathcal{R}$ is a 4-tuple $\mathcal{R} = (\Sigma, E, L, R)$ where Σ is a ranked alphabet of function symbols, E is a set of Σ-equations, L is a set of *labels*, and R is a set of pairs $R \subseteq L \times (T_{\Sigma,E}(X)^2)$ whose first component is a label and whose second component is a pair of E-equivalence classes of terms, with $X = \{x_1, \ldots, x_n, \ldots\}$ a countably infinite set of variables. Elements of R are called *rewrite rules*.[11] We understand a rule $(r, ([t], [t']))$ as a labelled

---

[11] To simplify the exposition the rules of the logic are given for the case of *unconditional* rewrite rules. However, all the ideas and results presented here have been extended to conditional rules in [25] with very general rules of the form

$$r : [t] \longrightarrow [t'] \; if \; [u_1] \longrightarrow [v_1] \wedge \ldots \wedge [u_k] \longrightarrow [v_k].$$

This of course increases considerably the expressive power of rewrite theories, as illustrated by several of the examples presented in this paper.

sequent and use for it the notation $r : [t] \longrightarrow [t']$. To indicate that $\{x_1, \ldots, x_n\}$ is the set of variables occurring in either t or t', we write $r : [t(x_1, \ldots, x_n)] \longrightarrow [t'(x_1, \ldots, x_n)]$, or in abbreviated notation $r : [t(\overline{x})] \longrightarrow [t'(\overline{x})]$.

Given a rewrite theory $\mathcal{R}$, we say that $\mathcal{R}$ *entails* a sequent $[t] \longrightarrow [t']$ and write $\mathcal{R} \vdash [t] \longrightarrow [t']$ if and only if $[t] \longrightarrow [t']$ can be obtained by finite application of the following *rules of deduction*:

1. **Reflexivity.** For each $[t] \in T_{\Sigma, E}(X)$,

$$\overline{[t] \longrightarrow [t]}$$

2. **Congruence.** For each $f \in \Sigma_n$, $n \in \mathbb{N}$,

$$\frac{[t_1] \longrightarrow [t'_1] \quad \ldots \quad [t_n] \longrightarrow [t'_n]}{[f(t_1, \ldots, t_n)] \longrightarrow [f(t'_1, \ldots, t'_n)]}$$

3. **Replacement.** For each rewrite rule $r : [t(x_1, \ldots, x_n)] \longrightarrow [t'(x_1, \ldots, x_n)]$ in R,

$$\frac{[w_1] \longrightarrow [w'_1] \quad \ldots \quad [w_n] \longrightarrow [w'_n]}{[t(\overline{w}/\overline{x})] \longrightarrow [t'(\overline{w'}/\overline{x})]}$$

4. **Transitivity.**

$$\frac{[t_1] \longrightarrow [t_2] \quad [t_2] \longrightarrow [t_3]}{[t_1] \longrightarrow [t_3]}$$

A nice consequence of having defined rewriting logic is that concurrent rewriting, rather than emerging as an operational notion, actually *coincides* with deduction in such a logic.

Definition 2. Given a rewrite theory $\mathcal{R} = (\Sigma, E, L, R)$, a (Σ, E)-sequent $[t] \longrightarrow [t']$ is called a *concurrent $\mathcal{R}$-rewrite* (or just a *rewrite*) iff it can be derived from $\mathcal{R}$ by finite application of the rules 1-4.

Type Inference of SELF

Analysis of Objects with Dynamic and Multiple Inheritance

Ole Agesen[*1], Jens Palsberg[2], Michael I. Schwartzbach[**2]

[1] Dept. of Computer Science, Stanford University, Stanford, CA 94305, USA,
agesen@self.stanford.edu
[2] Computer Science Dept., Aarhus University, Ny Munkegade, DK-8000 Århus C,
Denmark, {palsberg,mis}@daimi.aau.dk

Abstract. We have designed and implemented a type inference algorithm for the full SELF language. The algorithm can guarantee the safety and disambiguity of message sends, and provide useful information for browsers and optimizing compilers.

SELF features objects with dynamic inheritance. This construct has until now been considered incompatible with type inference because it allows the inheritance graph to change dynamically. Our algorithm handles this by deriving and solving type constraints that simultaneously define supersets of both the possible values of expressions and of the possible inheritance graphs. The apparent circularity is resolved by computing a global fixed-point, in polynomial time.

The algorithm has been implemented and can successfully handle the SELF benchmark programs, which exist in the "standard SELF world" of more than 40,000 lines of code.

Keywords: Languages and their implementation, tools and environments.

1 Introduction

The choice between static and dynamic typing involves a choice between safety and flexibility. The flexibility offered by dynamically typed object-oriented languages is useful in exploratory programming but may also be a hindrance to safety checking and optimization when delivering products.

Henry Lieberman [8] and Alan Borning [2] developed the notion of object-oriented languages based on prototypes. The absence of classes and types in these languages yields a considerable flexibility which may be significantly increased by the notions of dynamic and multiple inheritance. These language constructs, however, make safety checking more difficult than for class-based languages.

* Generously supported by National Science Foundation Presidential Young Investigator Grant #CCR-8657631, by Sun Microsystems, IBM, Apple Computer, Cray Laboratories, Tandem Computers, NCR, Texas Instruments, DEC, by a research fellowship from the Natural Science Faculty of Aarhus University, and by the Danish Research Academy.
** Partially supported by the Danish Research Council, DART Project (5.21.08.03).

O.M. Nierstrasz (Ed.): ECOOP '93, LNCS 707, pp. 247-267, 1993.
© Springer-Verlag Berlin Heidelberg 1993

This paper presents a type inference algorithm for the SELF language [13]. SELF is a prototype-based dynamically typed object-oriented language featuring dynamic and multiple inheritance. Our algorithm can guarantee the safety and disambiguity of message sends, and provide useful information for tools such as browsers and optimizing compilers. Although we focus on SELF our work applies to other languages as well.

Our approach to type inference is based on constraints, like in our previous papers on an idealized subset of SMALLTALK. In [10] we defined the basic type inference framework, and in [9] we demonstrated an efficient implementation.

Dynamic inheritance has until now been considered incompatible with type inference because it allows the inheritance graph to change dynamically. Our algorithm handles this by deriving and solving type constraints that simultaneously define supersets of both the possible values of expressions and of the possible inheritance graphs. The apparent circularity is resolved by computing a global fixed-point, in polynomial time.

In most other type inference algorithms for object-oriented languages, for example that of Graver and Johnson [7, 6] and our own [10, 9], inheritance is expanded away rather than dealt with directly. Using prototypes, however, expansion is impossible, since a parent may have an independent state. This paper demonstrates how to handle inheritance without expansion. It also shows how to handle blocks with non-local return.

In the following Section we give an overview of the required type constraints. In Section 3 we present example runs of our implementation, and in Section 4 we discuss details of our algorithm and implementation. Finally, in Section 5 we summarize our results and conclusions.

2 Type Constraints

SELF [13] resembles SMALLTALK [5] on the surface. However, there are major differences that make SELF a particularly interesting language to analyze: SELF has no classes, instantiation is object cloning, inheritance is between objects having independent state and identity, and the inheritance may be both dynamic and multiple. Dynamic inheritance allows the inheritance graph to change during program execution. The dynamic nature of SELF makes it harder to obtain non-trivial type information for SELF programs than for, say, SMALLTALK programs. It also makes such information immediately useful in browsers and optimizing compilers.

Below we describe our approach to type inference for SELF. We will use the SELF-terminology without explanation.

2.1 Constraint-Based Analysis

Our approach to type inference is based on constraints, like in our previous papers on an idealized subset of SMALLTALK. The main idea in constraint-based analysis [15, 12, 11] is as follows. First, define type variables for the unknown type information. Second, derive constraints on these variables from the given program. Third, solve the resulting constraints to obtain the desired information.

The algorithms in [10, 9] had safety checking as an integral part of the type constraints. As a result, type information could not be inferred for incorrect programs that could provoke a msgNotUnderstood error. The approach in this paper is more liberal, so type information can be computed for *all* programs. This may be useful during program development and debugging, since information about a partially correct program can be obtained. When a guarantee against msgNotUnderstood or ambiguousSend errors is desired, it can be provided by a tool that inspects the computed type information (although it is straightforward to implement these tools, we haven't done it yet).

2.2 Types and Type Variables

Any given SELF program contains a fixed number of *objects* (some of which are "block objects") and *methods* (which are either "normal methods" or "block methods"). We introduce a unique *token* for each of these: $\omega_1, \ldots, \omega_n$ for the objects and $\mu_1, \ldots, \mu_m$ for the methods. We use τ to denote the token for any object or method.

For every expression in a program we want to infer its *type*. The type of an expression is a set of tokens indicating the objects to which the expression may evaluate in any execution of the program. Since exact information is uncomputable in general, we will be satisfied with a (hopefully small) superset.

We now assign every expression a *type variable* $[\![E]\!]_\tau$. Here E is the syntax of the expression and τ is the token for the nearest enclosing object or method. The intuition is that $[\![E]\!]_\tau$ denotes the type of the expression E in the object or method τ. In our previous papers, constraint variables simply looked like $[\![E]\!]$ (without the index); this was possible since we, unlike in this approach, were able to expand away inheritance. We have a similar type variable $[\![x]\!]_\tau$ for every argument, variable, or parent slot x. There is also an auxiliary type variable $[\![\mu]\!]$ for each method μ. $[\![\mu]\!]$ denotes the type of the values that μ may return. The auxiliary type variables are needed to handle non-local returns. All type variables range over sets of tokens.

2.3 Constraints for SELF

From the syntax of the given program we generate and solve a finite collection of *constraints*. These constraints, which are presented by means of a *trace graph* [10, 9], are all conditional set inclusions. Using the trace graph technique, we need only define constraints for local situations; the corresponding global constraints will then automatically be derived, as described below.

We have a trace graph *node* for each object and method in the program. The MAIN node of the trace graph is the node corresponding to the initial method in the program being analyzed (in a C program this would be the main function). Each trace graph node contains *local constraints* which are generated from the syntax; some examples are shown in Figure 1. The local constraints are quite straightforward. They directly reflect the semantics of the corresponding constructs, constraining the types of expressions in a bottom-up fashion. For slots, 1), 2), and 3), ω is an object and μ is a method. The first constraint is associated with a dynamic parent slot. The constraint says that the initial object in the slot is included in the slot's type. The second constraint is analogous, but for a variable slot. The third constraint is associated with a method slot and it lifts the type of the method, $[\![\mu]\!]$, to the type of the slot, $[\![\mathrm{Id}]\!]$. Constraint 4) specifies that the type of a sequence of expressions is determined by the type of the last expression in the sequence. 5) is for a primitive, _Clone. The constraint says that a clone of an object has the same type as the object. There are of course many more primitives—a few hundred in fact—so the type inference implementation has a database of primitive local constraints currently covering the 100 most important primitives. Constraints 6) and 7) reflect the fact that an object literal evaluates to itself.

Slots:		Constraint:
1)	$\mathrm{Id}^* \leftarrow \omega$	$[\![\mathrm{Id}]\!]_\tau \supseteq \{\omega\}$
2)	$\mathrm{Id} \leftarrow \omega$	$[\![\mathrm{Id}]\!]_\tau \supseteq \{\omega\}$
3)	$\mathrm{Id} = \mu = (\mid S \mid E)$	$[\![\mathrm{Id}]\!]_\tau \supseteq [\![\mu]\!] \supseteq [\![E]\!]_\mu$
	Expression:	**Constraint:**
4)	$E_1 \cdot E_2$	$[\![E_1 \cdot E_2]\!]_\tau \supseteq [\![E_2]\!]_\tau$
5)	E _Clone	$[\![E \text{ _Clone}]\!]_\tau \supseteq [\![E]\!]_\tau$
6)	$(\mid S \mid)$	$[\![(\mid S \mid)]\!]_\tau \supseteq \{\text{the token for this object}\}$
7)	$[\mid S \mid \dots]$	$[\![[\mid S \mid \dots]]\!]_\tau \supseteq \{\text{the token for this block}\}$

Fig. 1. Some local constraints for SELF.

When defining the local constraints we are fortunate that SELF is a minimal language in which most mechanisms are coded in the language itself, starting with only a small core. For example, control structures such as ifTrue:False:, do:, and whileTrue: are implemented by normal SELF methods and objects. However, we pay a daunting price for this simplicity, since *any* program being analyzed is likely to use several of these control structures which are unseparable from the standard SELF world of more than 40,000 lines of code. Our experiences with this are detailed in Section 3.

Trace graph *edges* describe possible message sends. There is an edge from node A to node B, if A may invoke B. Each edge is decorated with *connecting constraints*, which reflect parameter passing during a message send. The crucial part in setting up this picture is to associate a *condition* with each edge. If all possible edges were taken seriously, then we would obtain only very pessimistic results from our type inference. It would correspond to the assumption that every object could send every possible message to every other object. However, if the condition of an edge is false, then it can safely be ignored.

Edge conditions must be *sound*, i.e., if some condition is false in the type analysis, then the corresponding message send must be impossible at run-time. There is a circularity between conditions and local constraints, in that conditions depend on type variables which are determined by local constraints, the relevance of which depends on conditions. We resolve this circularity by a global fixed-point computation.

The trace graph technique derives *global* constraints by considering all paths without repeating edges from the MAIN node; they correspond to abstract traces of a possible execution. Each such path yields a conditional constraint. The condition is the conjunction of the individual conditions on the edges, and the constraint is the conjunction of both the local constraints in the node to which the path leads and the connecting constraints of the final edge of the path. Such a global constraint means intuitively that if this trace is possible during execution, then these constraints must hold. For further details about the trace graph technique and how to derive global constraints, see [10, 9].

The circularity between conditions and constraints is fairly simple for a language like SMALLTALK, which has *dynamic* dispatch but *static* inheritance. When we include dynamic and multiple inheritance, several further complications arise. The conditions now have to soundly reflect possible searches through parent chains existing only at run-time, and they should of course be as restrictive as possible. This development is detailed below.

For SELF, there are several different kinds of edges, reflecting that the uniform message send syntax is (intentionally) overloaded to do several semantically different things. An edge kind is determined by two orthogonal choices:

- The kind of send. In SELF there are four kinds of sends: send to implicit self, send to an explicit receiver, undirected resend (super), and directed resend (delegation).
- The kind of slot that is "invoked" by the send. In SELF, message sends are used to invoke normal methods, invoke block methods, read variables, and write variables. Furthermore block methods come in two flavors: with and without non-local return.

These 4×5 choices have many things in common, but no two of them have the exact same semantics. Hence, our approach involves 20 different kinds of edges.

In the following we will restrict our attention to a send of the form "E_1 id: E_2", i.e., a send to an explicit receiver. Furthermore, we will only look at the cases where a normal method or a block method (with and without non-local return) is invoked. The last simplification we have made is to consider only a send with a single argument; the situations trivially generalize to an arbitrary number of arguments. We first present the edges for the case where the send invokes a normal method. Then we present the edges for invoking block methods. The remaining 17 cases are all quite analogous to the three we show.

Normal method invocation. The edge in Figure 2 describes invocation of a normal method. The expression above the arrow is the condition; the subset

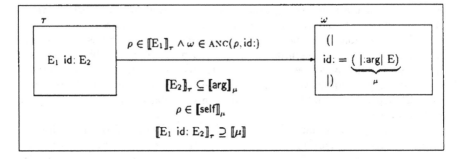

Fig. 2. Edge for invoking a normal method.

relations below the arrow are the constraints that must be respected if the condition becomes satisfied. The method being invoked is μ. It is found in a slot named "id:" in the object ω. The sender is τ, a block or normal method that contains the send "E_1 id: E_2". Finally, ρ is an object in the type of the receiver expression $[\![E_1]\!]_\tau$. We have the obvious connecting constraints for the argument and the result, plus one for maintaining the self parent in the invoked method μ. Because of dynamic and multiple inheritance, the condition involves the function ANC(ρ,id:) which computes the ancestors of ρ that the message "id:" can reach. This is done by directly expressing the lookup algorithm of SELF, but performing the search in the domain of type variables rather than objects (which do not exist until run-time), see Figure 3. We obtain a great deal of modularity in this manner, since changes in the definition of the lookup algorithm need only be reflected in the ANC function; in all other respects the constraints can be left unchanged. This has already been verified in practice since parent priorities were recently eliminated from SELF. The code in Figure 3, though, applies to the old semantics of SELF as found in release 2.0.1 [1]. For simplicity, the code in Figure 3 ignores privacy of methods and detection of cycles (SELF allows cyclic inheritance graphs).

Block method invocation. Block methods are different from normal methods in two major aspects. First, instead of a self parent they have an anonymous parent that refers to the lexically enclosing method. Second, they may have a non-local return. It is of minor importance for our work that block methods are only found in block objects, and that they are always in slots whose names start with value.

The edge for invoking a block method without a non-local return is shown in Figure 4. We have renamed the send to "E_1 value: E_2". The condition reflects that the send is subject to the full lookup, e.g. in the "worst" case the block method may be inherited through dynamic parents. Comparing with the edge for invoking a normal method, we note that there is no constraint involving self. This is because block methods have no self slot of their own; rather they *inherit* the lexically enclosing method's self slot through their lexical parent, and the invocation of the block method does not affect self. Otherwise the two kinds of

```
Algorithm LOOKUP(obj: object; id: string)   Algorithm ANC(obj: token; id: string)
  var m0, m: object;                           var found, f: boolean;
                                                var res: set of token;
  if obj has id slot then                       if obj has id slot then
    return obj                                    return {obj}
  end;                                          end;
  for i := 1 to MaxPriority do                  for i := 1 to MaxPriority do
    m0 := nil;                                     found := false; res := {};
    for all parent slots p                         for all parent slots p
        of priority i in obj do                        of priority i in obj do
      m := LOOKUP(contents(p),id);                   f := true;
      if m = ambiguousSend then                      for all a in [p] do
        return m                                        f := f ∧ ANC(a,id) ≠ {};
      end;                                             res := res ∪ ANC(a,id)
      if m ≠ msgNotUnderstood then                  end;
        if m0 ≠ nil ∧ m0 ≠ m then                    found := found ∨ f
          return ambiguousSend                     end;
        else                                       if found then return res end
          m0 := m                                end;
        end                                      return res
      end                                      end ANC.
    end;
    if m0 ≠ nil then return m0 end;
  end;
  return msgNotUnderstood
end LOOKUP.
```

Fig. 3. Method lookup in SELF release 2.0.1 and the derived ANC function.

edges have the same connecting constraints and conditions.

The edge for invoking a block method with a non-local return is shown in Figure 5. The block method being invoked is again labeled μ. The "↑" designates that the following expression, E', is returned non-locally. A non-local return in SELF, as in SMALLTALK, does not return to the point of the send that invoked the block method, but to the point of the send that invoked the method in which the block is contained. The edge in Figure 5 differs by a single constraint from the edge in Figure 4. The constraint involving the type of the send expression is missing, because invocation of a block method with non-local return does not return to the send point that invoked the block method.

Non-local return. Independently of these edges, we have some unconditional non-local connecting constraints, which reflect the possible control flow of non-local returns. One such is shown in Figure 6: the result of a block method, μ_{block}, with non-local return can become the result of the enclosing normal method object, μ_{normal}.

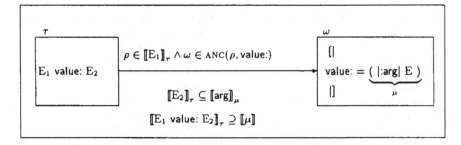

Fig. 4. Edge for invoking a block method.

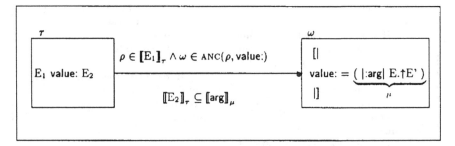

Fig. 5. Edge for invoking a block method with non-local return.

2.4 Code Duplication

As suggested in [10, 9], it is often necessary to duplicate code to obtain sufficiently precise types. The idea is for each method to make individual copies for every syntactic invocation. These copies can then be separately analyzed, so that unwanted "cross-constraints" can be avoided.

This process can be iterated to yield ever more precise type information, but at a huge cost since a single copying of all methods may square the size of the program. The need for code duplication may vary greatly from method to method; thus, a good implementation must include sensible heuristics for deciding when to duplicate the code for a method. We have been quite successful in finding such heuristics for the SELF analysis; see Section 4 for further details.

$$
\mu_{\text{normal}} : (\quad \vdots \\
\qquad\qquad \mu_{\text{block}} : [\,\cdots\uparrow\cdots\,] \\
\qquad\qquad \vdots \\
\qquad)\\
\qquad [\![\mu_{\text{block}}]\!] \subseteq [\![\mu_{\text{normal}}]\!]
$$

Fig. 6. Non-local connecting constraint.

2.5 Constraint Solving

All the global type constraints, derived from the trace graph, can be written as:

$$c_1 \wedge \ldots \wedge c_n \implies X \subseteq V$$

where V is a type variable, X is either a type variable or a constant set of tokens, and the c_i's is are *monotonic* conditions. Monotonicity of a condition simply means that it can never be true for a particular assignment of types to variables and false for a strictly larger one. In our case, assignments are ordered by variable-wise set inclusion.

In [10] it is shown that if the type constraints are monotonic, they have a unique minimal solution, which is also computable. To see that our constraints for SELF are monotonic, we look at a typical condition c_i which has the form

$$\rho \in [\![E]\!]_\tau \wedge \omega \in \text{ANC}(\rho, id).$$

Conjunction preserves monotonicity, so it is enough to ensure that each conjunct is monotonic. The first conjunct obviously is. The second conjunct is monotonic if a larger assignment of types to variables will result in a larger set of ancestors being returned by ANC. This property of ANC is of course dependent on the particular lookup strategy that ANC is derived from. However, any reasonable strategy will likely share this property and indeed the one we study does. This can be informally seen as follows. Imagine first executing ANC for one type assignment and then later executing it for a larger type assignment, see Figure 3. The second execution will perform more iterations in the innermost loop, since $[\![p]\!]$ will be larger, (by induction) causing a larger res set to be accumulated. Furthermore, searching more parents in the inner loop will never cause the search to be terminated at a higher parent priority (i.e., earlier), since there are more chances for the control variable f to become false, hence found will become true no sooner.

In Section 4 we describe how to obtain an efficient, polynomial-time algorithm for solving monotonic type constraints. It is similar to the one presented in [9], in using a lazy, incremental strategy; however, the new algorithm is a drastic improvement. Early experiments with the old algorithm, adapted to the SELF language, showed an unacceptable performance.

3 Examples

A good illustration of *both* the strengths and weaknesses of our type inference technique is obtained by looking at examples. Illustrating the capabilities of the technique has been our first goal when choosing the examples. Our second goal has been to show that our approach is realistic. This has had three consequences:

- All our examples are "real" in the sense that they are part of the standard SELF system. The code has not been (re)written or modified in any way whatsoever for the purpose of being analyzed. If desired, the test programs can be studied in context, by obtaining a copy of the SELF system by anonymous ftp from self.stanford.edu. The only pieces of code that we have written are a few message sends to invoke the main body of the code.

- The code being analyzed is not self-contained: it is an integrated part of a large body of code, the SELF world. Previous work on type inference has mainly analyzed self-contained code. Analyzing a 200 line program of which 100 lines implement a unary representation of natural numbers is not as interesting, or challenging, as analyzing 200 lines of code that just assume and use a fully developed implementation of numbers, collection classes, and other data structures.

- Previous articles [10, 9] have listed small programs, the derived constraints, and their minimal solution as found by a particular constraint solving algorithm. Since the constraints are hard to read and we want to scale towards analyzing realistically sized programs which produce *thousands* of constraints, we do not list any constraints in this section.

We present three concrete examples, each focusing on different aspects of both the type inference and the SELF system. The first example shows how tightly coupled much of the SELF code is. The second example illustrates the capabilities of a browser based on type inference. The third example deals with dynamic inheritance.

3.1 The Tangled Web: Simple Arithmetic

Our first example is conceptually the simplest, yet it illustrates very well just how tightly integrated the code in the SELF world is. We start with almost the simplest possible expressions and observe how a plethora of methods and objects come into play.

SELF has a hierarchy of number objects, the leaves of which are: smallInt which are limited to 30 bits precision, bigInt which have unlimited precision, and float. Mixed representation arithmetic is supported via dynamic dispatching and implicit coercions. For example, if an operation on smallInt overflows, the objects will transparently be coerced to bigInt and the operation will be retried. The consequence is that understanding how a simple expression such as 3+4 is computed is not trivial.

We have defined a small object with messages performing various arithmetic operations, some of which will fail if executed; the object is shown in Figure 7. We have performed type inference on this object in several different configurations; observations about this are listed in Figure 8, where, e.g., the column labeled "standard system" shows the results of inferring types in the standard SELF system. Each cell in the table shows the inferred type of the expression analyzed, the number of trace graph edges involved, the number of methods analyzed, and

```
example1Object = ( |
  parent* = traits oddball.             "Inherit default behavior."
  test1 = ( 3    +   4 ).               "Result: 7"
  test2 = ( 3.5 +   4 ).                "Result: 7.5"
  test3 = ( 3    + 4.5 ).               "Result: 7.5"
  test4 = ( 3.5 + 4.5 ).                "Result: 8.0"
  test5 = ( nil + 4.5 ).                "Result: error"
  test6 = ( 3    + 'random string' ).   "Result: error"
| ).
```

Fig. 7. Arithmetic operations.

the time it took to infer the types on a SPARCstation 2 (we will comment briefly on the execution times in Section 4).

First look at the "standard system" column. Several interesting points should be noted:

- This is the exact output as produced by the type inference implementation, except for a nicer write-up.
- Our type inference does no range analysis or constant folding, so it cannot determine if overflows occur. This is why bigInt shows up e.g. in test1, even though 3+4 will never overflow.
- Why does bigInt show up in test3? Inspection of the code reveals that adding a float to a smallInt can never result in a bigInt. The reason that the type inference cannot determine this is related to a single primitive message send, see Figure 9. The algorithm infers that the primitive send may fail, hence it analyzes the fail block. The fail block handles two failure modes: overflow (adding too big a smallInt) and badTypeError (e.g. adding a float to a smallInt). The two failure modes cannot be distinguished by looking at type information only. The fail block distinguishes them by comparing *values*, not types (specifically string prefix tests are used). Being limited to types, the inference algorithm must assume that both failure modes are possible, hence it cannot determine that the bigInt case never occurs.
- The empty types, inferred for the last two tests, indicate that an error will occur with certainty. The trace graph can be analyzed, and the exact send(s) that will fail can be identified.
- Of the two empty types inferred, one is a lot harder to infer than the other. In test5 there is only a single message send that has a matching slot: this is the send of nil to implicit self that is matched by a slot in an ancestor. The next send, +, finds no matching slot in nil or any of nil's ancestors and hence the type inference is completed. The contrast is test6: to determine that a string is not a good argument to give the + method of smallInt requires a detailed analysis of this and many other methods.
- The number of edges and nodes is very large; each edge corresponds to a possible message send, each node corresponds to a method that was analyzed (of course, the large numbers are partially caused by the code duplication

Method	Standard system	No bigInt	No bigInt or isPrefixOf:
test1 = (3 + 4)	{ smallInt, bigInt } 16,757 edges 4,969 nodes 60 seconds	{ smallInt } 2,444 edges 874 nodes 8 seconds	{ smallInt } 91 edges 41 nodes 0 seconds
test2 = (3.5 + 4)	{ float } 16,763 edges 4,972 nodes 60 seconds	{ float } 2,490 edges 894 nodes 9 seconds	{ float } 76 edges 34 nodes 0 seconds
test3 = (3 + 4.5)	{ float, bigInt } 16,782 edges 4,979 nodes 60 seconds	{ float } 2,509 edges 904 nodes 8 seconds	{ float } 123 edges 58 nodes 0 seconds
test4 = (3.5 + 4.5)	{ float } 16,742 edges 4,964 nodes 60 seconds	{ float } 2,468 edges 885 nodes 8 seconds	{ float } 54 edges 25 nodes 0 seconds
test5 = (nil + 4.5)	{ } 1 edge 1 node 0 seconds	{ } 1 edge 1 node 0 seconds	{ } 1 edge 1 node 0 seconds
test6 = (3 + 'str')	{ } 16,755 edges 4,969 nodes 61 seconds	{ } 2,520 edges 905 nodes 9 seconds	{ } 2,434 edges 880 nodes 9 seconds

Fig. 8. Type inference of arithmetic operations.

being done internally by the type inference algorithm, see sections 2.4 and 4).

In order to explain how a simple addition can potentially result in so much code being executed, the type inference was repeated in a world without bigInt. The result is shown in the "no bigInt" column of Figure 8.

The inferred types are not surprising, but the number of edges, although lower, is still high. The explanation is found in the fail block; Figure 9 shows a fragment of code which is the core of the smallInt addition (file smallInt.self, line 18). Virtual machine primitives in SELF have the same syntax as "real" message sends, but have names starting with "_" such as _IntAdd:IfFail:. The last argument is a "fail block". It is invoked to produce the result of the primitive send, if the virtual machine is unable to complete the primitive operation, e.g. because it is given an object of type float where it expects a smallInt. The test isPrefixOf: is complex because it uses general collection behavior to analyze if one sequence (here a string) is a prefix of another. The type inference algorithm precisely infers that the result of isPrefixOf: is true or false, but has to do a non-trivial amount of analysis. Short-circuiting the isPrefixOf: method and performing the

```
^ + a = (asSmallInteger _IntAdd: a IfFail: [| :error. :name. |
          ('badTypeError' isPrefixOf: error) ifTrue: [
            " use double dispatching "
            a addSmallInteger: asSmallInteger ] False: [
          ('overflowError' isPrefixOf: error) ifTrue: [
            " retry after coercing to bigInts "
            asBigInteger + a asBigInteger ] False: [
          primitiveFailedError: error Name: name ]]]).
```

Fig. 9. Core of smallInt addition.

inference again shows that we have indeed found the correct explanation for the many edges. The data are shown in the last column of Figure 8. We anticipate that the results of this analysis might lead to redesign of the primitive failure blocks in the future.

The latter example shows that the analysis of failure code significantly complicates the task of type inference. Previous type inference algorithms for object-oriented languages either assume that failures such as overflow are impossible, or treat them as fatal, i.e., the effect of failures is not propagated into the following code. We believe that for a type inference technique to be practical, it *must* be able to precisely analyze failures, not just "normal" execution.

For the last two examples we return to analyzing the standard system, i.e., with bigInt defined and no short-circuiting of any message.

3.2 Browsing Programs: Towers of Hanoi

To gather data for our second example we ran the type inference algorithm on a program that solves the well-known "Towers of Hanoi" problem. The program itself has a long history. Originally, it was written in PASCAL and included in the "Stanford Integer Benchmarks" suite collected by John Hennessy. Later the benchmarks were translated to SELF and used to characterize the run-time performance of the SELF system [3].

Now we use the towers_oo program to illustrate how a browser may combine program text with inferred types, to make program understanding easier. We call such a browser a "hyperbrowser" and, although we haven't implemented it yet, we believe that the following scenario is realistic, since it is directly based upon information computed by the type inference algorithm.

We use this example to illustrate two things. First, we show how the raw type information computed by the type inference algorithm is useful when a programmer is trying to understand object-oriented programs. Second, we show how control flow information that can be derived from the type information can be equally useful in the same situations.

The complete program text for the Towers of Hanoi program and selected type annotations produced by the hyperbrowser are shown in Figure 10. Let us look at the annotations one at a time. The paragraph numbers below refer to the numbers next to the annotations in the figure.

1. The runBenchmark method is the "main" method of the program. It is sending various messages to implicit self. Most of the sends ignore the return value and have constant arguments, i.e., their types are manifest from the program text. movesdone is the only exception so we "click" on it to see what information the hyperbrowser can give us. The result is the "balloon" labeled 1: movesdone has type {nil, smallInt, bigInt}. If we want to know which methods the send may invoke (including which variables it may read or write) we can ask the browser for "forward control flow" information. The answer is that the movesdone send will always be answered by reading a variable in a towers_oo object.

   The type of the send includes nil because movesdone is not initialized (see line 3 of the program): by combining type inference with data flow analysis, types can be improved in such situations [14]. The fact that nil shows up in the type could alternatively be attributed to "bad" programming style: prototype objects should have their slots initialized with proper prototypical objects, else they are not prototypical. In the specific case this means that movesdone should be initialized with an integer object. The towers_oo benchmark probably does not follow this style in order to be as similar as possible to the original PASCAL program.

2. Next we focus on the tower:I:J:K: method. Again, in such a simple program it is hard to find interesting questions to ask, but at least it is not obvious what the method returns. A click on the selector of the method brings up balloon 2 which shows that the method will always return a towers_oo object, i.e., it returns self.

3. Continuing our exploration we focus on the pop: method. First, what is the type of the argument? This question is easily answered, see balloon 3, but there is the annoying nil again! If we wanted to explore the nil issue further, we could ask the browser for "backward control flow", and be shown all the sends that invoke pop:. We could even ask to see only the sends that invoke pop: with an argument that *may* be nil. This would quickly reveal that nil is here because of another uninitialized variable: other in the towerI:J:K: method.

4. We now look at the return type of pop:. The disc and sentinel objects in balloon 4 seem reasonable, and by now we have learned that the author of the program has a lenient attitude towards nil, so we decide to get an answer to the question: "why can a string be returned?"

5. Our first attempt to answer this question is to "click" on the result send which, being the last in the method, produces the return value. No luck here, though, since there is no string in the resulting balloon 5.

6. Going back to balloon 4 and asking for control information, the browser resolves the mystery: balloon 6 pops up and shows us that string is injected into the return type by the block doing a non-local return. It could be claimed that we have found a bug in the program: error: should not return a string; in fact it should not return at all.

```
benchmark2 towers_oo _Define: ( |
    parent*    = traits benchmarks.
    movesdone.
    stackrange = 3.
    stack      = vector copySize: "stackrange" 3.
    discSize: i = (disc copy discSize: i).
    error: emsg = ( 'Error in towers_oo: ' print emsg printLine. ).
    makenull: s = ( stack at: s Put: sentinel ).
    disc = ( | parent** = traits clonable. "Disc object prototype."
            discSize.
            next. | ).
    pop: s = ( | result |
        sentinel = (stack at: s) ifTrue: [↑error: 'nothing to pop'] .
        result: stack at: s.
        stack at: s Put: result next.
        result ).
    push: d OnTo: s = ( | locale1 |
        locale1: stack at: s.
        d discSize > locale1 discSize ifTrue: [↑error: 'disc size error'].
        stack at: s Put: d next: locale1.
        self).
    init: s To: n = (
        n downTo: 1 Do: [ | :discctr |
            push: (discSize: discctr) OnTo: s. ] ).
    moveFrom: s1 To: s2 = (
        push: (pop: s1) OnTo: s2.
        movesdone: movesdone successor. ).
    towerI: i J: j K: k = (
        k = 1 ifTrue: [
            moveFrom: i To: j.
        ] False: [ | other |
            other: 3 - i - j.
            towerI: i J: other K: k predecessor.
            moveFrom: i To: j.
            towerI: other J: j K: k predecessor.
        ] ).
    runBenchmark = (
        makenull: 0.
        makenull: 1.
        makenull: 2.
        init: 0 To: 14.
        movesdone: 0.
        towerI: 0 J: 1 K: 14.
        movesdone = 16383 ifFalse: [ 'Error in towers.' printLine ].
        self ).
| )
benchmarks towers_oo _AddSlots: ( |
    sentinel = benchmarks towers_oo discSize: 15.
| )
```

6:
{string}

3:
{smallInt,bigInt,nil}
Senders: moveFrom:To:

2:
towers_oo

4:
{disc,sentinel,nil,string}

5:
{disc,sentinel,nil}

1:
{nil,bigInt,smallInt}
Slot read: towers_oo

Fig. 10. Program to solve the Towers of Hanoi problem.

By now it should be clear that the type inference algorithm computes detailed and precise information whose application includes, but goes beyond, simply establishing safety guarantees for programs.

3.3 Mastering Dynamic Inheritance: Binary Search Trees

The previous example illustrated how a hyperbrowser can provide assistance in understanding the control flow of programs that use dynamic dispatching. Dynamic inheritance, while providing the ultimate in expressive power, also provides the ultimate in control flow confusion in the sense that even if the exact receiver type of a send is known, it is still not possible to determine which method is invoked. Fortunately, type inference provides the kind of information that programmers need in order to curb the complexity of dynamic inheritance. Our final example demonstrates this.

One use of dynamic inheritance is to implement objects with modal behavior. The canonical example in the SELF system is the implementation of an ordered set data type using binary search trees. A tree is identified by a single node. Nodes are either leaves which contain no elements (e.g., the empty tree is a single leaf node) or they are interior nodes which contain an element and two subtrees. The behavior of any given node is determined by a *dynamic* parent. The parent will switch during execution whenever a node changes status from interior to leaf or vice versa.

Figure 11 shows selected parts of the SELF implementation of trees. Due to lack of space, we are unable to list the entire implementation which consists of some 300 lines of code. To simplify further, we have also removed a level of inheritance that is only used because the objects implement both sets and multisets. The figure shows three objects: traits emptyTrees which holds behavior for leaves, traits treeNodes which holds behavior for interior nodes, and treeNode which has a dynamic parent that initially holds traits emptyTrees.

The includesKey: methods search a tree for a given key. Since treeNode inherits this method through the dynamic parent, the result of sending includesKey: to a treeNode depends on the object in the parent slot.

The key to understanding a program that uses dynamic inheritance, is to understand *all* the behavioral modes. This requires knowing all the possible objects that can occur in the dynamic parent slots. Unfortunately, finding these objects is not easy: for example, with incomplete knowledge about the set of parents, the programmer has incomplete knowledge about the assignments that change the dynamic parents. Breaking this circularity is not trivial. Merely executing the program and observing the contents of the dynamic parent slots is not sufficient, since the programmer can never be sure that a new type of parent will not show up next time the program is executed. The strong guarantees that the programmer needs to reason correctly about the behavior of the program cannot be provided by the subsets of actual types that are the result of observing dynamic behavior. In contrast, type inference, which computes supersets, directly

```
traits emptyTrees _Define: ( |
    parent* = traits tree.
    add: x = (parent: nodeProto nodeCopyKey: x Contents: x).
    includesKey: k = ( false ).
    removeAll = (self).
    ...
| )

traits treeNodes _Define: ( |
    parent* = traits tree.
    includesKey: x = (
      findKey: x
          IfHere: true
            IfNot: [ | :subTree | subTree includesKey: x ] ).

    removeAll = ( parent: emptyTreeTraits ).
    left  <- treeSet copy.
    right <- treeSet copy.
    key.
    ...
| )

treeNode _Define: ( |
    parent* <- traits emptyTrees.
| )
```

Fig. 11. Binary search tree implementation using dynamic inheritance.

provides such guarantees: if a type T is inferred for a dynamic parent slot S, the programmer knows that in *any* execution of the program, the contents of S will always be (a clone of) one of the objects found in T. Another way of looking at this is that the fixed-point computation performed during type inference breaks the above-mentioned circularity.

To be concrete, we have inferred types for an example program that uses the (non-simplified) search trees taken from the SELF world. The analysis—as usual—computes a type for every expression and slot in the program, but in this case we focus on a single question: "what are the possible parents of treeNode objects?" The answer is decisive:

$$[parent]_{treeNode} = \{ \text{ traits emptyTrees, traits treeNode } \}.$$

That is, the type analysis has inferred the precise behavioral modes for tree nodes. Having access to the types of all dynamic parents, the hyperbrowser could also provide control flow information, including information for sends that are looked up through dynamic parents. Furthermore, since the inferred types are precise, so will the control flow information be. We will not go into details with this since it is similar to the Hanoi browsing scenario.

4 Algorithm and Implementation

The problem with a naive implementation of the constraint solver is that an explicit construction of the trace graph will be much too costly for programs of realistic sizes. In [9] this was remedied by an incremental computation of both the trace graph and its minimal solution. Starting with the MAIN node, the general situation would be that a connected part of the graph had been constructed and its solution computed. All outgoing edges from this fragment of the full trace graph were stored in a data structure along with their conditions. If any such condition was satisfied in the current minimal solution, then the local constraints of the targeted node were included, and a new, larger solution was computed. This technique works as long as the conditions are monotonic, as explained in Section 2.5, and it will ensure a polynomial running time.

In the present situation, with thousands of methods, even the collection of outgoing edges is too colossal to manage. Hence we have developed an even more frugal strategy, where we only generate those edges whose conditions are true in the current minimal solution. As the solution increases over time, we may have to go back to earlier processed nodes and include more edges whose conditions have now become true. In particular, we may have to go back and extend previously computed ANC sets, when new tokens are added to type variables associated with assignable parents. Adhering to this strategy leads to an acceptable performance.

As indicated earlier, the quality of the inferred types depends on finding good heuristics for duplicating the code of methods. For example, if no duplication is done, the inferred type of 3+4 degrades to a set of nineteen tokens, rather than the optimal two which our current heuristic can infer.

The problem can be described by looking at the message send in Figure 2, where we must choose whether to create a duplicate of the method μ. If we always duplicated, then the type inference algorithm might never terminate since, for example, a recursive method would result in an infinite number of duplicates being produced during the analysis. In [9] we created one duplicate for every syntactic message send with selector id: in the original program. In the SELF algorithm we apply a "hash function" and create a duplicate if none already exists with the same hash value. Since there are only finitely many different hash values, termination is ensured. The hash value of the situation in Figure 2 is a triple:

$$\text{(parse tree node for the send, origin}(\tau), \rho).$$

Here, the origin(τ) indicates the original version of the τ method (τ may of course itself be a duplicate). The intuition behind this hash function has two parts. The last component, ρ, ensures that each new receiver type will get its own duplicate, resulting in a duplication strategy akin to customization [3]. The first two components of the hash function refines this strategy to ensure that sends that are different in the original program will invoke different duplicates, even if the sends have the same receiver. This is useful because different sends often supply arguments of different types. The situation is somewhat different for resends, but we will not elaborate this further.

We cannot use type information as part of the hash value, since this has not been computed yet when the hash function must be applied. To compensate for this, a small carefully selected set of methods from the standard SELF world is *always* duplicated, independently of what the hash value recommends. Part of the careful selection is to guarantee termination of the algorithm. The selected methods that are always duplicated include ifTrue:False: and other methods in booleans, some double-dispatching methods (to preserve the type information of the arguments through the second dispatch), and a few "cascading" sends.

The type inference implementation is written in 4.000 lines of SELF. Currently it uses a lot of memory; the examples in Section 3 were running in a 30 Mbyte heap. The main reason for this voracity is that the implementation has not been optimized for space. In practice, run time seems to be proportional to the number of edges and the total size of all type variables. For the execution times of the arithmetic examples, see Figure 8. The measurements were done on a SPARCstation 2. The Hanoi and Search Tree examples have similar execution times as those found in the first column of Figure 8, since in all these cases the dominating factor is the bigInt arithmetic. Specifically, inferring types for the Hanoi example involves 17,380 edges, 5,143 nodes, and takes 93 seconds.

5   Conclusion

We have developed and efficiently implemented a powerful type inference algorithm for SELF. Our algorithm involves a novel way of defining and solving constraints that describe a dynamically changing inheritance graph. To the best of our knowledge, our type inference algorithm is the first algorithm to simultaneously handle dynamic inheritance, multiple inheritance, object based inheritance, and blocks with non-local returns. Furthermore, we have shown that it can handle real programs such as the standard SELF benchmarks, including the traditionally difficult (and often ignored) constructs of primitive failures and user-defined control structures. Our algorithm provides detailed information even for partial and incorrect programs rather than merely rejecting them; for this reason it can be useful as a basis for various advanced tools.

The tools that can be based on the type information include a msgNotUnderstood-checker and an ambiguousSend-checker. Since the computed type information is a precise and conservative approximation, the tools will be correspondingly precise and conservative.

We have also presented a scenario in which a programmer uses an interactive hyperbrowser that draws extensively on the type information inferred by our algorithm to answer queries about types and control flow in a program.

Another possible tool could use the type information to identify unused (dead) code. Dead code detection is important for generating stand-alone applications. Without type inference, one would have to include the entire standard world since it would be hard to determine which parts could not possibly be required at run-time. Using type information, a conservative (but quite precise) approximation to code liveness could be computed, and methods and objects that are deemed dead by this information could safely be omitted from the application.

A further potential gain is particular to the SELF technique of dynamic compilation. The result of type inference gives an upper bound on the methods that must be compiled; thus, these methods could be pre-compiled, obviating the need for dynamic compilation and allowing the compiler to be omitted from stand-alone applications.

The version of SELF that we have described in this paper is the version that was publicly released in the Fall of 1992 (release 2.0.1). It is both a simple and a complex language. Simple, e.g., because it does not have classes and meta-classes, but complex, e.g., because it has complicated inheritance rules [4]. The type inference work has focused attention on many of the complexities, providing input to an ongoing attempt to further simplify SELF. One example is the recent elimination of parent priorities.

The SELF language is less amenable to type inference than many other object-oriented languages, yet we have obtained promising results. We believe that our algorithm is adaptable to other languages, including typed ones like C++. In the latter case, our types would provide more precision than the type declarations written by the programmer. Furthermore, since our algorithm could infer concrete (implementation-level) types for each call site, it could be used as the basis for compiler optimizations such as the inlining of virtual function calls.

Acknowledgement. The authors thank David Ungar, Randall Smith, Lars Bak, Craig Chambers, Bay-Wei Chang, Urs Hölzle, and John Maloney for helpful comments on a draft of the paper. The first author would also like to thank Sun Microsystems Laboratories for its support.

References

1. Ole Agesen, Lars Bak, Craig Chambers, Bay-Wei Chang, Urs Hölzle, John Maloney, Randall B. Smith, and David Ungar. The SELF programmer's reference manual, version 2.0. Technical report, Sun Microsystems, Inc, 2550 Garcia Avenue, Mountain View, CA 94043, USA, 1992. SMLI document 93-0056. Available by anonymous ftp from self.stanford.edu.
2. Alan H. Borning. Classes versus prototypes in object-oriented languages. In *ACM/IEEE Fall Joint Computer Conference,* pages 36–40, 1986.
3. Craig Chambers and David Ungar. Making pure object-oriented languages practical. In *Proc. OOPSLA '91, ACM SIGPLAN Sixth Annual Conference on Object-Oriented Programming Systems, Languages and Applications,* pages 1–15, 1991.
4. Craig Chambers, David Ungar, Bay-Wei Chang, and Urs Hölzle. Parents are Shared Parts of Objects: Inheritance and Encapsulation in SELF. In *Lisp and Symbolic Computation* 4(3), pages 207–222, Kluwer Acadamic Publishers, June 1991.
5. Adele Goldberg and David Robson. *Smalltalk-80—The Language and its Implementation.* Addison-Wesley, 1983.
6. Justin O. Graver and Ralph E. Johnson. A type system for Smalltalk. In *Seventeenth Symposium on Principles of Programming Languages,* pages 136–150. ACM Press, January 1990.

7. Justin Owen Graver. *Type-Checking and Type-Inference for Object-Oriented Programming Languages*. PhD thesis, Department of Computer Science. University of Illinois at Urbana-Champaign, August 1989. UIUCD-R-89-1539.

8. Henry Lieberman. Using prototypical objects to implement shared behavior in object-oriented systems. In *Proc. OOPSLA '86, Object-Oriented Programming Systems, Languages and Applications*, pages 214–223. Sigplan Notices, 21(11), November 1986.

9. Nicholas Oxhøj, Jens Palsberg, and Michael I. Schwartzbach. Making type inference practical. In *Proc. ECOOP'92, Sixth European Conference on Object-Oriented Programming*, pages 329–349. Springer-Verlag (*LNCS* 615), Utrecht, The Netherlands, July 1992.

10. Jens Palsberg and Michael I. Schwartzbach. Object-oriented type inference. In *Proc. OOPSLA '91, ACM SIGPLAN Sixth Annual Conference on Object-Oriented Programming Systems, Languages and Applications*, pages 146–161, Phoenix, Arizona, October 1991.

11. Jens Palsberg and Michael I. Schwartzbach. Safety analysis versus type inference for partial types. *Information Processing Letters*, 43:175–180, 1992.

12. Michael I. Schwartzbach. Type inference with inequalities. In *Proc. TAPSOFT'91*, pages 441–455. Springer-Verlag (*LNCS* 493), 1991.

13. David Ungar and Randall B. Smith. SELF: The power of simplicity. In *Proc. OOPSLA '87, Object-Oriented Programming Systems, Languages and Applications*, pages 227–241, 1987. Also published in Lisp and Symbolic Computation 4(3), Kluwer Academic Publishers, June, 1991.

14. Jan Vitek, R. Nigel Horspool, and James S. Uhl. Compile-time analysis of object-oriented programs. In *Proc. CC'92, 4th International Conference on Compiler Construction, Paderborn, Germany*, pages 236–250. Springer-Verlag (*LNCS* 641), 1992.

15. Mitchell Wand. A simple algorithm and proof for type inference. *Fundamentae Informaticae*, X:115–122, 1987.

Predicate Classes

Craig Chambers

Department of Computer Science and Engineering
University of Washington

Abstract. Predicate classes are a new linguistic construct designed to complement normal classes in object-oriented languages. Like a normal class, a predicate class has a set of superclasses, methods, and instance variables. However, unlike a normal class, an object is automatically an instance of a predicate class whenever it satisfies a predicate expression associated with the predicate class. The predicate expression can test the value or state of the object, thus supporting a form of implicit property-based classification that augments the explicit type-based classification provided by normal classes. By associating methods with predicate classes, method lookup can depend not only on the dynamic class of an argument but also on its dynamic value or state. If an object is modified, the property-based classification of an object can change over time, implementing shifts in major behavior modes of the object. A version of predicate classes has been designed and implemented in the context of the Cecil language.

1 Introduction

One of the chief strengths of object-oriented languages is the ability of methods to describe the circumstances for which they are intended to be used. In singly-dispatched (receiver-based) object-oriented languages, methods are placed within a class, and only apply for objects that inherit from that class. In multiply-dispatched languages, a multi-method's argument specializers describe the kinds of arguments for which it should be used. Method lookup uses the dynamic type of the actual arguments of a message to select the right method to invoke. From another standpoint, this dynamic dispatching mechanism is an important piece of infrastructure that supports the improved modelling capabilities of object-oriented languages: classes represent entities in the application domain, and methods attached to classes implement the operations on the entities. Classes and inheritance help to model natural specialization hierarchies in the application domain and support better factoring of the implementation of the application-domain entities.

Traditional object-oriented languages can model and implement various sorts of static type-based classifications of objects using classes and inheritance. However, some kinds of classifications escape these linguistic constructs. For example, few object-oriented languages can reify the concept of an empty collection in such a way that whenever a collection is empty, any methods attached to the empty-collection concept would apply, but when the collection is mutated to become non-empty, the empty-collection behavior would no longer apply. Few object-oriented languages allow methods to specialize on the identity or state of an argument, in addition to its dynamic type.

O.M. Nierstrasz (Ed.): ECOOP '93, LNCS 707, pp. 268–296, 1993.
© Springer-Verlag Berlin Heidelberg 1993

Predicate classes extend the standard object-oriented modelling constructs by reifying transient states or behavior modes of objects. A predicate class has all the properties of a normal class, including a name, a set of superclasses, a set of methods, and a set of instance variables. Additionally, a predicate class has an associated predicate expression. A predicate class represents the subset of the instances of its superclass(es) that also satisfy the predicate. Whenever an object is an instance of the superclasses of the predicate class, and the predicate expression evaluates to true when invoked on the object, the object will automatically be considered to inherit from the predicate class as well. While the object inherits from a predicate class, it inherits all the methods and instance variables of the predicate class. If the object's state later changes and the predicate expression no longer evaluates to true, the inheritance of the object will be revised to exclude the predicate class. Predicate classes thus support a form of automatic, dynamic classification of objects, based on their run-time value, state, or other user-defined properties. To the extent that these transient states are important in the application domain, predicate classes can help in modelling and implementing them.

Predicate classes are a relatively language-independent idea. For concreteness, however, we have been exploring them in the context of the Cecil language [Chambers 92b, Chambers 93]. The next section of this paper presents a brief overview of Cecil. Section 3 then describes in more detail the semantics of predicate classes as included in Cecil, and section 4 presents several examples of predicate objects at work. Section 5 discusses related work.

2 Cecil

Cecil is a purely object-oriented language based on multi-methods. Static type declarations are optional in Cecil. Where present, types are checked statically; otherwise, type checking is done dynamically as messages are sent to objects. For most of this paper, we will concentrate on the dynamically-typed core of Cecil.

The following Cecil example (not using predicate classes) implements simple linked lists:

```
object list isa collection;

object nil isa list;
method length(n@nil) { 0 }
method do(n@nil, closure) {}

object cons isa list;
field head(c@cons);
field tail(c@cons) := nil;
method length(c@cons) { 1 + c.tail.length }
method do(c@cons, closure) {
    eval(closure, c.head); do(c.tail, closure); }

method prepend(x, l@list) {
    object isa cons { head := x, tail := l } }
```

```
method print(c@collection) {
    print("[");
    do(c, &(elem){
        print("\t"); print(elem); print("\n");
    });
    print("]"); }
```

The constructs in this example are explained briefly in the following subsections. More information on the Cecil language is available in other papers [Chambers 92b, Chambers 93].

2.1 Objects

Cecil is classless, associating methods directly with objects and allowing objects to inherit directly from other objects. In general, new named objects (akin to classes or one-of-a-kind global objects) are created using the general form:

> **object** *name* **isa** *parent$_1$, ..., parent$_n$;*

where the *parent$_i$* name the object's parents. An object's parents act roughly like superclasses: the object inherits methods and fields (instance and class variables) from its parents. Zero or more parents are allowed. New anonymous objects, such as those created at run-time, use a similar syntax but omit the object name, as with the object created in the prepend method.

2.2 Methods

Methods are defined using the general form:

> **method** *name* (*formal$_1$@obj$_1$, ..., formal$_n$@obj$_n$*) { *statements* }

Any of the @*obj$_i$* may be omitted. Where present, these *argument specializers* indicate that the method is defined only for message arguments that are descendants[1] of the object named *obj$_i$*. Unspecialized formals are treated as specialized to a "top" object that is implicitly an ancestor of all other objects, allowing unspecialized formals to accept any argument. By specializing on exactly the first argument, traditional singly-dispatched methods can be simulated. Specializing on no arguments allows normal procedures or default routines to be implemented. Argument specializers are viewed as attaching the multi-method to the specializing object(s), much as methods are defined inside a class in a singly-dispatched language.

To select the method invoked by a message send, the system first finds all methods that have the same name and number of arguments as the message and whose argument specializers are (improper) ancestors of the corresponding actuals; these are the *applicable methods* for the message. The system then orders the applicable methods according to specificity: one method M is more specific than another method N exactly when each of M's argument specializers is an (improper) descendant N's corresponding argument specializer and at least one of M's argument specializers is a proper descendant of N's corresponding argument specializer. Finally, the system selects the

---

1. The *descendant* relation is the reflexive, transitive closure of the *child* relation; an object is considered a descendant of itself. The *ancestor* relation is the inverse of the *descendant* relation. To reinforce the fact that the descendant and ancestor relations are reflexive, we will sometimes describe the relation as "improper."

single most specific method as the target of the message. If the system finds no applicable methods, it reports a "message not understood" error. If the system finds several applicable methods, but no single method is more specific than all other applicable methods, then it reports a "message ambiguous" error. Otherwise, the system has successfully located the single most applicable method for the message. The method is invoked and the result of its last statement is returned as the result of the message.

Unlike other languages with multi-methods, no ordering of parents or arguments is used to automatically resolve ambiguities. Cecil includes a resend mechanism, inspired by SELF's resend mechanism and similar to Smalltalk's super, CLOS's call-next-method, and C++'s qualified messages, that allows a method to invoke the method it is overriding and to explicitly resolve ambiguities among several inherited methods.

Argument specializers are not type declarations. Argument specializers are used to determine the outcome of method lookup. After method lookup is resolved, any type declarations attached to the formal parameters are checked (this checking is done statically before the program is run). Type declarations do not influence method lookup.

Methods can be encapsulated within an object despite the presence of multi-methods. If a method is prefixed with the private keyword, access to the method is restricted to methods associated with its argument specializers. Details on encapsulation and the intended programming model for Cecil may be found in an earlier paper [Chambers 92b].

2.3 Fields

Instance variables and class variables are realized in Cecil using the field construct. A field is defined using a notation similar to that used to define a method:

> **field** *field-name* (*formal@obj*) := *expr*;

where *obj* names the object containing the new instance variable and *expr*, if present, provides an initial value for the field. Objects inheriting from *obj* receive their own copies of the *field-name* instance variable. If the field declaration is prefixed with the shared keyword, all inheriting objects share a single memory location, much like a class variable. Non-shared fields of newly-created objects may be provided an initial value as part of the object creation operation, by suffixing the object creation expression with initialization code of the following form:

> ... {*field-name$_1$* := *expr$_1$*, ..., *field-name$_n$* := *expr$_n$*}

A field may be restricted to be immutable. Fields prefixed with the read_only annotation are shared fields that cannot be modified. Fields prefixed with the init_only annotation are object-specific fields that cannot be modified after the containing object is created.

Fields are accessed solely through message sends, enabling fields to be overridden with methods and vice versa. To make accessing fields syntactically convenient, dot-notation syntactic sugar exists for messages of the following forms:

- *expr.name* is sugar for *name* (*expr*)
- *expr.name* := *expr2* is sugar for set_*name* (*expr*, *expr2*)

Any message of either of the above forms may be sugared, irrespective of whether it invokes a field accessor method or a normal method. Fields may be encapsulated within an abstraction in the same way that methods are encapsulated.

2.4 Closures

Closure objects are analogous to blocks in Smalltalk and first-class functions in other languages. Closures are heavily used in Cecil programs as arguments to user-defined control structures and to handle exceptions. A closure object is created with an expression of the following form:

    & *(formal₁, ..., formalₙ)* { *statements* }

Such an expression constructs a new object that inherits from the built-in `closure` object (upon which operations such as `loop` and `while` are defined). The new closure object also has an attached method named `eval` of the following form:

    method `eval` *(<anon>@<the_closure>, formal₁, ..., formalₙ)* { *statements* }

The body of the `eval` method executes in a context that is nested within the closure's lexically-enclosing context. Thus, to "invoke" a closure, the `eval` message is sent to the closure along with any additional arguments expected by the closure. Closures are first-class and may be returned upwards out of their enclosing scope. An example of a closure constructor expression appears in the `print` method defined earlier.

When invoked, a closure may either return normally to the sender of the `eval` message or force a *non-local return* from the closure's lexically-enclosing method. Such a non-local return is analogous to a non-local return from a block in Smalltalk or a `return` statement in a traditional language.

3 Predicate Objects

Because Cecil is object-based rather than class-based, the adaptation of the general idea of predicate classes to Cecil's object model is called *predicate objects*. The next several subsections describe how predicate objects are declared in Cecil and how they interact with normal objects, methods, and fields. Subsection 3.7 describes support for static type checking of predicate objects, and subsection 3.8 sketches some implementation strategies.

3.1 Predicate Objects

A predicate object is defined much like a normal object, except that a predicate object is introduced with the keyword `pred` and may have an additional when clause:

    pred *name* **isa** *parent₁, ..., parentₙ* **when** *predicate-expr;*

For normal objects, one object is a child of another object exactly when the relationship is declared explicitly through `isa` declarations by the programmer. Predicate objects, on the other hand, support a form of automatic property-based classification: an object *O* is automatically considered a child of a predicate object *P* exactly when the following two conditions are satisfied:

- the object *O* is an (improper) descendant of each of the parents of the predicate object *P*, and

- the predicate expression of the predicate object *P* evaluates to true, when evaluated in a scope where each of the *parent$_i$* names is bound to the object *O*.

By evaluating the predicate expression in a context where the parent names refer to the object being tested, the predicate expression can query the value or state of the object.

For example, the following predicate objects describe various important conditions of collections:

```
pred empty_collection isa collection
   when collection.length = 0;
pred non_empty_collection isa collection
   when collection.length > 0;
pred singleton_collection isa non_empty_collection
   when non_empty_collection.length = 1;
pred multiple_collection isa non_empty_collection
   when non_empty_collection.length > 1;
```

The object `nil` defined earlier in section 2 would be implicitly a child of the `empty_collection` predicate object, since `nil` is also a descendant of `empty_collection`'s parent (`collection`) and evaluating the expression "`collection.length = 0`" in a context where the name `collection` is bound to `nil` returns true. Similarly, a `cons` object would be considered a child of `non_empty_collection`. A particular `cons` object would also be a child of either `singleton_collection` or `multiple_collection`, depending on the length of the list at run-time. The following diagram illustrates the inheritance graph of the list example extended with these predicate object classifications:

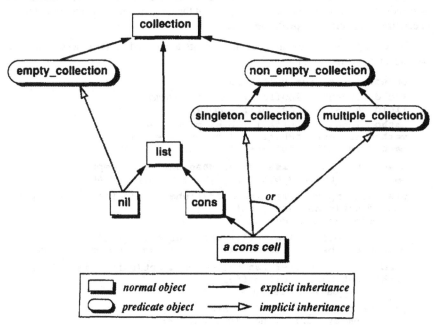

An object may inherit explicitly from a predicate object, with the implication that the predicate expression will always evaluate to true for the child object; the system verifies this assertion dynamically. In the above example, `singleton_collection` is declared to inherit from the predicate object `non_empty_collection`. This implies that any object that is a `singleton_collection` is also a `non_empty_collection`. For this simple case, one might expect the Cecil system to deduce automatically that the predicate "`non_empty_collection.length = 1`" implies the predicate "`collection.length > 0`," and so infer the inheritance link from `singleton_collection` to `non_empty_collection` automatically. However, in Cecil, nearly all operations, including basic operations such as comparisons, are user-defined, and the system cannot reason about the semantics of these operations in general. Consequently, the programmer must explicitly declare any such implications among predicate classes. Section 5 describes some other systems that restrict predicates to using only built-in operations in order to infer these inheritance relations automatically.

3.2 Predicate Objects and Methods

Predicate objects become more useful once methods and fields are associated with them. Predicate objects can be argument specializers just like normal objects. The method lookup rules remain the same: a method is applicable for a message when each actual argument object is a descendant of the corresponding argument specializer (independent of whether the specializer is a normal object or a predicate object), and one method is considered more specific than another when its argument specializers are descendants of the corresponding specializers of the other method, whether or not those specializers are normal or predicate objects.

For example, the following code implements a bounded buffer object with state-dependent behavior modes:

```
object buffer isa collection;
field elements(b@buffer);    -- a queue of elements
field max_size(b@buffer);    -- an integer
method length(b@buffer)  { b.elements.length }
method is_empty(b@buffer)  { b.length = 0 }
method is_full(b@buffer)   { b.length = b.max_size }

pred empty_buffer isa buffer when buffer.is_empty;
method get(b@empty_buffer) { ... }  -- raise error or block caller

pred non_empty_buffer isa buffer when not(buffer.is_empty);
method get(b@non_empty_buffer) {
   remove_from_front(b.elements) }

pred full_buffer isa buffer when buffer.is_full;
method put(b@full_buffer, x) { ... }  -- raise error or block caller

pred non_full_buffer isa buffer when not(buffer.is_full);
method put(b@non_full_buffer, x) {
   add_to_back(b.elements, x); }

pred partially_full_buffer isa
   non_empty_buffer, non_full_buffer;
```

The following diagram illustrates the inheritance hierarchy created by this example (the explicit inheritance link from the buffer object to `buffer` is omitted):

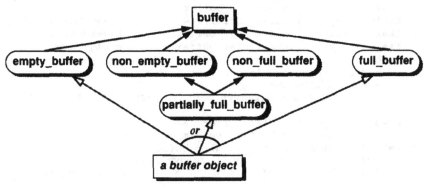

Predicate objects increase expressiveness for this example in two ways. First, important states of bounded buffers, e.g., empty and full states, are explicitly identified in the program and named. Besides documenting the important conditions of a bounded buffer, the predicate objects remind the programmer of the special situations that code must handle. This can be particularly useful during maintenance phases as code is later extended with new functionality. Second, attaching methods directly to states supports better factoring of code and eliminates `if` and `case` statements, much as does distributing methods among classes in a traditional object-oriented language. In the absence of predicate objects, a method whose behavior depended on the state of an argument object would include an `if` or `case` statement to identify and branch to the appropriate case; predicate objects eliminate the clutter of these tests and clearly separate the code for each case. In a more complete example, several methods might be associated with each special state of the buffer. By factoring the code, separating out all the code associated with a particular state or behavior mode, we hope to improve the readability and maintainability of the code.

The `partially_full_buffer` predicate object defined above illustrates that a predicate object declaration need not specify its own predicate expression. Such a predicate object may still depend on a condition if at least one of its ancestors is a predicate object. In the above example, the `partially_full_buffer` predicate object has no explicit predicate expression, yet since an object only inherits from `partially_full_buffer` whenever it already inherits from both `non_empty_buffer` and `non_full_buffer`, the `partially_full_-buffer` predicate object effectively repeats the conjunction of the predicate expressions of its parents, in this case that the buffer be neither empty nor full.

3.3   Predicate Objects and Inheritance

Predicate objects are intended to interact well with normal inheritance. If an abstraction is implemented by inheriting from some other implementation, any predicate objects that specialize the parent implementation will automatically specialize the child implementation whenever it is in the appropriate state. For example, a new implementation of bounded buffers could be built that used a fixed-length array with insert and remove positions that cycle around the array:

```
object circular_buffer isa buffer;
field array(b@circular_buffer); -- a fixed-length array of elements
field insert_pos(b@circular_buffer); -- an index into the array
field remove_pos(b@circular_buffer); -- another integer index
method max_size(b@circular_buffer) { b.array.length }
method length(b@circular_buffer) {
   -- % is modulus operator
   (b.insert_pos - b.remove_pos) % b.array.length }

pred non_empty_circular_buffer isa
        circular_buffer, non_empty_buffer;
method get(b@non_empty_circular_buffer) {
   var x := fetch(b.array, b.remove_pos);
   b.remove_pos := (b.remove_pos + 1) % b.array.length;
   x }

pred non_full_circular_buffer isa
        circular_buffer, non_full_buffer;
method put(b@non_full_circular_buffer, x) {
   store(b.array, b.insert_pos, x);
   b.insert_pos := (b.insert_pos + 1) % b.array.length; }
```

The following diagram illustrates the extended inheritance graph for bounded and circular buffers (the partially_full_buffer predicate object is omitted):

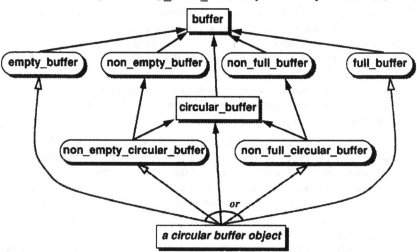

Since the circular_buffer implementation inherits from the original buffer object, a circular_buffer object will automatically inherit from the empty_buffer or full_buffer predicate object whenever the circular_buffer happens to be in one of those states. No empty_circular_buffer or full_circular_buffer objects need to be implemented if specialized behavior is not needed. The non_empty_circular_buffer and non_full_circular_buffer predicate objects are needed to override the default get and put methods in the non-blocking states. Any object that inherits from circular_buffer and that also satisfies the predicate associated with non_empty_buffer will automatically be classified as a non_empty_circular_buffer.

The specification of when an object inherits from a predicate object implicitly places a predicate object just below its immediate parents and after all other normal children of the parents. For example, consider an empty circular buffer object. Both the buffer object and its parent, the circular_buffer object, will be considered to inherit from the empty_buffer predicate object. Because circular_buffer is considered to inherit from empty_buffer, any methods attached to circular_buffer will override methods attached to empty_buffer. Often this is the desired behavior, but at other times it might be preferable for methods attached to predicate objects to override methods attached to "cousin" normal objects.[1] If this were the case, then the buffer code could be simplified somewhat, as follows:

```
object buffer isa collection;
... -- elements, length, etc.
method get(b@buffer) { remove_from_front(b.elements) }
method put(b@buffer, x) { add_to_back(b.elements, x); }

pred empty_buffer isa buffer when buffer.is_empty;
method get(b@empty_buffer) { ... } -- raise error or block caller

pred full_buffer isa buffer when buffer.is_full;
method put(b@full_buffer, x) { ... } -- raise error or block caller

object circular_buffer isa buffer;
... -- array, insert_pos, length, etc.
method get(b@circular_buffer) {
    var x := fetch(b.array, b.remove_pos);
    b.remove_pos := (b.remove_pos + 1) % b.array.length;
    x }
method put(b@circular_buffer, x) {
    store(b.array, b.insert_pos, x);
    b.insert_pos := (b.insert_pos + 1) % b.array.length; }
```

The non-blocking versions of get and put would be associated with the buffer object directly, and the non_empty_buffer, non_full_buffer, and partially_full_buffer predicate objects could be removed (if desired). The non-blocking get and put routines for circular buffers would similarly be moved up to the circular_buffer object itself, with the non_empty_circular-_buffer and non_full_circular_buffer predicate objects being removed also. If the methods attached to the empty_buffer object were considered to override those of the circular_buffer object, then sending get to a circular buffer that was empty would (correctly) invoke the empty_buffer implementation. In the current semantics of predicate objects in Cecil, however, the circular_buffer's implementation of get would be invoked, leading to an error.

---

1. One object is a cousin of another if they share a common ancestor but are otherwise unrelated.

A third potential semantics would be to consider the predicate object to be unordered with respect to "cousin" objects, and methods defined on two cousins to be mutually ambiguous. An important area of continuing work is determining whether one semantics is most helpful or if the programmer needs to use different rules in different circumstances.

3.4 Dynamic Reclassification of Objects

Since the state of an object can change over time (fields can be mutable), the results of predicate expressions evaluated on the object can change. If this happens, the system will automatically reclassify the object, recomputing its implicit inheritance links. For example, when a buffer object becomes full, the predicates associated with the non_full_buffer and full_buffer predicate objects both change, and the inheritance graph of the buffer object is updated. As a result, different methods may be used to respond to messages, such as the put message in the filled buffer example.

Semantically, predicate expressions are evaluated lazily as part of method lookup, rather than eagerly as the state of an object changes. Only when the value of some predicate expression is needed to determine the outcome of method lookup is the predicate evaluated. Since predicate expressions are expected to be pure functions, the exact time of evaluation of predicate expressions can usually be ignored. In any case, implementations are free to evaluate predicate expressions at other times, as described in section 3.8, as long as the externally-visible semantics is unchanged.

3.5 Predicate Objects and Fields

Fields may be associated with a predicate object. The semantics of accessing a field attached to a predicate object has already been specified: fields are accessed solely through message sends, and method lookup in the presence of predicate objects has been defined. However, the *contents* of a field inherited from a predicate object is less obvious. Several questions arise: does the field exist only when the controlling predicate evaluates to true? Does its value persist while the predicate evaluates to false? How does such a field get initialized?

In our version of predicate objects in Cecil, objects reserve space for any fields that *might* be inherited from a predicate object, i.e., those fields inherited by an object assuming all predicate expressions evaluate to true. The value stored in a field of an object persists even when the controlling predicate evaluates to false and the field is inaccessible. When the field becomes accessible again, its value will be the same as when it was last visible. At object-creation time, an initial value may be provided for fields inherited from predicate objects, even if those fields may not be visible in the newly-created object.

The following example exploits this semantics to implement a graphical window object that can be either expanded or iconified. Each of the two important states of the window remembers its own screen location (using a field named position in both cases), plus some other mode-specific information such as the text in the window and the bitmap of the icon, and this data persists across openings and closings of the window:

```
object window isa interactive_graphical_object;
field iconified(@window) := false;
method display(w@window) {
    -- draw window using w.position
    ... }
method erase(w@window) {
    -- clear space where window is
    ... }
method move(w@window, new_position) {
    -- works for both expanded and iconified windows!
    w.erase; w.position := new_position; w.display; }

pred expanded_window isa window when not(window.iconified);
field position(@expanded_window) := upper_left;
field text(@expanded_window);
method iconify(w@expanded_window) {
    w.erase; w.iconified := true; w.display; }

pred iconified_window isa window when window.iconified;
field position(@iconfied_window) := lower_right;
field icon(@iconified_window);
method open(w@iconified_window) {
    w.erase; w.iconified := false; w.display; }

method create_window(open_position, iconified_position,
                     text, icon) {
    object isa window { iconified := false,
        position@open_window := open_position,
        position@iconified_window := iconified_position,
        text := text, icon := icon } }
```

A window object has two position fields, but only one is visible at a time. This allows the display, erase, and move routines to send the message position as part of their implementation, without needing to know whether the window is open or closed. The create_window method initializes both position fields when the window is created, even though the position of the icon is not visible initially. The position@*object* notation used in the field initialization resolves the ambiguity between the two position fields.

3.6 Predicates on Methods

A predicate object characterizes the value or state of a single object. By using a predicate object as an argument specializer, a method can restrict its applicability to arguments in a particular state. In some cases, however, a method's applicability might be conditional on some predicate defined over all of its arguments as a group. For example, one early motivation for predicates in Cecil was to be able to write code like the following, which implements iterating through two lists in parallel:

```
method pair_do(l1@cons, l2@cons, closure) {
    eval(closure, l1.head, l2.head);
    pair_do(l1.tail, l2.tail, closure); }
method pair_do(l1@list, l2@list, closure)
    when l1@nil | l2@nil {}
```

The predicate restricts the second pair_do method to those cases where either or both of the list arguments are nil. Without the predicate expression, the code would be less robust to future programming extensions. If a new implementation of lists were added later, such as a special representation for singleton lists, but appropriate pair_do methods for singleton lists were accidentally omitted, the system would silently use the second "default" pair_do method when iterating through a singleton list, rather than signalling a "message not understood" error. To achieve this level of robustness without using a method predicate expression, the second pair_do method would need to be written using three separate methods:

```
method pair_do(l1@nil, l2@list, closure) {}
method pair_do(l1@list, l2@nil,  closure) {}
method pair_do(l1@nil, l2@nil,   closure) {}
```

The third method is needed to resolve the ambiguity between the first two methods when iterating through two nil objects; method lookup in Cecil does not prioritize arguments based on position.

One open issue with method predicate expressions is how to order predicated methods according to specificity. Method lookup depends on being able to order the applicable methods by specificity, raising an "ambiguous message" error if a single most specific method cannot be identified. For predicate objects, explicit inheritance declarations between two predicate objects can reflect when one predicate expression implies another, but methods cannot be named so easily in order to express an ordering.

At present, our extension of Cecil does not include predicated methods. Predicate objects already handle many practical cases simply and clearly. We prefer to gain experience with predicate objects before considering extensions such as predicated methods.

3.7   Static Type Checking

Cecil supports a static type system that can guarantee at program definition time that no "message not understood," "message ambiguous," "private method accessed," or "uninitialized field accessed" error messages can occur at run-time. When extended with predicate objects, these same guarantees should be preserved. The central type-checking problem introduced by predicate objects is that an object's inheritance graph, and consequently the set of methods inherited by an object, can change at run-time. To guarantee type safety, the type checker must verify that for each message declared in the interface of some object O:

- at all times there is an implementation of the message inherited by the object O, and

- at no time are there several mutually ambiguous implementations of the message inherited by the object O.

The set of methods inherited by the object O from normal objects is fixed at program-definition time and can be type-checked in the standard way. Methods inherited from predicate objects pose more of a problem. If two predicate objects might be inherited simultaneously by an object, either one predicate object must be known to override the other or they must have disjoint method names. For example, in the bounded buffer implementation, since an object can inherit from both the non_empty_buffer and the `non_full_buffer` predicate objects, they cannot implement methods with the same name. Similarly, if the only implementations of some message are in some set of predicate objects, then one of the predicate objects must always be inherited for the message to be guaranteed to be understood. In other words, the checker needs to know when one predicate object *implies* another, when two predicate objects are *mutually exclusive*, and when a group of predicate objects is *exhaustive*. Once these relationships among predicate objects are determined, the rest of type-checking becomes straightforward.

Ideally, the system would be able to determine all these relationships automatically by examining the predicate expressions attached to the various predicate objects. However, as described earlier in section 3.1, predicate expressions in Cecil can run arbitrary user-defined code, and consequently the system would have a hard time automatically inferring implication, mutual exclusion, and exhaustiveness. Consequently, we rely on explicit user declarations to determine the relationships among predicate objects; the system can verify dynamically that these declarations are correct. Section 5 describes some other systems that can infer some of the relationships automatically by restricting the form of the predicate expressions.

A declaration already exists to describe when one predicate object implies another: the `isa` declaration. If one predicate object explicitly inherits from another, then the first object's predicate is assumed to imply the second object's predicate. Any methods in the child predicate object override those in the ancestor, resolving any ambiguities between them. For example, a method associated with `non_empty_circular_buffer` overrides a method associated with `non_empty_buffer`, since `non_empty_circular_buffer` inherits explicitly from `non_empty_buffer`.

Mutual exclusion among a group of predicate objects is declared using the following notation:

disjoint $object_1,$ ..., $object_n;$

The predicate objects named by each of the $object_i$ are assumed by the static type checker to never be inherited simultaneously, i.e., that at most one of their predicate expressions will evaluate to true at any given time. Mutual exclusion of two predicate objects implies that the type checker should not be concerned if both predicate objects define methods with the same name, since they cannot both be inherited by an object. To illustrate, the following declarations extend earlier predicate objects with mutual exclusion information:

```
disjoint empty_collection, non_empty_collection;
disjoint singleton_collection, multiple_collection;
disjoint empty_buffer, non_empty_buffer;
disjoint full_buffer, non_full_buffer;
```

The system can infer that `empty_collection` is mutually exclusive with `singleton_collection` and `multiple_collection`, since `singleton_collection` and `multiple_collection` both inherit from `non_empty_collection`. A similar inference determines that `empty_buffer` and `full_buffer` are mutually exclusive with `partially_full_buffer`. Note that `empty_buffer` and `full_buffer` are not necessarily exclusive.

A final declaration asserts that a group of predicate objects exhaustively cover the possible states of some other object, using the following notation:

cover *object* **by** *object$_1$*, ..., *object$_n$*;

This declaration implies that whenever an object O descends from *object*, the object O will also descend from at least one of the *object$_i$* predicate objects; each of the *object$_i$* are expected to descend from *object* already. Exhaustiveness implies that if all of the *object$_i$* implement some message, then any object inheriting from *object* will understand the message. For example, the following coverage declarations extend the earlier predicate objects:

```
cover collection by empty_collection, non_empty_collection;
cover non_empty_collection by singleton_collection,
                               multiple_collection;
cover buffer by empty_buffer,
               partially_full_buffer,
               full_buffer;
```

Often a group of predicate objects divide an abstraction into a set of exhaustive, mutually-exclusive subcases. To make specifying such situations easier, the following declaration is syntactic sugar for a cover declaration and a disjoint declaration:

divide *object* **into** *object$_1$*, ..., *object$_n$*;

Using this declaration, we can compress the above disjoint and cover declarations as follows:

```
divide collection into empty_collection,
                       non_empty_collection;
divide non_empty_collection into singleton_collection,
                                 multiple_collection;
divide buffer into empty_buffer,
                   partially_full_buffer,
                   full_buffer;
disjoint empty_buffer, non_empty_buffer;
disjoint full_buffer, non_full_buffer;
```

We believe that adding the extra disjoint, cover, and divide declarations will not be too burdensome for the programmer. In addition to supporting static type checking of predicate objects with arbitrary predicate expressions, the declarations help to document the code. Furthermore, type declarations and type checking are optional in Cecil, helping to support both exploratory and production programming within the same language, and disjoint, cover, and divide declarations may similarly be omitted during exploratory programming.

Since fields are accessed solely through accessor methods, checking accesses to fields in predicate objects reduces to checking legality of messages in the presence of predicate objects, as described above. To ensure that fields are always initialized before being accessed, the type checker simply checks that the values of all fields potentially inherited by an object are initialized either at the declaration of the field or at the creation of the object. While this check is overly conservative (it does not take into account assignments to a field immediately after it comes into scope), it is sufficient, simple, and, we hope, not too restrictive.

Static type checking as described above ensures that a uniform interface is provided by an object, no matter what its state happens to be at run-time. An interesting, less restrictive approach to type checking would allow different states of an object to have different interfaces. For example, a stack object might be subdivided into empty_stack and non_empty_stack predicate objects, but only the non_empty_stack predicate object would support a pop operation. Type checking with such state-dependent interfaces might require some more interesting analysis akin to typestate checking in the Hermes language [Strom & Yemini 86, Strom *et al.* 91] or would fall back on run-time checking for state-dependent operations. Lea is exploring a similar idea which he calls fine-grained types [Lea 92].

3.8 Implementation Strategies

A straightforward implementation of predicate objects is not difficult. Each object allocates enough space for any field it might inherit from a predicate object, and method lookup is augmented with additional evaluations of predicate expressions for methods attached to predicate objects. This approach has comparable performance to what the programmer would likely have implemented in the absence of predicate objects: methods would have extra tests and case statements in them to evaluate the requisite predicate expressions, and objects would include all instance variables that might end up being needed. We followed this strategy in our initial implementation of predicate objects in our Cecil interpreter. As of this writing, the dynamically-typed portion of predicate objects has been running for several months, but the extensions to the static type system have not yet been implemented.

Several techniques can be used to improve the performance of predicate objects:

- The system can attempt to evaluate predicate expressions eagerly and to cache the results of these evaluations. For most simple predicates, the system can determine that they have no side-effects and therefore will not need to be reevaluated upon each method lookup. Instead, the result of the predicate can be stored with the object. A straightforward way of caching the result of a predicate is in a hidden instance variable, but a more efficient way is by replacing the class[1] of the object with a special internal subclass that represents the outcome of evaluating the predicate. Method lookup for one of these internal subclasses would bypass evaluation of the predicate, consequently running just as fast as normal method lookup. To record the outcomes of multiple independent predicates, internal combination subclasses can be constructed lazily as needed. For attributes that may vary during the lifetime of an object, assignments to the attribute would change the object's class to a generic class. Method lookup on the generic class would first evaluate all necessary predicate expressions, change the class of the object to record the predicates' results, and then resend the message to the new class to invoke the proper method. Newly-created objects would start out as instances of the generic class.

In the absence of predicate objects, programmers sometimes generate state-specific subclasses by hand. However, hand-written simulations become difficult to maintain with multiple independent predicates, and time-varying predicates are not amenable

---

1. In a classless language like Cecil, the implementation can maintain internal data structures that act like classes, as is done in the SELF implementation [Chambers *et al.* 89, Chambers 92a].

to this approach (since programmers normally cannot change the class of an object at run-time).

- Space for fields used solely as boolean or enumerated values governing selection of one of several possible predicate classes, such as the iconified attribute defined for window objects, can be reclaimed if the value of the attribute is encoded in the internal class of the object as described above. Similarly, if a predicate expression is constant for a particular object, space for fields associated with mutually exclusive (and so unreachable) predicates can be reclaimed.

These optimizations could make predicate classes *more* efficient than hand-written code not using predicate classes, since the system can perform optimizations, such as changing the class of an object dynamically, that the programmer could not emulate in most object-oriented languages.

4 Additional Examples

This section contains additional examples illustrating the usefulness of predicate objects in Cecil. Each example highlights some strengths and/or weaknesses of predicate objects not previously addressed.

4.1 Pattern Matching-Style Functions

Predicate objects can be used to emulate some of the functionality of pattern matching-based function definitions, as found in functional languages such as Standard ML [Milner *et al.* 90] and Haskell [Hudak *et al.* 92]. With pattern matching, a programmer can write multiple versions of a function, with the system automatically selecting the proper version of the function to call based on the dynamic value of the function arguments. Patterns can range from constants through partial descriptions of structured types through variable names which match any actual. For example, the following Haskell examples define some standard operations on numbers and lists:

```
-- return the sign of the argument
sign x | x <  0 = -1
       | x == 0 =  0
       | x >  0 =  1


-- map the unary function f over the argument list, returning a list of results
map f []     = []
map f (x:xs) = f x : map f xs


-- take a pair of lists of equal length and return a list of pairs
zip []     []     = []
zip (x:xs) (y:ys) = (x,y) : zip xs ys
zip xs     ys     = error "cannot zip lists of unequal length"


-- reduce the non-empty argument list using the binary function f
reduce f []       = error "cannot reduce an empty list"
reduce f [x]      = x
reduce f (x:y:zs) = f x (reduce f (y:zs))
```

The ability of pattern matching to select the function to call based on the dynamic value or state of the argument is absent from most object-oriented languages. Using predicate objects, however, we are able to capture this finer sort of dispatching:

```
pred negative isa number when number < 0;[1]
pred zero     isa number when number = 0;
pred positive isa number when number > 0;
method sign(n@negative) { -1 }
method sign(n@zero)     {  0 }
method sign(n@positive) {  1 }

method map(f, c@empty_collection) { nil }
method map(f, c@non_empty_collection) {
   prepend(eval(f, c.first), map(f, c.rest)) }

method zip(c1@empty_collection, c2@empty_collection) { nil }
method zip(c1@non_empty_collection,
           c2@non_empty_collection) {
   prepend([c1.first, c2.first],  -- an array constructor
           zip(c1.rest, c2.rest)) }
method zip(c1@collection, c2@collection) {
   error("cannot zip lists of unequal length"); }

method reduce(f, c@empty_collection) {
   error("cannot reduce an empty list"); }
method reduce(f, c@singleton_collection) { c.first }
method reduce(f, c@multiple_collection) {
   eval(f, c.first, reduce(f, c.rest)) }
```

Pattern matching provides additional facilities not supported by predicate objects. For example, pattern matching allows names to be bound to subcomponents of an object, such as in the pattern $(x:xs)$, which binds x to the head of the list and xs to the tail of the list. Also, patterns are very concise and readable syntactically, while predicate objects are somewhat more verbose.

Predicate objects have several advantages over pattern matching, however:

- The methods written using predicate objects are more general than those written using concrete patterns. Any representation of collections satisfying the predicate associated with empty_collection can invoke the corresponding map method, for instance, not just the one empty list object. Similarly, patterns can only range over concrete data types, not abstract data types, although Wadler has proposed an extension of pattern matching to support abstract data types [Wadler 87].

- Predicate objects can be ordered in terms of specificity, and the system with use this information to determine the most appropriate implementation of a method to call. Functional languages typically try functions in the order they were defined, invoking the first version whose patterns match.

- Predicate objects give a name to the interesting condition and can be used to group functions that operate on the same condition, potentially increasing the readability of the resulting code.

---

1. Recall that in the predicate "number < 0", the name number is bound to the descendant of number being considered, i.e., the number itself.

- With predicate objects, dispatching based on value or state is integrated with dispatching based on dynamic type. Pattern matching cannot select the version of the function based on the dynamic type of the argument.

- Predicate objects can be extended with new specialized cases as the system evolves. The versions of a function defined by pattern matching often must be defined as a group, and they cannot be extended later with new alternatives without editing the original function definition. Pattern matching in dynamically-typed logic languages usually does not suffer from this limitation.

In part, these examples are easy to write because Cecil provides the ability to add methods to an object without needing to modify the object's definition. Traditional singly-dispatched languages cannot achieve this kind of easy extension because the methods of a class are part of the class definition, which would need to be edited to add new methods to the class. To compensate for the extra separation between objects and methods, Cecil relies on the programming environment to show a view of the program in which methods are directly associated with their specializing objects [Chambers 92b].

4.2 Attributes of People

Predicate objects can help organize code for an abstraction that can be considered to have multiple independent attributes and behavior that depends on the state of the attributes. For example, a person object might have several independent fields such as sex and age, and some of the methods on person might depend on the values of the fields:

```
object person;
field sex(@person);
field age(@person);
method bedtime(@person) { "10pm" }
method long_lived(p@person) { p.age > p.expected_lifespan }
method have_birthday(p@person) { p.age := p.age + 1; }

pred male isa person when person.sex = "male";
method expected_lifespan(@male) { 70 }

pred female isa person when person.sex = "female";
method expected_lifespan(@female) { 74 }

pred child isa person when person.age <= 12;
method bedtime(@child) { "8pm" }

pred teenager isa person
        when person.age >= 13 & person.age <= 19;
method bedtime(@teenager) { "12am" }

pred boy isa male, child;
pred girl isa female, child;

method make_person(sex, age) {
    object isa person { sex := sex, age := age } }
```

Predicate objects provide a direct way of associating behavior with particular values of the object's attributes. In a traditional language without predicate objects, the programmer must choose between two different ways of implementing an attribute and its connected behavior:

- If the attribute is constant, it can be represented by instantiating a specialized subclass of the `person` class. For example, the `sex` attribute could be replaced with `male` and `female` subclasses. The programmer then could factor state-specific methods into the appropriate subclass. Unfortunately, in the presence of multiple independent attributes, this strategy suffers from a combinatorial explosion of combining subclasses. Also, object creations must name the appropriate subclass statically, which can be awkward if the corresponding attribute is a computed expression rather than a constant.

- The attribute could be represented as an instance variable. Behavior dependent on the attribute must be written in one place and be sprinkled with tests of the attribute value. Programmers usually have no choice but to implement time-varying attributes this way.

With predicate objects, attributes can be implemented using the first approach without fear of combinatorial explosions and without excluding time-varying attributes. Attributes still can be manipulated like instance variables when convenient: new people are created as children of the generic `person` object irrespective of their sex or age, and attributes can be queried and modified directly.

A similar example is found in several papers on mixins and object-oriented programming: windows that may have titles and/or borders. Conventional approaches implement titled-window and bordered-window subclasses, plus their combination class. In Cecil with predicate objects, a single `window` object would be defined with `has_title` and `has_border` fields. Predicate objects inheriting from `window` and conditional on the presence or absence of titles and/or borders would contain the code responsible for the two independent extensions. One complexity with this design is that in Cecil there is no automatic method combination: if a window has both a title and a border, and both predicate objects define a method such as `display`, the programmer must explicitly provide a `titled_bordered_window` predicate object that overrides the two others and resolves the ambiguity, perhaps by calling both `display` methods sequentially. The difficulty arises because the titled and bordered attributes are not truly independent; they interact for displaying behavior.

4.3   Squares, Rectangles, and Polygons

A classic example of object-oriented programming is a hierarchy of geometric shapes, such as would appear in a drawing editor. For example, the following code implements a fragment of a standard hierarchy of graphical shapes:

```
object polygon isa shape;
field vertices(@polygon);
method draw(p@polygon) { ... }
method add_vertex(p@polygon, vertex) { ... }

object rectangle isa polygon;
method length(r@rectangle) { ... } --compute from vertices
method set_length(r@rectangle, new_length) { ... }
method draw(r@rectangle) { ... }
method widen(r@rectangle, factor) {
    r.length := r.length * factor; }

object square isa rectangle;
method draw(s@square) { ... }
```

According to mathematical definitions, all squares are rectangles, and all rectangles are polygons, so this inheritance hierarchy is desirable from a modelling viewpoint. However, if the user invokes the add_vertex method (which modifies the polygon in place) on a rectangle, the object will no longer be a rectangle. Similarly, invoking the widen operation on a square will violate the specification of the square.

In the Eiffel community, the recommended solution is to *undefine* the add_vertex operation in the rectangle class and to undefine the widen operation in the square class, thus disallowing illegal modifications [Meyer 91]. However, this has two undesirable consequences. First, static type checking of operations in the presence of the undefine construct is quite difficult [Cook 89], leading to a complex, two-phase typing algorithm [Meyer 92]. Second, the drawing editor application either must realize that certain kinds of polygons cannot have vertices added to them (as must users of the application), or the editor must construct only polygons, forgoing any functionality and performance advantages of the more specialized subclasses.

With predicate objects, this example can be reimplemented with rectangle and square treated as predicate objects:

```
object polygon isa shape;
method is_rectangle(p@polygon) { ... }
   ...

pred rectangle isa polygon when polygon.is_rectangle;
method is_square(r@rectangle) { r.length = r.width }
   ...

pred square isa rectangle when rectangle.is_square;
   ...
```

Whenever a polygon satisfies the restrictions of rectangles or squares, the specialized implementations of the operations suitable to those kinds of objects are used. If a vertex is added to an object classified as a rectangle, it will be automatically reclassified as a general polygon. Non-predicate versions of rectangle and square are not needed. If an object inherits directly from the square predicate object, for instance, this informs the system that the object will always remain a square, and consequently the object will act just as if it inherited from a non-predicate version of square. The implementation strategies described in section 3.8 can make the implementation just as efficient as if square were a normal non-predicate object.

4.4 Mutable Binary Trees

Predicate objects can be used to represent distinct behavior modes of an object. The window example from section 3.5 illustrates this application, where the two distinct behavior modes are expanded and iconified windows. As a second example, the code below implements mutable binary trees, where the distinct behavior modes are empty and non-empty trees:

```
object tree isa collection;
field is_empty(@tree) := true;

pred empty_tree isa tree when tree.is_empty;
method insert(t@empty_tree, x) {
    t.is_empty := false;
    t.left   := object isa tree;  -- create a new, empty tree
    t.right  := object isa tree;
    t.contents := x; }
method do(t@empty_tree, closure) {}

pred non_empty_tree isa tree when not(tree.is_empty);
field left(@non_empty_tree);
field right(@non_empty_tree);
field contents(@non_empty_tree);
method insert(t@non_empty_tree, x) {
    if(x < t.contents,    -- if(,,) is a user-defined control structure
        { insert(t.left, x); },
        { insert(t.right, x); }); }
method do(t@non_empty_tree, closure) {
    do(t.left, closure);
    eval(closure, t.contents);
    do(t.right, closure); }
```

All trees understand the insert and do messages, but the implementation of these two messages is completely different for the two behavior modes, and predicate objects allow the two modes to be factored apart. Additionally, the state specific to non-empty trees is associated only with the non_empty_tree object. Optimizations described in section 3.8 can eliminate the storage space for the is_empty field by creating two internal subclasses of tree and changing the internal "class pointer" of a tree instance to implement assignment to the is_empty field.

Much of this example could be implemented without predicate objects. One approach would make empty_tree and non_empty_tree normal subclasses of the tree class. However, this approach would preclude adding in place to an empty tree, since the class of the tree cannot change. Alternatively, a single tree class could be defined without state-specific subclasses, but this approach would sacrifice the factoring of code, require is_empty checks in the implementation of insert and do, and expose the left, right, and contents fields even in empty trees. The solution with predicate objects supports both state-based factoring of code and mutating trees in place from one state to another.

5 Related Work

5.1 Value-Based Dispatching in Other Object-Oriented Languages

Object-oriented languages support one kind of dynamic binding of messages to methods, where the method to run can depend on the run-time class or type of the message receiver (for singly-dispatched languages) or for some subset of the message arguments (for multiply-dispatched languages). A few object-oriented languages, such as CLOS [Bobrow *et al.* 88] and Dylan [Apple 92], can dispatch on the identity of an argument, but cannot easily dispatch on a more general condition of an argument, such as being a negative number or an iconified window; prototype-based languages are similar in this regard.

5.2 Sets and Polymethods in LAURE

The LAURE language is an unusual hybrid language with object-oriented, rule-based, and constraint-based features [Caseau 91, Caseau & Silverstein 92, Caseau & Perron 93]. Of particular interest is LAURE's ability to define sets of objects and to associate methods (called *polymethods*) with all members of a set. For example, the following two polymethods define LAURE's fibonacci function:

```
[define fib(x:{0,1}) polymethod => 1]
[define fib(x:{integer & {sign as +}}) polymethod =>
    fib(x - 1) + fib(x - 2)]
```

A set in LAURE can describe a fixed list of objects, all the members of a particular class, or all the objects having a particular attribute with a particular value. Sets can be combined using intersection to form new sets, much as multiple inheritance is used to combine classes, but LAURE sets also may be combined using the union and power-set operators. Methods can be associated with arbitrary set specifications, not just classes, as in the f i b example. LAURE uses the specifications of the sets to automatically construct a lattice over the sets, ordered by set inclusion, and this lattice is used like an inheritance graph to resolve conflicts among methods whenever more than one method applies. A set specification is reevaluated whenever necessary to determine whether some object is currently a member of the specified set.

Sets in LAURE share many of the characteristics of predicate classes. Both describe the objects contained by (descended from) them, and this collection of objects can vary dynamically. Methods are attached to sets directly, as methods are attached to predicate classes. LAURE uses special kinds of inheritance operators to describe exhaustive or mutually-exclusive sets: a closed union implies that its subclasses are exhaustive, while a closed intersection somewhat counter-intuitively specifies that its superclasses are mutually exclusive.

LAURE's sets and predicate classes have some differences. Sets in LAURE may be specified using a fixed group of set construction operations and base sets, while predicate classes can be defined with arbitrary predicates. In LAURE, some of the specificity relationships among sets (the subsumption relation) is inferred automatically based on the structure of the set specifications, while all inheritance relationships among predicate classes must be specified explicitly.

5.3 Classifiers in Kea

The Kea language is a functional object-oriented language based on multiple dispatching [Mugridge *et al.* 91, Hamer 92]. Kea supports a notion of *dynamic classification* of objects. A class may be explicitly divided into a group of mutually-exclusive subclasses, and instances of the class can be classified into one of the disjoint subclasses. For example, a List class may be classified into EmptyList and NonEmptyList subclasses. Multiple independent classifiers may be used for any class. For example, a Person class may be classified into Male and Female subclasses as well as independent Young, MiddleAged, and Old subclasses. This approach avoids the need for creating a combinatorially-exploding number of combining classes (e.g., a YoungMale class, an OldFemale class, etc.), as these combination subclasses become implicit. The example in section 4.2 was inspired by a similar example presented in Kea.

Classifiers in Kea are similar to predicate classes. Both support automatic attribute-based classification of objects, and operations can be associated with the classified subclasses. Classifiers, however, appear to subdivide a class into a set of exhaustive, mutually-exclusive subclasses, with the particular subclass for an object determined either by the value of a single attribute (whose type must be some enumerated type) of the object or by explicit instantiation of a particular subclass. Predicate classes support arbitrary predicates and non-exhaustive and overlapping classifications, as illustrated by the buffer example in section 3.2. Since Kea is a functional language, it does not address the issue of an object whose classification varies over time.

5.4 Term Classification

Yelland developed an experimental extension of Smalltalk that supported *term classification* [Yelland 92]. Yelland introduced two new kinds of class-like constructs into Smalltalk: *primitive concepts* and *defined concepts*:

- Primitive concepts are used for explicit classification of objects. An object is a member of a primitive concept only when explicitly stated.

- Defined concepts are used for implicit property-based classification. An object is a member of a defined concept whenever its attributes (called *roles*) satisfy certain *role restrictions*. Only a few kinds of role restrictions are allowed, such as checking for an attribute being an instance of a particular class or concept, being within some integer range, or being an element of some fixed set. In return, Yelland's system will automatically compute the subsumption relationships among concepts (i.e., when one concept "inherits" from another) based on the structure of the role restrictions.

Methods and instance variables may be attached to both kinds of concepts just as with regular classes.

An object in Yelland's system may be a member of several independent defined concepts. Yelland's experimental system creates internal combination subclasses, and uses a single combination subclass to record that an object is a member of several independent concepts simultaneously. Since Smalltalk is imperative, an object's properties can change at run-time, and thus the object's classification can become out-of-date. Yelland describes problems that can occur if an object is eagerly reclassified immediately when its state changes, such as when an object temporarily violates its role restrictions while its state is being updated. Consequently, in Yelland's system, objects are reclassified only when explicitly requested by the program.

Yelland's system is similar to LAURE and Kea in that the system is responsible for automatically determining the "inheritance" relationships among concepts, at the cost of limiting the form of the role restrictions. The predicate expressions of predicate classes can be any boolean-valued expression, at the cost of requiring explicit programmer declaration of the inheritance relationships. To avoid problems with eager reclassification of objects while keeping automatic reclassification in the system, Cecil re-evaluates predicate expressions lazily as needed to resolve method lookup. As described in section 3.8, an optimizing implementation might choose to track inheritance from predicate classes in other ways for faster method lookup.

5.5   Dynamic Inheritance in SELF and Garnet

SELF is a prototype-based language with a simple and uniform object model [Ungar & Smith 87, Hölzle et al. 91]. One consequence of SELF's uniformity is that an object's parent slots, like other data slots, may be assigned new values at run-time. An assignment to a parent slot effectively changes an object's inheritance at run-time. Consequently, the object can inherit different methods and exhibit different behavior. This *dynamic inheritance* allows part of an object's implementation to change at run-time. Dynamic inheritance has been used in SELF to implement mutable objects with several distinct behavior modes, such as binary trees with empty and non-empty states [Ungar et al. 91]. The example in section 4.4 was inspired by this use of dynamic inheritance in SELF.

The Garnet system [Myers et al. 92] includes a similar mechanism, also called dynamic inheritance but implemented differently, to effect wholesale changes in the implementation of an object's behavior. This feature has been used in Garnet to capture the significant changes in a user-interface object's behavior when switching between build mode and test mode in an application builder tool.

Predicate classes can emulate some of the functionality of dynamic inheritance as found in SELF or Garnet. Where a SELF program would have an assignable parent slot and a group of parent objects that could be swapped in and out of the parent slot, Cecil with predicate objects would have an assignable field and a group of predicate objects whose predicates test the value of the field. However, dynamic inheritance is more powerful than are predicate objects in Cecil. Predicate objects support associating state and behavior with possibly time-varying behavior modes of an object. Dynamic inheritance can do the same, but dynamic inheritance also allows an object to inherit from other run-time objects with their own run-time state; Cecil today only supports inheritance from statically-defined objects. Dynamic inheritance is rather unstructured, and often it is difficult to determine the behavior of an object with assignable parents, since any object conceivably could be assigned as a parent. The set of potential predicate descendants of an object, in contrast, are statically determined (at link-time), and we hope are easier to reason about. In those situations where predicate objects provide sufficient functionality, we believe they are preferable to dynamic inheritance since the purpose and dynamic behavior of predicate objects is clearer.

A related mechanism is the become: primitive in Smalltalk-80[1] [Goldberg & Robson 83]. This operation allows the identities of two objects to be swapped, and so is more than powerful enough to change the representation and implementation of an object. The become: operation thus is even more powerful and unstructured than dynamic inheritance, and is likely to be at least as difficult to reason about if used extensively. Additionally, become: is difficult to implement efficiently without slowing down other basic operations of the system.

5.6   Other Related Work

Several other systems have constructs similar to aspects of predicate classes. Boolean classes [McAllester & Zabih 86], Exemplars [LaLonde *et al.* 86], and Clovers [Stein 91] all address the issue of forming automatic combination or union subclasses to avoid combinatorial explosion and better organize methods; in none of these systems is the classification based on an object's state, however. Some knowledge representation systems address many of the same issues as predicate classes, though usually more from a representation or modelling viewpoint than from a linguistic viewpoint. Many specification systems restrict the applicability of operations using preconditions and many concurrent systems allow operations to be conditional on guard expressions. Exception handling mechanisms share predicate classes' goal of factoring cases, although from an entirely different vantage point.

6   Conclusion

Predicate classes provide a descriptive and modelling capability absent from most object-oriented languages. Predicate classes identify and name important states or behavior modes of objects, describe relations among these behavior modes, and associate state and behavior with these modes. By factoring the implementation of a class into a group of state-specific subclasses, we hope to make code clearer and easier to modify and extend. Predicate classes complement normal classes, providing a form of automatic property-based classification that is compatible with the explicit classification supported by normal classes.

Predicate classes enable programmers to resolve the tension between representing state as data and representing state through subclasses. Programmers can factor state-dependent behavior into specialized subclasses without incurring the maintenance headaches caused by a combinatorial explosion of multiple, independent subclasses and without restricting the state represented by the subclass to be immutable or creating difficult type-checking problems. Predicate classes support clean solutions to existing "benchmark" problems such as representing multiple attributes of people and representing hierarchies of mutable geometric shapes.

Predicate objects are an adaptation of the general idea of predicate classes to the Cecil language. Predicate objects can be associated with arbitrary *time-varying*

---

1. Smalltalk-80 is a trademark of ParcPlace Systems, Inc.

predicates defined over the state of an object. The relationships among predicate objects are specified explicitly by the programmer through inheritance declarations and disjoint, cover, and divide declarations; these declarations help method lookup find the most specific method and help the static type checker suppress spurious type errors. Predicate objects can have methods and fields associated with them just like normal objects, helping to integrate predicate objects into the rest of the language.

Several areas of predicate objects in Cecil need further study. Interesting interactions between predicate objects and inheritance and fields were described earlier in the paper. Predicated methods appear to generalize the idea of predicate objects to groups of objects. Strategies for efficient implementation of predicate objects need to be implemented and measured. Finally, predicate objects encourage a new kind of type checking to be investigated where the interface exported by an object depends on its current state.

Predicate classes would probably be easy to incorporate into other object-oriented languages in a similar fashion, although multiple inheritance appears to be required and the ability to add methods to a previously-declared predicate class would be helpful. We believe that the potential increased expressiveness of predicate classes and their easy integration within other object-oriented programming models merits further experimentation and study.

Acknowledgments

We thank Alan Borning, Miles Ohlrich, Jeff Dean, Kevin Sullivan, Stuart Williams, Christine Ahrens, Doug Lea, and the anonymous reviewers for their helpful comments on earlier drafts of this paper. This research has been generously supported by a National Science Foundation Research Initiation Award (contract number CCR-9210990), a University of Washington Graduate School Research Fund grant, and several gifts from Sun Microsystems, Inc.

References

[Apple 92] *Dylan, an Object-Oriented Dynamic Language*. Apple Computer, April, 1992.

[Bobrow *et al.* 88] D. G. Bobrow, L. G. DeMichiel, R. P. Gabriel, S. E. Keene, G. Kiczales, D. A. Moon. Common Lisp Object System Specification X3J13. In *SIGPLAN Notices 23(Special Issue)*, September, 1988.

[Caseau 91] Yves Caseau. An Object-Oriented Language for Advanced Applications. In *Proceedings of TOOLS USA '91*, 1991.

[Caseau & Silverstein 92] Yves Caseau and Glenn Silverstein. Some Original Features of the LAURE Language. In *Proceedings of the OOPSLA '92 Workshop on Object-Oriented Programming Languages: The Next Generation*, pp. 35-43, Vancouver, Canada, October, 1992.

[Caseau & Perron 93] Yves Caseau and Laurent Perron. Attaching Second-Order Types to Methods in an Object-Oriented Language. In In *ECOOP '93 Conference Proceedings*, Kaiserslautern, Germany, July, 1993.

[Chambers et al. 89] Craig Chambers, David Ungar, and Elgin Lee. An Efficient Implementation of SELF, a Dynamically-Typed Object-Oriented Language Based on Prototypes. In *OOPSLA '89 Conference Proceedings*, pp. 49-70, New Orleans, LA, October, 1989. Published as *SIGPLAN Notices 24(10)*, October, 1989. Also published in *Lisp and Symbolic Computation 4(3)*, Kluwer Academic Publishers, June, 1991.

[Chambers & Ungar 91] Craig Chambers and David Ungar. Making Pure Object-Oriented Languages Practical. In *OOPSLA '91 Conference Proceedings*, pp. 1-15, Phoenix, AZ, October, 1991. Published as *SIGPLAN Notices 26(10)*, October, 1991.

[Chambers 92a] Craig Chambers. *The Design and Implementation of the SELF Compiler, an Optimizing Compiler for Object-Oriented Programming Languages*. Ph.D. thesis, Department of Computer Science, Stanford University, report STAN-CS-92-1420, March, 1992.

[Chambers 92b] Craig Chambers. Object-Oriented Multi-Methods in Cecil. In *ECOOP '92 Conference Proceedings*, pp. 33-56, Utrecht, the Netherlands, June/July, 1992. Published as *Lecture Notes in Computer Science 615*, Springer-Verlag, Berlin, 1992.

[Chambers 93] Craig Chambers. The Cecil Language: Specification and Rationale. Technical report #93-03-05, Department of Computer Science and Engineering, University of Washington, March, 1993.

[Cook 89] W. R. Cook. A Proposal for Making Eiffel Type-Safe. In *ECOOP '89 Conference Proceedings*, pp. 57-70, Cambridge University Press, July, 1989.

[Goldberg & Robson 83] Adele Goldberg and David Robson. *Smalltalk-80: The Language and Its Implementation*. Addison-Wesley, Reading, MA, 1983.

[Hamer 92] John Hamer. Un-Mixing Inheritance with Classifiers. In *Multiple Inheritance and Multiple Subtyping: Position Papers of the ECOOP '92 Workshop W1*, pp. 6-9, Utrect, the Netherlands, June/July, 1992. Also available as working paper WP-23, Markku Sakkinen, ed., Dept. of Computer Science and Information Systems, University of Jyväskylä, Finland, May, 1992.

[Hölzle et al. 91] Urs Hölzle, Bay-Wei Chang, Craig Chambers, Ole Agesen, and David Ungar. *The SELF Manual, Version 1.1*. Unpublished manual, February, 1991.

[Hudak et al. 92] Paul Hudak, Simon Peyton Jones, Philip Wadler, Brian Boutel, Jon Fairbairn, Joseph Fasel, María M. Guzmán, Kevin Hammond, John Hughes, Thomas Johnsson, Dick Kieburtz, Rishiyur Nikhil, Will Partain, and John Peterson. *Report on the Programming Language Haskell, Version 1.2*. In *SIGPLAN Notices 27(5)*, May, 1992.

[LaLonde et al. 86] Wilf R. LaLonde, Dave A. Thomas, and John R. Pugh. An Exemplar Based Smalltalk. In *OOPSLA '86 Conference Proceedings*, pp. 322-330, Portland, OR, September, 1986. Published as *SIGPLAN Notices 21(11)*, November, 1986.

[Lea 92] Doug Lea. Personal communication. December, 1992.

[McAllester & Zabih 86] David McAllester and Ramin Zabih. Boolean Classes. In *OOPSLA '86 Conference Proceedings*, pp. 417-428, Portland, OR, September, 1986. Published as *SIGPLAN Notices 21(11)*, November, 1986.

[Meyer 91] Bertrand Meyer. Static Typing for Eiffel. In *An Eiffel Collection*. Technical report #TR-EI-20/EC, Interactive Software Engineering, Goleta, California, 1991.

[Meyer 92] Bertrand Meyer. *Eiffel: The Language*. Prentice Hall, New York, 1992.

[Milner et al. 90] Robin Milner, Mads Tofte, and Robert Harper. *The Definition of Standard ML*. MIT Press, Cambridge, MA, 1990.

[Mugridge *et al.* 91] W. B. Mugridge, J. G. Hosking, and J. Hamer. Multi-Methods in a Statically-Typed Programming Language. Technical report #50, Department of Computer Science, University of Auckland, 1991. A later version published in *ECOOP '91 Conference Proceedings*, Geneva, Switzerland, July, 1991.

[Myers *et al.* 92] Brad A. Myers, Dario A. Giuse, and Brad Vander Zanden. Declarative Programming in a Prototype-Instance System: Object-Oriented Programming Without Writing Methods. In *OOPSLA '92 Conference Proceedings*, pp. 184-200, Vancouver, Canada, October, 1992. Published as *SIGPLAN Notices 27(10)*, October, 1992.

[Stein 91] Lynn A. Stein. A Unified Methodology for Object-Oriented Programming. In *Inheritance Hierarchies in Knowledge Representation and Programming Languages*, John Wiley & Sons, 1991.

[Strom & Yemini 86] Robert E. Strom and Shaula Alexander Yemini. Typestate: A Programming Language Concept for Enhancing Software Reliability. In *IEEE Transactions on Software Engineering 12(1)*, pp. 157-171, January, 1986.

[Strom *et al.* 91] Robert E. Strom, David F. Bacon, Arthur P. Goldberg, Andy Lowry, Daniel M. Yellin, Shaula Alexander Yemini. *Hermes, A Language for Distributed Computing*. Prentice Hall, Englewood Cliffs, NJ, 1991.

[Touretzky 86] D. Touretzky. *The Mathematics of Inheritance Systems*. Morgan-Kaufmann, 1986.

[Ungar & Smith 87] David Ungar and Randall B. Smith. SELF: The Power of Simplicity. In *OOPSLA '87 Conference Proceedings*, pp. 227-241, Orlando, FL, October, 1987. Published as *SIGPLAN Notices 22(12)*, December, 1987. Also published in *Lisp and Symbolic Computation 4(3)*, Kluwer Academic Publishers, June, 1991.

[Ungar *et al.* 91] David Ungar, Craig Chambers, Bay-Wei Chang, and Urs Hölzle. Organizing Programs without Classes. In *Lisp and Symbolic Computation 4(3)*, Kluwer Academic Publishers, June, 1991.

[Wadler 87] Phillip Wadler. Views: A Way for Pattern Matching to Cohabit with Data Abstraction. In *Proceedings of the Fourteenth ACM Conference on Principles of Programming Languages*. Munich, Germany, January, 1987.

[Yelland 92] Phillip M. Yelland. Experimental Classification Facilities for Smalltalk. In *OOPSLA '92 Conference Proceedings*, pp. 235-246, Vancouver, Canada, October, 1992. Published as *SIGPLAN Notices 27(10)*, October, 1992.

TOOA: A Temporal Object-Oriented Algebra

Ellen Rose[1] and *Arie Segev*[2]
The University of Toledo[1]
Toledo, OH 43606 and
Information and Computing Sciences Division
Lawrence Berkeley Laboratory

Walter A. Haas School of Business[2]
The University of California and
Information and Computing Sciences Division
Lawrence Berkeley Laboratory
Berkeley, California 94720

ABSTRACT

In this paper, we present a temporal, object-oriented algebra which serves as a formal basis for the query language of a temporal, object-oriented data model. Our algebra is a superset of the relational algebra in that it provides support for manipulating temporal objects, temporal types, type hierarchies and class lattices, multiple time-lines, and correction sequences in addition to supporting the five relational algebra operators. Graphs are used as the visual representations of both the schema and the object instances. The algebra provides constructs to modify and manipulate the schema graph and its extension, the object graph. The algebra operates on a collection or collections of objects and returns a collection of objects. This algebra is a first step in providing a formal foundation for query processing and optimizing in a temporal, object-oriented data model.

This work was supported by an NSF Grant Number IRI-9000619 and by the Applied Mathematical Sciences Research Program of the Office of Energy Research, U.S. Department of Energy under Contract DE-AC03-76SF00098.

O.M. Nierstrasz (Ed.): ECOOP '93, LNCS 707, pp. 297-325, 1993.
© Springer-Verlag Berlin Heidelberg 1993

1. Introduction

The increase in complexity of new applications such as computer aided design, office information systems, scientific databases and multimedia databases has pressed the limits of the relational model and led to research into next-generation data models. These new data models must capture the semantics of complex objects and treat time as a basic component versus as an additional attribute in order to build more accurate models. New primitives to handle temporal data and complex types need to be incorporated into the query and specification languages of these models. An algebra to transform these temporal, object-oriented model queries into a more efficient form for execution is the focus of this paper.

The approach taken herein evolved from the integration of research on extensions of the relational model to include temporal semantics and complex objects and the recent work on object-oriented models. The literature on temporal extensions to the relational model proposes adding temporal semantics through tuple or attribute versioning. Research in these directions includes: [Clifford & Warren 83], [Clifford & Croker 87], [Snodgrass 87], [Segev & Shoshani 87], [Gadia 88b], [Gadia & Yeung 88] and [Navathe & Ahmed 89]. A good summary of temporal extensions to the relational algebra can be found in [McKenzie & Snodgrass 91]. [Tuzhilin & Clifford 90] propose an algebra that is restricted to temporal relational models which support a linear, discrete bounded model of time and propose a new linear recursive operator. Generalized logical temporal models have been proposed by [Ariav 86] and [Segev & Shoshani 87]. A comprehensive bibliography on temporal databases and references to three previous bibliographies can be found in [Soo 91]. Extensions to the Entity-Relationship model incorporate time as either an entity or attribute and include [Klopprogge & Lockemann 83], [Ferg 85] and [Elmasri & Wuu 90].

Recent work on object-oriented algebras include OQL and its algebra in [Alashqur etal 89] and [Guo etal 91] respectively. OQL operates on sets of association patterns which are derived from a graph of object instances. OQL includes a non-association operator and can operate on heterogeneous sets of objects. Our approach is most similar to that found in [Guo etal 91]. [Shaw & Zdonik 90] developed a query language and algebra for ENCORE which supports object identity and the creation of new objects and types. EXTRA [Carey etal 88] and its query language EXCESS were developed using a database generator EXODUS. EXCESS supports querying nested or un-nested sets, arrays, tuples and individual objects similar to O_2 and user-defined functions as in POSTGRES. The above list of OO-Algebras is not meant to be exhaustive but rather to mention those algebras which have features which are more closely related to TOOA.

Research on schema evolution has taken two forms: single-schema modification and schema versioning. Most proposals [Banerjee, etal 88], and [Penny & Stein 87] take the single-schema approach. Disadvantages of this approach include the loss of historical values when an attribute is dropped and the forcing of all users in a multi-user environment to accept all schema changes as part of their view. Schema versioning in the ENCORE system [Skarra & Zdonik

86] and in ORION [Kim & Chou 88] [Kim etal 89] doesn't have the aforementioned problems since it allows any user to view any data base through the schema version of their choice. [Skarra & Zdonik 86] deal with versioning class types, not an entire database schema. Any change to a class type creates a new version of the type and its sub-types. Therefore, the schema of the database at any moment will consist of the selected version of each type and the links between them. [Kim & Chou 88] [Kim etal 89] and [Andany etal 91] are the only papers found which deal with database schema versioning. In any version of the database schema, only one version of each distinct class object is allowed. [Kim & Chou 88] develop a model of database versions based on [Chou 88]'s model of object versions and provide implementation techniques to support database schema versioning. The basic premise of their proposal is to allow derived schema versions to inherit all the objects of the schema version from which they are derived. The user is allowed to specify if the objects will be inherited and whether or not they can be updated through the parent. In this approach, any change to the database schema creates a new version of the database schema which can lead to the problem of managing a large number of versions. [Andany etal 91] elaborate on the alternative approach of handling schema modification using view definitions proposed in [Kim & Chou 88] in the Farandole 2 model. In this approach the concept of a context, a connected subgraph of the database schema graph, is used as the level of granularity for versioning. Whereas, the previous approaches look only at structural consistency, [Zicari 91] also looks at consistency in the behaviour of methods after a schema change has occurred. To date, no database systems have incorporated schema versioning [Kim 90]. Our approach is one of schema histories at the type level using the time-sequence concept.

Several papers which focus on temporal, object-oriented models have recently appeared in the literature. [Kafer & Schoning 92] extend a complex object model, adding the following attributes: references to the previous and next tuple, a boolean existence attribute, a transaction time attribute, an object identifier and a valid time point. This model is actually a nested relational model which adopts tuple timestamping and therefore does not allow cyclic queries. [Su & Chen 91] proposed an object-based temporal knowledge representation model called OSAM*/T and query language called OQL/T. Here rules are used to capture temporal semantics other than the valid start and end times of a tuple. [Wuu & Dayal 91] add temporal semantics to OODAPLEX. In this model, a POINT type is the supertype of the TIME and VERSION types. Time varying properties are modeled as functions that map time objects to non-temporal snapshot values. A more detailed comparison with these other works is given in section 6 after the features of TOODM have been explained.

In this paper, a temporal, object-oriented algebra (called TOOA) for the manipulation of the intension (types) and extension (objects) of a temporal, object-oriented data model is proposed. The time-sequence collection type [Rose & Segev 91] is used to model histories of attribute values of objects and histories of the set of properties which define an object's type. Each time-sequence has an associated sequence of corrections which can be merged with the original history.

Multiple time-lines are used in the time-sequence collection type to allow for both historical and rollback queries.

The remainder of this paper is organized as follows. Section 2 presents an example which is used to discuss the basic concepts of the data model (TOODM) for which the algebra is designed. Section 3 gives an overview of the algebra, its notations and assumptions. Section 4 outlines the object level operators and section 5 describes the schema level update operators. It should be noted that the algebra only applies to retrieval operators not to the update operators. Finally, section 6 concludes the paper with a discussion of how our proposal compares with other temporal extensions of object-oriented data models and also delineates future work.

2. Motivating Example and Data Model

The model upon which our algebra operates is the temporal, object-oriented data model (TOODM) in [Rose & Segev 91]. In TOODM, a class is viewed as the extension of the type of an object instance, hereafter referred to as object. A type serves as a template to encapsulate the structure (attributes), behavior (messages/methods) and constraints of an object. Each object has a globally unique system generated identifier that is independent of the object's state or physical location. The state of an object is described by the values held by its attributes. New types must be defined as a subtype of existing types in the type hierarchy. A subtype inherits the properties of its supertypes. Figure 1 shows the types which have been defined in the type hierarchy for our social security database example as well as the system-defined types. This database would track individuals as they progress from childhood to adulthood, old age, retirement and death. At each point in an individual's life, a different set of relevant information may be required. An individual may be described by a different type template at different stages of their life and belong to different classes simultaneously (e.g. every adult is also a person) or at different time points (e.g. a person can't be both a child and an adult simultaneously).

User-defined COMPLEX TYPES such as PERSON are defined as subtypes of V-TYPE which means versionable type. A history is kept of the type definition of all types defined as subtypes of V-TYPE. META-DATA are subtypes of NV-TYPE, meaning non-versionable type, since a history of their type definitions is not maintained. The instances of a subtype of NV-TYPE are versionable. PTYPE, primitive types, (e.g. integers, time, etc.) have atomic values and a set of operators. Collection types, such as SET, TUPLE, SEQUENCE, and LIST are parameterized types used to build the extensions of other types. A special collection type called time-sequence,[1] $TS[O_i]$ is illustrated in Figure 2. $TS[O_i]$ has the type O_i as its parameter. Each time sequence object has the history and correction history (corr-history) properties which each contain a sequence of (A; TL) pairs. "A" represents a tuple of attribute values and "TL" represents a tuple of time-line values, (TL_i), having type time (T_i) or one of its specializations. Valid time (vt)

---

[1] The time-sequence object and some of its operators are based on concepts from [Segev & Shoshani 87].

Figure 1 - Type Hierarchy for Social Security Database

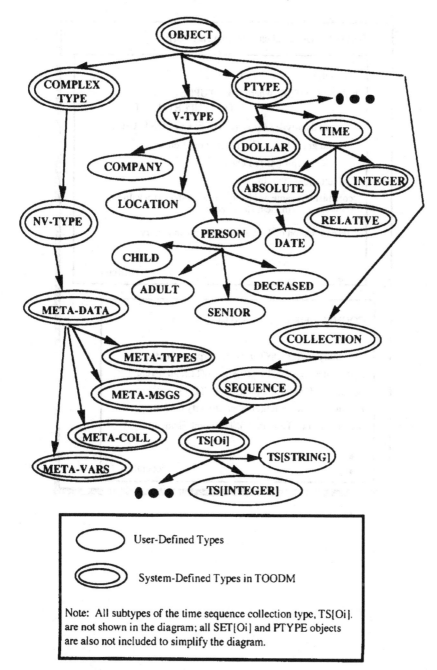

User-Defined Types

System-Defined Types in TOODM

Note: All subtypes of the time sequence collection type, TS[Oi].
are not shown in the diagram; all SET[Oi] and PTYPE objects
are also not included to simplify the diagram.

302

Figure 2 - Time Sequence Collection Type, TS [Oi]

Define TS [Oi] as subclass of Sequence [Oi]

surr: OID

history: {(A;TL)} where   A = TUPLE (Ai)

$\qquad\qquad\qquad\qquad$ TL = TUPLE (TLi : Ti)

and data-type (Ai) : {SWC, Event, CONT, User}

and gran (TLi) : CalendarSet or Ordinal

and interp-f (Ai) : Functions

default-order: TLi in TL

corr-history: same as history except value(tt) > value(tt)
$\qquad\qquad\qquad$ in the history sequence

lifespan: Union of Temporal Elements in history

•
•
$\qquad\qquad\qquad\qquad\qquad\qquad$ attributes
•

COUNT( ) FIRST( )   LAST( )   Nth ( )

Accumulate(Agg-Op(Target-Ai),Grp(acc-pred))

Aggregate(Agg-Op(Target-Ai),Grp(TLi, gran-value)

Select (LIST[Ai], Conditions(Ai or TLi))

Restrict (TS, condition(another property of Oi))

Merge (History-TS,Corr-TS, Temporal Element)

•
•
$\qquad\qquad\qquad\qquad\qquad\qquad$ operators
•

and transaction time (tt) are mandatory members of this tuple. Each attribute A_i has a data-type which is step-wise constant (SWC), event, continuous (CONT) or user-defined. If the data-type is user-defined, an interpolation function (interp-f) should be provided to determine values for time points which are not recorded as data points. Each time-line, TL_i has a granularity which may be a calendar time (CalenderSet) or an ordinal number. The transaction time value for a correction history element is restricted to be greater than that of the objects in the associated history sequence.

The lifespan attribute is defined as a possibly (but not necessarily) non-contiguous union of temporal elements of the history property. Temporal elements [Gadia 88a] are finite unions of time-lines. Temporal elements are closed under intersection, complement and union. An object's lifespan is the union of it's lifespans in all classes in which it has participated.

The operators in [Segev & Shoshani 87] are defined for time-sequences with one or more attributes but only one time-line, vt. These operators are extended to handle multiple time-lines in TOODM through the representation of TL_i as a tuple of time-lines. Since information can be viewed with and without corrections taken into consideration, a merge operator was developed in TOODM. Count( ), First( ), Last( ) and Nth ( ) return the number of data points in the sequence, the first pair, last pair and nth pair respectively.

Figure 3 shows example type definitions for META-DATA and user-defined types in the example. Only the attributes of the user-defined types are shown to simplify the diagram. Attributes of meta-data types, except the object identifier, take values from time-sequence classes so the database schema can contain different sets of types, constraints, etc. at different time points. The class SET[PERSON] has a set structure and the value structure of one of its instances would be a set of PERSON identifiers. INV indicates that the employer property of Adult and the employees property of Company are inverses representing a relationship.

2.1. Schema Graph

The schema graph, SG, in Figure 4 is a graphical representation of the user-defined properties in Figure 3. Unlabeled arcs represent is-a links directed from a super-type (e.g. PERSON) to its subtypes (e.g. CHILD, ADULT, SENIOR and DECEASED). The schema graph serves as the logical representation of the database. It consists of a set of nodes (types) and a set of links (properties of the types). The set of types is a disjoint union of the set of Primitive Types (PTYPE) and the set of COMPLEX TYPES. Each complex type has an identifier, attributes, a supertype list, operations and constraints. This information is stored in the extensions of the meta-data types shown in Figure 3. If a property is single-valued, its values are stored as a $TS[O_i]$. If the property is multi-valued its values are stored as TS[SET or LIST[O_i]].

A link in the schema graph represents a property and is directed from its defining object type to its domain. Since more than one link can exist between the same two types, all link types have a unique name. For example, $L_{PERSON,LOCATION}^{residence}$

Figure 3 - Type Definitions of Meta-Data and User-Defined Types

Define Meta-Types as subclass of Meta-Data
   Type_Oid: OID
     Type_Name: TS |String|
     Superclasses: TS | LIST |Meta_Types| |
     Subclasses: TS | SET |Meta_Types| |
     Attributes: TS |Set [Meta_Vars] |
     Operations: TS |Set [Meta_Msgs] |
     Class_Attributes: TS |Set |Meta_Class_Vars| |
     Relationships: TS |Set [Meta_Rels] |
     Constraints: TS| Set |BOOL| |

Define Meta-Vars as subclass of Meta-Data
   var-oid: OID
   var-signature: TS [<var-name:String,
     var-parent:Meta-Type,
     var-creator : UserID,
     var-type: Meta-Types> |
   constraints: TS| Set [BOOL] |

Define Meta-Msgs as subclass of Meta-Data
   msg-oid: OID
   msg-signature: TS | <msg-name:String,
     msg-parent: Meta-Types,
     msg-creator: UserID,
     msg-params: Set |Params|,
     msg-code:<Code,Userid> > |
   pre-conditions: TS|Set [BOOL] |
   post-conditions: TS| Set [BOOL] |

Define Meta-Coll as subclass of Meta-Data
   coll-oid: OID
   coll-name: String
   operators: TS |SET |Operators|
   constraints: TS [Set |BOOL | |

Define Person as SubType of V-Type
   soc-sec#: TS |String|
   pname: TS |String|
   birthdate: TS |Date|
   residence: TS |Location |

Define Child as SubType of Person
   guardians: TS | SET |Person| |
   school: TS |School|

Define Adult as SubType of Person
   employer: TS |Company|
     INV is Company.employees
   salary: TS |Dollar|
   dependents: TS |SET |Person| |

Define Senior as SubType of Person
   pension: TS |Dollar|

Define Deceased as SubType of Person
   cause: TS |String |
   beneficiaries: TS |SET |Person| |

Define Company as SubType of V-Type
   cname: TS |String|
   employees: TS |SET |Person| |
     INV is Adult.employer
   location: TS |Location |

Define Location as SubType of V-Type
   city: TS | String |
   state: TS | String |

Figure 4 - Schema Graph of Figure 3 User-Defined Types

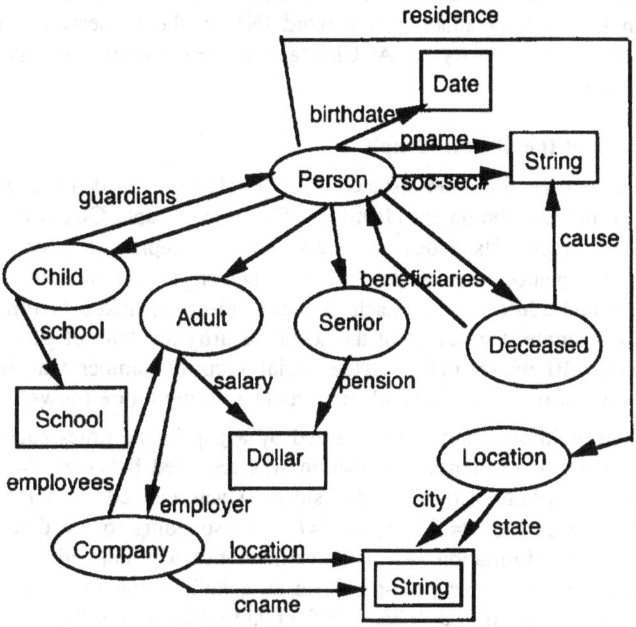

Note 1: unlabeled arcs are is-a relationships and the String type only appears once but was drawn twice for clarity of the diagram.

Note 2: each arc has a lifespan indicating when it was a property of the type it is directed from; lifespans are temporal elements and may be non-contiguous

indicates that each PERSON has a residence whose value is in the class LOCA-
TION and a time-sequence of the location values is kept. Properties with primitive
domains can't be represented as inverse links. Recall that relationships are
described in the type by attaching the word INV to the property as in Figure 3
where the employer property of ADULT and the employees property of COM-
PANY are inverses.

2.2. Objects and the Object Graph

Each object has a unique instance identifier (IID) which is a concatenation of
the type identifier and the object identifier. The object graph, OG, is the extension
of the schema graph. Its nodes are IID's and links represent associations from
IID's to time-sequence objects. In Figure 5, person_1 (p1) has subtype objects
child_1 (ch1) and adult_1 (a1). Each of these objects is linked to time-sequence
objects. For example, the values of the social-security attribute of p1 are found in
time-sequence ts10 which indicates the social security number was recorded as
"333-33-3333" at tt=71 and is valid from vt=71 into the future (now+).

Deletion of information is represented by a gap in the time-sequence values
as in ts33 where no residence information was recorded between vt=[71,75]. In
Figure 6, ts68, attribute variable (V4=residence) was deleted from Person's type
definition for the period vt=[71,75] at tt=71 corresponding to the deleted data in
Figure 5. If the information was not available but was defined in the type, it
would have appeared in the time-sequence as a null[2] value for vt=[71,75]. The
residence link for p3 has a lifespan of <60,[36,70]> $\cup$ <76, [71,76]>. The
lifespan of a link in the object graph is the same as the lifespan of its time-
sequence object. The transaction time associated with a period where no value
was recorded is the previous transaction time where the association existed.

Relationships are constrained in terms of lifespans of the participants. For
instance, the values of company c5 in Figure 5 appear in ts41 through the employees link instance which has a lifespan of [66,86]. The first pair in ts41 associates
person p2 with the time [66,80], the second pair associates p1 and p2 with time
[81,84] and the third pair associates p2 with time [85,86]. Since the employer link
is an inverse in the schema graph, c5 must appear in each pair in ts16 (p1's
employer link) which has a valid time that intersects with [81,84] and in each pair
in ts26 (p2's employer link) that intersects with [66,86].

Non-temporal data is a degenerative case where the lifespan of the link consists of a single element of its time-sequence object. The end point of the valid
time interval would be now+ as in the cause of death property.

---

[2] Different representations for nulls including not-available and unknown can be used.

Figure 5 - Object Graph of Some Instances of User-Defined Types

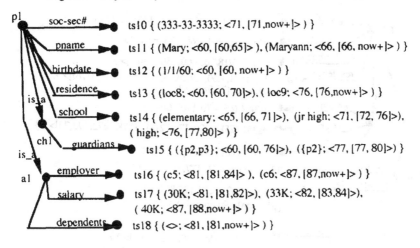

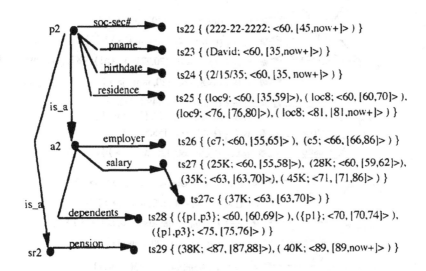

Note:
The time sequence instances "ts", are sequences of pairs (attribute-tuple:
time-line tuple), where the first element of the time-line tuple is record time
and the second is valid time.

pi - person i, ai - adult i, chi - child i, sri - senior i, tsi - time sequence i,
di - deceased i, ci - company i, loci - location i

308

Figure 5 - Object Graph of Some Instances of User-Defined Types

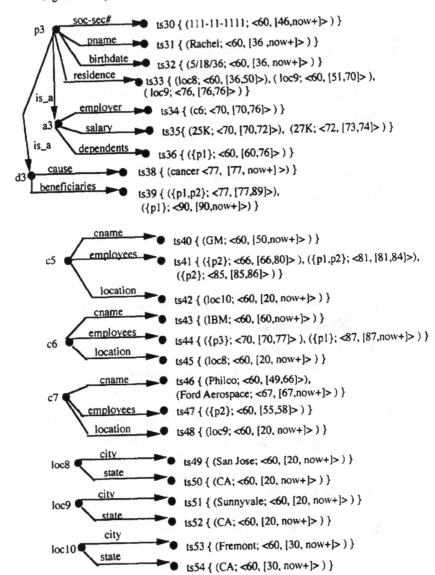

3. An Overview of TOOA

3.1. Assumptions

Events are viewed as durationless and cause an object to change state. The taxonomy of time given in [Snodgrass & Ahn 85] for valid time (vt) and transaction time (tt) is adopted here. The state of an object persists over some duration of time and is represented by the values held by the attributes of the object over this time duration. The time period over which a state holds is the valid time. The transaction time refers to when an object was recorded. Time is represented as a primitive type which is independent of events. Time can be subtyped into absolute and relative time values as well as specialized time types with different orderings. A partial ordering is useful in representing alternate versions of design objects.

The semantics of existing operations -- retrievals, corrections and updates differ in TOODM. Retrievals can result in a time-sequence of values. Corrections are illustrated in Figure 5 where ts27c is the corr-history for ts27. The query, "Find David's salary at vt=64 as seen from tt=69 accounting for corrections made during tt=[64,69]", can be answered by doing merge(ts27,ts27c,[64,69]). The result with corrections is 37K whereas it would be 35K without. Updates (add, change, delete) also differ from those of a static data model. For instance, changing an existing attribute's value means adding an element to the time-sequence of values representing the attribute. Changes to an existing object implies ending its valid time interval one unit prior to the time of the change, at t-1 and starting the valid time interval of the new value at time t. The end point of the new value's valid time interval could be a specific time point or now+ if it is assumed to hold in the future and present. Adding a new object to a class requires creating time-sequence objects to represent each of its properties. Deletion of an object implies the end of its lifespan without the removal of the information from the database and that the object can't be referenced by any other objects from the time of deletion forward until the time if any that the object re-enters the system.[3] These operators are defined in the type called OBJECT in Figure 1.

3.2. Overview of the Operators

Operations can be applied to a class or the hierarchy rooted at a class, meaning the result may contain heterogeneous objects with different sets of properties. This is different from the relational algebra which only allows operations on homogeneous sets of objects, specifically sets of tuples where all tuples in a particular relation have the same set of attributes. The following two sections discuss the object level and schema level operators in terms of the example instances found in Figures 5 and 6.

---

[3] Historical information for "deleted" objects can be queried since the history of the object's past states prior to the deletion exists in the database.

310

Figure 6 - Object Graph of Some Instances of Meta-Types

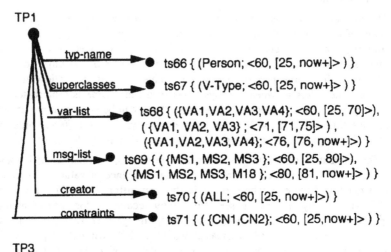

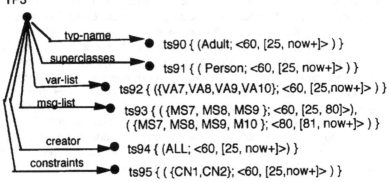

Note: The time sequence instances "ts", are sequences of pairs (attribute-tuple; time-line tuple), where the first element of the time-line tuple is record time and the second is valid time.

VA1 = soc-sec#, VA2 = pname, VA3 = birthdate, VA4 = residence, VA5 = school, VA6 = guardians, VA7 = employer, VA8= salary, VA9 = dependents, VA10 = cname, VA11 = employees and VA12 = location, TPi - Type i, MSi - Message i, VAi - Variable i, tsi - time sequence i, CNi - Constraint i

4. Object Level Operators

4.1. Objects with Tuple Values

1) $\bullet_T^k$, Temporal Association

This binary operator returns a collection of graphs of objects. For each graph in the result, an instance of the class or class hierarchy specified by the first operand is associated through link k with an instance or instances of the class or hierarchy rooted at the class in the second operand at time T. If the class represented by the second operand is not primitive, then the association operator can be applied again to retrieve a value of an attribute of that class. We can think of the association operator as a navigational operator that allows us to specify a path through the schema graph that existed at some time T for each link. This means that T must be contained in the lifespan of link k for the operation to be valid since the link is only defined during its lifespan. For example, we can specify a path from the class Adult to Company to String where the link between Adult and Company is employer and the link between Company and String is cname and T is specified as [74,76] for both links. The result of the following is shown in Figure 7a: $Adult \bullet_{[74,76]}^{employer} Company \bullet_{[74,76]}^{cname} String$

2) $|_T$, Temporal Complement

Whereas the previous operator returns a TS[values] that are associated with an object through one of its attributes, this operator returns the members of the second operand that were not associated with the objects belonging to the first operand during time T. For example, we can retrieve the adults who were not employed according to their employment history in the database at time T = [85,87]. We also need to know when this property was defined in the type definition. From Figure 6, we see the employer property (VA7) was defined for type Adult (TP3) at transaction time 60 and was retroactively valid from time 25 to now+. This means that T = [85,87] is valid since it is contained in the lifespan of the property employer for type Adult in the schema. From Figure 5, we see that a_1 was not employed during [85,86], a2 was not employed during [87,now+] and a3 was not employed during [60,69] and only the first two adults were not employed during time T. Note that a3's lifespan ends prior to T and therefore has no employment history after her death. We can express this Temporal Complement operation as follows: $Adult \mid_{[85,87]}^{employer} Company$ where the result appears in Figure 7b.

3) $\sigma\text{-}IF_{TP}$, Temporal Selection Using a Temporal Predicate

Select-IF is a unary operator which returns the set of objects that meet the temporal predicate condition specified by TP. The temporal predicate consists of a non-temporal FOL predicate (NTP), a quantifier (Q) over time (for all or for some) and a temporal element (T) over which the selection is to be taken. The NTP can consist of several predicates combined with the boolean connectives: "and", "or" and "not". Comparisons must be made between objects of the same type: primitive to primitive or IID to IID. The result of a temporal select-IF is shown in Figure 7c where we select those Adults who were employed by IBM some time in the last 2 years. The time period during which the specified condition must exist is used to restrict the objects in the result as follows:

Figure 7 - Operator Examples

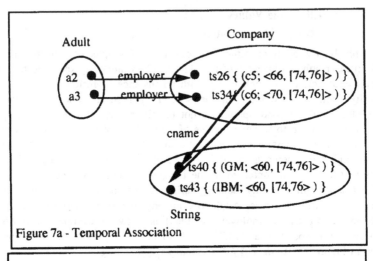

Figure 7a - Temporal Association

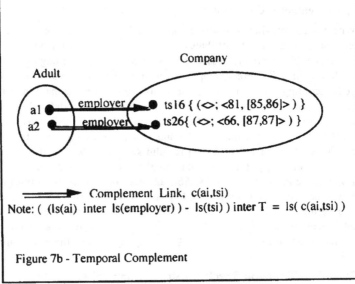

Complement Link, c(ai,tsi)

Note: ((ls(ai) inter ls(employer)) - ls(tsi)) inter T = ls(c(ai,tsi))

Figure 7b - Temporal Complement

Figure 7 - Operator Examples

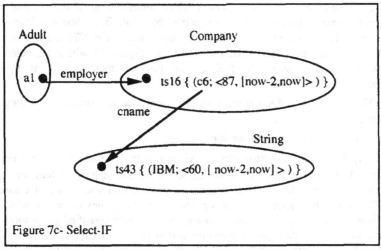

Figure 7c- Select-IF

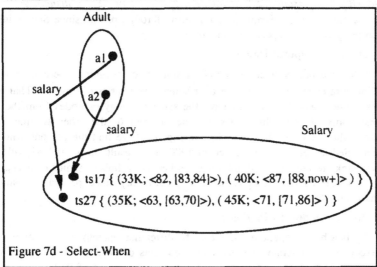

Figure 7d - Select-When

$\sigma-IF_{[cname\,=IBM,\,exists,\,[now-2,now]}(\,Adult\,\cdot\,Company\,\cdot\,String\,)$

4) $\sigma-WHEN_{NTP}$, Temporal Selection Using a Non-Temporal Predicate

Select-WHEN is a unary operator which returns a set of objects that meet the non-temporal predicate condition specified by NTP. The lifespan of the resultant objects is the set of times when the object meets the NTP condition. The result of a temporal select-WHEN is shown in Figure 7d where we select the Adults who had a salary > 30K at sometime in their history as follows:
$\sigma-WHEN_{[salary>30K]}(Adult)$

The lifespan of the resulting objects would be the times when they had salaries greater than 30K.

5) $\cap_T$, Temporal Intersection

$\cap_T$ is a binary operator which is similar to the join operator in a relational algebra. The result only exists if the graphs to be joined have at least one node class in common. The result of a temporal intersection over a set of classes at time T is given in Figure 7e where we get the current names of people who were guardians of children in 1980 and who are also currently classified as seniors. The set of classes in this case just contains the primitive class String.
$(Child\,\cdot\,^{guardians}_{1980}\,Person\,\cdot\,^{pname}_{now}\,String\,)\,\cap^{\{String\}}_{now}\,(Senior\,\cdot\,^{pname}_{now}\,String\,).$
Note, we can associate Senior to class String through pname since Senior inherits this property from its supertype, Person.

6) $\cup_T$, Temporal Union

$\cup_T$ is a binary operator which is similar to the union operator in a relational algebra except it can operate over heterogeneous sets of objects. That is, the graphs in the operands need not have the same topology or nodes from the same classes. Only objects which exist in one operand or the other at time T will appear in the resulting set of graphs. In Figure 7f we find the persons who were not classified as seniors or deceased in 1980. This results in p1 and p2 with complement links to both sr1 and sr2 since neither had a link to senior or deceased in 1980. p3 will have a complement link to sr3 only since p3 was classified as deceased in 1980.

7) $-_T$, Temporal Difference

$-_T$ is a binary operator similar to the difference operator in a relational algebra except it can operate over heterogeneous sets of objects. Any objects which exist in the first operand at time T and contain an element of the second operand that exists in it at time T, will not appear in the result. In Figure 7g we find existing adults who were not part of the group of adults who were not linked to a Company in [85,87] by subtracting the result of 7b) from the set of adults. This gives us the adults who did not have a period of unemployment in their employment history. We express this operation as follows:
$Adult\,-^{\{Adult\}}_{now}\,(Adult\,\mid\,^{employer}_{[85,87]}\,Company\,)$

Figure 7 - Operator Examples

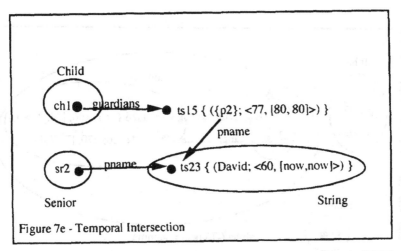

Figure 7e - Temporal Intersection

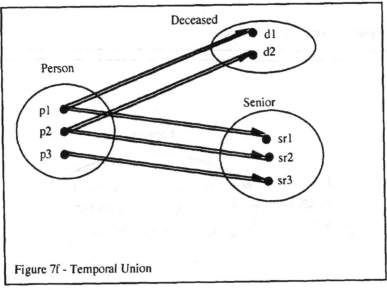

Figure 7f - Temporal Union

Figure 7 - Operator Examples

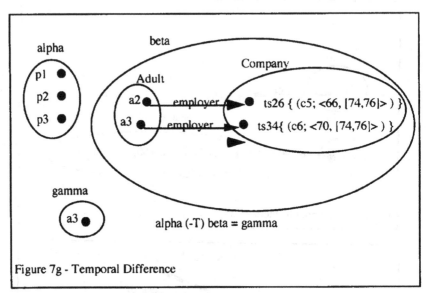

Figure 7g - Temporal Difference

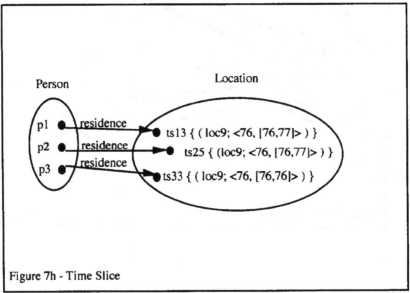

Figure 7h - Time Slice

8) *Time – Slice$_T$*

This operator reduces the objects in the time dimension just as the relational project reduces relations in the attribute dimension and the relational select reduces relations in the value dimension. It returns a snapshot of the object graph at time T. In Figure 7h we find each person's residence in T = [76,77] as follows:

$Time – Slice_{[76,77]}^{\{Location\}} (Person \bullet^{residence} Location)$

9) *Rollback$_T$*

This operator produces a snapshot of the database as it existed at some previous transaction time T. Note that the previous operators used T with valid time semantics. In Figure 7i we get the history of dependents for each adult as recorded in the database in 1962. This operation is expressed as follows:

$Rollback_{1962}^{Person} (Adult \bullet^{dependents} Person)$

Only the portion of the time-sequence where transaction time is less than or equal to T is retained in the result. No restrictions are placed on the relationship between tt and vt.

10) π_T, **Temporal Projection**

This operator is the counterpart of the relational project in that it returns objects which contain some subset of the object's properties. The difference is it returns a history of the values of each of those properties. For example, each person has four associated attributes in our example database and we may only want to return the history of their residence property if they have ever lived in Sunnyvale. The result of the following expression appears in Figure 7j:

$\pi (Person \bullet^{residence} \sigma-IF_{[city = Sunnyvale, exists,]} (Location \bullet^{city} String)) [Location]$

where the temporal element is left out since we are requesting the entire history.

The unary operators have precedence over the binary operators and the ordering for the binary operators is: $\bullet_T$, $|_T$, $\cap_T$, $-_T$ and $\cup_T$. Parentheses can be used to create other orderings.

4.2. Set and List Structures

Set structures have the operations: $\in$, $\cap$, *minus*, $\cup$, *count*. List structures have the operators: *ith* $\in$, *sublist*, *concat* and *count*. Other aggregate operators such as max, min and *avg* can be added to collections of objects of type SET[T] or LIST[T] when T is a numeric type.

4.3. Time Sequence Structures

The time-sequence structure is used to model histories of attributes of complex objects. The operators defined in the time-sequence type are only briefly discussed here due to space limitations. These operators include: $\in$, *ith*, *merge*, restriction over a time-line or by values of the attributes in the time-sequence pairs and accumulation over time. These operators are described in [Segev & Shoshani 87]. We have also extended the select, aggregate, accumulate and restrict operators to handle multiple time-lines as discussed in Figure 2 where TL_i can be any time-line. For example, one could request the average salary of adults grouped on valid time with a granularity of year by sending the following message where Result is a keyword in the data manipulation language used to indicate a collection

Figure 7 - Operator Examples

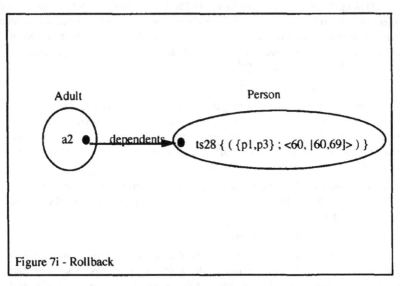

Figure 7i - Rollback

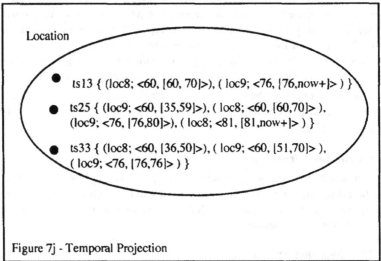

Figure 7j - Temporal Projection

where the result of the operation is stored: Result :=
Aggregate(AVG(salary),GRP(vt,year)) Similarly, one could request the average
salary of adults grouped by transaction time with a granularity of year as follows:
Result := Aggregate(AVG(salary),GRP(tt,year))

4.4. Update Operators

The following operators are defined in COMPLEX TYPE and are inherited
by all user-defined types except subtypes of primitive types and collection types.

Add_Obj_Instance(o, A)

Adding an object o to the EXT(A) where A is the defining type of object o
involves creation of an IID for the object where the class part of the IID is the
identifier for type A. The user must supply the valid time interval for each property and transaction time will be the current time. A time-sequence object is
created for each property of the new object.

Del_Obj_Instance(o, A)

Deleting an object o from the EXT(A) where A is the object's defining type
involves ending the lifespans of all properties of the object. Since relationships are
stored as properties their lifespan is also ended. The inverse attribute in the other
type participating in the relationship will have the last (A,T) pair[4] in its time
sequence which includes the IID of the deleted object adjusted in one of the following ways. If the time-sequence (TS) stores a set or list of values of type A
then a new (A,T) pair is added to the TS which does not include the deleted object
and the lifespan of the previous element is ended. If the TS object stores a single
value the lifespan of the last (A,T) pair is ended.

Mod_Obj_Instance(o, A, [List of property:value])

Modification of an object o in the EXT(A) involves updating the TS associated with each property in the list. The end point of the previous (A,T) object's
valid time interval will be set to the current time or a user-specified time and the
start time of the new (A,T) object's valid time will be set to that time plus one
time unit. The transaction time of the new object is set to the current time. Since
relationships between this object and others are by reference and only involve its
IID, no other updates are required. Any values in the list can not violate conditions in the set of constraints associated with object type A.

5. Schema Level Operators

The domain for the schema operators is the extension of the meta-data types.
These classes contain instances of type definitions, variable definitions, operation
(message) definitions and collection definitions. The meta-data classes can be
queried using the operators defined at the object level since they are treated in the
same way as the data. Therefore, we just define the update operators in this section. Operators for adding/deleting/renaming types, instance variables (attributes),

---

[4] (A,T) pair is used to refer to a time-sequence pair or element. TS refers to a time-sequence.

messages, and constraints are defined. Operators to add/delete a supertype from a type's list of supertypes, to modify an attribute's domain, parent or creator and to modify a message's parent, creator, parameters and code module are defined as well. We don't include transaction time in the operator's parameters since it is automatically recorded by the system.

1)   Add_Type   (Name,   LIST[O_i],   TUPLE[Meta-Vars],   SET[Meta-Msgs], UserID, SET[BOOL], vt)

The user supplies a string-value for Name, a list of existing identifiers indicating the new type's supertype list his/her userid and the valid time when the type is allowed to be used. The valid time is restricted to be greater than or equal to the time when the type is recorded (tt) since a type can not have an extension until it exists in the database. Next, the user is asked to define the instance variables that will represent the structure of the object and the messages and constraints that will define its behavior. This operator results in the creation of an instance of Meta-Types, a set of instances of Meta-Vars, a set of instances of Meta-Msgs and a class object called SET[Name] to represent the extension of the new type.

2)   Del_Type(OID, Name, UserID, END(vt))

The user supplies the name of the type to delete, his/her userid and the date when the deletion will become effective - END(vt). Names of types must be unique so the name can be used to find the OID of the type to be deleted. The lifespans of all properties associated with the instance of Meta-Types with this OID will be ended with the time END(vt). All the lifespans of the properties of the corresponding Meta-Vars and Meta-Msgs instances will be ended with the same time. These properties will no longer be inherited by the deleted type's sub-types as of END(vt). The supertype lists of the deleted type's subtypes must be updated to exclude the deleted type as of END(vt). This entails terminating the last element of the supertype list time-sequence at END(vt) and adding a new element that doesn't contain the deleted type whose valid start time is END(vt) + 1 where 1 has the same granularity as vt. The endpoint of the new interval is defined as now+. The lifespan of the extension of the deleted type, SET[Name] must also be ended at END(vt).

3)   Rename_Type(OID, Old_Name,New_Name, UserID,vt)

Adds a new element to the time-sequence associated with the typ-name property of the Meta-Type instance whose typ-name = Old_Name and creator = UserID. The new element will have New_Name and UserId as its attribute values. It will become valid at time vt.

4)   Add_Var(Type-OID,   Name,   Parent,   UserID,   Domain, SET[BOOL], vt)

The user supplies the OID of the type to which the variable is to be added, the name of the variable, the parent it is inherited from, his/her userid, the domain type from which the variable will get its values, constraints on the variable and the time when the definition becomes valid. This results in the creation of a new instance of Meta-Vars and adds an element to the time-sequence associated with the instance of Meta-Types that has the given OID.

5)   Del_Var(Type-OID, Var-OID, vt)

The lifespan of the last element in the time-sequence associated with the var-list property of the Meta-Type instance with Type-OID as its identifier will be ended at vt. A new element will be started which does not contain the OID of the deleted instance variable. The lifespans of all properties of the instance of Meta-Vars with the identifier Var-OID will also be ended at time vt. If the variable is an inverse, the same procedure must be done for the instance of Meta-Vars representing the inverse variable.

6)   Add_Msg(Type-OID, Name, Parent, UserID, SET[Param], Code, vt, SET[BOOL])

This operator creates an instance of Meta-Msgs using the user-supplied values. Pre- and Post-condition constraints for the use of the messages can also be specified as a set of boolean conditions. The last element of the time sequence associated with the msg-list property of the instance of meta-types identified by Type-OID has its lifespan ended at vt and a new element which includes the new message is added to the sequence as in the previous add operations. Parameters in the new message are restricted to represent existing variables during the message's lifespan.

7)   Del_Msg(Type-OID, Msg-OID, vt)

The lifespan of the last element in the time-sequence associated with the msg-list property of the Meta-Type instance with Type-OID as its identifier will be ended at vt. A new element will be started which does not contain the OID of the deleted instance variable. The lifespans of all properties of the instance of Meta-Msgs with the identifier Msg-OID will also be ended at time vt.

8)   Add_Bool(Type-OID,{Var-OID| Msg-ID| Coll-ID}, BOOL, vt)

This operator creates an instance of type Boolean using the expression, BOOL, supplied by the user. The last element of the time sequence associated with the constraints property of the instance of meta-types identified by Type-OID has its lifespan ended at vt and a new element which includes the new constraint is added to the sequence as in the previous add operations. If a variable, message or collection OID is specified as the second parameter, the previous operation is carried out on the constraint (pre-/post-conditions) property of the appropriate instance.

9)   Del_Bool(Type-OID,{Var-OID| Msg-ID| Coll-ID}, BOOL-OID, vt)

The lifespan of the last element in the time-sequence associated with the constraint (pre-/post-condition) property of the specified instance will be ended at vt. A new element will be started which does not contain the OID of the deleted constraint.

10)   Add_SuperT($Type_i$, $Type_j$, position, vt)

This operator says to make $Type_j$ a supertype of $Type_i$ and to add $Type_j$ to the supertype list of $Type_i$ at position. This operation entails ending the lifespan of the last element in the time-sequence associated with the superclasses property of $Type_i$ at time vt and adding a new element which includes the new supertype.

Type$_j$

and *Type$_i$* must both be pre-defined in order to perform this operation.

11)   **Del_SuperT(*Type$_i$* , *Type$_j$* , position, vt)**

This operator says to delete *Type$_j$* from the supertype list of *Type$_i$* at position. This operation entails ending the lifespan of the last element in the time-sequence associated with the superclasses property of *Type$_i$* at time vt and adding a new element which excludes the supertype to be deleted. *Type$_j$* and *Type$_i$* must both be pre-defined in order to perform this operation.

12)   **Mod_Var_Signature(Var-OID, Name, Parent, UserID, Domain, vt)**

This operator lets the user change the name, parent, userid and/or domain associated with the variable identified by Var-OID. The last element of the time sequence associated with the var-signature property of the instance of meta-vars identified by Var-OID has its lifespan ended at vt and a new element which includes the new signature values is added to the sequence.

13)   **Mod_Msg_Signature(Msg-OID,   Name,   Parent,   UserID, SET[Param], Code, vt)**

This operator lets the user change the name, parent, userid parameters and/or code associated with the message identified by Msg-OID. The last element of the time sequence associated with the msg-signature property of the instance of meta-msgs identified by Msg-OID has its lifespan ended at vt and a new element which includes the new signature values is added to the sequence. Parameters in the new message are restricted to represent existing variables during the message's lifespan.

6. Summary and Future Work

Unlike the three temporal object-oriented models described in the introduction, TOODM supports type definition histories and makes use of the time-sequence construct shown in Figure 2. [Wuu & Dayal 91] and TOODM use attribute time-stamping whereas the other two papers time-stamp at the object instance level. TOODM allows a lifespan to be a finite union of non-contiguous intervals whereas [Wuu & Dayal 91] require contiguous intervals which does not allow for the case where a particular attribute may have been part of a type definition, then removed from it and later added back. [Su & Chen 91] do not directly support tt in their data model, rather they require the user to define rules to handle tt. Neither [Wuu & Dayal 91], [Su & Chen 91] or [Kafer & Schoning 92] include a discussion of a temporal object-oriented algebera with their data model.

In this paper, we developed a temporal, object-oriented algebra (called TOOA) for the manipulation of the intension and extension of a temporal, object-oriented data model. The time-sequence collection type was used to model histories of attribute values of objects and histories of the set of properties defining an object type. The paper makes the following contributions. First, it provides an algebra that operates on collections of object graphs. Second, it provides sets of update operators for both object histories and type definition histories. Third, it provides a merge operator for time-sequence objects to filter in or leave out corrections. The algebra includes a rollback operator to allow reversion back to a previous state of the recorded model as well as operators that retrieve values based on when they were valid. The separation of recorded values from their corrections also allows us to maintain an audit trail which could prove useful in accounting applications and in duplicating the results of previous analyses. Our operators also allow us to specify a different time period for each property of an object through the use of the associate/non-associate operators.

The next step in the development of this model will be to map the algebra to a higher-level, SQL-like syntax. Formal proofs to establish the equivalence properties will be used to determine transformations that will optimize query processing. Constraints are also being developed for the model to provide a means of doing semantic query optimization by transforming the query into a syntactically different but semantically same query which may have a more efficient execution plan. Implementing the optimizer as a rule-based system would make it more extensible, providing a means for adding new information and optimization methods. We will also need to investigate the trade-offs between optimizing the time to execute a query and the time to select the best query execution plan. Determining access patterns and indexes to facilitate those patterns will also be investigated through the development of a graphical front-end to the POSTGRES extended relational system.

REFERENCES

[Alashqur etal 89] A.M. Alashqur, S.Y.W. Su and H. Lam, OQL: A Query Language for Manipulating Object-Oriented Databases, *Proceedings of the 5th International Conference on Very Large Data Bases,* Amsterdam, The Netherlands, 1989, pp. 433-442.

[Andany etal 91] J. Andany, M. Leonard and C. Palisser, Management of Schema Evolution in Databases, *Proceedings of the 17th International Conference on Very Large Data Bases,* Barcelona, Spain, September 1991, pp. 161-170.

[Ariav 86] G. Ariav, A Temporally Oriented Data Model, *ACM Transactions on Database Systems,* V. 11, N. 4, December 1986, pp. 499-527.

[Banerjee etal 88] J. Banerjee, W. Kim, and K.C. Kim, Queries in Object-Oriented Databases, *Proceedings of the 4th International Conference on Data Engineering,* Los Angeles, California, February 1988, pp. 31-38.

[Clifford & Warren 83] J. Clifford and D.S. Warren, Formal Semantics for Time in Databases, *ACM Transactions on Database Systems,* V.8, N. 2, June 1983, pp. 214-254.

[Carey etal 88] M.J. Carey, D.J. DeWitt and S.L. Vandenberg, A Data Model and Query Language for EXODUS, *Proceedings of the ACM SIGMOD International Conference on the Management of Data,* June 1988, pp. 413-423.

[Clifford & Croker 87] J. Clifford and A. Croker, The Historical Data Model (HRDM) and Algebra Based on Lifespans, *Proceedings of the 3rd*

International Conference on Data Engineering, Los Angeles, California, February 1987, pp. 528-537.

[Elmasri & Wuu 90] R. Elmasri and G.T.J. Wuu, A Temporal Model and Query Language for ER Databases, *Proceedings of the 6th International Conference on Data Engineering,* May 1990, pp. 76-83.

[Ferg 85] S. Ferg, Modeling the Time Dimension in an Entity-Relationship Diagram, *Proceedings of the 4th International Conference on the ER Approach. In Entity-Relationship Approach,* Ed. Chen, P.P.S., Elsevier Science Publishers B.V. North-Holland, 1985, pp. 280-286.

[Gadia 88a] S.K. Gadia, The Role of Temporal Elements in Temporal Databases, *Database Engineering,* V 7, 1988, pp. 197-203.

[Gadia 88b] S.K. Gadia, A Homogeneous Relational Model and Query Language for Temporal Databases, *ACM Transactions on Database Systems* V. 13, N. 4, December 1988, pp. 418-448.

[Gadia & Yeung 88] S.K. Gadia and C.S. Yeung, A Generalized Model for a Relational Temporal Database, *Proceedings of ACM SIGMOD International Conference on the Management of Data,* V. 17, N. 3, June 1988, pp. 251-259.

[Guo etal 91] M. Guo, S.Y.W. Su and H. Lam, An Association-Algebra for Processing Object-Oriented Databases, *Proceedings of the 7th International Conference on Data Engineering,* Kobe, Japan, April 1991, pp. 23-32.

[Kafer & Schoning 92] W. Kafer and and H. Schoning, Realizing a Temporal Complex-Object Data Model, to appear in *Proceedings of the ACM SIGMOD International Conference on the Management of Data,* San Diego, California, June 1992.

[Kim & Chou 88] W. Kim and H.T. Chou, Versions of Schema for Object-Oriented Databases, *Proceedings of the 14th International Conference on Very Large Data Bases,* Los Angeles, California, 1988, pp. 148-159.

[Klopprogge & Lockemann 83] M.R. Klopprogge and P.C. Lockemann, Modeling Information Preserving Databases: Consequences of the Concept of Time, *Proceedings of the 9th International Conference on Very Large Data Bases,* Florence, Italy, 1983, pp. 399-416.

[McKenzie & Snodgrass 91] E. McKenzie and R. Snodgrass, Evaluation of Relational Algebras Incorporating the Time Dimension in Databases, *ACM Computing Surveys,* V. 23, N. 4, December 1991, pp. 501-543.

[Navathe & Ahmed 89] S.B. Navathe and R. Ahmed, A Temporal Relational Model and Query Language, *Information Sciences,* V. 49, 1989, pp. 147-175.

[Rose & Segev 91] E. Rose and A. Segev, TOODM - A Temporal, Object-Oriented Data Model with Temporal Constraints, *Proceedings of the 10th International Conference on the Entity-Relationship Approach,* San Mateo, California, 1991, pp. 205-229.

325

[Segev & Shoshani 87] A. Segev and A. Shoshani, Logical Modeling of Temporal Databases, *Proceedings of ACM SIGMOD International Conference on the Management of Data*, May 1987, pp. 454-466.

[Shaw & Zdonic 90] G.M. Shaw and S.B. Zdonic, A Query Algebra for Object-Oriented Databases, *Proceedings of the 6th International Conference on Data Engineering*, Vol. 12, No. 3, February 1990, pp. 154-162

[Skarra & Zdonik 86] A.H. Skarra and S.B. Zdonik, The Management of Changing Types in an Object-Oriented Database, *Procceedings of the OOPSLA Conference*, Portland, Oregon, September 1986, pp. 483-495.

[Soo 91] M.D. Soo, Bibliography on Temporal Databases, *SIGMOD Record*, V. 20, N. 1, March 1991, pp. 14-23.

[Snodgrass & Ahn 85] R. Snodgrass and I. Ahn, A Taxonomy of Time in Databases, *Proceedings of ACM SIGMOD International Conference on the Management of Data*, May 1985, pp. 236-246.

[Snodgrass 87] R. Snodgrass, The Temporal Query Language TQUEL, *ACM Transactions on Database Systems*, V. 12, N. 2, June 1987, pp. 247-298.

[Su & Chen 91] S.Y.W. Su and H.M. Chen, A Temporal Knowledge Representation Model OSAM*/T and Its Query Language OQL/T, *Proceedings of the 17th International Conference on Very Large Data Bases*, Barcelona, Spain, September 1991, pp. 431-442.

[Tuzhilin & Clifford 90] A. Tuzhilin and J. Clifford, A Temporal Relational Algebra as a Basis for Temporal Relational Completeness, *Proceedings of the 16th International Conference on Very Large Data Bases*, 1990, pp. 13-23.

[Wuu & Dayal 91] G. Wuu and U. Dayal, A Uniform Model for Temporal Object-Oriented Databases, *Proceedings of the 8th International Conference on Data Engineering* February 1991, pp. 584-593.

[Zicari 91] R. Zicari, A Framework for Schema Updates In An Object-Oriented Database System, *Proceedings of the 7th International Conference on Data Engineering*, Kobe, Japan, April 1991, pp. 2-13.

A Timed Calculus for
Distributed Objects with Clocks

Ichiro Satoh* and Mario Tokoro**

Department of Computer Science, Keio University
3-14-1, Hiyoshi, Kohoku-ku, Yokohama, 223, Japan

Abstract. This paper proposes a formalism for reasoning about distributed object-oriented computations. The formalism is an extension of Milner's CCS with the notion of local time. It allows to describe and analyze both locally temporal and behavioral properties of distributed objects and interactions among them. We introduce timed bisimulations with respect to local time. These bisimulations equate distributed objects if and only if their behaviors are completely matched and their timings are within a given bound. The bisimulations provide a method to verify distributed objects with temporal uncertainties and real-time objects with non-strict time constraints.

1 Introduction

Distributed systems consist of more than one processor loosely coupled by communication networks with inherent delay[3]. The notion of concurrent object-oriented computation [25] is considered as a powerful means to design and develop distributed systems. This is because objects are logically self-contained active entities interacting with one another through message passing. Recently, many programming languages for distributed systems were developed based on this notion [1, 22].

Communication delay is the most featuring characteristic of distributed systems. It prevents objects from sharing a global clock among all processors. Many distributed systems need real-time facilities to manage time critical responses and interactions with the real world. These facilities have to be materialized by clocks on local processors instead of the shared global clock. However, such clocks can never run at the same rate. Relative differences among clocks that cannot be ignored may lead cooperations among local processors to failure. In order to develop correct programs for distributed systems, we must take this problem into consideration. Hence, we need a theoretical model for describing and analyzing both locally temporal properties and functionally behavioral properties of distributed object-oriented computing.

---

* Email: *satoh@mt.cs.keio.ac.jp*

** Email: *mario@mt.cs.keio.ac.jp*, Also with Sony Computer Science Laboratory Inc. 3-14-13 Higashi-Gotanda, Shinagawa-ku, Tokyo, 141, Japan.

[3] Geographical distance between processors manifests in communication delay.

O.M. Nierstrasz (Ed.): ECOOP '93, LNCS 707, pp. 326-345, 1993.
© Springer-Verlag Berlin Heidelberg 1993

A number of computing models for describing and verifying distributed systems have been proposed based on temporal logic, automata, and process calculi. However, most of them are intended to model only behavioral aspects in distributed computing and thus lack in the ability of representing temporal properties. Others can manage only temporal properties based on the global time which cannot be essentially realized in distributed systems. Consequently, they can not model the notion of local time in distributed systems. In the fields of artificial intelligence and real-time systems, some logical systems to deal with different time scales have been proposed in [4, 7, 16]. However they cannot sufficiently model time based on local clocks which may drift in distributed systems. Also, some researchers have explored methods for agreement on processes' time by using clock synchronization [10, 13] and for maintaining local time based on causality by using time-stamps [9, 12]. However the former methods cannot cope with systems where communication delay is unpredictable. The latter methods lose real-time duration between events.

The goal of this paper is to develop a formalism for reasoning about distributed object-oriented computations, in particular, local time properties in computation. The formalism is based on an existing process calculus, CCS [14]. This is because CCS allows us to easily model many features of concurrent objects by means of its powerful expressive capabilities [8, 18]. For example, objects can be viewed as processes; interactions among objects can be seen as communications; and encapsulation can be modeled by the restriction of visible communications. However, CCS essentially lacks in the notion of local time and thus we need to extend CCS with it. Indeed the authors introduced a timed extended process calculus, called RtCCS, for real-time concurrent (but non-distributed) object-oriented computing in an earlier paper [21]. RtCCS is an extension of CCS [14] with timeout operator and timed observation equivalences. The extensions make RtCCS unique among other timed process calculi [5, 6, 15, 17, 24]. However, the extensions are based on the global time and thus RtCCS, like other timed calculi, cannot represent the notion of local time in distributed systems. In this paper, we develop a process calculus called DtCCS (*Distributed timed Calculus of Communication Systems*), by extending CCS with the notion of local time in order to explicitly describe and analyze both temporal properties based on local time and behavioral properties in distributed object-oriented computing[4]. Based on DtCCS, we furthermore develop theoretical proof techniques for distributed objects.

The organization of this paper is as follows: in the next section, we first informally introduce our approach to extend CCS with the notion of local time. Section 3 defines the syntax and the semantics of DtCCS and then presents how to describe distributed objects along with some examples in DtCCS. In Section 4 we present timed bisimulations based on local time and study their basic theoretical properties, and then we present some examples to demonstrate the usefulness of our formalism. The final section contains some concluding remarks and future works.

---

[4] There have indeed been some process calculi for distributed computing [2, 3, 11] but they are extensions of CCS with the concept of process locations and not local time.

2 Basic Framework

In this section, we present a brief introduction to our formalism.

2.1 Time in Distributed Computing

Before giving an exposition of our formalism, we first present the basic idea for modeling local time. If relative motion of all processors is negligible, from Einstein's Relativity, the passage of physical *time* in every processor elapses at the same rate. On the other hand, each local *clock* progresses at its own rate. Clock rates are different from each other and these rate may vary within a certain bound. Hence, we can envisage local clocks as follows: each actual local clock reads its own current time by translating the passage of the global time into its own time coordinate according to its own measurement rate. Therefore, local times which are measured by different clocks may be different from one another, although the clocks share the same global time. Summarizing this discussion, we give the following two basic assumptions on time in distributed computing: (1) *all processors in a distributed system share the conceptual global time*, and (2) *the local clock of each processor measures the global time according to its own time unit and precision*. We will hereafter call a clock running at a given constant rate as a *constant clock*, and call a clock running at a dynamically drifting rate within a given bound as a *variable clock*.

2.2 Extensions of CCS

According to the above assumptions, we develop a formalism for reasoning about behavioral and temporal properties of distributed objects by using a language based on CCS. In order to represent the temporal properties of distributed systems, we need to extend CCS with the ability of representing local time properties in distributed systems. To do this, we introduce three temporal primitives: *timed behavior*, *global time*, and *local clock*. We briefly summarize these extensions[5] as follows:

- *Timed Behavior.* The behavior of distributed systems is dependent on the passage of time, such as delaying process and timeout handling. Particularly, in distributed systems timeout handling is a crucial part for failure detection in communication network and other processors. Therefore, we introduce a special binary operator having the semantics of timeout handling, written as $\langle \ , \ \rangle_t$, and called a *timeout* operator. For instance, $\langle P, Q \rangle_t$ behaves as P if P can execute an initial transition within t units of time, and behaves as Q if P does not perform any action within t units of time.

---

[5] The extensions, except for local clock, are essentially equivalent to ones in RtCCS in [21].

- *Global Time.* We assume that all processors share the conceptual global time. The passage of the global time is represented as a special action. The action is a synchronous broadcast message over all objects and corresponds to the passage of one unit of the global time. It is described as a $\sqrt{}$. called a *tick* action. Please note that, in our formalism, the existence of the global time does not implies the existence of an actual global clock: it only provides the time that each local clock may measure.

- *Local Clock.* Local clocks are given as special mappings from time instants on local time into corresponding time instants on the global time, according to its own time unit and precision. The mapping defines how many time instants on the global time corresponds to the length of one time unit in the local time. Conversely, local time on each processor is given as a collection of all the time instants which can be translated into the global time by the mapping. In order to represent a variable clock, the clock may be given as a non-deterministic mapping.

In our formalism, descriptions of objects with respect to local times are translated into ones in the global time. The descriptions are interpreted based only on the global time. Thus, we obtain a uniform way to easily analyze distributed objects with their own local times. As a result, we can use many pleasant properties of timed process calculi based on global time, including the proof techniques of RtCCS presented in [21]. The translation maps time values with respect to local time in the descriptions into values with respect to the global time. Our method of interpreting the descriptions on local time may seem to be similar to that of [4, 16]. However, the latter is intended to deal with different time scales in specification and cannot sufficiently model time based on variable clocks in distributed systems.

3 Definition

This section first presents the basic definitions for time related notations and then defines the syntax and the semantics of our calculus.

3.1 Time Domain

In our formalism, time is represented as a time domain composed of time instants. An instant represents a time interval from an initial time and we restrict the instants to be discrete, instead of continuous. Each time domain corresponds to a local time measured by one local clock. We assume a special time domain which is a finest and absolute reference time basis for all local times and is called the *global time domain*.

Definition 3.1 Let T denote the set of the positive integers including 0. We call T a *time domain*.

$$T \equiv \mathcal{N} \cup \{0\} \quad \text{where } \mathcal{N} \text{ is a set of natural numbers.}$$

Especially, the global time domain is denoted as T_G. □

All occurrences of any instant times on local time domains correspond to instant times in the global time domain. The linkage between a local time domain and the global time domain is given as the following mapping.

Definition 3.2   Let T_l be a local time domain and $\delta_{min}, \delta_{max} \in T_G : 0 < \delta_{min} \leq \delta_{max}$. A clock mapping $\theta : T_l \rightarrow T_G$ is defined as follows: for all $t \in T_l$,

$$\theta(t) \overset{\text{def}}{=} \begin{cases} 0 & \text{if } t = 0 \\ \theta(t-1) + \delta & \text{if } t > 0 \end{cases} \text{ where } \delta \in \{ d \in T_G \mid \delta_{min} \leq d \leq \delta_{max} \}$$

where we call θ a *clock mapping*, or simply a *clock*. We let $\{\theta(t)\}$ denote $\{ t_G \mid \forall t_G \in T_G : t_G = \theta(t)\}$. Particularly, if $\delta_{min} = \delta_{max}$, we call θ a *constant clock* and hereafter will sometimes abbreviate the definition of θ as $\theta(t) \overset{\text{def}}{=} \delta t$. □

In above definition, δ corresponds to the interval of one time unit on the local time domain according to the global time domain. δ_{min} is the lower bound of that interval and δ_{max} the upper bound of that interval. Also $\{\theta(t)\}$ means the set of the whole time values can be evaluated in $\theta(t)$.

We present some examples of clock mappings.

Example 3.3   *Examples of clock mappings*

(1) The clock mapping of a constant clock whose time units is three units of the global time, is denoted as follows: $\theta(t) \overset{\text{def}}{=} 3t$.

(2) The clock mapping of a variable clock whose time unit varies from two to four units of the global time is given as follows:

$$\theta(t) \overset{\text{def}}{=} \begin{cases} 0 & \text{if } t = 0 \\ \theta(t-1) + \delta & \text{if } t > 0 \end{cases} \text{ where } \delta \in \{2, 3, 4\}$$

□

As previously mentioned, time is discrete in our formalism. Therefore, if an event is executed between two consecutive time instants, we say that the event occurs at the earlier time instant. Also, if two or more events occur between two consecutive time instants, we say that the events occur at the same time.

Here, we present the inverse of clock mapping. It maps a time instant on global time into the coordinates of local time.

Definition 3.4   The inverse mapping of $\theta: T_l \rightarrow T_G$ is defined as follows:

$$\{\theta^{-1}(t_G)\} \overset{\text{def}}{=} \{ t \mid \forall t \in T_l : \min\{\theta(t)\} \leq t_G < \max\{\theta(t+1)\} \}$$

where $t_G \in T_G$. □

To demonstrate how $\theta^{-1}(t)$ works, we show an inverse mappings.

Example 3.5 *Examples of clock inverse mappings*
Recall θ in (2) of Example 3.3. We present a few of the possible results of its inverse mapping $\theta^{-1}(t)$ as follows: $\{\theta^{-1}(1)\} = \{0\}, \{\theta^{-1}(2)\} = \{0,1\}, \{\theta^{-1}(3)\} = \{0,1\}, \{\theta^{-1}(4)\} = \{1,2\}, \{\theta^{-1}(6)\} = \{1,2,3\}, \{\theta^{-1}(8)\} = \{2,3,4\}, \ldots$ □

We show an alternative definition of the inverse mapping below.

Proposition 3.6 Let $\theta \colon T_\ell \to T_G$ and $\dot\phi : T_G \to T_\ell$ be the following functions. We have that for all $t_G \in T_G$: $\{\phi(t_G)\}$ is equivalent to $\{\theta^{-1}(t_G)\}$.

$$\theta(t) \stackrel{\text{def}}{=} \begin{cases} 0 & \text{if } t = 0 \\ \theta(t-1) + \delta & \text{if } t > 0 \end{cases} \quad \text{where } \delta \in \{ \, d \in T_G \mid \delta_{min} \le d \le \delta_{max} \, \}$$

$$\{\phi(t_G)\} \stackrel{\text{def}}{=} \{ \, t \mid \forall t \in T_\ell : \lfloor t_G / \delta_{max} \rfloor \le t \le \lfloor t_G / \delta_{min} \rfloor \, \}$$

where $\delta_{min}, \delta_{max} \in T_G : 0 < \delta_{min} \le \delta_{max}$. □

Note that the definitions of the clock mapping and its inverse mapping are different from that of usual functions in mathematics.

3.2 Notation and Syntax

Here we present the syntax of DtCCS. The syntax is an extension of Milner's CCS [14] by introducing a tick action, a timeout operator, and clock translation rules.

A few preliminary definitions are needed before giving the definition of the syntax. We first define notation conventions which we will follow hereafter.

Definition 3.7

- Let $\mathcal{A}$ be an infinite set of communication action names, ranged over by $a, b, \ldots$.
- Let $\overline{\mathcal{A}}$ be the set of co-names, ranged over by $\overline{a}, \overline{b}, \ldots$ where an action $\overline{a}$ is the complementary action of a, and $\overline{\overline{a}} \equiv a$.
- Let $\mathcal{L} \equiv \mathcal{A} \cup \overline{\mathcal{A}}$ be a set of action labels, ranged over by $\ell, \ell', \ldots$.
- Let τ denote an internal action which is unobservable from the outside.
- Let $\sqrt{}$ denote a tick action which represents the passage of one time unit.
- Let $Act \equiv \mathcal{L} \cup \{\tau\}$ be the set of behavior actions, ranged over by $\alpha, \beta, \ldots$.
- Let $Act_T \equiv Act \cup \{\sqrt{}\}$ be the set of actions, ranged over by $\mu, \nu, \ldots$.

□

In our formalism, distributed objects are described by means of expressions as defined below. In order to clarify our exposition, we divide the expressions into two groups: sequential expressions for describing objects on a processor (or a node) with one local clock, and interacting expressions for describing interactions among distributed objects following different clocks.

Definition 3.8 The set S of sequential expressions, ranged over by $S, S_1, S_2, ..$ is the smallest set which contains the following expressions:

$$
\begin{array}{lll}
S ::= & \mathbf{0} & (\textit{Terminated Process}) \\
& | \quad X & (\textit{Process Variable}) \\
& | \quad \alpha.S & (\textit{Sequential Execution}) \\
& | \quad S_1 + S_2 & (\textit{Alternative Choice}) \\
& | \quad \mathbf{rec}\, X : S & (\textit{Recursive Definition}) \\
& | \quad \langle S_1, S_2 \rangle_t & (\textit{Timeout})
\end{array}
$$

where t is an element of a time domain. We assume that X is always *guarded* [6]. We shall often use the more readable notation $X \overset{\text{def}}{=} S$ instead of **rec** $X : S$. □

Intuitively, the meaning of constructors on S are as follows: $\mathbf{0}$ represents a terminated and deadlocked object; $\alpha.S$ performs an action α and then behaves like S; $S_1 + S_2$ represents an object which may behave as either S_1 or S_2; **rec** $X : S$ binds the free occurrences of X in S; $\langle S_1, S_2 \rangle_t$ represents an object such that it behaves as S_1 if S_1 can execute an initial transition within t time units, whereas it behaves as S_2 if S_1 does not perform any action within t time units.

We now define the syntax of expressions for interactions among different processors with local clocks as shown below. We assume that $[\![\cdot]\!]_\theta$ is a clock translation mapping which will be defined later. It allows sequential expressions following a local clock θ to be translated into expressions on the global time domain T_G.

Definition 3.9 The set $\mathcal{P}$ of interacting expressions on local time, ranged over by $P, P_1, P_2, ..$ is defined by the following grammar:

$$
\begin{array}{lll}
P ::= & [\![S]\!]_\theta & (\textit{Local Object}) \\
& | \quad P_1 | P_2 & (\textit{Parallel Composition}) \\
& | \quad P[f] & (\textit{Relabeling}) \\
& | \quad P \setminus L & (\textit{Encapsulation})
\end{array}
$$

where θ is a clock mapping. We assume that $f \in Act \rightarrow Act$, $\overline{f(\ell)} = f(\overline{\ell})$, $f(\tau) = \tau$, and $L \subseteq Act$. □

---

[6] X is *guarded* in S if each occurrence of X is only within some subexpressions $\alpha.S'$ in S where α is not an empty element; c.f. *unguarded* expressions, e.g. **rec** $X : X$ or **rec** $X : X + S$.

The informal meaning of constructors of $\mathcal{P}$ is as follows: $[\![S]\!]_\theta$ represents a sequential expression S executed on a processor (or a node) with a local clock θ; $P_1|P_2$ allows P_1 and P_2 to execute in parallel; $P[f]$ behaves like P but with the actions in P relabeled by function f; $P \setminus L$ behaves like P but with actions in $L \cup \bar{L}$ prohibited.

3.3 Semantics

As we noted already, the definition of the semantics of DtCCS consists of two parts: clock translation rules, written as $[\![S]\!]_\theta$, which translate expressions on a local time into expressions on the global time, and structural transition rules which define the mean of all constructors in expressions on the global time.

Expressions on Local Time

We here define the clock translation rules $[\![S]\!]_\theta$. We first present the key idea of the rules. In order to translate expressions on local time into expressions on the global time, we translate all local time values in expressions on local time into time values on the global time. In our formalism only the deadline time of the timeout operator corresponds to such time values. We introduce special translation rules which map each deadline time on local clocks in expressions into deadline time based on the global time, by using the clock mapping.

Definition 3.10 Let $\mathcal{T}_\ell$ be a local time domain and θ be a clock mapping from $\mathcal{T}_\ell$ to $\mathcal{T}_G$. The clock translation rule $[\![\cdot]\!]_\theta$ is recursively defined by the following syntactic rewriting rules.

$$[\![0]\!]_\theta \longrightarrow 0$$
$$[\![X]\!]_\theta \longrightarrow X$$
$$[\![\alpha.S]\!]_\theta \longrightarrow \alpha.[\![S]\!]_{\theta'}$$
$$[\![S_1 + S_2]\!]_\theta \longrightarrow [\![S_1]\!]_{\theta'} + [\![S_2]\!]_{\theta'}$$
$$[\![\mathbf{rec}\,X : S]\!]_\theta \longrightarrow \mathbf{rec}\,X : [\![S]\!]_{\theta'}$$
$$[\![\langle S_1, S_2 \rangle_t]\!]_\theta \longrightarrow \langle [\![S_1]\!]_{\theta'}, [\![S_2]\!]_{\theta''} \rangle_{\theta'(t)}$$

where $\theta', \theta'' \stackrel{\text{def}}{=} \theta$ such that $\forall t_\ell \in \mathcal{T}_\ell : \theta'(t_\ell) = \theta(t_\ell), \theta''(t_\ell) + \theta(t) = \theta(t_\ell + t)$. $\square$

We briefly explain the intuitive meaning of the main rules. The third rule translates an unpredictable synchronization time for waiting for α into an unpredictable time on the global time domain. The fourth rule shows that all alternative subsequences in a processor share the same clock. The last rule means that the deadline time t on local clock θ is mapped into deadline time on the global time.

We show some notable points on the above clock translation rules.

- Hereafter we will often omit the —→ translation if it is understood from the context.

- By the definition of $\mathcal{P}$, expressions applicable to $[\![\cdot]\!]_\theta$ are restricted to expressions in $\mathcal{S}$. This means that expressions to model internal interactions, such as concurrency and encapsulation, among objects sharing the same clock cannot be translated into the global time by $[\![\cdot]\!]_\theta$. However, this restriction never results in unavoidable difficulties in describing distributed systems. This is because any expression for interaction on the same clock can be reduced to an equivalent sequential expression in $\mathcal{S}$ by using the expansion rules shown in Corollary 1 and Proposition 10 of [21]. Therefore, we first translate expressions for interacting objects following the same clock into expressions in $\mathcal{S}$ using the expansion rules and then we can apply $[\![\cdot]\!]_\theta$ to the translated expressions.

Expressions on Global Time

The clock translation rules can completely eliminate all $[\![\cdot]\!]_\theta$ from expressions in $\mathcal{P}$. Therefore, in order to define the operational semantics of DtCCS, we need to give semantics to all syntactical constructors in $\mathcal{P}$ except $[\![\cdot]\!]_\theta$. The semantics is given in terms of a labeled transition system [20]. The operational semantics of the language which consists of the translated expressions on the global time, is given as a labeled transition system $\langle \mathcal{P},\ Act_T,\ \{\ \xrightarrow{\mu}\ |\ \mu \in Act_T\ \}\ \rangle$ where $\xrightarrow{\mu}$ is a transition relation ($\xrightarrow{\mu}\subseteq \mathcal{P} \times \mathcal{P}$ where $\mathcal{P}$ contains no constructor $[\![S]\!]_\theta$). The definition of the semantics is structurally given in two phases. The first phase defines the relations $\xrightarrow{\alpha}$ for each $\alpha \in Act$. The inference rules determining $\xrightarrow{\alpha}$ are given in Fig. 1. This is based on the standard operational semantics for CCS except for the addition of the timeout operator. The new action $\sqrt{}$ does not effect any rule. The second phase defines the relation $\xrightarrow{\sqrt{}}$ by inference rules given in Fig. 2.

Let us give some remarks on the definition of the semantics.

- The syntax and the semantics of the translated expressions on the global time domain essentially coincide with these of RtCCS [21]. Therefore, the translated expressions enjoy proof techniques presented in [21] for RtCCS, such as timed strong equivalence and timed observation equivalence.

- As previously mentioned, there have been many time extended process calculi. The syntax and the semantics of the expressions translated into the global time domain (i.e. RtCCS) are somewhat similar to some of them. Detail comparisons can be found in [21].

- In DtCCS, external actions cannot be performed before their partner actions in other objects are ready to communicate it. Objects must perform $\sqrt{}$ actions, while waiting for partner actions corresponding to their external actions. If an object can perform any executable communication (including τ), it must perform the communication immediately, instead of idling unnecessarily.

$$\alpha.P \xrightarrow{\alpha} P$$

$$P_1 \xrightarrow{\alpha} P_1' \qquad \text{implies } P_1 + P_2 \xrightarrow{\alpha} P_1', \; P_2 + P_1 \xrightarrow{\alpha} P_1'$$

$$P_1 \xrightarrow{\alpha} P_1' \qquad \text{implies } P_1|P_2 \xrightarrow{\alpha} P_1'|P_2, \; P_2|P_1 \xrightarrow{\alpha} P_2|P_1'$$

$$P_1 \xrightarrow{\alpha} P_1', \; P_2 \xrightarrow{\overline{\alpha}} P_2' \qquad \text{implies } P_1|P_2 \xrightarrow{\tau} P_1'|P_2'$$

$$P \xrightarrow{\alpha} P' \qquad \text{implies } P[f] \xrightarrow{f(\alpha)} P'[f]$$

$$P \xrightarrow{\alpha} P', \; \alpha \notin L \cup \overline{L} \qquad \text{implies } P \setminus L \xrightarrow{\alpha} P' \setminus L$$

$$P\{\text{rec } X : P/X\} \xrightarrow{\alpha} P' \text{ implies rec } X : P \xrightarrow{\alpha} P'$$

$$P_1 \xrightarrow{\alpha} P_1', \; t > 0 \qquad \text{implies } \langle P_1, P_2 \rangle_t \xrightarrow{\alpha} P_1'$$

$$P_2 \xrightarrow{\alpha} P_2' \qquad \text{implies } \langle P_1, P_2 \rangle_0 \xrightarrow{\alpha} P_2'$$

Fig. 1. Operational Rules of $\mathcal{P}$ on Global Time

$$0 \xrightarrow{\surd} 0$$

$$\ell.P \xrightarrow{\surd} \ell.P$$

$$P_1 \xrightarrow{\surd} P_1', \; P_2 \xrightarrow{\surd} P_2' \qquad \text{implies } P_1 + P_2 \xrightarrow{\surd} P_1' + P_2'$$

$$P_1 \xrightarrow{\surd} P_1', \; P_2 \xrightarrow{\surd} P_2', \; P_1|P_2 \not\xrightarrow{\tau} \text{ implies } P_1|P_2 \xrightarrow{\surd} P_1'|P_2'$$

$$P \xrightarrow{\surd} P' \qquad \text{implies } P[f] \xrightarrow{\surd} P'[f]$$

$$P \xrightarrow{\surd} P' \qquad \text{implies } P \setminus L \xrightarrow{\surd} P' \setminus L$$

$$P\{\text{rec } X : P/X\} \xrightarrow{\surd} P' \qquad \text{implies rec } X : P \xrightarrow{\surd} P'$$

$$P_1 \xrightarrow{\surd} P_1', \; t > 0 \qquad \text{implies } \langle P_1, P_2 \rangle_t \xrightarrow{\surd} \langle P_1', P_2 \rangle_{t-1}$$

$$P_2 \xrightarrow{\surd} P_2' \qquad \text{implies } \langle P_1, P_2 \rangle_0 \xrightarrow{\surd} P_2'$$

Fig. 2. Temporal Rules of $\mathcal{P}$ on Global Time

3.4 Examples on Description of Distributed Objects

In order to illustrate how to describe distributed object in DtCCS, we present some simple examples.

Example 3.11 *Interaction between Distributed Objects*
We suppose interaction between a client object and a sever object on different processors by means of *remote procedure call*.

- The client object (*Client*) sends a request message ($\overline{req}$) and then waits for a return message (*ret*). If the return message is not received within 6 units of local time, then it sends the request message again.
- Upon reception of a request message (*req*), the server object (*Server*) sends a return message ($\overline{ret}$) after an internal execution of 5 units of local time.

These objects are denoted as follows:

$$Client \stackrel{\text{def}}{=} \overline{req}.\langle ret.0, Client\rangle_6$$

$$Server \stackrel{\text{def}}{=} req.\langle 0, \overline{ret}.Server\rangle_5$$

We assume that the client and server objects are allocated to different processors. The time unit of variable clock θ_c for the client varies from 4 to 6 units of the global time. The time unit of variable clock θ_s for the server varies from 3 to 5 units of the global time. θ_c and θ_s are defined as follows:

$$\theta_c(t) \stackrel{\text{def}}{=} \begin{cases} 0 & \text{if } t = 0 \\ \theta_c(t-1) + \delta_c & \text{if } t > 0 \end{cases} \quad \text{where } \delta_c \in \{4,5,6\}$$

$$\theta_s(t) \stackrel{\text{def}}{=} \begin{cases} 0 & \text{if } t = 0 \\ \theta_s(t-1) + \delta_s & \text{if } t > 0 \end{cases} \quad \text{where } \delta_s \in \{3,4,5\}$$

By $[\![\cdot]\!]_\theta$ mapping rules, the client and the server are mapped on the global time domain as shown below. From the definition of θ_c and θ_s, there are multiple results for $\theta_c(6) \in \{24, 25, ..36\}$ and $\theta_s(5) \in \{15, 16, ..25\}$:

$$[\![Client]\!]_{\theta_c} \longrightarrow \cdots \longrightarrow \overline{req}.\langle ret.0, [\![Client]\!]_{\theta_c}\rangle_{\theta_c(6)}$$

$$[\![Server]\!]_{\theta_s} \longrightarrow \cdots \longrightarrow req.\langle 0, \overline{ret}.[\![Server]\!]_{\theta_s}\rangle_{\theta_s(5)}$$

The interaction between the objects is described as the following parallel composition:

$$([\![Client]\!]_{\theta_c} | [\![Server]\!]_{\theta_s}) \setminus \{req, ret\}$$

where $\setminus\{req, ret\}$ makes internal communications encapsulated from the environment. The result of the interaction is dependent on the evaluated values of $\theta_c(6)$ and $\theta_s(5)$. Here we show some of the possible results:

(1) In the case of $\theta_c(6) = 30$ and $\theta_s(5) = 20$:

$$([\![Client]\!]_{\theta_c} | [\![Server]\!]_{\theta_s}) \setminus \{req, ret\}$$
$$\stackrel{\tau}{\longrightarrow} (\langle ret.0, [\![Client]\!]_{\theta_c}\rangle_{30} | \langle 0, \overline{ret}.[\![Server]\!]_{\theta_s}\rangle_{20}) \setminus \{req, ret\}$$
$$(\stackrel{\checkmark}{\longrightarrow})^{20} (\langle ret.0, [\![Client]\!]_{\theta_c}\rangle_{10} | \overline{ret}.[\![Server]\!]_{\theta_s}) \setminus \{req, ret\}$$
$$\stackrel{\tau}{\longrightarrow} (0 | [\![Server]\!]_{\theta_s}) \setminus \{req, ret\}$$
$$(successful)$$

In the above case (i.e. $\theta_c(6) > \theta_s(5)$), the client can always receive the return message before it goes into timeout.

(2) In the case of $\theta_c(6) = 24$ and $\theta_s(5) = 25$:

$$([\![Client]\!]_{\theta_c} | [\![Server]\!]_{\theta_s}) \setminus \{req, ret\}$$
$$\stackrel{\tau}{\longrightarrow} (\langle ret.0, [\![Client]\!]_{\theta_c}\rangle_{24} | \langle 0, \overline{ret}.[\![Server]\!]_{\theta_s}\rangle_{25}) \setminus \{req, ret\}$$
$$(\stackrel{\checkmark}{\longrightarrow})^{24} ([\![Client]\!]_{\theta_c} | \langle 0, \overline{ret}.[\![Server]\!]_{\theta_s}\rangle_1) \setminus \{req, ret\}$$
$$(\stackrel{\checkmark}{\longrightarrow})^1 ([\![Client]\!]_{\theta_c} | \overline{ret}.[\![Server]\!]_{\theta_s}) \setminus \{req, ret\}$$
$$(failure)$$

In the above case, the client goes into timeout before receiving a return message *ret* because of $\theta_c(6) \leq \theta_s(5)$. Thus, the objects goes into a deadlock.

DtCCS allows us to analyze explicitly how the differences among local clocks affect the result of interactions in distributed computing. □

Note that the deadline time of the timeout operator in *Server* means execution steps for handling the request in the server. θ_s in $[Server]_{\theta_s}$ represents an index on the performance of a processor executing the server. For example, the larger δ_s in θ_s is, the faster the processor is. The result shows that the clock translation rules $[\cdot]_{\theta}$ allows us to represent differences among processors' performances as well as differences among processors' clocks.

Example 3.12 *Embedding Asynchronous Communication with Delay*
We illustrate an embedding of an asynchronous communication mechanism in DtCCS. The key idea of the embedding is to express asynchronous communication in terms of synchronous communication and a messenger creation, i.e. asynchronous message sending is represented by creating a process which can engage only in an input action with the same name of the message. Note that this embedding is very similar to the ways to express asynchronous communication developed in [8, 11].

Let $\uparrow a.P$ and $\downarrow a.P$ denote asynchronous sending and receiving expressions, respectively. $\uparrow a.P$ sends a message to the target name a and continues to execute P without waiting the reception of the message. $\downarrow a.P$ behaves like P after receiving a message with a target name a. These expressions are encoded by expressions of DtCCS as follows:

(1) First we describe the case we can neglect the transmission delay of the communication.

$$\uparrow a.P \equiv (\overline{c}.P | c.\overline{a}.0) \setminus \{c\} \qquad (Asynchronous\ Sending)$$
$$\downarrow a.P \equiv a.P \qquad (Receiving)$$

where we assume that newly introduced name c does not appear in P.

Note that $\uparrow a.P$ can continue to execute P without blocking before $\uparrow a$ is received by another object.

(2) Next we take communication delay into consideration. In the above expression $c.\overline{a}.0$ corresponds to a communication channel for the message and thus we extend $c.\overline{a}.0$.

$$\uparrow a.P \equiv (\overline{c}.P | [c.\langle 0, \overline{a}.0 \rangle_1]_{\theta_d}) \setminus \{c\} \qquad (Asynchronous\ Sending)$$

$$\theta_d(t) \stackrel{\text{def}}{=} \begin{cases} 0 & \text{if } t = 0 \\ \theta_d(t-1) + \delta_d & \text{if } t > 0 \end{cases} \qquad \text{where } \delta_d \in \{ d \mid d_{min} \leq d \leq d_{max} \}$$

where d_{min} and d_{max} correspond to the minimum and maximal delay of the transmission, respectively. The multiple results of $\theta_d(1)$ allows us to model uncertain delay time within a given bound ($d_{min} \leq d \leq d_{max}$).

(3) We extend the server object of Example 3.11 with asynchronous communication.

$$Server \stackrel{\text{def}}{=} \lfloor req.\langle 0, \uparrow ret.Server \rangle_5$$

We derive an expansion of $Server$ as follows:

$$
\begin{aligned}
[\![Server]\!]_{\theta_s} &\equiv & req.\langle 0, (\overline{c}.[\![Server]\!]_{\theta_s} | c.\langle 0, \overline{ret}.0 \rangle_{\theta_d(1)}) \setminus \{c\} \rangle_{\theta_s(5)} \\
&\xrightarrow{req} & \langle 0, (\overline{c}.[\![Server]\!]_{\theta_s} | c.\langle 0, \overline{ret}.0 \rangle_{\theta_d(1)}) \setminus \{c\} \rangle_{\theta_s(5)} \\
&(\xrightarrow{\checkmark})^{\theta_s(5)} & (\overline{c}.[\![Server]\!]_{\theta_s} | c.\langle 0, \overline{ret}.0 \rangle_{\theta_d(1)}) \setminus \{c\} \\
&\xrightarrow{\tau} & ([\![Server]\!]_{\theta_s} | \langle 0, \overline{ret}.0 \rangle_{\theta_d(1)}) \setminus \{c\} \\
&\xrightarrow{req} & \cdots
\end{aligned}
$$

where θ_s were already defined in Example 3.11.

The server can receive the next req message while $\overline{ret}$ is being transmitted, and thus not yet received. $\quad\square$

4 Bisimulation Based on Local Time

This section defines two timed bisimulations. In the earlier paper [21], the author provided temporally strict equivalences in which timed equivalent objects must *completely* match their time properties as well as their functional behaviors. However, the temporal properties of any two distributed objects may not completely match one another because local processors may not compute at exactly the same speed and local clocks may not run at the same rate. It is natural and practical that two objects on different processors can be treated as equivalent only if their behaviors are completely matched and differences in their timings are within a given bound. Therefore, we develop such equivalences by extending the notion of bisimulation [19, 14] and study some theoretical properties of them. Hereafter we will only deal with expressions with no occurrences of free[7] process variables.

Definition 4.1 *Optimistically Timed Bisimulation*
A binary relation $\mathcal{R}_\theta$ is a *optimistically timed bisimulation* on clock θ ($\theta : T_\ell \rightarrow T_G$) if $(P, Q) \in \mathcal{R}_\theta$ implies, for all $\alpha \in Act$,

(i) $\forall m \in T_G, \forall P': P(\xrightarrow{\checkmark})^m \xrightarrow{\alpha} P' \supset \exists n \in T_G, \exists Q': Q(\xrightarrow{\checkmark})^n \xrightarrow{\alpha} Q'$
   $\wedge \{\theta^{-1}(m)\} \cap \{\theta^{-1}(n)\} \neq \emptyset \wedge (P', Q') \in \mathcal{R}_\theta.$

---

[7] An occurrence of a variable X in an expression $P \in \mathcal{P}$ is called *bounded* if it occurs in a subexpression of the form $rec\, X : P'$. Otherwise it is called *free*.

(ii) $\forall n \in T_G,\ \forall Q'\colon Q(\xrightarrow{\checkmark})^n \xrightarrow{\alpha} Q' \supset \exists m \in T_G,\ \exists P'\colon P(\xrightarrow{\checkmark})^m \xrightarrow{\alpha} P'$
$\wedge\ \{\theta^{-1}(m)\} \cap \{\theta^{-1}(n)\} \neq \emptyset \wedge (P',Q') \in \mathcal{R}_\theta.$

We let "$\sim_\theta$" denote the largest optimistically timed bisimulation, and call P and Q *optimistically timed bisimilar* if $P \sim_\theta Q$. Also if $\theta(t) \stackrel{\mathrm{def}}{=} t$, we let $\sim$ denote $\sim_\theta$. □

Let us describe the informal meaning of $\sim_\theta$. If $P \sim_\theta Q$, an observer following clock θ cannot distinguish between the behavioral contents and the timings of P and Q. Especially, when the running rate of the clock drifts, there may be measurement errors due to the drift. The observer leaves these errors out of consideration. Therefore, $\sim_\theta$ optimistically equates the temporal properties of two objects.

Proposition 4.2 $\forall S_1, S_2 \in \mathcal{S},\quad S_1 \sim S_2 \quad iff \quad [\![S_1]\!]_\theta \sim_\theta [\![S_2]\!]_\theta$ □

This proposition shows a relationship between the optimistically timed bisimilarity and the clock translation rules.

Next we define the pessimistic counterpart of $\sim_\theta$.

Definition 4.3   *Pessimistically Timed Bisimulation*
A binary relation $\mathcal{R}_\theta$ is a *pessimistically timed bisimulation* on clock θ ($\theta : T_\ell \to T_G$ and $\forall t \in T_\ell : \max\{\theta(t)\} \leq \min\{\theta(t+1)\}$) if $(P,Q) \in \mathcal{R}_\theta$ implies, for all $\alpha \in Act$,

(i) $\forall m \in T_G, \forall i \in \{\theta^{-1}(m)\},\ \forall P'\colon P(\xrightarrow{\checkmark})^m \xrightarrow{\alpha} P' \supset \exists n \in T_G, \exists Q'\colon Q$
$(\xrightarrow{\checkmark})^n \xrightarrow{\alpha} Q' \wedge \max\{\theta(i)\} \leq n < \min\{\theta(i+1)\} \wedge (P',Q') \in \mathcal{R}_\theta.$

(ii) $\forall n \in T_G, \forall j \in \{\theta^{-1}(n)\},\ \forall Q'\colon Q(\xrightarrow{\checkmark})^n \xrightarrow{\alpha} Q' \supset \exists m \in T_G, \exists P'\colon P$
$(\xrightarrow{\checkmark})^m \xrightarrow{\alpha} P' \wedge \max\{\theta(j)\} \leq m < \min\{\theta(j+1)\} \wedge (P',Q') \in \mathcal{R}_\theta.$

We let "$\simeq_\theta$" denote the largest pessimistically timed bisimulation, and call P and Q *pessimistically timed bisimilar* if $P \simeq_\theta Q$. Also if $\theta(t) \stackrel{\mathrm{def}}{=} t$, we let $\simeq$ denote $\simeq_\theta$. □

We show the informal meaning of $\simeq_\theta$. If P and Q are pessimistically timed bisimilar on θ, an observer according to clock θ cannot distinguish between their behavioral contents and between their timings. When θ is a variable clock, there may be measurement errors due to the drift of θ. The observer in $\simeq_\theta$ takes these errors into consideration and equates only objects whose temporal and behavioral properties cannot constantly be distinguished by the observer, regardless of whether the errors affect the measurement result of θ or not. Hence, $\simeq_\theta$ pessimistically equates the temporal properties of two objects.

Since $\simeq_\theta$ is a particular instance of $\sim_\theta$, we have the following relationship between $\sim_\theta$ and $\simeq_\theta$

Proposition 4.4 $\forall P_1, P_2 \in \mathcal{P}$, *If* $P_1 \simeq_\theta P_2$, *then* $P_1 \sim_\theta P_2$. ◻

The above proposition shows that $\simeq_\theta$ is more strict than $\sim_\theta$. Another interesting fact is that $\sim_\theta$ coincides with $\simeq_\theta$ if clock θ is a constant clock.

We show some useful relations for proving substitutability between two distributed objects.

Proposition 4.5 $\forall P_1, P_2 \in \mathcal{P} : P_1 \sim_\theta P_2$, $\forall Q \in \mathcal{P}$ such that $Q \in \mathcal{P}$ contains no timeout operator.

(1)	$\alpha.P_1 \sim_\theta \alpha.P_2$	(2)	$P_1 + Q \sim_\theta P_2 + Q$
(3)	$P_1 \setminus L \sim_\theta P_2 \setminus L$	(4)	$P_1[f] \sim_\theta P_2[f]$
(5)	$P_1|Q \sim_\theta P_2|Q$		

where the same results holds for $\simeq_\theta$. ◻

Since distributed object-oriented computing is based on interaction among objects executing concurrently, the following substitutability for parallel composition provides a method to verify interactions among distributed objects.

Proposition 4.6 $\forall P_1, P_2 \in \mathcal{P}$, $\forall S \in \mathcal{S}$,

$$\text{If } P_1 \simeq_\theta P_2, \text{ then } P_1|[S]_\theta \sim_\theta P_2|[S]_\theta$$

◻

This proposition shows that if an object according a clock θ interacts with one of two objects which cannot be distinguished by an observer following the same clock θ, the object itself cannot notice any difference in its interactions with either object.

Preorder on Clocks

It is well known that any actual clocks are different in their measurement unit and precision. Based on such unit and precision, we here formulate some order relations over local clocks and further study interesting relationships between the preorders and the timed bisimulations.

We define order relations over clock functions.

Definition 4.7 Let T_1, T_2, T_ℓ be local time domains,

(i) *Granularity Preorder* Let $\theta_1 : T_1 \to T_G$ and $\theta_2 : T_2 \to T_G$.
If $\forall t_2 \in T_2, \exists t_1 \in T_1 : \{\theta_1(t_1)\} = \{\theta_2(t_2)\}$, *then* θ_1 *is finer than* θ_2, *written as* $\theta_1 \unlhd \theta_2$.

(ii) *Precision Preorder* Let $\theta_1 : T_\ell \to T_G$, and $\theta_2 : T_\ell \to T_G$.
If $\forall t_\ell \in T_\ell : \{\theta_1(t_\ell)\} \subseteq \{\theta_2(t_\ell)\}$, *then* θ_1 *is more precise than* θ_2, *written as* $\theta_1 \sqsubseteq \theta_2$. ◻

Intuitively, $\theta_1 \unlhd \theta_2$ means that one time unit of θ_2 corresponds to more than one time unit of θ_1. $\theta_1 \sqsubseteq \theta_2$ means that θ_2 is less accurate than θ_1.

Proposition 4.8 $\unlhd$ and $\sqsubseteq$ are preorder relations. □

We here show relationships between $\unlhd$ and timed bisimilarities.

Proposition 4.9 $\forall P_1, P_2 \in \mathcal{P}, \theta_1 \unlhd \theta_2$, then

(1) If $P_1 \sim_{\theta_1} P_2$, then $P_1 \sim_{\theta_2} P_2$
(2) If $P_1 \simeq_{\theta_1} P_2$, then $P_1 \simeq_{\theta_2} P_2$ □

Intuitively, this property will be exemplified by the following example: if two objects cannot be distinguished by an observer following an accurate clock whose time unit is one second, then they cannot be distinguished by another observer having an accurate clock with the unit of one minute.

Below we present relationships between $\sqsubseteq$ and timed bisimilarities.

Proposition 4.10 $\forall P_1, P_2 \in \mathcal{P}, \theta_1 \sqsubseteq \theta_2$, then

(1) If $P_1 \sim_{\theta_1} P_2$, then $P_1 \sim_{\theta_2} P_2$
(2) If $P_1 \simeq_{\theta_2} P_2$, then $P_1 \simeq_{\theta_1} P_2$ □

From Proposition 4.9 and 4.10, we assume $\theta_1 \unlhd \theta_2$ and $\theta_2 \sqsubseteq \theta_3$, then for any P and Q, if $P_1 \sim_{\theta_1} P_2$ then $P_1 \sim_{\theta_3} P_2$.

The strictness of $\sim_\theta$ (and $\simeq_\theta$) depends on clock θ. The orders of clocks are available in specifications with respect to different time scales and precisions.

Example 4.11 We suppose two clocks $\theta_{\pm 5\%}$ and $\theta_{\pm 10\%}$ whose worst measurement errors are $\pm 5\%$ and $\pm 10\%$ respectively.

$$\theta_{\pm 5\%}(t) \stackrel{\text{def}}{=} \begin{cases} 0 & \text{if } t = 0 \\ \theta_{\pm 5\%}(t-1) + \delta_{\pm 5\%} & \text{if } t > 0 \end{cases} \quad \delta_{\pm 5\%} \in \{95, ..100, ..105\}$$

$$\theta_{\pm 10\%}(t) \stackrel{\text{def}}{=} \begin{cases} 0 & \text{if } t = 0 \\ \theta_{\pm 10\%}(t-1) + \delta_{\pm 10\%} & \text{if } t > 0 \end{cases} \quad \delta_{\pm 10\%} \in \{90, ..100, ..110\}$$

Immediately we have $\theta_{\pm 5\%} \sqsubseteq \theta_{\pm 10\%}$. Also, from Proposition 4.10, $\sim_{\theta_{\pm 5\%}}$ is more strict than $\sim_{\theta_{\pm 10\%}}$. We have for any P_1 and P_2, if $P_1 \sim_{\theta_{\pm 5\%}} P_2$, then $P_1 \sim_{\theta_{\pm 10\%}} P_2$. Clearly the converse is not true. □

Examples on Verification of Distributed Objects

For the remainder of this section we will present some examples of verification of distributed objects by using the timed bisimilarities. We first illustrate how to equate two objects whose temporal properties are different.

Example 4.12 *Verification for Real-Time Objects*
We consider two server objects as given below. The informal exposition of the objects has already been described in Example 3.11.

$$Server_A \stackrel{\text{def}}{=} req.\langle 0, \overline{ret}.Server_A\rangle_8$$

$$Server_B \stackrel{\text{def}}{=} req.\langle 0, \overline{ret}.Server_B\rangle_9$$

We assume a constant clock $\theta(t) \stackrel{\text{def}}{=} 6t$. An observer according to θ cannot distinguish between temporal properties of the objects, i.e. their execution times of 8 and 9 time units, because of $\{\theta^{-1}(8)\}, \{\theta^{-1}(9)\} = \{1\}$. Hence, $\sim_\theta$ can equate them even if their temporal properties are different.

$$Server_A \sim_\theta Server_B \quad c.f. \quad Server_A \not\sim Server_B$$

This holds on $\simeq_\theta$ as well as $\sim_\theta$.   □

- $\sim_\theta$ (and $\simeq_\theta$) provides a useful method to verify real-time objects with non-strict time constraints. For example, let $Server_A$ be a specification of the server object and $Server_B$ be an implementation of the object. The above result shows that the implementation completely satisfies the behavioral requirements in the specification, and that the temporal differences between them is within a permissible bound specified in terms of θ.

- Let us suppose a clock θ' such that $\theta \trianglelefteq \theta'$. By Proposition 4.9 we can easily prove $Server_A \sim_{\theta'} Server_B$. For example, let $\hat{\theta}(t) \stackrel{\text{def}}{=} 12t$ then $\theta \trianglelefteq \hat{\theta}$. Hence, we have $Server_A \sim_{\hat{\theta}} Server_B$.

Next we show an example to illustrate how to equate distributed objects following different clocks.

Example 4.13 *Verification for Distributed Objects with Variable Clocks*
Let the client object be as follows:

$$Client \stackrel{\text{def}}{=} \overline{req}.\langle ret.0, Client\rangle_2$$

We assume that the program is allocated on two processors with local clocks, θ_1 and θ_2, whose time unit may vary from 9 to 11 and from 10 to 12, respectively.

$$\theta_1(t) \stackrel{\text{def}}{=} \begin{cases} 0 & \text{if } t = 0 \\ \theta_1(t-1) + \delta_1 & \text{if } t > 0 \end{cases} \qquad \theta_2(t) \stackrel{\text{def}}{=} \begin{cases} 0 & \text{if } t = 0 \\ \theta_2(t-1) + \delta_2 & \text{if } t > 0 \end{cases}$$

$$\text{where } \delta_1 \in \{9, 10, 11\} \qquad\qquad \text{where } \delta_2 \in \{10, 11, 12\}$$

An observer according to the following variable clock $\theta'(t)$ equates these objects.

$$\theta'(t) \stackrel{\text{def}}{=} \begin{cases} 0 & \text{if } t = 0 \\ \theta'(t-1) + \delta' & \text{if } t > 0 \end{cases} \quad \text{where} \quad \delta' \in \{14, 15, 16\}$$

$$[\![Client]\!]_{\theta_1} \sim_{\theta'} [\![Client]\!]_{\theta_2} \quad c.f. \quad [\![Client]\!]_{\theta_1} \not\sim [\![Client]\!]_{\theta_2}$$

This result shows that the timed bisimilarities can equate two distributed objects even if the units and precisions of their clocks are different. □

We illustrate how to verify whether distributed objects can be substituted for each other.

Example 4.14 *Substitutability between Distributed Objects*
Recall the two clients $[\![Client]\!]_{\theta_1}$ and $[\![Client]\!]_{\theta_2}$, and clock θ' already presented in Example 4.13. We have:

$$[\![Client]\!]_{\theta_1} \simeq_{\theta'} [\![Client]\!]_{\theta_2}$$

We suppose a server object being executed by a processor having the clock θ'. From Proposition 4.6, we have:

$$Server \stackrel{\text{def}}{=} req.\langle 0, \overline{rel}.Server \rangle_1$$

$$[\![Client]\!]_{\theta_1} | [\![Server]\!]_{\theta'} \sim_{\theta'} [\![Client]\!]_{\theta_2} | [\![Server]\!]_{\theta'}$$

Two pessimistically timed bisimilar objects on θ can be substitutable for each other as long as they interact with any objects on the local clock θ. Therefore the timed bisimilarities provide a method to verify reusability and substitutability for distributed objects. □

5 Conclusion

In this paper we have seen a way to formulate local time properties in distributed computing, along with developing a formalism based on a minor temporal extension of CCS [14]. The extension is based on the notion of local time and thus allows us to model various local time aspects in distributed computing, such as inaccurate clocks on local processors and timeout handling. The formalism provides a theoretical framework to describe and analyze both temporal and behavioral properties of distributed objects with temporal uncertainties and interactions among them.

Based on the notion of bisimulation [14, 19], we defined bisimulations with respect to local time. These bisimulations can equate two objects whose functional behaviors completely match and whose timings are different within a given bound. The bisimulations are appropriate and useful to verify distributed objects and real-time objects with non-strict time constraints.

Finally, we would like to point out some further issues. The formalism is based on synchronous communication but in many distributed systems asynchronous communication may seem more appropriate. We plan to develop a calculus based on asynchronous communication. Particularly, we believe that the study of time properties for asynchronous communications will provide us with concepts for programming languages for distributed systems[8]. We are interested in investigating timed bisimulation based on observation concept which can ignore internal behavior, i.e. τ-transition. Besides, the extension for representing local time presented in this paper is essentially independent of DtCCS. We are interested in whether the extension can be applied to other timed formalisms based on global time, such as other timed calculi, real-time temporal logic, and timed Petri nets.

Acknowledgements

We would like to thank an anonymous referee for providing many constructive and valuable suggestions. We also thank Professor S. Matsuoka, and R. Pareschi for significant suggestions. We are grateful to K. Takashio for stimulating comments and discussions. We heartily thank V. Vasconcelos for very insightful comments on an earlier version of this paper.

References

1. Black, A., Hutchinson, N., July, E., and Levy, H., *Object Structure in the Emerald System*, Proceedings of ACM OOPSLA'86, November, p78-86, 1986.
2. Boudol, G., Castellani, I., Hennessy, M., and Kiehn, A., *A Theory of Processes with Localities*, Proceedings of CONCUR'92, LNCS 630, p108-122, August, 1992.
3. Castellani, H., and Hennessy, M., *Distributed Bisimulation*, Journal of ACM, Vol.36, No.4, p887-911, 1989.
4. Corsetti, E., Montanari, A., and Ratto, E., *Dealing with Different Granularities in Formal Specifications of Real-Time Systems*, Real-Time Systems, Vol.3, No.2, p191-215, May, 1991.
5. Hansson, H., and Jonsson, B., *A Calculus of Communicating Systems with Time and Probabilities*, Proceedings of 11th IEEE Real-Time Systems Symposium, p278-287, December, 1990.
6. Hennessy, M., *On Timed Process Algebra: a Tutorial*, Technical Report 2/93, University of Sussex, 1993
7. Hobbs, J. R., *Granularity*, Proceedings of 9th International Joint Conference Artificial Intelligence, p432-435, August, 1985.
8. Honda, K., and Tokoro, M., *An Object Calculus for Asynchronous Communication*, Proceedings of ECOOP'91, LNCS 512, p133-147, June, 1991.
9. Jefferson, D. R., *Virtual Time*, ACM TOPLAS, Vol.7, No.3, 1985.
10. Kopetz, H., *Clock Synchronization in Distributed Real-Time Systems*, IEEE Transactions on Computers, Vol.36, No.8, p933-940, August, 1987.
11. Krishnan, P., *Distributed CCS*, Proceedings of CONCUR'91, LNCS 527, p393-407, August, 1991.

---

[8] The reader may refer to the authors' preliminary work in this context, e.g. [23].

12. Lamport, L., *Time, Clocks, and the Ordering of Events in a Distributed System* Communication of the ACM, Vol.21, No.7, p558-565, July, 1978.

13. Lundelius, J., and Lynch, N., *An Upper and Lower Bound for Clock Synchronization,* Information and Control, Vol.62, p190-204, 1984.

14. Milner, R., *Communication and Concurrency,* Prentice Hall, 1989.

15. Moller, F., and Tofts, C., *A Temporal Calculus of Communicating Systems,* Proceedings of CONCUR'90, LNCS 458, p401-415, August, 1990.

16. Montanari, A., Ratto, E., Corsetti, E., and Morzeniti, A., *Embedding Time Granularity in Logical Specification of Real-Time Systems,* Proceedings of EUROMICOR'91, Workshop on Real-Time Systems, p88-97, June, 1991.

17. Nicollin, X., and Sifakis, J., *The Algebra of Timed Process ATP: Theory and Applications,* IMAG Technical Report, RT-C26, 1990.

18. Nierstrasz, O. M., and Papathomas, M., *Viewing Objects as Patterns of Communicating Agents,* Proceedings of ECOOP/OOPSLA'90, October, p38-43, 1990.

19. Park, D., *Concurrency and Automata on Infinite Sequences,* Proceedings of Theoretical Computer Science, LNCS 104, p167-187, 1981.

20. Plotkin, G. D, *A Structural Approach to Operational Semantics,* Technical Report, Department of Computer Science, Arhus University, Denmark, 1981.

21. Satoh, I., and Tokoro, M., *A Formalism for Real-Time Concurrent Object-Oriented Computing,* Proceedings of ACM OOPSLA'92, p315-326, October, 1992.

22. Takashio, K., and Tokoro, M., *DROL: An Object-Oriented Programming Language for Distributed Real-time Systems,* Proceedings of ACM OOPSLA'92, p276-294, October, 1992.

23. Tokoro, M., and Satoh, I., *Asynchrony and Real-Time in Distributed Systems,* US/Japan Seminar on Parallel Symbolic Computing, October, 1992.

24. Yi, W., *CCS + Time = an Interleaving Model for Real Time Systems,* Proceedings of Automata, Languages and Programming'91, LNCS 510, p217-228, 1991.

25. Yonezawa, A., and Tokoro, M., editors, *Object-Oriented Concurrent Programming,* MIT Press, 1987.

A Language Framework
for Multi-Object Coordination

Svend Frølund and Gul Agha

Department of Computer Science
1304 W. Springfield Avenue
University of Illinois at Urbana-Champaign
Urbana, IL 61801, USA

Email: { frolund | agha }@cs.uiuc.edu

Abstract. We have developed language support for the expression of multi-object coordination. In our language, coordination patterns can be specified abstractly, independent of the protocols needed to implement them. Coordination patterns are expressed in the form of constraints that restrict invocation of a group of objects. Constraints are defined in terms of the interface of the objects being invoked rather than their internal representation. Invocation constraints enforce properties, such as temporal ordering and atomicity, that hold when invoking objects in a group. A constraint can *permanently* control access to a group of objects, thereby expressing an inherent access restriction associated with the group. Furthermore, a constraint can *temporarily* enforce access restrictions during the activity of individual clients. In that way, constraints can express specialized access schemes required by a group of clients.

1 Motivation

Coordination of activities is a fundamental aspect of programming languages for concurrent and distributed systems. In existing languages, multi-object coordination is expressed in terms of explicit communication protocols such as two-phase commit; it is not possible to express coordination patterns independent of their implementation. The inability to abstract over multi-object coordination results in low level specification and reasoning. As a consequence, it is not possible to compose multiple coordination patterns without changing their implementation. Moreover, it is difficult to modify and customize the implementation of coordination patterns since the involved protocols are hard-wired into applications.

Our approach is to express coordination patterns in the form of *multi-object constraints*. A multi-object constraint maintains certain properties such as temporal ordering and atomicity associated with invocations processed by a group of objects. Multi-object constraints are specified abstractly and independent of the protocols required to implement the enforced properties. A multi-object constraint restricts the freedom of objects to process invocations: whether or not an object may process an invocation depends on the current status and invoca-

O.M. Nierstrasz (Ed.): ECOOP '93, LNCS 707, pp. 346-360, 1993.
© Springer-Verlag Berlin Heidelberg 1993

tion history of a group of objects. Enforced restrictions capture a large class of multi-object coordination schemes. Consider the following examples:

- A group of resource administrators must adhere to a common allocation policy. An example of a common policy is a limit on the total number of resources the administrators may collectively allocate. Enforcement of a common policy can be expressed as a constraint on invocations that allocate resources: an allocation request can only be serviced if the total number of allocated resources minus the total number of released resources is below the enforced limit.

- A group of dining philosophers share a number of chopsticks. The number of philosophers is equal to the number of chopsticks and a philosopher needs two chopsticks in order to eat. A coordination scheme should (at least) prevent deadlock when philosophers attempt to pick up chopsticks. Deadlocks can be avoided by a multi-object constraint that enforces atomic invocation of the pick method in two chopstick objects: each philosopher picks up either both or neither chopstick that he needs.

Our constructs build on the observation that multi-object constraints can be specified independent of the representation of the constrained objects. Specifying multi-object constraints in terms of the interface of the constrained objects enables better description, reasoning and modification of multi-object constraints. Only utilizing knowledge of interfaces when describing multi-object constraints separates coordination and object functionality. This separation enables system design with a larger potential for reuse. Objects may be reused independent of how they are coordinated; conversely, multi-object coordination patterns may be reused on different groups of objects. In particular, it is possible to abstract over coordination patterns and factor out generic coordination structures. As noted in [AB92], separation also gives a more natural way of expressing the coordination schemes found in many problem domains.

Multi-object constraints are described in the form of *synchronizers*. Conceptually, a synchronizer is a special object that observes and limits the invocations accepted by a set of ordinary objects that are being constrained. Synchronizers may overlap: multiple, separately specified, synchronizers can constrain the same objects. Operationally, the compiler translates synchronizers into message-passing between the constrained objects. The advantage of synchronizers is that the involved message-passing is transparent to the programmer who specifies multi-object constraints in a high-level and abstract way. The implementation of synchronizers can involve direct communication between the constrained objects, indirect communication with a central "coordinator" or a hybrid. Utilizing a high-level specification of multi-object constraints it is possible to map the same multi-object constraint to different implementations.

In object-based concurrent computing it has become commonplace to describe per object coordination in the form of synchronization constraints [Nie87, TS89, Neu91, AGMB91, MWBD91, Frø92]. Both synchronizers and synchronization constraints are based on conditions which are verified prior to the processing of invocations. The conditions of synchronization constraints are expressed in terms of the encapsulated state of individual objects, e.g. in the form of boolean predicates. The conditions associated with synchronizers involve the status and invocation history of a group of objects.

As we explain in the related work section (Section 5), existing approaches to multi-object coordination do not take local coordination such as synchronization constraints into account. For example, transactions are meant to coordinate access to passive records not active objects. On the other hand, synchronizers are designed to integrate with local synchronization constraints: conceptually, synchronizers supplement synchronization constraints with additional conditions that must be met for invocations to be legal. With synchronizers, the programmer can specify per object coordination and multi-object coordination using similar concepts.

In the following sections we give more details about synchronizers. In Section 2, we introduce a notation for describing synchronizers. The introduced notation is applied in a number of examples in Section 3 and Section 4. Section 5 gives an overview of related work and Section 6 concludes with a discussion of our approach.

2 Basic Concepts and Notation

For simplicity we assume that synchronizers are integrated with an object-oriented concurrent language that adheres to the Actor [Agh86] model of computation. Specifically this implies that message-passing is asynchronous so that sending objects are not blocked by enforced synchronizers. Although our development is based on Actors, we believe the concepts behind synchronizers can be integrated with most concurrent object-oriented languages.

It is important to note that our notation only constitutes the "core" functionality of a framework for describing multi-object constraints. The purpose of this paper is to promote the *concept* of synchronizers, their separate specification and high-level expression of multi-object coordination. The main objective of providing a notation for multi-object constraints is to give the principles a concrete form and allow the description of example constraints.

Figure 1 gives an abstract syntax for synchronizers. In the following we will give an informal description of the semantics of synchronizers. The structure of a synchronizer is specified using the { ... } constructor. Such constructors are named, allowing instantiation of synchronizers with similar structure. A constructor has a list of formal parameters that are bound to actual values when synchronizers are instantiated. The init part of a synchronizer declares a list of local names that hold the state of a synchronizer.

Synchronizers are instantiated by ordinary objects. In that way, objects can enforce constraints on other objects. In our framework, enforcing a constraint on an object requires a reference to that object. However, it is possible to employ other models of locality for constraint enforcement. For example, objects could be required to have certain capabilities in order to enforce constraints on other

binding	::= *name* := *exp*	
	binding$_1$; *binding$_2$*	
pattern	::= *object.name*	
	object.name(*name$_1$* , ... , *name$_n$*)	
	pattern$_1$ or *pattern$_2$*	
	pattern where *exp*	
relation	::= *pattern* updates *binding*	
	exp disables *pattern*	
	atomic(*pattern$_1$* , ... , *pattern$_i$*)	
	pattern stops	
	relation$_1$, *relation$_2$*	
synchronizer ::= *name*(*name$_1$* , ... , *name$_n$*)		
{ [init *binding*]		
relation		
}		

Fig. 1. Abstract syntax for synchronizers.

objects. Furthermore, constraints could be specified for groups of objects that are defined using patterns rather than identities [AC93].

A synchronizer is a special kind of object that observes and limits invocation of other objects: a synchronizer cannot be accessed directly using message-based communication.[1] The invocations observed and limited by a synchronizer are identified using pattern matching. Pattern matching is defined by the following rules:

- The pattern *o.n* matches all messages invoking method *n* in object *o*.
- The pattern *o.n*(x_1 , ... , x_n) matches all messages matched by the pattern *o.n* and binds the actual values of a matching message to the names x_1 , ... , x_n.
- The pattern p_1 or p_2 matches messages that match either p_1 or p_2.
- A message matches the pattern *p* where *exp* if the message matches the pattern *p* and the boolean expression *exp* evaluates to true. The expression is side-effect free and evaluated in a context including the names bound in *p*.

Since we assume an object-oriented invocation model, each message invokes a specific method in a specific object. The or combinator allows the definition of patterns that cover multiple methods in multiple objects. In that way, messages

---

[1] There is nothing inherent in the synchronizer concept that prevents direct communication. Our convention merely reflects a design choice that, for pedagogical reasons, makes a clear distinction between synchronizers and objects.

sent to different objects may match the same pattern. Notice that a corresponding and combinator can be expressed by a boolean predicate in a where clause.

Having explained patterns, we are now in a position to describe the semantics of the relation part of a synchronizer. A relation that contains the updates operator can be used to observe specific invocations of specific objects. In particular, relations of the form *pattern* updates *binding* changes the state of the enclosing synchronizer according to *binding* each time an object is invoked by a message that matches *pattern*. In order to maintain consistency of synchronizers, bindings are established as atomic actions. If an invocation matches the pattern of multiple updates relations, the corresponding bindings are made in some indeterminate order after the pattern matching is complete.

Observations made by a synchronizer are consistent with the temporal and causal ordering between the observed invocations. For example, if an object is invoked by the message m_2 after the message m_1, synchronizers will observe m_2 after m_1. Using the updates operator, a synchronizer can record the invocation history of objects.

The disables operator is used to prevent invocations. The relation *exp* disables *pattern* prevents acceptance of messages that match *pattern* if the expression *exp* evaluates to true in the current state of the enclosing synchronizer. Relations that contain the disables operator define conditions that must be met before an object can be invoked by certain messages. Prevented invocations are delayed at the receiver if the enforced multi-object constraints are not satisfied.

Synchronizers that contain both updates and disables relations can enforce temporal ordering where the legality of invocations is determined by the past invocation history. A given message can match the pattern of both updates and disables relations in the same synchronizer. For such messages, there is exclusive access to the state of the enclosing synchronizer during evaluation of the expression associated with disables relations and a possible subsequent binding caused by an updates relation. Hence, a combination of updates and disables operators can express mutual exclusion and exclusive choice involving sets of invocations.

Certain coordination schemes require the expression of atomicity constraints, i.e. multiple invocations that occur without any observable temporal ordering. The relation atomic($pattern_1, \ldots, pattern_i$) involves i kinds of messages which match the patterns $pattern_1, \ldots, pattern_i$, respectively. The relation ensures that acceptance of a message from either kind occurs along with acceptance of messages from the other $i - 1$ kinds without any observable middle states where only part of the messages have been accepted. Regardless of the observing context, either all or none of the patterns are matched and there is no temporal ordering between the matching invocations.

The atomic operator gives rise to indivisible scheduling of multiple invocations at multiple objects. In our framework, a set of invocations scheduled atomically cannot contain multiple invocations of the same object. Consequently, atomicity of a set of invocations can be ensured prior to the processing of the invocations. This is in contrast to transactions that provide atomicity relative to the transitive effect of invocations. Our notion of atomicity is cheaper to implement and can be combined with temporal constraints. For example, it is possible to describe temporal ordering as well as exclusive choice between sets of invocations that are scheduled atomically.

Once instantiated, a synchronizer remains in effect until observing an invocation that matches the pattern of a stops relation. The relation *pattern* stops implies that acceptance of a message that matches *pattern* terminates the enclosing synchronizer. A synchronizer without a stops operator remains in effect permanently. In practice, more sophisticated control over the duration of synchronizers may be needed. We simply want to make the case for dynamic enforcement of synchronizers and we incorporate the stops relation as a simple way of achieving dynamic constraint enforcement.

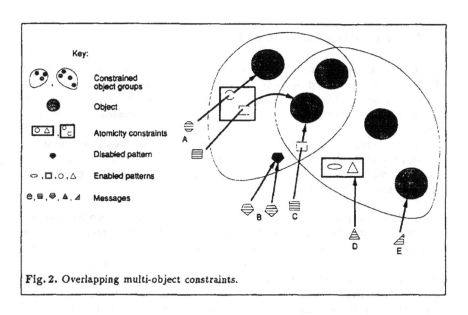

Fig. 2. Overlapping multi-object constraints.

In summary, a synchronizer coordinates a group of objects by enforcing temporal and atomicity properties on certain patterns of invocations processed by the group. The groups being coordinated can overlap and the coordination may be initiated and terminated dynamically. Figure 2 illustrates the functionality of synchronizers. In that figure, pattern matching is depicted as matching shapes between patterns and messages. Synchronizers may disable certain patterns: disabled patterns are black and enabled patterns are white. Arrows illustrate the status of messages: an arrow that ends at an object starts at an enabled message and an arrow that ends at a pattern starts at a disabled message. Objects that are not pointed to by an arrow have no messages to process in the current system state. The messages at B are disabled whereas the message at C is enabled. The E message is unconstrained since it does not match any pattern. Patterns may be grouped together into atomicity constraints that ensure that multiple invocations are scheduled as an atomic action. Grouping of patterns into atomicity constraints is depicted by boxes around the groups. The messages at A satisfy the atomicity constraint whereas the message at D is blocked waiting for another message before both can be scheduled atomically.

Having introduced the core principles of synchronizers, the following two sections illustrate the use of synchronizers. We believe that synchronizers can be used to express many different aspects of multi-object coordination within the same basic framework. Much of the generality of synchronizers stem from the flexible binding scheme between constraints and constrained invocations. Section 3 provides examples of constraints that express logical grouping and interdependence between objects. The constraints of Section 4 capture specialized access schemes defined and enforced by clients.

3 Coordinating Groups of Objects

In this section we demonstrate how certain kinds of interdependence between objects can be represented by means of synchronizers that permanently constrain a group of objects. Synchronizers can express interdependence relations that take the form of properties that must hold for invocations processed by a group of objects.

The cooperating resource administrators mentioned in the introduction is a prototypical example of interdependent objects. In Example 1 below, we illustrate how our notation can capture the dependence between the cooperating administrators.

Example 1 (*Cooperating Resource Administrators*). Consider two resource administrators that allocate different kinds of resources, e.g. printers and disks. Each administrator has a local synchronization constraint that prevents allocation of more resources than the system provides. In addition to the local constraint the administrators may be subject to a collective constraint on the number of resources they allocate collectively. For example, enforcing a collective constraint may be necessary if the allocated resources are external devices and the bus that interconnects the devices has a maximum capacity.

```
AllocationPolicy(adm1,adm2,max)
{ init prev := 0

    prev >= max disables (adm1.request or adm2.request),
    (adm1.request or adm2.request) updates prev := prev + 1,
    (adm1.release or adm2.release) updates prev := prev - 1
}
```

Fig. 3. A Synchronizer that enforces collective bound on allocated resources.

Maintenance of a collective bound on allocated resources can be described external to the administrators as a synchronizer. Figure 3 contains a synchronizer that prevents collective allocation of more than **max** resources by the two administrators. The names **adm1** and **adm2** are references to the two constrained administrators and the variable **prev** holds the total number of resources that have previously been allocated and not yet released. □

Synchronizers give flexible ways of describing coordination relations between shared servers. With synchronizers, coordination is expressed independent of the representation of the involved servers. The resulting modularity makes it possible to modify the coordination scheme without changing the servers and vice versa. In particular, it is possible to dynamically add new servers to an existing coordinated group by instantiating a new synchronizer. Furthermore, synchronizers allow the description of overlapping groups of interdependent servers.

A part-whole hierarchy is another structure that gives rise to permanent enforcement of constraints on a group of objects. A part-whole hierarchy contains a set of objects that are related by an *is-component-of* relation. A part-whole hierarchy induces consistency constraints on its members: the independence of individual parts is limited by the fact that they are parts of a containing entity. As we illustrate in the following example, synchronizers can be used to capture consistency constraints of concurrent part-whole hierarchies.

Example 2 (*Vending Machine*). A vending machine is an example of a concurrent part-whole hierarchy with a consistency constraint. A vending machine has a number of parts: a coin accepter into which coins can be inserted and a number of slots that each contain a piece of fruit. The parts of a vending machine are subject to a consistency requirement in order for the vending machine to have the desired functionality: insert enough money and get back a piece of fruit from one of the slots. When a sufficient amount of money has been inserted into the coin accepter, one or more of the slots are available for opening (each slot may be priced differently). Opening one of the slots will remove the inserted money from the coin accepter and prevent other slots from being opened. Pushing a special button on the coin accepter, it is possible to get a refund.

Assume that each part of the vending machine is represented as a separate object. The constraint of a vending machine hierarchy can be modeled as a synchronizer that enforces a constraint on the parts of the vending machine. Figure 4 contains a synchronizer which reflects the functionality of a vending machine constraint. The vending machine in Figure 4 has two slots: one for apples and one for bananas. The name **apples** refers to the apple slot and the name **apple_price** is the price of apples and vice versa for bananas.[2] The name **accepter** refers to an object representing the coin accepter. The methods of

---

[2] In practice, the constraint in Figure 4 would be parameterized with an arbitrary set of slot objects that has an associated price. We have ignored such parameterization issues in order to focus on the essential aspects of multi-object constraints. Note that price changes could easily be incorporated by having the synchronizer observe **change_price** requests sent to such slot objects.

```
VendingMachine(accepter,apples,bananas,apple_price,banana_price)
{   init amount := 0

    amount < apple_price   disables apples.open,
    amount < banana_price  disables bananas.open,
    accepter.insert(v)  updates amount := amount + v,
    (accepter.refund  or  apples.open  or  bananas.open)
        updates amount := 0
}
```

Fig. 4. A Synchronizer that coordinates access to the parts of a vending machine.

a coin accepter are insert() and refund(). The apple and banana slots each have an open operation that can be invoked if the accepter contains enough money.

In Figure 4, the variable amount holds the amount of money that is available in the coin accepter. Insertion of money into the coin accepter increments the variable amount. Opening any slot or requesting a refund clears the coin accepter and binds the value 0 to the amount variable; for simplicity we have ignored the issue of giving back change. Since constraint evaluation and state mutation associated with the same message is done as an atomic action, only one slot can be opened before the coin accepter is cleared.

Without synchronizers it would be necessary to explicitly implement the consensus protocol between the slot objects so that only one slot can be opened. Similar to the cooperating resource administrators, the consensus protocol could be implemented centrally with a coordinator, distributed by explicit message-passing, or some hybrid scheme could be used. In all cases, explicit implementation would require construction of complicated and inflexible code. □

The vending machine example illustrates an important real-world property: the behaviors of objects depend on the context in which they exist. Synchronizers allow us to express the contextual constraints of a part-whole hierarchy as an aspect of the *hierarchy*, not an aspect of the parts. With synchronizers, it is easier to reason about context constraints since they are expressed more directly. Furthermore, it is possible to exchange parts without affecting the consistency constraint of the containing hierarchy.

4   Customized Access Schemes

In this section we present constraints that are defined and enforced by clients that access a number of shared objects. Such client based constraints express customized access schemes utilized by individual clients; they are temporary in nature, enforced for a specific set of invocations issued by one or more clients.

Synchronizers give a flexible and expressive model for describing access restrictions such as atomicity, mutual exclusion and temporal ordering. We use the dining philosophers problem to illustrate constraints used as access restrictions.

Example 3 (*Dining Philosophers*). The dining philosophers is a classical example from the literature on concurrent systems. A group of philosophers (processes) need to coordinate their access to a number of chopsticks (resources). The number of chopsticks and the number of philosophers is the same and a philosopher needs two chopsticks in order to eat. Access to the chopsticks needs to be regulated in order to avoid deadlock and starvation. The constraint that each philosopher picks up two chopsticks atomically ensures absence of deadlock. Note that this multi-object constraint does not explicitly guarantee freedom from starvation; that condition may be ensured by fairness in the implementation of synchronizers.

```
PickUpConstraint(c1,c2,phil)
{
    atomic( (c1.pick(sender) where sender = phil),
            (c2.pick(sender) where sender = phil) ),
    (c1.pick where sender = phil) stops
}
```

Fig. 5. A synchronizer giving atomic access of chopsticks.

Each philosopher has an **eat** method that is called when the philosopher is hungry. The **eat** method attempts to pick up two chopsticks by sending a **pick** message to the two chopsticks. The **eat** method is parameterized by the two chopsticks that must be picked up in order to eat. The **eat** method instantiates a synchronizer with a structure similar to the synchronizer depicted in Figure 5. The synchronizer is parameterized with the two chopsticks (**c1** and **c2**) and the philosopher who accesses the chopsticks (**phil**). The synchronizer only applies to **pick** messages sent by the philosopher referred by the name **phil**. We assume that the **eat** method concurrently invokes **pick** on each of the needed chopsticks. The instantiated synchronizer guarantees that the access to the chopsticks occurs atomically. When both chopsticks have been acquired, the eat method starts using the chopsticks and releases them when done eating. When the philosopher has successfully acquired both chopsticks, the constraint is terminated.

A chopstick can only be picked up by one client (philosopher) at a time. The local synchronization constraints of a chopstick will disable the **pick** method after a successful pick up. When the **put** method is invoked, **pick** is enabled again. Note that a chopstick may be subject to additional local synchronization constraints. One local constraint could be that a chopstick is washed after being put down. While being washed, a chopstick cannot be picked up. Conventional methods for solving the dining philosophers problem cannot be combined with such local constraints in a modular fashion. □

Synchronizers support a wide range of access restrictions. Example 3 focussed on atomicity. Other examples include exclusive access and temporal ordering imposed on sets of invocations. For example, it is possible to describe exclusive choice where clients issue a number of requests under the constraint that only one of the requests are processed by the receiver.

As the above example shows, synchronizers allow access restrictions to be specified *separate* from the accessed objects. Separation makes it possible to access groups of objects in ways that were not anticipated when the group was instantiated. Thus, synchronizers provide an extensible way of describing access constraints.

5 Related Work

In existing languages and systems, client enforced access restrictions can be specified using synchronous communication, transactions or atomic broadcasts. The temporal constraints of synchronizers are more abstract and expressive than the temporal constraints expressible by synchronous communication. Transactions provide atomicity in a number of systems [LS82, WL88, DHW88, KHPW90, GCLR92, WY91]. As we have already mentioned, transactions cannot be combined with temporal constraints. Furthermore, the atomicity provided by the atomic operator is cheaper to implement. It should be emphasized that we do not perceive synchronizers as a substitute for transaction systems: we think of synchronizers as a structuring tool that can supplement transactions in an orthogonal and non-interfering way.

A number of systems provide broadcasts with different delivery guarantees. Examples are ISIS [BJ87], Consul [MPS91] and the notion of Interface Groups proposed in [OOW91]. In such systems, it is possible to ensure certain properties for the reception of broadcast messages. None of the broadcast systems deal with objects that have local synchronization constraints: the guarantees provided are relative to delivery, not acceptance.

Neither synchronous communication, transactions or broadcast protocols can be used to describe constraints permanently associated with object groups. In all three cases, the constraints expressible are associated with individual clients.

The constraints of Kaleidoscope [FBB92] capture numerical relations between instance variables of multiple objects. Kaleidoscope emphasizes state-consistency by propagating updates. In contrast, synchronizers express invocation consistency by request scheduling. Synchronizers and the constraints of kaleidoscope capture fundamentally different aspects of multi-object consistency.

The constraints of Procol [vdBL91] and RAPIDE [LVB+92] provide triggering of activities based on observation of events. The constraints of Procol and RAPIDE can only observe, not limit invocations.

Several attempts have been made at documenting multi-object coordination at an abstract level. In [Ara91], a temporal logic framework is used for assertions about the message passing behavior of objects. The notion of a *contract* is proposed in [HHG90, Hol92]. Contracts extend the notion of type to capture the message passing obligations fulfilled by objects. In [CI92] a mix of path-expressions, data-flow and control-flow is used to capture coordination between objects comprising a sub system. The above approaches to multi-object interactions *describe* rather than *prescribe* multi-object coordination. The expression of multi-object coordination serves to document and verify the coordination behavior of a set of interacting objects. The coordination behavior is realized by traditional means such as explicit message passing between the objects. In contrast to the above approaches, synchronizers are executable specifications of multi-object coordination.

In the Dragoon language [RdPG91, AGMB91], synchronization constraints are specified external to the constrained objects. Constraints are general specifications that can be mixed-in with class definitions yielding a class with synchronization constraints. The common factor between Dragoon and synchronizers is that coordination and computation are two distinct aspects that are combined in a flexible way. A major difference is that the Dragoon specifications of coordination only cover single objects.

6 Discussion

We have introduced synchronizers as tools for coordinating access to multiple objects. Compared to existing schemes where multi-object constraints are implemented by explicit communication, synchronizers provide abstraction, modularity and integration with synchronization constraints. Modularity enables a compositional approach to multi-object coordination: multiple synchronizers can be imposed on the same set of constrained objects, composing multiple constraint specifications. Consequently, synchronizers support system design that emphasizes physical separation of logically distinct aspects.

It should be emphasized that we do not consider synchronizers the complete answer to the challenge of describing multi-object coordination. The primary purpose of this paper is to promote constraints as a means of describing multi-object coordination. Furthermore, the principles presented in this paper only constitute the core of a language for describing multi-object constraints. Due to space limitations we have focused on the essential principles. For example, in practice it might be desirable for synchronizers to be able to receive messages as well as trigger new activities. The ability to trigger activities would provide an elegant way of extending the vending machine in Example 2 to give back change: successful opening of a slot triggers a refund of the money remaining in the accepter.

In order to gain more experience with the proposed concepts, we are currently developing a prototype implementation and semantic foundation for synchronizers. We are experimenting with different protocols for constraint evaluation and enforcement. An interesting aspect that we are investigating is the price paid for composition and fairness. Synchronizers can be implemented in numerous ways, e.g. purely distributed, with a central coordinator or some hybrid. Which implementation to choose depends on application specific characteristics. Therefore, it may be necessary to extend the language so that the choice of implementation is guided to a certain extent by the application programmer. One possible model for customization of implementation is to use reflection along the lines pointed out in [YMFT91, AFPS93]. Synchronizers make it feasible to customize the implementation of multi-object coordination since the coordination protocols are no longer hard-wired into applications but specified separately.

Acknowledgments

The first author is supported in part by the Danish Research Academy and a research fellowship from the Natural Science Faculty of Århus University in Denmark.

The research described in this paper was carried out at the University of Illinois Open Systems Laboratory (OSL). The work at OSL is supported by grants from the Office of Naval Research (ONR contract number N00014-90-J-1899), Digital Equipment Corporation, and by joint support from the Defense Advanced Research Projects Agency and the National Science Foundation (NSF CCR 90-07195).

The authors wish to thank Carolyn Talcott and Shingo Fukui as well as past and present members of OSL for reading and commenting on manuscript versions of this paper.

References

[AB92]   M. Aksit and L. Bergmans. Obstacles in Object-Oriented Software Development. In *Proceedings OOPSLA 92*. ACM, October 1992.

[AC93]   G. Agha and C.J. Callsen. ActorSpace: An Open Distributed Programming Paradigm. In *1993 ACM Conference on Principles and Practice of Parallel Programming (PPOPP)*, 1993. (To be published).

[AFPS93] G. Agha, S. Frølund, R. Panwar, and D. Sturman. A Linguistic Framework for Dynamic Composition of Dependability Protocols. In *Dependable Computing for Critical Applications III*. International Federation of Information Processing Societies (IFIP), Elsevier Science Publisher, 1993. (To be published).

[Agh86]   G. Agha. *Actors: A Model of Concurrent Computation in Distributed Systems*. MIT Press, 1986.

[AGMB91] C. Atkinson, S. Goldsack, A. D. Maio, and R. Bayan. Object-Oriented Concurrency and Distribution in DRAGOON. *Journal of Object-Oriented Programming*, March/April 1991.

[Ara91]   C. Arapis. Specifying Object Interactions. In D. Tsichritzis, editor, *Object Composition*. University of Geneva, 1991.

[BJ87]   K. P. Birman and T. A. Joseph. Communication Support for Reliable Dis-
             tributed Computing. In *Fault-tolerant Distributed Computing*. Springer-
             Verlag, 1987. LNCS.

[CI92]   R. H. Campbell and N. Islam. A Technique for Documenting the Frame-
             work of an Object-Oriented System. In *Proceedings of the Second Interna-
             tional Workshop on Object Orientation in Operating Systems*, September
             1992.

[DHW88]   D. L. Detlefs, M. P. Herlihy, and J. M. Wing. Inheritance of Synchroniza-
             tion and Recovery Properties in Avalon/C++. *IEEE Computer*, 21(12):57-
             69, December 1988.

[FBB92]   Bjorn N. Freeman-Benson and Alan Borning. Integrating Constraints with
             an Object-Oriented Language. In O. Lehrmann Madsen, editor, *Proceed-
             ings ECOOP '92*, LNCS 615, pages 268-286, Utrecht, The Netherlands,
             July 1992. Springer-Verlag.

[Frø92]   Svend Frølund. Inheritance of Synchronization Constraints in Concurrent
             Object-Oriented Programming Languages. In O. Lehrmann Madsen, ed-
             itor, *Proceedings ECOOP '92*, LNCS 615, pages 185-196, Utrecht, The
             Netherlands, July 1992. Springer-Verlag.

[GCLR92]   Rachid Guerraoui, Riccardo Capobianchi, Agnes Lanusse, and Pierre Roux.
             Nesting Actions through Asynchronous Message Passing: the ACS Proto-
             col. In O. Lehrmann Madsen, editor, *Proceedings ECOOP '92*, LNCS 615,
             pages 170-184, Utrecht, The Netherlands, July 1992. Springer-Verlag.

[HHG90]   Richard Helm, Ian M. Holland, and Dipayan Gangopadhyay. Contracts:
             Specifying Behavioral Compositions in Object-Oriented Systems. In *Pro-
             ceedings OOPSLA/ECOOP '90*, pages 169-180, October 1990. Published
             as ACM SIGPLAN Notices, volume 25, number 10.

[Hol92]   Ian M. Holland. Specifying Reusable Components Using Contracts. In
             O. Lehrmann Madsen, editor, *Proceedings ECOOP '92*, LNCS 615, pages
             287-308, Utrecht, The Netherlands, July 1992. Springer-Verlag.

[KHPW90]   G. E. Kaiser, W. Hseush, S. S. Popovich, and S. F. Wu. Multiple Con-
             currency Control Policies in an Object-Oriented Programming System. In
             *Proceedings of the Second Symposium on Parallel and Distributed Process-
             ing, Dallas Texas*. IEEE, December 1990.

[LS82]   Barbara Liskov and Robert Scheifler. Guardians and Actions: Linguistic
             Support for Robust, Distributed Programs. In *Conference Record of the
             Ninth Annual ACM Symposium on Principles of Programming Languages*,
             pages 7-19, Albuquerque, New Mexico, January 1982. ACM.

[LVB+92]   D. C. Luckham, J. Vera, D. Bryan, L. Augustin, and F. Belz. Partial Or-
             derings of Event Sets and Their Application to Prototyping Concurrent
             Timed Systems. In *Proceedings of the 1992 DARPA Software Technology
             Conference*, April 1992.

[MPS91]   S. Mishra, L. L. Peterson, and R. D. Schlichting. Consul: A Communica-
             tion Substrate for Fault-Tolerant Distributed Programs. Technical report,
             University of Arizona, Tucson, 1991.

[MWBD91]   C. McHale, B. Walsh, S. Baker, and A. Donnelly. Scheduling Predicates.
             In M. Tokoro, O. Nierstrasz, and P. Wegner, editors, *Object-Based Con-
             current Computing*, pages 177 - 193. Springer-Verlag, July 1991. LNCS
             612.

[Neu91]   Christian Neusius. Synchronizing Actions. In P. America, editor, *Proceed-
             ings ECOOP '91, LNCS 512, pages 118-132, Geneva, Switzerland, July
             1991. Springer-Verlag*.

[Nie87]   Oscar Nierstrasz. Active Objects in Hybrid. In *Proceedings OOPSLA '87*, pages 243–253, December 1987. Published as ACM SIGPLAN Notices, volume 22, number 12.

[OOW91]   M. H. Olsen, E. Oskiewicz, and J. P. Warne. A Model for Interface Groups. In *Tenth Symposium on Reliable Distributed Systems*, Pisa, Italy, 1991. IEEE.

[RdPG91]   Stefano Crespi Reghizzi, Guido Galli de Paratesi, and Stefano Genolini. Definition of Reusable Concurrent Software Components. In P. America, editor, *Proceedings ECOOP '91*, LNCS 512, pages 148–166, Geneva, Switzerland, July 1991. Springer-Verlag.

[TS89]   Chris Tomlinson and Vineet Singh. Inheritance and Synchronization with Enabled Sets. In *Proceedings OOPSLA '89*, pages 103–112, October 1989. Published as ACM SIGPLAN Notices, volume 24, number 10.

[vdBL91]   J. van den Bos and C. Laffra. PROCOL, a Concurrent Object-Oriented Language with Protocols Delegation and Constraints. *Acta Informatica*, 28:511 – 538, 1991.

[WL88]   C. T. Wilkes and R. J. LeBlanc. Distributed Locking: A Mechanism for Constructing Highly Available Objects. In *Seventh Symposium on Reliable Distributed Systems*, Ohio State University, Columbus, Ohio, 1988. IEEE.

[WY91]   K. Wakita and A. Yonezawa. Linguistic Supports for Development of Distributed Organizational Information Systems in Object-Oriented Concurrent Computation Frameworks. In *Proceedings of the First Conference on Organizational Computing Systems, Atlanta Georgia*. ACM, September 1991.

[YMFT91]   Y. Yokote, A. Mitsuzawa, N. Fujinami, and M. Tokoro. Reflective Object Management in the Muse Operating System. In *Proceedings of the 1991 International Workshop on Object Orientation in Operating Systems*, Palo Alto, California, October 1991.

PANDA — Supporting Distributed Programming in C++

H. Assenmacher, T. Breitbach, P. Buhler, V. Hübsch, R. Schwarz

Department of Computer Science, University of Kaiserslautern
P.O. Box 3049, W - 6750 Kaiserslautern
Germany

Abstract: PANDA is a run-time package based on a very small operating system kernel which supports distributed applications written in C++. It provides powerful abstractions such as very efficient user-level threads, a uniform global address space, object and thread mobility, garbage collection, and persistent objects. The paper discusses the design rationales underlying the PANDA system. The fundamental features of PANDA are surveyed, and their implementation in the current prototype environment is outlined.

1. Introduction

Systems for parallel and distributed object-oriented programming can be classified into two basic categories. Firstly, there is a variety of programming languages developed especially to serve experimental purposes. Different object models for parallel and distributed programming can be investigated by designing and working with such systems. Some examples of languages in this area are Emerald [Jul el al. 88], Pool [America and van der Linden 90], Sloop [Lucco 87], and Orca [Bal et al. 92]. In contrast, systems belonging to the second category provide support for parallelism and distribution in the environment of an existing object-oriented programming language. In this type of systems, the corresponding mechanisms must fit into the framework of the underlying language, while in the first case no restrictions exist for system development. An advantage of a system embedded into an existing language environment is that the programming tools of the environment and existing software components can still be used. Furthermore, with the increasing acceptance of C++ [Stroustrup 86] — especially in the area of system programming — there is a growing need for systems providing support for programming of parallel and distributed applications in this language. Representative systems in this research area are, among others, Amber [Chase et al. 89], Cool/C++ [Habert et al. 90], and DC++ implemented on top of Clouds [Dasgupta et al. 91].

In C++, programming support for parallel and distributed applications can be realized by a library of classes providing the required functionality, and a run-time system to execute these functions. Important qualities of such systems which do not rely on compiler extension are their portability, extensibility, and ease of modification, as has been shown, for instance, by Presto [Bershad et al. 88]. The behavior of every system object can be redefined, allowing to adapt it to changing requirements. On the other hand, however, several mechanisms proposed to handle parallelism and concurrency control in the object-oriented setting can be implemented only by introducing special language constructs [Gehani and Roome 88, Nierstrasz and Papathomas 90, Saleh and Gautron 91]; thus, they are not applicable in this case.

O.M. Nierstrasz (Ed.): ECOOP '93, LNCS 707, pp. 361-383, 1993.
© Springer-Verlag Berlin Heidelberg 1993

Furthermore, providing distribution support in C++ is — to a large extend — a problem because of its "C-isms". Restricting the language would facilitate this work but it would conflict with the user requirements concerning software re-use. Full language support ensures that software developed for centralized systems can be used in a distributed environment with an acceptable amount of adaptation.

The goal of PANDA is to provide an environment for parallel and distributed programming in C++, imposing as little as possible restrictions on the use of the language. This work is based on the experience which we obtained in previous projects where experimental distributed programming languages and environments were developed [Wybranietz and Buhler 89, Buhler 90]. PANDA's basic library consists of classes which address the issues of parallelism, distribution, object persistence, and garbage collection. These classes can be used directly for building an application, or — alternatively — as a basis for more specialized programming systems, since the user is free to define new abstractions by customizing the PANDA classes. A fundamental part of PANDA is a thread package which provides mechanisms for expressing and handling parallelism in the user space. Here, the crucial issue is performance. The cost of parallelism determines its grain and has thus a strong influence on the programming style. As has been shown by FastThreads [Anderson et al. 89] and Presto [Faust and Levy 90], high performance and flexibility of parallelism support can be achieved by a *user-level* thread implementation.

PANDA has been designed for a hardware platform consisting of a network of homogenous processors. It addresses the issue of distribution by the concepts of single global address space, distributed shared memory, and thread migration. Similar to Amber [Chase et al. 89], all nodes of a PANDA system share a single virtual address space managed globally. Thus, a virtual address can be used as a system-wide unique identifier. References transmitted across node boundaries do not lose their meaning. This concept has serious limitations in the case of 32-bit addressing, which makes virtual addresses to a scarce resource. The wider virtual addresses of emerging 64-bit architectures, however, will support such a system organization, as stated in [Chase et al. 92, Garrett et al. 92].

This paper surveys the PANDA system. Section 2 describes the PANDA interface from the application programmer's point of view, and it discusses the underlying design rationales. The implementation of the fundamental features of our programming environment is briefly outlined. In particular, the thread package, distribution and mobility concepts, as well as the integration of persistence and garbage collection are presented. Section 3 describes the system layers of the PANDA run-time environment. In Section 4, the current status of our prototype implementation is presented. Finally, the main results are summarized, and the direction of future work is indicated.

2. Programming in PANDA

The PANDA system architecture is based on a C++ class hierarchy, and it provides an object-oriented application interface. The system levels of PANDA are especially designed to get high performance at the application level. Our design has been influenced by new trends of hardware architectures and operating systems.

The system supports standard C++; no extensions to the original language are required. This decision was influenced by our goal to be highly portable. However, we use C++ precompiling to simplify the user's task of encoding. This precompiler inserts source code fragments at specified places. This is, for example, useful when a class should be protected against concurrent activation. Without a precompiler the programmer would have to insert a mutual-exclusion semaphore in every method. Instead of this, only a hint in the class definition is necessary, and the precompiler can do this instrumentation. The precompiler frees the programmer from the burden of such routine work, but it is not essential for the concepts that are described in the sequel.

2.1 Thread Package

Activities in a system are called processes or *threads*. In a usual C++ program there exists only one thread. Figure 1 depicts what happens during program execution. A single thread "runs" sequentially through objects and their methods.

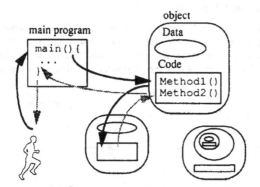

Fig. 1.   "Running" thread in a sequential C++ program

To create a parallel program where several threads operate in one application, the programming model has to offer certain functionality to handle concurrency. In PANDA, the basic mechanisms for thread management are provided by the system class UserThread. An instantiation of this class generates a new activity. The advantage of this approach is that concurrency support can benefit from the object-oriented environment. By deriving new classes from UserThread, various types of active objects may be defined. An example illustrates the usage of PANDA threads:

The following declaration specifies a thread which periodically increments its private variable number:

```
class Increaser : UserThread {
  public:
    Increaser (int StartValue) { number = StartValue; }

    void code() {
      for (;;) {
        Delay(1sec); //method of UserThread
        number = number + 1;
      }
    }
  private:
    int number;
};
```

Creation of threads is now performed by:

```
main{
  incPtr1 = new Increaser (10);
  incPtr2 = new Increaser (500);
  incPtr3 = new Increaser (1000);
}
```

Just before the closing bracket three parallel threads exist in the system, each represented by an Increaser object (Figure 2).

Note that the Increaser class has a special method code. On instantiation, the invocation of Increaser's constructor creates a new thread which executes the code method. The constructor is executed in the creator's context and it is guaranteed that this constructor has finished before the new thread is actually activated, so that parameters may be passed safely.

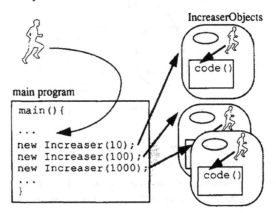

Fig. 2. Active objects obtained by derivation from *UserThread*

PANDA threads are realized by a thread package implemented in user space [Assenmacher 92]. The underlying operating system kernel has no notion of PANDA threads. Management and scheduling of threads is done in non-privileged user mode. Threads which are managed in this way are called *user-level threads* [Bershad et al. 88, Marsh et al. 91]. Our implementation offers very fast thread management. Creation and deletion of threads is extremely fast, causing an overhead within only one order of magnitude compared to a procedure call, see Table 1 in Section 4.

In a system with concurrent activities which act on non-disjunctive object sets, mechanisms for synchronization are required. PANDA offers synchronization objects such as semaphores, distributed read/write semaphores, and signals. To protect objects against concurrent access, a class may be turned into a monitor. For this purpose, the PANDA precompiler may be instructed to add mutual-exclusion semaphores to every method, thus saving a lot of encoding work.

2.2 Distribution

Recall that one of our main goals was to support programming in a distributed environment. Consequently, the question arises how PANDA manages to link the remote components of a distributed application together. In particular, what provisions are taken to ensure that a thread can visit and enter not only local, but also remote objects? This question is central to our model. In this chapter, we address this issue and discuss the different ways to solve the problem.

Three fundamental mechanisms can be employed to provide activities which are able to span several nodes:

As a first alternative (Figure 3), we may simply rely on message passing to cross node boundaries if an invocation is made to a remote object. In essence this type of remote object invocation corresponds to the well-known *remote procedure call (RPC)* mechanism which has been discussed in great detail in the literature [Birrell and Nelson 84]. In order to provide a transparent interface, each caller and

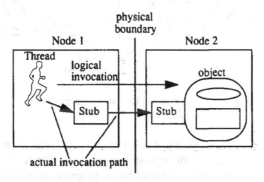

Fig. 3.   Supporting remote object invocation

each remotely accessible object has to be equipped with an appropriate RPC stub, and parameter marshalling has to be done on every invocation of a non-local method. In the object-oriented setting, the functionality of RPC stubs may be provided by so-called *proxies* [Shapiro 86], i.e., local representatives of remote objects. Typically, marshalling is based on some preprocessing of the source code. However, providing perfect transparency in a language like C++ is rather difficult. For instance, it is difficult to handle pointers which may occur in the parameter list of a method. Also, it should be noted that RPC supports a slightly asymmetric model of computation. Most applications based on RPC make an explicit distinction between *clients* on the one hand, and *servers* on the other — at least at the conceptual level. In some applications, such an asymmetry appears to be artificial, and is only an artifact of the underlying RPC mechanism. These subtleties diminish the location transparency which can be achieved with RPC.

Therefore, a more natural approach to the distribution problem is to create the illusion of a single, global object and thread space, i.e., to hide the node boundaries from the application programmer. To this end, the system has to ensure that all operations — local or remote — are eventually carried out locally. On the conceptual level, this can be achieved with two different strategies [Jul et al. 88, Chase et al. 89, Dasgupta et al. 91], one based on object mobility, the other on thread mobility. In Figure 4, the system migrates the object to its invoking thread as soon as a non-local invocation is encountered. After the object has been moved to the node on which the thread resides, the remote object invocation turns into a local call. Figure 5 shows the dual solution. Instead of moving the object, the system migrates the invoking thread, again turning the remote invocation into a local one.

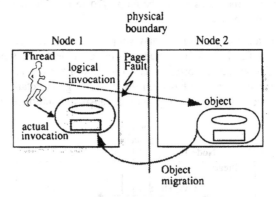

Fig. 4. Object migration based on page-fault mechanism

The solutions depicted in Figures 4 and 5 are very attractive from a programmer's point of view. They do not distinguish between the caller (client) and the called (server), and they need not be reflected by the program code. In principle, the program could be completely unaware of the distributed nature of the underlying hardware. This is a highly desirable property. For example, an application could be im-

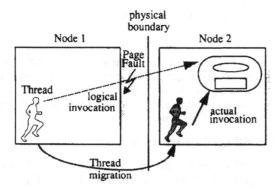

Fig. 5. Thread migration based on page-fault mechanism

plemented and tested in a centralized system; distribution may then be realized by simply spreading the different components of the application to different nodes of the distributed system, without any need to change the code of the various program modules. In most application domains, this view is, of course, too optimistic — efficiency considerations typically preclude a thoughtless distribution and require a careful decomposition of the system into (relatively independent) components. Nevertheless, location transparency is at least a first step in the direction of this ideal, and it helps to reduce the complexity of the application code.

Actually, both object and thread mobility have proved their value in practical implementations [Ananthanarayanan et al. 90, Bennett et al. 90, Chase et al. 92b, Garrett et al. 92, Nitzberg and Lo 91]. The approach depicted in Figure 4 is generally described in more abstract terms, disregarding the object structure of the data. Transparent access to remote memory locations based on moving the respective data to the requestor is usually referred to as *distributed shared memory* (DSM). In PANDA, DSM is provided to support object mobility.

Providing Distributed Shared Memory

One possible way to achieve perfect location transparency in a distributed environment would be to completely re-implement the memory management layer of the underlying C++ run-time system, and to base the execution of all programs exclusively on a DSM mechanism. Unfortunately, however, in many situations DSM turns out to be a rather expensive mechanism; a thoughtless use of shared memory objects may lead to permanent thrashing, intolerably reducing the efficiency of the program execution. Therefore, PANDA provides DSM only if the programmer explicitly requests for it.

From the programmer's perspective, the allocation of an object in the DSM address space is straightforward. The following code fragment illustrates how it is done:

```
class Any; //Arbitrary user class
...
Any *pointer = new DSM Any;
```

All that has to be done is to insert the preprocessor directive 'DSM' between the new operator and the object class name; the preprocessor replaces this by a special parameter which is handed to the new allocation routine. The PANDA run-time support system takes this as a hint, and ensures that the newly created object instance resides in the DSM where it is accessible from all nodes of the system.

Implementation of the DSM Mechanism

Basically, the PANDA implementation of DSM is as follows. A global virtual address space is assigned to the Panda application. As shown in Figure 6, this address space is statically partitioned into several, disjoint memory partitions, (at least) one private partition for each node of the distributed system, and (at least) one shared partition per node. The private partition assigned to a node contains all private objects of that node. Such objects are not shared but can only be accessed by the threads running on the owner node of the respective partition. Consequently, the pages of the private partitions are only mapped into the address space of their respective owner node; remote nodes are not allowed to reference these memory locations. The second partition, however, comprises the DSM address space and contains those objects which are shared by all nodes; the pages of all shared partitions are mapped into the address space of all processes. Thus, every node may access any shared location.

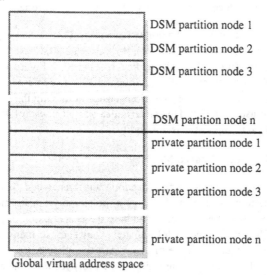

Fig. 6.   Statically partitioning of memory

Note that a static partitioning of the address space is only feasible if the address space is sufficiently large. With the advent 64-bit architectures which is the emerging technology, spending some available memory addresses (recall that the virtual addresses of the private partitions assigned to the remote nodes are lost on the local host) in order to obtain a simpler and more efficient realization of the memory management mechanisms seems reasonable [Chase et al. 92, Chase et al. 92b, Garrett et al. 92].

Having partitioned the address space as described above, DSM memory management is now straightforward. All pages which are currently not available are read-write protected by the memory management unit. Whenever a thread tries to access an object which is not locally available, a page fault occurs. This page fault is handled by an appropriate page fault handler. If the address that caused the page fault refers to a private memory partition, this shows that a remote private partition has been referenced. As objects within such a non-local partition are not remotely accessible, access cannot be granted locally, that is, an exception has to be raised to indicate an access violation, or — depending on circumstances — the system may try to migrate the thread that caused the page fault to the node which owns the referenced partition (see below).

If the address that caused the page fault refers to a DSM partition, a different strategy applies. As DSM partitions are shared between all nodes, an access to an arbitrary DSM partition is always permissible, and should therefore always be granted. To this end, the page fault handler follows some protocol which links together the distributed physical DSM memory pages to a single virtual shared memory.

In the PANDA system, managing distributed memory and reacting to page faults is particularly easy, due to the static partitioning strategy that is applied. Note that for each virtual memory address, the system can immediately determine the corresponding partition. This knowledge helps to simplify the DSM protocol. For example, we can easily determine the node which is responsible for each partition, and that node can coordinate all activities related to the management of the partition's virtual pages, for example, their retrieval, and the invalidation of read copies.

In principle, the PANDA system is open to all DSM protocols that are known from the literature [Nitzberg and Lo 91]. However, an appropriate page fault handler has to be provided which implements the chosen strategy. In the current PANDA prototype system, a simple approach (exclusive-read-exclusive-write) has been chosen, mainly because we were able to provide this functionality with a trivial DSM manager (approximately 150 lines of code). Currently, we are about to realize several more sophisticated DSM protocols and to study their performance benefits.

Providing Thread Mobility

An approach to achieve location transparency which is dual to DSM is based on thread mobility. Instead of moving the object to the thread where it is needed (*data shipping*), we may as well move the thread to the object (*function shipping*). None of these approaches is superior to the other in general; their appropriateness depends on the actual object and thread granularity, and also on the object reference patterns that occur in the application at hand [Ananthanarayanan et al. 90, Dasgupta et al. 91, Jul et al. 88].

In PANDA, thread migration is performed by a method of the already mentioned class UserThread. This class provides the method migrate at its interface:

```
class UserThread {
  public:
    ...      // Constructor, code() etc. ...
    void migrate (destination);
};
```

Conceptually, invoking this method interrupts the thread's execution, transfers its stack segment to the appropriate partition on the specified remote node, moves its thread control block to the same destination, and inserts it into the appropriate queue of the destination node's scheduler. After this has been done, the thread's execution can be resumed. In practice, slight variations on this scheme are feasible to increase the efficiency of thread migration. For example, one might postpone the transfer of the stack segment and provide its memory pages only on demand.

From an abstract point of view, thread mobility is a possible realization of function shipping. In Figure 5, we showed how function shipping may serve to provide location transparency, i.e., to create the illusion of a single, global address space which can be accessed from each node in the system. The basic idea is to provide a page fault handler which — on receiving a page fault interrupt — determines the current location of the referenced memory page, and then migrates the requestor to that location. This approach provides an alternative to the DSM mechanism discussed in the previous sections.

One could also imagine to combine data shipping with function shipping by simply providing both strategies within a single page fault handler. Based on the type of object that is requested, the type of thread which made the request, and on global load conditions in the system, the handler could decide on each page fault whether to move the object to the thread, or whether to move the thread to the object. We will further pursue such strategies in the future.

2.3   Persistent Objects

In conventional programming languages data is transient. Its lifetime maximally spans the program's execution. Very often, preserving data across multiple invocations of several programs is required. Moreover, some data should even survive system failures. Data having these properties is called *persistent*. In conventional environments, persistence is typically realized with the help of file systems or database interfaces. But the lack of integration makes these realizations rather difficult to handle. Using the file system to make data persistent imposes a lot of additional encoding work on the programmer. He has to "flatten" his data structures to make them storable and re-readable. If a database interface is used, the user has to learn a database language, and he has to fit his data structures into the model provided by the database. New approaches in object-oriented databases [ODeux et al. 91, Lamb et al. 91] try to better bridge the gap between programming languages and databases. A database, however, is rather resource intensive, and therefore probably not adequate for those applications which do not require its functionality to the full extent.

Thus, the integration of persistence mechanisms into the run-time environment of the language seems to be a reasonable alternative. Such an approach has been pursued — in particular — in systems designed for fault tolerant computing [Ahamad et al. 90, Liskov 88, Shrivastava et al. 91].

In PANDA, an integrated persistence mechanism has been realized. Persistence is modelled as an additional object attribute which is orthogonal to the existing features of the C++ language. Persistent objects are remotely accessible.

If a class is intended to be persistent in PANDA, the precompiler directive "persistent" has to be placed in front of its definition:

```
persistent class Confer {
  public:
    Confer (int year) { date = year; }
  private:
    int date;
};
```

Creation of a persistent instance of such a class is done by:

```
Confer *con = new "ECOOP" Confer(93);
```

Finding an existing persistent object is performed by:

```
Confer *con2 = new "ECOOP";
```

One major problem concerning persistent objects is how to maintain their consistency in the presence of concurrent access and node failures. An abstraction which guarantees this requirement is the transaction principle.

PANDA offers distributed transaction support, restricted to persistent objects. By default, transaction brackets are automatically inserted by the precompiler at the beginning and the end of each method of a persistent class. However, there exists a precompiler directive which suppresses this default to allow manual instrumentation. Currently, nested transactions are not supported; recursive invocations are, of course, feasible. If a failure occurs, always the outermost transaction bracket is aborted. Only persistent objects are recovered. Our implementation of transactions is based on the page-fault mechanism. Shadow copies of modified pages are managed. Pages are stored on a simple block-oriented file system. Distributed transactions are based on two-phase-commit.

2.4 Garbage Collection

It is generally claimed that environments which support applications comprising a changing set of dynamically allocated objects have an urgent demand for automatic garbage collection. Distributed garbage collection has been intensively studied in the literature, in particular in the context of functional programming environments where dynamically allocated data is ubiquitous [Rudalics 88].

In imperative programming languages such as C++, however, an excessive use of dynamically allocated data is less common, and it is always explicitly requested by the programmer. Due to the language's block structure, most of the volatile data can simply be declared within the block scope, i.e., on the invocation stack; such *stack objects* are removed on block exit. In C++, true *heap objects* tend to be rather long-lived. Empirical studies have shown, however, that long-lived objects are rarely subject to garbage collection [Hayes 91, Sharma and Soffa 91]. As the application programmer is generally well aware of their existence, and of their lifetime, manual deletion is probably most effective.

The potential benefits of garbage collection may be further restricted if there is a shared access to complex dynamic data structures. Figure 7 shows an example. Sup-

Shared linked list object

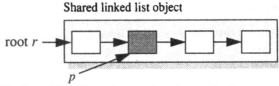

Fig. 7.   Limitations of automatic garbage collection

pose that several threads share a common linked list, reachable via the root pointer *r*. One of these threads may call some list operation *drop(p)* to declare *p as "no longer in use" from its local perspective. However, *p cannot so easily be discarded, without knowing whether *all* other threads have also dropped *p*. Consequently, *p has to remain in the list until it is certain that it has *semantically* turned into garbage. Unfortunately, the notion of semantical reachability is not adequately matched by the criterion of physical reachability on which all garbage collectors are based. Note that all list items will always remain *physically* reachable via *r* unless they are explicitly removed by the list management. Obviously, automatic garbage collection is of little help in such cases; instead, an explicit agreement protocol for the identification of garbage has to be provided by the programmer. Situations similar to our example are quite common in concurrent applications sharing linked data structures. Similar observations have been reported from systems based on an actor model [Kafura and Washabaugh 90].

Design Rationales

For efficiency reasons, PANDA supports a *co-existence* of ordinary objects with objects that are automatically garbage-collected. This means that a garbage-collectable object can be declared and used in roughly the same way as any other object. Being garbage-collectable should be mostly *orthogonal* to existing features of the C++ programming language [Detlefs 92, Edelson 90]. This rules out any form of added formalism deviating from normal C++ syntax.

We currently pursue a telecommunication exchange system application. There, *responsiveness* — i.e., the ability to react to incoming stimuli within a short and predictable interval of time — is one of the most stringent requirements, even more important than efficiency. Unfortunately, many of the most efficient distributed collectors known from the literature exhibit a stop-and-collect behavior which conflicts with the requirements of responsiveness. What is needed is an *incremental* garbage collection scheme which collects garbage on the fly. So-called *reference counting collectors* are well suited for that purpose [Bevan 89, Piquer 91, Rudalics 88], in particular because they can easily handle *references in transit* which are a major source of difficulties in distributed garbage collection schemes.

Another reason why stop-and-collect approaches are probably not an adequate choice is because they tend to leave garbage objects in the system for a substantial amount of time before they actually delete them. This may conflict with C++ *destructors*, methods which are called when their corresponding object is deleted. If (as it is often the case) a garbage collector treats garbage as a single, uniform memory space without considering the individual garbage objects, then this may completely preclude the invocation of any destructors [Edelson 90]. But even if the individual garbage objects *are* identified, but their deletion is delayed until the next detection phase, this conflicts with the semantics of destructors which are assumed to be *instantaneously* called on deletion (and may cause relevant side effects that must not suffer from any delays). These subtle requirements originating from C++ as well as the demand for responsiveness were our main motivation for choosing a simple reference counting scheme.

Language-Based Implementation

To support reference counting in C++, the method at hand is to employ so-called *smart pointers* [Detlefs 92, Edelson 92], i.e., reference objects which provide all basic functionality of an ordinary pointer, but transparently carry out additional semantic operations. This can be put nicely into practice, based only on features which are provided by C++.

We included two different garbage collection schemes in our PANDA run-time support system. The first follows the classical *reference counting* approach. The second strategy is based on positive weights which are assigned to each garbage-collectable object, and to each reference to such an object [Bevan 89].

The idea is to maintain the following invariant: The sum of the weight of an object and of the weights of all references that point to that object is a known constant *CONST*. To satisfy this invariant, an object and its original reference is initially equipped with a weight of *CONST*/2 each. Whenever a weighted reference to an object is copied, its weight is split into two shares. One share is handed back to the original reference, the other is assigned to the newly created reference. Accordingly, as soon as a reference is removed or overwritten, its current weight is returned to the object. Obviously, as soon as the weight of the object increases to *CONST*, all its references must have been deleted, and the object is garbage. For more details, the interested reader is referred to [Bevan 89] and [Schwarz 92]. The potential benefit of this scheme is that reference copying only involves the original reference and its copy, but not the (potentially remote) object. This may help to save communication bandwidth and copying delay.

PANDA supplies a base class GC_obj which provides the basic functionality required for (weighted) reference counting. An object class is made garbage-collectable simply by deriving it from GC_obj. All other objects (probably, the ma-

```
class UserType: public GC_obj {
  ...// add internals, e.g.:
  char *name;
};

UserType obj1, obj2;
GC_ref<UserType> ref1, ref2;

ref1 = ref2 = new UserType;

ref1->name = "AnyName";
obj2 = *ref1;
if (ref2 == 0) cerr << "???\n";

ref1 = 0;// implicit deletion;
ref2 = &obj1;// implicit deletion:
        // *** collection ***
```

Fig. 8.   A code fragment showing the application of
garbage collection

jority) are by no means affected by garbage collection. We regard this as an essential feature. Probably only a small fraction of all objects is subject to garbage collection. This will drastically reduce the computational overhead and the storage requirements of reference counting. Figure 10 shows a code fragment which illustrates how garbage collection can be applied. Note that garbage-collectable references — implemented by the template class GC_ref<...> — may be assigned, compared, and dereferenced like any ordinary pointer of the C++ language.

Potential Problems

Garbage collection based on smart pointers is subject to certain limitations. This general observation is particularly true for C++ which suffers from the burden of several C anachronisms. In [Edelson 92], the author discusses the weaknesses of smart pointers in C++. The three main sources of potential trouble are: Smart pointers to constant objects, implicit type casting and "pointer leakage".

The first problem — the difficulty to provide the smart pointer equivalent of a const Type pointer — does not so much affect the functionality of smart pointers, but is just desirable for documenting and structuring reasons, and to provide a more rigorous compile-time checking of the application code. Edelson presents a solution to this problem which causes, however, some inconvenience for the application programmer.

The inability to extend the implicit type casting rules of C++ to smart pointers has more significant consequences. For example, ambiguous function calls are often made unambiguous by comparing the argument types with the signatures of the functions in question. This procedure depends on a number of implicit type conversion rules which the C++ compiler automatically applies to the function arguments. With smart pointers, such implicit casts are no longer feasible. In most cases, however, the programmer can simply specify an explicit type conversion to resolve ambiguous (or otherwise even illegal) situations. This may be inconvenient, but it is not a fatal handicap.

So-called pointer leakage [Edelson 92] is another potential pitfall. Note that the overloaded "->" operator must return an *ordinary* pointer. Therefore, once a temporary smart pointer has been dereferenced and "->" has returned an ordinary pointer, the smart pointer is no longer needed and may be destroyed. If it was the only reference to an object, then the object might be subject to garbage collection, although the ordinary pointer returned by "->" is still in use. The danger of pointer leakage can be reduced by careful encoding; unfortunately, aggressive optimizing compilers may sometimes try to eliminate "superfluous" intermediate variables, thus destroying the last smart pointer to an object.

Besides these shortcomings which are inherent to C++ and the smart pointer approach, the main weakness of our (weighted) reference counting strategy is its inability to identify cyclical garbage structures. On the other hand, a cyclical structure often represents *one* entity of the application domain which should rather be represented by an *atomic* object providing a specialized delete operation. A trick that might sometimes help to combine user-defined destructors with automatic garbage collection is illustrated in Figure 9. The basic idea is to exploit the compatibility between ordinary pointers and reference objects, and to break the cycle by inserting at least one simple pointer in the reference chain.

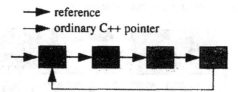

Fig. 9.   Breaking cycles by mixing references with ordinary pointers

Despite of the problems mentioned above, we think that the advantages of our solution outweigh its potential drawbacks:

- Only garbage-collectable objects are penalized by the collector.
- Garbage is eliminated incrementally.
- The overhead is proportional to the access frequency to garbage-collectable objects.
- Our strategy complies with the semantics of C++ destructors.
- Our approach does not depend on any special system support, and it is applicable in a parallel and distributed setting.

3.   System Architecture

The design of our system very much benefits from current hardware trends, which will have a major impact on future system architectures in general [Karshmer and

Nehmer 91]. We expect that multiprocessor workstations connected by a high-speed network capable of a bandwidth of 1 GB/s will soon become the standard working environment. The availability of 64-bit wide machine addresses will allow the use of a global address space shared by several applications [Chase et al. 92].

Object-Oriented System Design

In order to maximize extensibility, exchangeability, maintainability, and to minimize development time, an object-oriented design of our system has been chosen. We regard it as an adequate approach to structure the operating system kernel, the run-time support, and also the applications. Hence, we focused on a single programming language for both application and system software. This approach prevents the obstacles and the performance penalties entailed by interface mismatch. Moreover, structuring the system in an object-oriented manner simplifies the replacement of its components, thus facilitating experiments regarding various system configurations. Derivation techniques in combination with dynamic binding and polymorphism allow a gradual refinement of system components and improve structural clarity.

Main Components

As shown in Figure 10, the system is divided up into three different layers: pico-kernel, run-time package, and application layer. The objects within each layer form a set of exchangeable building blocks. This technique simplifies maintenance and the integration of new or customized components.

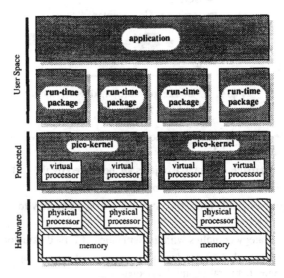

Fig. 10. PANDA system layers

A single application may span several run-time packages. There is a one-to-one mapping between run-time packages and virtual processors. Several virtual processors may share a single physical processor, whereby scheduling is done on a preemptive single-priority FIFO basis. This policy prevents an application from processor monopolization. The current scheduling policy can, however, easily be adapted to specialized application domains. For example, a fixed time slot may be assigned to a virtual processor in order to meet the requirements of real-time systems.

The pico-kernel offers only those hardware abstractions which are critical in respect to protection and monopolization considerations: protection domain management and virtual processor scheduling. The code size of the pico-kernel is reduced to an absolute minimum because only those functions remain in the kernel which actually require the privileged instructions of the processor.

All kernel calls are non-blocking. This allows the continuation of user-level threads within the run-time package. No thread will ever block within the kernel stopping the whole run-time package. For a further discussion of problems related to the implementation of user-level threads, the reader is referred to [Anderson et al. 92, Draves et al. 91, Marsh et al. 91].

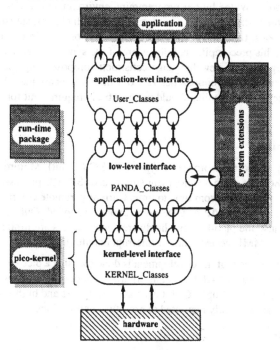

Fig. 11. PANDA interfaces

At the first glance, assigning only one virtual processors to each run-time package seems to be restrictive. Note that it precludes true parallelism between threads within the same run-time package. On the other hand, scheduling a single virtual processor can be accomplished without additional overhead for locking. This eliminates the need for special multiprocessor mechanisms, discussed, e.g., in [Anderson et al. 89]. By saving the synchronization costs in this critical code section, substantial performance gains are obtained. An application may still benefit from a multiprocessor platform by simply employing several run-time packages. One drawback of this approach is that it is up to the application to evenly distribute load over the available processors. However, global load distribution may be implemented by using thread migration between the run-time packages.

System support such as communication service, different DSM services, migration service, or persistence service are realized as exchangeable components of the run-time package. Most of these servers are hidden from the application by higher-level abstractions. In general, an application uses the *application-level interface*. It may, however, also access the *low level interface*, but only "applications" meant as system extensions — such as a load distribution facility — are encouraged to do so. The three different interfaces are provided by corresponding class families (see Figure 10).

A valuable tool provided by our programming environment is a C++ precompiler. It facilitates the instrumentation of programs with stub classes, statistical counters, monitoring hooks, transaction brackets, method add-ons etc. In contrast to a mere preprocessor, this precompiler is fully aware of the syntactical structure, which allows the integration of new language constructs, proposed, e.g., in [Gehani and Roome 88, Buhr and Stroobosscher 92]. But this is a technique which we try to avoid because the precompiler should not be a basic requirement for our system.

4. Status

We currently support the processor types SPARC (32 bit), Motorola 680xx, and Intel i386/i486. The main development stream uses SPARC processors, the others are updated and adopted from time to time. Currently, remote communication via a raw Ethernet and a TCP/IP or UDP connection is supplied. Our system is highly portable because the pico-kernel's hardware dependencies are limited to a context switch facility, MMU access, and the interrupt handler interface.

For convenience, most of the development is done by using a pico-kernel emulation on top of UNIX (SunOS 4.1.1). As this environment does not yet reflect new hardware trends like, for example, 64-bit wide address spaces and high-speed local area networks, we are currently restricted to prototype applications.

Performance

In order to put the PANDA system into perspective, some preliminary performance measurements are listed in Table 1. Our results compare quite well with the performance of FastThreads [Anderson et al. 92], Presto [Faust and Levy 90], and Psyche [Marsh et al. 91]. The measurements were carried out on Sun SPARC-2 workstations connected by a 10 Mb/s Ethernet, with a pico-kernel emulation on top of SunOS 4.1.1. Comparing the null procedure with a null process (creation, context switch, null execution, and deletion), it should be taken into account that the SPARC

Benchmark operation	Time
Thread creation, null execution, and deletion (with/ without lazy stack allocation)	15.1 μs / 10.7 μs
Context switch	17.7 μs
Remote message (8 bytes) transfer (ping / burst)	1.8 ms / 0.3 ms
Local memory allocation and deletion	1.5 μs
Remote memory access via DSM page transfer	9.6 ms
Null procedure call (with / without register window overflow)	7.1 μs / 0.31μs

Tab. 1. Performance of the PANDA prototype

architecture is particularly tuned to allow extremely fast procedure calls; context switches, on the other hand, are relatively slow, and only poor support for user-level threads is provided [Anderson et al. 91].

5.   Conclusions and Future Work

The results gained so far are encouraging. PANDA has proved to be a practical and efficient support for parallel and distributed programming. Due to our compliance with standard C++, an industrial partner is seriously considering our system as a platform for telecommunication software, and is currently employing it for prototype implementations. Thus, we are able to obtain valuable feedback regarding our design choices.

We also explore PANDA's capability to serve as a base for various concurrent and distributed programming models. To this end, we implemented a run-time support layer for COIN [Buhler 90], a programming language especially designed for parallel and distributed applications. As expected, PANDA's low-level interface provided a suitable set of abstractions for this purpose, and no major performance penalties had to be payed due to interface mismatch.

Our experience with C++ is twofold. On the one hand, it is an emerging standard which provides access to a variety of software, and which allows very efficient system programming. On the other hand, it has definite disadvantages as far as concurrency and distribution are concerned. We are well aware of the fact that C++ is probably not an ideal language to address these issues. Therefore, our work is directed towards two main goals. First, we would like to enhance our environment by adding C++ classes to deal with problems related to — in particular — robustness and persistence. Second, we will also investigate how the aspects of parallelism, distribution, and persistence can be more suitably reflected in an object-oriented programming language.

Acknowledgments

We would like to thank Peter Sturm for many fruitful discussions, and Thomas Gauweiler for his technical help.

References

[Ahamad et al. 90] M. Ahamad, P. Dasgupta, and R.J. Leblanc, Jr. *Fault-tolerant Atomic Computations in an Object-Based Distributed System.* Distributed Computing, Vol. 4, pp. 69-80, 1990.

[America and van der Linden 90] P.H.M. America and F. van der Linden. *A Parallel Object-Oriented Language with Inheritance and Subtyping.* Proc. of European Conference on Object-Oriented Programming and ACM Conference on Object-Oriented Programming: Systems, Languages, and Applications (Ottawa, Canada, Oct. 21-25), ACM, New York, pp. 161-168, 1990.

[Ananthanarayanan et al. 90] R. Ananthanarayanan et al. *Experiences in Integrating Distributed Shared Memory With Virtual Memory Management.* Technical Report GIT-CC-90/40, Georgia Institute of Technology, College of Computing, Atlanta, GA, 1990.

[Anderson et al. 89] T.E. Anderson, E.D. Lazowska, and H. Levy. *The Performance Implications of Thread Management Alternatives for Shared-Memory Multiprocessors.* IEEE Trans. Comput. 38, 12 (Dec.), pp. 1631-1644, 1989.

[Anderson et al. 91] T.E. Anderson, H.M. Levy, B.N. Bershad, and E.D. Lazowska. *The Interaction of Architecture and Operating System Design.* Proc. ACM SIGOPS '91, 1991.

[Anderson et al. 92] T.E. Anderson, B.N. Bershad, E.D. Lazowska, H.M. Levy. *Scheduler Activations: Effective Kernel Support for the User-Level Management of Parallelism.* ACM Transactions on Computer Systems, Vol. 10, No. 1, Feb. 1992.

[Assenmacher 92] H. Assenmacher. *The PANDA Run-time Package.* Technical Report, Department of Computer Science, University of Kaiserslautern, Germany, 1992.

[Bal et al. 92] H.E. Bal, M.F. Kaashoek, and A. S. Tanenbaum. *Orca: A Language for Parallel Programming of Distributed Systems.* IEEE Trans. Softw. Eng. 18(3), pp. 190-205, March 1992.

[Bennett et al. 90] J.K. Bennet, J.B. Carter, W. Zwaenepoel. *Adaptive Software Cache Management for Distributed Shared Memory Architecture.* Proc. 17th Annual Int. Symposium on Computer Architecture, Seattle, Washington, pp. 125-134, May 1990.

[Bershad et al. 88] B.N. Bershad, E.D. Lazowska, H.M. Levy, and D. Wagner. *An Open Environment for Building Parallel Programming Systems.* Proc. of the ACM SIPLAN PPEALS - Parallel Programming: Experience with Applications, Languages, and Systems, (July 19-21), pp. 1-9, July 1988.

[Bevan 89] D.I. Bevan. *An Efficient Reference Counting Solution to the Distributed Garbage Collection Problem.* Parallel Computing 9, pp. 179-192, 1989.

[Birrell and Nelson 84] A.D. Birrell and B.J. Nelson. *Implementing Remote Procedure Calls*. ACM Transactions on Computer Systems, 2(1), Feb. 1984.

[Buhler 90] P. Buhler. *The COIN Model for Concurrent Computation and its Implementation*. Microprocessing and Microprogramming 30, No. 1-5, North Holland, pp. 577-584, 1990.

[Buhr and Stroobosscher 92] P.A. Buhr and R.A. Stroobosscher. *μC++ Annotated Reference Manual*. University of Waterloo, Canada, Aug. 1992.

[Chase et al. 89] J.S. Chase, F.G. Amador, E.D. Lazowska, H.M. Levy, and R.J. Littlefield. *The Amber System: Parallel Programming on a Network of Multiprocessors*. Proc. of the 12th ACM Symposium on Operating Systems Principles, pp. 147-158, 1989.

[Chase et al. 92] J.S. Chase et al. *How to Use a 64-Bit Virtual Address Space*. Technical Report 92-03-02, Department of Computer Science and Engineering, University of Washington, Seattle, WA, 1992

[Chase et al. 92b] J.S. Chase et al. *Lightweight Shared Objects in a 64-Bit Operating System*. Technical Report 92-03-09, Department of Computer Science and Engineering, University of Washington, Seattle, WA, 1992.

[Dasgupta et al. 91] P. Dasgupta, R.J. LeBlanc, M. Ahamad, and U. Ramachandran. *The Clouds Distributed Operating System*. IEEE Computer, pp. 34-44, Nov. 1991

[Detlefs 92] D. Detlefs. *Garbage Collection and Run-time Typing as a C++ Library*. Proc. USENIX C++ Conference, Portland, Oregon, Aug. 1992.

[Draves et al. 91] R.P. Draves, B.N. Bershad, R.F. Rashid, and R.W. Dean. *Using Continuations to Implement Thread Management and Communication in Operating Systems*. Proc. of the 13th ACM Symposium on Operating Systems Principles, Oct. 1991.

[Edelson 90] D.R. Edelson. *Dynamic Storage Reclamation in C++*. Technical Report UCSC-CRL-90-19, University of California at Santa Cruz, CA, June 1990.

[Edelson 92] D.R. Edelson. *Smart Pointers: They're Smart, but They're Not Pointers*. Proc. USENIX C++ Conference, Portland, Oregon, pp. 1-19, Aug. 1992.

[Ellis and Stroustrup 90] M. Ellis and B. Stroustrup. *The Annotated C++ Reference Manual*. Addison-Wesley, 1990.

[Faust and Levy 90] J.E. Faust and H.M. Levy. *The Performance of an Object-Oriented Thread Package*. Proc. of European Conference on Object-Oriented Programming and ACM Conference on Object-Oriented Programming: Systems, Languages, and Applications (Ottawa, Canada, Oct. 21-25), ACM, New York, pp. 278-288, Oct. 1990.

[Garrett et al. 92] W. E. Garrett, R. Bianchini, L. Kontothanassis, R.A. McCallum, J. Thomas, R. Wisniewski, and M.L. Scott. *Dynamic Sharing and Backward Compatibility on 64-Bit Machines*. TR 418, University of Rochester, Computer Science Department, Rochester, NY, April 1992.

[Gehani and Roome 88] N.H. Gehani and W.D. Roome. *Concurrent C++: Concurrent Programming with Class(es)*. Software — Practice and Experience 18(12), pp. 1157-1177, Dec. 1988.

[Habert et al. 90] S. Habert, L. Mosseri, and V. Abrossimov. *Cool: Kernel Support for Object-Oriented Environments*. Proc. of European Conference on Object-Oriented Programming and ACM Conference on Object-Oriented Programming: Systems, Languages, and Applications (Ottawa, Canada, Oct. 21-25), ACM, New York, pp. 269-277, Oct. 1990.

[Hayes 91] B. Hayes. *Using Key Object Opportunism to Collect Old Objects*. Proc. OOP-SLA'91, Phoenix, Arizona, Oct. 1991.

[Jul el al. 88] E. Jul, H. Levy, N. Hutchinson, and A. Black. *Fine-grained Mobility in the Emerald System*. ACM Trans. Comput. Syst. 6(1), pp. 109-133, Feb. 1988.

[Kafura and Washabaugh 90] D. Kafura and D. Washabaugh. *Garbage Collection of Actors*. Proc. ECOOP/OOPSLA'90, pp. 126-134, Oct. 1990.

[Karshmer and Nehmer 91] A. Karshmer and J. Nehmer (eds.). *Operting Systems of the 90s and Beyond*. LNCS 563, Springer-Verlag, 1991.

[Lamb et al 91] C. Lamb, G. Landis, J. Orenstein, D. Weinreb. *The Objectstore Database System*. Communications of the ACM, Vol. 34, No. 10, pp. 50-63, Oct. 1991.

[Liskov 88] B. Liskov. *Distributed Programming in ARGUS*. Comm, ACM, Vol. 31, No. 3, pp. 300-312, March 1988.

[Lucco 87] S.E. Lucco. *Parallel Programming in a Virtual Object Space*. Proc. of ACM Conference on Object-Oriented Programming: Systems, Languages, and Applications (Orlando, Fla., Oct. 4-8). ACM, New York, pp. 26-34, Oct. 1987.

[Marsh et al. 91] B. D. Marsh, M.L. Scott, T.J. LeBlanc, and E.P.Markatos. *First-Class User-Level Threads*. Proc. of the 13th Symp. on Operating Systems Principles, Pacific Grove (California), pp. 110-121, Oct. 1991.

[Nierstrasz and Papathomas 90] O.M. Nierstrasz and M. Papathomas. *Viewing Objects as Patterns of Communicating Agents*. Proc. of European Conference on Object-Oriented Programming and ACM Conference on Object-Oriented Programming: Systems, Languages, and Applications (Ottawa, Canada, Oct. 21-25), ACM, New York, pp. 38-42, 1990.

[Nitzberg and Lo 91] Nill Nitzberg and Virginia Lo. *Distributed Shared Memory: A Survey of Issues and Algorithms*. IEEE Computer, pp. 52-60, Aug. 1991.

[ODeux et al. 91] O. Deux et al. *The O_2 System*. ACM Communications of the ACM, Vol. 34, No. 10, pp. 34-48, Oct., 1991.

[Piquer 91] J. Piquer. *Indirect Reference Counting: A Distributed Garbage Collection Algorithm*. In: LNCS 505, E.H.L. Aarts, J. van Leeuwen, M. Rem (eds.), Springer-Verlag, pp. 150-165, 1991.

[Rudalics 88] M. Rudalics. *Multiprocessor List Memory Management*. Technical Report RISC-88-87.0, Research Institute for Symbolic Computation, J. Kepler University, Linz, Austria, 1988.

[Saleh and Gautron 91] H. Saleh and P. Gautron. *A Concurrency Control Mechanism for C++ Objects*. Proc. of the ECOOP '91 Workshop on Object-Based Concurrent Computing (Geneva, Switzerland, July 15-16), LNCS 612, Springer-Verlag, pp. 95-210, 1991.

[Schwarz 92] R. Schwarz. *Language-based Garbage Collection in the PANDA System*. Internal Report, Department of Computer Science, University of Kaiserslautern, Germany, 1992.

[Sharma and Soffa 91] R. Sharma and M. L. Soffa. *Parallel Generational Garbage Collection*. Proc. OOPSLA'91, Phoenix, Arizona, Oct. 1991.

[Shapiro 86] M. Shapiro. *Structure and Encapsulation in Distributed Systems: The Proxy Principle*. Proc. 6th Int. Conference on Distributed Computer Systems, pp. 198-204, Cambridge, MA, May 1986.

[Shrivastava et al. 91] S.K. Shrivastava, G.N. Dixon, G.D. Parrington. *An Overview of the ARJUNA Distributed Programming System*. IEEE Software, pp. 66-73, Jan. 1991.

[Stroustrup 86] B. Stroustrup. *The C++ Programming Language*. Addison-Wesley, Reading, MA, 1986.

[Wybranietz and Buhler 89] D. Wybranietz and P. Buhler. *The LADY Programming Environment for Distributed Operating Systems*. Proc. of the PARLE'89 Conference, Eindhoven, Holland, Juni 1989. Springer-Verlag, LNCS 365, pp. 100-117, 1989.

Transparent parallelisation through reuse: between a compiler and a library approach

J.-M. JÉZÉQUEL

I.R.I.S.A. Campus de Beaulieu
F-35042 RENNES CEDEX, FRANCE
E-mail: jezequel@irisa.fr
Tel: +33 99 84 71 92 ; Fax: +33 99 38 38 32

Abstract. Software environments for commercially available Distributed Memory Parallel Computers (DMPCs) mainly consist of libraries of routines to handle communications between processes written in sequential languages such as C or Fortran. This approach makes it difficult to program massively parallel systems in both an easy and efficient way. Another approach relies on (semi-)automatic parallelizing compilers but it has its own drawbacks. We propose to tackle this problem at an intermediate level (i.e. between high level parallelizing compilers and raw libraries), using Object Oriented (OO) technologies. We show that existing OO techniques based on the reuse of carefully designed software components can be applied with satisfactory results to the large scale scientific computation field. We propose to use a form of parallelism, known as data parallelism, and to embed it in a pure sequential OOL (Eiffel). We illustrate on several examples how sequential components and frameworks can be modified for parallel execution on DMPCs to allow for transparent parallelisation of classes using these components and frameworks.

Keywords: Distribution, Data Parallelism, Reuse, Components and Frameworks

1 Introduction

The large scale scientific computation field is looking for ever growing performances that only Distributed Memory Parallel Computers (DMPCs) could provide. The spreading of DMPCs in this user community is hampered by the fact that writing or porting application programs to these architectures is a difficult, time-consuming and error-prone task. Nowadays software environments for commercially available DMPCs mainly consist of libraries of routines to handle communications between processes resulting from the execution of programs written in sequential languages such as C and Fortran.

For instance, since its introduction in the late 50's, Fortran has been widely used for programming sequential numerical algorithms of engineering and science. Naturally, Fortran users wished to program DMPCs that way. But as if it weren't complex enough to program large (and even very large) applications with such an ill designed language, application programmers also had to deal with the whole task of parallelisation, distribution, process creation, communication management, and eventually very long debugging sessions.

O.M. Nierstrasz (Ed.): ECOOP '93, LNCS 707, pp. 384–405, 1993.
© Springer-Verlag Berlin Heidelberg 1993

In order to abstract Fortran programs toward parallel and massively parallel architectures, leading industries and academics launched the so-called High Performance Fortran Forum bound to deliver a new release of Fortran called High Performance Fortran (HPF). It is based on the so-called data-parallelism model where the set of data involved in a computation is split into partitions, to which processes are associated: this makes it possible to benefit from one of the fundamental aspects of scientific applications which is the use of repetitive computations on a large data space. HPF extends Fortran 90 (which contains itself Fortran 77 as a proper subset) by means of syntactically distinguished directives. Most representative among them are directives to specify data alignment and distribution. When coupled with array operations of Fortran 90, they would enable compilers endowed with sophisticated dependence analysis and MIMD parallelisation techniques to produce message passing code efficiently utilizing DMPCs. But there is a long way to go before such semi-automatic tools are made available. Presently available commercial tools such as MIMDizer [17] only help the user to decompose, distribute and parallelize his program interactively. Anyway, even future tools emerging from either US big companies or European Esprit projects (like the PREPARE Project) will still require the user to define (at least) his data partitions, thus altering the original sequential program either interactively or through the use of compiler directives.

Furthermore, this kind of compiler must still have a wide know-how about algorithmic parallelisation rules for the distributed data structures (actually only arrays) on which it works, and thus will be able to generate efficient code for a limited set of well known problems only: if the programmer faces a new problem, the only solution for him/her would be to get back to low level message passing Fortran, with all its drawbacks.

Another important thing to be highlighted is that data distribution compiler directives change the program semantics in such a way that it is not easily manageable outside of the compiler itself. Linking a program with HPF object code in libraries poses several problems, because some data distribution information must exist at runtime but cannot be encapsulated (in a compiler independant fashion) with subroutines performing operations on the distributed data structure, as it could be if modular or object oriented languages were used. Hence new runtime format standards or external tools such as databases holding this information will be needed, thus bringing compatibility and/or coherence problems; and adding complexity to already overwhelming complex environments.

We claim that no library level approach can solve easily the problem of code reuse on a DMPC. In this paper, we propose to tackle all these problems at an intermediate level (i.e. between high level parallelizing compilers and raw libraries), using OO technologies. We show that existing OO techniques based on the reuse of carefully designed software components can be applied to this field with good results.

We are not the first at thinking that the reuse of software components could help to manage the complexity of concurrent programming. For example in [6] it is proposed to derive parallel programs from sequential ones just by introducing asynchronous (inter-object) message passing along with the *wait by necessity* mechanism. Then *had-hoc* synchronization features encapsulated in classes allow for a customizable and versatile reuse of sequential code for safe concurrent execution. In a similar way, it is shown in [9] how synchronization constraints can be encapsulated in classes and reused (and customized) through inheritance.

We consider these approaches as very valuable and promising, but we think they lack the scalability that would make them efficient in the context of DMPCs with hundreds of processors. Actually this kind of parallelism is of a functional nature and thus it is not scalable: the definition of processes is determined by the sub-task decomposition and does not allow an efficient mapping onto the very high number of processors that may be available in a DMPC.

In a rather orthogonal way, our approach aims at embedding the scalable data parallelism programming model in an OOL, Eiffel in our case. This is presented in the next section. In the third section, we describe main reuse techniques, both within and outside of the object oriented context. Then we show how they can be applied in a distributed framework: this leads us to define reusable parallel abstractions that we illustrate on a toy example. In the fourth section, we describe how these reusable parallel abstractions can be applied to the large scale scientific computation field, and we study their performance overhead. Some implementation related remarks are made before we conclude on our experiment.

2 Programming Massively Parallel Architectures with Sequential Object Oriented Languages

2.1 Embedding data parallelism in an OOL

In our opinion a programming language should be kept as small as possible, and most notably should leave data structures and their access procedures and functions outside. So logically, we propose to conceptually remove the parallelisation know-how existing for example in a parallelizing FORTRAN compiler, and to encapsulate this know-how with the data structure to which it applies. Our approach at encapsulating parallelism can be compared to the encapsulation of tricky pointer manipulations within a linked list class, thus providing the abstraction *list* without annoying the user with pointer related notions.

Opposite to OOL where objects can be made active and methods invocations can result in actual message passing communications (sometimes referred as functional parallelism as implemented in POOL-T [1], ELLIE [2], ABCL/1 [20], Emerald [5], COOL [7] or PRESTO [4] for example), we focus on the data parallelism model associated with a SPMD (Single Program Multiple Data) mode of execution, we no longer map the object oriented message passing paradigm onto actual interprocess communications, because our goal is to completely hide the parallelism to the user (*i.e.* the application programmer).

This approach seems to be rather natural in an OO context, since object oriented programming usually focuses on data rather than on functions. Furthermore, the SPMD mode of execution appears as an attractive one because it offers the conceptual simplicity of the sequential instruction flow, while exploiting the fact that most of the problems running on DMPCs involve large amounts of data (in order to generate usefull parallelism). Each process executes the same program, corresponding to the initial user-defined sequential program, on its own data partition. The application programmer view of his program is still a sequential one and the parallelism is automatically derived from the data decomposition, leading to a regular and scalable kind of parallelism.

In [12], we have described how a sequential Object Oriented Language (OOL) can embed data parallelism in a clean and elegant way —without any language extensions— to exploit the potential power of massively parallel systems. The encapsulation of all the methods of a given object allow us to precisely know the structure of the data accesses and to define appropriate parallel techniques accordingly: parallelism is thus hidden in classes describing the low level accesses to data structures without altering their interface. These "distributed" classes are also compilation units (like any normal class), thus there are no more problems to link separately compiled modules: this is a major advantage with respect to FORTRAN-like appoaches. The modularity encourages the construction of methods by refinement. At first, a simple implementation using the pure SPMD model is realized, reusing sequential classes in this parallel context. Optimizations may then be added for each method separately: this allows an incremental porting of already existing applications to DMPCs.

2.2 The Eiffel Parallel Execution Environment

We implemented these ideas in EPEE (Eiffel Parallel Execution Environment): data distribution and parallelism are totally embedded in standard language structures (classes) using nothing but already existing language constructions. EPEE is based on Eiffel because Eiffel offers all the concepts we need, using a clearly defined syntax and semantics. However our approach is not strongly dependent on Eiffel; it could be implemented in any OOL featuring strong encapsulation (and static type checking), multiple inheritance, dynamic binding and some kind of genericity.

An EPEE prototype is available for Intel iPSC computers (iPSC/2 or iPSC/860) and networks of workstations above TCP/IP. We validated our approach through an experimentation with an implementation of distributed matrix using EPEE, and got interesting results [11].

We distinguish two levels of programming in EPEE: the class user (or *client*) level and the parallelized class designer level. Our aim is that at the client level, nothing but performance improvements appear when running an application program on a DMPC. We would like these performance improvements to be proportional to the number of processors of the DMPC (linear speed-up), which would guarantee scalability.

The designer of a parallelized class is responsible for implementing general data distribution and parallelisation rules, thus ensuring portability, efficiency and scalability, while preserving a "sequential-like" interface for the user. If a class already has a specification —and/or a sequential implementation— the parallel implementation should have the same semantics: each parallelized method should leave an object in the same abstract state as the corresponding sequential one.

To implement that, a designer selects interesting classes to be data parallelized, *i.e.* classes aggregating large amounts of data, such as classes based on *arrays, sets, trees, lists...* Then, for each such class, one or more distribution policies are to be chosen and data access methods redefined accordingly, using the abstractions provided in the EPEE distributed aggregate class (referred as DISTAGG in the following). Our distributed aggregate concept is not unrelated to the notion proposed in [8]: it is an abstract aggregate of generic data that is spread across a DMPC, together with a set of methods to access its data transparently, to redistribute it, to perform a method on each of its elements, and to compute any associative function on the aggregate.

3 Towards reusing software components for parallelism

3.1 Classical approach of reuse

Reuse is not a new idea in software engineering (see for instance [13]). However, attempts to go beyond the reuse of source code and the reuse of personnel (*i.e.* reuse of the know-how of a given software engineer) are plagued by the "Not Invented Here" complex and/or lack of flexibility of existing software components.

Still, building and using libraries of (sub)routines is a classical technique that is quite successful in the scientific computation field. According to [14], this is mainly because every instance of each problem can be identified with a small set of parameters and is quite independent from other problems, and also because few complex data structures are actually involved beyond arrays. However, in the context of DMPC programming, these assumptions no longer hold —for the reasons explained in the introduction. One must rely on more modern and flexible reuse techniques.

One of the key issue in reuse is the aptitude to parameterize general purpose algorithms of data structures traversing with the "actions" to be performed at each step. In ML (actually CAML, an ML dialect [19]) we can find for example the function map:

```
map : (('a -> 'b) -> 'a list -> 'b list)
```

which applies its first argument (the function ('a -> 'b) taking as input an object of type a and returning an object of type b) to a list of type a objects and returns a list of type b objects. If one wants to build a list of squares from a list of integers, one should just call:

```
# let square x = x * x;;
Value square is <fun> : int -> int
# map square [1; 2; 3; 4; 5];;
[1; 4; 9; 16; 25] : int list
```

In a language such as ANSI-*C*, this could be emulated through the use of function pointers (see figure 1).

However, *C* has not the secured flexibility of something like ML: if one wants to introduce some kind of parameterization (genericity), one must use the principle of *type coercion* which is widely known as a very unsafe feature (it can lead to runtime type errors that crash the program).

Anyway, ML and *C* (along with other languages like Smalltalk) are languages where routines are *first-class objects*, *i.e.* can be handled at runtime with dedicated language constructs. Whereas first-class objects provide a great deal of flexibility

```
#include <stdio.h>
#define MAXT 5
void print_square (int *n) {  printf("%d\n",*n**n); }

void apply (void (*f) (int *n), int *t)
{
   int i;
   for (i=0;i<MAXT;i++) { (*f)(&t[i]);}
}

main(void)
{
   int tab[MAXT]={1,2,3,4,5};
   apply(print_square,tab);
}
```

Fig. 1. Applying a function in C

(which does not always preclude type checking security: cf. CAML), this feature generally requires costly run time support: in high level languages (i.e. not C for that matter) the run-time data structure representing a routine is substantially more complicated than the sole address of an entry point in the code. In this context, it seems that we have to trade efficiency (a C like approach) for type checking security (CAML). One way to cumulate efficiency and type checking security is to make use of the feature characterizing OOL vs. modular languages like Modula or Ada, that is to say, *inheritance*.

3.2 A key towards reuse in OOL: inheritance

A large amount of numeric computations involves algorithms performing data structure walking (think of matrix operations for example). These are the computations we are actually interested in parallelizing on DMPCs, because here lies the main kind of scalable parallelism. Actually, not every program can be parallelized in a scalable way, *i.e.* its parallelisation does not necessarily bring significant performance improvement when adding more processors. To formalize that, Valiant proposed in [18] the BSP model (Block Synchronous Parallel). A computation fits the BSP model if it can be seen as a succession of parallel phases separated by synchronization barriers and sequential phases. In this model, a computation can be efficiently parallelized only if the cost of synchronization, communications and other processing paid for managing parallelism is compensated by the performance improvement brought by the parallelisation. We will get speed-up greater than one only if the size of the data structure is large enough, and our speed-up will increase with the ratio computation time vs. communication time.

In the following, we focus on this kind of algorithms (*i.e.* those performing walking across data structure big enough); and we show how well-designed sequential

```
deferred Class ENUMERABLE [E]
    -- E is a formal generic parameter
    -- identifying the type of the ENUMERABLE elements
feature
    start is deferred end;          -- Move to some arbitrary first element
    forth is deferred end;          -- Advance to a not yet enumerated element
    off : boolean is deferred end;  -- Is there not a current item?

    item : E is
            -- Current item of the enumerable data structure.          10
        require not_off: not off
        deferred
        end;
    put ( new : E ) is
            -- Change the current item of the enumerable data structure with new
        require not_off: not off
        deferred
        ensure item = new
        end;
end; -- class ENUMERABLE [E]                                           20
```

Fig. 2. The generic deferred ENUMERABLE class

frameworks can be reused for parallel execution on DMPCs in a transparent way. Basically, there are two kinds of such algorithms:

- those applying a given action to each (or some of the) elements of the data structure
- and those computing an associative function based on each (or some of the) element of the data structure (much like the APL *reduce* operator).

The first step is to specify the data structures where walking algorithms can be defined at the most abstract level. We could think of abstract data types allowing some kind of finite *enumeration*, *i.e.* let us take an element, then another one, etc. until we reach the last one. It is convenient to make this abstract data type (called ENUMERABLE in the following) hold the abstract notion of *cursor*, which could be a kind of window focusing on at most one element of the ENUMERABLE object. Then an ENUMERABLE would offer the following operations:

item to look at the element under the cursor
put to change the value of the element under the cursor
start to move the cursor to an arbitrary first element
forth to advance to a not yet enumerated element
off to tell whether there is an element under the cursor

Using the Eiffel syntax, this ENUMERABLE abstract data type could be defined as described in figure 2.

This class ENUMERABLE is declared as *deferred* because it declares features without giving any implementation (deferred features): these features will be given actual definitions (*effected*) in classes inheriting from ENUMERABLE. Eiffel also allows the specification of pre-conditions (keyword **require**) and postconditions (keyword **ensure**) in the abstract data type classical way.

Our class ENUMERABLE can be seen as a generalization of the ISE Eiffel V2.3 library class called TRAVERSABLE, and will be the basis of our construction. Actually, if we need a kind of class ENUMERABLE where we can *apply* a given *action* to each element, we can define a class APPLIABLE as displayed in figure 3.

```
deferred Class APPLIABLE [E]
  inherit ENUMERABLE [E]
feature
  apply is
    do
      from start until off
        loop action; forth end
    end;
  action is do end;
end; -- APPLIABLE [E]                                           10
```

Fig. 3. The generic deferred APPLIABLE class

By mean of multiple inheritance, this class APPLIABLE could be used in a class LIST of INTEGER in the following way:

```
Class LISTINT
export squarelist, repeat FIXED_LIST      -- specify the class interface
inherit
  FIXED_LIST [INTEGER];
  APPLIABLE [INTEGER]
    rename action as square,              -- Give a more significant name
           apply as squarelist            --    to action and apply
    define start, forth, off, item, put   -- Merge APPLIABLE features with
                                          -- corresponding ones in FIXED_LIST
    redefine square;                      -- Give a new definition for square
feature
  square is do put (item * item) end;
end;
```

```
deferred Class REDUCIBLE [E,F]
inherit
  ENUMERABLE [E]
feature
  reduce : F is
    do
      Result := initialisation;
      from start until off
        loop Result := function (Result); forth end;
      end;                                                      10
    function (accumulator : F) : F is do end;
    initialisation : F is do end;
end; -- REDUCIBLE [E,F]
```

Fig. 4. The generic deferred REDUCIBLE class

A client would just call **MyIntList.squarelist** to apply the square function to each element of its list.

For the reader not fluent in Eiffel, the main rules driving multiple inheritance are recalled below, (in agreement with [16]):

- If various features are inherited under the same final name f in class C, then they are said to be *shared*, i.e. C has only one feature named f. At most one instance of the features named f can be effected (at least all but one must be deferred) or else there is a name conflict (detected by the compiler) that must be remove through renaming.
- If two features are inherited under different final names in class C, then they are said to be *duplicated*, i.e. C has two distinct features

In LISTINT, the features **start, forth, off, item, put** exist in a single instance, and their implementation is the one found in FIXED_LIST.

In a similar way, if our client wish to call something like **MyIntList.maxelem** to know the higher element of the list (thus performing a *reduce* operation on the list), the class LISTINT should be modified as follow:

```
Class LISTINT
export maxelem ...
inherit
  ...
  REDUCIBLE [INTEGER,INTEGER]
    rename function as sup,            -- Give a more significant name
           initialisation as neg_infinite, -- to function, initialisation
           reduce as maxelem               --   and reduce
```

```
  define start, forth, off, item, put      -- Merge REDUCIBLE features with
                                           -- corresponding ones in FIXED_LIS
    redefine sup, neg_infinite;            -- Give a new definition for these
...
feature
...
  sup (max : INTEGER) : INTEGER is
    do if item>max then Result := item  else Result := max end; end;
  neg_infinite : INTEGER is -2147483648;
...
```

where the class REDUCIBLE is as displayed in figure 4.

But now, what if we want to have another reduce-like function (say total, which computes the sum of the elements) on this list? We simply have to inherit again from REDUCIBLE, directly using the *repeated inheritance* mechanism of Eiffel: the inheritance graph for class LISTINT is displayed in figure 5, where deferred features are marked with an asterisk". Again, features with the same final name will be merged, whereas features with differing final names will be duplicated (for example, total and maxelem are both renamed instances of the reduce feature). Here is the final text of our LISTINT class:

```
Class LISTINT
export squarelist, maxelem, total, repeat FIXED_LIST
inherit
  FIXED_LIST [INTEGER]
    rename Create as fixed_list_Create;     -- Hold fixed_list constructor
  APPLIABLE [INTEGER]
    rename action as square,                -- Give a more significant name
           apply as squarelist              --    to action and apply
    define start, forth, off, item, put     -- Merge APPLIABLE features with
                                            -- corresponding ones in FIXED_LIST
    redefine square;                        -- Give a new definition for square
  REDUCIBLE [INTEGER,INTEGER]
    rename function as sup,                  -- Give a more significant name
           initialisation as neg_infinite, --   to function, initialisation
           reduce as maxelem                --    and reduce
    define start, forth, off, item, put     -- Merge REDUCIBLE features with
                                            -- corresponding ones in FIXED_LIST
    redefine sup, neg_infinite;             -- Give a new definition for these
  REDUCIBLE [INTEGER,INTEGER]
    rename function as plus,                 -- Give a more significant name
           reduce as total                  --   to function and reduce
    define start, forth, off, item, put     -- Merge REDUCIBLE features with
                                            -- corresponding ones in FIXED_LIST
    redefine plus;                          -- Give a new definition for plus
feature
  Create (n: INTEGER) is do fixed_list_Create(n) end;
```

```
square is do put (item * item) end; '
sup (max : INTEGER) : INTEGER is
  do if item>max then Result := item  else Result := max end; end;
neg_infinite : INTEGER is -2147483648;
plus (acc : INTEGER) : INTEGER is do Result := acc + item end;
positive (acc : BOOLEAN) : BOOLEAN is do Result := item>0 or else acc end;
end; -- LISTINT
```

It may look complicated, but one has to keep in mind that a client of this class only has to look at the class interface (directly provided by the *short* command), whereas a descendant can get a flat view of the inheritance graph through the *flat* command.

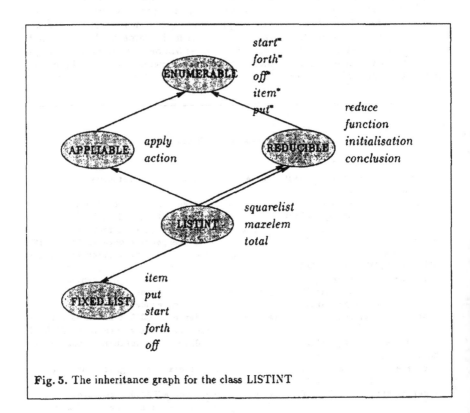

Fig. 5. The inheritance graph for the class LISTINT

We can see that the frame of the **reduce** operation has been actually reused twice (in **total** and **maxelem**) and could be still reused several times, thus achieving sequential reuse. If we can give a distributed version of this kind of reusable operation, we can achieve the transparent reuse of this distributed version by already defined features (like **total** and **maxelem**). This is the aim of the next section.

3.3 Reusing sequential code for a parallel execution

Distributed Enumerable Objects We want to reuse our class LISTINT for execution on a DMPC. The basic idea is to change the meaning of our ENUMERABLE, REDUCIBLE and APPLIABLE abstractions to deal with ENUMERABLE objects distributed across a DMPC. These distributed objects are split across the DMPC (each processor has only a piece of the object), and operations are implemented using the SPMD programming model along with the *owner-compute rule* principle. This principle assesses that an assignment is only run by the process on which the left hand side variable is located. To deal with remote accesses, a data belonging to a distributed object is *Refreshed* before any reading attempt, i.e. the owner of this data broadcasts it to the other processors (see [3] for more details).

By definition, the class APPLIABLE makes use of local assignments only (an *action* can only be applied on the item under the cursor position), so we do not need to change it. On the contrary, the reduce function of the class REDUCIBLE is meant to access each item of the ENUMERABLE object. But if we would use the version of reduce directly as described above, each reduce function would only compute on each node a local result on the locally available items. To compute the global result from these local ones, we have to append a *conclusion* to this reduce function (this is why the computed function has to be associative: the order of evaluation may be different between a sequential execution and the distributed one). A simple minded implementation of this *conclusion* would be to have each processor send its local result to a master processor, which would then compute the global result and broadcast it. But as the number of processors of the DMPC grows, this simple minded implementation shows its performance limitations. We could choose more sophisticated algorithms, using for example minimal spanning tree algorithms where each processor computes its result with the values received from its childs on the tree, sends it to its father, and so on until the root is reached. The global result can then be sent back along the tree or simply broadcasted. We could also use a built-in system level function of the DMPC when available (on the Intel iPSC/2 for example).

A Distributed List example Our idea is to realize one (careful, robust, efficient) distributed implementation of some general purpose data structure walking algorithms that distributed implementations of sequential classes can reuse in a transparent way.

To achieve that on our example, we create a new class, DLISTINT, which has the very same interface as LISTINT but with such a distributed implementation. A client of the class LISTINT wishing to take advantage of a distributed implementation would just use DLISTINT instead of LISTINT, without altering its code in any other way. The only difference we could see would be the improvement of performances when running on a DMPC.

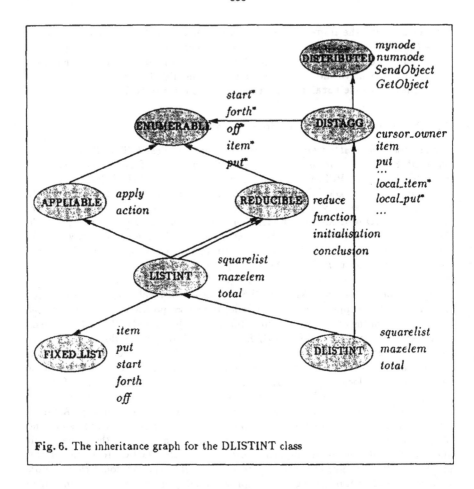

Fig. 6. The inheritance graph for the DLISTINT class

The multiple inheritance feature makes it possible to express that this distributed DLISTINT is both a LISTINT and a distributed aggregate of integers as described in DISTAGG [INTEGER]: see on figure 6 how we update the inheritance graph.

In DLISTINT, the only way to assign a value to an element of the list is to call the feature *put*. To implement the *owner-compute rule* principle for this class, we need to give a new definition of this feature, so to make it store the required value only if the processor trying to execute the assignment owns the relevant part of the list, i.e. if it owns the cursor. Symetrically, the feature *item* is the only way to access an element of the list. We give a new definition of *item* to implement the *Refresh* operation as defined above. As this is general for every distributed aggregate, these features are actually defined in the class DISTAGG in the following way:

```
deferred Class DISTAGG [E->ANY]
  -- E is a formal generic parameter
  -- identifying the type of the DISTAGG elements
inherit
  DISTRIBUTED;   -- Imports low level features like mynode, numnode...
  ENUMERABLE [E] -- DISTAGG is a special case of ENUMERABLE made of the
                 -- union accross the DMPC of "local" ENUMERABLE pieces
    define start, forth, item, put;
                 -- Give a global SPMD meaning for those
                 -- while letting off deferred
feature
  owner_of_cursor : INTEGER is deferred end;
  cursor_owner : BOOLEAN is do Result := owner_of_cursor = mynode end;
  item : E is
    do
      if cursor_owner
        then SendObject(local_item,-1); Result := local_item
        else Result ?= GetExpandedObject (owner_of_cursor)
      end
    end;
  put (v: like item) is do if cursor_owner then local_put(v) end end;
  start is
    do cursor_start; if cursor_owner then local_start end end;
  forth is
    local previous_owner : INTEGER;
    do
      previous_owner := owner_of_cursor;
      if cursor_owner then local_forth end;
      cursor_forth;
      if cursor_owner and then previous_owner /= owner_of_cursor
        then local_start end
    end;

  cursor_start is deferred end;
  cursor_forth is deferred end;
  local_start is deferred end; -- Move to arbitrary local first element
  local_forth is deferred end; -- Go to a not yet enumerated local element
  local_off : boolean is deferred end; -- Is there not a current local_item?
  local_item : like item is deferred end;
  local_put (v: like item) is deferred end;
end; -- DISTAGG
```

We can see that features dealing with the cursor (start, forth, off) are also given new meanings, according to their global semantics in our SPMD programming model. Actually we want every exported (public) feature of DLISTINT to have exactly the same semantics as in LISTINT, so that a client can use DLISTINT instead of

LISTINT transparently. The global version implementation can be given for **start**
and **forth** using the local (deferred) definitions. Thus an actual heir of DISTAGG
is left to *effect* the feature **off**, the local versions of cursor features (**local_start**,
local_forth, **local_off**), along with those dealing with distribution policies (for
instance **owner_of_cursor**).

To implement DLISTINT we choose a very simple distribution scheme: we cut the
list in parts of more or less the same size, and allocate them to consecutive processors
(as shown below in the Create feature), so that it is easy to compute the owner of
a list item (see the **owner_of_cursor** feature below). To implement local versions of
cursor features, we use the LISTINT cursor features: we have just to rename them as
local_start, **local_forth**, and **local_off**. Finally, the global cursor abstraction is
implemented by mean of an INTEGER (cursor), and deferred cursor related features
are given a definition accordingly. The class DLISTINT eventually looks like:

```
Class DLISTINT
    export repeat LISTINT
            -- Same interface than LISTINT
    inherit DISTAGG [INTEGER]
                define local_item, local_put, local_start,
                       local_forth, local_off    -- to be merged with
                                                  --    LISTINT features
              LISTINT
                rename  Create as Listint_Create,
                        item as local_item,        -- Merge with
                        put as local_put           --    DISTAGG features
                        start as local_start,
                        forth as local_forth,
                        off as local_off;

    feature
      cursor : INTEGER;          -- implements the global cursor abstraction
      cursor_start is do cursor := 1 end;
      cursor_forth is do cursor := cursor + 1 end;
      cardinal : INTEGER;        -- The total number of items in the list
      owner_of_cursor : INTEGER -- A simple distribution scheme
        is do Result:= (cursor*numnode-1) div cardinal end;
      off : BOOLEAN is
        do Result := (cursor = 0) or else (cursor > cardinal) end;
      Create (n: INTEGER) is     -- Creates just the local part of the list
        do
          cardinal := n;
          if cardinal mod numnode > mynode
            then Listint_Create(cardinal div numnode + 1)
            else Listint_Create(cardinal div numnode + 1)
          end
      end;
```

When a client is calling MyDListInt.total for example, it is actually the distributed version of reduce which is called: transparent parallelisation is achieved through reuse.

4 A realistic example

4.1 Generality of the method

These ideas have also been applied to more realistic heirs of ENUMERABLE, like the class MATRIX encapsulating the abstract data type matrix of real, with such operations as reading, addition, multiplication, inversion, and trace (sum of the elements on the diagonal). These features have been implemented by means of the APPLIABLE and REDUCIBLE ones. However, whereas the class LISTINT had the very notion of a cursor already available through the features start, forth, and off (inherited from the library class LIST), other ENUMERABLE heirs may not have it. We must provide it when it is not available. Since a MATRIX element is usually accessed by means of a pair of indexes (i,j), we can encapsulate this in a class called INDEXABLE2D and say a MATRIX is an INDEXABLE2D (i.e. inherit from it). Figure 7 shows a possible definition of INDEXABLE2D.

```
deferred Class INDEXABLE2D [E]
  inherit ENUMERABLE [E] -- An enumerable with 2D indexes
  feature
    i, j: INTEGER;
    start_i is do i := 1 end;
    start_j is do j := 1 end;
    start is do start_i; start_j end;

    forth_i is do i := i + 1 end;
    forth_j is do j := j + 1 end;                          10
    forth is do forth_j; if off_j then start_j; forth_i end end;

    off_i : BOOLEAN is do Result := i > bsup_i end;
    off_j : BOOLEAN is do Result := j > bsup_j end;
    off   : BOOLEAN is do Result := off_i end;

    bsup_i : INTEGER is deferred end;
    bsup_j : INTEGER is deferred end;
  end;
```

Fig. 7. The generic deferred INDEXABLE2D class

We also added new features to deal with the potentially different signatures of apply and action, as for example when only one parameter is needed:

```
deferred Class APPLIABLE [E]
...
feature
...
  apply1 (other : like Current) is
    do
      from start until off
        loop action1(other.item); forth; other.forth  end
    end;
...
```

Then the addition operation `M1.add(M2)` can be implemented as follow:

```
  inherit
    ARRAY2[REAL]
      rename Create as Array2_Create,
             item as item2d,    -- Avoid name clashes between default ARRAY2
             put as put2d;      -- features and ENUMERABLE ones
    INDEXABLE2D                 -- implementing the cursor (i,j)
      rename bsup_i as height,  -- merge the upper limits of iterations
             bsup_j as width    -- with the numbers of lines and columns
      define height, width;     -- of ARRAY2
    APPLIABLE [REAL]
      rename action1 as add_item,
             apply1 as add
      define start, forth, off, item, put
      redefine add_item;
...
  feature
    item : REAL is do Result := item2d(i,j) end;
    put (v: like item) is do put (v,i,j) end;
    add_item(other_item: REAL) is do put(item+other_item) end;
...
```

Then this feature add may be reused "as it is" in a Class DistributedMatrix implemented the same way the DLISTINT was.

4.2 Customized walks

One point of interest appears when we need to perform a customized walk through the data structure, like for the implementation of the **trace** operation. Instead of using the common implementation for cursor moves (start, forth, off), we rename and redefine these to implement the customized walk we need:

```
...
  inherit
    REDUCIBLE [REAL]
      rename reduce as trace,
             function as plus
             forth as diagonal_forth, -- customizes REDUCIBLE with the new
                                       -- meaning for forth, as defined below
      define start, diagonal_forth, off, item, put
      redefine plus;
...
    plus (acc : REAL) : REAL is do Result := acc + item end;
    diagonal_forth is do forth_i ; forth_j end;
...
```

When the feature trace is called, it is actually reduce that is invoked, but a version of reduce modified so that it calls diag_forth instead of the default forth.

4.3 Reusing the class Matrix to build a class DistributedMatrix

We proceed the same way as for building a class DLISTINT from the LISTINT one. First we express that a distributed Matrix is both a Matrix and a distributed aggregate:

```
Class DMATRIX
    export repeat MATRIX
             -- Same interface than MATRIX
             -- inherit from both ancestors
    inherit DISTAGG [REAL];
           MATRIX
```

The Distributed Matrix constructor (Create feature in Eiffel) can be defined so that it splits the Matrix onto the various nodes of the DMPC, using the Distributed Aggregate features. As we work in a SPMD model, each processor executes the creation instruction, but creates only its own part of the matrix. Then as the only way MATRIX elements are accessed is through the features item and put, these features are renamed and given a new definition exactly the same way as for corresponding features in DLISTINT, i.e. using the global versions available in DISTAGG.

4.4 A comment on the efficiency of this approach

Since we are using rather advanced features of Eiffel (repeated inheritance, subtle use of the rename clause to manage feature duplication or merging), the question of their efficient implementation arises. It is even crucial for us, as our main rationale to use DMPCs lies in their potential computing power. If we would end up with a parallelized code running slower than the (best) sequential one, we would have completely missed the point. Fortunately, it is not so.

The first thing to be highlighted is that most of the feature name resolutions can usually be done at compile time. If a matrix M is declared of type DMATRIX (and if DMATRIX has no descendant), *every* feature call on M can be identified statically: the general dynamic binding mechanism can be discarded and replaced with a mere procedure call. For instance, the compiler can realize that the addition operation (as in `M1.add(M2)`) invoked in some client is in fact the renamed form of the `apply1` feature of the APPLIABLE class, with `action` (re-)defined in MATRIX, and `start`, `forth`, and `off` features defined in INDEXABLE2D: the direct procedure calls can be generated accordingly.

Then it is possible to avoid the overhead of procedure calls through inline expansions: the ISE Eiffel compiler can do it automatically when it finds it interesting. Finally, with all this OO stuff removed from the intermediate code, state-of-the-art compiling techniques can be used to implement loop merging, common sub-expression eliminations, etc. and to generate code as efficient as a hand-written equivalent in FORTRAN.

Since the features taking advantage of the parallelism of the DMPC can rely on the reuse of the implementations of features such as `reduce` and `apply`, the final code running on the DMPC could be as efficient as the best hand-coded one (i.e. at the message passing level). As an example, we can say that our feature `add` (from class DMATRIX) is optimal because it involves absolutely no (machine level) message exchange: the better FORTRAN hand-written version would have exactly the same behavior and performance.

4.5 Implementation comments and results

EPEE (Eiffel Parallel Execution Environment) is actually made of three main parts:

- the DISTAGG generic class, encapsulating the distributed aggregate abstraction and the DISTRIBUTED class, which is a normal Eiffel class making heavy usage of external C functions calls. This class must be inherited by each Eiffel class willing to take advantage of parallelism and distribution features within EPEE.
- a set of interface modules (written in C), built on top of the ECHIDNA experimentation environment [10] to provide an homogeneous and instrumented interface to the Distributed Aggregate Class. At present, modules for Intel iPSC/2, iPSC/860 and Sun networks are available.
- a set of tools to facilitate cross-compilation and distributed experimentation of an Eiffel program in EPEE.

We experimented our ideas through the implementation of prototype classes (Matrix and Distributed Matrix), using the ISE Eiffel compiler (V.2.3) which allows the production of portable C packages.

It is worth insisting that with EPEE, a pure Eiffel program is compiled, with the full sequential semantics of Eiffel. However, we currently have a limitation: we do not handle non-fatal exceptions properly, so the Eiffel *rescue* mechanism cannot always be used safely. The only other visible difference when executed on a DMPC is an increase of performances.

We led some performance measurements of our implementation on an Intel hypercube iPSC/2 with 32 processors. For various cube sizes, we measured execution times of various methods of the class DMATRIX. We compared these results to their best sequential counterparts (i.e from the class MATRIX) run on one iPSC/2 node, thus allowing a speed-up evaluation. We got nearly linear speed-up (presented in [11]), that is to say that when problems are large enough, we can half the computing time by doubling the number of processors.

4.6 Problems and limitations

We found two kinds of problem while implementing our ideas. First, conceptual problems that limit the expressiveness and ease of use of our approach:

- Not all operation can be expressed in terms of the few reusable parallel abstractions (apply, reduce, etc.) we provide: a real implementation should be much more complete.
- Full automatic parallelism is obtained only for the features making use of our reusable parallel abstractions: other feature will also work in parallel, but no performance improvement will be obtained. However, critical methods (in terms of efficiency) can be redefined, using the SPMD programming model to take advantage of a specific data distribution. The general methods defined in the classes DISTRIBUTED and DISTAGG are to be used to hide the underlying system.
- features such as apply must be provided with at least three signatures: apply without parameter, with one, and with a list of parameters. This can be tedious, as the code is essentially the same. Furthermore, each APPLIABLE descendant class would have these three features, even if only one is needed. A possible solution would be to have three classes (APPLIABLE, APPLIABLE1, and APPLIABLEn) with only one apply feature in each of them.

We also found problems linked to the version 2.3 of the Eiffel language and its compiler:

- The Eiffel concept of genericity is very powerful, and works very well in general. However, it is not totally orthogonal to the rest of the language: we got problems when trying to mix genericity and expanded types (mostly for I/O and interprocessor communications).
- In case of complex occurrences of repeated inheritance and renaming, the compiler does not always give the expected results, and tools like *flat* can be fooled. Furthermore, the current syntactic mechanism driving the merging or the duplication of features does not have all the expressive power that we would have liked, so in a few cases, we had to hack the design of our reusable classes to make them pass through the compilation process.

On these two points, the next version of Eiffel (as described in the book *Eiffel: The Language* [15]) will bring significant improvements: expanded types should be much better integrated in the language, and a more expressive syntax will be available to drive renaming, merging, selection and even undefinition of features.

5 Conclusion

We have proposed a method based on the reuse of carefully designed software components to allow the programming of DMPCs in an easy and efficient way. A prototype of a software environment (EPEE) has been developed, implemented and experimented on real DMPCs with satisfying performances.

EPEE facilitates DMPC programming at both user and class designer levels. While providing a SPMD programming model to the designer of distributed classes, EPEE presents a sequential model to the user, so the DMPC is only seen as a powerful processor whose architecture details are hidden. Furthermore, EPEE makes it possible to reuse already existing Eiffel sequential classes in a parallel context, with a transparent gain in performances for features using our data structure walking abstractions.

However our prototype is just a first step demonstrating the interest of programming DMPCs at the right level, using the versatile features of OOL: we have shown there is an interesting intermediate level between full (semi-)automatic parallelizing compilers and raw message passing libraries. We currently try to extend it through experimentations with other domains, like sparse matrix operations, with promising results. But much more work is still necessary before we have some really operational and efficient object oriented environment available for the programming of DMPCs.

References

1. P. America. Pool-t: a parallel object-oriented programming. In A. Yonezawa, editor, *Object-Oriented Concurrent Programming*, pages 199–220, The MITI Press, Yonezawa A.Tokoro M., "Object-Oriented Concurrent Programming", Cambridge, MA, 1987.
2. Birger Andersen. Ellie language definition report. *Sigplan Notices*, 25(11):45–64, November 1990.
3. Françoise André, Jean-Louis Pazat, and Henry Thomas. Pandore : A system to manage Data Distribution. In *International Conference on Supercomputing*, ACM, June 11–15 1990.
4. Briand N. Bershad, Edward D. Lazowska, and Henry M. Levy. Presto: a system for object-oriented parallel programming. In *Software-Practice and Experience*, February 1988.
5. Andrew P. et al. Black. Emerald: a general-purpose programming language. *Software-Practice and Experience*, 21(1):91–118, January 1991.
6. D. Caromel. Concurrency and reusability: from sequential to parallel. *Journal of Object-Oriented Programming*, 3(3):34–42, September 1990.
7. Rohit Chandra, Anoop Gupta, and John L Hennessy. *COOL: a Language for Parallel Programming*, chapter 8. MIT Press, 1990.
8. A. A. Chien and W. J. Dally. Concurrent aggregates (ca). In *Proc. of the Second ACM Sigplan Symposium on Principles and Practice of Parallel Programming*, March 1991.
9. J.-F. Colin and J.-M. Geib. Eiffel classes for concurrent programming. In J. Bezivin et al. (eds.), editor, *TOOLS 4*, pages 23–34, Prentice Hall, 1991.
10. C. Jard and J.-M. Jézéquel. A multi-processor Estelle to C compiler to experiment distributed algorithms on parallel machines. In *Proc. of the 9th IFIP International Workshop on Protocol Specification, Testing and Verification, University of Twente, The Netherlands*, North Holland, 1989.

11. J.-M. Jézéquel. EPEE: an Eiffel environment to program distributed memory parallel computers. In *ECOOP'92 proceedings*, Lecture Notes in Computer Science, Springer Verlag, (also to appear in the Journal of Object Oriented Programming, 1993), July 1992.

12. J.-M. Jézéquel, F. André, and F. Bergheul. A parallel execution environment for a sequential object oriented language. In *ICS'92 proceedings*, ACM, July 1992.

13. M. D. McIlroy. Mass-produced software components. In P. Naur J.M. Buxton and B. Randell, editors, *Software Engineering Concepts and techniques (1968 NATO conference of Software Engineering)*, 1976.

14. B. Meyer. Reusability: the case for object-oriented design. *IEEE SOFTWARE*, (3):50–64, March 1987.

15. Bertrand Meyer. *Eiffel: The Language*. Prentice-Hall, 1992.

16. Bertrand Meyer. *Object-Oriented Software Construction*. Prentice-Hall, 1988.

17. MIMDizer user's guide. *Version 7.02*. Technical Report, Pacific Sierra Research Corporation, 1991.

18. Leslie G. Valiant. A bridging model for parallel computation. *CACM*, 33(8), Aug 1990.

19. P. Weis, M.V. Aponte, A. Laville, M. Mauny, and A. Suárez. *The CAML reference manual*. Rapport Technique 121, INRIA, septembre 1990.

20. Akinori Yonezawa, Jean-Pierre Briot, and Etsuya Shibayama. Object-oriented concurrent programming in ABCL/1. In *OOPSLA'86 Proceedings*, September 1986.

Design Patterns: Abstraction and Reuse of Object-Oriented Design

Erich Gamma[1*], Richard Helm[2], Ralph Johnson[3], John Vlissides[2]

[1] Taligent, Inc.
10725 N. De Anza Blvd., Cupertino, CA 95014-2000 USA

[2] I.B.M. Thomas J. Watson Research Center
P.O. Box 704, Yorktown Heights, NY 10598 USA

[3] Department of Computer Science
University of Illinois at Urbana-Champaign
1034 W. Springfield Ave., Urbana, IL 61801 USA

Abstract. We propose **design patterns** as a new mechanism for expressing object-oriented design experience. Design patterns identify, name, and abstract common themes in object-oriented design. They capture the intent behind a design by identifying objects, their collaborations, and the distribution of responsibilities. Design patterns play many roles in the object-oriented development process: they provide a common vocabulary for design, they reduce system complexity by naming and defining abstractions, they constitute a base of experience for building reusable software, and they act as building blocks from which more complex designs can be built. Design patterns can be considered reusable micro-architectures that contribute to an overall system architecture. We describe how to express and organize design patterns and introduce a catalog of design patterns. We also describe our experience in applying design patterns to the design of object-oriented systems.

1 Introduction

Design methods are supposed to promote good design, to teach new designers how to design well, and to standardize the way designs are developed. Typically, a design method comprises a set of syntactic notations (usually graphical) and a set of rules that govern how and when to use each notation. It will also describe problems that occur in a design, how to fix them, and how to evaluate a design. Studies of expert programmers for conventional languages, however, have shown that knowledge is not organized simply around syntax, but in larger conceptual structures such as algorithms, data structures and idioms [1, 7, 9, 27], and plans that indicate steps necessary to fulfill a particular goal [26]. It is likely that designers do not think about the notation they are using for recording the design. Rather, they look for patterns to match against plans, algorithms, data structures, and idioms they have learned in the past. Good designers, it appears, rely

---

* Work performed while at UBILAB, Union Bank of Switzerland, Zurich, Switzerland.

O.M. Nierstrasz (Ed.): ECOOP '93, LNCS 707, pp. 406-431, 1993.
© Springer-Verlag Berlin Heidelberg 1993

on large amounts of design experience, and this experience is just as important as the notations for recording designs and the rules for using those notations.

Our experience with the design of object-oriented systems and frameworks [15, 17, 22, 30, 31] bears out this observation. We have found that there exist idiomatic class and object structures that help make designs more flexible, reusable, and elegant. For example, the Model-View-Controller (MVC) paradigm from Smalltalk [19] is a design structure that separates representation from presentation. MVC promotes flexibility in the choice of views, independent of the model. Abstract factories [10] hide concrete subclasses from the applications that use them so that class names are not hard-wired into an application.

Well-defined design structures like these have a positive impact on software development. A software architect who is familiar with a good set of design structures can apply them immediately to design problems without having to rediscover them. Design structures also facilitate the reuse of successful architectures—expressing proven techniques as design structures makes them more readily accessible to developers of new systems. Design structures can even improve the documentation and maintenance of existing systems by furnishing an explicit specification of class and object interactions and their underlying intent.

To this end we propose **design patterns**, a new mechanism for expressing design structures. Design patterns identify, name, and abstract common themes in object-oriented design. They preserve design information by capturing the intent behind a design. They identify classes, instances, their roles, collaborations, and the distribution of responsibilities. Design patterns have many uses in the object-oriented development process:

- Design patterns provide a common vocabulary for designers to communicate, document, and explore design alternatives. They reduce system complexity by naming and defining abstractions that are above classes and instances. A good set of design patterns effectively raises the level at which one programs.
- Design patterns constitute a reusable base of experience for building reusable software. They distill and provide a means to reuse the design knowledge gained by experienced practitioners. Design patterns act as building blocks for constructing more complex designs; they can be considered **micro-architectures** that contribute to overall system architecture.
- Design patterns help reduce the learning time for a class library. Once a library consumer has learned the design patterns in one library, he can reuse this experience when learning a new class library. Design patterns help a novice perform more like an expert.
- Design patterns provide a target for the reorganization or refactoring of class hierarchies [23]. Moreover, by using design patterns early in the lifecycle, one can avert refactoring at later stages of design.

The major contributions of this paper are: a definition of design patterns, a means to describe them, a system for their classification, and most importantly, a catalog containing patterns we have discovered while building our own class libraries and patterns we have collected from the literature. This work has its roots in Gamma's thesis [11], which abstracted design patterns from the ET++ framework. Since then the work has been refined and extended based on our collective experience. Our thinking has also been influenced and inspired by discussions within the Architecture Handbook Workshops at recent OOPSLA conferences [3, 4].

This paper has two parts. The first introduces design patterns and explains techniques to describe them. Next we present a classification system that characterizes common aspects of patterns. This classification will serve to structure the catalog of patterns presented in the second part of this paper. We discuss how design patterns impact object-oriented programming and design. We also review related work.

The second part of this paper (the Appendix) describes our current catalog of design patterns. As we cannot include the complete catalog in this paper (it currently runs over 90 pages [12]), we give instead a brief summary and include a few abridged patterns. Each pattern in this catalog is representative of what we judge to be good object-oriented design. We have tried to reduce the subjectivity of this judgment by including only design patterns that have seen practical application. Every design pattern we have included works—most have been used at least twice and have either been discovered independently or have been used in a variety of application domains.

2 Design Patterns

A design pattern consists of three essential parts:

1. An abstract description of a class or object collaboration and its structure. The description is abstract because it concerns abstract design, not a particular design.
2. The issue in system design addressed by the abstract structure. This determines the circumstances in which the design pattern is applicable.
3. The consequences of applying the abstract structure to a system's architecture. These determine if the pattern should be applied in view of other design constraints.

Design patterns are defined in terms of object-oriented concepts. They are sufficiently abstract to avoid specifying implementation details, thereby ensuring wide applicability, but a pattern may provide hints about potential implementation issues.

We can think of a design pattern as a micro-architecture. It is an architecture in that it serves as a blueprint that may have several realizations. It is "micro" in that it defines something less than a complete application or library. To be useful, a design pattern should be applicable to more than a few problem domains; thus design patterns tend to be relatively small in size and scope. A design pattern can also be considered a transformation of system structure. It defines the context for the transformation, the change to be made, and the consequences of this transformation.

To help readers understand patterns, each entry in the catalog also includes detailed descriptions and examples. We use a template (Figure 1) to structure our descriptions and to ensure uniformity between entries in the catalog. This template also explains the motivation behind its structure. The Appendix contains three design patterns that use the template. We urge readers to study the patterns in the Appendix as they are referenced in the following text.

3 Categorizing Design Patterns

Design patterns vary in their granularity and level of abstraction. They are numerous and have common properties. Because there are many design patterns, we need a way to organize them. This section introduces a classification system for design patterns. This classification makes it easy to refer to families of related patterns, to learn the patterns in the catalog, and to find new patterns.

		Characterization		
		Creational	Structural	Behavioral
Jurisdiction	Class	Factory Method	Adapter (class) Bridge (class)	Template Method
	Object	Abstract Factory Prototype Solitaire	Adapter (object) Bridge (object) Flyweight Glue Proxy	Chain of Responsibility Command Iterator (object) Mediator Memento Observer State Strategy
	Compound	Builder	Composite Wrapper	Interpreter Iterator (compound) Walker

Table 1. Design Pattern Space

We can think of the set of all design patterns in terms of two orthogonal criteria, **jurisdiction** and **characterization**. Table 1 organizes our current set of patterns according to these criteria.

Jurisdiction is the domain over which a pattern applies. Patterns having **class** jurisdiction deal with relationships between base classes and their subclasses;

DESIGN PATTERN NAME   Jurisdiction Characterization

What is the pattern's name and classification? The name should convey the pattern's essence succinctly. A good name is vital, as it will become part of the design vocabulary.

Intent

What does the design pattern do? What is its rationale and intent? What particular design issue or problem does it address?

Motivation

A scenario in which the pattern is applicable, the particular design problem or issue the pattern addresses, and the class and object structures that address this issue. This information will help the reader understand the more abstract description of the pattern that follows.

Applicability

What are the situations in which the design pattern can be applied? What are examples of poor designs that the pattern can address? How can one recognize these situations?

Participants

Describe the classes and/or objects participating in the design pattern and their responsibilities using CRC conventions [5].

Collaborations

Describe how the participants collaborate to carry out their responsibilities.

Diagram

A graphical representation of the pattern using a notation based on the Object Modeling Technique (OMT) [25], to which we have added method pseudo-code.

Consequences

How does the pattern support its objectives? What are the trade-offs and results of using the pattern? What does the design pattern objectify? What aspect of system structure does it allow to be varied independently?

Implementation

What pitfalls, hints, or techniques should one be aware of when implementing the pattern? Are there language-specific issues?

Examples

This section presents examples from real systems. We try to include at least two examples from different domains.

See Also

What design patterns have closely related intent? What are the important differences? With which other patterns should this one be used?

Fig. 1. Basic Design Pattern Template

class jurisdiction covers static semantics. The **object** jurisdiction concerns relationships between peer objects. Patterns having **compound** jurisdiction deal with recursive object structures. Some patterns capture concepts that span jurisdictions. For example, iteration applies both to collections of objects (i.e., object jurisdiction) and to recursive object structures (compound jurisdiction). Thus there are both object and compound versions of the Iterator pattern.

Characterization reflects what a pattern does. Patterns can be characterized as either **creational**, **structural**, or **behavioral**. Creational patterns concern the process of object creation. Structural patterns deal with the composition of classes or objects. Behavioral patterns characterize the ways in which classes or objects interact and distribute responsibility.

The following sections describe pattern jurisdictions in greater detail for each characterization using examples from our catalog.

3.1 Class Jurisdiction

Class Creational. Creational patterns abstract how objects are instantiated by hiding the specifics of the creation process. They are useful because it is often undesirable to specify a class name explicitly when instantiating an object. Doing so limits flexibility; it forces the programmer to commit to a particular class instead of a particular protocol. If one avoids hard-coding the class, then it becomes possible to defer class selection to run-time.

Creational class patterns in particular defer some part of object creation to subclasses. An example is the Factory Method, an abstract method that is called by a base class but defined in subclasses. The subclass methods create instances whose type depends on the subclass in which each method is implemented. In this way the base class does not hard-code the class name of the created object. Factory Methods are commonly used to instantiate members in base classes with objects created by subclasses.

For example, an abstract Application class needs to create application-specific documents that conform to the Document type. Application instantiates these Document objects by calling the factory method DoMakeDocument. This method is overridden in classes derived from Application. The subclass DrawApplication, say, overrides DoMakeDocument to return a DrawDocument object.

Class Structural. Structural class patterns use inheritance to compose protocols or code. As a simple example, consider using multiple inheritance to mix two or more classes into one. The result is an amalgam class that unites the semantics of the base classes. This trivial pattern is quite useful in making independently-developed class libraries work together [15].

Another example is the class-jurisdictional form of the Adapter pattern. In general, an Adapter makes one interface (the adaptee's) conform to another, thereby providing a uniform abstraction of different interfaces. A class Adapter accomplishes this by inheriting privately from an adaptee class. The Adapter then expresses its interface in terms of the adaptee's.

Class Behavioral. Behavioral class patterns capture how classes cooperate with their subclasses to fulfill their semantics. Template Method is a simple and well-known behavioral class pattern [32]. Template methods define algorithms step by step. Each step can invoke an abstract method (which the subclass must define) or a base method. The purpose of a template method is to provide an abstract definition of an algorithm. The subclass must implement specific behavior to provide the services required by the algorithm.

3.2 Object Jurisdiction

Object patterns all apply various forms of non-recursive object composition. Object composition represents the most powerful form of reusability—a collection of objects are most easily reused through variations on how they are composed rather than how they are subclassed.

Object Creational. Creational object patterns abstract how sets of objects are created. The Abstract Factory pattern (page 18) is a creational object pattern. It describes how to create "product" objects through an generic interface. Subclasses may manufacture specialized versions or compositions of objects as permitted by this interface. In turn, clients can use abstract factories to avoid making assumptions about what classes to instantiate. Factories can be composed to create larger factories whose structure can be modified at run-time to change the semantics of object creation. The factory may manufacture a custom composition of instances, a shared or one-of-a-kind instance, or anything else that can be computed at run-time, so long as it conforms to the abstract creation protocol.

For example, consider a user interface toolkit that provides two types of scroll bars, one for Motif and another for Open Look. An application programmer may not want to hard-code one or the other into the application—the choice of scroll bar will be determined by, say, an environment variable. The code that creates the scroll bar can be encapsulated in the class Kit, an abstract factory that abstracts the specific type of scroll bar to instantiate. Kit defines a protocol for creating scroll bars and other user interface elements. Subclasses of Kit redefine operations in the protocol to return specialized types of scroll bars. A MotifKit's scroll bar operation would instantiate and return a Motif scroll bar, while the corresponding OpenLookKit operation would return an Open Look scroll bar.

Object Structural. Structural object patterns describe ways to assemble objects to realize new functionality. The added flexibility inherent in object composition stems from the ability to change the composition at run-time, which is impossible with static class composition[4].

Proxy is an example of a structural object pattern. A proxy acts as a convenient surrogate or placeholder for another object. A proxy can be used as a

---

[4] However, object models that support dynamic inheritance, most notably Self [29], are as flexible as object composition in theory.

local representative for an object in a different address space (remote proxy), to represent a large object that should be loaded on demand (virtual proxy), or to protect access to the original object (protected proxy). Proxies provide a level of indirection to particular properties of objects. Thus they can restrict, enhance, or alter an object's properties.

The Flyweight pattern is concerned with object sharing. Objects are shared for at least two reasons: efficiency and consistency. Applications that use large quantities of objects must pay careful attention to the cost of each object. Substantial savings can accrue by sharing objects instead of replicating them. However, objects can only be shared if they do not define context-dependent state. Flyweights have no context-dependent state. Any additional information they need to perform their task is passed to them when needed. With no context-dependent state, flyweights may be shared freely. Moreover, it may be necessary to ensure that all copies of an object stay consistent when one of the copies changes. Sharing provides an automatic way to maintain this consistency.

Object Behavioral. Behavioral object patterns describe how a group of peer objects cooperate to perform a task that no single object can carry out by itself. For example, patterns such as Mediator and Chain of Responsibility abstract control flow. They call for objects that exist solely to redirect the flow of messages. The redirection may simply notify another object, or it may involve complex computation and buffering. The Observer pattern abstracts the synchronization of state or behavior. Entities that are co-dependent to the extent that their state must remain synchronized may exploit Observer. The classic example is the model-view pattern, in which multiple views of the model are notified whenever the model's state changes.

The Strategy pattern (page 21) objectifies an algorithm. For example, a text composition object may need to support different line breaking algorithms. It is infeasible to hard-wire all such algorithms into the text composition class and subclasses. An alternative is to objectify different algorithms and provide them as **Compositor** subclasses. The interface for Compositors is defined by the abstract Compositor class, and its derived classes provide different layout strategies, such as simple line breaks or full page justification. Instances of the Compositor subclasses can be coupled with the text composition at run-time to provide the appropriate text layout. Whenever a text composition has to find line breaks, it forwards this responsibility to its current Compositor object.

3.3 Compound Jurisdiction

In contrast to patterns having object jurisdiction, which concern peer objects, patterns with compound jurisdiction affect recursive object structures.

Compound Creational. Creational compound patterns are concerned with the creation of recursive object structures. An example is the Builder pattern. A Builder base class defines a generic interface for incrementally constructing recursive object structures. The Builder hides details of how objects in the structure are created, represented, and composed so that changing or adding a new representation only requires defining a new Builder class. Clients will be unaffected by changes to Builder.

Consider a parser for the RTF (Rich Text Format) document exchange format that should be able to perform multiple format conversions. The parser might convert RTF documents into (1) plain ASCII text and (2) a text object that can be edited in a text viewer object. The problem is how to make the parser independent of these different conversions.

The solution is to create an RTFReader class that takes a Builder object as an argument. The RTFReader knows how to parse the RTF format and notifies the Builder whenever it recognizes text or an RTF control word. The builder is responsible for creating the corresponding data structure. It separates the parsing algorithm from the creation of the structure that results from the parsing process. The parsing algorithm can then be reused to create any number of different data representations. For example, an ASCII builder ignores all notifications except plain text, while a Text builder uses the notifications to create a more complex text structure.

Compound Structural. Structural compound patterns capture techniques for structuring recursive object structures. A simple example is the Composite pattern. A Composite is a recursive composition of one or more other Composites. A Composite treats multiple, recursively composed objects as a single object.

The Wrapper pattern (page 24) describes how to flexibly attach additional properties and services to an object. Wrappers can be nested recursively and can therefore be used to compose more complex object structures. For example, a Wrapper containing a single user interface component can add decorations such as borders, shadows, scroll bars, or services like scrolling and zooming. To do this, the Wrapper must conform to the interface of its wrapped component and forward messages to it. The Wrapper can perform additional actions (such as drawing a border around the component) either before or after forwarding a message.

Compound Behavioral. Finally, behavioral compound patterns deal with behavior in recursive object structures. Iteration over a recursive structure is a common activity captured by the Iterator pattern. Rather than encoding and distributing the traversal strategy in each class in the structure, it can be extracted and implemented in an Iterator class. Iterators objectify traversal algorithms over recursive structures. Different iterators can implement pre-order, in-order, or post-order traversals. All that is required is that nodes in the structure provide services to enumerate their sub-structures. This avoids hard-wiring traversal algorithms throughout the classes of objects in a composite structure. Iterators may be replaced at run-time to provide alternative traversals.

4 Experience with Design Patterns

We have applied design patterns to the design and construction of a several systems. We briefly describe two of these systems and our experience.

4.1 ET++SwapsManager

The ET++SwapsManager [10] is a highly interactive tool that lets traders value, price, and perform what-if analyses for a financial instrument called a swap. During this project the developers had to first learn the ET++ class library, then implement the tool, and finally design a framework for creating "calculation engines" for different financial instruments. While teaching ET++ we emphasized not only learning the class library but also describing the applied design patterns. We noticed that design patterns reduced the effort required to learn ET++. Patterns also proved helpful during development in design and code reviews. Patterns provided a common vocabulary to discuss a design. Whenever we encountered problems in the design, patterns helped us explore design alternatives and find solutions.

4.2 QOCA: A Constraint Solving Toolkit

QOCA (Quadratic Optimization Constraint Architecture) [14, 15] is a new object-oriented constraint-solving toolkit developed at IBM Research. QOCA leverages recent results in symbolic computation and geometry to support efficient incremental and interactive constraint manipulation. QOCA's architecture is designed to be flexible. It permits experimentation with different classes of constraints and domains (e.g., reals, booleans, etc.), different constraint-solving algorithms for these domains, and different representations (doubles, infinite precision) for objects in these domains. QOCA's object-oriented design allows parts of the system to be varied independently of others. This flexibility was achieved, for example, by using Strategy patterns to factor out constraint solving algorithms and Bridges to factor out domains and representations of variables. In addition, the Observable pattern is used to propagate notifications when variables change their values.

4.3 Summary of Observations

The following points summarize the major observations we have made while applying design patterns:

- Design patterns motivate developers to go beyond concrete objects; that is, they objectify concepts that are not immediately apparent as objects in the problem domain.
- Choosing intuitive class names is important but also difficult. We have found that design patterns can help name classes. In the ET++SwapsManager's calculation engine framework we encoded the name of the design pattern

in the class name (for example CalculationStrategy or TableAdaptor). This convention results in longer class names, but it gives clients of these classes a hint about their purpose.

- We often apply design patterns *after* the first implementation of an architecture to improve its design. For example, it is easier to apply the Strategy pattern after the initial implementation to create objects for more abstract notions like a calculation engine or constraint solver. Patterns were also used as targets for class refactorings. We often find ourselves saying, "Make this part of a class into a Strategy," or, "Let's split the implementation portion of this class into a Bridge."

- Presenting design patterns together with examples of their application turned out to be an effective way to teach object-oriented design by example.

- An important issue with any reuse technology is how a reusable component can be adapted to create a problem-specific component. Design patterns are particularly suited to reuse because they are abstract. Though a concrete class structure may not be reusable, the design pattern underlying it often is.

- Design patterns also reduce the effort required to learn a class library. Each class library has a certain design "culture" characterized by the set of patterns used implicitly by its developers. A specific design pattern is typically reused in different places in the library. A client should therefore learn these patterns as a first step in learning the library. Once they are familiar with the patterns, they can reuse this understanding. Moreover, because some patterns appear in other class libraries, it is possible to reuse the knowledge about patterns when learning other libraries as well.

5 Related Work

Design patterns are an approach to software reuse. Krueger [20] introduces the following taxonomy to characterize different reuse approaches: software component reuse, software schemas, application generators, transformation systems, and software architectures. Design patterns are related to both software schemas and reusable software architectures. Software schemas emphasize reusing abstract algorithms and data structures. These abstractions are represented formally so they can be instantiated automatically. The Paris system [18] is representative of schema technology. Design patterns are higher-level than schemas; they focus on design structures at the level of collaborating classes and not at the algorithmic level. In addition, design patterns are not formal descriptions and cannot be instantiated directly. We therefore prefer to view design patterns as reusable software architectures. However, the examples Krueger lists in this category (blackboard architectures for expert systems, adaptable database subsystems) are all coarse-grained architectures. Design patterns are finer-grained and therefore can be characterized as reusable micro-architectures.

Most research into patterns in the software engineering community has been geared towards building knowledge-based assistants for automating the application of patterns for synthesis (that is, to write programs) and analysis (in debugging, for example) [13, 24]. The major difference between our work and that of the knowledge-based assistant community is that design patterns encode higher-level expertise. Their work has tended to focus on patterns like enumeration and selection, which can be expressed directly as reusable components in most existing object-oriented languages. We believe that characterizing and cataloging higher-level patterns that designers already use informally has an immediate benefit in teaching and communicating designs.

A common approach for reusing object-oriented software architectures are object-oriented frameworks [32]. A framework is a codified architecture for a problem domain that can be adapted to solve specific problems. A framework makes it possible to reuse an architecture together with a partial concrete implementation. In contrast to frameworks, design patterns allow only the reuse of abstract micro-architectures without a concrete implementation. However, design patterns can help define and develop frameworks. Mature frameworks usually reuse several design patterns. An important distinction between frameworks and design patterns is that frameworks are implemented in a programming language. Our patterns are ways of *using* a programming language. In this sense frameworks are more concrete than design patterns.

Design patterns are also related to the idioms introduced by Coplien [7]. These idioms are concrete design solutions in the context of C++. Coplien "focuses on idioms that make C++ programs more expressive." In contrast, design patterns are more abstract and higher-level than idioms. Patterns try to abstract design rather than programming techniques. Moreover, design patterns are usually independent of the implementation language.

There has been interest recently within the object-oriented community [8] in pattern languages for the architecture of buildings and communities as advocated by Christopher Alexander in *The Timeless Way of Building* [2]. Alexander's patterns consist of three parts:

- A context that describes when a pattern is applicable.
- The problem (or "system of conflicting forces") that the pattern resolves in that context.
- A configuration that describes physical relationships that solve the problem.

Both design patterns and Alexander's patterns share the notion of context/problem/configuration, but our patterns currently do not form a complete system of patterns and so do not strictly define a pattern language. This may be because object-oriented design is still a young technology—we may not have had enough experience in what constitutes good design to extract design patterns that cover all phases of the design process. Or this may be simply because the problems encountered in software design are different from those found in architecture and are not amenable to solution by pattern languages.

Recently, Johnson has advocated pattern languages to describe how to use use object-oriented frameworks [16]. Johnson uses a pattern language to explain how to extend and customize the Hotdraw drawing editor framework. However, these patterns are not design patterns; they are more descriptions of how to reuse existing components and frameworks instead of rules for generating new designs.

Coad's recent paper on object-oriented patterns [6] is also motivated by Alexander's work but is more closely related to our work. The paper has seven patterns: "Broadcast" is the same as Observer, but the other patterns are different from ours. In general, Coad's patterns seem to be more closely related to analysis than design. Design patterns like Wrapper and Flyweight are unlikely to be generated naturally during analysis unless the analyst knows these patterns well and thinks in terms of them. Coad's patterns could naturally arise from a simple attempt to model a problem. In fact, it is hard to see how any large model could avoid using patterns like "State Across a Collection" (which explains how to use aggregation) or "Behavior Across a Collection" (which describes how to distribute responsibility among objects in an aggregate). The patterns in our catalog are typical of a mature object-oriented design, one that has departed from the original analysis model in an attempt to make a system of reusable objects. In practice, both types of patterns are probably useful.

6 Conclusion

Design patterns have revolutionized the way we think about, design, and teach object-oriented systems. We have found them applicable in many stages of the design process—initial design, reuse, refactoring. They have given us a new level of abstraction for system design.

New levels of abstraction often afford opportunities for increased automation. We are investigating how interactive tools can take advantage of design patterns. One of these tools lets a user explore the space of objects in a running program and watch their interaction. Through observation the user may discover existing or entirely new patterns; the tool lets the user record and catalog his observations. The user may thus gain a better understanding of the application, the libraries on which it is based, and design in general.

Design patterns may have an even more profound impact on how object-oriented systems are designed than we have discussed. Common to most patterns is that they permit certain aspects of a system to be varied independently. This leads to thinking about design in terms of "What aspect of a design should be variable?" Answers to this question lead to certain applicable design patterns, and their application leads subsequently to modification of a design. We refer to this design activity as **variation-oriented design** and discuss it more fully in the catalog of patterns [12].

But some caveats are in order. Design patterns should not be applied indiscriminately. They typically achieve flexibility and variability by introducing additional levels of indirection and can therefore complicate a design. A design pattern should only be applied when the flexibility it affords is actually needed. The consequences described in a pattern help determine this. Moreover, one is often tempted to brand any new programming trick a new design pattern. A true design pattern will be non-trivial and will have had more than one application. We hope that the design patterns described in this paper and in the companion catalog will provide the object-oriented community both a common design terminology and a repertoire of reusable designs. Moreover, we hope the catalog will motivate others to describe their systems in terms of design patterns and develop their own design patterns for others to reuse.

7 Acknowledgements

The authors wish to thank Doug Lea and Kent Beck for detailed comments and discussions about this work, and Bruce Anderson and the participants of the Architecture Handbook workshops at OOPSLA '91 and '92.

References

1. B. Adelson and Soloway E. The role of domain experience in software design. *IEEE Transactions on Software Engineering*, 11(11):1351–1360, 1985.
2. Christopher Alexander. *The Timeless Way of Building*. Oxford University Press, New York, 1979.
3. Association for Computing Machinery. *Addendum to the Proceedings, Object-Oriented Programming Systems, Languages, and Applications Conference*, Phoenix, AZ, October 1991.
4. Association for Computing Machinery. *Addendum to the Proceedings, Object-Oriented Programming Systems, Languages, and Applications Conference*, Vancouver, British Columbia, October 1992.
5. Kent Beck and Ward Cunningham. A laboratory for teaching object-oriented thinking. In *Object-Oriented Programming Systems, Languages, and Applications Conference Proceedings*, pages 1–6, New Orleans, LA, October 1989.
6. Peter Coad. Object-oriented patterns. *Communications of the ACM*, 35(9):152–159, September 1992.
7. James O. Coplien. *Advanced C++ Programming Styles and Idioms*. Addison-Wesley, Reading, Massachusetts, 1992.
8. Ward Cunningham and Kent Beck. Constructing abstractions for object-oriented applications. Technical Report CR-87-25, Computer Research Laboratory, Tektronix, Inc., 1987.
9. Bill Curtis. Cognitive issues in reusing software artifacts. In Ted J. Biggerstaff and Alan J. Perlis, editors, *Software Reusability, Volume II*, pages 269–287. Addison-Wesley, 1989.
10. Thomas Eggenschwiler and Erich Gamma. The ET++SwapsManager: Using object technology in the financial engineering domain. In *Object-Oriented Programming Systems, Languages, and Applications Conference Proceedings*, pages 166–178, Vancouver, British Columbia, October 1992.
11. Erich Gamma. *Objektorientierte Software-Entwicklung am Beispiel von ET++: Design-Muster, Klassenbibliothek, Werkzeuge*. Springer-Verlag, Berlin, 1992.
12. Erich Gamma, Richard Helm, Ralph Johnson, and John Vlissides. A catalog of object-oriented design patterns. Technical Report in preparation, IBM Research Division, 1992.

13. Mehdi T. Harandi and Frank H. Young. Software design using reusable algorithm abstraction. In *In Proc. 2nd IEEE/BCS Conf. on Software Engineering*, pages 94–97, 1985.

14. Richard Helm, Tien Huynh, Catherine Lassez, and Kim Marriott. A linear constraint technology for user interfaces. In *Graphics Interface*, pages 301–309, Vancouver, British Columbia, 1992.

15. Richard Helm, Tien Huynh, Kim Marriott, and John Vlissides. An object-oriented architecture for constraint-based graphical editing. In *Proceedings of the Third Eurographics Workshop on Object-Oriented Graphics*, pages 1–22, Champéry, Switzerland, October 1992. Also available as IBM Research Division Technical Report RC 18524 (79392).

16. Ralph Johnson. Documenting frameworks using patterns. In *Object-Oriented Programming Systems, Languages, and Applications Conference Proceedings*, pages 63–76, Vancouver, BC, October 1992.

17. Ralph E. Johnson, Carl McConnell, and J. Michael Lake. The RTL system: A framework for code optimization. In Robert Giegerich and Susan L. Graham, editors, *Code Generation—Concepts, Tools, Techniques. Proceedings of the International Workshop on Code Generation*, pages 255–274, Dagstuhl, Germany, 1992. Springer-Verlag.

18. S. Katz, C.A. Richter, and K.-S. The. Paris: A system for reusing partially interpreted schemas. In *Proc. of the Ninth International Conference on Software Engineering*, 1987.

19. Glenn E. Krasner and Stephen T. Pope. A cookbook for using the model-view controller user interface paradigm in Smalltalk-80. *Journal of Object-Oriented Programming*, 1(3):26–49, August/September 1988.

20. Charles W. Krueger. Software reuse. *ACM Computing Surveys*, 24(2), June 1992.

21. Mark A. Linton. Encapsulating a C++ library. In *Proceedings of the 1992 USENIX C++ Conference*, pages 57–66, Portland, OR, August 1992.

22. Mark A. Linton, John M. Vlissides, and Paul R. Calder. Composing user interfaces with InterViews. *Computer*, 22(2):8–22, February 1989.

23. William F. Opdyke and Ralph E. Johnson. Refactoring: An aid in designing application frameworks and evolving object-oriented systems. In *SOOPPA Conference Proceedings*, pages 145–161, Marist College, Poughkeepsie, NY, September 1990.

24. Charles Rich and Richard C. Waters. Formalizing reusable software components in the programmer's apprentice. In Ted J. Biggerstaff and Alan J. Perlis, editors, *Software Reusability, Volume II*, pages 313–343. Addison-Wesley, 1989.

25. James Rumbaugh, Michael Blaha, William Premerlani, Frederick Eddy, and William Lorenson. *Object-Oriented Modeling and Design*. Prentice Hall, Englewood Cliffs, New Jersey, 1991.

26. Elliot Soloway and Kate Ehrlich. Empirical studies of programming knowledge. *IEEE Transactions on Software Engineering*, 10(5), September 1984.

27. James C. Spohrer and Elliot Soloway. Novice mistakes: Are the folk wisdoms correct? *Communications of the ACM*, 29(7):624–632, July 1992.

28. ParcPlace Systems. *ParcPlace Systems, Objectworks/Smalltalk Release 4 Users Guide*. Mountain View, California, 1990.

29. David Ungar and Randall B. Smith. Self: The power of simplicity. In *Object-Oriented Programming Systems, Languages, and Applications Conference Proceedings*, pages 227–242, Orlando, Florida, October 1987.

30. John M. Vlissides and Mark A. Linton. Unidraw: A framework for building domain-specific graphical editors. *ACM Transactions on Information Systems*, 8(3):237-268, July 1990.

31. André Weinand, Erich Gamma, and Rudolf Marty. ET++—An object-oriented application framework in C++. In *Object-Oriented Programming Systems, Languages, and Applications Conference Proceedings*, pages 46-57, San Diego, CA, September 1988.

32. Rebecca Wirfs-Brock and Ralph E. Johnson. A survey of current research in object-oriented design. *Communications of the ACM*, 33(9):104-124, 1990.

A Catalog Overview

The following summarizes the patterns in our current catalog.

Abstract Factory provides an interface for creating generic product objects. It removes dependencies on concrete product classes from clients that create product objects.

Adapter makes the protocol of one class conform to the protocol of another.

Bridge separates an abstraction from its implementation. The abstraction may vary its implementations transparently and dynamically.

Builder provides a generic interface for incrementally constructing aggregate objects. A Builder hides details of how objects in the aggregate are created, represented, and composed.

Command objectifies the request for a service. It decouples the creator of the request for a service from the executor of that service.

Composite treats multiple, recursively-composed objects as a single object.

Chain of Responsibility defines a hierarchy of objects, typically arranged from more specific to more general, having responsibility for handling a request.

Factory Method lets base classes create instances of subclass-dependent objects.

Flyweight defines how objects can be shared. Flyweights support object abstraction at the finest granularity.

Glue defines a single point of access to objects in a subsystem. It provides a higher level of encapsulation for objects in the subsystem.

Interpreter defines how to represent the grammar, abstract syntax tree, and interpreter for simple languages.

Iterator objectifies traversal algorithms over object structures.

Mediator decouples and manages the collaboration between objects.

Memento opaquely encapsulates a snapshot of the internal state of an object and is used to restore the object to its original state.

Observer enforces synchronization, coordination, and consistency constraints between objects.

Prototype creates new objects by cloning a prototypical instance. Prototypes permit clients to install and configure dynamically the instances of particular classes they need to instantiate.

Proxy acts as a convenient surrogate or placeholder for another object. Proxies can restrict, enhance, or alter an object's properties.

Solitaire defines a one-of-a-kind object that provides access to unique or well-known services and variables.

State lets an object change its behavior when its internal state changes, effectively changing its class.

Strategy objectifies an algorithm or behavior.

Template Method implements an abstract algorithm, deferring specific steps to subclass methods.

Walker centralizes operations on object structures in one class so that these operations can be changed independently of the classes defining the structure.

Wrapper attaches additional services, properties, or behavior to objects. Wrappers can be nested recursively to attach multiple properties to objects.

ABSTRACT FACTORY Object Creational

Intent

Abstract Factory provides an interface for creating generic product objects. It removes dependencies on concrete product classes from clients that create product objects.

Motivation

Consider a user interface toolkit that supports multiple standard look-and-feels, say, Motif and Open Look, and provides different scroll bars for each. It is undesirable to hard-code dependencies on either standard into the application—the choice of look-and-feel and hence scroll bar may be deferred until run-time. Specifying the class of scroll bar limits flexibility and reusability by forcing a commitment to a particular class instead of a particular protocol. An Abstract Factory avoids this commitment.

An abstract base class WindowKit declares services for creating scroll bars and other controls. Controls for Motif and Open Look are derived from common abstract classes. For each look-and-feel there is a concrete subclass of WindowKit that defines services to create the appropriate control. For example, the Create-ScrollBar() operation on the MotifKit would instantiate and return a Motif scroll bar, while the corresponding operation on the OpenLookKit returns an Open Look scroll bar. Clients access a specific kit through the interface declared by the Window-Kit class, and they access the controls created by a kit only by their generic interface.

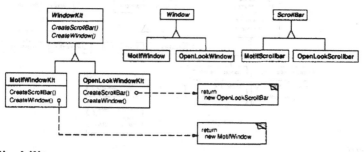

Applicability

When the classes of the product objects are variable, and dependencies on these classes must be removed from a client application.

When variations on the creation, composition, or representation of aggregate objects or subsystems must be removed from a client application. Differences in configuration can be obtained by using different concrete factories. Clients do not explicitly create and configure the aggregate or subsystem but defer this responsibility to an AbstractFactory class. Clients instead call a method of the Abstract-Factory that returns an object providing access to the aggregate or subsystem.

Participants

- **AbstractFactory**

  - declares a generic interface for operations that create generic product objects.

- **ConcreteFactory**

  - defines the operations that create specific product objects.

- **GenericProduct**

  - declares a generic interface for product objects.

- **SpecificProduct**

  - defines a product object created by the corresponding concrete factory.

  - all product classes must conform to the generic product interface.

Collaborations

- Usually a single instance of a ConcreteFactory class is created at run-time. This concrete factory creates product objects having a particular implementation. To use different product objects, clients must be configured to use a different concrete factory.
- AbstractFactory defers creation of product objects to its ConcreteFactory subclasses.

Diagram

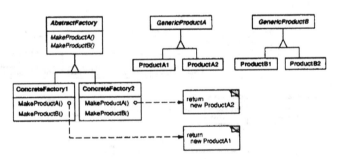

Consequences

Abstract Factory provides a focus during development for changing and controlling the types of objects created by clients. Because a factory objectifies the responsibility for and the process of creating product objects, it isolates clients from implementation classes. Only generic interfaces are visible to clients. Implementation class names do not appear in client code. Clients can be defined and implemented solely in terms of protocols instead of classes.

Abstract factories that encode class names in operation signatures can be difficult to extend with new kinds of product objects. This can require redeclaring the AbstractFactory and all ConcreteFactories. Abstract factories can be composed with subordinate factory objects. Responsibility for creating objects is delegated to these sub-factories. Composition of abstract factories provides a simple way to extend the kinds of objects a factory is responsible for creating.

Examples

InterViews uses the "Kit" suffix [21] to denote abstract factory classes. It defines WidgetKit and DialogKit abstract factories for generating look-and-feel-specific user interface objects. InterViews also includes a LayoutKit that generates different composition objects depending on the layout desired.

ET++ [31] employs the Abstract Factory pattern to achieve portability across different window systems (X Windows and SunView, for example). The WindowSystem abstract base class defines the interface for creating objects representing window system resources (for example, MakeWindow, MakeFont, MakeColor). Concrete subclasses implement the interfaces for a specific window system. At runtime ET++ creates an instance of a concrete WindowSystem subclass that creates system resource objects.

Implementation

A novel implementation is possible in Smalltalk. Because classes are first-class objects, it is not necessary to have distinct ConcreteFactory subclasses to create the variations in products. Instead, it is possible to store classes that create these products in variables inside a concrete factory. These classes create new instances on behalf of the concrete factory. This technique permits variation in product objects at finer levels of granularity than by using distinct concrete factories. Only the classes kept in variables need to be changed.

See Also

Factory Method: Abstract Factories are often implemented using Factory Methods.

Intent

A Strategy objectifies an algorithm or behavior, allowing the algorithm or behavior to be varied independently of its clients.

Motivation

There are many algorithms for breaking a text stream into lines. It is impossible to hard-wire all such algorithms into the classes that require them. Different algorithms might be appropriate at different times.

One way to address this problem is by defining separate classes that encapsulate the different linebreaking algorithms. An algorithm objectified in this way is called a Strategy. InterViews [22] and ET++ [31] use this approach.

Suppose a Composition class is responsible for maintaining and updating the line breaks of text displayed in a text viewer. Linebreaking strategies are not implemented by the class Composition. Instead, they are implemented separately by subclasses of the Compositor class. Compositor subclasses implement different strategies as follows:

- **SimpleCompositor** implements a simple strategy that determines line breaks one at a time.

- **TeXCompositor** implements the TEXalgorithm for finding line breaks. This strategy tries to optimize line breaks globally, that is, one paragraph at a time.

- **ArrayCompositor** implements a strategy that is used not for text but for breaking a collection of icons into rows. It selects breaks so that each row has a fixed number of items.

A Composition maintains a reference to a Compositor object. Whenever a Composition is required to find line breaks, it forwards this responsibility to its current Compositor object. The client of Composition specifies which Compositor should be used by installing the corresponding Compositor into the Composition (see the diagram below).

Applicability

Whenever an algorithm or behavior should be selectable and replaceable at runtime, or when there exist variations in the implementation of the algorithm, reflecting different space-time tradeoffs, for example.

Use a Strategy whenever many related classes differ only in their behavior. Strategies provide a way to configure a single class with one of many behaviors.

Participants

- **Strategy**

    - objectifies and encapsulates an algorithm or behavior.

- **StrategyContext**

    - maintains a reference to a Strategy object.
    - maintains the state manipulated by the Strategy.
    - can be configured by passing it an appropriate Strategy object.

Collaborations

- Strategy manipulates the StrategyContext. The StrategyContext normally passes itself as an argument to the Strategy's methods. This allows the Strategy to call back the StrategyContext as required.
- StrategyContext forwards requests from its clients to the Strategy. Usually clients pass Strategy objects to the StrategyContext. Thereafter clients only interact with the StrategyContext. There is often a family of Strategy classes from which a client can choose.

Diagram

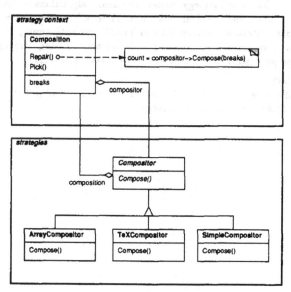

Consequences

Strategies can define a family of policies that a StrategyContext can reuse. Separating a Strategy from its context increases reusability, because the Strategy may vary independently from the StrategyContext.

Variations on an algorithm can also be implemented with inheritance, that is, with an abstract class and subclasses that implement different behaviors. However, this hard-wires the implementation into a specific class; it is not possible to change behaviors dynamically. This results in many related classes that differ only in some behavior. It is often better to break out the variations of behavior into their own classes. The Strategy pattern thus increases modularity by localizing complex behavior. The typical alternative is to scatter conditional statements throughout the code that select the behavior to be performed.

Implementation

The interface of a Strategy and the common functionality among Strategies is often factored out in an abstract class. Strategies should avoid maintaining state across invocations so that they can be used repeatedly and in multiple contexts.

Examples

In the RTL System for compiler code optimization [17], Strategies define different register allocation schemes (RegisterAllocator) and different instruction set scheduling policies (RISCscheduler, CISCscheduler). This gives flexibility in targeting the optimizer for different machine architectures.

The ET++SwapsManager calculation engine framework [10] computes prices for different financial instruments. Its key abstractions are Instrument and Yield-Curve. Different instruments are implemented as subclasses of Instrument. The YieldCurve calculates discount factors to present value future cash flows. Both of these classes delegate some behavior to Strategy objects. The framework provides a family of Strategy classes that define algorithms to generate cash flows, to value swaps, and to calculate discount factors. New calculation engines are created by parameterizing Instrument and YieldCurve with appropriate Strategy objects. This approach supports mixing and matching existing Strategy implementations while permitting the definition of new Strategy objects.

See Also

Walker often implements algorithms over recursive object structures. Walkers can be considered compound strategies.

Intent

A Wrapper attaches additional services, properties, or behavior to objects. Wrappers can be nested recursively to attach multiple properties to objects.

Motivation

Sometimes it is desirable to attach properties to individual objects instead of classes. In a graphical user interface toolkit, for example, properties such as borders or services like scrolling should be freely attachable to any user interface component.

One way to attach properties to components is via inheritance. Inheriting a border from a base class will give all instances of its derived classes a border. This is inflexible because the choice of border is made statically. It is more flexible to let a client decide how and when to decorate the component with a border.

This can be achieved by enclosing the component in another object that adds the border. The enclosing object, which must be transparent to clients of the component, is called a Wrapper. This transparency is the key for nesting Wrappers recursively to construct more complex user interface components. A Wrapper forwards requests to its enclosed user interface component. The Wrapper may perform additional actions before or after forwarding the request, such as drawing a border around a user interface component.

Typical properties or services provided by user interface Wrappers are:

− decorations like borders, shadows, or scroll bars; or

− services like scrolling or zooming.

The following diagram illustrates the composition of a TextView with a Border-Wrapper and a ScrollWrapper to produce a bordered, scrollable TextView.

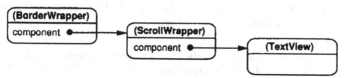

Applicability

When properties or behaviors should be attachable to individual objects dynamically and transparently.

When there is a need to extend classes in an inheritance hierarchy. Rather than modifying their base class, instances are enclosed in a Wrapper that adds the additional behavior and properties. Wrappers thus provide an alternative to extending the base class without requiring its modification. This is of particular concern when the base class comes from a class library that cannot be modified.

Participants

- **Component**
  - the object to which additional properties or behaviors are attached.

- **Wrapper**
  - encapsulates and enhances its Component. It defines an interface that conforms to its Component's.
  - Wrapper maintains a reference to its Component.

Collaborations

- Wrapper forwards requests to its Component. It may optionally perform additional operations before and after forwarding the request.

Diagram

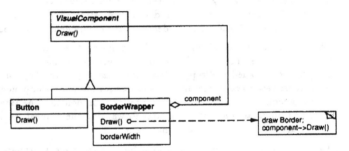

Consequences

Using Wrappers to add properties is more flexible than using inheritance. With Wrappers, properties can be attached and detached at run-time simply by changing the Wrapper. Inheritance would require creating a new class for each property composition (for example, BorderdScrollableTextView, BorderedTextView). This clutters the name space of classes unnecessarily and should be avoided. Moreover, providing different Wrapper classes for a specific Component class allows mixing and matching behaviors and properties.

Examples

Most object-oriented user interface toolkits use Wrappers to add graphical embellishments to widgets. Examples include InterViews [22], ET++ [31], and the ParcPlace Smalltalk class library [28]. More exotic applications of Wrappers are the DebuggingGlyph from InterViews and the PassivityWrapper from ParcPlace Smalltalk. A DebuggingGlyph prints out debugging information before and after it forwards a layout request to its enclosed object. This trace information can be used to analyze and debug the layout behavior of objects in a complex object composition. The PassivityWrapper can enable or disable user interactions with the enclosed object.

Implementation

Implementation of a set of Wrapper classes is simplified by an abstract base class, which forwards all requests to its component. Derived classes can then override only those operations for which they want to add behavior. The abstract base class ensures that all other requests are passed automatically to the Component.

See Also

Adapter: A Wrapper is different from an Adapter, because a Wrapper only changes an object's properties and not its interface; an Adapter will give an object a completely new interface.

Composite: A Wrapper can be considered a degenerate Composite with only one component. However, a Wrapper adds additional services—it is not intented for object aggregation.

Objchart: Tangible Specification of Reactive Object Behavior*

Dipayan Gangopadhyay
I.B.M. Thomas J. Watson Research Center
P.O. Box 704, Yorktown Heights, NY 10598
dipayan@watson.ibm.com

Subrata Mitra
Department of Computer Science
University of Illinois at Urbana-Champaign
1304 West Springfield Avenue
Urbana, Illinois 61801, USA.
mitra@cs.uiuc.edu

Abstract

ObjChart is a new visual formalism to specify objects and their reactive behavior. A system is specified as a collection of asynchronously communicating objects arranged in a part-of hierarchy, where the reactive behavior of each object is described by a finite state machine. Value propagation is effected using *functional invariants* over attributes of objects. A compositional semantics for concurrent object behavior is sketched using the equational framework of Misra.

In contrast to other Object Oriented modeling notations, ObjChart uses object decomposition as the single refinement paradigm, maintains *orthogonality* between control flow and value propagation, introduces *Sequence* object which embodies structural induction, and allows tracing causality chains in time linear in the size of the system. ObjChart's minimality of notations and precise semantics make ObjChart models of systems coherent and executable.

1 Introduction

Specifying reactive systems is an important problem [Pnu86, Har87]. A large body of literature exists on various specification formalisms, for example see [MP92, CM89]. These, however, demand enough formal sophistication of a practitioner. CASE notations [Boo91, SM88], on the other hand, attempt to use pictorial descriptions to capture specifiers' conceptualization of a system under design. As Harel ([Har88a]) has eloquently argued, unless these pictorial notations are backed up by precise semantics, they remain only pretty pictures. Thus, combining the intuitive appeal of

---

*The term ObjChart was introduced in a video tutorial (Object-oriented paradigm, IEEE Video Press, No. 2096AV, May 1990).

O.M. Nierstrasz (Ed.): ECOOP '93, LNCS 707, pp. 432-457, 1993.
© Springer-Verlag Berlin Heidelberg 1993

visual notations with the precision of formal specification languages is an important goal.

Towards this end, we present ObjChart, a new set of visual notations for describing objects and their reactive behavior, and precise compositional semantics of behavior of ObjChart Objects.

In ObjChart formalism, a system under design is conceptualized by a set of concurrently interacting *objects* and a set of *relations* among these objects. Structurally, each object can have a set of attributes and a set of ports. An object can be decomposed into a hierarchy of constituent sub-objects. The attributes of an object or attributes of sibling objects (i.e., sub-objects within a common parent object) may be be related via *functional relations*. Each such relation is a set of functional constraints (invariants) over the related attributes.

The reactive behavior of each object is specified by associating an extended finite-state machine (FSM) with it. An FSM of an object captures the reactions of this object to received messages. Receipt of a message is treated as an event, which may cause a state transition, concomitantly initiating the reactions; reactions being asynchronous messages with limited scope. An object can send messages to itself, its immediate sub-objects, its parent object or to its ports. Ports of sibling objects can be connected by *behavioral relations*, each of which has an FSM controlling the message exchanges over these connected ports. Thus, a typical ObjChart model is a part-of hierarchy of objects with relations (both behavioral and functional) among siblings and the behavior of these objects is controlled by FSMs.

We provide compositional semantics for ObjChart objects. Although behavior of each object is controlled by a deterministic state machine, any composite object has non-deterministic behavior due to internal concurrency, with and among its sub-objects. Thus, the output reaction of a composite object cannot be expressed as a function of its input stimuli. We circumvent this problem by adopting Misra's framework of equational reasoning [Mis90]. Semantics of an ObjChart object is given by a set of equations relating functions on traces over a set of ports—i.e., sequences of observable messages received and sent by an object via these ports. Behavior of an object is the set of *smooth solutions* each of which is a trace obeying certain causality ordering[1].

Compared to the plethora of visual notations for Object-Oriented Analysis, the advantage of ObjChart formalism is that it comprises of only a minimal set of notations and the notations have precise semantics. Minimality and precision make ObjChart models *coherent and executable* – the latter property is the key to understanding and experimentation with objects and their behavior early in the analysis phase of system development. In fact, our rationale for naming ObjChart models as "tangible" is the fact that the models directly represent the conceptual entities visually and the inter-entity cause and effect relations can be perceived by observing the execution of the ObjChart models. Few of the notation-heavy modeling disciplines lend themselves easily to executable models.

In recent years, several proposals have used state machines for capturing reactive behavior of objects. For example, ObjectChart and OMT use Statechart of Harel for behavioral specification. The StateChart paradigm aims to manage state explosion

---

[1]Smoothness formalizes the notion that the output message of an object can depend only on the input received *prior to* sending this output.

problem of FSM based system descriptions, by structuring system description into "OR" and "AND" compositions of smaller FSMs. ObjChart models structure system behavior by object decomposition, each object requiring a small FSM. Thus, we achieve the same goals as Statecharts. Moreover, as a detailed comparison in Section 5 will show, ObjCharts have simpler semantics and much better performance in analysis—linear as opposed to exponential as compared to Statecharts.

Furthermore, treating the denotation of objects as a set of equations provides an elegant and simple framework for defining substitution and composition of objects. Behavioral equivalence can be thought of as equivalence of the sets of solutions for the respective equations. Composition by containment is given by the union of such equations. Composition by interconnection becomes union of equations with suitable port name unification. Substitution and composition are important for developing theory of types and subtypes for concurrent objects.

The rest of the paper is organized as follows. In Section 2 we introduce the constructs of ObjChart informally and illustrate them with a small example. Section 3.1 presents precisely the compositional semantics of reactive behavior of ObjChart objects using the equational framework of Misra. There we also discuss how the same framework can be used to define precisely subsumption and composition of reactive behavior. Thereafter, in Section 4, we discuss how ObjChart notations help one structure system specifications naturally by object hierarchies. We also observe how tracing causality chains along the same object hierarchy helps one organize reasoning about system behavior. In Section 5 we compare our work with other approaches that use state machines for describing object behavior.

2 ObjChart Notations

In this section, we introduce the notations of ObjChart using an example of a system to keep track of checkbook balances. All the visual notations are summarized in Figure 1.

Object

The primary construct of ObjChart is an *object* with a name and optionally with a type[2]. An object can have a set of *attributes*, each of which can hold a value of some type. An attribute a of object O can be queried and updated, respectively, by the following two constructs: $O \ll getValue(a, V)$[3], abbreviated optionally as $O.a(V)$, retrieves the value of a into the variable V, while $O \ll setValue(a, v)$ (optionally abbreviated as $O.a := v$) sets the attribute to value v. In addition, objects may have a set of named *ports* through which it sends and receives messages (to other objects). Visual notation of objects and attributes is exemplified in Figure 2. Here, the object a_RegisterEntry, modeling a typical entry in a checkbook register, has the attributes old-balance, amount and new-balance.

---

[2] Types in this context are just user-defined words.

[3] $a \ll m(Args)$ denotes sending a message $m(Args)$ to a target object a

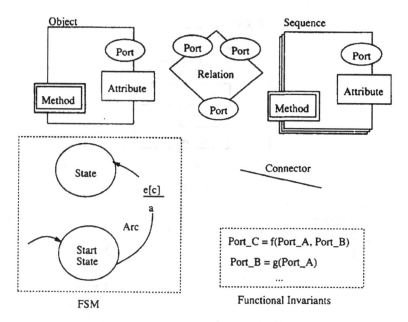

Figure 1: Basic Constructs of ObjChart

Relations

In ObjChart, *relation* objects can be used to depict both behavioral and computational dependencies among objects. In the former case, a relation object may be connected between the ports of objects, while, for the latter, attributes of objects can be connected via relations.

A relation has a set of typed *ports* and semantically embodies either some *behavioral constraint* or a set of *functional invariants* among these ports. Behavioral constraints are described using state machines (refer to the section below for details), whereas, a functional invariant is an equation of the form $p_j = f(p_1 \cdots p_k)$ which states that the value of the port p_j is a function f of the values of other ports $p_i, 1 \le i \le k$ and $i \ne j$. Connection of an attribute a_j to a port p_j of a relation R depicts substitution of a_j for p_j in all functional invariants for R.

Figure 3 shows an example of a relationship among attributes. The attribute new-balance is the difference of old-balance and amount for the object a_RegisterEntry. This is depicted by the relation subtract with ports A, B and C and a functional invariant $C = A - B$ among them.

State Machines

Behavior of an object is defined either by associating a *finite state machine* (FSM) or by defining *methods* in some 3GL. It can be shown that the combination of FSM used here and the functional invariants is adequate for writing any method; thus without loss of generality, we shall concentrate on behavior definition involving FSMs alone

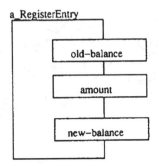

Figure 2: Object and Attribute

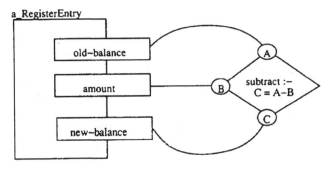

Figure 3: Functional Invariant

and use methods as "short-hand" for FSMs.

FSMs could be used either as controllers for single objects, or to coordinate message interchange between a set of sibling objects. An FSM of an individual object is meant to capture what its reactions are to the receipt of messages: the object may make state transitions and concomitantly may generate a set of other messages. On the other hand, a behavioral relation object, connecting several sibling objects, coordinates message exchanges among the connected objects by embodying a FSM. The FSM in such a relation object defines the reaction to the receipt of a message from one connected object via a port; the reaction may include a state transition and generation of messages to other ports of the relation i.e., to other connected objects.

The transitions of an FSM are depicted as labels on arcs between states. An arc label is a triple of the form (Event, Condition, Actions), usually written in the following syntax in our formalism:

$$\frac{Event[Condition]}{Actions}.$$

The presence of an arc labeled $\langle e, c, \bar{a} \rangle$ with source state s_1 and destination state s_2 for an object O means: If O is in state s_1 when it receives the message e, and the condition c "holds," then the object undergoes a state transition (to state s_2), sending the set of messages $\bar{a}$.

Figure 4 shows an example state machine for a single object, a register-entry; in reaction to the message setAmount(A), a register entry becomes "filled" by making a transition from the "blank" state, simultaneously generating a message to itself[4] to set its amount attribute. This depicts a *behavioral protocol* that a register entry, once made, cannot be altered.

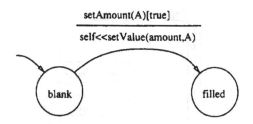

Figure 4: State Machine of a typical Register Entry

The inter-object messaging paradigm of ObjChart is as follows.

- The messages in the action part of an arc label, are *asynchronously* sent to the target objects without the sender waiting for their reply. Thus the sender is free to react to other input messages.

- The messages in the action part of an arc label can be executed in any order and the sender does not care about the order. These two aspects of ObjChart's messaging paradigm result in its ability to model object-level concurrency.

- Each recipient object process messages in a FIFO fashion. If a message is received when the object is not in the appropriate state, the message is lost.

The *condition* part of an arc label is a boolean expression involving conjunction, disjunction or negation of *predicates*. A predicate can be a simple relational comparison such as $X \leq Y$ or a *query predicate*. A query predicate is of the form $O.p(Args)$ which is true if the object O has the property $p(Args)$ for suitable bindings of the $Args$; O is limited to be one of the immediate sub-objects or an argument of the event for the arc in question. It is to be noted that such query predicates are evaluated *synchronously*, i.e., the calling object waits until a corresponding acknowledgement is received.

Both the FSM-s (i.e., actions and conditions in arc labels) and the methods of an object are restricted to having scopes only *local* to the object. These can refer to only the object itself (self), its environment (parent), its sub-objects, its ports and attributes. Furthermore, FSM-s of objects can query objects which are explicitly passed as arguments of its events during their event evaluations. Due to this locality restriction, ObjChart description of objects are very modular and are easier to analyze.

Sequence

ObjChart provides the construct *Sequence* object as a short-hand for an ordered set of identical objects. A Sequence is defined in terms of a distinguished object, its

---

[4]The distinguished word self denotes the object itself.

representative element; all elements of the sequence are structurally and behaviorally similar to the representative element. Visually a Sequence is shown as a stack of objects, where the top of the stack is the representative element. As an example, a set of register entries can be specified by a Sequence RegisterEntries where the representative element denotes a typical register-entry as shown in Figure 5.

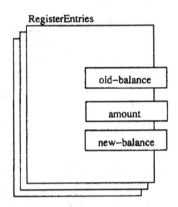

RegisterEntries

Figure 5: Sequence of Register Entries

By defining a Sequence in terms of its representative element, one can express in ObjChart an abstract schemata for potentially infinite set of objects. Moreover, ObjChart allows definition of relations between the ith and $(i + k)^{th}$ elements of the sequence (for any constant k). The functional invariants specified through these relations hold at creation and update of elements. As an example, the fact that in a checkbook register, the old-balance of $(i + 1)^{th}$ entry is equal to the new-balance of the ith entry (for all i), is expressed via the eqBal relation in Figure 6.

The ability to define functional invariants over the representative element permits elegant reasoning on structure, using induction.

Sequences support the following built-in messages: The $O \ll newElement$ message can be used to create a new element of the Sequence O. Elements of the sequence are numbered (starting at 0). $O \ll getCount(C)$ returns the number of elements currently present in the sequence O. The N-th element of a Sequence O is referenced in ObjChart notations as $O(N)$.

Object Decomposition

In any large modeling effort, one would like to define objects at an abstract level first and progressively refine them into greater details incrementally. ObjChart promotes such "step-wise refinement" by decomposing objects into sub-parts. The sub-objects are only accessible via the containing composite object. In view of our previous discussion on communication ports of objects, this translates to having named communication ports between any object and its parent, and all its subcomponents. (Note that these are the ports which define the part-of hierarchy. There may be other ports which allow sideways communication between sibling objects, using behavioral relations.) As an example of object decomposition, referring to Figure 7, the checkbook

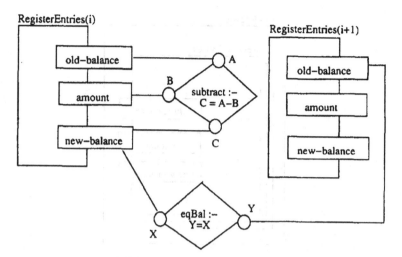

Figure 6: Dependencies between elements of RegisterEntries

register is modeled as an Object CheckRegister whose sub-objects are the elements of the Sequence RegisterEntries.

Model Execution

ObjChart models of systems are executable. Essentially execution involves interpretations of the FSMs and functional invariants, invoking the builtin messages of the various ObjChart Constructs employed. For example, the checkbook register model defined above, is executable: a setAmount(A) message sent to an element RegisterEntry(i) will compute the new-balance attribute of the element and set the old-balance attribute of the element RegisterEntry(i+1). ObjChart Builder, described in [GMD93], is an environment to execute and experiment with ObjChart models.

3 Behavioral Semantics of ObjChart Objects

In this section, we provide an equational framework for defining compositional semantics of reactive behavior of ObjChart objects. We use this equational framework to define the precise meaning of behavioral subsumption of concurrent objects. Finally, we indicate how the same framework can be used to provide a semantics for Contracts.

3.1 The Equational Framework

Reactive behavior of an object is controlled by its state machine. An object may receive messages from its parent, itself, from one of its sub-objects or via one of its ports. For each such message received, its state machine determines the outcome (resulting output messages to parent, children and so forth). Furthermore, the object

CheckRegister

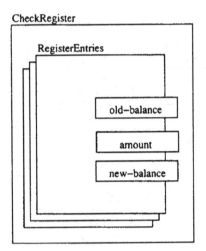

RegisterEntries

old—balance

amount

new—balance

Figure 7: CheckRegister Object

may undergo state change in this process. Externally observable behavior is the relationship among the messages received from and sent to the object's environment, that is, its parent and ports, as shown in Figure 8. Each object O can communicate with its parent (through channel P for input, and P' for output), itself (through the channel marked *self*), all its sub-objects (using channels C_i for output to and channel C'_i for input from the ith sub-object), and other sibling objects via named ports (which get connected to such ports of other objects using relations which describe behavioral dependencies as explained in Section 2). The external behavior of an object is the relation between the sequence of messages on channels $P \cup Ports$ and $P' \cup Ports'$. Evidently, to give a compositional semantics, this relation must be definable in terms of those for the sub-objects, and the description of the object's state machine.

Defining compositional semantics of ObjChart objects is not easy because their external behavior is in general non-functional. The main difficulty comes from their inherent non-deterministic behavior. Since in our model every object executes concurrently with others, the outcome of a given sequence of input messages may be different depending on the possible interleaving of messages from the sub-objects with the input sequence, and the order in which messages in the *action* part of an arc get executed. It is well-known that input-output relation between message sequences on channels $P \cup Ports$ and $P' \cup Ports'$ cannot be expressed functionally. In fact, there have been several proposals made in the literature of non-deterministic data-flow networks to provide compositional semantics in the presence of non-determinism, including [Jon89, Mis90]. In this section we show that these results can be adapted to provide a compositional behavioral semantics for ObjChart objects.

In the remainder of our discussion on this issue, we follow Misra ([Mis90]) more closely. Misra characterizes each component by a set of equations of the form $f(\overline{C}) \leftarrow g(\overline{C})$ ($f \leftarrow g$ for short), where $\overline{C}$ is the set of channels connected to the component of interest, and f and g are continuous functions over the traces on these channels. The behavior itself is one of the so-called *smooth solutions* of the set of equations.

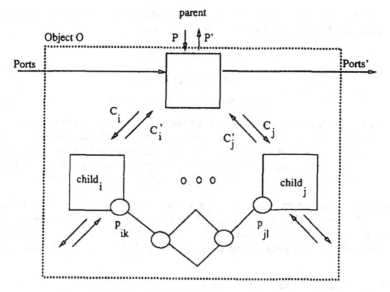

Figure 8: Object Model for Behavioral Specifications

Moreover, for deterministic components, there is a unique smooth solution, which is the least fixpoint of the equations. Given two descriptions of components $f_1 \leftarrow g_1$ and $f_2 \leftarrow g_2$, their combined description is given by $f \leftarrow g$, where f is the tuple consisting of f_1 and f_2, and similarly for g.

Following the work on nondeterministic dataflow networks, we provide the description of each ObjChart object as a network of subcomponents as shown in Figure 9. From Figure 9 we see that each object has three sub-parts (or sub-processes in the

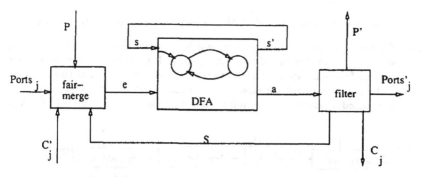

Figure 9: Subcomponents of an ObjChart Object

data-flow network terminology), namely:

Fair-merge This is a non-deterministic process which gets input from the *parent, self* and $C'_j, 1 \leq j \leq n$ channels, and merges them to produce a sequence of events (e)

for the state machine of the object under consideration. The following equations define the Misra style behavior of this component:

$$\text{select}(parent, e) \leftarrow P,$$

$$\text{select}(self, e) \leftarrow S,$$

$$\text{select}(child_j, e) \leftarrow C'_j, 1 \leq j \leq n.$$

Here we have assumed that each of the channels have a sequence of values, and *select* is a function which gives the subsequence in which each element has the tag given by the first argument. Note that there have to be more components to actually attach and remove tags from the channel values, which we do not specify for simplicity. See Section 4.10 of [Mis90] for complete details.

DFA This process implements the transition table for the deterministic state machine for the current object. The actual description is given in Table 1 below. We write $\langle s, e, c, a, s' \rangle \in \text{transitions}(O)$ whenever there is an arc with event e, condition c and actions a from state s to state s'. Here σ is a substitution for

DFA : $State \times Event \rightarrow State \times Actions$
$\text{DFA}_O(\bot, e) = \langle \bot, \{\} \rangle$
$\text{DFA}_O(s, e) =$
    if $\exists.\langle s, e', c, a, s' \rangle \in \text{transitions}(O)$
        such that $\exists \sigma : e'.\sigma \equiv e$ **and** $c.\sigma$ **holds, then**
        $\langle s', a.\sigma \rangle$
    else
        $\langle \bot, \{\} \rangle$

Table 1: Transition Table for DFA

the parametric variables in e' which is a matching of e' with e (i.e., $e'.\sigma \equiv e$).

Filter This is a non-deterministic process, which receives a sequence of sets as input; each set contains elements of the form $O_j \ll e_j$. It produces a non-deterministic sequence from each such set and outputs the relevant portions of this sequence on the output channel corresponding to each target object. Figure 10 gives the detailed description of the sub-processes required for the purpose. We now

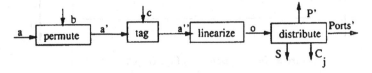

Figure 10: Description of Filter

provide the necessary equations (in the figure, we use b as a sequence of random numbers ([Mis90]), and c as a sequence of natural numbers, which is easy to generate using a counter):

$$a' \leftarrow permute(b, a),$$

$$a'' \leftarrow \langle c, a' \rangle.$$

In this description, *tag* uses natural numbers to tag its input messages such that each input set gets a unique tag, while *permute* generates a random permutation of its input set, and *linearize* is defined as in Table 2.

$$linearize(Tag, Set) =$$
$$\langle Tag, e_1 \rangle, \ldots, \langle Tag, e_n \rangle$$
$$(where\ e_j, 1 \leq j \leq n\ is\ the\ j^{th}\ element\ of\ Set)$$

Table 2: Description of Linearize

Finally, *distribute* strips off the tags and the preceding object identifier O_j; it then sends the event (e_j) on the channel for O_j (which could be one of *parent*, *self*, any C_i for a child or $Ports'_j$ for a port).

Note that *fair-merge* and *filter* are non-deterministic. This coincides with our intuition that the essential non-determinism for an object is due to (1) the potential interleaving of message sequences from its parent, its sub-objects and its ports; and (2) the order in which messages in the actions get executed. Furthermore, *fair-merge* and *filter* are duals of each other, since one merges input events to the state machine, while the other distributes outgoing actions. However, their equational descriptions are somewhat different since we are dealing with single messages for the event part, and with sets of messages for the action part.

Finally, we provide a description of the relation object (for behavioral dependencies using state machines) as shown in Figure 11. Note that this description is in fact a

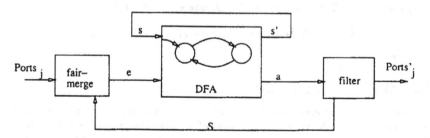

Figure 11: Description of Behavioral Relation

simplification of the one for an ObjChart object, as shown in Figure 9.

We are now ready to describe the behavioral semantics in terms of traces. A *trace* on a set of K channels is a sequence (possibly infinite) of pairs of the form $\langle c, v \rangle$, where v is a value appearing on the channel c. The *description* of an ObjChart object is the set of equations for its network of components as defined by Figures 8 and 9. The *behavioral denotation* of the object is the set of all *smooth solutions* ([Mis90]), that is, the admissible traces, of its description. The *external behavior* of an object is the projection of its behavioral denotation onto the channels $P \cup Ports$ and $P' \cup Ports'$.

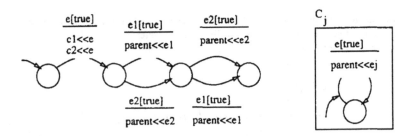

Figure 12: Example of the Trace Model

Example 1. *Consider the state machine of an object as shown in Figure 12, where the state machine on the left is for the object O which has two sub-objects $(C_j, j \in \{1,2\})$, each of which has a state machine as shown on the right. For this collection, one smooth solution is given by:*

$$\langle P, e \rangle, \langle C_1, e \rangle, \langle C_2, e \rangle, \langle C_2', e_2 \rangle, \langle P', e_2 \rangle, \langle C_1', e_1 \rangle, \langle P', e_1 \rangle,$$

which means that for the object O, the external behavior is given by:

$$\langle P, e \rangle, \langle P', e_2 \rangle, \langle P', e_1 \rangle.$$

Theorem 1 (Composition,[Mis90]). *Consider an object O with N sub-objects and M behavioral dependency relations between them, such that the ith sub-object has a description $f_i \leftarrow g_i$ and the jth relation has a description $f_{rel_j} \leftarrow g_{rel_j}$. Furthermore, let $f_{fair\text{-}merge} \leftarrow g_{fair\text{-}merge}$ be the description of the fair-merge component of O, $f_{DFA} \leftarrow g_{DFA}$ of the DFA component of O and $f_{filter} \leftarrow g_{filter}$ of the filter component of O. Then $f \leftarrow g$ describes O, where f is the tuple*

$$\langle f_1, \ldots, f_N, f_{rel_1}, \ldots, f_{rel_M}, f_{fair\text{-}merge}, f_{DFA}, f_{filter} \rangle$$

(and similarly g).

3.2 Object Subsumption

The equational framework presented above gives us an intuitive and elegant way to talk about substitutability and subsumption of objects. The general denotation of an object is a triple, with a structure component, a behavior component and a component for functional invariants. Since we have used equations to define both behavior (due to Misra) and functional invariants, we can in essence treat ObjChart objects as *collections of equations*, and therefore, we define object equivalence (subsumption) as the equivalence (subsumption) of the sets of solutions of these equation. That is, for two ObjChart objects O_1 and O_2, we say that O_2 subsumes O_1 if and only if the following conditions hold:

Attribute The set of external attributes of O_2 subsume those for O_1. In other words, for each attribute of O_1, O_2 has an attribute which accepts the same "type" of values.

Port The set of ports of O_2 subsume those for O_1. In other words, for each port of O_1, O_2 has a port which accepts the same "type" of messages.

Behavior Every *smooth* solution of O_1 (refer to Section 3.1) is also a smooth solution for O_2. In other words, O_2 has at least the same set of legal traces as O_1.

Functional Invariants The solutions (least fixpoint) of each functional invariant of O_1 is also a solution to the corresponding functional invariant of O_2.

From the above definition it is clear that in general it may not be possible to algorithmically decide if an object subsumes another, since we are using semantic equivalence for both behavior and functional invariants. However, we now identify a useful class of subsumption, where the subsuming object is obtained by copying and extending the subsumed object, by adding attributes, states, arcs, or actions. For such a case, it is easy to show that the subsumption problem is decidable, by comparing the two structures in question.

We illustrate this idea with a simple example, in which we extend the state machine of an alarm clock to produce one which also has the "snooze" feature, as shown in Figure 13.

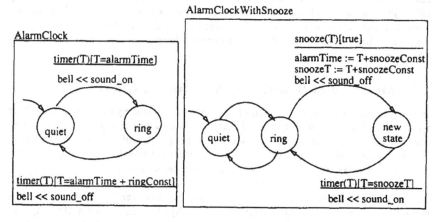

Figure 13: Alarm Clock with and without Snooze

The *copy-and-extend* paradigm exemplified here, is quite useful for the system designer, because it shows that a system may be developed incrementally by reusing and extending previously defined models. The ability to check subsumption algorithmically for such cases enable us ascertain that incrementally extended models are indeed semantically proper extension of the original ones.

3.3 Semantics of Contracts

"Contracts" was introduced in an earlier paper [HHG90] as a way of capturing multi-object behavioral collaboration. That paper did not, however, provide a precise semantics for Contracts.

The equational framework described here can provide precise semantics for Contracts. A Contract is intended to express a set of constraints on the order of message exchanges among a set of participants. These constraints are precisely the set of equations over traces where the participants are the channel names. Contract composition becomes union of the set of equations for the sub-Contracts (with possible channel name unification, whenever the output of one channel is connected to the input of another). Contract refinement has the same semantics as that of object subsumption discussed in Section 3.2.

In the visual notations of ObjChart, Contracts are depicted by the behavioral relation construct, such that the typed ports represent the Contract participant roles, and the constraints are defined by the relation's state machine. In effect, the state machine of the Contract controls the order of message exchanges between the objects connected to the ports.

4 Specification Structuring and Reasoning

This section discusses how ObjChart notations help structure system specifications naturally, using object hierarchies. We also observe how tracing causality chains along this object hierarchy helps organize reasoning about system behavior. Subsection 4.1 presents an ObjChart specification of a version of the Elevator Control System problem and Subsections 4.2 and 4.3 makes several observations about reasoning with ObjChart models.

4.1 Modeling of Reactive Systems in ObjChart

In this section we specify a version of an Elevator Control System using ObjChart notations. This example is typical of reactive systems and has been used as a test problem for judging efficacy of specification languages [Dav89]. The example shows that *hierarchical object based decomposition provides a natural structure of the specification, and keeps the state machines under manageable size.*

We first model the overall system structure as Building object, as shown in Figure 14. Building is decomposed into its sub-objects, Elevators and the floors. The floors themselves are decomposed into their sub-objects, namely the buttons up and down. Note that the terminal floors, floor(0) and floor(m), are modeled separately, since terminal floors have one button each.

We represent the assembly *Elevators* as a Sequence, in which the representative element specifies an elevator, as shown in Figure 15. Each elevator has three attributes: current-direction of movement, current-floor recording the current floor number and door keeping the status information about its door, whether opened or closed.

Each elevator is further decomposed into its sub-objects, a set of internal buttons (button_set) and a request queue (request_queue). The request queue has the

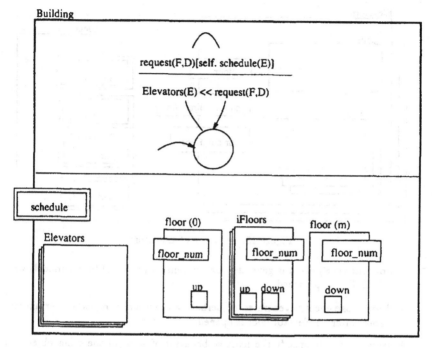

Figure 14: Overall System Structure

following four methods:

- **pending?(F,D)** queries if a particular request from a Floor F and direction D is in the queue.

- **toMove?(D)** determines if there are further requests for going in the Direction D. This method essentially implements the elevator sweeping algorithm.

- **enq(F,D)** adds to the queue the request from Floor F for going in direction D.

- **deq(F,D)** removes the request from Floor F for direction D from the queue.

Next, the state machine of Figure 16 models the reactive behavior of an elevator. An elevator could be in one of three states, namely: **dead** (this is a quiescence situation in which there are no requests to be satisfied), **stopped** (an elevator is in this state when it is actually servicing a request) and **moving** (in which the elevator is using its sweeping algorithm to continually service requests for a particular direction). The events handled by the state machine are the following:

- **request(F,D)** event denotes a request to go to floor F and direction D. These events are generated by either pushing the floor buttons or by pushing the buttons inside the elevators.

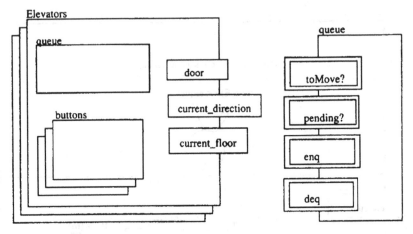

Figure 15: Sequence of Elevators

- floor_near(F) event is generated by the sensors (external to our model) when a floor F is approached.

- door_close event is generated by perhaps an external timer when certain time elapses after an elevator door is opened.

Finally, we briefly specify the reactive behavior of some of the other objects, as shown in Figure 17.

This section highlights how specification of a system is structured easily and naturally into the specifications of its constituent objects. Stepwise decomposition of objects into sub-objects results in each object with a very local scope. Such locality enables one to specify the objects independently and simply. For example, the FSM of an elevator is specified using only 3 states and is independent of the state machines of the elevator's buttons. In the next sub-section, we shall see how reasoning about a system under modeling is structured very naturally along inspecting objects locally.

4.2 Reasoning with ObjChart Models

In this section we use the elevator example developed in Section 4.1 to illustrate that in ObjChart reasoning about properties of a model can be done at a very intuitive level. *The structure of such reasoning arguments follow closely the system structure.* A typical such reasoning process about a reactive system involves making eventuality arguments and ascertaining safety properties. Eventuality arguments are effected by following causality chains through the communicating state machines, showing that progress making states are entered eventually. Safety properties of an object, on the other hand, being invariants, are established by examining all states of an object.

Consider the elevator model described in Section 4.1. A natural desire of the system analyst may be to prove the following property about the model:

If an *up* button is pressed at floor f, eventually some elevator comes to the floor and opens the door.

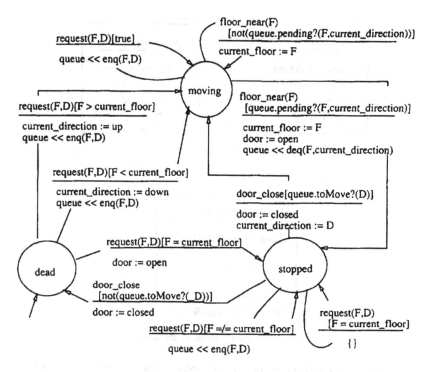

Figure 16: State machine for an individual elevator

We proceed by breaking this top-level goal into various smaller sub-goals which we solve one at a time:

1. **Every button push reaches some elevator** E. To establish this, one can trace the causality chain from the individual button (for floor f, and direction up), and establish that when this button is pressed, some elevator (say E) eventually gets $request(f, up)$. For example, one possible such chain could be

$$push \leadsto floor_f \ll dir(up)$$

$$floor_f \ll dir(up) \leadsto Building \ll request(f, up)$$

$$Building \ll request(f, up) \leadsto Elevators(E) \ll request(f, up),$$

i.e., eventually, elevator E will receive the request (some scheduling algorithm is employed by the *building* to determine the actual value of E).[5] Refer to Figures 14 and 17 of Section 4.1 for more details on the actual structure of the model. Note that, in general, it will be necessary to establish that each object in such a causality chain is indeed in a state in which it is ready for the corresponding

---

[5]The notation $a \leadsto b$ means that a causes b and in fact, a is an event and b is an action in some arc label of an FSM.

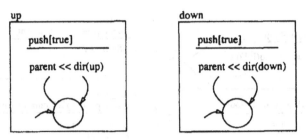

FSM of the individual buttons

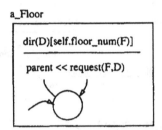

FSM of an individual floor

Figure 17: Specification of Behavior

message. For our example, all the intermediate objects involved, from a floor-button to an elevator, have a single state in their state machine, and so this fact is easy to ascertain.

2. **Elevator E services the message $request(f, up)$ eventually.** To do so, however, we have to consider the following sub-goals:

(a) **Elevator E never loses any request.** This is a *safety* property that can be established by inspecting all the states of the elevator (Figure 16), and noting that in each state the message $request(f, up)$ is handled. Hence, the request gets immediately satisfied if E was in "dead" state at floor f or the request gets queued if the elevator was in either "moving" or "stopped" states.

(b) **Whenever elevator E has a non-empty queue, it returns to the "moving" state.** This can be deduced from the facts that (i) *toMove?* would always hold whenever the queue is non-empty, and (ii) whenever the elevator enters the "stopped" state a *door_close* event occurs eventually. Furthermore, if the elevator was in a "dead" state, a request will send it to the "moving" state.

(c) **In the "moving" state, the elevator makes finite progress towards satisfying $request(f, up)$.** For this we assume receipt of a correct sequence of *floor_near* events whenever the elevator is in the "moving" state. As a result, the elevator may either transit to the "stopped" state or may continue in the "moving" state. In the former case, we use the previous argument to show that either the request has been satisfied, or the elevator must return to "moving" state again. In the latter case, we say that we have progressed one step closer to satisfying the request under consideration. Note that it may be the case that the elevator is actually moving away from the request under consideration, however, this is still progress, because the elevator is getting closer to its next sweep (i.e., direction change) in which the current request would be serviced.

The above arguments assume:

- All the methods of the *queue* object work correctly. In particular, the query *toMove?* is assumed to evaluate to true when the queue is non-empty. In fact, if we did specify the *queue* object completely, using its state machine, then we could have actually established this fact using similar causality argument about that state machine. However, in this paper, due to lack of space, we have simply assumed that the interface for queue is pre-defined in terms of methods which satisfy certain specifications.

- The external events (*door_close* and *floor_near*) arrive correctly whenever required.

This example shows that the ObjChart formalism allows system modelers to intuitively reason about their models by inspecting *causality chains* among the FSM-s of the objects under consideration. Furthermore, hierarchical decomposition modularizes, in most cases, such reasoning to inspecting a single object.

4.3 Orthogonality of Functional Invariants from Causality Chains

In this section we describe an example to show that our method for specifying functional invariants obviates the need of reasoning with explicit pre- and post-conditions. This example also illustrates that reasoning with functional invariants is orthogonal to reasoning with the causality chains.

The example involves specifying a bicycle, as shown in Figure 18. In our partial description of the system we have two objects, called rear and front which denote the wheels of the cycle. Each wheel has three attributes, namely: omega (for angular velocity), radius and velocity. The functional invariants describe the relation among angular and linear velocities of each wheel and the fact that the linear velocities of the two wheels must be equal. Furthermore, the WheelAssembly responds to a rotate message (which is generated from the pedal object in a more detailed scenario).

Suppose we want to establish that turning the pedal at an angular velocity W, will turn the front wheel at angular velocity $W * rear.radius/front.radius$.

This can be accomplished using the following two orthogonal steps:

- establish that pedal's message rotate(W) will set the value of rear object's omega attribute. That is, $rear.omega = W$. This is done by inspecting causality chain from pedal to WheelAssembly's FSM.

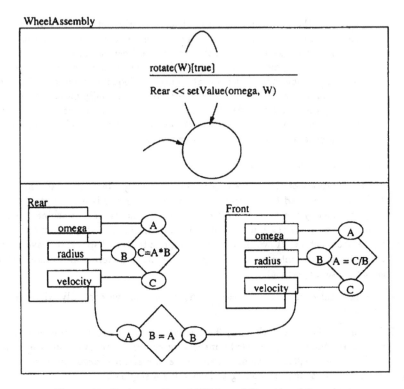

Figure 18: Orthogonality of FSMs and Functional Invariants

- establish that the angular velocities of two wheels are inversely proportional to their radii. That is, $front.omega = rear.omega * rear.radius/front.radius$. This can be established by following the chain of functional invariants.

This example illustrates the fact that reasoning about an ObjChart model is a truly orthogonal process: Follow a causality chain (any system trace) to find messages requesting value change and reason about the value network separately using techniques like function composition. In contrast, in some systems one has to explicitly deal with pre- and post-conditions in order to establish that a particular trace is valid for the object under consideration. We believe such orthogonality simplifies reasoning tremendously.

5 Comparison

In contrast to other state machine based behavior modeling languages, ObjChart uses object decomposition as the single system refinement paradigm, maintains orthogonality between control flow and value propagation, introduces *Sequence* object which embodies structural induction, and allows tracing causality chains in time linear in the size of the system. We elaborate these issues in the following sections.

5.1 Statechart

Statechart [Har87] proposes an elegant extension to FSMs so as to allow hierarchic refinement of states, decomposition of the system state machine into a set of orthogonal sub-component FSMs and multilevel concurrency utilizing broadcast communication of events among component state machines. Due to the hierarchy of states and substates, Statechart has also the notion of history nodes which remember the sub-state from the previous entry. Furthermore, chain reactions of internal events, triggered by a single external event, cannot interleave with arrival of further external events [HPSS87]. These two features seemingly complicate the semantics of Statechart—see Section 3 of [HPSS87].

In contrast, we use hierarchical object decomposition in lieu of orthogonal components for keeping the state machine of each object simple. We also use directed communication, unlike broadcast, along the decomposition hierarchy.

As shown in Section 4.2, typical reasoning for reactive systems involve chasing causality chains. Hierarchically directed communication of ObjChart allows us to analyze the effect of a chain reaction, caused by an external event, by considering only affected objects as opposed to all the objects in the system. For example, for a system of N objects where each object has at most c sub-objects, a k-step transition sequence may involve $O(c^{k+2}) = O(N)$ objects, i.e., number of inspections is linear in the size of the system. In contrast, for Statechart, analyzing a $k-$step chain reaction (i.e., a k-step micro-step sequence) requires exponentially many ($O(N^k)$) inspections. To see this consider a system which has N "AND" components. An external event e may cause state transition for any of these N subcomponent. Furthermore, each such transition may generate new events, which may cause transitions for all the N components again. Thus, each event has the potential to cause transitions for any of the N objects, and therefore, for every event one may potentially have to look at the entire system to find its effect, and thus the result. Finally, in ObjChart, communication between two objects in different parts of the hierarchy may need $O(logN)$ steps, and thus involve $O(logN)$ components. In Statecharts, although the same communication may be accomplished in a single step due to broadcast, it would still require inspections of all N components to find its effect.

Moreover, our semantics is relatively simple due to the following two facts. First, since hierarchically decomposed objects in practice need very few states, we do not have "OR" decomposition and thus, we do not have the complications due to History Nodes. Second, since we allow interleaving of external messages with those from the sub-objects, our semantics is free from the complications due to the asymmetry of macro and micro steps.

Thus, ObjChart accomplishes the same objectives as Statechart by using the object decomposition paradigm with a simpler semantics and a much better time complexity in analyzing system models.

5.2 ObjectChart

ObjectChart [BCHA90, CHB92] retains the traditional notion of classes and uses Statecharts to define the behavior of classes. They have used both "AND" and "OR" decomposition of Statecharts. It is not apparent how the orthogonal components of a Statechart within a single class can communicate and synchronize without broadcast, because their claimed directed communication is only for sending messages from one object to another and not for communication among orthogonal components within a single class.

As for operational semantics, ObjectChart is very restrictive: execution of each message (called an interaction) has to complete before the next one begins in the entire system. Moreover, execution of a service request cannot involve a nested request for another service. Thus, the concurrency allowed in Statechart formalism is not even utilized in ObjectChart's semantics.

ObjectChart also allows annotating states by state invariants (i.e., conditions holding at a given state) and associating pre- and post-conditions with service requests (message executions) in order to reason with the effects of these service requests. However, ObjectChart models have *not* achieved *orthogonality*—a trace derived from the state machines may still be disallowed if the necessary pre-conditions of the constituent service requests are not satisfied. Therefore, dealing with pre- and post-conditions destroys the intuitive simplicity of reasoning with state machines.

In contrast, we treat value propagation by functional invariants. The beauty of this approach is that these invariants always hold and therefore, any causality chain determined from inspecting state machines alone is always legal for the system. The result is that reasoning with ObjChart models consists of two truly orthogonal phases: follow a causality chain to identify any value update and then use functional invariants to determine consequent value propagation (see Section 4.3 for an example).

Finally, ObjectChart, being class based, does not directly support part-of decomposition at the object level. As such, the flatness of the traditional class model makes it difficult to express hierarchical layering of a system [BBJS92].

5.3 OMT

OMT uses three facets to describe a system, namely: the object model (E-R diagram), the dynamic model (Statechart) and the functional model (DFD). They have two major problems for describing large systems: First, their dynamic descriptions are at the class level, and therefore, like ObjectChart, the flat structure of classes is inelegant for describing hierarchically layered systems. Second, a system description gets refined along these three separate models, thus making it difficult to maintain coherence between these models [BBJS92, HC91].

As such, any system design methodology employing separate refinement hierarchies, for example, [Boo91, Har88b] and a list of others, have this inherent impediment of maintaining coherence among the different models. On the contrary, in ObjChart, object decomposition is the only system refinement paradigm. We believe that object is the fundamental element in any object oriented system, and therefore, object decomposition must be the predominant (and perhaps the sole) system refinement discipline.

6 Conclusion

In summary, ObjChart formalism aims to combine the intuitive appeal of visual notations with preciseness of formal methods. The constructs have been carefully designed, on one hand, to promote the tangible thinking in terms of objects as the sole system building-blocks and, on the other hand, to provide facilities such as functional invariants and structural induction (via Sequence object) which are found useful in reasoning.

By modeling many examples in ObjChart, we have made several encouraging observations: (1) system specifications are structured naturally as the objects of the system and (2) the same object structure is useful in guiding the reasoning process in a natural fashion. In many cases, such reasoning is very *local*, requiring inspections only within an object. Furthermore, we observe that causality chains of message passing can be reasoned *orthogonally* from reasoning with networks of functional invariants. Finally, tracing causality chains is the corner stone for reasoning with ObjChart models and can be accomplished in time linear in the size of the system. All these factors lay the foundations for reasoning with ObjChart models to scale up to practically sized systems. However, much more work is needed to realize these potentials.

Currently, we have built a prototype environment, called ObjChart Builder [GMD93], to create, edit, reuse and execute ObjChart models. In practical terms, execution of ObjChart models enable one to understand the cause and effect relations among objects. ObjChart Builder enables a system analyst to debug the conceptualization of a system directly at the level of ObjChart models by execution and inspection of the states of the objects.

In developing ObjChart notations, we have focused on object-level dynamics as the key component of system modeling and have not emphasised the static modeling features typical of class-based notations. For example, we cannot express, in ObjChart notations, disjunctive facts such as "Vehicles are either Cars or Trucks". Extending the Sequence Object construct by allowing alternative representative elements will be a potential solution.

Finally, using equations over traces as the denotation of objects provided us with an elegant framework to define object substitution and composition. However, the current framework is based on a fixed network of components and cannot handle the semantics of dynamic object creation. Semantics of Actors, on the other hand, can handle dynamic creation; however, the semantics is operational in nature. We believe that extension of the concept of smooth solutions to equations involving higher order functions may provide a general framework in which dynamic object creation can be handled.

Acknowledgement

The authors wish to thank several people who have, over the years, been involved in the Tangible Programming Project — Mukesh Dalal, Ashish Gupta, Constantine Laufer and Richard Helm. They all helped directly or indirectly in developing the ideas presented here, although the authors remain responsible for any remaining flaws. We would like to thank Rajendra Panwar and Jarir Chaar for proof-reading earlier versions of this paper. We are also indebted to Satbir S. Dhaliwal, who implemented a major portion of ObjChart Builder in C++.

References

[BCHA90] S. Bear, D. Coleman, F. Hayes and P. Allen. Graphical specification of object-oriented systems. In *Proc. OOPSLA/ECOOP '90* Vol. 25, No. 10, pages 28–37, 1990.

[Boo91] G. Booch. *Object-oriented design with applications*. The Benjamin Cummings Publishing Company Inc., 1991.

[BA81] J. D. Brock and W. B. Ackerman. Scenarios: a model of nondeterminate computation. In *Formalization of programming concepts*, LNCS 107, pages 252–259, 1981.

[BBJS92] B. Bruegge, J. Blythe, J. Jackson and J. Shufelt. Object-oriented system modeling with OMT. In *Proc. OOPSLA '92* Vol. 27, No. 10, pages 359–376, 1992.

[CM89] K. M. Chandy and J. Misra. *Parallel program design*. Addison-Wesley, 1989.

[CHB92] D. Coleman, F. Hayes and S. Bear. Introducing ObjectCharts or how to use Statecharts in object-oriented design. IEEE Transactions on Software Engineering, Vol. 18, No. 1, 1992.

[Dav89] N. Davis. Problem Set for the Fourth Int. Workshop on Software Specification and Design. In *Proc. of the Fourth IEEE Int. Workshop on Software Specification and Design*, Monterey, USA, 1989.

[GMD93] D. Gangopadhyay, S. Mitra and S. S. Dhaliwal. ObjChart-Builder: An environment for executing visual object models. IBM Technical Report. Submitted for publication. 1993.

[Har87] D. Harel. Statecharts: A visual formalism for complex systems. Science of Computer Programming, Vol. 8, pages 231–274, 1987.

[HPSS87] D. Harel, A. Pnueli, J. P. Schmidt and R. Sherman. On the formal semantics of Statecharts. In *Proc. of the Second IEEE Symp. on Logic in Computer Science*, pages 54–64, 1987.

[Har88a] D. Harel. On visual formalisms. Communications of the ACM, Vol. 31 (5).

[Har88b] D. Harel et al. Statemate: A working environment for the development of complex reactive systems. In Proc. of the Tenth Int. Conf. on Software Engg., pages 396–406, 1988.

[HC91] F. Hayes and D. Coleman. Coherent models for object-oriented analysis. In *Proc. OOPSLA '91*, Vol. 26, No. 11, pages 171-183, 1991.

[HHG90] R. Helm, I. M. Holland and D. Gangopadhyay. Contracts: specifying behavioral compositions in object-oriented systems. In *Proc. OOPSLA/ECOOP '90*, Vol. 25, No. 10, pages 169–180, 1990.

[Jon89] B. Jonsson. A Fully Abstract Trace Model for Dataflow Networks. In *Proceedings of the sixteenth annual Symposium on Principles of Programming Languages*, pages 155–165, 1989.

[MP92] Z. Manna and A. Pnueli. *The temporal logic of reactive and concurrent Systems*. Springer-Verlag, 1992.

[Mis90] J. Misra. Equational reasoning about nondeterministic processes. *Formal Aspects of Computing*, Vol. 2, pages 167–195, 1990.

[Pnu86] A. Pnueli. Application of temporal logic to the specification and verification of reactive systems: A survey of current trends. In *Current Trends in Concurrency*, LNCS 224, pages 510–584, 1986.

[RBPEL91] J. Rumbaugh, M. Blaha, W. Premerlani, F. Eddy and W. Lorensen. *Object-oriented modeling and design*. Prentice-Hall, 1991.

[SM88] S. Shlaer and S. Mellor. *Object-oriented systems analysis*. Yourdon Press, 1988.

O-O Requirements Analysis: an Agent Perspective

Eric Dubois, Philippe Du Bois and Michaël Petit

Institut d'Informatique
Facultés Universitaires de Namur
Rue Grandgagnage, 21
B-5000 Namur (Belgium)

{edu, pdu, mpe} @info.fundp.ac.be

ABSTRACT : In this paper, we present a formal object-oriented specification
language designed for capturing requirements expressed on composite real-
time systems. The specification describes the system as a society of 'agents',
each of them being characterised (i) by its responsibility with respect to actions happening in the system and (ii) by its time-varying perception of the
behaviour of the other agents. On top of the language, we also suggest some
methodological guidance by considering a general strategy based on a progressive assignment of responsibilities to agents.

KEYWORDS : O-O requirements analysis, agents, actions, formal language, first-
order, temporal and deontic logic, elaboration of the requirements document.

1 Introduction

Requirements Analysis (also called Requirement Engineering) is now widely
recognised as a critical activity in the context of software development.

Some languages where proved useful to express requirements. These include,
e.g., PSL/PSA [TH77], SADT [Ros77], MERISE [TRC83] or IDA [BP83]. Languages of that family have a rigorous syntax but suffer from a lack of formal
semantics. This fact leads to the development of new languages based on formal
grounds like, e.g., RML [GBM86], GIST [Fea87], ERAE [DHR91] and TELOS
[MBJK90].

The common characteristic of all these languages is the existence of a logical /
mathematical semantics which permits unambiguous and consistent expression
of requirements together with a formal framework for a rigorous investigation
of the R.A. process (see, e.g. [JF90]). Differences exist between these languages
and are inherent to their *expressive* power (i.e. the level of requirements that
can be captured using the language) and the nature of the available *structuring mechanisms* (i.e. mechanisms which help in organizing large requirements
documents).

O.M. Nierstrasz (Ed.): ECOOP '93, LNCS 707, pp. 458-481, 1993.
© Springer-Verlag Berlin Heidelberg 1993

In the last years, the O-O paradigm has been adopted at the level of programming and design specification languages. OBLOG [SSE89], Larch [GHW85], Object-Z [DKRS91] and OOZE [AG91] are examples of formal design languages supporting the O-O paradigm. Recent approaches (e.g. [CY91], [SM88]) consider the application of this paradigm at the requirements analysis level. Our paper goes along this direction but emphasises the need for formality in OORA.

We propose a formal O-O language designed for supporting requirement engineering. Our language aims at supporting the expression of (i) statements about real-world entities, (ii) performances requirements and (iii) visibility and reliability requirements. More precisely, the proposed language can be seen as an extension of the ERAE language [DHR91] complemented with:

- the concept of *agent* (as introduced for programming languages in [Sho90]). This concept, which can be seen as a specialization of the concept of *object*, is needed for structuring the requirements document according to the contractual responsibilities attached with each agent (a manual procedure, a device or a software component) with respect to the information it manages, accesses and modifies in the system;
- the concept of *action* (see, e.g., MAL [FP87]), introduced to define the role of agents w.r.t. changes happening in the system. Secondarily, the introduction of this concept is also motivated by our aim to overcome the *frame problem* existing in a declarative language [BMR92];
- the concept of *perception*, introduced to model the knowledge the agent has about its environment (i.e. the behaviour of other agents).

In Sect.2, the requirements engineering activity is first described and the concept of "composite system" is introduced.

The language itself is presented in Sect.3. It is called ALBERT (an acronym for "Agent-oriented Language for Building and Eliciting Requirements for real-Time systems") and supports the possibility of writing *graphical* declarations and complement them with *textual* constraints.

On top of a language, one definitively requires some *methodological* guidance for an incremental elaboration of a complex requirements document (see, e.g. [Fea89, FF89]). In Sect.2, we briefly describe a general strategy where the progressive elicitation of requirements is supported by identifying the *goals* of the system first before to refine them in terms of local responsibilities attached to each individual agent. In Sect.4, we illustrate how this strategy is supported in our language.

All along this paper, we will illustrate our ideas on a simplified fragment of a Computer Integrated Manufacturing (C.I.M.) application.

Requirements are associated with a specific *cell* being part of a complex production system. This cell is in charge of the production of a *bolt* when a production request is issued. A bolt results from the transformation of a *rivet* through a given process. More specifically, the cell (see Fig.1) is made of:
- the rivets stock. Rivets are produced by another cell and put in this stock waiting for their processing;

- the **bolts stock**. Bolts are the resulting products of the cell activity and are stored in a stock. Bolts remain in the stock until their use for activities performed in other cells;
- the **lathe**. It is the machine transforming a rivet into a bolt by producing a thread on the rivet;
- the **robot** equipped with a gripper. Its role is twofold : on the one hand, it transports a rivet from its stock to the lathe machine; on the other hand, it transports a bolt from the lathe which produces it to the stock of bolts.

Finally, there is a performance constraint imposing that a bolt must be produced within 10 minutes.

Cell

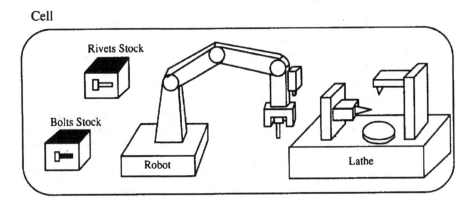

Fig. 1. The C.I.M. case study

2 Requirements Engineering of Composite Systems

In this section, we briefly details the activity of requirements engineering and its role within the software life-cycle; then we will define the concept of composite systems.

2.1 Requirements Engineering vs. Software Engineering

The majority of recent software development methods distinguish between two basic activities : *requirements engineering* and *software engineering* (see Fig.2). The former starts from informal wishes expressed by one or several customers and elaborates a so-called *requirements document* where the system to be developed is defined in a precise way. This document is the starting point of the software engineering (or design) activity, which develops a software system meeting the requirements in an efficient way.

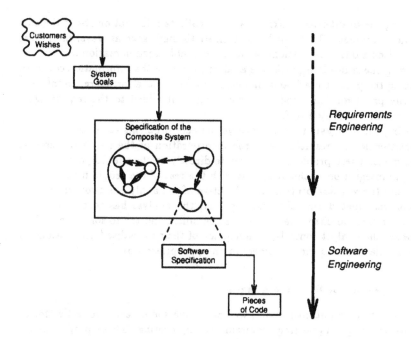

Fig. 2. Requirements Engineering vs. Software Engineering

2.2 The Four Tasks of Requirements Engineering

The requirements engineering (R.E.) activity is not as trivial as writing down the customers' wishes because these wishes are often unprecise, incomplete, ill-structured, and even inconsistent. Therefore requirement engineering implies a constant interaction between the customers and the analyst in order to progressively clarify the requirements.

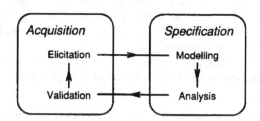

Fig. 3. Tasks of the R.E. activity

As suggested on Fig.3, R.E. can be subdivided in four interacting tasks [DHR91]:

- During the **elicitation** task, the analyst collects information about the customers' problem. This can be performed through several ways: interviews and discussions, observations, study of available documentation,...
- During the **modelling** task, the analyst processes the information collected during the previous task and elaborates a model, i.e. a formal representation of the problem. This model is a new fragment added to the requirements document elaborated so far.
- During the **analysis** task, the analyst detects problems (contradictions, inconsistencies,...) resulting from the incorporation of the new requirements fragment. These problems either relate directly to the the fragment itself or to the integration of this fragment with the rest of the requirements.
- During the **validation** task, the objective of the analyst is twofold. If problems were met during the analysis task, the analyst has to communicate them in a comprehensible way to the customers and try to solve them. Otherwise, the analyst controls the adequacy of their formalised descriptions by reformulating it to the customers in an appropriate way.

2.3 Properties of R.E. Languages

From the activities outlined above, we can derive some basic properties for an adequate language supporting requirements engineering. These properties are *expressiveness*, *structuring* and *formality*.

Expressiveness. To support effectively the elicitation and also the validation task, a language should be sufficiently expressive to support a natural mapping between all kind of things that should be described in a requirements document and the various concepts available in the language. Definitely, capturing requirements should not be a cumbersome coding task.

Structuring. Requirements documents are often quite large and, thereby, complex interactions exist between different pieces of descriptions. To facilitate the modelling task and to make the resulting document manageable, requirements should be organised into separable units which can be combined in a controllable way to yield to the complete specification.

Moreover, structuring mechanisms are also essential to support the reuse of specification components and the maintenance of requirements documents.

Formality. The formal aspect of a language depends on the availability of rigorous rules of interpretation which guarantee the absence of ambiguity. Besides, rules of deductive inference are needed to make possible the derivation of new statements from the given ones.

The deductive power of a language allows the development of tools supporting the analysis task (semantic checkers) and the validation task (prototype generators and inference tools).

2.4 Composite Systems

In the context of the development of real-time software and information systems, the requirements document, in its final stage of elaboration, should include not only specifications on the software piece to be implemented but also on the *environment* around this software as well as the nature of the interactions taking place between both (see, e.g., [Bjø92]). Let us consider two specific examples:

- in the context of an information system, requirements may include references to manual procedures to be installed (like, "this department is in charge of encoding the orders within the day of their arrival") or to real-world entities (like the following *accuracy* requirement [MCN92]: "the stocks quantities recorded in the information system should reflect the real-world stocks quantities with some delta").
- In the context of real-time software, requirements may include references to specific hardware/devices to be used (like, "the existence of an analog device which measures pulse and skin resistance in a patient monitoring system" [Fea89]) or to *performance* requirements (like, "in a furnace system, when the water temperature exceeds 100°C degrees, the alarm has to be triggered on within a 10 seconds delay").

In this paper, we consider requirements associated with the kind of systems described above that are sometimes referred as **composite systems** [Fea87] made of multiple *agents*. For example, one may think about a composite system including manual procedures, hardware, specific devices and software components interacting together. For example, in the context of the C.I.M. case study introduced in Sect.1, one may envisage (i), at the higher level, the system as being made of *Cell* agents and an *Environment* agent, and (ii), at a lower level, each cell as being made of multiple agents, viz the *Rivets container*, the *Bolts container*, the *Robot*, the *Lathe* and the *Controller*. The last three agents play an active role in the *Cell*. This is especially the case for the *Controller* which is in charge of synchronising and controlling the whole production process. Conversely, the two first agents (viz the Rivets and Bolts containers) have a more passive role restricted to stock keeping (see Fig.4).

In the final version of the requirements document for a composite system, we have to be able to identify *responsibilities* attached with the different agents (computerised or not) and make them precise because they form a contractual part for the designers (not only the software designer) in charge of implementing them and guaranteeing their desired behaviour.

On top of the detailed behaviour attached to each agent identified, we also need to have a more abstract view of the global *goals* [Dub89, DFHF91], i.e. objectives associated with the system considered as a whole (black box approach). Goals are expressed in terms of system-wide properties, regardless of how responsibility is decomposed among agents.

The requirements engineering activity should thus encompass a phase of "organisational design", i.e. the work of organising a system into agents (subsystems), assigning responsibilities to them and describing their interconnections.

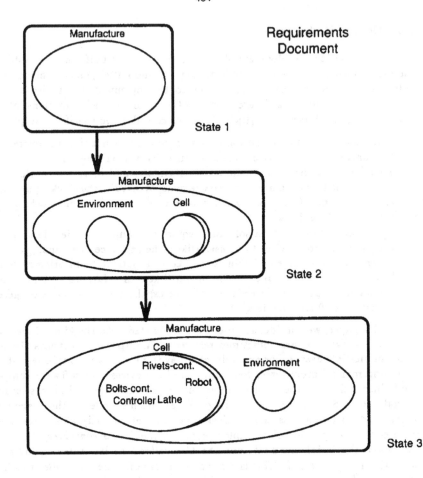

Fig. 4. Development of the Requirements Document

To conclude, we plead that an adequate method for supporting the gradual elaboration of the requirements document should include:

1. the specification of the *problem* expressed in terms of goals associated with the whole system to be developed;
2. the specification of a *solution* to the problem in terms of the description of a composite system where the set of requirements attached to individual agents meet the goals introduced.

In Sect. 4, we will further detail the set of activities supporting the model sketched above.

3 ALBERT: the Language

3.1 Models of a specification

The purpose of our requirements language is to define admissible behaviours of a composite system. This description, which must abstract of irrelevant details, is usually called a *model* of the system. A specification language is best characterized by the structure of models it is meant to describe.

The rules for deriving the set of admissible models from a given specification expressed in the formal language are defined in [Du 92]. Their comprehensive presentation is however beyond the scope of this paper, which will remain informal.

In order to master their complexity, models of a specification are derived at two levels:

- at the agent level: a set of possible behaviours is associated with each agent without any regard to the behaviour of the other agents;
- at the society level: interactions between agents are taken into account and lead to additional restrictions on each individual agent behaviour.

The specification describes an agent by defining a set of possible *lives* modelling all its possible behaviours. A life is an (in)finite alternate sequence of *changes* and *states*; each state is labelled by a time value which increases all along the life (see Fig.5).

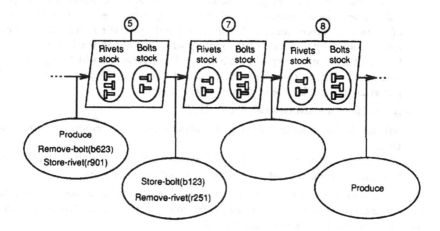

Fig. 5. A possible life of the *Cell* agent

The term "*history*" refers to the sequence of changes which occur in a possible life of the agent. A change is composed of several occurrences of simultaneous *actions* (the absence of action is also considered as a change). In our terminology we use the word 'action' both for denoting:

- happenings having an effect on the state where it occurs (called *actions* in some existing specification languages: e.g. [RFM91], [JSS91]);
- happenings with no direct influence on the state (called *events* in some other specification languages: e.g. [DHR91]).

The term *"trace"* refers to a sequence of states being part of a possible life of the agent. A state is structured according to the information handled in the considered application. In the case study, a specific state structure is associated with the *Cell* agent (see Sect.3.3).

The value of a state at a given time in a certain life can always be derived from the sub-history containing the changes occurred so far.

3.2 Language Constructs

Basically, the formal language that we propose is based on a variant of *temporal logic* [GB91], a mathematical language particularly suited for describing histories. This logic is itself an extension of multi-sorted first order logic, still based on the concepts of variables, predicates and functions. In this paper, three extensions are taken into account:

1. the introduction of **actions** to overcome the well-known *frame* problem [BMR92, HR92], a typical problem resulting from the use of a declarative specification language;
2. the introduction of **agents** together with their properties (responsibilities for actions, for providing perceptions, ...). This object-oriented concept can also be seen as a possible way of structuring large specifications in terms of more finer pieces, each of them corresponding to the specification of an agent guaranteeing a part of the global behaviour of the whole system;
3. the identification of **typical patterns of constraints** which support the analyst in writing complex and consistent formulas. In particular, typical patterns of formulas are associated with actions.

Using the language involves two activities:

- writing *declarations* introducing the vocabulary of the considered application,
- expressing *constraints*, i.e. logical statements which identify possible behaviours of the composite system and exclude unwanted ones.

A graphical syntax (with a textual counterpart) is used to introduce *declarations* and to express some typical *constraints* frequently encountered. The expression of the other constraints is purely textual.

3.3 Declarations

The declaration part of an agent consists in the description of its states structure and the list the actions its history can be made of.

Agents are considered as *specialised* objects; therefore, our modelling of a state structure is largely inspired by recent results in O-O conceptual modelling (see, e.g., OBLOG [SSE89] and O* [Bru91]).

The state is defined by its components which can be *individuals* or *populations*. Usually populations are *sets* of individuals but they can also be structured in *sequences* or *tables*. Components can be time-varying or constant. Elements of components are typed using:

- predefined elementary data types (like, *STRING, BOOLEAN, INTEGER,...*) equipped with their usual operations [1];
- elementary types defined by the analyst (like, *BOLT* and *RIVET* in our example), those are types for which no structure is given, they are only equipped with equality;
- more complex types built by the analyst using a set of predefined type constructors like set, list, Cartesian product,... (see, e.g. [BJ78]) and elementary types; on top of operations inherited from their structure, new operations can be defined on these new types;
- types corresponding to agent identifier.
  Agents includes a key mechanism that allows the identification of the different instances. A type is automatically associated to each class of agent. This correspond to the type of agents identifiers within that class. E.g., each *Cell* agent has an identifier of type *CELL* [2] [3].

Figure 6 proposes the graphical diagram associated with the declaration of the state structure of the *Cell* where:

- *Input-stock* and *Output-stock* are considered as two set populations, respectively of type *RIVET* and *BOLT*;
- *Produce, Store-rivet, Remove-bolt, Remove-rivet* and *Store-bolt* are five actions which may happen in a *Cell* history. Actions can have arguments[4]; for example, each occurrence of the *Store-rivet* action has an instance of type *RIVET* as argument.

The diagram also includes graphical notations making possible (i) to distinguish between internal and external actions and (ii) to express the visibility relationships linking the agent to the outside (*Importation* and *Exportation* mechanisms):

(i) Information within the parallelogram is under the control of the described agent (the *Cell*) while information outside from the parallelogram denotes elements (state components or actions) which are imported from other agents of the society the agent belongs to. From the graphical declaration, it can be

---

[1] Operations on data types should not be confused with actions of agents: operations denote only mathematical functions, they may be used to simplify expressions in constraints but cannot be used to model the dynamic behaviour of systems (i.e. agents)

[2] When an agent is unique (like, e.g., the *Environment* agent), then a constant is also automatically defined to refer to the identifier of that agent (*envt* in our case study).

[3] Inside the description of an agent, the *self* constant refers to the proper identifier of the described agent.

[4] Arguments may be regarded as input or output arguments but there is no difference on a semantics point of view.

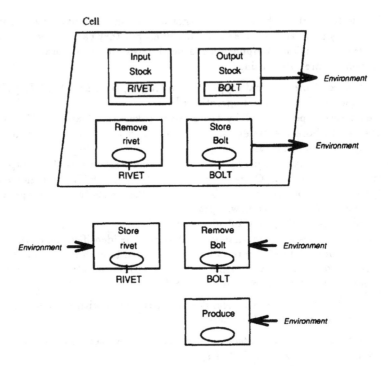

Fig. 6. Declaration associated with the *Cell* agent

read that *Cell* has the initiative for *Remove-rivet* and *Store-bolt* actions while it lets the *Environment* having the initiative of *Store-rivet* and *Remove-bolt* actions [5];

(ii) For information in the parallelogram, boxes without arrow indicate that this information is not visible from the outside. Conversely, boxes with arrow denote information which are exported to the outside. From the graphical declaration, it can be read that the *Environment* may have knowledge of the *Output-stock* state and of the *Store-bolt* actions.

Importation and *Exportation* are static properties; *Perception* and *Publicity* are their dynamic counterparts and provides the analyst with a finer way of controlling how agents can see information inside each other (perception and publicity constraints will be discussed in the next section).

---

[5] In the textual part of the specification, external actions will be referred prefixed with the identifier of the agent responsible for it

3.4 Constraints

Constraints are used for pruning the (usually) infinite set of possible lives of an agent.

Unlike in O-O design languages, e.g. OBLOG, the Albert semantics is not operational. A life must be extensively be considered before it can be classified as possible or not, i.e. adding new states and changes at the end of a possible life does not necessarily result in a possible life.

Figure 7 introduces the specification associated with the behaviour of the *Cell* agent and refers to the graphical declaration introduced in Fig.6.

| Cell |

STATE BEHAVIOUR

$\neg$ *Empty(Input-stock)*
In(Input-stock,r) $\implies$ $\lozenge$ $\neg$ *In(Input-stock,r)*

EFFECTS OF ACTIONS

Remove-rivet(r): Input-stock = Remove(Input-stock,r)
Store-bolt(b): Output-stock = Add(Output-stock,b)
envt.Remove-bolt(b): Output-stock = Remove(Output-stock,b)
envt.Store-rivet(r): Input-stock = Add(Input-stock,r)

COMMITMENTS

envt.Produce $\overset{\lozenge \leq 10min}{\longrightarrow}$ *Remove-rivet(r); Store-bolt(b)*

RESPONSIBILITY

PERCEPTION

F(envt.Remove-bolt / Empty(Output-stock))
X(envt.Produce / $\neg$ Empty(Input-stock))

PUBLICITY

X(Output-stock.{envt} / $\neg$ Empty(Output-stock))

Fig. 7. Constraints on the *Cell* agent

In order to provide some methodological guidance to the analyst, properties are grouped under six different headings: **State Behaviour, Effects of
Actions, Responsibility, Perception, Publicity, and Commitments.**

State Behaviour. Constraints under this heading express properties of the
states or properties linking states in an admissible life of an agent.

First of all, there are constraints which are true in all states of the possible
traces of an agent (see the first constraint on Fig.7 expressing that the input stock
may never be empty). These constraints are written according to the usual rules
of strongly typed first order logic. In particular, they are formed by means of
logical connectives ¬ (not), ∧ (and), ∨ (or), ⇒ (implies), ⇔ (if and only if),
∀ (for all), ∃ (there exists). The outermost universal quantification of formulas
can be omitted. The rule is that any variable, which is not in the scope of a
quantifier, is universally quantified outside of the formula.

On top of constraints which are true in all states (usually referred as *invariants*), there are constraints on the evolution of the system (like, e.g. if this
property holds in this state, then it holds in all future ones) or referring states
at the different times (see the second constraint on Fig.7 expressing that a rivet
may not stay indefinitely in the input stock). Writing these constraints require
to be able to refer to more than one state at a time. This is done in our language by using additional temporal connectives which are prefixing statements
to be interpreted in different states. The following table introduces these operators (inspired from temporal logic, see e.g. [Ser80, TLW91]) and their intuitive
meaning (ϕ and ψ are statements):

$\lozenge \, \phi$ ϕ is true sometimes in the future (including the present)
$\blacklozenge \, \phi$ ϕ is true sometimes in the past (including the present)
$\square \, \phi$ ϕ is always true in the future (including the present)
$\blacksquare \, \phi$ ϕ is always true in the past (including the present)
$\phi \, \mathcal{U} \, \psi$ ϕ is true from the present until ψ is true (strict)
$\phi \, \mathcal{S} \, \psi$ ϕ is true back from the present since ψ was true (strict)

There are constraints related to the expression of real-time properties. They are
needed to describe delays or time-outs (like, e.g., "an element has to be removed
from its population within 15 minutes") and are expressed by subscripting temporal connectives with a time period. This time period is made precise by using
usual time units: *Sec, Min, Hours, Days,* ... [KVdR89].

Effects of Actions. Beyond this heading, we describe the effects of actions[6]
which may alter states in lives (see on Fig.7 how, e.g., an occurrence of the
Store-bolt(b) action alters the output stock). Only actions which bring a traceable
change are described here (for example, we do not describe the role of the *Produce*
action).

---

[6] This heading contains constraints which describe both effects of internal actions as
and effects of actions perceived from the outside.

In the description of the effect of an action, we use an implicit *frame rule* saying that states components for which no effect of actions are specified do not change their value in the state following the happening of a change.

The effect of an action is expressed in terms of a property characterising the state which follows the occurrence of the action. The value of a state component in the resulting state is characterised in terms of a relationship referring to (i) the action arguments, (ii) the agent responsible for this action (if this action is an external one, the name of the agent is prefixing the action) and (iii) the previous state in the history.

In the last statement of the "Effects" clause on Fig.7, we express that the effect associated with the action *Store-rivet* issued by the external agent *Environment* is to add a rivet in the *Input-stock* of the *Cell*. In the pattern associated with the definition of an action, the left hand side of the equation characterises the state as it results from the occurrence of the action while the right hand side refers to the state as it is before the occurrence of the action.

Responsibility. Under this heading, we describe the role of the agent with respect to the occurrence of its own actions. To this end, we are still using an additional extension of the classical first-order and temporal logic by making possible to express *permissions* associated with an agent. To this end, we consider three specific connectives allowing the expression of *obligations*, *preventions* and *exclusive obligations* (respectively the O, the F and the X connectives). The study of these connectives has been heavily influenced by some work performed in the area of *Deontic Logic* (see, e.g. [FM90], [Dub91]).

The pattern for an obligation "$O(\ <internal\text{-}action> / <situation>\ )$" expresses that the action has to occur if the circumstances expressed in the situation are matched (these circumstances refer to conditions on the current state).

The pattern for a prevention "$F(\ <internal\text{-}action> / <situation>\ )$" expresses that the action is forbidden when the circumstances expressed in the situation are matched (e.g. "the cell cannot remove a rivet from the stock when the stock is empty", in other words, it is forbidden to the cell to produce the *Remove-rivet* action when the stock is empty).

The pattern "$X(\ <internal\text{-}action> / <situation>\ )$" is used to express exclusive obligation, it is a shorthand for the combination of "$O(\ <internal\text{-}action> / <situation>\ )$ and $F(\ <internal\text{-}action> /\neg\ <situation>\ )$".

The default rule is that all actions are *permitted* whatever the situation.

Using these connectives makes possible to express the control that the agent has with respect to its internal actions.

Perception. Beyond this heading we define how the agent is sensitive to the outside (i.e. to changes or state components which are made available to it by other agents belonging to the same society).

Perceptions are also specified using the O, F and X connectives.

The pattern "$O(\ <external\text{-}action> / <situation>\ )$" defines the situation where, if an action is issued by the external agent, the behaviour of the current agent's state is influenced. For example, in our case study, one may think about the following constraint: "the cell is obliged to take into account a production request issued by the environment when the input stock is not empty" (in other words, *Produce* actions occurring in the environment has necessarily to affect the history of the cell when the input stock is not empty).

The pattern "*F(<external-action> / <situation>)*" defines the situation where, if such action is issued by the external agent, it has no influence on the current agent's behaviour (e.g. "the cell cannot remove a rivet from the stock when the stock is empty", in other words, it is forbidden to the cell to produce the *Remove-rivet* action when the stock is empty).

The "*X*" connective is defined for perceptions in the same way as for responsibilities.

The default rule is that all all imported elements available may be perceived whatever the situation.

Publicity. Constraints under this heading specify how information (i.e. occurrences of actions or state components) is made available by an agent to other agents belonging to the same society. This is also a dynamic property and is expressed using the O, F and X connectives introduced above.

For example, one may imagine that, in our case study, "the storing of a bolt is made visible to the environment if it happens between 9AM and 12AM" and the publicity statement on Fig.7 expresses that the *Environment* agent has no access to the "Output-stock" component of the *Cell* agent state when that stock is empty.

Commitments. This heading is related to the *causality* relationship existing between some occurrences of actions.

Expressing causality rules with usual temporal connectives may appear very cumbersome (see, e.g., motivations given by [FS86]). To this end, our language is enriched with specific connectives which allow to specify, for example, that an action has to be issued by the agent as a unique response to the occurrence of another action (brought or not by the agent). A common pattern is based on the use of the "$\longrightarrow$" symbol which is not to be confused with the usual "$\Longrightarrow$" logical symbol. In our case, we want to denote some form of *entailment*, as it exists in Modal Logic [HC68].

In the case study, an example of causality exists between the *Produce*, the *Remove-rivet* and the *Store-bolt* actions. It relies upon the necessity of having a unique occurrence of the *Remove-rivet* and of the *Store-bolt* action (in that order) in response to each occurrence of the *Produce* action (see Fig.7).

The "$\longrightarrow$" symbol can be quantified by a temporal operator to express performances constraints (e.g. the "$\overset{\Diamond \leq 10min}{\longrightarrow}$" symbol in the commitment on Fig.7 means that the occurrence of the *Store-bolt* action has to happen within a 10 minutes interval after the occurrence of the *Produce* action).

The right part of a commitment (the *reaction*) may only refer actions which are issued by the agent (i.e. actions which are not prefixed).

Left and right parts of a commitment may be composed of one or more occurrences of actions. In case of more than one, occurrences may be composed in the following ways:

- "act1 ; act2" which means "an occurrence act1 followed by an occurrence act2";
- "act1 ∥ act2" which means "an occurrence act1 and an occurrence act2 (in any order)";
- "act1 ⊕ act2" which means "an occurrence act1 or an occurrence act2 (exclusive or)".

Some more complex expressions are provided to model iterations.

3.5 Complex Agents

The specification of a composite system is made of the specification of several agents. To be more precise, we propose to organise these in terms of a *hierarchy* where we distinguish between :

- *complex agents* corresponding to the nodes in the hierarchy and made of finer agents;
- *individual agents* corresponding to leaves in the hierarchy and which are not further decomposed.

In the sequel, we describe the *declarations* and *constraints* that can be associated with complex agents. In the next section, we will. make precise the role played by complex agents during the elaboration of a requirements document.

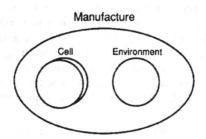

Fig. 8. Declaration associated with the *Manufacture* agent

Declarations of Complex Agents. Figure 8 proposes the graphical declaration associated with the CIM case study where *Manufacture* is a complex agent while *Cell* and *Environment* are individual agents. The *Environment* agent has been introduced for sake of simplicity but a more realistic specification would have considered *Environment* as being itself composed of a *Production & Planning* unit, a *Quality Assurance* unit,...).

The existing hierarchy among agents is expressed in term of two combinators: Cartesian Product and Set. In our specific case, the *Manufacture* agent is an aggregate of one *Environment* agent and several *Cell* agents (which form a "class").

Constraints on Complex Agents. A complex agent has no specific behaviour except the aggregation of the local behaviours of individual agents which it is composed of.

In the specification associated with a complex agent, we will only express global properties derived from properties attached to individual agents. These properties are called **goals** and correspond to the declarative part of the statements presented in the previous sub-section, viz constraints expressed under the **State Behaviour** and the **Commitments** headings.

On Fig.8, it would have been possible to attach *goals* to the *Manufacture*. The concept of *goals* will be illustrated in the next section.

4 The Elaboration of the Requirements Document

4.1 The Elaboration Process

The requirements document, in its final stage of elaboration, is usually a complex document due to the number of individual agents belonging to the composite system and the complexity of the interactions taking place among these agents. Therefore, one cannot imagine that the R.E. activity performed by the specifier only consists in the transcription of the customers' wishes in terms of the requirements document. It is essential to provide some methodological guidance in the *process* of a progressive elaboration of the requirements document.

The elaboration of a specification can be seen as a sequence of development steps, each step being defined by the application of a transformation on the current state of the requirements document and resulting in a new state of this document [DvL87]. The application of a transformation at some stage of the development depends on some strategies followed by the specifier.

In some recent work [Dub91, DDR92], we have proposed the following strategy:

1. Express specifications on the problem, i.e. on the system considered as a monolithic one (i.e. black-box approach).
2. Identify new sub-systems and attach to each of them their responsibilities so that the refinement preserves the original prescribed behaviour.
3. Apply recursively the step 2 up to the identification of 'terminal' sub-systems, i.e. components for which designers (see Sect.2) agree on the implementation of their attached properties.

Applying this strategy to the *Manufacture* application results in the possible sequence of development steps already suggested on Fig.4 where:

- in state 1, the *Manufacture* is considered as an individual agent in our language;

- in state 2, the *Environment* and *Cell's* are the individual agents, the *Manu-facture* is now considered as a complex agent;
- in state 3, the final version identifies new individual agents composing the *Cell* agents (now considered as complex agents).

In the next sub-section, we further detail the process followed by the specifier when he/she goes from the state 2 to the state 3 of the requirements document.

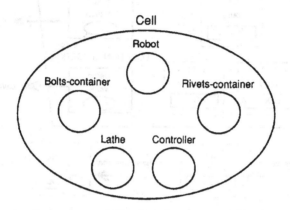

Fig. 9. Declaration associated with the *Cell* agent (II)

4.2 Identifying Agents Responsibilities

In the previous section, we introduced Fig.8 which represents the state of the requirements document at the state 2 of the process. This specification is not a terminal one because the cell is more a "virtual" agent rather than a "concrete" one (i.e. which can be implemented by a designer). To this end, the specifier has to follow a *refinement* process (analogously to the one followed in software design, see, e.g., [BJ78]) which will result in the final version of document presented on Fig.9.

At this level, five new terminal agents are identified:

1. the *lathe* corresponds to the machine in charge of the transformation of a rivet into the bolt. This agent is a device;
2. the *Input-container* is a passive agent in charge of keeping rivets stored on it;
3. the *Output-container* is a passive agent with a role similar to the previous one, viz a bolts keeper;
4. the *Robot* is an active agent in charge of transporting rivets and bolts between containers and the lathe machine;

5. the *Controller* is the software piece which plays the important role of managing the other agents so that the production goal attached to the cell is reached.

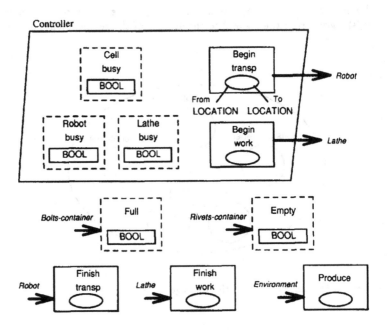

Fig. 10. Declaration associated with the *Controller* agent

For lack of place, the formal specification characterising the behaviour of each agent is not further detailed. On Fig.10 and Fig.11, we are just making precise the role of the *Controller*. From this specification, it results that the controller is in charge of managing the *Produce* orders by issuing the appropriate orders to the different other agents and by controlling their behaviour. For example, the *Controller* is issuing transportation orders to the *Robot* and is aware of the emptiness of the *Rivets-container* (which is equipped with a sensor).

4.3 Reasoning on Agents Responsibilities

In the specification presented on Fig.9, *Cell* is identified as a complex agent and thereby *goals* are associated with it. These goals correspond to a subset of the specification presented on Fig.7 and restricted to declarative constraints (**State Behaviour** and **Commitments**).

The refinement process followed by the specifier is a *correct* one if the goals attached with the *Cell* complex agent are met by the joint behaviour of the

---

Controller

STATE BEHAVIOUR

$\neg$ (Lathe-busy $\wedge$ Robot-busy)
(Lathe-busy $\vee$ Robot-busy) $\implies$ Cell-busy

EFFECTS OF ACTIONS

Begin-transp(o,d): Robot-busy = true
Begin-work: Lathe-busy = true
envt.Produce: Cell-busy = true
robot.Finish-transp(o,d): Robot-busy = false
robot.Finish-transp(lathe,bolts-shelf): Cell-busy = false
lathe.Finish-work: Lathe-busy = false

COMMITMENTS

envt.Produce $\xrightarrow{\Diamond \leq 10min}$ Begin-transp(rivets-shelf,lathe);
Begin-work;
Begin-transp(lathe,bolts-shelf)

RESPONSIBILITY

F(Begin-transp(o,d) / Robot-busy $\vee \neg$ Cell-busy)
F(Begin-work / Lathe-busy $\vee \neg$ Cell-busy)

PERCEPTION

X(envt.Produce / $\neg$ Cell-busy $\wedge \neg$ rivets-shelf.Empty $\wedge \neg$ bolts-shelf.Full)
X(robot.Finish-transp / Cell-busy $\wedge$ Robot-busy)
X(lathe.Finish-work / Cell-busy $\wedge$ Lathe-busy)

PUBLICITY

Fig. 11. Constraints on the *Controller* agent

five individual agents [FH91]. For example, the goal of *"producing a bolt within 10 minutes after a request"* has to be achieved through the combination of the individual actions made by the *Controller, Robot* and *Lathe*.

Due to the formality of our language, a formal proof can be exhibited. For sake of brevity, it is not detailed in this paper but the interested reader may refer to [Dub89] for further discussion.

5   Conclusion

Analogously to some recent contributions in Distributed Artificial Intelligence [Hew91] or in the Design of Distributed Software [SSE89, FM90], we claim that a formal language for capturing requirements should encompass the specification of a composite system, i.e. a system made of multiple agents. Different authors propose different concepts for modelling agents and reasoning on their properties (see, e.g. [Fea87, Bjø92, DFvL91]). In this paper, we introduce ALBERT, a formal language for capturing some of them. This language includes a certain number of features also proved useful in languages like TROLL [JSS91] or DAL [RFM91]. It also incorporates recent results gathered in O-O conceptual modelling by considering agents as a specialization of the object concept (agents being characterized by some specific dynamic properties).

For lack of place, we have not illustrated the structuring mechanisms (based on parameterization and inheritance) which can be used to achieve (i) a better structuring of the requirements document (in particular, by defining a specific vocabulary for some application domain) and (ii) the reuse of existing specification fragments. More details on that topic can be found in [DDR92].

Within the framework of an Esprit II project, a semantics has been given to our language in terms of GLIDER [DDRW91] (A General Language for an Incremental Definition and Elaboration of Requirements). The GLIDER language is based on a so-called *loose (algebraic) semantics* [OSC89] which supports the expression of constraints using, among other things, typed first-order formulas and *streams* (i.e. infinite sequences). In this project, a set of supporting tools are also under development including, in particular, a graphical editor for our language. Finally, our research plans are in three directions:

- the validation of the language concepts and the enhancement of the proposed methodology through the study of conclusions from large industrial experiments currently done in a Computer-Integrated-Manufacturing (C.I.M.) environment and in the field of advanced communications applications;
- at the product level, the identification of a set of orthogonal patterns supporting the expression of different forms of *commitments*;
- at the process level, the study and the formalisation of a set of typical *transformations* and of their *strategies* of use. Examples of them include the development of specifications for non reliable agents and/or non omniscient agents.

Acknowledgement: This work was partially supported by the European Community under Project 2537 (ICARUS) of the European Strategic Program for

Research and development in Information Technology (ESPRIT). The authors wish to thank Marc Derroitte and Robert Darimont for helpful discussions and critical comments.

References

[AG91]   A.J. Alencar and J.A. Goguen. Ooze: An object oriented Z environment. In P. America, editor, *Proc. of the 5th european conference on object-oriented programming – ECOOP'91*, pages 180–199. LNCS 512, Springer-Verlag, 1991.

[BJ78]   D. Bjørner and C.B. Jones. *The Vienna Development Method. The meta-language*, volume 61 of *LNCS*. Springer-Verlag, 1978.

[Bjø92] D. Bjørner. Trusted computing systems: The procos experience. In *Proc. of the 14th international conference on software engineering*, pages 15–34, Melbourne (Australia), May 11–15, 1992. IEEE, ACM Press.

[BMR92] A. Borgida, J. Mylopoulos, and R. Reiter. ...and nothing else changes : The frame problem in procedure specifications. Technical Report DCS-TR-281, Dept. of Computer Science, Rutgers University, 1992.

[BP83]   F. Bodart and Y. Pigneur. *Conception assistée des applications informatiques. Première partie: Etude d'opportunité et analyse conceptuelle.* Masson, Paris, 1983.

[Bru91] J. Brunet. Modelling the world with semantic objects. In *Proc. of the working conference on the object-oriented approach in information systems*, Québec, 1991.

[CY91]   P. Coad and E Yourdon. *Object-Oriented Design.* Prentice-Hall, Englewood Cliffs, New Jersey, 1991.

[DDR92] Eric Dubois, Philippe Du Bois, and André Rifaut. Elaborating, structuring and expressing formal requirements of composite systems. In P. Loucopoulos, editor, *Proc. of the 4th conference on advanced information systems engineering – CAiSE'92*, pages 327–347, Manchester (UK), May12–15, 1992. LNCS 593, Springer-Verlag.

[DDRW91] Eric Dubois, Philippe Du Bois, André Rifaut, and Pierre Wodon. Glider user manual. Intermediate Deliverable SpecFunc-028-R, ESPRIT Project Icarus 2537, June 1991.

[DFHF91] E. Doerry, S. Fickas, R. Helm, and M. Feather. A model for composite system design. In *Proc. of the 6th international workshop on software specification and design*, Milano, October 1991.

[DFvL91] A. Dardenne, S. Fickas, and A. van Lamsweerde. Goal-directed concept acquisition in requirements elicitation. In *Proc. of the 6th international workshop on software specification and design*, Milano, October 1991.

[DHR91] Eric Dubois, Jacques Hagelstein, and André Rifaut. A formal language for the requirements engineering of computer systems. In André Thayse, editor, *From natural language processing to logic for expert systems*, chapter 6. Wiley, 1991.

[DKRS91] Roger Duke, Paul King, Gordon Rose, and Graeme Smith. The object-z specification language – version 1. Technical report 91-1, SVRC, Dept. of Computer Science, The University of Queensland, Queensland (Australia), May 1991.

[Du 92]   Philippe Du Bois. Using glider for the formal definition of a requirements
            language for specifying composite systems. Technical report, Computer
            Science Department, University of Namur, Namur (Belgium), May 1992.

[Dub89]   Eric Dubois. A logic of action for supporting goal-oriented elaborations of
            requirements. In *Proceedings of the 5th international workshop on software
            specification and design*, pages 160–168, Pittsburgh PA, May 19-20, 1989.
            IEEE, CS Press.

[Dub91]   Eric Dubois. Use of deontic logic in the requirements engineering of com-
            posite systems. In J.J. Meyer and R.J. Wieringa, editors, *Proc. of the first
            international workshop on deontic logic in computer science*, Amsterdam
            (The Netherlands), December 11-13, 1991.

[DvL87]   Eric Dubois and Axel van Lamsweerde. Making specification processes
            explicit. In *Proceedings of the 4th international workshop on software spec-
            ification and design*, pages 161–168, Monterey CA, April 3-4, 1987. IEEE,
            CS Press.

[Fea87]   Martin S. Feather. Language support for the specification and development
            of composite systems. *ACM Transactions on programming languages and
            systems*, 9(2):198–234, April 1987.

[Fea89]   Martin S. Feather. Constructing specifications by combining parallel elab-
            orations. *IEEE Transactions on software engineering*, SE-15(2), February
            1989.

[FF89]   Anthony Finkelstein and Hugo Fuks. Multi-party specification. In *Proceed-
            ings of the 5th international workshop on software specification and design*,
            pages 185–195, Pittsburgh PA, May 19-20, 1989. IEEE, CS Press.

[FH91]   Stephen Fickas and Rob Helm. Acting responsibly : Reasoning about agents
            in a multi-agent system. Technical Report CIS-TR-91-02, Dept. of Com-
            puter and Information Science, University of Oregon, Eugene OR, 1991.

[FM90]   Jose Fiadeiro and Tom Maibaum. Describing, structuring and imple-
            menting objects. In *Foundations of Object-Oriented Languages - REX
            School/Workshop*, pages 275–310, Noordwijkerhout (The Netherlands),
            May 28 - June 1, 1990. LNCS 489, Springer-Verlag.

[FP87]   Anthony Finkelstein and Colin Potts. Building formal specifications using
            "structured common sense". In *Proceedings of the 4th international work-
            shop on software specification and design*, pages 108–113, Monterey CA,
            April 3-4, 1987. IEEE, CS Press.

[FS86]   Jose Fiadeiro and Amilcar Sernadas. Linear tense propositional logic. *In-
            formation Systems*, 11(1):61–85, 1986.

[GB91]   D. Gabbay and P. Mc Brien. Temporal logic and historical databases.
            In *Proc. of the 17th international conference on very large databases*,
            Barcelona, September 1991.

[GBM86]   Sol J. Greenspan, Alexander Borgida, and John Mylopoulos. A require-
            ments modeling language and its logic. In M.L. Bodie and J. Mylopoulos,
            editors, *On knowledge base managment systems*, Topics in information sys-
            tems, pages 471–502. Springer-Verlag, 1986.

[GHW85]   John V. Guttag, James J. Horning, and Jeannette M. Wing. Larch in five
            easy pieces. Technical Report 5, Digital systems research center, Palo Alto
            CA, July 1985.

[HC68]   G.E. Hughes and M.J. Cresswell. *An introduction to modal logic*. Methuen
            and Co., London, 1968.

[Hew91] C. Hewitt. DAI betwist and between: open systems science and/or intelligent agents. In J. Mylopoulos and R. Balzer, editors, *Proc. of the international workshop on the development of intelligent information systems*, Niagara-on-the-Lake (Canada), April 21-23, 1991.

[HR92] Jacques Hagelstein and Dominique Roelants. Reconciling operational and declarative specifications. In P. Loucopoulos, editor, *Proc. of the 4th conference on advanced information systems engineering - CAiSE'92*, pages 221-238, Manchester (UK), May12-15, 1992. LNCS 593, Springer-Verlag.

[JF90] W. Lewis Johnson and Martin Feather. Building an evolution transformation library. In *Proceedings of the 12th international conference on software engineering*, Nice (France), March 1990. IEEE.

[JSS91] R. Jungclaus, G. Saake, and C. Sernadas. Formal specification of object systems. In S. Abramsky and T. Maibaum, editors, *Proc. of TAPSOFT'91 Vol.2*, pages 60-82, Brighton (UK), 1991. LNCS 494, Springer-Verlag.

[KVdR89] R. Koymans, J. Vytopil, and W. de Roever. Specifying message passing and time-critical systems with temporal logic. Doctoral dissertation, Eindhoven University of Technology, Eindhoven (The Netherlands), 1989.

[MBJK90] J. Mylopoulos, A. Borgida, M. Jarke, and M. Koubarakis. Telos: A language for representing knowledge about information systems. *ACM Transansaction on Information Systems*, 8(4):325-362, 1990.

[MCN92] J. Mylopoulos, L. Chung, and B. Nixon. Representing and using non-functional requirements: a process-oriented approach. *IEEE Transactions on software engineering*, SE-18, June 1992.

[OSC89] F. Orejas, V. Sacristan, and S. Clerici. Development of algebraic specifications with constraints. In *Proc. of the workshop in categorical methods in computer science*. LNCS 393, Springer-Verlag, 1989.

[RFM91] Mark D. Ryan, Jose Fiadeiro, and Tom Maibaum. Sharing actions and attributes in modal action logic. In T. Ito and A. Meyer, editors, *Theoretical Aspects of Computer Software*. Springer-Verlag, 1991.

[Ros77] Douglas T. Ross. Structured analysis (sa): a language for communicating ideas. *IEEE Transactions on software engineering*, SE-3(1):16-34, January 1977.

[Ser80] Amilcar Sernadas. Temporal aspects of logic procedure definition. *Information Systems*, 5:167-187, 1980.

[Sho90] Y. Shoham. Agent-oriented programming. Technical report STAN-CS-90-1335, Robotics Laboratory, Computer Science Dept, Stanford University, Stanford CA, 1990.

[SM88] S. Shlaer and S.J. Mellor. *Object-oriented systems analysis: modelling the world in data*. Yourdon Press: Prentice-Hall, Englewood Cliffs, New Jersey, 1988.

[SSE89] A. Sernadas, C. Sernadas, and H.-D. Ehrich. Abstract object types: a temporal perspective. In B. Banieqbal, H. Barringer, and A. Pnueli, editors, *Proc. of the colloquium on temporal logic and specification*, pages 324-350. LNCS 398, Springer-Verlag, 1989.

[TH77] D. Teichroew and E. Hershey. A computer-aided technique for structured documentation and analysis of information processing systems. *IEEE Transactions on software engineering*, SE-3:41-48, 1977.

[TLW91] C. Theodoulidis, P. Loucopoulos, and B. Wangler. A conceptual modelling formalism for temporal database applications. *Information Systems*, 16(4):401-416, 1991.

[TRC83] H. Tardieu, A. Rochfeld, and R. Colletti. *La méthode MERISE: principes et outils*. Les Editions d'Organisation, Paris (France), 1983.

Designing an Extensible Distributed Language with a Meta-Level Architecture

Shigeru Chiba* and Takashi Masuda

Department of Information Science, The University of Tokyo
7-3-1 Hongo, Bunkyo-ku, Tokyo 113, Japan
E-mail: {chiba,masuda}@is.s.u-tokyo.ac.jp

Abstract. This paper presents a methodology for designing extensible languages for distributed computing. As a sample product of this methodology, which is based on a meta-level (or reflective) technique, this paper describes a variant of C++ called *Open C++*, in which the programmer can alter the implementation of method calls to obtain new language functionalities suitable for the programmer's applications. This paper also presents a framework called *Object Communities*, which is used to help obtain various functionalities for distributed computing on top of Open C++. Because the overhead due to the meta level computation is negligible in distributed computing, this methodology is applicable to practical programming.

1 Introduction

Languages for distributed computing have been designed mostly to provide a general functionality that can be used in a broad range of application domains. Designers of these languages have developed numerous language primitives or functionalities, such as Ada's rendezvous [26], the remote procedure call [2], and Orca's shared data-object [1]. Each of these functionalities has its own most suitable domain of applications, so a language that has a single one of these functionalities will be small and simple but will not be suitable for some applications. It is, on the other hand, possible to design a language that has many or all such functionalities, but such a language would be large and awkward.

The goal of this paper is to demonstrate another approach, which is to make a language extensible. By this approach, we have been able to design a language that is, at the same time, simple, elegant, and applicable in a wide range of domains. A programmer can tailor the language to exploit various functionalities. Language extensibility has long been an important issue, and Kiczales et al., for example, have recently discussed the designing of extensible class libraries [11]. A typical approach to supporting various functionalities within a single language is to provide a set of reusable code, called a library program, that implements functionalities that are not supported by the language alone. Although functionalities implemented by this approach may show lower performance than

---

* JSPS (Japan Society for the Promotion of Science) Fellow-DC

O.M. Nierstrasz (Ed.): ECOOP '93, LNCS 707, pp. 482-501, 1993.
© Springer-Verlag Berlin Heidelberg 1993

ones implemented by altering the language system such as the compiler, this approach is broadly employed because sufficient performance is usually obtained by this approach in practice. The library-program approach, however, is limited in that it cannot implement a functionality that deals with non-first-class entities of the language.

This paper proposes methodology using an object-oriented meta-level technique in designing of an extensible language for distributed computing. To demonstrate the use of this methodology, we present *Open C++*, which is a C++ [23] variant including a simple *metaobject protocol* (MOP) [10]. In Open C++ the implementation of a method call (or in the object-oriented terminology, message passing) is made open-ended by that MOP. To obtain a new functionality that fits the application, the programmer can easily extend the implementation within Open C++ itself. Performance overheads are one of major issues in meta-level techniques, but they are not critical in domains such as distributed computing, which Open C++ deals with. The seriousness of the overheads depends on the inherent cost of functionalities achieved with the meta-level technique. Since the overhead of Open C++ is negligible in comparison with the implemented functionalities, we believe that our approach is — like the library-program approach, which is useful in spite of its relative slowness — applicable to actual problems.

As with other systems using meta-level techniques, an extension of Open C++ is described in meta code (meta-level program). Although meta code is usually written only by a system specialist because MOP would be often complicated and extension was not frequent, we expect normal programmers (who are not "wizards") to write meta code in Open C++ whenever a new functionality is required for their applications. The Open C++ MOP is therefore designed to provide an abstraction that encapsulates implementation details unnecessary to the extension of a method call. To facilitate extension by normal programmers, this paper also provides a framework, called *Object Communities*, that includes some basic functionalities for extending a method call for distributed computing. With this framework, normal programmers can easily obtain various functionalities for distributed computing on top of Open C++.

2 Open C++: A Simple MOP for C++

In most imperative languages for distributed computing, procedure calls (or in the object-oriented terminology, method calls) are extended to support remote communication across a network. Those extended method calls provide not only a functionality invoking a procedure (or a method) at a remote machine, but also a functionality synchronizing multiple threads of control. In Ada [26] and Concurrent C [5], for example, a statement syntactically similar to a procedure call is used for executing a rendezvous, and a procedure call is extended to block the sender thread until the receiver is ready. In ConcurrentSmalltalk [28], a method call of Smalltalk-80 [6] is extended to be synchronous or asynchronous: an *asynchronous method call* lets a sender thread continue its execution without blocking, whereas a *synchronous method call* blocks the sender thread until the receiver thread finishes a requested task.

By using a meta-level or so-called reflection technique [21], Open C++ offers normal programmers the ability to extend a method call. Normal programmers can modify the implementation of a method call within a user program to obtain various functionalities for remote communication. The implementation of a method call is exposed to programmers as a *metaobject* [15], which is an abstract model of that implementation and conceals implementation details unnecessary to the extension. A metaobject is almost the same as a normal object, but its behavior corresponds to the actual execution of the method call. An object at the *base level* has its metaobject at the *meta level*, and the execution of its methods is controlled by the metaobject. If a method of the object is invoked, the specific method of the metaobject, instead of a default implementation embedded in the compiler, is used to execute the invoked method. Since a metaobject is defined in C++, the programmer can alter the implementation of a method call by defining another metaobject and then substituting it. Our approach does not require rebuilding the compiler but is done within a user program.

2.1 Base-Level Directives

Open C++ provides a very simple MOP (metaobject protocol[2]) to make a method call extensible. The objects controlled by metaobjects are called *reflective objects*. Because control by a metaobject imposes some performance and memory overhead in Open C++, the programmer can specify whether or not an object is reflective. A nonreflective object is compiled to be a normal C++ object, which has no metaobject, so that it is executed without overhead. To distinguish between reflective and nonreflective objects, a reflective object is identified by a different class name. If the class of an object that may be reflective is X, then a reflective object is refl_X and a nonreflective object is still X. In the current implementation, the class refl_X is a subclass of X.

To create a reflective object, the class of the object and its metaobject must be declared with special directives, which are C++ comments that start with //MOP. Note that even if a program includes the directives of Open C++, that program is still a valid C++ program. The declaration of a reflective object takes the form

```
//MOP reflect class X : M;
```

This declaration means that an object of the class refl_X is a reflective object controlled by a metaobject of the class M. Note that it never means that the classes X or refl_X are subclasses of M. The class M is a normal C++ class except that it must inherit from the class MetaObj. To extend its implementation of a method call, a metaobject can be a reflective object that is controlled by a meta-metaobject. Open C++ allows such an ascending tower of metaobjects.

---

[2] A metaobject protocol is a meta-protocol organized using object-oriented techniques. Here a meta-protocol is a protocol about the behavior and implementation of another protocol, such as interface and functionality.

The methods of a reflective object are divided into two groups, depending on whether the invocation of the method is controlled by its metaobject. The methods controlled by the metaobject are called reflect methods, and although reflect methods are invoked in an extended manner, the other methods are invoked according to the plain C++ method call semantics. The following is an example of specifying a reflect method.

```
class X {
public:
    X();
//MOP reflect:
    int func(int);
private:
    int p;
};
```

The methods following the directive "//MOP reflect:" are specified as reflect methods. Here, for example, func() is a reflect method. Such methods may have a category name to enable their metaobject to recognize a role of the methods. A metaobject may alter the execution of a method call according to the category name. Consider the following example: The method update() has a category name "write".

```
class Y {
public:
    ...
//MOP reflect(write):
    int update(int);

//MOP reflect(metamethod):
    void Meta_operation();
    ...
```

The category name "metamethod" has a special meaning: it is used to call meta-methods of a metaobject from the base level across the boundary of the levels. Calling a reflect method in this category is regarded as calling a meta-method that has the same *method* name. The reflect methods having the category name "metamethod" themselves are never executed.

2.2 Metaobject Protocol

When a reflect method is called, its execution is controlled by its metaobject. A metaobject is defined in C++, and its class must inherit from the base class MetaObj, which mainly defines the following two methods.

- void Meta_MethodCall(Id method, Id category, ArgPack& args,
                                              ArgPack& reply);
  This method implements a method call at the base level. It is invoked if a reflect method is called.

- void Meta_HandleMethodCall(Id method, ArgPac& args,
                                               ArgPac& reply);

This method is used to actually execute a reflect method.

To alter the implementation of a method call, the programmer defines a subclass of MetaObj in which those methods are redefined so that the metaobject acts in the intended way.

Suppose that a reflect method f() is called. If the method f() is called, then the method Meta_MethodCall() is instead invoked at the meta level. The first argument of the method Meta_MethodCall() is bound to the integer identifier of the called method f() (the type Id represents integers), and the second argument represents the category name of the method f(). The actual arguments of the method call to f() are passed as the third argument, args. Note that within a metaobject, the actual argument list of a method call is a first-class entity because the third argument, args, is a normal C++ object whose class is ArgPac. The argument args has the same interface as a stack so that the programmer can access any actual argument stored in args. The programmer can also transfer the argument args to another metaobject that may reside on a different machine. Converting the actual arguments to an ArgPac-class object corresponds to the *reifying* process. which is impossible in C++ alone without support of the Open C++ compiler.

The method Meta_MethodCall() carries out certain computation and stores the result into the forth argument, reply. The stored result is returned as a return value to the caller that calls the reflect method f(). The method Meta_MethodCall() usually uses the method Meta_HandleMethodCall() to compute the result value. This method takes a method identifier and an actual argument list, and it returns the result value of the specified method. This method allows any reflect method to be executed at any time. In the example above, the metaobject can execute another reflect method as well as f() to compute the result value.

To illustrate the Open C++ MOP, consider a simple example in which this metaobject prints a message before executing a reflect method called at the base level:

```
class VerboseMetaObj : public MetaObj {
public:
    void Meta_MethodCall(Id method, Id category,
                         ArgPac& args, ArgPac& reply){
        printf("***reflect method %s was called.\n",
               Meta_GetMethodName(method));
        Meta_HandleMethodCall(method, args, reply);
    };
};
```

If a metaobject of the class VerboseMetaObj is specified, a message is printed on the console every time a reflect method is called. The method Meta_Method-Call() specifies that this metaobject prints the name of the called method before actually executing that method. Note that if we eliminate the line "printf(...);" from this method, the implementation of a method call by this metaobject becomes the same as the implementation in plain C++. Figure 1 shows how a metaobject of the class VerboseMetaObj controls a method call. The metaobject controls an object of the class refl_X (as previously shown, a reflective object of the class X). When a reflect method func() of that object is called, the metaobject traps that method call and executes the method func() according to the method Meta_MethodCall().

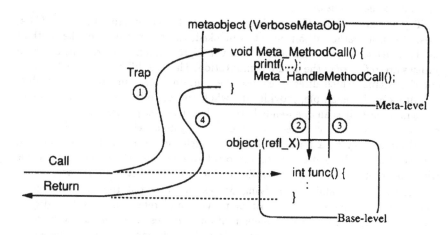

Fig. 1. Metaobject protocol of Open C++

Converting the actual arguments to an ArgPac-class object is similar to the marshaling/unmarshaling process in remote procedure calls. In the current implementation, the class refl_X (which the Open C++ compiler generates) redefines a reflect method so that the method carries out such conversion and then invokes the method Meta_MethodCall() of its metaobject. The current Open C++ compiler converts some atomic types (integers, pointers, etc.) implicitly but does not class types (i.e., objects). The class types that can be an argument of a reflect method must have some specific methods for the conversion. A similar limitation also appears in the marshaling/unmarshaling process because the efficiency of converting complex data, such as an object, often depends on the program semantics. Such conversion should be under programmer's control [8]. Open C++, however, provides a convenient library to implement the methods for the conversion, and it also provides some predefined classes that facilitate to use a character string etc. as an argument of a reflect method. Thereby, the limitation on argument types of reflect methods is not awkward.

2.3   Why Meta? Pros and Cons

Open C++ does not expose the implementation of a method call directly, but through an abstract interface. Although the original implementation of a method call, which is embedded in the compiler, is described in assembly code, the programmer who attempts to extend the method call describes a new implementation of C++ methods such as Meta_MethodCall() instead of assembly code. Because of the description through the abstract interface, the programmer need not consider such details of the implementation as a stack image and the number of arguments. The programmer can thus concentrate on matters strongly relevant to the extension.

This feature of Open C++ is due to the meta-level technique that Open C++ uses. When a method of an object is invoked, the computation of the method call is *reified* to be entities available in a C++ program, and operations on these entities are *reflected* in the actual computation. This is a difference from "pseudo-open" systems, which directly expose their internal structure to be extensible. Smalltalk-80, for example, provides the whole source code of its runtime system. Thus in a sense, it is an open-ended system because user programmers can freely modify classes of kernel objects to extend the system behavior. This feature of Smalltalk-80 may be a kind of reflection[3]. Such modification of kernel objects, however, can easily lead the system into collapse because the programmer deals with the complicated kernel code directly, without an abstract interface.

On the other hand, the reifying process implies that the performance of Open C++ degenerates. The cost of reifying and reflecting is not negligible compared with the original implementation fully described in assembly code. This is because the reifying process bridges the wide gap between the assembly level and the C++ level. The higher the abstract interface Open C++ provides for extension, the bigger the performance degeneration of the reifying process will be. This degeneration is negligible, however, when Open C++ is used for distributed computing. The method call extended for distributed computing is so slow that the performance degeneration becomes relatively insignificant. This issue is discussed in detail in Section 5.

Another benefit of Open C++ is that meta code defines the extension independently of each object so that meta code has high reusability. The same meta code can be used to extend method calls to different objects. Because meta code is organized according to the metaobject protocol, furthermore, part of it is also reusable by class inheritance.

Open C++ improves the expressive power of a class library, which is also a technique for supporting various functionalities within a single language. If a functionality like remote method calls is implemented solely by means of class libraries, the translation of an argument list into a network message becomes responsibility to the programmer. This is because the class library alone cannot deal with any entities except these available at the base level, and an argument

---

[3] Peter Deutsch pointed this out at the BOF session in the '92 workshop on reflection and meta-level architecture.

list is available not at the base level but at the meta level. On the other hand, Open C++ enables a class library to deal with an entity available at the meta level through a metaobject. For example, it can use a metaobject for transferring an argument list to a different machine and can execute a remote method.

3 Object Communities — An Additional MOP for Distributed Computing

Because a method call is a good basis of functionalities for distributed computing, various functionalities can be implemented on top of Open C++. Most imperative languages include a method call statement, and it has been used to implement a lot of existing functionalities for distributed computing. A method call can be extended to support not only a remote method call but also asynchronous message passing and message broadcasting. It can also be extended to be a synchronization mechanism such as a rendezvous or a distributed semaphore.

To obtain a functionality suitable for the application, normal programmers should themselves describe meta code to extend a method call. Although previous systems usually expected meta code to be written only by a specialist, the simple MOP of Open C++ makes meta programming possible for programmers with little knowledge as well as for specialists. The MOP of Open C++, however, does not in itself support distributed computing; it only provides a platform on top of which a functionality for distributed computing is implemented. This section proposes a framework, called *Object Communities*, that facilitates to implement such a functionality on top of Open C++. This framework is a class library of metaobjects and includes facilities that are commonly used to extend a method call. *Object Communities* add a layered protocol onto the MOP of Open C++. It provides the classes of metaobjects that implement some typical functionalities for distributed computing so that programmers can obtain functionalities tailored to their applications by redefining some methods of those classes.

3.1 Background Problem

Object Communities are designed to be a framework for implementing various application-specific functionalities for distributed computing, such as distributed shared data, distributed transactions, remote procedure calls. Such a framework must provide a facility managing computation distributed to multiple processes on different machines. A simple client-server framework based on remote procedure calls is not sufficient as such a framework because although it can request computation to another process, it cannot synchronize computation between processes.

The simple client-server framework, for example, cannot in an easily understandable way implement the functionality required by groupware[4] (or multiuser applications), which supports collaborative work by multiple users. The essential feature of groupware is that an application program consists of multiple *autonomous* processes that are responsible for interaction with each user. Those processes interfere with each other because the users manipulate shared entities, such as shared documents and pictures, and their actions are therefore restricted by the actions of other users. The processes may also notify each other when shared entities are updated and they can request computation, such as redrawing the displays, in order to keep consistent images of the entities on the displays. To do these things, the application needs a functionality that makes it possible to block the execution of other processes as well as to request computation to other processes.

3.2 Overview of Object Communities

The fundamental functionality of *Object Communities* is the management of a group of objects distributed in different machines. Such a group is called *an object community* (Figure 2). We assume that each object belongs to a single process that has its own address space separated from others and communicates with other processes across a network. A process is invoked explicitly by the user, and it performs cooperatively with other processes in the same application.

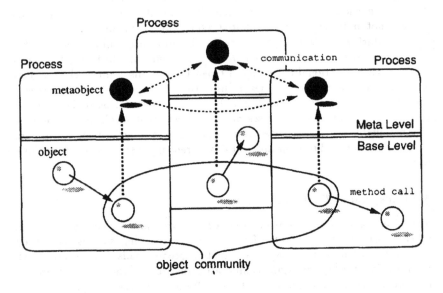

Fig. 2. An object community

Each object of an object community acts in a manner that depends on behavior of other objects of that object community. The method calls to the objects are executed cooperatively by the metaobjects so that the objects provide a certain functionality for distributed computing. Note that although a group of objects as a whole provides some functionality, the definition of the objects does not include any distributed concepts: these appear only in the definition of the metaobjects. The functionality provided is implemented at the meta level, and the base-level programmer has only to know how a method call is extended at the base level. *Object Communities* provide a clear separation between distributed computation and the substantial computation executed in the application.

In *Object Communities*, a metaobject has the following additional abilities.

- *Concurrency Control.* A metaobject controls the internal concurrency of its object. It can ignore and delay execution of a called method of the object until some condition is satisfied. A metaobject can also execute multiple methods of its object concurrently. And a metaobject can execute a method of its object when other metaobjects request that the method be executed.
- *Communication.* A metaobject has two means of communicating with other metaobjects of the same object community: a remote method call and message broadcasting. A metaobject can call a remote method of other metaobjects. This is done in a manner similar to that of a local method call. The caller metaobject is blocked until a reply is returned from the called object. A metaobject can also send a message to all metaobjects of the same object community. Because broadcast messages are serialized by the underlying system, all metaobjects receive the messages in the same order. A broadcast message is also delivered to the metaobject that sent the message.

Although a metaobject controls the internal concurrency of its object, there is with few exceptions no internal concurrency of the metaobject by default. The methods of a metaobject are executed sequentially, so the behavior of a metaobject is easily understandable. If internal concurrency of a metaobject is necessary, it must be controlled by an explicitly specified meta-metaobject.

3.3 MOP of Object Communities

To append the *Concurrency Control* and *Communication* abilities, *Object Communities* provide the class OcCoreMetaObj, which is a subclass of MetaObj, and the other classes of metaobjects that implement functionalities based on *Object Communities* must inherit from this subclass.

The class OcCoreMetaObj defines some methods for manipulating an object community, for network communication, for controlling concurrency, and so on. The following methods are to manipulate an object community.

- Meta_CreateOc(...) creates an object community.
- Meta_DestroyOc(...) destroys an existing object community.
- Meta_Join(...) lets an object join a specified object community.
- Meta_Leave(...) lets an object leave a specified object community.

An object community is treated if it were a communication channel. An object can join or leave an object community at any time, but the object community remains even if no object belongs to it. It exists until it is destroyed explicitly.

To give initial information to a metaobject that joins an object community, the underlying system holds an initializing message for each object community. This message, which can be dynamically updated by a metaobject, is passed to a metaobject when its object joins to an object community.

The class `OcCoreMetaObj` defines three methods for communication with other metaobjects.

- `Meta_EventNotify(...)` broadcasts a message to the other metaobjects of the same object community.
- `Meta_Query(...)` calls a method of other metaobjects in a manner like that of the remote procedure call. The metaobject is blocked until a reply message arrives.
- `Meta_WaitForEvent(...)` blocks a metaobject until it is ready to receive a broadcast message. A metaobject can use this method to wait for a message broadcast by itself.

A message sent with the first two methods must be a pair consisting of an method identifier (`Id`) and an actual argument list (`ArgPac`). By sending a message, a metaobject requests other metaobjects to execute a method of their object so that the methods are executed cooperatively.

The behavior of a metaobject receiving a message is defined by the following methods. The class `OcCoreMetaObj` only declares these methods; their bodies are defined in its subclasses to alter the behavior of each metaobject.

- `Meta_EventCallbackBody(...)` is executed when a broadcast message is received.
- `Meta_SelfEventCallbackBody(...)` is executed when a broadcast message that the metaobject itself sent is received.
- `Meta_ReplyQueryBody(...)` is a method exported to other metaobjects. This method can be called by other metaobjects with the method `Meta_-Query()`.

Although basically there is no internal concurrency of a metaobject, these three methods may be executed concurrently when the metaobject is blocked by either the method `Meta_Query()` or `Meta_WaitForEvent()`. This exception is necessary to prevent a deadlock.

The current implementation of *Object Communities* does not provide a pre-emptive scheduler. The programmer must therefore voluntarily cause a context switch at short intervals. The class `OcCoreMetaObj` defines methods like `WakeupTaskSv()` and `RecvMessage()` to cause a context switch. Note that implementing a preemptive scheduler is possible, and that a preemptive scheduler can, in fact, be obtained if a timer-signal handler is available. The reason that a nonpreemptive scheduler is selected is to prevent the internal concurrency of a metaobject that has no meta-metaobject. The methods of a metaobject are executed atomically; they are not preempted.

4 Examples of Method-Call Extension

Many functionalities for distributed computing can be implemented as a group of objects on different machines. Since *Object Communities* provide the ability to manage a group of objects, such a functionality is implemented on top of Open C++ by defining a subclass of the class OcCoreMetaObj. In fact, *Object Communities* already include some subclasses of OcCoreMetaObj, which implement various functionalities for distributed computing. Figure 3 illustrates the class hierarchy of metaobjects provided by *Object Communities* in default.

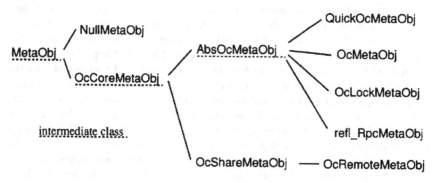

Fig. 3. Class hierarchy of metaobjects

The class NullMetaObj is irrelevant to *Object Communities*: it implements a method call that is done in the original manner of C++ method calls. The other subclasses correspond to various functionalities. They implement distributed shared data, transactions, and remote procedure calls. They also implement remote object pointers with which an object can transparently call a method of an object on a different machine. The implementation of remote object pointers exploits other programming techniques such as "smart pointers" [23] so that remote object pointers are naturally available in C++. Furthermore, another subclass implements persistent objects by using the ability of Open C++ to deal with instance variables of an object by the metaobject. Because of space limitation, the details of this ability are not given here; we will present them in another paper.

Here we explain two of the subclasses of *Object Communities*: distributed shared data and transactions. Distributed shared data are implemented by the class OcMetaObj. The shared data are replicated and held by the objects that belong to the same object community. The metaobjects control those objects to hold consistent values of the shared data. Suppose that the shared data is an integer and is represented as a variable p of the class SharedData at the base level. To update the variable p, the class SharedData has a method Update(). If the variable p is updated, this method redraws a graphical display according to the new value of p:

```
class SharedData {
    ...
public:
//MOP reflect:
    void Update(int new_p) { p = new_p; RedrawDisplay(); }
private:
    void RedrawDisplay();
    int  p;        // inaccessible from the outside of the object
};

//MOP reflect class SharedData : OcMetaObj;
```

An object of the class SharedData can be a reflective object, and the class of the metaobject is OcMetaObj. The method Update() is a reflect method. If an object of the class refl_SharedData is created, the metaobject makes the object join the specified object community. Then the variable p of the object is maintained by the metaobject to hold the same value as the values of p of the other objects of the same object community. If the method Update() is called, the metaobject requests the other metaobjects to use the same argument new_p, and execute the same method of their objects. Thus if the method Update() of an object of the object community is called, then the methods of all the objects are executed and the values of p are updated keeping consistency. Note that the definition of the class SharedData does not include any code concerning distributed computation; such code is in the definition of the metaobject. Methods of the metaobject are defined as follows:

```
void OcMetaObj::Meta_MethodCall(Id method_id, Id category,
                                ArgPack args, ArgPack reply){
    // notifying others of a method call
    Id event = Meta_EventNotify(method_id, args);
    // waiting until that notification is serialized
    Meta_WaitForEvent(event, args);
    // executing the called method actually
    Meta_HandleMethodCall(method_id, args, reply);
}

void OcMetaObj::Meta_EventCallbackBody(Id method_id,
                                ArgPack args, ArgPack reply){
    // if other metaobjects report a method call,
    // the metaobject executes the called method.
    Meta_HandleMethodCall(method_id, args, reply);
}
```

The consistency between the values of p is guaranteed even if two metaobjects attempt to execute the method Update(). This is because the notifications by those metaobjects are serialized so that every metaobject receives the notifications in the same order.

Since there is no restriction in terms of the definition of the method Update(), the programmer can define any action that is executed whenever the shared data are updated. This kind of processing cannot be adequately treated by other mechanisms for distributed shared data, such as distributed shared memory [13], because they do not support a functionality that invokes user-defined actions on each machine that shares the data.

Although in the example above other metaobjects are notified of a method call immediately, some mechanisms for distributed shared data improve performance by using an algorithm in which the notification is delayed [24]. Such an algorithm is also available in Open C++ if the programmer defines a subclass of OcMetaObj to implement it. When implementing such an algorithm, it is necessary to distinguish methods that modify the shared data from methods that simply read the data. Category names of reflect methods are useful for this. For example,

```
class SharedData2 {
    ...
public:
//MOP reflect(write):
    void Update(int new_p) { p = new_p; RedrawDisplay(); }
//MOP reflect(read):
    int Get() { return p; }
    ...
};
```

The category names let the metaobject identify the method Update() as a "write" method, and the method Get() as a "read" one.

Next we show another subclass of *Object Communities*. The class OcLockMetaObj of metaobjects implements atomic transactions. Although the concept of atomic transactions includes recoverability (a transaction causes no side-effect if it fails), the class OcLockMetaObj does not support recoverability. It only guarantees atomicity; the sequence of the operations in a transaction is executed continuously. The method Meta_MethodCall() of the class OcLockMetaObj is as follows.

```
void OcLockMetaObj::Meta_MethodCall(Id method_id, Id category,
                        ArgPac& args, ArgPac& reply){
    while(locked)
        Meta_WaitForEvent();      // block until a lock is released.

    // the following is the same as the method of OcMetaObj
    Id event = Meta_EventNotify(method_id, args);
    Meta_WaitForEvent(event, args);
    Meta_HandleMethodCall(method_id, args, reply);
}
```

The metaobject of the class OcLockMetaObj delays the method execution while the execution is locked. To begin a transaction, the programmer calls a method of the metaobject, which locks method execution with a broadcast message. Receiving the message, the other metaobjects of the same object community stop method execution until that metaobject releases the lock. The variable lock indicates whether execution is locked or unlocked. It is maintained by messages between metaobjects.

5 Overheads due to having a Meta Level

Efficient implementation of meta-level techniques is a major research topic. Because execution of a reflective object in Open C++ is partly interpreted by a metaobject, its execution is slower than that of a nonreflective object. This section briefly shows the result of measurements in terms of the execution speed.

The current Open C++ compiler is a preprocessor of the C++ compiler. Because no modification is added to the C++ compiler, an Open C++ program is translated into a plain C++ code. Calling a reflect method thus imposes some overhead that by some standards is not small.[4] We show the result of performance measurements of method calls.

Table 1. Average Latency (μsec.) of a null method call

number of arguments	0	1	5	5 × double
C++ function	0.3	0.6	1.3	2.1
C++ virtual method	0.8	1.0	1.8	2.2
reflect method	1.8	6.3	13.8	21.7
reflect/virtual ratio	2.3	6.3	7.7	9.9

SPARC 40 MHz (28.5 MIPS) and Sun C++ 2.1

Table 1 lists latency time for three kinds of null method calls. These values were measured on a SPARC station 2 (SunOS 4.1.1), and the compiler was Sun C++ 2.1. The latency was measured for different numbers of arguments. The type of arguments was int except for the data of the rightmost column, for which the type was double. Although the 0-argument method does not return anything, the other methods return an int value. A method that takes 5 double arguments returns a double value. The three kinds of null method calls are a C++ function, a virtual method, and a reflect method. The first two are supported by both C++ and Open C++, whereas the last is available only in Open C++. A C++ function call is to call a method of an object pointed to by a variable. This takes a form like ptr->func(). A virtual method call is to call a method of an object whose class is unknown at compile time; a method name is dynamically bound to a method body. A reflect method call is one controlled by a metaobject of the class NullMetaObj, which implements a method call so that its behavior is the same as that of a C++ function call.

The last line of the table shows the ratio of the latency of a reflect method call to that of a virtual method call. This ratio increases with the number of arguments because the overhead of a reflect method call is mainly due to the

---

[4] The initial version of the Open C++ compiler showed that a reflect method call was 100 times slower than a virtual method call of C++.

reifying process of the argument list of the method call. Arguments are copied to an `ArgPac` class object separately when the `reflect` method is called. The overhead for this copying increases in proportion to the number of arguments. Since the 0-argument method takes no argument, its overhead is smaller than that of the other methods.

The result of these measurements shows that a `reflect` method call is 6 to 8 times slower than a `virtual` method call. Although this overhead seems important, it is actually negligible if Open C++ is used for distributed computing, since the network latency time is between several hundred microseconds and several milliseconds. The overhead is also reduced by a proper designing of the applications. In carefully designed applications, distributed computation is localized in a small number of objects, which would be reflective, and the other objects are executed without overhead since Open C++ allows to specify whether or not an object is reflective. We believe that meta-level techniques are already applicable to practical programming if the programmer selects a domain in which the overhead is negligible in comparison with the overhead for performance of a functionality implemented with the meta-level technique.

Furthermore, from the viewpoint of distributed computing, the overhead of Open C++ is due to the cost of the marshaling/unmarshaling process, in which transferred data are converted into a network message. Because this process commonly appears in distributed computing, the overhead of Open C++ is almost equivalent to that of other approaches such as Sun's RPC [25]. When Sun's RPC library is used, each conversion of an `int` argument takes a few microseconds because that library is a general one, and a few nested function calls are needed whenever a converting routine (an XDR routine) is called.

If the increased overhead of a meta-level technique is limited to within a factor of 10, then the advantage of that meta-level technique is worthwhile. In the concurrent language ABCL/R2 [17], for example, the execution that involves a meta-level operation is 6 or 7 times slower than a normal execution [16]. As in Open C++. the programmer can select whether or not an object is controlled by a metaobject. As a result, ABCL/R2 improves the execution speed of a program by a meta-level technique.

6 Related Work

C++ provides some meta-level operations. The macro set of handling a variable argument list can be considered to provide a few restricted meta-level operations. It allows the programmer to traverse an argument list whose length and element types are variable, as if the argument list were a first-class entity. Operator overloading is also a meta-level operation because it enables the replacement of predefined operators, such as + and ->, with user-defined procedures. No meta-level information is available in a overloading procedure, however, because operator overloading is not implemented by using the concept of reflection.

The stub generator [2] of remote procedure calls, such as Sun's `rpcgen` [25], has a functionality similar to that of the Open C++ compiler. It reads the description file of a remote procedure and then generates a stub routine, which is a utility routine for calling the remote procedure. Unlike the Open C++ compiler, however, the stub generator does not expose the inside of a stub routine, so the programmer cannot alter the implementation of a stub routine in a well-organized manner. The FOG compiler [7] provides the ability of extending a generated code. It allows to use in C++ a fragmented object (FO), which is a distributed object. In the FOG compiler, the programmer can specify a communication protocol of a remote procedure call.

Meta-level (or reflection) techniques have been applied in various domains and they are still an active area of research. CLOS MOP [10] is the first try to apply the meta-level techniques to a practical language. It provides an extensible implementation of CLOS [22]: all specifications of CLOS are modifiable. The mechanism for method lookup, for example, is extensible by a metaobject. There are several reflective language systems other than CLOS MOP. ABCL/R2 applies a meta-level technique to parallel computation, and RbCl [9] tries to minimize the run-time kernel that is not extensible. AL1/D [18] provides multiple abstract models for each aspect of the implementation, and this is effective when many aspects of the implementation are exposed. The programmer can alter each aspect independently, without considering other aspects.

Meta-level techniques are also beginning to be used for commercial systems. The Meta-Information-Protocol (MIP) [3] used in some commercial systems, is a mechanism for accessing the type information of a C++ object at run time. It represents type information by a metaobject so that typesafe downcast is available in C++. Because a metaobject in the MIP exposes internal information but a change of the metaobject does not influence behavior of an object, the overheads of the MIP is obviously small with respect to execution speed compared with Open C++. Meta-level techniques are also used for developing systems other than languages, such as an operating system and a window system. Apertos [27] is an operating system completely based on a meta-level technique, and Silica [19] is a window system with which the programmer can alter how the system draws an image on a window, how the relationship of windows is maintained, and so on. The Choices operating system uses a meta-level technique to implement its kernel and subsystems [14]. Using macros and programmer conventions, Choices exploits a meta-level technique within the confines of plain C++.

Some researchers try to reduce the cost associated with having the meta level. CLOS MOP, for example, has no costs beyond these of plain CLOS. This is achieved by careful protocol design and by implementation devices in which, for example, calls to the meta-level functions are partially evaluated. Because the execution mechanism of CLOS has inherent complexity and costs, the cost due to the meta level can be recovered by those techniques. On the other hand, C++ is designed so that the program is directly translated into efficient assembly code. The C++ method call, for example, is compiled into a few machine instructions. The techniques used for CLOS MOP are therefore insufficient to implement Open C++ MOP without overhead.

Anibus [20] and Intrigue [12] support "compile-time" MOPs to reduce the cost due to the meta level. They are Lisp compilers that are extensible according to MOP. The "compile-time" MOPs modify the compilers to compile a program in a different scheme. Because a meta code replaces an internal code of the compilers instead of a compiled code, this approach, like that of CLOS MOP, does not generate overheads. In this approach, however, meta code must describe not how an object behaves, but how the compiler generates compiled code that makes an object behave according to the programmer's intention. Although this approach has no overhead, its meta code is less straightforward than those in CLOS MOP and Open C++.

7 Conclusion

This paper described Open C++ in order to demonstrate a methodology for designing extensible languages for distributed computing. Open C++ is designed on the basis of an object-oriented meta-level (or reflection) technique so that the implementation of a method call is made open-ended. The programmer can alter the implementation of a method call according to a simple metaobject protocol (MOP), and obtain on top of Open C++ a new language functionality for distributed computing. Open C++ MOP is made so simple and easily understandable that programmers who are not familiar with the meta system can implement a new functionality effortlessly on top of Open C++. The MOP exposes the implementation of a method call with some abstraction. Open C++ also provides *Object Communities*, which is a framework that facilitates meta-level programming for implementing a functionality for distributed computing.

Open C++ clearly separates distributed computation from the other computation that is more substantial to the programmer. Computation concerning communication and synchronization notions appears only at the meta level, and need not be considered by the programmer writing a program at the base level. This feature of Open C++ makes a program more understandable and easier to describe.

The overhead associated with Open C++ MOP is negligible when Open C++ is used for distributed computing, since even though it is not small, it is negligible in comparison with network latency time. How much performance the system using the MOP must achieve depends on the operations controlled by the MOP. Although meta-level techniques are still difficult to implement efficiently, they are already applicable to practical programming if the domain is selected properly.

Unlike CLOS MOP, Open C++ introduces a meta-level technique into a compiler-based language. Because Open C++ must bridge an abstraction gap between C++ and an assembly language, its design considered implementation issues that the design of CLOS MOP did not. It restricts the extensible part of the language specifications in order to reduce the cost associated with the meta level. The entities that the MOP reifies are only those necessary for distributed computing. To apply Open C++ in application domains such as parallel comput-

ing as well as distributed computing, however, the overhead due to extensibility
needs to be further reduced.

Acknowledgments

We thank Satoshi Matsuoka for his suggestions on clarifying and organizing
this work. We also thank Gregor Kiczales, Hidehiko Masuhara, and Frank
Buschmann for their helpful comments on earlier drafts of this paper.

References

1. Bal, H. E., M. F. Kaashoek, and A. S. Tanenbaum, "Orca: A Language For Parallel Programming of Distributed Systems," *IEEE Trans. Softw. Eng.*, vol. 18, no. 3, pp. 190–205, 1992.
2. Birrell, A. D. and B. J. Nelson, "Implementing Remote Procedure Calls," *ACM Trans. Comp. Syst.*, vol. 2, no. 1, pp. 39–59, 1984.
3. Buschmann, F., K. Kiefer, F. Paulisch, and M. Stal, "The Meta-Information-Protocol: Run-Time Type Information for C++," in *Proc. of the Int'l Workshop on Reflection and Meta-Level Architecture* (A. Yonezawa and B. C. Smith, eds.), pp. 82–87, 1992.
4. Ellis, C., S. Gibbs, and G. Rein, "Groupware –Some Issues and Experiences," *Commun. of the ACM*, vol. 34, no. 1, pp. 38–58, 1991.
5. Gehani, N. and W. Roome, "Concurrent C," *Software-Practice and Experience*, vol. 16, no. 9, pp. 821–844, 1986.
6. Goldberg, A. and D. Robson, *Smalltalk-80: The Language and Its Implementation.* Addison-Wesley, 1983.
7. Gourhant, Y. and M. Shapiro, "FOG/C++: a Fragmented-Object Generator," in *Proc. of USENIX C++ Conference*, pp. 63–74, 1990.
8. Herlihy, M. and B. Liskov, "A Value Transmission Method for Abstract Data Types," *ACM Trans. Prog. Lang. Syst.*, vol. 4, no. 4, pp. 527–551, 1982.
9. Ichisugi, Y., S. Matsuoka, and A. Yonezawa, "RbCl: A Reflective Object-Oriented Concurrent Language without a Run-time Kernel," in *Proc. of the Int'l Workshop on Reflection and Meta-Level Architecture* (A. Yonezawa and B. C. Smith, eds.), pp. 24–35, 1992.
10. Kiczales, G., J. des Rivières, and D. G. Bobrow, *The Art of the Metaobject Protocol.* The MIT Press, 1991.
11. Kiczales, G. and J. Lamping, "Issues in the Design and Specification of Class Libraries," in *Proc. of ACM Conf. on Object-Oriented Programming Systems, Languages, and Applications*, pp. 435–451, 1992.
12. Lamping, J., G. Kiczales, L. Rodriguez, and E. Ruf, "An Architecture for an Open Compiler," in *Proc. of the Int'l Workshop on Reflection and Meta-Level Architecture* (A. Yonezawa and B. C. Smith, eds.), pp. 95–106, 1992.
13. Li, K., *Shared Virtual Memory on Loosely Coupled Multiprocessors.* PhD thesis, Dept. of Computer Science, Yale Univ., 1986.
14. Madany, P., P. Kougiouris, N. Islam, and R. H. Campbell, "Practical Examples of Reification and Reflection in C++," in *Proc. of the Int'l Workshop on Reflection and Meta-Level Architecture* (A. Yonezawa and B. C. Smith, eds.), pp. 76–81, 1992.

15. Maes, P., "Concepts and Experiments in Computational Reflection," in *Proc. of ACM Conf. on Object-Oriented Programming Systems, Languages, and Applications*, pp. 147–155, 1987.

16. Masuhara, H., S. Matsuoka, T. Watanabe, and A. Yonezawa, "Object-Oriented Concurrent Reflective Languages can be Implemented Efficiently," in *Proc. of ACM Conf. on Object-Oriented Programming Systems, Languages, and Applications*, pp. 127–144, 1992.

17. Matsuoka, S., T. Watanabe, and A. Yonezawa, "Hybrid Group Reflective Architecture for Object-Oriented Concurrent Reflective Programming," in *Proc. of European Conf. on Object-Oriented Programming '91*, no. 512 in LNCS, pp. 231–250, Springer-Verlag, 1991.

18. Okamura, H., Y. Ishikawa, and M. Tokoro, "AL-1/D: A Distributed Programming System with Multi-Model Reflection Framework," in *Proc. of the Int'l Workshop on Reflection and Meta-Level Architecture* (A. Yonezawa and B. C. Smith, eds.), pp. 36–47, 1992.

19. Rao, R., "Implementational Reflection in Silica," in *Proc. of European Conf. on Object-Oriented Programming '91*, no. 512 in LNCS, pp. 251–267, Springer-Verlag, 1991.

20. Rodriguez Jr., L. H., "Coarse-Grained Parallelism Using Metaobject Protocols," Techincal Report SSL-91-61, XEROX PARC, Palo Alto, CA, 1991.

21. Smith, B. C., "Reflection and Semantics in Lisp," in *Proc. of ACM Symp. on Principles of Programming Languages*, pp. 23–35, 1984.

22. Steele, G., *Common Lisp: The Language*. Digital Press, 2nd ed., 1990.

23. Stroustrup, B., *The C++ Programming Language*. Addison-Wesley, 2nd ed., 1991.

24. Stumm, M. and S. Zhou, "Algorithms Implementing Distributed Shared Memory," *IEEE Computer*, vol. 23, no. 5, pp. 54–64, 1990.

25. Sun Microsystems, *Network Programming Guide*. Sun Microsystems, Inc., 1990.

26. U.S. Dept. of Defense, *Reference Manual for the Ada Programming Language*. ANSI/MIL-STD-1815A, 1983.

27. Yokote, Y., "The Apertos Reflective Operating System: The Concept and Its Implementation," in *Proc. of ACM Conf. on Object-Oriented Programming Systems, Languages, and Applications*, pp. 414–434, 1992.

28. Yokote, Y. and M. Tokoro, "The Design and Implementation of Concurrent-Smalltalk," in *Proc. of ACM Conf. on Object-Oriented Programming Systems, Languages, and Applications*, pp. 331–340, 1986.

MetaFlex:
A Flexible Metaclass Generator

Richard Johnson and Murugappan Palaniappan
Aldus Corporation
411 First Avenue South
Seattle, WA 98104-2871 USA
muru@aldus.com, richj@aldus.com

Abstract

Motivated to support the needs of component-based applications, we have developed a system called MetaFlex that generates metaclasses to extend the behavior of our C++ classes without inventing variants of the original classes. We make the case that a flexible metaclass generator service that allows developers to freely choose the kind and degree of detail for each metaclass is needed and present our architecture for making this specification. We also illustrate a powerful use of this technique with a scripting extension to our application framework. With an evaluation of our current MetaFlex implementation and its use with the scripting extension, we conclude that this service is best provided by compiler vendors.

Introduction

The 1980s was a period where many organizations developed application frameworks. We can expect the 1990s to be a period where development of component-based application frameworks will be prevalent. An industrial strength, platform independent application framework developed in C++ by Aldus was presented in [Ferrel89]. The next evolutionary step towards development of a C++ component-based application framework is presented in [Christiansen92]. This article describes one of the major issues in achieving the componentization goal - the need for accessing information about classes, usually lost during compilation, at run-time.

Component-based application frameworks allow users to construct an application dynamically to best meet their needs . By construct, we mean that users can install a set of components, at run-time, from a list of published components. A component can be as simple as a single drawing tool or as complicated as a page-layout application. The application framework provides the necessary glue for components to work together as an application. The glue is developed without knowing what kinds of components would be developed and published.

As part of the componentization goals, we desire the ability to dynamically extend an application. An extension, in our sense, is the ability to add behavior to a class either statically or dynamically without structurally modifying the nature of the original class

O.M. Nierstrasz (Ed.): ECOOP '93, LNCS 707, pp. 502-527, 1993.
© Springer-Verlag Berlin Heidelberg 1993

being extended. Examples of extensions include:

- **Scripting.** Usually there is a delay between application functionality development and the development of end-user scripting access to this functionality due to the orthogonal nature of scripting development and application functionality development. By using parser technology for generating an application's metaclass hierarchy, it is easy to expose the application functionality during its development for end-user scripting.

- **Database access control.** In terms of the access protocol to a database, the primary difference between single-user databases and multi-user databases is the need for transaction serialization and user access privilege management. Database access control semantics are orthogonal to this base functionality and are appropriately added as extensions.

- **Test monitors.** Unobtrusive introduction of "up-stream" quality assurance methods may be one of the most important usages of our proposed extension architecture. There are countless applications, including test coverage tools, memory and performance profiling, semantic assertion checking, message flow monitors for dynamic program behavior analysis, and object inspectors.

We have implemented a scripting extension as part of our component-based application framework development and will use it for the case study presented in this paper. We wanted to build a scripting scaffold into the application framework such that the code can manipulate object types that are not known at compile-time but can be determined at run-time. Object types refer to information like the addresses of the objects' class methods and member variable map information. While not universally true, many typed language implementations, including most commercial versions of C++, do not preserve the class type information. By discarding it, they effectively freeze, at compile time, the data maps and functions that operate on it.

To overcome this limitation, we developed a tool architecture called MetaFlex, and have a production version of it by the same name. MetaFlex is a *metaclass* generator that is built on top of a C++ parser. Metaclass refers to the type information of a class extracted at compile time and made available at run-time.

The focus of this paper is to describe the MetaFlex architecture and the experiences we had in achieving the scripting extension goal of the application framework using MetaFlex. Two additional capabilities, though not implemented in the production version of our current MetaFlex tool, are described: 1) a means of specifying what type information should be made available in the application on a class by class basis, and 2) a mechanism for dynamically attaching code and data to extend class behavior.

MetaFlex is more general than the metaclass notion in Smalltalk [Goldberg83] and the factory notion in Objective C [Cox86]. MetaFlex allows extension developers to specify exactly what type information is needed and how much is needed, properly gauged to the application being developed whereas Smalltalk and Objective C automatically generate metaclass (or factory) information for all classes of the application being developed. We argue that a MetaFlex-like tool is needed for creating the types of extensions we are suggesting because a) the metaclass requirements for one extension may be quite different from that of another, b) we agree with [Stroustrup92], that it is not possible to generate an "ideal" metaclass, and c) the generated metaclass information should be as small as possible to reduce the size of the final executable. This final point, while perhaps less an issue on sixty-four megabyte workstations, is definitely a problem when the target environment is a PC class machine.

With this context in mind, the goals of this paper are to:

- Make the case that a flexible metaclass generator service is needed that will allow developers to freely choose the kind and degree of detail for each metaclass to be made part of an application.

- Explain how the use of a generated metaclass offers the developer a means to dynamically add orthogonal extensions of class behavior with mixin classes, minimizing the need to develop specialized versions of the class.

- Describe the architecture we have used to design and implement a flexible metaclass generator service, highlighting issues that may be useful for other developers of metaclass generator services. An architectural description is included of a proposed metaclass specification grammar.

- Illustrate a powerful use of this technique with a scripting extension to an application framework.

We first present related work in the area of metaclass generation services and extension application examples. Then, we present our design of the MetaFlex architecture which includes a description of our specification language. We next describe the scripting application we use as a case study of an extension application, followed by a description of the MetaFlex implementation for the scripting application. We conclude with an evaluation of our implementation, highlighting issues that may be useful for developers of metaclass generation services.

Related Work

Cointe's notes that metaclasses provide meta-tools to build open-ended architecture [Cointe87]:

> "From an implementor's point of view, metaclasses are very powerful because they provide hooks to extend or modify an existing kernel. Metaclass allows the programmer to provide a flexible means to introduce inherited behavior in a system, including single and multiple inheritance as well as method wrapping."

Since our applications are primarily developed in C++, we can also choose whether these extensions are to be dynamically bound to the application at execution time or are generated, compiled and made a static part of the system. This flexibility is possible because of the nature of our metaclass design.

The creators of C++, in the process of developing their own run-time type system implementation, acknowledge the predicament of creating a metaclass that would meet all engineering needs [Stroustrup92]:

> "... the likelihood that someone can come up with a set of (run-time type) information that satisfies all users is zero".

For the most common computing platforms found in use today, it is too expensive in terms of time and space to make all possible type information about a class available at run-time. More importantly, the requirement for *what* type information is needed by a given application is highly dependent upon the application being built.

Although primarily focused on database extensions, a similar architecture is suggested for extending class behavior [Wells92a]:

- Use a meta-architecture consisting of a collection of glue modules and definitions to provide the infrastructure for specifying/implementing event extensions and regularizing interfaces between modules.

- Develop an extensible collection of extender modules that implement OODB functionality via behavioral extensions.

Our metaclass architecture roughly corresponds to the authors' notion of glue modules while our Extension classes roughly corresponds to their notion of extender modules. The authors see a robust implementation of their Open OODB architecture having extenders for transactions and access policy management, distributed access to objects, object versioning, and database index maintenance, among others. This is on target from our perspective, but stops short in that it constrains the domain of usage of this mechanism to database functionality. Their initial implementation of the glue is the notion of a wrapper class that will assume the role of the class being modeled in the system. These role player classes are derived from base class Sentry, which duplicates the public interface of the modeled class as well as having metaclass protocol for installing, de-installing, and manipulating the extensions.

In discussing her work with the 3KRS language environment, Maes observes that the "extra structure and computation necessary to provide objects with special features such as documentation, constraints, or attachment (of other behavior) do not have to be supported for all objects in the system, but can be provided on a local basis" [Maes87].

This is a key architectural goal of MetaFlex. Why generate metaclass containers for types that are not to be extended?

Maes also explains that either an object can call upon its meta-object to extend or modify its overall behavior (conscious reflection), or presumably, other knowledgeable system objects can call upon an object's meta-object to modify the behavior of the object it models.

Our architecture differs from the 3KRS language environment in that we generate only one metaclass for each class. Although we have organized our metaclasses as first class objects, we don't create one for each class instance created.

One of the thrusts in our business of software development is to somehow reduce the tremendous expense associated with testing our applications before they are sold. In their work, Böcker and Herczeg introduce un-obtrusive tracing and profiling facilities to monitor the application developer's code [Böcker90]. The authors point out it is hard to make the tracing tools found in the marketplace "provide just the right amount of information at a level of detail that is just about right for the problem at hand." They recommend direct control over the specification of what to view and what to trace. At the same time, they recommend the extended methods be hidden from the programmer. In our architecture, these test monitors would be mixed in as extensions in the metaclass.

Kleyn describes a tracing tool that allows developers a means of visualizing the message passing between objects in their system [Kleyn88]. This application would make use not only of the metaclass extension architecture and the type information of the class being modeled, but also use the class hierarchy / lattice information collected by it or some other parser based application.

Palay describes ΔC++ [Palay92], a C++ system that permits the developer to release new compatible versions of libraries or dynamically loaded components without recompiling portions of the system that make use of the classes defined in these new components. The stated purpose of the work is to develop an environment that supports the full C++ language specification as well as dynamic loading of new functionality without performance degradation.

Achieving flexibility without performance penalty is one of our key requirements as well. Palay points out the ability to extend behavior dynamically allows one to quickly respond to changing application requirements, and that these extensions can be codified in a more optimal implementation later.

Murray describes Alf [Murray92], a system that represents C++ programs as trees of abstract objects. These abstract objects encapsulate the syntax tree complexities (offering a surrounding infrastructure) tailored for access by tools that use the trees as their input. Tools may attach tool-specific attributes to the Alf abstract objects, without affecting other tools that may have interest in the same abstract objects. Alf maintains these trees permanently. The conventional file based organization of C++ source code is replaced. Incremental compilation and editing is implemented without compromising the static semantic analysis properties found in a conventional C++ compiler.

Although MetaFlex doe not work off a database, the notion of marking classes of interest with an Alf-like attribute is functionally equivalent to the metaclass specification we are suggesting in this paper.

In the next section, we first present the motivation for developing MetaFlex. Following it, we describe our parser architecture that constructs syntax trees of C++ source code. We then describe the MetaFlex architecture that generates metaclass information for a specific extension, based on the syntax trees it provides. The architecture section concludes with a description of our metaclass specification language.

Architecture

Motivation

Consider the bottom half of Diagram 1, below the dotted line. It depicts how a linker would statically compose a component based application. Nothing precludes dynamic system composition, however. If one were to replace the linker with a loader component that was part of a component framework kernel, it is not difficult to see how a component based system could be dynamically composed at execution time. The description of how the loader component might work is beyond the scope of this paper.

In our architecture, an extendible application, whether created statically or dynamically, is made with the following ingredients:

- metaclass library of the extendible classes (compiled metaclasses of the application)
- metaclass run-time library (various styles of function dictionaries, field dictionaries, component loaders, etc.)
- application libraries (statically or dynamically installable components, framework libraries)
- extension code (behavioral extensions to a class)

In both the static and dynamic cases, the key ingredient that supplies the necessary flexibility and extensibility properties is the run-time type information, or metaclasses for the application. The source of the metaclasses is depicted in the top half of Diagram 1, the MetaFlex generator, and shall be discussed in the next several sections.

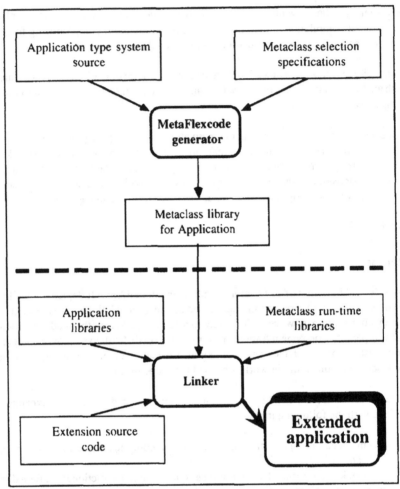

Diagram 1 - Basic flow of MetaFlex metaclass information collection for statically linked component based application.

The MetaFlex Parser

In order to generally analyze and interpret C++ source code for purposes other than generating machine instructions (e.g., MetaFlex), one needs a C++ parser. In 1990, the availability of an inexpensive, commercial C++ parser for these purposes was non-existent. Those available were not able to deal with the full language syntax. In particular, we needed a parser that was capable of dealing with old-style K&R grammars through C++ 2.x grammars [Ellis90].

Since C++ is not an LALR(1) grammar, YACC can not be easily used to generate a parser directly for C++. The solution that we selected was to use YACC to generate a parser for a modified version of its own grammar definition language. The generated parser will then read the C++ language expressed with this grammar, generating the parse tables that represent the follow symbol sets that guide the match process.

The parser we have built can be characterized as top-down, *for the most part predictive*, recursive descent. The *for the most part predictive* description is needed, since the parser does back-track in several situations. To minimize back-tracking during the match process, a dependency mechanism is employed. Dependent functions gain control at propitious moments. With the ability to freely access information in the token stream, symbol tables, and current syntax tree state, these functions force pre-mature match failures, whenever it can be determined that pursuing some sub-tree would be pointless.

Rather than mangle type names in the system and maintain a flat symbol table, we chose to implement a scoped symbol table, implemented as a stack of symbol tables built for the types previously seen in the input stream. These tables are pushed and popped from the scoped symbol table as needed.

The parser engine automatically traverses matched syntax trees for each compilation unit, giving control at the appropriate moments to the attached applications. The architecture of the parser permits multiple applications to be hosted or attached to it. Attachment consists of a parser application showing interest in a particular syntax tree node by adding an instance of itself to one of the node's dependency lists. Dependency list support is available on all node types, including rules, productions, and production symbols. It is possible to attach applications *before* a node or *after* it. This means that as the parser traverses a parse tree for its attached applications, these applications can receive control just before or just after a given sub-tree has been traversed. Furthermore, each application can show interest in more than one syntax tree node. This makes it convenient to collect information in complicated trees.

For certain C++ productions, parser information collection applications are implemented as part of the standard parser. In particular, the class declaration receives this treatment. For each class, an ordered collection of class member information is organized. Standard information, such as member name and base type of the member are always extracted, available through simple access protocol in the class information collector. If necessary, however, an application is able to access the syntax trees directly through the ordered collection member.

MetaFlex Source Code Generation

Built upon the parser described, we designed and implemented a flexible metaclass generator called MetaFlex to support the extension behavior of C++ classes. It uses the class declaration of a marked class to automatically generate code for a companion metaclass class. This metaclass class models the type information of its counterpart, the selected class. Although not part of our current implementation, our architecture plans for specification of extension installation as well. These extensions may be used to either replace or extend the modeled class' behavior. An application's metaclass organization is similar to the Smalltalk approach, except that not all classes necessarily have metaclasses prepared for them. The application developers must explicitly choose which of the classes or class hierarchies need to be modeled with metaclasses.

Perhaps the key distinction to be made here is that the developer may not only specify which classes shall have metaclasses, but also choose which type information properties are to be generated for a given application class. For those properties selected for inclusion in the generated metaclass, it is possible to plug in different type information property representations for them. Different representations are desirable to avoid carrying large amounts of detail, when it is not needed or used in the application. For example, class type properties such as its method addresses and instance variable map information are available in several styles, selectable by the developer.

The following list summarizes the sorts of behavior for which we feel the metaclass should be responsible:

- the ability to create an object by name
- offer dynamic method dispatching by name to methods of a given class.
- the ability to extend and even change the behavior of one or more methods found in a given class.
- the ability to broadcast messages to all instances of a given class.
- offer tailorable class structural information to support service extensions, such as general purpose object streaming, persistent object management functionality, and scripting.

The metaclass instance creation protocol can be used to create instances of the type being modeled. If specified, the instances created by this protocol can be registered in an instance collection. No provisions in the architecture are made for registering instances of the objects created in the traditional manner, via the *new* operator. To make use of the registration service, the client must use the object creation service provided in the metaclass. Like other type information, instance registration service may be included on a case by case basis.

Code is generated by MetaFlex that automatically registers generated metaclasses in an application's metaclass dictionary, each entry keyed by the class name it models. This makes it possible to polymorphically create metaclass modeled objects (i.e. create these objects by class name), potentially by objects or processes external to the application. Polymorphic instance creation is part of the minimal, or what we refer to as the *vanilla* MetaFlex metaclass behavior.

In addition to flexible specification of the type system information to be included in the metaclass, a dependency list mechanism is provided by MetaFlex, similar in functionality to the *Object* dependency list behavior in Smalltalk. It is used to add *Extension class* derivatives to the Metaclass instance modeling a given class. As with the other type information, the presence of this feature is specified with instructions to the MetaFlex metaclass generator.

Extension class derivatives allow the developer to implement orthogonal behavior that extend the MetaFlex modeled class in some way. Since this extension is added to the class' metaclass, and not directly to the class itself, the original semantics of the class remain pure to their original purpose. Much as the Smalltalk View subclasses explicitly know everything about the Model subclasses they depend upon, the Extension class derivative has explicit access not only to the class instance being modeled, but also explicit access to the type information available in the metaclass as well. The reverse is not necessarily true. Nothing precludes an extended class from explicitly knowing about its extensions, but typically an omniscient configuration/policy object is given the responsibility to activate and deactivate the extended behavior.

Rather than create derived classes from a base Metaclass class to add extended type information about classes, we have chosen to develop a MetaInfo hierarchy instead. Each Metaclass *has a* MetaInfo. The MetaInfo contains references to the extended type information and developer supplied extensions required by the application. Diagram 2 illustrates the general relationships of the class, its Metaclass, its MetaInfo, extended type information, and developer-supplied extensions. The Class has a reference to its Metaclass. In our system, this is implemented as a class variable (i.e., a static variable in class scope). A reference to the metaclass of the modeled class' superclass(es) is also maintained in each metaclass. The MetaInfo instance may contain references to class extensions, class function information, class field information, and class instances. In order to be generated, the Metaclass, its MetaInfo, and the aspects of the MetaInfo must be specified to the MetaFlex code generator for the class in question.

Although it is not shown for each instance of the Extension classes in the MetaInfo's Extensions collection, there is a reference to the MetaInfo (and therefore Metaclass) for each Extension instance. We see most extensions being heavy users of a class' type information to perform its tasks. Applications like those suggested in [Richardson92], [Wells92b], [Pérez92], [Böcker90], [Voss92], and [Voss93] could be implemented as kinds of class Extension. These applications all use the type information of the class to which they are attached.

We have described the internal MetaFlex architecture in this section. In the next section, the external interface of MetaFlex is explained. This is the interface that extension developers will use to specify what types of meta-information they need.

Metaclass Specification Language

The following description of the Metaclass Specification Language is a suggested design and, at the time of this writing, has not been implemented in our existing MetaFlex tool. These notions, however, get at the details of what we think is needed.

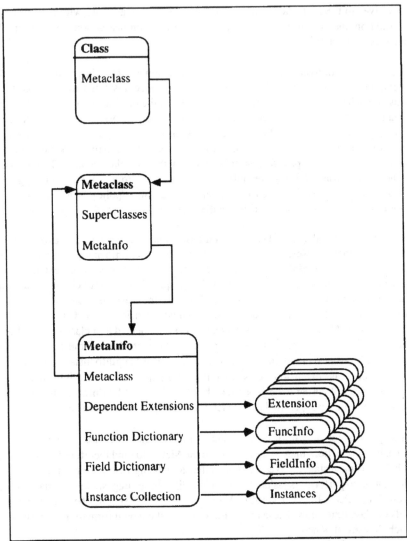

Diagram2 - Relationships of the class, its metaclass, extensions and other type information.

The specification of metaclass requirements to MetaFlex has been one of the more difficult areas for us. These requirements are ideally directly associated with the class declaration to be modeled with a metaclass. It is also desirable that these metaclass specifications do not interfere with the readability of the class declaration and its semantics. The reasoning here is that although a class can have explicit knowledge of its metaclass, as is suggested in Diagram 2, the knowledge is not necessary to understand the core abstractions the class provides its users.

Clearly, development environment support for viewing class declarations with and without the metaclass specifications is desirable. We also feel it would be useful to view all metaclass specifications together as a whole for an application. Such support does not exist commercially for C++. User definable attributes on ALF trees, as discussed in [Murray92], coupled with multiple view support on the class trees to which they are attached, would provide the sort of facility needed.

To control the composition of Metaclass derivatives a MetaFlex tool creates for us, we have developed a small metaclass specification language expressed in a YACC-like grammar as shown in Diagram 3. The grammar is admittedly elementary, using a simple keyword-value approach. It doesn't capture all of the possibilities by any means, but offers the reader a structured means of thinking about metaclass specification.

Given this language, the following four examples are representative metaclass specifications:

1. MakeMetaClassFor	Class	DatabaseObject
	Support	FunctionDictionary Style
		FunctionAddressesOnly
	Install	DBAccessPolicyManager

2. MakeMetaClassFor	Class	ApplicationKernel
	Support	InstanceCollection
	Install	ScriptingExtension

3. MakeMetaClassFor	AllDerivedClassesOf	Command
	Support	FunctionDictionary Style
		FunctionDispatching
	AllowAccessTo	PublicMembers

| 4. MakeMetaClassFor | Class | EventHandler |

In the first example, a class named DatabaseObject will have Metaclass and MetaInfo class derivatives prepared for it. The MetaInfo class is created, since support for a function dictionary and a behavioral extension have been requested. The particular implementation of the FuncDict to be generated contains the address of the functions in the class for each member, but no extensive argument and return type information needed by applications such as scripting.

An instance of the Extension class derivative called DBAccessPolicyManager is to be added to the Extensions list in the MetaInfo object. Assuming an access policy manager design similar to that discussed in [Richardson92], the function dictionary with function address availability for each dictionary member would be needed to create the necessary method wrappers for the DatabaseObject member function protocol.

translationUnit	:	metaClassSpecifications
	;	
metaClassSpecifications	:	metaClassSpecification metaClassSpecifications
	|	metaClassSpecification
	;	
metaClassSpecification	:	MakeMetaClassFor classParm specificationParms
	;	
specificationParms	:	specificationParm specificationParms
	|	specificationParm
	;	
specificationParm	:	Support supportValues styleParms_opt accessParms_opt
	|	Install extensionClassName
	;	
classParm	:	Class CLASS_NAME
	|	AllDerivedClassesOf CLASS_NAME
	;	
styleParms	:	Style styles
	;	
styles	:	functionDictionaryStyles
	|	fieldDictionaryStyles
	;	
accessParms	:	AllowAccessTo accessControl
	;	
accessControl	:	PublicMembers
	|	ProtectedMembers
	|	AllMembers
	;	
extensionClassName	:	CLASS_NAME
	;	
supportValues	:	NoMetaInfo
	|	FunctionDictionary
	|	FieldDictionary
	|	InstanceCollection
	;	
functionDictionaryStyles	:	RespondsToSupportOnly
	|	FunctionAddressesOnly
	|	FunctionDispatching
	;	
fieldDictionaryStyles	:	OffsetsAndLengthsOnly
	|	FullFieldInformation
	;	

Diagram 3 - Metaclass style specification grammar. Note that all grammar rules start in lower case. Grammar tokens all start in upper case. The _opt suffix on the end of several symbols is meant to suggest that occurrences of this symbol are optional.

In the second example, a class named ApplicationKernel will have Metaclass and MetaInfo class derivatives prepared for it. The MetaInfo is needed to support an InstanceCollection and ScriptingExtension extension instance.

The third example shows how metaclass requirements might be set for all classes derived from a given class. In this case, all derivatives of class Command will have a Metaclass and MetaInfo built for them. The MetaInfo will have a function dictionary capable of supporting function dispatching. Notice that more type information is required to support function dispatching than offered by the other function dictionary styles. Only the public members of the Command class derivatives will have their functions included in this dictionary.

The fourth example illustrates the case where vanilla Metaclass services (e.g., instance creation by name, instance type identification, instance length) are needed for a class named EventHandler, but no additional MetaInfo is required. Consequently, MetaInfo will not be generated for this class by MetaFlex.

In all examples, the application using the metaclass system, and in particular, the type of extensions attached to a given class' meta information, highly influence what sorts of type information should be made available at run-time.

Nothing in this architectural description precludes the use of dynamic loading of the meta information or developer-supplied extensions at run-time. In particular, the Extension, FuncDict, and FieldDict derived class instances could be streamed in from persistent storage. We see this architecture unifying the platform specific techniques used today to load class dynamic behavior.

In the next section, a description of the scripting application that uses the MetaFlex tool is presented, followed by a description of the MetaFlex tool currently in use.

Case Study: Scripting Enabled Applications

As part of the development of our component-based application framework, we wanted to provide scripting support for applications at the framework-level. An application-framework class, called the ScriptManager, provides the necessary support for processing end-user scripts to access, create, and change the contents of applications. If additional scripting functionality is required by an application that is not defined in the framework, it can bring along its own custom scripting.

In our application framework, we established ground rules for applications where all creation or content change operations are done through commands whereas content accesses of an object are done through directly though their method invocation.

At the time of writing this paper, we have implemented support for Apple Events [Apple91]. End users can use scripting applications such as AppleScript and Frontier (they translate scripts to Apple Events) to access and manipulate applications. The three major Apple Events supported by the Script Manager, but developed without knowing the scripting requirements of the applications are:

- **Set event** - changes content of applications. For example, "set object foo to move:{10, 15}" is an instruction to the Script Manager to access object foo and dispatch a message to move it by the specified amount. The Script Manager translates this instruction to create a MoveCmd(foo, Point(10, 15)) and invoking its DoIt() method. In the DoIt() method, the command sends the message, foo-> Move(Point(10,15)).
- **Get event** - accesses content of applications. For example, "get fontSize of object 4" is an instruction to access object 4 for its fontSize. This instruction translates to dispatching the message return(object 4->GetFontSize()).
- **Create event** - create contents in applications. For example, "create new line with color: green" is an instruction to create an object of type *line* and set its color to green. This instruction translates to creating a CreateCmd(newLine), invoking its DoIt() method. In the DoIt() method, the command created a newLine object and returns it to the Script Manager. Once the newLine is created, the Script Manager creates a ColorCmd(line, green) and invokes its DoIt() method. In the DoIt() method, the command sends the message, newLine->DoIt(green).

In the examples above, the complication is once the target object is accessed, the Script Manager needs a mechanism to determine whether the object will "understand" the message that will be sent to it. In the first example, whether object foo will understand the message Move() and in the second example, whether object 4 will understand the message GetFontSize().

In order to accomplish the goal of type-independent script dispatching by the Script Manager, we chose to use the MetaFlex tool to generate metaclasses for these objects. From the generated metaclass information made available at run-time by MetaFlex, the Script Manager uses the type information about an object to choose the correct command to change/create content or to access content of an object through its method invocation.

The following code fragments illustrate the interface between the Script Manager and the metaclass, generated by MetaFlex. What is shown in the code segment is only the interface between the Script Manager and MetaFlex and not the error checking or other processing that happens in the code. The first segment shows the Set event handler, next the Get event handler, and finally the Create event handler.

- **Set event** - changes content of applications.

```
{
    // Non-metaclass related code

    // Do the command dispatching by "Make"ing the command through its
```

```
        // metaclass.  Since it is a command, call its DoIt() method....
        // Note: NumArgs + 1 is passed in to specify the number of data values
        // plus the object descriptor
        Metaclass* aMeta = gTheApp->GetMetaclass(cmdName);
        MetaInfo* anInfo = (aMeta ) ?
                        (aMeta ->GetMetaInfo()) : (MetaInfo*)NULL;
        if(anInfo){
                aCmd = (UndoableCmd*) anInfo->Make(numArgs+1,argv);
                if(aCmd) {
                        aCmd->DoIt();
                }
        }
        // Non-metaclass related code
}


• Get event - accesses content of applications.
        {
        // Non-metaclass related code here ...
        // anObj is the object from which we want to access the information
        // cmdName is the method name to invoke in the object
        Metaclass* aMeta =anObj->GetMetaclass();
        MetaInfo* anInfo = (aMeta ) ?
                        (aMeta ->GetMetaInfo()) : (MetaInfo*)NULL;
        FuncDict* aDict = (anInfo ) ?
                        (anInfo ->GetFunctionDictionary()) :
                        (FuncDict*)NULL;
        if (aDict) {
                void* buffer = (void*)
                        (aDict->Execute(anObj,cmdName,numArgs,argv));
        }
        // Non-metaclass related code
}


• Create event - create contents in applications.
        {
        // Non-metaclass related code here ...
        // Get the command that will create one of this object
        Metaclass* aMeta = (Metaclass*)(gTheApp->GetMetaclass
                                        (theCmdName));
        MetaInfo* anInfo = (aFact) ?
                        (aMeta ->GetMetaInfo()) : (MetaInfo*)NULL;
        if(anInfo){
                aCmd = (UndoableCmd*) anInfo->Make(numArgs+1,argv);
                if(aCmd) {
                        aCmd->DoIt();
                }
        }
        // Non-metaclass related code
}
```

The interface requirements specified by the scripting application to the MetaFlex are:
- generate metaclasses for specified commands and objects
- provide ways of querying which methods are understood by a given class
- determine return type, function name, and argument types for all functions found in classes modeled by metaclasses.
- provide an interface to create commands and initialize them
- provide an interface to execute a method of a selected object and return its value

As we had not implemented the metaclass specification language described in the architecture section, we used a macro DEFINE_METACLASS to make the specification to MetaFlex. This macro introduced the static variable gMetaclass into the declaration, and is the key used by MetaFlex to decide whether or not to generate a Metaclass derivative for the class. From the application developers' perspective, all they need to do is mark which commands and objects they want to give access to end-users, with the macro.

MetaFlex Tool Implementation for the Scripting Application

Compile-time Description

Metaclass class declarations for the specified (i.e., marked with the DEFINE_METACLASS macro) classes of the scripting application are generated by the current version of MetaFlex. MetaFlex generates several source code files containing the metaclasses. Depending upon the number of classes specified to have metaclasses generated for them, more than one source file may be generated to hold the metaclass declarations, definitions, and instantiation code. This feature was added due to compiler capacity limitations. These source files are then compiled with the regular C++ compiler. The compiled object code is linked with the application's object code created from the original source, to form the extended application. The generated source for the scripting application is described in the remainder of this section.

Since function dispatching by name is the key functionality needed by the scripting application, MetaFlex generates MetaInfo class declarations containing references to function dictionaries. The type of function dictionary generated is able to dispatch the functions of the class it is modeling. Field dictionaries, instance collections, or the Extension class described in the architectural section are not used. Function dispatching is done on behalf of the Script Manager by explicitly accessing the object's function dictionary found in its MetaInfo instance.

Beside generating class declarations and their implementations, MetaFlex also generates instantiation code, that can create instances of the Metaclass, MetaInfo and FuncDict classes. Of particular note here is a C function generated for each FuncDict initialization. Initialization of the function dictionary is done at its first access to minimize the application startup time. The initialization process consists of loading the FuncInfo elements with the function member information of the class, including the function address. For example, given the member function declaration of class foo,

      void   Init (type1 var1, type2 var2);

the following pointer to member function variable [Ellis90], named ptrMem, is generated by MetaFlex:

      void (foo::*ptrMem)(type1,type2)   =   &&foo :: Init;

To support function dispatching, MetaFlex must do a reasonably good job understanding the types used in the member function declarations that are being included in the function dictionary. Not only the string representations of a member function's base type and argument types must be known, but the base type of all typedefs used must be understood as well. The base type understanding is needed to determine argument lengths and whether they are references.

Run-time Description

The run-time support provided by MetaFlex for the scripting application uses two of the features discussed in the architecture: 1) instance creation by name, and 2) function dispatching by name.

The Metaflex generated metaclass instance supplies instance creation by name, and the function dictionary supplies the function dispatching. An instance of class FuncDict provides the following services:

> **Lookup services.** Function information can be looked up by exact key (the simple name and argument type list), by simple name alone, or by using a name that is comprised of the simple name and first part of the argument type list. For example, the key "Lookup(char*,i" would uniquely identify the second Lookup function in the list below. When there is ambiguity, it is possible to have a collection of all matching function members returned. For example, a call to the first LookupAll function below with "LookupAll" as the argument would return an OrderedCollection with FuncInfo instances for the two LookupAll functions below.

FuncInfo*	Lookup (char* pszNameNPartOfArgs);
FuncInfo*	Lookup (char* pszSimpleName, int iArgCnt);
OrderedCollection*	LookupAll (char* pszWithThisSimpleNm);
OrderedCollection*	LookupAll (char* pszWithThisSimpleNm,int iArgCnt);
char*	GetFullName (char* pszWithThisSimpleNm);
char*	GetFullName (char* pszWithThisSimpleNm , int iArgCnt);

> **Function dispatch service.** The function specified in the name key (2nd argument) is dispatched for the client to the instance of this class that "understands" this protocol (1st

argument). The number of arguments and their values are passed as the third and fourth arguments, respectively. The ArgV (4th argument) is an array of the arguments corresponding to the formal parameters of the function to be dispatched. The function dispatcher in the function dictionary uses this information to properly construct the stack frame for the function call.

```
void      *Execute (void *anInstanceOfThisClass
                   ,char *pszSimpleFuncName  // or pszNameNPartOfArgs
                   ,int iArgCnt
                   ,void **ArgV);
```

Each FuncDict contains a number of FuncInfo instances, one for each method that is part of the class being modeled with the Metaclass information. The following information is provided for each member function in an instance of class FuncInfo:

- Full function name (e.g. "foo(int, Ferrengi*, Bar&)"), a human readable version of the part of the member function declaration that is used by the compilers to generate unique ("mangled") names for a function.
- Simple name (e.g. "foo")
- Whether its virtual or non-virtual
- Its address (or virtual table offset)
- The number of arguments for this member function
- An encoded representation of the function's return type and arguments used to understand the length of things.
- The string representation of the return type of the function, that may be used to access its metaclass services (assuming it is a type for which a metaclass has been defined).

In this section, we have described the compile and run time responsibilities of the MetaFlex implementation to support extension of the scripting application. In the next section, we will evaluate our implementation, highlighting issues that may be helpful to others who may choose to implement a flexible metaclass generator service.

Evaluation

Without an automation tool like MetaFlex, we would not have been able to generally extend the scripting application in our application framework. Specifically, the ability to delegate the responsibility of responding to scripting requests (the Script Manager) and dispatching functions (to the function dictionaries generated for various application classes) from the system's application objects would not be possible. Without metaclass support, application objects would have to be explicitly knowledgeable about scripting, making them generally un-wieldy and less useful. With the MetaFlex generated support, these objects can be manipulated through scripts without compromising the original object semantics.

A number of key issues raised during our development are covered in the following sub-sections.

Specifying Metaclasses

In our early implementations, MetaFlex generated metaclasses for all classes in an application. To reduce the amount of generated code, a simple, but expressive scheme was needed for programmers to selectively choose which classes should have metaclasses generated for them by MetaFlex. Unfortunately, *simple* and *expressive* are competing goals.

With this in mind, we considered three ways for the engineers to specify their metaclass requirements:

1)   Mark individual class declarations.
2)   Mark a root class so that all derived classes from that root class will have metaclasses generated.
3)   Specify an application's metaclass requirements in a separate file.

For the scripting application, the first approach was selected, primarily because this method did not explicitly interfere with the current development practices of the engineers, some of whom were already comfortable using a macro based metaclass solution for generating the vanilla metaclass functionality. The MetaFlex system is keyed on declarations these macros were generating in the expanded source input stream. Macros are difficult to maintain, however, compared to other specification methods. The macro approach, while capable of implementing the specification language we suggest, suffers from un-readability.

The second approach seems attractive, since it would require less effort to mark the classes that MetaFlex would act upon. It suffers, however, in that the metaclass specification for a class is isolated from it - in the declaration(s) of its parent class(es), which are typically found in a different file(s). Furthermore, there is a distinct possibility that all classes in the hierarchy would not necessarily require the same metaclass implementation. In our application framework, however, we do have a class hierarchy where this approach would work nicely. As a result, the metaclass specification language has support for this possibility.

The third approach, like the second, also suffers from the locality of reference problem. Unlike the first solution, it forces engineers to have explicit knowledge about the complexities of modeling type information, when all they really wanted to do was ask about what kind of object they have. More sophisticated means of expressing systems becomes available at the price of increased complexity. Being specified in a separate file is also attractive, in that one is able to manage the metaclass specification in one place, even though it describes classes that are defined elsewhere. For these reasons, this is the likely approach we will pursue if we continue to use our own MetaFlex tool to generate metaclasses for our applications' type systems.

Another dimension to the specification problem is whether a function dictionary should model all the methods in a class, once it has been determined that a metaclass should be generated. In the MetaFlex implementation we are currently using for scripting, meta-information for all methods in a class are generated and made accessible. This is a violation of the private and protected notions in C++. Ideally, access patterns should follow the same semantics as set forth in [Ellis90]. To support this variation, access control syntax has been added to the metaclass specification grammar described in the architecture section of this paper.

It ultimately may be desirable for engineers to explicitly choose which class members should be exposed for access by external applications. For example, for several classes in our scripting application, we would have liked to create function dictionary entries for only those methods that permit query access to end users. This not only reduces the size of the function dictionary considerably, but places further control over what an external scripting environment can do to internal application objects.

Type Checking

Better type checking from MetaFlex is desirable for the scripting application. After parsing end-user scripts, the Script Manager constructs the script parameters as an array of arguments of type *void** and invokes MetaFlex. MetaFlex, at present, checks to see the number of arguments in the supplied array and the number of arguments needed in the command initialization are the same. No additional checking is currently done, however, to see if the types match between each argument in the array and the corresponding type information of the function dictionary member to be dispatched. In order to make the system robust, better type checking is a must before command dispatching.

Type checking by MetaFlex can be done by querying the *isA* relationship of the arguments supplied in the array. For example, a command's initialization method declared as Init(Window*, Rct*, int) is supplied the array (void* val1, void* val2, void* val3). Since MetaFlex already maintains type information of the arguments in the command's metaclass, all it needs to do is to check that val1 isA Window and val2 isA Rct, before dispatching the command. If MetaFlex were to use this approach, however, it could only check the argument types that also have metaclasses created for them.

Name Overloading

To reliably disambiguate overloaded method names, the full specification of the name is often necessary for MetaFlex to be able to dispatch the correct function. Consider the example where there are two initialization methods of a class with the same number of arguments: Init(Window*, Foo*, Bar*) and Init(Window*, Foo*, FooBar*). In order for MetaFlex to select the correct method, the Script Manager could request MetaFlex to return both the initialization methods and then decide which method was appropriate, based upon information in its possession. Alternatively, the Script Manager could supply sufficient argument type names in its method lookup key to choose the appropriate method. At worst, all argument types need to be supplied.

In the context of component-based systems, possibly supplied by different software companies, the name disambiguation problem becomes even more complex. Without planning and cooperation, it is possible that classes in different components will be created with the same names. While this may be the intent in some situations, some orderly means of introducing new as well as replacement components is needed. Although we did not resolve this issue in our implementation, one suggestion we came up with is to assign a unique identifier to every command, possibly using an Internet-like addressing scheme. For example, a N-byte identifier might be used that identifies the software company developing the component, the component type, the command identifier, and version of the command. A scripting extension, like the one described in this paper, could then use this command identifier to dispatch the correct command. ISO and ANSI committees are actively investigating solutions to this complex problem.

MetaFlex Maintenance and Performance

As previously mentioned, our early implementation of MetaFlex generated metaclasses for all classes in an application. This initially did not pose a problem for the MPW compiler, but, caused both the MPW lib and linker utilities to choke as the generated amount of code exceeded their segment limits. To overcome these limits, we modified MetaFlex to automatically split the metaclass implementations such that no more than X number of them were put into any one code segment. Later, as the number of metaclasses grew, the compiler limits were exceeded as well. To manage this limitation, generated source was divided into files with no more than Y class implementations per file. Both of these values may be overridden at the invocation of MetaFlex.

With each revision of the C++ grammar, the change in its parser semantics needs to be updated in MetaFlex's parser - this is a challenging task. During our development of the scripting application, we noticed that component developers used C++ syntax that would not cause an error during regular C++ compilation but would break when we run it through the parser in MetaFlex. The reason is C++ compilers allow archaic C expressions not defined in ANSI C++ BNR forms. To accommodate these expressions, we had to fix the parser used by MetaFlex.

In general, performance was a drawback to our implementation of MetaFlex. At this writing, nearly seventy classes are having metaclasses with function dictionary dispatching capabilities prepared form them. MetaFlex generates approximately 620 K-Bytes of source code for them. This process, in turn, adds nearly thirty minutes to the build cycle for our script-aware application.

We have preliminary designs for several parser speed-ups that would mitigate this situation, but frankly, would prefer that the compiler vendors incorporate the ideas expressed in this paper into their compilers. If C++ compilers provided a MetaFlex-like service, significant performance gains should be achieved, if for no other reason than the code would not have to be parsed twice.

Metaclass Specification Recommendation

In the final analysis, we would prefer that the compiler vendors implement a metaclass specification mechanism in their respective compilers that has all of the characteristics we have discussed here. For example, it would not be too difficult to imagine that the metaclass specification language, offered in this paper, could be implemented as a set of _keywords, or perhaps with the use of pragmas. These methods offer two ways of extending the C++ language. Both of these techniques potentially could be employed. In our metaclass specification grammar, nearly twenty tokens are introduced, and we don't think that the grammar is complete. Since it is difficult to have even one new language keyword adopted, it would be prudent to use the #pragma construct to implement most, if not all, of the metaclass specification.

The MakeMetaClassFor term in our grammar could be transformed into _MakeMeta keyword or #pragma declaration. For example, the first example in our specification language section, presented earlier, might be implemented as follows:

```
#pragma MakeMeta     Class DatabaseObject
                     Support FDict Style AddrsOnly
                     Install DBAccessPolicyManager
```

Our recommendation to compiler vendors is to allow developers to site metaclass specifications anywhere in the type system. Some developers will find it most attractive to co-locate their metaclass specification in the class being modeled. Others may want to co-locate all metaclass specifications in one file, as we suggested in the evaluation above. This may add some complexity to the problem (e.g., Which specification takes precedence when more than one are present in the type system for a given class? Do standard scoping rules apply?), but offers the greatest flexibility and customer satisfaction.

Conclusions

We have presented the need for a flexible metaclass generator to build extensions to applications. A number of extensions that would benefit from such a service were illustrated, including a detailed case study on a scripting application that is part of our component based application framework. Since the MetaFlex service is not commercially available in C++ compilers, we were forced to develop an in-house solution that served our needs. Through an evaluation of the MetaFlex generation service, we highlighted a number of issues we faced in our development and discussed the relative merits of possible solutions.

From our experience, it has become quite clear that it is impossible to build an ideal metaclass that suit the needs of all extensible applications. To mitigate this difficulty, we presented a metaclass specification language that allows software developers the means to engineer appropriate run-time type information, tailored to the application's needs. We recognize that the grammar presented is, by no means, a complete elaboration of what may be required, but does offer an organized view of the issues surrounding metaclass specification.

It is our belief that compiler developers should provide flexible metaclass generation capabilities to model an application's type system, and that vendors who provide such a service, will have a competitive edge for supporting the current trend of building extensible applications. It would be best if the development environments provided a graphical interface that allows developers to specify which classes, or roots of classes, should have metaclasses built for them.

Acknowledgments

We would like to acknowledge Roger Voss, Jim Murphy, and Krishna Uppala for their valuable critique of our paper. A special recognition goes to Krishna Uppala who played a principal role in the development of the C++ parser. We also recognize the valuable contribution that Jim Murphy made by introducing the notion of metaclass to the engineering teams at Aldus. Pat Ferrel, Erik Christiansen, Robert Meyer, Scott Moody, and Murugappan Palaniappan developed the component based application framework.

References

[Apple91]   Apple Computer, Inc, *Inside Macintosh Volume VI*, Addison-Wesley, Reading, MA, 1991.

[Böcker90]   Heinz-Dieter Böcker, Jürgen Herczeg, "What Tracers Are Made Of" *OOPSLA/ECOOP '90 Proceedings*, 21-25 October, 1990.

[Christiansen92]   Erik Christiansen, Mark Cutter, Pat Ferrel, Robert Meyer, Scott Moody, Murugappan Palaniappan, "Platypus: Aldus Scalable Component Architecture," Aldus Technical Report (1992).

[Cointe87]   Pierre Cointe, "Metaclasses are First Class: the ObjVlisp Model," *Conference Proceedings of OOPSLA '87*, October 4-8, 1987.

[Cox86]   Brad Cox, *Object-Oriented Programming: An Evolutionary Approach*, Addison-Wesley, Reading, MA, 1986.

[Ellis90]   Margaret A. Ellis, Bjarne Stroustrup, *The Annotated C++ Reference Manual*, Addison-Wesley, Reading, MA, 1990.

[Ferrel89]   Patrick J. Ferrel, Robert F. Meyer, "Vamp: The Aldus Application Framework," *Conference Proceedings of OOPSLA '89*, October 1-6, 1989.

[Goldberg83]   Adele Goldberg, David Robson, *Smalltalk-80: The Language and Its Implementation*, Addison-Wesley, Reading, MA, 1983.

[Kleyn88]   Michael F. Kleyn, Paul C. Gingrich, "GraphTrace - Understanding Object-Oriented Systems Using Concurrently Animated Views," *Conference Proceedings of OOPSLA '88*, September 25-30, 1988.

[Maes87]   Pattie Maes, "Concepts and Experiments in Computational Reflections," *Conference Proceedings of OOPSLA '87*, October 4-8, 1987.

[Murray92]   Robert B. Murray, "A Statically Typed Abstract Representation for C++ Programs," *Usenix C++ Conference Proceedings*, USENIX Association, August 10-13, 1992.

[Palay92]   Andrew J. Palay, "C++ in a Changing Environment," *Usenix C++ Conference Proceedings*, USENIX Association, August 10-13, 1992.

[Pérez92]   Edward R. Pérez, Moira Mallison, "Sentries and Policy Managers: Providing Extended Operations for Objects," Texas Instruments Inc, October 16, 1992.

[Richardson92]   Joel Richardson, Peter Schwarz, Luis Felipé Cabrera, "CACL: Efficient Fine Grained Protection for Objects" *Conference Proceedings of OOPSLA '92*, Andreas Paepcke, ed. (1992).

[Stroustrup92]   Bjarne Stroustrup, "Run Time Type Identification for C++," *Usenix C++ Conference Proceedings*, USENIX Association (1992).

[Voss92]   Roger Voss, "Virtual Member Function Dispatching for C++ Evolvable Classes," Aldus Technical Report (1992).

[Voss93]   Roger Voss, "C++ Evolvable Base Classes Residing In Dynamic Link Libraries," To appear in *C++ Journal*, Vol. 3, No. 1 (1993).

[Wells92a] David L. Wells, José A. Blakeley, Craig W. Thompson, "Architecture of an Open Object-Oriented Database Management System," *IEEE Computer*, Vol. 25, No. 10 (1992).

[Wells92b] David L. Wells, Moira Mallison, Edward R. Pérez, "Behavioral Extension Mechanisms in Open Object-Oriented Database System," Texas Instruments Inc. (1992).

Panel:
Aims, Means, and Futures of
Object-Oriented Languages

Mike Banahan, Chairman of the European C++ User Group
L. Peter Deutsch, Sun Microsystems Laboratories Inc.
Boris Magnusson, University of Lund
Jens Palsberg, moderator, Aarhus University

Abstract. Panelists will compare and assess the strengths and weaknesses of major object-oriented languages. They will also comment on the possible development and use of those languages and their related tools.

1 Background

Many object-oriented languages are in use today. From the programmer's perspective, they differ both when comparing language features and tool support. These differences have impact on programming style and programmer productivity, and also on how well a language is suited for a particular development project.

This panel focuses on three major object-oriented languages, namely Simula, Smalltalk, and C++. We will compare and assess their strengths and weaknesses, and hazard guesses about future developments of the languages themselves and their related tools.

2 Mike Banahan

The C++ language is currently receiving a lot of attention, especially in the PC and Unix communities who view it as a natural fit to many of the problems of their environments. C++ is viewed as an easy migration path from the most common language already in use there (C), since it is almost entirely upwards-compatible with C and yet offers the promise of stronger type checking, better encapsulation and the chance to implement Object Oriented Concepts. All at the same time!

C++ sets out to do much more than C. It is a considerably larger language and requires a different approach to development than does C. As many organisations have discovered, using a particular language does not guarantee that the software developed will necessarily make the best use of the facilities available.

Strong type checking and Object Orientation sound like a good combination of buzz-words. There is much to be said for it, and the wise use of C++ can be extremely powerful. Working together, those notions force designers to think

O.M. Nierstrasz (Ed.): ECOOP '93, LNCS 707, pp. 528-530, 1993.
© Springer-Verlag Berlin Heidelberg 1993

hard about the nature of type relationships within program designs. The availability of generic types and exception handling takes the language out of the realm of concepts familiar to most procedural programmers.

As a result, there is not only a new language to learn, but also many programming techniques which are new, exciting and difficult.

Your speaker will be happy to share the insights that he has been able to gain during his eight years' of using C++.

3 Boris Magnusson

Simula was the first object-oriented language and introduced all the now popular concepts associated with o-o (and a few more). The language and its implementations are stable, efficient and reliable and thus provides the framework for many projects. From the language point of view, some of the strength of Simula comes from the combination of o-o constructs it offers. In this company (with C++ and Smalltalk) its tempting to mention compile time typing *and* garbage collection. Simula also offers important unusual mechanisms as unlimited *nesting* of constructs (classes defined inside classes as procedures inside procedures in many procedural languages) and *processes* (co-routines, lightweight processes). Nesting is important to cope with large applications. Processes are important to deal with external communication as in user interfaces and in client-server applications. There are thus mature o-o systems available.

Implementations of o-o languages using traditional techniques and conventional tools in the bottom, such as text editors, linkers and Unix utilities exhibit some common problems:

- Selective loading from libraries does not work so well, since all possible virtual implementations will be included (back side of the coin of dynamic binding)
- More compilation module dependencies means more re-compilations (back side of inheritance and re-use). This can to some extent be fought by fast compilers but as programs grow...
- Utilities such as "grep" does not work so well with o-o languages since it will find all implementations of a procedure (not just the one called from here (back side of several names-spaces created by encapsulation).

These new problems (compared to procedural languages) call for more research in implementation techniques. Tight integration incremental techniques such as those developed in the Smalltalk environment and in the Mjolner project gives some answers, but much more remains to be done before these techniques are in common use.

"SIMULA—Common Base Language" was the title of the definition. Already here we are given a hint of another important direction in o-o development— to see o-o languages as specialized application languages. This is an extremely important way to fight the complexity of large systems—reducing their size by increasing the level of the language used (to say more per source line, in some sense this is what language development is all about). To make this a viable technique it must be fairly easy to define and implement such application languages, as easy as doing conventional programming.

Author Index

Bruno Achauer 103
Ole Agesen 247
Gul Agha 346
Holger Assenmacher 361
Herman Balsters 161
Mike Banahan 528
Andreas Birrer 21
Andrew P. Black 57
Thomas Breitbach 361
Peter Buhler 361
John M. Carroll 4
Yves Caseau 142
Craig Chambers 268
Shigeru Chiba 482
Wim Codenie 197
Theo D'Hondt 197
Rolf A. de By 161
Koen De Hondt 197
L. Peter Deutsch 528
Philippe Du Bois 458
Eric Dubois 458
Thomas Eggenschwiler 21
Svend Frølund 346
Erich Gamma 406
Dipayan Gangopadhyay 432
Urs Hölzle 36
Volker Hübsch 361
Richard Helm 406

Mark P. Immel 57
Jean-Marc Jézéquel 384
Ralph E. Johnson 406
Richard Johnson 502
Dimitri Konstantas 80
Michael G. Lamming 1
Barbara Liskov 118
Carine Lucas 197
Boris Magnusson 528
Takashi Masuda 482
José Meseguer 220
Subrata Mitra 432
Murugappan Palaniappan 502
Jens Palsberg 247
Laurent Perron 142
Michaël Petit 458
Ellen Rose 297
Mary Beth Rosson 4
Ichiro Satoh 326
Michael I. Schwartzbach 247
Reinhard Schwarz 361
Arie Segev 297
Patrick Steyaert 197
Mario Tokoro 326
Marc Van Limberghen 197
John Vlissides 406
Jeannette M. Wing 118
Roberto Zicari 161

Springer-Verlag
and the Environment

We at Springer-Verlag firmly believe that an international science publisher has a special obligation to the environment, and our corporate policies consistently reflect this conviction.

We also expect our business partners – paper mills, printers, packaging manufacturers, etc. – to commit themselves to using environmentally friendly materials and production processes.

The paper in this book is made from low- or no-chlorine pulp and is acid free, in conformance with international standards for paper permanency.

Lecture Notes in Computer Science

For information about Vols. 1–629
please contact your bookseller or Springer-Verlag

Vol. 630: W. R. Cleaveland (Ed.), CONCUR '92. Proceedings. X, 580 pages. 1992.

Vol. 631: M. Bruynooghe, M. Wirsing (Eds.), Programming Language Implementation and Logic Programming. Proceedings, 1992. XI, 492 pages. 1992.

Vol. 632: H. Kirchner, G. Levi (Eds.), Algebraic and Logic Programming. Proceedings, 1992. IX, 457 pages. 1992.

Vol. 633: D. Pearce, G. Wagner (Eds.), Logics in AI. Proceedings. VIII, 410 pages. 1992. (Subseries LNAI).

Vol. 634: L. Bougé, M. Cosnard, Y. Robert, D. Trystram (Eds.), Parallel Processing: CONPAR 92 – VAPP V. Proceedings. XVII, 853 pages. 1992.

Vol. 635: J. C. Derniame (Ed.), Software Process Technology. Proceedings, 1992. VIII, 253 pages. 1992.

Vol. 636: G. Comyn, N. E. Fuchs, M. J. Ratcliffe (Eds.), Logic Programming in Action. Proceedings, 1992. X, 324 pages. 1992. (Subseries LNAI).

Vol. 637: Y. Bekkers, J. Cohen (Eds.), Memory Management. Proceedings, 1992. XI, 525 pages. 1992.

Vol. 639: A. U. Frank, I. Campari, U. Formentini (Eds.), Theories and Methods of Spatio-Temporal Reasoning in Geographic Space. Proceedings, 1992. XI, 431 pages. 1992.

Vol. 640: C. Sledge (Ed.), Software Engineering Education. Proceedings, 1992. X, 451 pages. 1992.

Vol. 641: U. Kastens, P. Pfahler (Eds.), Compiler Construction. Proceedings, 1992. VIII, 320 pages. 1992.

Vol. 642: K. P. Jantke (Ed.), Analogical and Inductive Inference. Proceedings, 1992. VIII, 319 pages. 1992. (Subseries LNAI).

Vol. 643: A. Habel, Hyperedge Replacement: Grammars and Languages. X, 214 pages. 1992.

Vol. 644: A. Apostolico, M. Crochemore, Z. Galil, U. Manber (Eds.), Combinatorial Pattern Matching. Proceedings, 1992. X, 287 pages. 1992.

Vol. 645: G. Pernul, A M. Tjoa (Eds.), Entity-Relationship Approach – ER '92. Proceedings, 1992. XI, 439 pages, 1992.

Vol. 646: J. Biskup, R. Hull (Eds.), Database Theory – ICDT '92. Proceedings, 1992. IX, 449 pages. 1992.

Vol. 647: A. Segall, S. Zaks (Eds.), Distributed Algorithms. X, 380 pages. 1992.

Vol. 648: Y. Deswarte, G. Eizenberg, J.-J. Quisquater (Eds.), Computer Security – ESORICS 92. Proceedings. XI, 451 pages. 1992.

Vol. 649: A. Pettorossi (Ed.), Meta-Programming in Logic. Proceedings, 1992. XII, 535 pages. 1992.

Vol. 650: T. Ibaraki, Y. Inagaki, K. Iwama, T. Nishizeki, M. Yamashita (Eds.), Algorithms and Computation. Proceedings, 1992. XI, 510 pages. 1992.

Vol. 651: R. Koymans, Specifying Message Passing and Time-Critical Systems with Temporal Logic. IX, 164 pages. 1992.

Vol. 652: R. Shyamasundar (Ed.), Foundations of Software Technology and Theoretical Computer Science. Proceedings, 1992. XIII, 405 pages. 1992.

Vol. 653: A. Bensoussan, J.-P. Verjus (Eds.), Future Tendencies in Computer Science, Control and Applied Mathematics. Proceedings, 1992. XV, 371 pages. 1992.

Vol. 654: A. Nakamura, M. Nivat, A. Saoudi, P. S. P. Wang, K. Inoue (Eds.), Parallel Image Analysis. Proceedings, 1992. VIII, 312 pages. 1992.

Vol. 655: M. Bidoit, C. Choppy (Eds.), Recent Trends in Data Type Specification. X, 344 pages. 1993.

Vol. 656: M. Rusinowitch, J. L. Rémy (Eds.), Conditional Term Rewriting Systems. Proceedings, 1992. XI, 501 pages. 1993.

Vol. 657: E. W. Mayr (Ed.), Graph-Theoretic Concepts in Computer Science. Proceedings, 1992. VIII, 350 pages. 1993.

Vol. 658: R. A. Rueppel (Ed.), Advances in Cryptology – EUROCRYPT '92. Proceedings, 1992. X, 493 pages. 1993.

Vol. 659: G. Brewka, K. P. Jantke, P. H. Schmitt (Eds.), Nonmonotonic and Inductive Logic. Proceedings, 1991. VIII, 332 pages. 1993. (Subseries LNAI).

Vol. 660: E. Lamma, P. Mello (Eds.), Extensions of Logic Programming. Proceedings, 1992. VIII, 417 pages. 1993. (Subseries LNAI).

Vol. 661: S. J. Hanson, W. Remmele, R. L. Rivest (Eds.), Machine Learning: From Theory to Applications. VIII, 271 pages. 1993.

Vol. 662: M. Nitzberg, D. Mumford, T. Shiota, Filtering, Segmentation and Depth. VIII, 143 pages. 1993.

Vol. 663: G. v. Bochmann, D. K. Probst (Eds.), Computer Aided Verification. Proceedings, 1992. IX, 422 pages. 1993.

Vol. 664: M. Bezem, J. F. Groote (Eds.), Typed Lambda Calculi and Applications. Proceedings, 1993. VIII, 433 pages. 1993.

Vol. 665: P. Enjalbert, A. Finkel, K. W. Wagner (Eds.), STACS 93. Proceedings, 1993. XIV, 724 pages. 1993.

Vol. 666: J. W. de Bakker, W.-P. de Roever, G. Rozenberg (Eds.), Semantics: Foundations and Applications. Proceedings, 1992. VIII, 659 pages. 1993.

Vol. 667: P. B. Brazdil (Ed.), Machine Learning: ECML – 93. Proceedings, 1993. XII, 471 pages. 1993. (Subseries LNAI).

Vol. 668: M.-C. Gaudel, J.-P. Jouannaud (Eds.), TAPSOFT '93: Theory and Practice of Software Development. Proceedings, 1993. XII, 762 pages. 1993.

Vol. 669: R. S. Bird, C. C. Morgan, J. C. P. Woodcock (Eds.), Mathematics of Program Construction. Proceedings, 1992. VIII, 378 pages. 1993.

Vol. 670: J. C. P. Woodcock, P. G. Larsen (Eds.), FME '93: Industrial-Strength Formal Methods. Proceedings, 1993. XI, 689 pages. 1993.

Vol. 671: H. J. Ohlbach (Ed.), GWAI-92: Advances in Artificial Intelligence. Proceedings, 1992. XI, 397 pages. 1993. (Subseries LNAI).

Vol. 672: A. Barak, S. Guday, R. G. Wheeler, The MOSIX Distributed Operating System. X, 221 pages. 1993.

Vol. 673: G. Cohen, T. Mora, O. Moreno (Eds.), Applied Algebra, Algebraic Algorithms and Error-Correcting Codes. Proceedings, 1993. X, 355 pages 1993.

Vol. 674: G. Rozenberg (Ed.), Advances in Petri Nets 1993. VII, 457 pages. 1993.

Vol. 675: A. Mulkers, Live Data Structures in Logic Programs. VIII, 220 pages. 1993.

Vol. 676: Th. H. Reiss, Recognizing Planar Objects Using Invariant Image Features. X, 180 pages. 1993.

Vol. 677: H. Abdulrab, J.-P. Pécuchet (Eds.), Word Equations and Related Topics. Proceedings, 1991. VII, 214 pages. 1993.

Vol. 678: F. Meyer auf der Heide, B. Monien, A. L. Rosenberg (Eds.), Parallel Architectures and Their Efficient Use. Proceedings, 1992. XII, 227 pages. 1993.

Vol. 679: C. Fermüller, A. Leitsch, T. Tammet, N. Zamov, Resolution Methods for the Decision Problem. VIII, 205 pages. 1993. (Subseries LNAI).

Vol. 680: B. Hoffmann, B. Krieg-Brückner (Eds.), Program Development by Specification and Transformation. XV, 623 pages. 1993.

Vol. 681: H. Wansing, The Logic of Information Structures. IX, 163 pages. 1993. (Subseries LNAI).

Vol. 682: B. Bouchon-Meunier, L. Valverde, R. R. Yager (Eds.), IPMU '92 – Advanced Methods in Artificial Intelligence. Proceedings, 1992. IX, 367 pages. 1993.

Vol. 683: G.J. Milne, L. Pierre (Eds.), Correct Hardware Design and Verification Methods. Proceedings, 1993. VIII, 270 Pages. 1993.

Vol. 684: A. Apostolico, M. Crochemore, Z. Galil, U. Manber (Eds.), Combinatorial Pattern Matching. Proceedings, 1993. VIII, 265 pages. 1993.

Vol. 685: C. Rolland, F. Bodart, C. Cauvet (Eds.), Advanced Information Systems Engineering. Proceedings, 1993. XI, 650 pages. 1993.

Vol. 686: J. Mira, J. Cabestany, A. Prieto (Eds.), New Trends in Neural Computation. Proceedings, 1993. XVII, 746 pages. 1993.

Vol. 687: H. H. Barrett, A. F. Gmitro (Eds.), Information Processing in Medical Imaging. Proceedings, 1993. XVI, 567 pages. 1993.

Vol. 688: M. Gauthier (Ed.), Ada-Europe '93. Proceedings, 1993. VIII, 353 pages. 1993.

Vol. 689: J. Komorowski, Z. W. Ras (Eds.), Methodologies for Intelligent Systems. Proceedings, 1993. XI, 653 pages. 1993. (Subseries LNAI).

Vol. 690: C. Kirchner (Ed.), Rewriting Techniques and Applications. Proceedings, 1993. XI, 488 pages. 1993.

Vol. 691: M. Ajmone Marsan (Ed.), Application and Theory of Petri Nets 1993. Proceedings, 1993. IX, 591 pages. 1993.

Vol. 692: D. Abel, B.C. Ooi (Eds.), Advances in Spatial Databases. Proceedings, 1993. XIII, 529 pages. 1993.

Vol. 693: P. E. Lauer (Ed.), Functional Programming, Concurrency, Simulation and Automated Reasoning. Proceedings, 1991/1992. XI, 398 pages. 1993.

Vol. 694: A. Bode, M. Reeve, G. Wolf (Eds.), PARLE '93. Parallel Architectures and Languages Europe. Proceedings, 1993. XVII, 770 pages. 1993.

Vol. 695: E. P. Klement, W. Slany (Eds.), Fuzzy Logic in Artificial Intelligence. Proceedings, 1993. VIII, 192 pages. 1993. (Subseries LNAI).

Vol. 696: M. Worboys, A. F. Grundy (Eds.), Advances in Databases. Proceedings, 1993. X, 276 pages. 1993.

Vol. 697: C. Courcoubetis (Ed.), Computer Aided Verification. Proceedings, 1993. IX, 504 pages. 1993.

Vol. 698: A. Voronkov (Ed.), Logic Programming and Automated Reasoning. Proceedings, 1993. XIII, 386 pages. 1993. (Subseries LNAI).

Vol. 699: G. W. Mineau, B. Moulin, J. F. Sowa (Eds.), Conceptual Graphs for Knowledge Representation. Proceedings, 1993. IX, 451 pages. 1993. (Subseries LNAI).

Vol. 700: A. Lingas, R. Karlsson, S. Carlsson (Eds.), Automata, Languages and Programming. Proceedings, 1993. XII, 697 pages. 1993.

Vol. 701: P. Atzeni (Ed.), LOGIDATA+: Deductive Databases with Complex Objects. VIII, 273 pages. 1993.

Vol. 702: E. Börger, G. Jäger, H. Kleine Büning, S. Martini, M. M. Richter (Eds.), Computer Science Logic. Proceedings, 1992. VIII, 439 pages. 1993.

Vol. 703: M. de Berg, Ray Shooting, Depth Orders and Hidden Surface Removal. X, 201 pages. 1993.

Vol. 704: F. N. Paulisch, The Design of an Extendible Graph Editor. XV, 184 pages. 1993.

Vol. 705: H. Grünbacher, R. W. Hartenstein (Eds.), Field-Programmable Gate Arrays. Proceedings, 1992. VIII, 218 pages. 1993.

Vol. 706: H. D. Rombach, V. R. Basili, R. W. Selby (Eds.), Experimental Software Engineering Issues. Proceedings, 1992. XVIII, 261 pages. 1993.

Vol. 707: O. M. Nierstrasz (Ed.), ECOOP '93 – Object-Oriented Programming. Proceedings, 1993. XI, 531 pages. 1993.